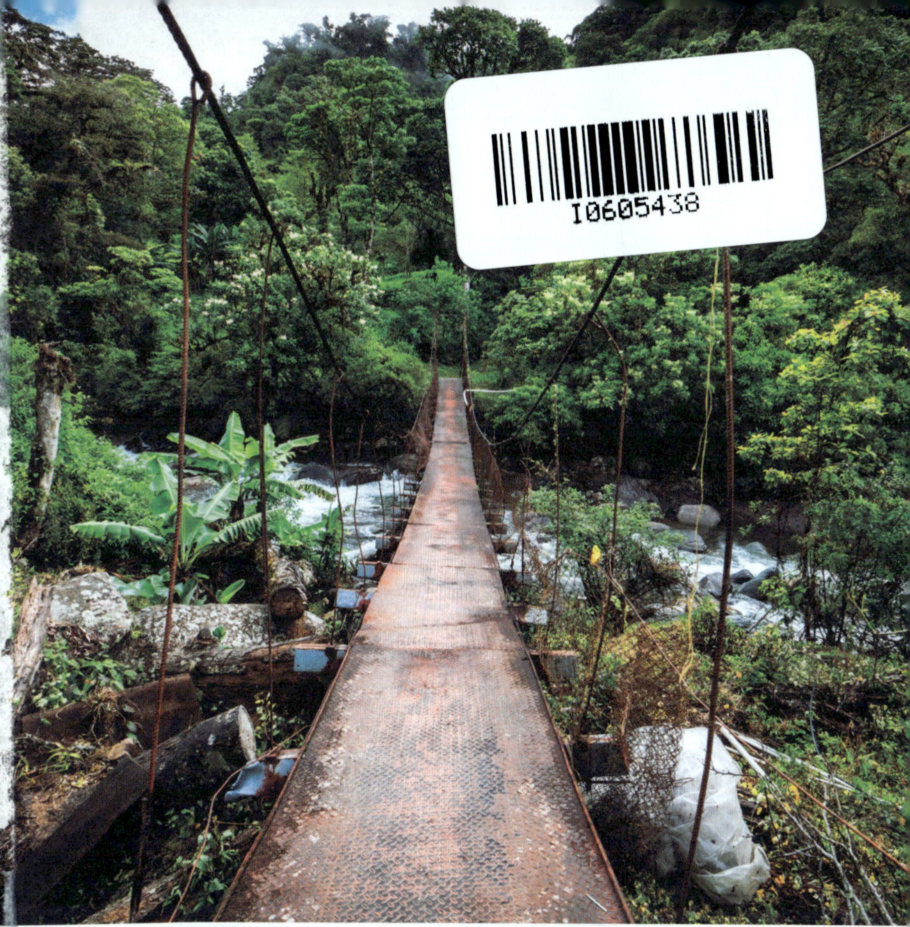

PANAMA

This fourth edition updated by
Sara Humphreys

with additional contributions by
Raffa Calvo

Contents

THREE-TOED SLOTH, ISLA COLÓN

Introduction to
Panama

Never has a country been so defined by its location. From the summit of Volcán Barú – Panama's highest peak – it's possible to watch the sun rise over both the Atlantic and Pacific oceans, light slowly spreading across the water to reveal two glittering archipelagos. For centuries this slender isthmus has provided an invaluable shortcut between the two seas; you can witness it yourself, tramping the old mule trails of the Spanish conquistadors or gliding past forested islands along the world's most famous canal. Panama is a "biological corridor", too, linking the vast land masses of the Americas, and harbours tremendous biodiversity within its cloud-forested highlands, glorious palm-fringed islands, vast mangrove tracts and towering rainforests. The country also boasts Central America's most ebullient capital city, and if you're after riotous partying, be it at a small village festival or throughout the hedonistic marathon of Carnaval, you're in the right place.

Panama's compact size means the vast majority of its sights are **easily accessible**. From the comfort of your hotel in the capital, you can head out in the morning to hike through spectacular, primate-packed rainforest, or explore crumbling colonial forts, and the same evening be swinging your hips to salsa or dining by candlelight in a downtown hot spot. The ancient and modern, artificial and natural are irresistibly juxtaposed: vast container ships transiting the Canal slice through primeval rainforests teeming with fluorescent frogs and elusive wild cats, just thirty minutes by dugout from where Emberá villagers practise subsistence agriculture. Visiting the country's fringes and interior, you can explore uninhabited islands and untracked jungle, basing yourself in small towns, friendly villages and remote ecolodges.

Despite these attractions, Panama has often been overlooked as a tourist destination, overshadowed by its neighbour Costa Rica, and sometimes mistakenly viewed as a US

BRIDGE OF THE AMERICA ACROSS THE PANAMA CANAL

annexe – thanks to the US occupation of the former Canal Zone and the dollarized economy. Add to that Panama's not entirely undeserved reputation for money-laundering and penchant for attracting North American retirees, and it's perhaps not surprising that tourists have been slow to appreciate the country's multifaceted identity and outstanding natural beauty. Yet the US is only one of many **cultural influences** – which derive from Spain and other parts of Europe, West Africa, the West Indies, China, India and the Middle East – fused with the fascinating heritage of the eight **indigenous peoples** that survived the Spanish Conquest. Many of these indigenous communities welcome tourists, sharing their traditional skills, customs and modern-day challenges.

Panama's complexities and contradictions confront you at every turn, which can intrigue and frustrate in equal measure. The Panamanian government is actively promoting international **tourism**, yet there's often very little information on offer. The colourful traditional attire of Panama's indigenous populations is used unashamedly in promotional images, but the people themselves are frequently ignored by their government. Many inhabit the tropical rainforests of Panama's national parks and reserves, which remain tantalizingly underdeveloped and desperately underfunded; covering more than a third of Panama's land and marine territory, these ostensibly protected areas are threatened by government-sanctioned

PANAMA

CARIBBEAN SEA
COSTA RICA
Guabito
Changuinola
Archipiélago de Bocas del Toro
Bocas Town
Almirante
P.N. LA AMISTAD
P.N. MARINO ISLA BASTIMENTOS
Río Sereno
Cerro Punta
Boquete
Volcán Barú
P.N. VOLCÁN BARÚ
Volcán
Chiriquí Grande
Golfo de los Mosquitos
San Miguel de la Borda
Coclé del Norte
Lago Gatún
P.N. OMAR TORRIJOS
P.N. ALTOS DE CAMPANA
P.N. SANTA FÉ
El Copé
El Valle
Penonomé
Antón
Paso Canoas
David
Santa Fé
San Félix
Aguadulce
Puerto Armuelles
Boca Chica
Las Lajas
INTERAMERICANA
Santiago
P.N. SARIGUA
Chitré
Punta Burica
P.N. MARINO GOLFO DE CHIRIQUÍ
Golfo de Chiriquí
Soná
Las Tablas
Mariato
P.N. COIBA
Santa Catalina
Peninsula de Azuero
Isla Coiba
Isla Cébaco
Tonosí
Isla de Cañas
Punta Mariato
P.N. CERRO HOYA

0 50
kilometres

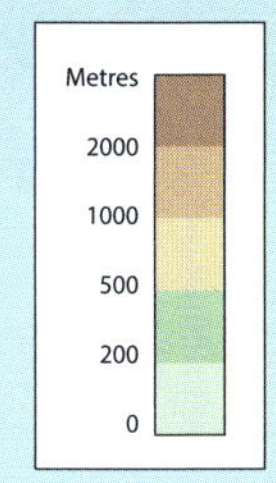
Metres
2000
1000
500
200
0
Isla Grande
P.N. PORTOBELO
Portobelo
El Porvenir
Archipiélago Gunayala (San Blas)
Cartí
Corazón de Jesús
Playón Chico
Colón
P.N. SOBERANÍA
P.N. CHAGRES
Chepo
Lago Bayano
Panama Canal
Gamboa
P.N. CAMINO DE CRUCES
PANAMA CITY
Balboa
INTERAMERICANA
Tubuala
La Chorrera
Isla Taboga
Isla Contadora
Metetí
Río Chucunaque
Puerto Obaldía
La Palma
Yaviza
El Real
Golfo de Panamá
Archipiélago de las Perlas
Garachiné
Río Sambú
Río Tuira
P.N. DARIÉN
Isla Iguana
Pedasí
Jaqué
COLOMBIA
PACIFIC OCEAN

FACT FILE

- Though Panama has enjoyed one of the highest average **GDP** growth rates in the world – around 5.7 percent 1990–2023 – and has reduced the numbers of people living in poverty, the levels of income **inequality** remain one of the highest in the world.
- Panama hosts over 1000 species of **bird**, including the odd-looking three-wattled bellbird, resident in the Chiriquí Highlands, whose extraordinary "bonk" call can be heard almost 1km away.
- Panama City's **metro** – the first in Central America – was inaugurated in 2014. The first two lines cost over $4 billion dollars to complete, and the third line, which travels under the canal, is estimated to cost $2.5 billion, and is due to open in 2028.
- The original **Panama Canal** took more than 60 million pounds of dynamite to blast through the isthmus; the ships laden with the explosives each contained twenty thousand boxes that all had to be unloaded by hand.
- The **Guna**, Panama's most high-profile indigenous people, have one of the highest rates of albinism in the world with one in 150 being born a "moon child".

hydroelectric and mining projects, as well as by land-hungry cattle-farmers.

It's hard to visit Panama and not be both amazed and perturbed by the pace of change in this small, young nation, as skyscrapers gobble up Panama City's skyline and new roads and farms push deeper into the forests. Outside the big attractions, though, it's easy enough to get off the beaten track. Seek out and spend time in the country's **less-visited corners** – far-flung islands, isolated mountain hamlets, remote indigenous communities and untamed national parks – and you'll be afforded greater insights into this compelling, beautiful and often surprising country.

Where to go

The vast majority of visitors fly in to cosmopolitan **Panama City**, where brash skyscrapers stare across the bay at the rocky peninsula of **Casco Viejo**, the city's regenerated colonial centre, whose elegantly restored mansions, churches and leafy plazas demand at least a day's leisurely exploration. If you're planning a short visit, it's easy to base yourself in the city and make daily forays to the monumental **Panama Canal** and the Spanish **colonial forts** of San Lorenzo and Portobelo. Should the frenetic energy and interminable traffic din of the city's clogged arteries get too much, an exhilarating excursion to the **Archipiélago de las Perlas**, or a relaxing outing birdwatching in the **Parque Nacional Soberanía** or kayaking down the **Río Chagres** are all possible without forgoing the epicurean delights of the capital's sophisticated bars and restaurants in the evening.

After Panama City, the country's most popular tourist area is the Caribbean archipelago of **Bocas del Toro**, close to the Costa Rican border. Its deserted stretches of sand, powerful surf and colourful coral reefs are matched by an often-forgotten mainland that offers spectacular wilderness hiking as well as wildlife viewing in the Parque Nacional Humedales de San San Pond Sak. Bocas's bohemian vibe and Afro-Caribbean culture contrasts with the vast archipelago of **Gunayala**, which extends for hundreds of kilometres along Panama's eastern Caribbean coast, and is home to

GUNA WOMAN SELLING HANDICRAFTS, GUNAYALA

ARTS AND CRAFTS IN PANAMA

It may not have the sprawling markets of Mexico or Guatemala, but Panama's arts and crafts are thriving, and reflect the country's multi-ethnic make-up. From appliqué textiles to coiled basketry, woodcarving to mask-making, here's our pick of the top five crafts:

Basketry and woodcarving Head for the Darién to pick up some exquisite Emberá basketry in villages such as Mogue and La Chunga, or smooth cocobolo and tagua carvings of animals in Wounaan communities such as Puerto Lara. See pages 287, 290 and 281.

Beaded necklaces Though once fashioned out of dyed pebbles, shells and bone worn by Ngäbe and Buglé warriors, these modern-day colourful *nguñunkua* (*chaquira* in Spanish) still make beautiful adornments. You'll find them sold in stalls along the Interamericana near Tolé, as well as in chic shops in Panama City. See page 205.

Devil masks Although made for festivals around the country, the most famous mask-makers hail from La Villa de los Santos and Chitré, their workshops stuffed full of terrifying salivating dragon or gargoyle-like monsters in kaleidoscopic colours. See page 159.

Molas Guna women's distinctive multicoloured, embroidered *molas* are transformed into everything from cushion covers to Christmas stockings using traditional geometric designs or modern-day icons such as Batman. They're widely available everywhere in Gunayala, and you'll find them on the street corners of Panama City. See pages 85, 136 and 257.

Straw hats Panama's hats may not be Panama hats – those are made in Ecuador – but some finely woven specimens are available: consider buying a *sombrero pintao* in La Pintada, or an *ocueño* in Ocu. See pages 143 and 161.

Panama's most politically independent and culturally distinct indigenous people, the Guna. Here you can live out your desert-island fantasies swinging in a hammock and sleeping in simple wooden *cabañas* on picture-postcard cays of white sand and coconut palms. With more time, you can experience the aquatic wonderlands off the Pacific coast, with world-class scuba diving, snorkelling and sport fishing in the mangrove-rich protected marine parks of the **Golfo de Chiriquí**, and **Coiba**, the penal colony turned wildlife reserve. The latter is generally reached from the laidback surfing hot spot and fishing village of **Santa Catalina**.

From there it's a short hop east to the rolling pastureland and quaint villages of the **Azuero Peninsula**, a region that revels in its colonial heritage. Once neglected by visitors, its joyous festivals, including the country's most ardent **Carnaval**, overflow with enthusiastic accordion and violin playing, colourful costumes, masks, rodeos and lashings of seco – Panama's potent national tipple – and provide ample opportunities to interact with the outgoing populace.

The dorsal mountain range dividing Panama's two coasts rises dramatically from the Pacific coastal plains that constitute the country's agricultural heartlands, with the most impressive peaks in the spectacular **national parks** of Chiriquí's **Western Highlands**, surrounding the alpine towns of **Boquete** and the less touristed **Cerro Punta**, which lie either side of brooding **Volcán Barú**. Here it's hard to resist the allure of verdant cloud forests filled with orchids, quetzals and hummingbirds, precision rows of shade-grown coffee plantations and fast-flowing rivers, perfect for whitewater rafting, and a range of adventure activities. Further east, the **Cordillera Central** hosts more parks and rainforested peaks laced with waterfalls above the small communities of **El Copé**, **Santa Fé** and **El Valle**, all of which offer rewarding hiking, birdwatching and horseriding.

Few visitors venture east of Panama City to the **Darién** jungle, which has gained almost mythical status, as much for FARC guerrillas and drug-traffickers as for its spectacular scenery and wildlife. Requiring patience, money and more than a smattering of Spanish, the rewards are ample: sinuous river journeys by dugout, great canopies of cathedral-like rainforests sheltering some of Panama's most spectacular fauna, and remote Emberá and Wounaan communities, keen to share their skills and culture with visitors.

ISLA TABOGA

When to go

Squeezed between seven and nine degrees north of the equator, Panama is located firmly within the **tropics**, with a climate to match: relentlessly hot and humid in the lowlands, cooling off fractionally to give balmy nights, whereas in the highlands, temperatures vary significantly with altitude, and can be chilly at night.

Most travellers visit during the shorter **dry season** (*verano*, "summer"), which runs from mid-December to the end of April, and with good reason. Azure skies predominate, at least on the drier Pacific plains, sheltered by Panama's mountainous spine. The firmer going underfoot makes it easier to travel on unpaved roads and explore the rainforests, and the reduced rainwater run-off ensures clearer waters to for swimming. The dry season also includes the lively holiday periods of Christmas, New Year, Carnaval and Holy Week, when flights and hotels in popular tourist spots are at a premium.

You'll avoid the crowds and the price hikes in the **rainy season** (*invierno*, "winter"), which stretches roughly from May to mid-December. Although the mountainous and rainforested regions in Panama are best avoided during the wettest months, since peaks are constantly swathed in cloud and tracks are boggy, if you stick to the lowland areas on the Pacific coast, the downpours, while frequent and intense, rarely last more than a few hours, leaving plenty of sunny, dry periods to enjoy. In particular, the otherwise parched Azuero Peninsula offers much more picturesque scenery during its understated rainy season.

By contrast, the **Caribbean coast** receives almost twice as much rain as the Pacific, with virtually no recognizable dry season. Regional variations impact here too: the trade winds (strongest Dec–Feb) make the water choppy and outer islands inaccessible in Bocas del Toro and Gunayala, while Bocas enjoys two relatively dry spells around March and October.

AVERAGE DAILY TEMPERATURES AND RAINFALL

	Jan	Feb	Mar	Apr	May	Jun	Jul	Aug	Sep	Oct	Nov	Dec
PANAMA CITY												
Max/min (°C)	30/22	31/22	32/23	32/23	31/24	30/23	30/23	31/23	30/23	30/23	30/23	30/23
Max/min (°F)	86/71	87/71	89/73	89/73	87/75	86/73	86/73	87/73	86/73	86/73	86/73	86/73
Rainfall (mm)	33	18	13	74	201	203	178	198	198	262	254	137
BOQUETE												
Max/min (°C)	25/13	27/13	28/14	29/14	28/15	27/14	27/14	27/14	27/14	28/14	27/14	27/13
Max/min (°F)	77/55	80/56	82/58	84/59	82/59	80/58	81/58	81/58	80/57	83/57	81/56	82/56
Rainfall (mm)	2.5	38	81	231	472	432	467	660	546	925	376	121
BOCAS DEL TORO												
Max/min (°C)	31/20	31/20	31/21	31/21	32/22	32/22	32/22	32/22	32/22	32/22	32/22	31/21
Max/min (°F)	88/68	88/68	88/70	88/70	90/72	90/72	90/72	90/72	90/72	90/72	90/72	88/70
Rainfall (mm)	204	235	188	323	273	287	387	346	254	219	390	485

Author picks

To research this guide, the authors spent countless hours hunched over in dugout canoes, tramping though steamy rainforests and fending off sandflies as they journeyed from the cocktail bars of Bocas to Emberá and Wounaan villages deep in the Darién. Here are some of their personal picks.

Thrilling boat trip The Parque Nacional Humedales de San San Pond Sak (see page 242) is at its best at sunrise as the mist clears; glide through the wetlands to see herons, hawks, sloths, snakes and the extraordinary-looking manatee.

Wow-factor birdwatching After a dawn hike through the Darién rainforest, and a lengthy stakeout of a nest, the sight of a majestic adult harpy eagle swooping down to feed its chick is truly special (see page 288).

Desert island delight Swinging in a hammock on Misdub, Gunayala (see page 261), will leave you gasping at the sparkling white sand fringed with coconut palms, with pelicans perched on the pier, surrounded by translucent turquoise shallows.

Panoramic views The vistas from the summit of Cerro Ancón (see page 69) take your breath away: on one side the city with its shimmering skyscrapers dwarfing the colonial architecture of Casco Viejo, on the other a procession of vast ships passing through the Panama Canal.

Challenging hike It's hard to beat the four-day trek across the cordillera from Boquete to Bocas (see page 187), hiking through cloud forest, traversing rivers and sleeping in Ngäbe villages, with the reward of a soak in the Caribbean at the end.

Fabulous fiesta While the extreme hedonism of Carnaval grabs the headlines, tiny Guararé's Festival de la Mejorana (see page 164) is a more mellow but equally joyous affair, including heavy doses of *pindín* – upbeat folk music featuring accordion-playing – and competitions in traditional skills.

Lipsmacking ice cream To alleviate the sweltering heat of Panama City, head to *Granclément* (see page 80): for mouthwatering sorbets and creamy chocolatey *helados*.

Our author recommendations don't end here. We've flagged up our favourite places – a perfectly sited hotel, an atmospheric café, a special restaurant – throughout the Guide, highlighted with the ★ symbol.

HARPY EAGLE IN THE DARIÉN RAINFOREST

VIEW OF PANAMA CITY FROM CERRO ANCÓN

15

things not to miss

It's not possible to see everything Panama has to offer in one trip – and we don't suggest you try. What follows, in no particular order, is a selective taste of the country's highlights: remote islands, vibrant cultures, great coffee, colonial architecture and unique wildlife. All highlights are colour-coded by chapter and have a page reference to take you straight into the Guide, where you can find out more.

1

2

3

4

5

1 FESTIVALS

See page 36

Fascinating festivals showcase Panama's diverse cultural heritage, from the hedonism of Carnaval to the vibrant, rebellious celebration of Afro-Panamanian Congo dancers, pictured here parading at the Desfilé de las Mil Polleras in Las Tablas.

2 STAY IN AN EMBERÁ VILLAGE

See pages 104 and 286

Experience village life with the Emberá and Wounaan in the forests of the Chagres and Darién, where traditional communities are adapting to modern-day challenges.

3 BIRDWATCHING

See page 37

Get close to the country's thousand-plus bird species – including dazzling hummingbirds, the resplendent quetzal and, pictured here, the blue-crowned motmot.

4 COLONIAL ARCHITECTURE

See pages 110 and 114

From Baroque Pacific churches to streets lined with attractive balconies, Panama possesses some fine colonial structures, including the crumbling fortresses at San Lorenzo and Portobelo.

5 CASCO VIEJO

See page 52

Hip bars and chic restaurants rub shoulders with colonial churches and leafy plazas in Panama City's historic centre.

6
7
HORIZON APHRODITE
8

6 SANTA FÉ DE VERAGUAS

See page 208

A fresh climate, picturesque waterfalls and an abundance of glorious orchids make this village an appealing retreat.

7 ISLAND LIFE IN GUNAYALA

See page 254

Sleep in a thatched wooden *cabaña* amid swaying coconut palms, and learn about the rich cultural traditions of the island-dwelling Guna.

8 PANAMA CANAL

See page 92

Experience the twentieth century's greatest engineering feat with a transit through the locks.

9 THE SOUTHERN AZUERO

See page 168

This peninsula's cost is full of treats, from the wildlife-rich island of Iguana, to the surfing splendour of Playa Venao and hidden coves round Cambutal.

10 THE CHIRIQUÍ HIGHLANDS

See page 183

Get up close to spectacular scenery – including moss-laden cloudforest, fast-flowing rivers and dazzling waterfalls.

11 SNORKELLING AND DIVING

See page 227

The coral reefs of the Caribbean offer superb snorkelling; for world-class diving, head to Isla Coiba.

12 COFFEE IN BOQUETE

See page 187

Learn to detect floral, caramel, citrus and spice aromas in some of the world's finest gourmet coffee estates.

13 CHILLING IN BOCAS

See page 221

Laidback bar-restaurants, windswept beaches, mellow lodges and Caribbean cuisine make Bocas a fine spot to let your hair down for a few days.

14 DARIÉN BOAT TRIPS

See page 278

Glide upriver into one of the world's last remaining wilderness areas, viewing vast buttress roots, tangled vines and the soaring forest canopy.

15 HIKING

See pages 38, 139 and 145

The combination of magnificent views, picturesque waterfalls and lush forest makes hiking in central and western Panama a constant delight.

11

12

13
PRIVADO
14
15

Itineraries

These itineraries cover the length and breadth of the isthmus, from idyllic Caribbean beaches to steaming rainforests. Limited roads and facilities in the Canal area and eastern Panama mean that in many cases the capital will necessarily serve as a hub, either as a base for day-trips or as a transit point during longer excursions.

THE GRAND TOUR

Use the capital as a base, with a few nights in appealing provincial towns and tropical beach hideaways. Doable in two weeks but for a richer experience, take it at a more leisurely pace.

❶ **Panama City** Get to know the vibrant capital, exploring its sights and nightlife and hopping out on a wealth of day-trips. See page 52

❷ **The Canal** Watch giant container ships squeeze through the locks, or experience a partial transit by boat. See page 92

❸ **Parque Nacional Soberanía** A short bus ride beyond the Miraflores Locks, this accessible park offers excellent rainforest hiking and birdwatching. See page 98

❹ **San Lorenzo** Yet another day-trip, if you want, the forts at Portobelo may boast more cannons, but San Lorenzo's atmospheric location, towering above the Río Chagres, is unbeatable. See page 110

❺ **Gunayala** Best as a three-day escape: stay in thatch *cabañas* on tranquil tropical beaches, and engage with Guna culture. See page 248

❻ **El Valle** Flower-filled crater town, surrounded by scenic hills, two hours west of Panama City by bus. An ideal place to unwind for a couple of days. See page 134

❼ **Boquete** Two bus changes away, in the Chiriquí Highlands, this scenic centre of gourmet coffee production and adventure activities merits at least three days. See page 184

❽ **Bocas del Toro** A trip across the cordillera takes you to bohemian Bocas – enjoy diving, surfing and snorkelling by day, and drinking, dining and partying by night. Great day-trips, too. See page 218

SAND, SEA AND SURF

Spend around sixteen days enjoying the best beaches, surf spots, islands and marine reserves of Panama's Caribbean and Pacific coastlines.

❶ **Playa Bluff** A flight or overnight bus trip from the capital takes you to Bocas Town; Playa Bluff is its finest beach. Relax in a Caribbean eco-retreat overlooking a 5km expanse of deserted sand and pounding surf, and in season watch turtles lay their eggs. See page 224

❷ **Golfo de Chiriquí** A lengthy bus journey across the cordillera brings you to Boca Chica village; book into a boutique lodging and kayak around the coastal mangroves and secluded coves of the nearby Pacific islands. See page 203

❸ **Santa Catalina** Panama's top surfing spot has a world-class break, a good beach for novices and a mellow après-surf scene. See page 211

❹ **Isla Coiba** A short boat trip away, Coiba is a diver's paradise, with great snorkelling too. See page 214

❺ **Playa Venao** At the southern tip of the Azuero, this glorious arc of sand hosts surfing and partying at one end, and a more laid-back eco-beach scene at the other end. See page 171

❻ **Archipiélago de las Perlas** Accessible by boat or plane from Panama City, beautiful Isla Contadora makes a good base for sailing out to deserted cays and islands. See page 104

❼ **Western Gunayala** Laze away your days on idyllic cays, palm-topped islands and translucent warm waters – the quintessential Caribbean paradise. See page 256

CULTURES AND CRAFTS

Swap modern hotel comforts for basic rural lodgings and gain great insights into Panama's cultural and colonial heritage. Count on two or three nights per stop, plus a five-day Emberá stay in the Darién if you're feeling adventurous.

❶ **Naso communities** The provincial town of Changuinola, a flight or lengthy bus ride away from Panama City, is the launch pad for trips up the Río Teribe to visit Seiyik, seat of the Naso monarch, and to float downriver on a bamboo raft. See page 243

❷ **Río Caña** Just along the coast, stay in traditional *cabañas* in this Ngäbe village, learning about traditional gastronomy and their turtle conservation programme, and visit Isla Escudo de Veraguas. See pages 235 and 238

❸ **Santa Fé de Veraguas** A long bus journey takes you to this delightful mountain village, where a tour of the coffee cooperative gives a taste of the community's history. See page 208

❹ **An Azuero festival** Head southeast to laidback Las Tablas, and aim to time your trip to coincide with one of the peninsula's many riotous festivals. See page 168

❺ **Azueran crafts** On your way back to Panama City, drop in to see the devil mask-makers of Chitré and the women's hat-making cooperative in nearby Ocú. See pages 159 and 161

❻ **Casco Viejo, Panama City** Steeped in colonial history, the old city centre is a great place to find jewellery, clothing, baskets, masks and carvings made in far-flung communities around the country. See page 55

❼ **Gunayala** After a challenging jeep ride to the *comarca* from the capital, experience first-hand how the women make their colourful *molas* and *winis*. See page 248

❽ **Emberá homestay** A full day's travel (by bus and dugout) brings you to the welcoming Darién communities of La Chunga, La Marea or Mogue, where you can sleep in an open-sided *bujia* (wooden house on stilts). See page 286

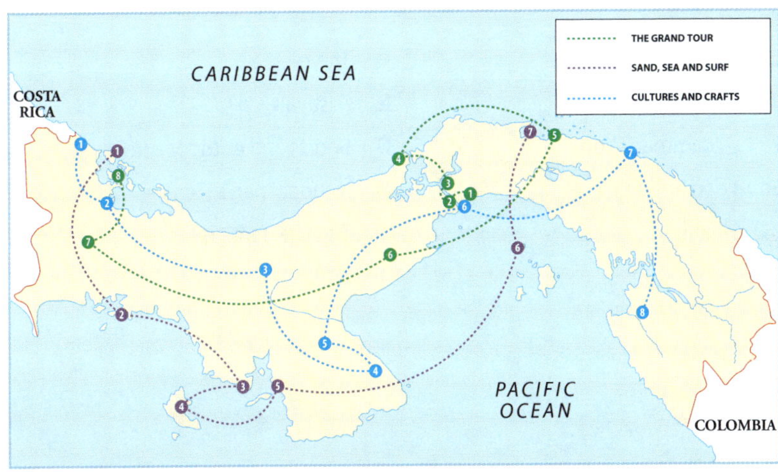

DIABLO ROJO IN PORTOBELO

Basics

Getting there

The vast majority of visitors to Panama arrive by air, landing at Tocumen International Airport in Panama City. Seats are generally more expensive and more heavily subscribed during the dry season (late Dec to April), especially the peak holiday periods of Christmas, Easter and Carnaval (usually in Feb) when many Panamanians living in the US return home. Thus, high season broadly counts as December through to the end of April, low season May to November. Though flights are easily booked online it is still sometimes cheaper to make arrangements via a travel agent – bearing in mind the crucial distinction between Panama City in Central America (airport code PTY) and the Panama City in Florida (airport code PFN).

Panama's reliable no-frills **national carrier**, Copa Airlines (ⓦcopaair.com), often offers the best rates and has an efficient online booking service. It flies to and from numerous US cities and destinations in Latin America and the Caribbean, with one to three connecting flights a day from Tocumen to the airport at David, capital of Chiriquí province, in the far west of the country. The new **Panamá Pacífico International Airport**, formerly the US Howard Air Force base in the Canal Zone, 9km southwest of Balboa, accommodates a couple of low-cost airlines and charter flights, including Copa's sibling Wingo (ⓦwingo.com), which operates flights to Colombia, Cuba and Costa Rica. Charter flights predominantly from Canada, also land at Río Hato – another former US military base – 120km southwest of Panama City (see page 24).

Visitors travelling down from **Central America** may choose to make the longer but cheaper bus journey through Costa Rica, either along the Pan-American Highway via the Pacific border crossing at Paso Canoas, or at Guabito on the Caribbean (or Atlantic) coast in Bocas del Toro, although there is a less used border at Río Sereno in the Western Highlands.

Alternatives to flying from **South America** are a great deal more complicated, involving several boat and bus journeys on the Caribbean side, and are only for the adventurous. Cruise ship visitors will dock at the cruise ship terminals in either Colón, at the Caribbean end of the Panama Canal, or on the Calzada de Amador (Amador Causeway) in Panama City, on the Pacific side. Sailing boats carrying backpackers from Cartagena usually unload passengers in Puerto Lindo or Portobelo, along the coast in Colón province, though some deposit travellers at Cartí in Gunayala. Other yacht arrivals will probably call in at the Balboa Yacht Club on the Calzada de Amador or at the Shelter Bay Marina west of Colón.

Visas and red tape

Tourists from **most European countries**, plus the US, Canada, Australia, New Zealand and South Africa, do not need a visa. They can get their passport stamped for ninety days on arrival (180 days in the case of Canada and the US) provided they can produce a passport valid for at least six months after departure, an onward (or return) bus or plane ticket and proof of funds (usually $500 or a credit card).

That said, check for the latest **regulations** at a Panamanian consulate in advance and don't forget that if you are transiting via the US, you will need a transit visa, or a visa waiver (ESTA) application in advance of travel (see ⓦusimmigrationsupport.org), as well as a machine-readable passport. The Panamanian immigration authorities' website is also worth checking (ⓦmigracion.gob.pa).

If you are arriving from one of the WHO-listed yellow fever countries you may be asked to produce your vaccination certificate (see page 33).

The only way to **extend your stay** is to pop over to Costa Rica for a couple of days before returning, brandishing a return bus ticket.

Flights from the US and Canada

There are numerous **direct flights**: Delta (ⓦdelta.com), United (ⓦunited.com) and American Airlines

A BETTER KIND OF TRAVEL

At Rough Guides we are passionately committed to travel. We believe it helps us understand the world we live in and the people we share it with – and of course tourism is vital to many developing economies. But the scale of modern tourism has also damaged some places irreparably, and climate change is accelerated by most forms of transport, especially flying. We encourage all our authors to consider the carbon footprint of the journeys they make in the course of researching our guides.

(Ⓦ aa.com) alongside Copa (Ⓦ copaair.com) fly daily to Panama City from numerous US cities, including Miami – the main portal, offering several daily connections – New York, Washington, Los Angeles and Chicago.

Including the relevant taxes, return **fares** from Miami, for example, range from US$350 (low season, only carry-on luggage) to US$700 (high season, one checked bag), from New York or Washington US$750–1400 and from Los Angeles US$750–1600.

Copa also offers direct flights from Toronto and Montréal in **Canada** with typical return prices of Can$900–1500. Cheaper charter flights are available in high season through Transat (Ⓦ transat.com) from Calgary, Montréal and Toronto or through Sunwing (Ⓦ sunwing.ca) from Montréal and Toronto to **Río Hato** airport at Playa Blanca, on the Pacific coast.

Flights from the UK and Ireland

Although there are currently no direct flights from the **UK** or **Ireland**, code-sharing flights (£750–1500) are offered with KLM (Ⓦ klm.com), which offers twice-weekly flights to Panama City from Amsterdam, and Air France (Ⓦ airfrance.com), which makes the trip five times a week from Paris. Iberia (Ⓦ iberia.com) has frequent departures from several Spanish cities. Another option is with German airline Condor (Ⓦ condor.com), which started operating two flights a week from Frankfurt in 2025, with Lufthansa providing affordable connections from London and Ireland, as well as from other European destinations. The cheapest route from the UK or Ireland is sometimes via the US with a US carrier (see above), though the lengthier flying time and the extra hassle of clearing US immigration generally makes this less appealing than flying via mainland Europe.

Flights from Australia, New Zealand and South Africa

It is a long, expensive haul to Panama from Australia, New Zealand and South Africa, with no direct flights. Most routes from **Australia** (Aus$3500–8000) and New Zealand (NZ$3000–9000) travel via the US, generally passing through Los Angeles, though flights via Santiago or Buenos Aires are also possible with the journey time (26hr-plus) staying much the same. From **South Africa** (30hr-plus), you can travel via Amsterdam or Paris, South America or the US (ZAR$27,000–37,000).

Flights from Central and South America

Various countries in **Latin America** have direct connections with Panama City, generally either through Avianca or, more usually, Copa, which connects with more than eighty destinations across Latin America and the Caribbean. In Costa Rica, Sansa offers flights three times a week from San José to Bocas del Toro (US$260 one-way). Copa's Colombian-owned low-cost airline, Wingo (Ⓦ wingo.com), offers cheap connections with several Colombian destinations, including Bogotá or Medellín (from $120 one-way, with just carry-on, for example) – note that flights land at **Panamá Pacífico** airport (see page 73). Other budget airlines also periodically offer flights here.

Buses from Central America

It is possible to travel overland along the **Pan-American Highway** from Tapachula in Mexico to Panama City (with drop-offs at David and Santiago), with **Ticabus** (Ⓦ tica-bus.com; around US$200 one way). Buses are comfortable and air-conditioned, offering the obligatory diet of Hollywood movies; they pick up (and drop off) passengers at the major Central American cities on the way, though you will have to spend a couple of nights in hotels, which increases the cost. **Agencia Tracopa** (Ⓦ tracopacr.com) operates a daily service from San José to David (US$21 one way).

Boats from Colombia

The only break in the 50,000km or so Pan-American Highway is an 87km stretch of swamp and mountainous jungle between Carepa on the Colombian border and Yaviza in Panama, in what is known as the Darién Gap (see pages 43 and 277). Up until the early 1990s, thrashing your way through here overland was a famous challenge for adventurers. However, crossing the Darién Gap has been forbidden for several years – the presence of drug-traffickers, Colombian paramilitaries, people traffickers and smugglers make it extremely dangerous, with the threat of death or kidnapping adding to the usual jungle hazards.

For those wanting to save money on air fares travelling by a series of speedboats along the Caribbean coast is an option, though if you are out of luck with the weather, timings and bookings, the overall saving is likely to be negligible. Still, an adventure of sorts is guaranteed. This route requires a reasonable command of Spanish or a travelling companion who can speak the language. A **multiday sailing trip** from Cartagena, Sapzurro, or Capurganá in Colombia to Colón province is another possibility (see box, page 25).

To make the coastal journey from Colombia, it is first necessary to get to **Turbo**, a small city in the Antioquia

SAILING BETWEEN COLOMBIA AND PANAMA – THE CLASSIC BACKPACKER ROUTE

A popular passage between Colombia and Panama involves a four- to five-day **sailing trip** between **Cartagena**, **Sapzurro** or **Capurganá** (close to the Colombia–Panama border) – taking in some of the more remote tropical islands of Gunayala – and **Cartí** (see page 259), from where it's another US$25 to reach Panama City; Portobelo (see page 112); or Puerto Lindo (see page 118). Typically backpacker rates are from around US$600 per person from Cartagena (US$550 from Sapzurro), including food and non-alcoholic drinks, though some deals require you to help around the ship, be it crewing or cooking. In addition to being cheaper, the Sapzurro or Capurganá route has the advantage of avoiding the roughest seas by hugging the coast, thereby affording more time to explore Gunayala. Be prepared to hang around at your departure point for a few days, since preparations can take some time. **Horror stories** abound of drunken captains and poorly maintained boats, so do your homework; hostel recommendations of particular captains can be helpful, but should be viewed critically since hostels usually receive commission for supplying passengers. You're best getting the lowdown from other people who have made the trip. Bear in mind, too, that this trip is **seasonal** – sailing between November and February can be dangerous with rough seas, so much so that some captains do not make the crossing during that period.

department on the Pan-American Highway (accessible by regular buses from Medellín, which are safe during the day), or **Necoclí**, which lies nearer Cartagena. Both have a regular morning launch (8–9am) to **Capurganá** – 2hr 30min from Turbo, 1hr 30min from Necoclí, a burgeoning low-key Caribbean resort unreachable by road. You should note, however, that in recent years Necoclí has also become a major centre in the migrant route to the US (see page 270), which can result in periodic suspensions of the boat service. Note also that in high season (Dec–April) there is usually more than one departure a day from Turbo. From Capurganá there is a speedboat connection with **Puerto Obaldía** (1hr; cost depends on numbers), a small military outpost across the border in Panama, at the eastern end of Gunayala. Note also that both sea crossings can be exceedingly rough (especially between Nov and Feb) and are not for the faint-hearted; the boats are small and the waves loom large, though life jackets are provided. A large plastic bag to cover your luggage is a must, as well as waterproof protection for yourself.

Moving on from Puerto Obaldía, the usual option (unless flights resume) is to book a seat in a speedboat bound for Cartí (from around 259), at the western end of Gunayala and the eight-hour trip can be horrifically uncomfortable if the waves are high.

Red tape

Before leaving Colombia, get an exit stamp from **immigration** at Capurganá (daily 9am–5pm) and an entry stamp for Panama on arrival in Puerto Obaldía (daily 8am–4pm). Military police will meet the boat and escort you to the relevant authorities. Your belongings will be thoroughly searched for drugs and you are likely to be required to show proof of onward travel, possibly a yellow fever vaccination certificate (see page 33), and sufficient funds (a credit card will do) to cover your stay.

Agents and operators

Only a handful of operators offer Panama-only tours; most combine a visit with Costa Rica or other countries in Central America. While packages are convenient, it's cheapest to book your flight to Panama using a regular travel agent and then arrange your itinerary with a Panama City-based tour operator (see page 77).

Audley Travel UK, Ⓦ audleytravel.com. Several packages to Panama (eleven to fifteen days), including birdwatching and a highlights tour taking in Panama City, the Canal, Bocas and Gunayala.

Journey Latin America UK, Ⓦ journeylatinamerica.com. Long-established UK-based tour operator offering tailor-made itineraries and tours; includes trips combining Panama with Costa Rica, as well as a Panama highlights package.

Responsible Travel UK, Ⓦ responsibletravel.com. Offers numerous itineraries round Panama as well as trips that include Costa Rica, family-oriented holidays and custom-made tours.

Rickshaw Travel UK, Ⓦ rickshawtravel.co.uk. Responsible travel agency offering several "bite-size"(two- or three-day) excursions within Panama, which can be collated to make a longer itinerary.

Wild Planet Adventures US, Ⓦ wildplanetadventures.com. Multi-award-winning company offering excellent wildlife-focused adventure holidays (nine or fourteen days) to Panama, led by naturalist guides. Also scuba diving in Coiba and tailor-made tours.

FINDING YOUR WAY

Panama is not without its frustrations: **streets** often have several names, rarely marked on a signpost; **telephone numbers** change frequently, especially for mobile phones and even for government offices; and **websites** are often not updated, or domain names left to lapse – all of which makes contacting people difficult. Moreover, the **pace of change** in some parts of Panama at the moment is phenomenal: following post-pandemic closures, new places to stay are mushrooming; bars, discos and restaurants, especially in Panama City and the main tourist areas, regularly open, close, move or change name, often lasting the summer partying and tourist season, but failing to make it through winter. This Guide will help you navigate this dynamic country, but it's always worth checking details on the ground.

Getting around

Panama has a fairly comprehensive and very efficient bus network, used by the majority of the population, which will get you around most of the mainland, though the level of comfort varies enormously. Along the western section of the Interamericana – the Panamanian section of the Pan-American Highway – luxury vehicles with reclinable seats, air conditioning, nonstop videos and on-board toilets speed along for several hours for a handful of dollars, while at the other end of the scale *chivas* – converted pickup trucks packed like the proverbial sardine can – grind their way up twisting mountain roads to remote villages for not a lot less.

There are many good paved **roads** in central and western Panama, even to small villages up in the mountains, and dirt roads are also generally well graded, though in the rainy season (roughly May to mid-Dec) they can soon become a quagmire. East of Panama City, beyond the Interamericana, are few roads of any description.

For the longer trips from Panama City – over the Cordillera Central to Bocas, down to the Azuero or across to the Western Highlands – an **internal flight** on **Air Panama** (Ⓦairpanama.com), Panama's main domestic airline, or the smaller **Fly Trip** (Ⓦflytrip.com.pa), will save a lot of time. And to hop from island to island in Bocas and Gunayala, or ease upriver to visit Emberá villages in the Darién, the main mode of transport is a fibreglass *lancha,* or, occasionally, a wooden dugout (*cayuco* or *piragua*).

By bus

The vast brick building fronted by battalions of buses just down the road from Albrook Airport on the edge of Panama City is the Gran Terminal de Transportes de Panamá – or **Albrook bus terminal –** the hub of the **national bus system**. Most of the capital's local transport and all international and regional buses leave from here (see page 74).

The main centres, such as Santiago, Chitré and David, also have large efficient **bus terminals** on the outskirts of town complete with toilets, left-luggage facilities and restaurants. From these, regional connections and local buses – usually a mixture of battered Toyota minivans with extra fold-down aisle seating and the more comfortable Coasters – head out into the countryside in centrifugal fashion. In the smaller settlements, minibuses or *chivas* hang out in the plaza or main street waiting for an adequate number of passengers. Generally, the more **rural** the location, the more laissez-faire the bus timetable and the more likely it is that passengers will be picked up anywhere along the route.

Along most regional **bus routes** from Panama City, transport runs from 5.30/6am until 7/8pm, whereas the first buses heading into the capital from the provinces may leave from 1 to 4am to ensure passengers arrive for the start of the commercial day. Local transport in the provinces usually peters out around 6.30 or 7pm. Unless stated otherwise, all the bus services we list throughout this Guide are **daily** – but note that departures are often less frequent at weekends and in very rural areas, the last bus may not leave at all. The **timetables** for many routes can be consulted online at Ⓦthebusschedule.com/pa, which is kept reasonably up to date.

The **Interamericana** is punctuated with official and unofficial (generally at a major intersection) bus stops where you can flag down transport. Bear in mind that on Friday and Sunday afternoons, and at either end of a holiday period, when buses are jam-packed, you might be left stranded for hours.

Ticket prices range from around $4 for a two-hour ride in moderate comfort to $19 for a relaxing uninterrupted six-hour recline from Panama City all the way to David. There are set prices for every route, often posted on the bus window, and tourists are rarely overcharged – if in doubt about a fare ask a local on the bus. **Luggage** generally goes for free, either on the roof or in the luggage compartment, although surfboards sometimes incur extra charges. Security is not usually an issue.

Booking ahead for busy holiday periods and international journeys is a must, though it is only possible for international and some long-haul domestic routes and generally only a couple of days in advance. You'll need to go in person to the travel company ticket office, usually in the bus terminal, in Panama City, David or Changuinola, to buy the ticket in cash.

By plane

Flying within Panama is a convenient and safe experience. The few internal flights almost all depart from or arrive at Marcos A. Gelabert Airport (Ⓣ524 9406), more commonly known as **Albrook Airport** (after the former US Air Force base it occupies), which lies 3km northwest of Panama City centre.

Air Panama (Ⓦairpanama.com), the country's main **domestic airline**, was only serving four destinations at the time of writing: Isla Colón in Bocas del Toro, Changuinola, David and Chitré. Propeller planes seating forty to fifty passengers are the norm.

Prices tend to reflect demand with the maximum one-way domestic fare currently around $180 (including taxes) and some much cheaper. Luggage allowances are 23kg plus 2.3kg carry-on, but full-size surfboards incur an extra charge. In 2023, charter airline Flytrip (Ⓦflytrip.com.pa) also started offering scheduled daily flights to Bocas del Toro, as well as more infrequent flights to Pedasí, Contadora and Guararé/Las Tablas, on small 9-seater or 12-seater planes.

Compared with the long-distance buses, plane **timetables** are less reliable. Flights fill quickly in advance of a holiday weekend.

By car

Away from the traffic hell that is Panama City, **driving** in Panama is generally fairly straightforward, with very good, well-signposted roads connecting the main urban centres, though it can be a different story in some of the more remote or mountainous areas.

The **Interamericana** (also called the Carretera Panamericana in Panama), Panama's main thoroughfare – part of the Pan-American Highway that travels almost 48,000km from Alaska to Chile – runs 486km from the Costa Rican border at Paso Canoas in the west, skirting several major cities, crossing the canal and bludgeoning its way through the capital before continuing another 282km and grinding to an abrupt halt in Yaviza in the eastern Darién.

Traffic for the Azuero Peninsula peels off onto the **Carretera Nacional** at Divisa, 34km east of Santiago, and branches off north across the Cordillera Central at Chiriquí for the sinuous journey across the continental divide down to the islands of Bocas del Toro on western Panama's only transisthmian route. Though an excellent paved road, it is sometimes blocked by landslides during the wettest months of the rainy season (roughly May to mid-Dec).

The only other routes across the isthmus lie east of the canal. The frequently log-jammed **Transístmica** links the capital with the country's second city of Colón; the faster **Autopista Panamá–Colón**, a toll road aimed at improving commercial traffic, runs parallel. An hour east of Panama City, beyond Chepo, a roller coaster of a road heads north from the Interamericana at El Llano, heading 40km over the mountains to Cartí, providing the only road link with Gunayala (though another link further east is under construction). It's accessible most of the year, but although it's paved, only 4WD vehicles are granted access. Further east, the final stretch of the Interamericana as far as **Yaviza** is also paved, but at the time of writing was severely potholed and every year after heavy rain a section or two gets severely damaged. Expect an increasing number of police **checkpoints** along this stretch of road, as well as along the western section of the Interamericana, as you near the Costa Rican border.

Despite Panama's decent road network, **driving at night** is best avoided because there's little illumination outside the urban centres, and drink driving, one of the main causes of accidents nationally, is common. Though there is a legal limit of 86mg, it is rarely adhered to or enforced.

If you are involved in a car **accident**, Panamanian law requires that you should not move the vehicles but should wait near them until the traffic police (*Transito*) arrive; a statement from them is required in order to file any insurance claim. Unless otherwise indicated, the **speed limits** are 40km/h in urban areas, 60km/h on secondary roads and 100km/h on primary roads but these limits are neither widely advertised nor followed. Two of the most **dangerous** roads are the Interamericana, along which copious buses and heavy trucks thunder, and the route across the Cordillera Central to Bocas del Toro, when bad weather can make the hairpin bends even more scary.

Hitching is possible, though with all the obvious attendant risks, on the main thoroughfares, but it is unlikely anyone will stop. In the very rural areas, where there is no or at best infrequent bus service, it is quite usual to thumb a lift, though you should offer to pay at least the equivalent of a bus fare.

Car rental

Renting a car makes it easier to explore some out-of-the-way spots – though if you're staying in Panama City and the Canal area, it's much more convenient to use buses, taxis and the metro. You'll find all the usual international **car rental firms** represented. The larger firms have their head offices at Tocumen International Airport, with many running a downtown office and sometimes branches at Albrook and David airports too. Some operators have offices in other major cities and tourist towns. Rental **costs** vary greatly, so shop around and note that rates fluctuate according to season and demand. You may get a better deal if you book online in advance.

Virtually all rental vehicles have air conditioning. A manual economy car is the cheapest option (from approximately $65/day, or $160/week, including taxes and insurance cover). For a 4WD, which is probably only necessary if you want to get off the beaten track and into the national parks, bank on paying almost double that. **Fuel** costs around $4.20 a gallon (less than a $1/litre) and petrol stations (often 24hr) are liberally sprinkled along the main roads.

The **minimum age** for most car rental companies is 25 but 23 will suffice for some firms provided a credit card is produced as security. A driving licence – international or from your country of origin – as well as a passport will need to be shown.

By taxi

Taxis, generally in the form of a 4WD twin cab, are also a practical way of reaching rural locations that are poorly served by public transport. Official cabs are yellow, with their licence number printed on the door, though in the countryside you may come across unofficial drivers whose service is generally just as reliable.

Taxis are widely available in most **urban centres** and can save you from melting in the heat. Panama City cabs ostensibly charge fixed rates according to zones (which are rarely adhered to) or generally agreed prices for particular routes (see page 76). Most central trips within the capital during the day should not exceed $3–4; in other urban centres it should not exceed a couple of dollars. Across the country, a small surcharge is added for more than two passengers and prices are higher at night. While most taxi drivers are very honest, in Panama City and tourist areas like Boquete some might try to take advantage – make local enquiries about the going rates and agree on a price before getting in. The establishment of an **Uber** system in Panama City and David has helped to curb some drivers overcharging.

Taxi drivers can also be hired as **tourist guides**, though most will only speak Spanish – ask at your accommodation for a recommended driver. There is no set charge, but around $15 an hour is the going rate in the capital for a driver who speaks English, $10–12 an hour for a driver who can only speak Spanish. Petrol costs also need to be factored in if you want to cover a substantial distance. A full day-trip round the Canal area (both Pacific and Atlantic sides), for example, might cost around $140 but you'll need to shop around.

By boat

Panama boasts more than 1500 islands so it's almost inevitable you'll require water transport at some stage, be it smooth sightseeing in a Canal transit or a bumpy water-taxi ride in Bocas. Fairly robust **ferries** equipped with life jackets and radio transmitters leave Panama City for Isla Taboga and the Archipiélago de las Perlas, according to regular timetables. In the remoter regions of eastern Gunayala, meanwhile, you could be seated on a plank in a leaking motorized **dugout** bailing out with a yoghurt carton, having spent a couple of hours asking round for a ride. Frequent **water-taxis** serve Bocas from Almirante for fixed fares ($6), whereas any trip to the Pacific island of Coiba may mean getting a group of interested people together and negotiating a deal with a fisher.

Travelling in a **skiff** (*panga*), is the norm among the communities of Gunayala and the Darién. If a boat is already heading the way you want to travel, as a **colectivo**, you can travel *como pasajero*, and the fare will be cheaper. Otherwise, private boat rental, or **viaje especial** (which needs to cover fuel and the boat operator's time), can be expensive; awareness of the going price for diesel will help when it comes to haggling, as will knowledge of the amount of fuel necessary to cover the distance given the size of the engine. Note that the seaworthiness of vessels varies enormously; some are overloaded and may lack sufficient life jackets even when heading for long trips on potentially hazardous waters. Every few months a boat somewhere sinks or capsizes and people **drown**. Make sure you check out your transport thoroughly before committing to a journey.

By bike

Away from the Interamericana and Panama City, **cycling** is pleasant – with wonderful views and quiet roads – and growing in popularity both as recreation and a means of transport (though you won't find cycle lanes or cycle routes). Mountain and e-bike **rental** is on the increase in tourist areas such as El Valle, Boquete, Bocas and Santa Fé, though the quality of the machine on offer and prices vary ($6–15/hr, $10–30/day). In Panama City you'll find rental places on the Cinta Costera and the Calzada de Amador, which both possess a cycle path, as well as on the fringes of Casco Viejo. Exodus (Ⓦexodustravels.com), Explore (Ⓦexplore.co.uk) and Responsible Travel (Ⓦresponsibletravel.com) offer **cycling holidays** from Nicaragua to Panama.

Accommodation

From secluded mountain ecolodges to thatched cane *cabañas* on deserted islands, and from backpackers' party hostels to smart boutique hotels, Panama offers a wide range of accommodation. Panama City has the greatest variety, though prices are generally a lot higher than elsewhere. In touristy areas such as Bocas and Boquete prices are also high, although a high price-tag is not always an indicator of quality. More lodgings now exist at the higher end of the market, with an increasing number of comfortable lodges, which are often foreign-owned, and B&Bs. However, beyond a couple of private islands, there is still little outside Panama City that could truly be described as luxury accommodation. In Gunayala you could just as likely be sleeping in a customary cane hut, while in the Darién you might be snoozing on a thin mattress on an open-sided raised traditional Emberá dwelling.

Types of lodging

Lodges usually offer a fair degree of comfort in pleasant natural surroundings, whereas places prefaced with **hospedaje**, **pensión** or **residencial** are generally much simpler small family-owned lodgings. The word **cabaña** may conjure up an image of a simple thatched hut in an idyllic natural setting, but can just as easily mean a dark, windowless cement cell in an unremarkable location. **Hostal** may signify a place with dorms for backpackers but is also a synonym for a family-run hotel. The term **hotel**, too, can cover a mixed bag from a plush international five-star high-rise to a dilapidated shack, and also includes the famous by-the-hour push-button motel, often referred to as "**un push**", which rents out rooms short-term for sexual liaisons. In no way unique to Panama, they are scattered all over the country, most visibly along the Interamericana, with such enticing names as *Sueño Lindo* (Sweet Dreams) or *Las Mil y Una Noches* (Thousand and One Nights). As for the much-abused prefix "**eco**", it may simply denote pleasant natural surroundings, and is no guarantee of sustainable environmental practices or social responsibility.

Finally, before committing to a weekend at a lodge or hotel in the countryside, especially one with a pool, check whether they also sell day passes (*pasadías*). With many mid-range lodgings still struggling to recover after the pandemic, some are offering day passes to help supplement their income. Although they try to minimize the disruption to the overnight guests by attempting to impose strict regulations about music and noise, it can mean that your relaxing retreat becomes a major pool- or picnic-party.

Facilities

Neither name nor price is much of an indication of what you'll get for your money, though a private **bathroom** is often squeezed into even rudimentary and minuscule lodgings. In the lowlands, even the cheapest establishments usually have **air conditioning**, though not

ACCOMMODATION PRICES

The accommodation price codes in this book refer to the cheapest rate for a **double room** (one double bed or *matrimonial*) for one night in high season (outside public holidays), including tourist tax (see page 30), with a private bathroom where available; we state in the reviews if only shared bathrooms are available. However, room prices are often negotiable, especially in low season. Dorm beds and camping are priced per person, unless otherwise stated, as are prices for **homestays**.

$ = $30 and under
$$ = $30–80
$$$ = $80–180
$$$$ = Over $180

necessarily **hot water**; in the highlands, air conditioning and fans are unnecessary and usually absent though hot water is almost always available. **Wi-fi** is widely available and free. Gunayala and the Darién are the two exceptions: in these areas coverage is limited and unreliable. As in most other Latin American countries, toilet paper should not be put down the **toilet**, but into the adjacent wastebasket, because it can clog the system in all but the most modern top-end hotels. If in doubt, enquire at reception.

Breakfast is not always provided, and where it is available, it may not be included in the rates. In our reviews and price coding we assume breakfast is not included unless otherwise stated.

Hostels

Panama's **hostel** scene took a hit during the Covid-19 pandemic when many hostels were forced to close down. Although new ones are beginning to open, international backpacker numbers have not yet reached pre-pandemic levels. Most hostels have common areas, shared kitchens, free wi-fi or internet access and bags of useful information about the surrounding area. Currently there are about two dozen in the country – mainly in Panama City, Bocas, Boquete, Playa Venao, David and Santa Catalina. Advance **booking**, where allowed, is advisable in high season. A dorm bunk varies in price from around \$11 to \$30, occasionally including coffee and/or a light breakfast, and, in lowland areas, may include air conditioning. Some establishments also offer private rooms at around \$30–40. Some of the **national parks** and protected areas offer dorm accommodation (usually \$15/person/night) and a shared kitchen.

Camping

There is virtually no organized **camping** in Panama, though a few lodgings allow tents if asked and some places provide tents to rent in summer (Dec–April). In rural communities you can almost always find someone willing to let you to camp on their land for a small fee. Alternatively, there are long swathes of empty beaches to pitch a tent on, although you should always seek local advice, since they are not universally safe; beach campers in touristy areas such as Santa Clara and Isla Bastimentos have periodically been subject to thefts and muggings. The **national parks** are more set up for camping, with set fees (usually \$6/person a night), but the sites rarely offer facilities beyond those shared with the park wardens at the park entrance: a toilet, cold-water shower and basic kitchen with limited utensils, though the current government is said to be undertaking changes to improve the situation.

Homestays

Homestays, a good budget accommodation option, often help the local economy more directly while providing an opportunity to engage in cross-cultural interaction. They may also be the only option during major fiestas in a town that is short of formal lodgings. In indigenous communities, such as in Gunayala and the Darién, a homestay is frequently the norm when overnighting in a village, away from the touristy western isles; you will need to arrange this with the chief or tourist coordinator on arrival (see pages 266 and 284).

Pricing and taxes

Most mid-range and high-end accommodation operates a dual **pricing system**: high-season rates (mid-Dec to April) generally coincide with the dry season, whereas the rest of the year counts as low season, when it's possible to find significant discounts, especially for online bookings. On top of high-season rates, some establishments in Panama City and the major holiday destinations hike their prices even higher for Carnaval, Easter (Semana Santa), Christmas and New Year. Some lodgings in places that are primarily weekend retreats, such as Isla Grande and El Valle, charge more from Friday to Sunday, occasionally demanding a two- or three-night minimum stay over the weekend.

Places with more than nine rooms are subject to a ten-percent **tourist tax** (though even smaller lodgings sometimes charge), which is not always included in the advertised rate. Note too that in mid-range hotels a double room often means a room with two double beds and you might have to specify one double bed (*una cama doble*, or *una cama matrimonial*) if you want to keep costs down, or ask about rooms with smaller, cheaper twin beds (*camas de tres cuartos*). Room costs are usually based on two people sharing, but many rooms have an extra single bed, which a third person can have for an extra \$15. Children under 12 are often allowed to stay for free.

Food and drink

Panamanian cuisine is infused with numerous culinary influences, notably Afro-Antillean, indigenous, Spanish, Chinese and American. Cosmopolitan Panama City offers the greatest variations

in terms of gastronomy and price, from an inexpensive plate of noodles and chicken in the public market to ornate fusion cuisine served on damask tablecloths. You can take your pick from a host of world cuisines, including American – and thankfully not just McDonald's and KFC.

In the capital, **Panamanian food** rarely features on the menus of the mid- to high-end restaurants, outside a few tourist-oriented venues, but in markets, hole-in-the-wall restaurants and out in the interior, it's much easier to find local specialities – often heavy on starch and frequently fried.

Outside the capital and the major tourist destinations of Boquete and Bocas, there is less variety and dining is often more informal and cheaper; travellers on a tight budget can easily find simple well-cooked food in *fondas* (basic restaurants), which offer *comida corriente* – also known as the *menú del día* – (meal of the day) for very little. Outside Panama City, vegetarians and vegans will be challenged since, as elsewhere in Central America, even the veggie staple of beans and rice can be cooked in pork fat. Your best bet is to head for a Chinese restaurant (*chifa*), which exist in most towns, or one of the proliferating pizzerias, or to stock up with the fresh fruit and vegetables that abound in local markets.

Predominantly self-service *cafeterías* – the Panamanian equivalent of American diners – keep going from around 6 or 7am until 11pm or midnight in the urban centres. Out in the countryside, local restaurants and *fondas* may also open for all three meals but shut shortly after nightfall, depending on demand.

Breakfast

Panama's filling **desayuno típico** (traditional breakfast) is aimed at sustaining workers for a hard day in the fields. Deep-fried favourites include tortillas (thick cornmeal cakes), *carimañolas* (mashed boiled yuca – cassava or manioc – stuffed with ground beef) and *hojaldres* (discs of sweetened leavened dough, which at best are delightfully crispy and tasty but at worst are chewy and dripping in grease). Costa Rica's national dish, *gallo pinto* (literally "speckled rooster"), is also popular, a moist rice, beans and onions mix often accompanied with a dollop of *natilla* – a local sour cream that is also lavished on strawberries in the Chiriquí Highlands. Fried or scrambled eggs are also frequently on offer.

For something lighter, head for a **panadería** (bakery) for a pastry and a shot of coffee, or pick up fresh fruit at the local market. In the more expensive hotels in Panama City and in European- or North American-owned establishments outside the capital, you can also expect combinations of cereals, fruit, yoghurt and toast, as well as fried or scrambled eggs.

RESTAURANT PRICES

The price codes used in this guide represent the cost of a two-course meal (including VAT), assuming an average-priced main from the menu, plus a drink. For cafés which do not sell full meals the price is more an indication of the relative cost of a coffee and cake in relation to other such cafés.

$ = $10 and under
$$ = $11–20
$$$ = $21–30
$$$$ = $31 and over

Lunch and dinner

Lunch in formal dining establishments is usually served from noon until 3pm, dinner from 6 or 7pm until around 10pm, with the midday meal usually offering better value for money.

While it's possible to grab a light **lunch** – a flaky *empanada* (pasty) with a beef-, pork-, chicken or cheese-based filling or an *emparedado* (sandwich) – in urban areas, for most Panamanians lunch is the main meal of the day. In the *fondas* and cheaper restaurants ordering an *almuerzo* or *menú del día* (lunch of the day) will get you a filling plate of chicken with rice, plus beans or lentils, or maybe fish and plantain down on the coast, for $5–6. Some places throw in a soup starter and dessert to give you a three-course set meal at very little extra cost. Posher restaurants in the city will sometimes offer a *menú ejecutivo* – a more fancy and slightly pricier set menu – but still good value – to their business clientele.

Set-meal **cenas** (dinner of the day) are available in the early evening in some places. Otherwise, **evening eating** is generally more low-key except in fancy urban restaurants.

Mid-range and high-end restaurants often add the seven-percent sales tax (ITBMS) on top of the bill, and some even add an obligatory ten-percent **service charge**, which is not always included on the menu price list. For our price codes in the Guide we have factored in these extra charges.

Street food and snacks

Street food, though not widespread, can range from chunks of fresh pineapple or watermelon to plantain

TRADITIONAL DISHES

PANAMANIAN MAINS

Non-vegetarians should not leave Panama without sampling the **national dish**, *sancocho*. Variations are served in many parts of Latin America and even within Panama the meal is prepared in numerous ways; essentially it's a hearty chicken-based soup with large chunks of yuca and other filling root vegetables, or maybe even plantain and sweetcorn, flavoured with culantro – a herb similar to coriander but more pungent – exemplifying the Caribbean culinary influence. Other Panamanian variations of ubiquitous **Latin dishes** include the unappetizing-sounding *ropa vieja* ("old clothes" – spicy shredded beef over rice), ceviche (white fish, shrimp or octopus marinated in lime juice with chopped onion and garlic, plus hot pepper and fresh coriander) and *mondongo* (a slow-cooked tripe- and chorizo-based stew with root vegetables, laced with garlic, and fresh coriander or culantro).

COASTAL CUISINE

Seafood is a Panamanian staple in both the Pacific and Caribbean lowlands. In the latter, the Afro-Antillean influence is dominant – typical dishes include rice cooked in coconut milk and seafood prepared with spices and judicious amounts of lime. *Corvina* (sea bass) is the most widely eaten fish, but you can also find snapper, grouper, dorado, shrimp, langoustines, crab and lobster, though you should refuse the last four if offered them during the closed season (Dec 1–April 15 in the Pearl Islands, March 1–June 30 along the Caribbean coast) unless you know they have come from a freezer. Locally farmed trout is a speciality of the Chiriquí Highlands.

GREENS AND SPICES

While starch and carbohydrates abound in most traditional foods, **greenery** is scarce. Don't be surprised if your salad accompaniment is merely a lettuce leaf supporting a slice of tomato and a couple of onion rings. Green vegetables are even conspicuous by their absence in many restaurants outside the capital, though they can often be found in local markets. Spices are generally used sparingly, but there's usually some *salsa picante* on the table to help add a kick.

crisps (*platanitos*) deep-fried on the spot. Small **roadside grills** often serve *carne en palito* (meat on a little stick) – fairly tiny kebabs comprising slivers of (occasionally spicy) marinated beef, which take the edge off your appetite. During the day, you'll also see men pushing carts laden with fluorescent liquids and blocks of ice around the main squares, peddling **raspados** – paper cones filled with shavings of ice, drizzled over with a sickly flavoured liquid, made still sweeter by a slurp of condensed milk and much loved by kids.

Alcoholic drinks

Beer is the most popular alcoholic drink; Panama's three main labels – Panamá, Balboa and Atlas – are all fairly inoffensive lagers, with Balboa, the current favourite, slightly more full-bodied. Balboa Ice, Panamá Lite, Atlas Golden Lite are low-alcohol additions to the range. Though none of these will set the pulses of beer aficionados racing, when ice-cold they do hit the spot. You'll pay a dollar to swig out of a bottle in a local *cantina*, and up to $6 to have your beer served in a frosted glass on a serviette in a plush restaurant. Imported beers such as Heineken and Budweiser, and even Guinness, are available in Panama City and tourist towns but are more expensive. Locally brewed craft beers are now widespread in the major tourist/expat areas; bank on paying from $4 upwards for beer on tap.

The national tipple, the transparent, throat-singeing **seco** (a rough sugar-cane spirit), is significantly more potent (35 percent) and more commonly consumed by men in the interior, particularly during fiestas – as is **rum**. **Chicha fuerte**, a potent fermented maize brew, is made in bulk for special celebrations, particularly among indigenous and *campesino* communities. Another lethal home-brew favoured by *campesinos* is **vino de palma**, made from fermented palm sap, whereas **guarapo** is sugar-cane juice distilled to knockout strength. **Wine** – usually Chilean or Californian – is widely available at reasonable prices in Panama City and in tourist areas such as Bocas and Boquete.

Non-alcoholic drinks

Fruit-based drinks feature prominently; in most parts of the country you can enjoy them with ice, safe in the knowledge that the water is drinkable (see page 33). Mango, pineapple, soursop, passion fruit, tamarind and a host of other fruits can be savoured in a range of forms: as a *jugo natural* (pure fruit juice), a *licuado* (a fresh fruit, water and sugar shake), a *batido* (a milk shake) or a *chicha* (a sweet maize-based fruit concoction, not to be confused with its alcoholic cousin *chicha fuerte*). The similar-sounding chicheme, a tasty Panamanian speciality of ground maize, milk, vanilla and cinnamon, most revered in La Chorrera, should be sampled, as should pipa – fresh coconut water sipped through a straw straight from the shell.

Outside the country, Panama's reputation as the world leader in producing gourmet **coffee** is a secret known only to connoisseurs; you can sample the most prized beans in Boquete and Panama City, though elsewhere you're more likely to be sipping the more mundane but perfectly satisfying Café Duran, which will be strong and is sometimes offered with condensed milk. While black **tea** is widely available in cities and tourist areas, tea lovers will usually have to content themselves with herbal varieties elsewhere – chamomile (*manzanilla*) or cinnamon (*canela*) are the most common.

Iced **tap water** is generally served on arrival in restaurants, except where water quality is poor – Bocas, the Darién and Gunayala – in which case you'll need to order mineral water.

Health

In the years when the transisthmus railroad and Canal were under construction, Panama was synonymous with disease, in particular yellow fever, malaria and cholera. Thankfully, times have changed, and most of Panama poses little threat to your health: yellow fever has been eradicated; malaria only persists in a few isolated areas; tap water is safe to drink in most of the country; and sophisticated medical care is widely available in the main population centres. Your most likely medical ailment will be travellers' diarrhoea from a change of diet and climate, or sunburn from overdoing it on the beach.

That said, you should ensure that your basic **inoculations** are up to date and consult a travel medical centre professional to help you decide what other precautions to take. If you intend only to explore the Canal area and chill on the beach, you'll probably need little more than sun block and insect repellent, but if you're bent on venturing into the Darién jungle, all kinds of insect- and water-borne hazards need to be considered. **Medical insurance** is essential (see page 35 and 44).

Inoculations

Most inoculations that involve multiple jabs need six to eight weeks to complete. There are no compulsory vaccinations to visit Panama but in addition to ensuring that your **routine injections** are current (tetanus, diphtheria and polio, and MMR), hepatitis A and typhoid are generally recommended, though you can also have a combined hepatitis A and B jab, advisable for long-term travellers. **Yellow fever** is nearly always flagged up as a hazard on health websites in relation to Panama, although the last documented case was in 1974. Nevertheless, there is still deemed to be a very slight risk of the disease in the Darién and remoter parts of Gunayala. Moreover, since November 2008 the Panamanian government has required travellers entering the country from countries where yellow fever is listed as endemic, such as Colombia and Brazil, to carry proof of vaccination at least ten days prior to entry – ironic given that Panama is also on the list – though this requirement is rarely enforced.

Rabies is another potential hazard, more from vampire bats in cattle-ranching areas than from feral dogs, and one that should only really be considered by travellers expecting to spend time in the remoter rural areas.

General precautions

A major plus is that **tap water** in most of Panama is safe to drink, which means the usual travel worries about avoiding ice in drinks and salads washed in ordinary water can be dispensed with. The exceptions are in Gunayala, much of the Darién and parts of Bocas. On the main tourist islands of Gunayala and Bocas bottled water, though expensive, is widely available, but it is less easily obtained in the Darién. That said, since disposing of non-organic waste such as plastic bottles is a particularly acute environmental issue in these areas, try to bring a water filter or use water purification tablets as much as possible. These are rarely available in Panama City (see page 38) so bring them with you. While vile-tasting chlorine or iodine tablets are still effective and widely available, most companies now produce tablets to neutralize the unpleasant aftertaste. Seek advice on the relative merits of chlorine versus iodine; the latter, for example, though considered more effective against giardia parasites, is generally not recommended for pregnant women. Campers with their own stove can of course boil water to sterilize it.

Since food safety is related to water safety and to food storage, exercise common sense when eating **salads** or **unpeeled fruit** in the few areas in Panama where the water is not potable. **Street food**, though frequently very tasty, is another potential minefield, particularly at fiestas when mounds of chicken and rice stand around in the hot sun for hours. Make sure the food is well cooked in front of you and, if the stall has been dishing up food all day, that any raw meat or fish has been stored in a cooler box with ice before cooking – and avoid anything swimming in mayonnaise.

Intestinal problems

Travellers' **diarrhoea** (TD) lasting a few days is the most common ailment encountered, as likely to be due to the change in diet and climate as to contaminated food or water-carrying bacteria, viruses or parasites. If you're afflicted by the runs, the best cure is to rest and rehydrate, drinking plenty of clean water with rehydration salts. Sachets of Dioralyte or Electolade are worth keeping in your first-aid kit, though equivalents are easily found in pharmacies in the major urban centres. Diarrhoea remedies such as Imodium and Lomotil should only be used in emergencies, such as when embarking on a long-distance plane journey or a jungle trek, since stopping the flow is not actually healthy. If symptoms persist, especially if there is blood in the stool or vomiting occurs, consult a doctor, who will probably prescribe a course of antibiotics.

Sunburn and dehydration

Skin cancer is on the increase, largely because of overexposure to UV radiation – indeed it is the most prevalent form of cancer in the US. In the fierce tropical sun of Panama, a high-factor sun cream (SPF 15 or higher with both UVA and UVB protection), a sun hat and sunglasses are an absolute must. Up to forty percent of the sun's rays can be reflected back up from water or sand, even if you're sitting in the shade; nor is an overcast day free from damaging UV light. When travelling in a dugout – a likely scenario if exploring the Darién or Gunayala – you could be faced with hours without any protection. Serious sunburn, sunstroke and heatstroke are therefore all very real health hazards and far more likely than catching a tropical disease. Keeping up your fluid intake to avoid **dehydration** is essential.

Malaria

There is low risk of **malaria** in more remote areas of the Caribbean lowlands in Bocas and Veraguas, and a slightly higher risk east of the Canal, in the Darién and in more isolated areas of Gunayala. Transmitted by a parasite in the saliva of an infected anopheles mosquito (active from dusk to dawn), its symptoms – fever, chills, headaches and muscle pains – are easily confused with flu.

It is most effectively combated through **prevention** – wearing long loose sleeves and trousers for protection, dousing yourself in repellent and sleeping under a mosquito net or in screened rooms. Most effective chemical insect **repellents** contain DEET, with the 25–35 percent varieties considered adequate for most needs. However, a few recent studies have started to raise questions about DEET's possible neurological side-effects as well as damage to the environment. Whatever the medical opinions on the subject, you have to wonder about a solution that will melt your pen if it gets too close. Recently, more organic, non-chemical products, based on oils such as eucalyptus, citronella, cedar or verbena, are appearing on the market. They are generally more expensive but give less fierce protection, which wears off much more quickly. They can be effective enough when used with other preventive measures, although if you are in a malarial area you might want to stick to DEET. Mosquito **coils** are widely available across Panama, even in small villages; if you're seeking a natural alternative, candles can help deter the insects. In neither case should they be used in enclosed indoor environments. It's a good idea to carry a travel mosquito **net** if you're intending to travel widely in the Darién or spend time in the national parks.

A range of **anti-malarial tablets** are on the market, all of which should be bought prior to arriving in Panama and started in advance of visiting the malarial area, though a public medical centre (*centro de salud*) in a malarial area should stock a supply for post-exposure treatment. West of the Canal, chloroquine is the drug of choice, generally taken once a week a fortnight in advance of entering a malarial area and for four weeks afterwards. East of the Canal, where mosquitoes are chloroquine-resistant, mefloquine (also known as Larium) is often prescribed, though it can have particularly severe side effects. Malarone is a less controversial alternative but is currently the most expensive anti-malarial drug on the market. It is taken daily only two days before entering an infected area, to be continued for a week after leaving. Whatever you choose, it is important to finish the course of anti-malarials because of the time lag between bite and infection. If you become ill with flu-like symptoms after returning home, consult a doctor and inform them you've been to a malarial risk area.

Other bites and stings

Taking steps to avoid being bitten by **insects** is of paramount importance (see page 34). In addition to malaria, mosquitoes can transmit **dengue fever**, which induces flu-like symptoms similar to malaria but with more extreme aches and has been on the increase in Central America and the Caribbean in recent years. **Sandflies** (*chitras*) are a more likely pest for travellers, proliferating during the rainy season (roughly May to mid-Dec), and not only at the beach; they're almost invisible, so you will become aware of them only when they bite. Sandfly bites itch more and for longer than mosquito bites – calamine lotion or antihistamine cream will usually reduce the aggravation. In various parts of Panama bites from an infected sandfly can cause cutaneous leishmaniasis, whose symptoms can remain dormant for several months before sores and swellings break out on the skin. Though there is no vaccine, the sores may disappear of their own volition though not for many months or even years. Specialist medical advice should be sought and the decision whether and how to treat the symptoms depends on a number of factors such as the strain of the leishmania, and the risk of it evolving into the more damaging mucosal leishmaniasis. The most common treatment is a multiday systemic intravenous treatment.

An overfamiliarity with Indiana Jones films can lead to the misconception that the greatest danger in the rainforest is a **snake bite**. While Panama has its share of venomous snakes – bushmaster, fer-de-lance and coral for starters – you are unlikely to see one, let alone get bitten. Nevertheless, donning long trousers and closed shoes, or (even better) boots, reduces the risk, as does avoiding walking in the forest at night. Should a snake manage to get its fangs into you, immobilize the affected area, apply a light-pressure bandage (not tourniquet) above and below the bite and seek immediate medical attention. Even a local medical centre should have some antivenin.

There's a whole host of **other beasts** on land that may bite or sting, but only when threatened – scorpions (more commonly seen at night) and some spiders, for example – while in the sea jellyfish, sting rays and fire coral can all be painful.

If you are prone to allergic reactions to bites and stings, make sure you carry some antihistamine tablets, which can reduce swelling and itchiness, as well as antihistamine cream or calamine lotion to cool and ease the pain.

Accessing medical care

Both state and private **medical care** is very good in Panama, particularly in Panama City; many doctors work in the public-sector hospitals in the morning and run private clinics in the afternoon. The main problem the public sector faces is a lack of resources, particularly in the more remote rural villages, so most Panamanians who can afford private health care, as well as almost all expats, will head for a **private clinic**, where service is likely to be more immediate. The average cost of a consultation with a private doctor starts at $50, provided no X-rays or laboratory tests need doing, whereas a doctor at the local government-run clinic will see you for under $10.

While **travel insurance** may cover costs, it will only do so after you file a claim on your return; you still need to be able to access sufficient funds to cover the bills at the time. Many doctors in the main cities have trained in the US at some stage and so speak good English. The US Embassy has a list of **bilingual doctors** in Panama City on its website (Ⓦpa.usembassy.gov/services).

Medical resources for travellers

There are several useful **online resources**, though their information may not be sufficiently nuanced for your needs. The websites listed here generally note travel medical centres, where you can get jabs, and give general advice on the most common ailments and diseases that you might encounter.

Travel medical centre professionals generally have access to more detailed and specific health information; you are strongly advised to consult them well in advance of your trip, as well as carrying out your own research.

US AND CANADA

Travel Health Ⓦcanada.ca/en/public-health/services/travel-health.html. Extensive list of travel health centres.

Centers for Disease Control and Prevention (CDC) Ⓦhttps://wwwnc.cdc.gov/travel. Official US government travel health site that's laden with info and runs a 24-hour hotline.

Public Health Agency of Canada Ⓦcanada.ca/en/public-health.html. Distributes free pamphlets on travel health and provides a comprehensive list of travel clinics in the country.

Travellers' Medical and Vaccination Centre Ⓦtmvc.com. List of travel health centres in Canada and vaccination costs plus brief travel health tips.

UK AND IRELAND

Fitfortravel Ⓦfitfortravel.nhs.uk. Excellent NHS (Scotland) public access site with country-specific advice, the latest health bulletins and information on immunizations.

Hospital for Tropical Diseases Travel Clinic UK Ⓦ uclh.nhs.uk. Offers private travel clinic services and is the place to go if you experience symptoms of a tropical disease on your return to the UK.
MASTA (Medical Advisory Service for Travellers Abroad) Ⓦ masta-travel-health.com. List of affiliated travel clinics where you can get vaccinations and detailed country-specific health briefs.
National Travel Health Network and Centre Ⓦ nathnac.net. Excellent website for health professionals and the travelling public providing factsheets on travel health risks and a free database of country-specific health info.
Tropical Medical Bureau Ⓦ tmb.ie. List of travel clinics in Ireland and country-specific info from US consular service.

AUSTRALASIA AND SOUTH AFRICA

South African Society of Travel Medicine Ⓦ sastm.org.za. Primarily aimed at medical professionals, it also provides information on common tropical diseases and news updates.
Travellers' Medical and Vaccination Centre Ⓦ traveldoctor.com.au. User-friendly site listing travel clinics in Australia and New Zealand plus accessible factsheets on travel health and postings of health alerts worldwide.

The media

Aside from one government TV channel and one radio station, the media in Panama is privately owned, and tends to consist of a diet of news, soap operas, reality TV, quiz shows and sport. The five national daily Spanish-language newspapers – and several Chinese-language papers, catering to the country's two-hundred-thousand-strong Chinese-Panamanian community – are available from street vendors in urban areas and in supermarkets countrywide, as well as online. It's hard to escape TV in Panama – screens adorn most eating and drinking establishments, even upmarket restaurants, and are standard in most hotel rooms.

Newspapers

Although the press is deemed free – especially in comparison to some other Latin American Countries – it is mostly owned by the country's elite, and journalists are increasingly self-censoring their coverage of government corruption and cover-ups for fear of legal prosecution. The most respected paper is the conservative *La Prensa* (Ⓦ prensa.com), which also produces informative supplements with in-depth writing and interesting features on tourism, history and culture. *La Estrella de Panamá* (Ⓦ laestrella.com.pa) and *Panamá América* (Ⓦ panamaamerica.com.pa) also count as "quality press", with *El Siglo* (Ⓦ elsiglo.com) and *La Crítica* (Ⓦ critica.com.pa) the popular tabloid options.

Given the large US expat population, there is no shortage of free English-language news aimed at, and primarily written by, ex-pats, such as *Panama Now Online* (Ⓦ panamanowonline.com), *Newsroom Panama* (Ⓦ newsroom panama.com) and, in Bocas del Toro, the *Bocas Breeze* (Ⓦ thebocasbreeze.com). They occasionally contain some useful listings.

Liberally sprinkled round hotel lobbies and restaurants around the country are: the free bilingual weekly *The Visitor/El Visitante* (Ⓦ thevisitorpanama.info), which offers a bland summary of Panamanian news, features and a decent listings section of events in the main tourist zones of Panama City, Bocas and Boquete.

TV and radio

On evenings in a bar or *cafetería* you're likely to catch an unremittingly awful soap opera (*telenovela*) on TV. The main terrestrial channels are TVN (government-owned), Telemetro and RPC. Many middle-class Panamanians have access to cable TV with channels in Spanish and English.

Festivals

Panama is awash with festivals and public holidays. Alongside the numerous commemorations of historical events, there are copious Catholic celebrations – including each town's patron-saint bash, agricultural fairs and cultural extravaganzas that reflect the country's ethnic diversity. Whatever the differences in the details, they all demand the ability to survive several days and nights of music, dancing and processions, fuelled on mountains of street food and gallons of booze. Head and shoulders above the rest stands Carnaval – generally referred to in the plural as Los Carnavales – a five-day marathon of hedonism at its most outlandish in the tiny Azuero town of Las Tablas (see box, page 167). Major festivals are listed opposite and in the relevant sections of the Guide. Public holidays are listed in our "Opening hours and public holidays" section (see page 47).

A festival calendar

JANUARY

Desfilé de las Mil Polleras 2nd Sat in Jan. A fabulous skirt-swishing musical parade in Las Tablas, with every kind of *pollera* imaginable on display, from the vibrant multi-coloured *pollera Congo* to the elaborate embroidered *pollera de gala*.

Feria de las Flores y del Café Mid-Jan. Ten-day celebration in Boquete to mark the coffee harvest with carpets of flowers, food and craft stalls. Daytime family entertainment is followed by night-time discos.

FEBRUARY

Revolución Dule Feb 25. Celebrates the Guna Revolution of 1925, their Independence Day, with colourful reenactments of battles against the Panamanian authorities held across the *comarca*.

Carnaval Five days ending at dawn on Ash Wednesday. Wild partying and processions – celebrated countrywide, but especially in Las Tablas and Panama City, with an aquatic parade on the Saturday in Penonomé.

MARCH

Semana Santa or Holy Week March–April. Celebrated everywhere, but most colourfully on the Azuero Peninsula.

Festival de la Pollera Congo, Máscaras y Bailes Some time in March or April. Annual weekend event in Portobelo, showcasing Afro-Colonial culture and resistance to the Spanish conquest.

APRIL

Feria de las Orquídeas Five days in early April. Boquete festival featuring copious orchids, craft stalls and cultural events.

Feria Internacional de Azuero Ten days in April. Major agricultural fair in La Villa de Los Santos with stalls, presentations and competitions reflecting the area's colonial and cattle-farming traditions.

MAY AND JUNE

Festival de Corpus Christi Late May/early June. Celebrated across the country but most spectacularly in La Villa de Los Santos, with processions and dramatic devil dances.

JULY

Fiestas Patronales de la Virgen del Carmen July 16. On Isla Taboga the Holy Virgin gets to circumnavigate the island in a procession of decorated boats.

Fiestas Patronales de la Santa Librada July 20–22. A mix of religious and folkloric parades in Las Tablas, incorporating the Festival de la Pollera, which showcases Panama's gorgeous national dress.

AUGUST

Festival del Manito Ocueño Thurs–Sun, dates vary. In Ocú, on the Azuero Peninsula, this lively folk festival features a mock duel and peasant wedding.

SEPTEMBER

Festival de la Mejorana Late Sept. Panama's premier folk festival, in Guararé, on the Azuero Peninsula, involving five days of music, dancing and parades.

OCTOBER

Feria de Río Tigre Mid-Oct. Multiday festivity of Guna culture, celebrated in Digir Dubbu (Isla Tigre) Gunayala.

Festival del Cristo Negro Oct 21. The most revered pilgrimage in the country, attracting thousands bedecked in purple robes to Portobelo.

NOVEMBER

Primer Grito de la Independencia Nov 10. The "First Cry of Independence", celebrated in La Villa de los Santos as part of "El Mes de la Patria". Patriotic flag-waving parades and marching bands, attended by the president.

Sports and outdoor activities

Both inside and outside the parks, Panama offers a host of outdoor activities, from swinging through the canopy on a zip line to tracking tapir prints in the mud of the Darién or lolling on a deserted beach. Some of these pursuits can be experienced as efficient packages from Panama City; others will need to be arranged more informally on the spot and a few require no organization whatsoever. Already renowned as a world-class birdwatching and sport fishing destination, Panama is also developing a reputation for outstanding diving, white-water rafting and wilderness hiking.

Several excellent **tour operators**, providing knowledgeable bilingual or multilingual naturalist guides work out of Panama City and offer tours around the country (see page 77), though for the more distant locations, such as Bocas del Toro, Boquete or Coiba, you are better off looking for operators closer to the destination; they are listed in the relevant chapters of the Guide.

Birdwatching

Panama offers first-class **birdwatching**. Boasting around a 1000 recorded species of bird, including 55 varieties of hummingbird and spectacular show birds such as the emerald-and-ruby resplendent quetzal (easy to see in the Chiriquí Highlands), the country also contains the world's largest concentration of harpy eagles (most likely to be spotted in the Darién or in Amistad). Though Panama acts as a magnet for serious twitchers laden with tripods, checklists and hefty avian tomes (see page 310), it might persuade even those who have viewed birdwatching as a dull pastime, involving hours of trying to identify one indistinguishable brown bird from another, to think again. It's hard not to be impressed by the dazzling flashes of parrots and macaws in flight or the ludicrous painted bills of toucans swooping across the treetops.

Since many of these glamorous birds spend much of their time tantalizingly high up in the canopy, it is worth splashing out on at least a small pair of binoculars, which will significantly enhance your birdwatching experience. So too will engaging a **guide**. Alongside the big-name tour operators in the capital (see page 77) there are small-scale specialists, such as Birding Panama (W birdingpanama.com) and Birding in Panama (W panamabirdguide.com), as well as numerous local residents scattered across the country, whose contact details are given in the relevant chapters of the Guide. Half-day rates for a professional bilingual naturalist guide contracted in the capital can range from $120–180 per person, partly depending on how far you travel, but if you want something less expensive or just want someone to be able to point out some of the more obvious species (not necessarily in English), engaging a local guide from one of the villages for a few hours can cost as little as $30–40. The Panama Audubon Society (T 232 5977, W audubonpanama.org) holds birding hikes around Panama City and the canal zone on the first Sunday morning of every month. These are advertised on their social media and are open to members and non-members (for a small charge).

Hiking

Panama also affords a myriad **hiking** opportunities. Vast wilderness areas such as La Amistad and the Darién are ideal for adventurous multiday hikes across the isthmus, often involving bivouacking, staying in indigenous villages, fording rivers and wading through metres of mud. Aside from the Panama City operators, guides can be engaged locally in places such as Santa Fé de Veraguas, Boquete and Cerro Punta, at far less cost, though you'll need some Spanish. If you fancy a more modest outing, parks in the canal basin offer a range of trails from a gentle circular route to a reasonably strenuous rainforest tramp following in the footsteps of the conquistadors. Note you'll need warm clothes for the chilly nights in the peaks of western Panama.

Basic hiking and camping gear can often be bought at any of the Novey (W novey.com.pa) or Do It Center (W doitceter.com.pa) shops in the main cities. **Outdoor Adventure** (W tiendasoutdoor.com) has a store in Albrook Mall, and several other shopping centres in Panama City, as well as in Penonomé, Chitré and Santiago; it offers a limited range of shoes, clothing and hiking and camping accessories. However, the best range is offered in Decathlon (W decathlon.com.pa), which has two stores in Panama City, and Wanderlust, an independent store in David (T 6267 8924).

Do It Center in Albrook Mall sometimes stocks water filters and water purification tablets, but you are better off bringing them with you.

Rafting and kayaking

The fast-flowing rivers that tumble down from the highlands of western and central Panama, carving their way through dramatic scenery, have put Panama on the map for **whitewater rafting** and **kayaking**, although damming for hydro-electric power stations and reservoirs, along with climate change, mean that at certain times river levels may be too low. The top destination is the Río Chiriquí Viejo, which runs parallel with the Costa Rican border. which can produce Category IV to V rapids depending upon conditions, but more often averages at Class III. The rivers are at their wildest during the heavy rains (roughly May to mid-Dec), but you'll manage to find enough water flowing somewhere to raft and kayak year-round. Boquete operators (see page 188) are best placed to organize Chiriquí destinations, while companies in the capital head for rivers in the Chagres basin or in neighbouring Coclé province.

Sea-kayaking is growing in popularity, offering a great way to explore rocky coastlines and mangroves, and to access remote beaches among the islands of Gunayala, or round Coiba and Boca Chica in Chiriquí, or round Portobelo or Bocas del Toro along the Caribbean coast.

Diving and snorkelling

Diving in the **Pacific** can be truly spectacular, particularly in the Golfo de Chiriquí and the Archipiélago de las Perlas. Pick the right time of year (see page 313) and you're likely to spot manta rays, moray eels, sharks, schools of dolphins and migrating humpback and sperm whales – some scuba operators offer whale-watching tours. Large pelagic fish such as marlin, sailfish, amberjack, dorado and tuna also abound, which reel in sport fishing enthusiasts too. The jewel in this marine crown is Isla Coiba; located on the edge of the second-largest reef on the Pacific side of the Americas, it offers world-class diving.

Among the coral reefs of Bocas and Portobelo on the **Caribbean** side, diving can also be enjoyable, if not as spectacular as at some other Caribbean destinations. Visibility can vary enormously, especially after heavy rain. However, the rainbow-coloured soft corals of Cayo Crawl off Isla Bastimentos make for breathtaking **snorkelling** and there are plenty of other fun spots to explore.

Reputable local **dive shops** operate out of Bocas, Portobelo, Santa Catalina, Isla Contadora and Pedasí, on the Azuero Peninsula, while Scuba Panama (T 261 3841, W scubapanama.com), the country's oldest outfit, organizes expeditions from Panama City.

Surfing

With two long coastlines, Panama offers waves of all kinds to suit novices and expert **surfers**. Away from the renowned hot spots you can have the beach almost to yourself, though the surfing infrastructure (hostels, bars, restaurants and regular public transport) may also be lacking.

Local surfers confined to Panama City tend to dash to the nearby Pacific beaches of Panama Oeste for a weekend escape, such as El Palmar and Playa Malibu. For top-drawer surfing on the **Pacific coast** (generally best May–Nov), head for the internationally renowned breaks round **Santa Catalina**. In October waves here can reach 2m or more, though when there is a swell a good ride is guaranteed year-round. **Playa Venao**, on the south coast of the Azuero Peninsula, arguably offers the country's best-known beach break, and also attracts international competitions; the more remote **Cambutal**, which has beach and point breaks, and can catch big waves, lies further west. On the eastern side of the peninsula, the small town of **Pedasí** is within reach of several surfing spots; **Playa Morrillo**, on the western flank, is up-and-coming.

On the **Caribbean coast** (best Dec–March), **Bocas del Toro** is the standout, offering varied breaks for beginners and experts – including the monster reef bottom wave of Silverbacks – plus welcoming bars and a decent après-surf scene. Less-well-known surfing spots lie **east of Portobelo**, such as Isla Grande or Nombre de Dios and Palenque.

W surfeapanama.com and the Panamanian surfing association's Facebook page, W facebook.com/surfAPS, offer **information** (in Spanish); check also Surf Captain (W surfcaptain.com), which also has an app, for the swell forecasts for the best-known spots.

Sport fishing

According to one reading of the indigenous language Cueva, Panama means "abundance of fish", so it is no surprise that the country offers some phenomenal **fishing**. The Bahía de Piñas on the Pacific coast of the Darién, location of the exclusive *Tropic Star Lodge* (W tropicstarlodge.com), is widely considered to be the world's top saltwater fishing destination, with the Golfo de Chiriquí, and Coiba in particular, a close second and the Islas Perlas not far behind.

Foreign-owned **fishing lodges** are mushrooming along the Pacific coast, most of which offer multiday package deals that cover accommodation, meals and fishing excursions costing up to several thousand dollars. Recommended outfits include Panama Big Game Fishing (W panama-sportfishing.com), Coiba Adventure Sportfishing (W marlinpanama.com) and Pesca Panama (W pescapanama.com).

Other activities

The Boquete Tree Trek (see page 186) can justifiably be considered the **canopy adventure** to top them all, boasting a dozen zip lines – more modest versions exist in El Valle (see page 137), near Portobelo (see box, page 117) and on Isla Bastimentos (see page 233). Similar adrenaline surges are guaranteed when **kitesurfing** at Punta Chame on the Pacific coast (see page 132).

Pass by any small fishing village and you can usually find a **boatman** willing to take you for a chug round the mangroves, drop you off for a laze on a deserted beach or even throw a line for a spot of fishing. Similarly relaxing is a plod along an empty beach or through the rainforest on **horseback**, which offers the chance to soak up the scenery without frightening the wildlife – though don't necessarily expect a safety helmet, or a saddle that fails to remind you what you've been doing for the next week.

Mountain-bikers in search of company might consider contacting Boa Panama (W facebook.com/groups/boapanama) for English- and Spanish-speaking contacts; this association of recreational off-road cycling enthusiasts organizes weekend outings. Rock-climbers and abseilers (rappellers) should head for Boquete, where the country's first rock-climbing school (W es-la.facebook.com/RockClimbingPanama.com) has taken off.

Panama's fabulous scenery can also be explored on horseback; popular destinations include Boquete and Santa Fé, or along the beaches of Bocas del Toro.

Spectator sports

With a highly ranked national team, and a number of successful major-league baseball stars to its credit, **baseball** is Panama's national sport. An inexpensive and captivating evening's entertainment awaits if you attend one of the fiercely contested national-league matches that take place in the dry season (late Dec to April) – check Ⓦfedebeis.com.pa for fixtures – particularly in the more intimate stadiums in the interior. Under the floodlights, a raucous spirit prevails, with people partying in the stands and screaming to the accompaniment of brass bands and drums, with plenty of tasty street-food on hand.

Close behind comes **boxing**, which has produced more Panamanian world champions than any other sport. Of these, three stand out: "Panama Al Brown", a bantamweight from Colón, who became the first Latin American world champion in 1929, Eusebio Pedroza, who remained world featherweight champion for nine years (1978–85), and Roberto Durán, who won numerous world titles at various weights during the 1970s and 80s. The stadium named after him (Arena Roberto Durán) is the venue for boxing fights and other events. A film of his life (entitled *Hands of Stone*, after his nickname) was made in 2016, with an all-star cast including Robert de Niro, Ruben Blades and Usher. In the 2024 Paris Olympics boxer Athena Bylon made history by winning Panama's first Olympic boxing medal and the first for a female athlete.

Less illustrious, though still given passionate support when the occasion demands, the men's national **football** team won its first international trophy in 2009, triumphing in the Central American championships. This was followed by qualification for the 2018 World Cup – a first which merited a public holiday. The women's team also managed to qualify for the World Cup in 2023. Generally, though, both teams can do

with all the help they can muster so if you fancy going to cheer them on, check out Ⓦfepafut.com, although the professional league matches played out in the low-key stadiums in the interior, at Santiago or David, may provide greater entertainment.

Panama also excels in **horse racing**, which you can see in Panama City (Ⓦhipodromo.com; see box, page 85).

National parks

Almost a quarter of Panama's land lies within the boundaries of its fourteen national parks – add in reserves, refuges and other protected areas, and the figure is more than a third. Under siege on all sides from urban development, pollution and deforestation (see page 314), these nevertheless constitute one of Panama's major attractions: you can trek through pristine rainforest, explore Spanish colonial forts, haul yourself up volcanic peaks or swim with sharks and manta rays. Some, such as the legendary Darién, Central America's largest wilderness, and Cerro Hoya, at the tip of the Azuero Peninsula, are particularly inaccessible and involve a lot of planning, perseverance and often money to reach; others, such as Camino de Cruces and Soberanía, are a stone's throw from Panama City,

making an easy day-trip and providing a great opportunity to see some of Panama's dazzling birdlife.

Panama's ecosystems are astonishingly diverse – little surprise given that the country stands at the crossroads of two oceans and two continents, a vital link in the biological corridor between North and South America. Since the country is so slender, many of the parks offer a hugely varied **topography**. Several straddle the continental divide, ranging from lofty moss-covered cloud forest pierced by rugged peaks to humid lowland rainforest; others protect dense swathes of mangrove, harbouring caimans, crocodiles and crustaceans while protecting vital mud flats for thousands of migratory birds. The three **marine parks** offer coral reefs, turquoise waters and islands encircled with sugar-sand beaches and coated in tropical forest that supports everything from fluorescent poison dart frogs to primordial iguanas. Ruined colonial fortresses, a crumbling Devil's Island penitentiary and a rare tract of dry tropical forest also lie within national park boundaries.

Visiting the parks

Panama's national parks are managed by the **Ministry of the Environment** (Ministerio de Ambiente), often referred to as **MiAmbiente**, or **MIA** (Ⓦmiambiente.gob.pa/ecoturismo360). Dealing with tourists is in theory the job of Panama's national tourist agency, the ATP (see page 49) but you are more likely to come into contact with the *guardaparques* (park wardens), who are often very helpful and likely to be of more direct use, though they will only speak Spanish.

MIA offices are generally open from Monday to Friday from 8am to 4pm, though if the office is located inside a park, there will be someone around all the time, even if the office is theoretically closed.

Park fees range from $20 per person for Isla Coiba, to $10 for Bastimentos, Isla Iguana and Isla Cañas, and $3–5 for the other national parks and protected areas. Rates are daily, and although some camping fees are indicated on the website, others are not. They are generally $6/person for most parks, but more for Coiba and Darién.

Travel essentials

Accessible travel

Organized tourism is in its infancy in Panama and awareness of the needs and rights of **people with disabilities** is a fairly recent phenomenon – they

PAYING NATIONAL PARK FEES

Since 2024, all visitors must pay park fees in advance of visiting the park, either by paying into the Mi Ambiente bank account (Mi Ambiente – Fondo de Ingreso, current account number: 010000163794, Banco Nacional de Panamá) or by wrestling with MIA's temperamental online payment system (Ⓦclickpago.merchantprocess.net/Clientv2/client/MiAmbienteAreasProtegidas). Ostensibly, the online system was to save paper (and the planet) and reduce bureaucracy; in practice it's a nightmare, and for international visitors paying with a credit card that charges for overseas transactions, it's an unnecessary additional expense. Take a screenshot as proof of online purchase.

In Coiba and Bastimentos, the tour operator will probably sort out the payment for you, though the park fees are rarely included in the tour rate – check in advance. For independent travellers who turn up at a park or reserve without having paid online or deposited the money into the MIA bank account, you may be refused entry – it all depends on the place and the wardens. If there's an internet connection, the park warden may ask you to pay online there and then; if there's no signal, they may just wave you in without paying, but tourists arriving in Isla Iguana, for example, have been turned away as they disembark from the boat if they can't provide proof of payment. In several places – along the Camino de Oleoducto in Soberanía, for example – you're unlikely to see a warden.

In terms of accommodation, several parks have bunkhouses (*refugios*) with bunk beds but no bedding ($15 per person per night), and the kitchen usually has basic utensils, for use by both visitors and the resident park wardens. Camping costs $6 per person per night. These costs also need to be paid in advance. Since trails are often not well signposted you may also need to hire the services of a park warden to act as a guide (around $30–35/person for a full day), which can be paid in cash on the day.

were only granted equal rights by law in 1999. As a result, Panama isn't really geared up to accommodate travellers with disabilities. That said, Tocumen International Airport and many mid-range and luxury hotels in Panama City have "wheelchair access", though none addresses the spectrum of special needs. The three resorts mentioned in our "Travelling with children" section (see below) also advertise "disabled access" (as in "wheelchair access") and most cruise ships that take in Panama tend to be suitably equipped. Eco-Adventure International (Ⓦeaiadventure.com), and DisabledHolidays.com (Ⓦdisabledholidays.com) both organize customized **tours** to Panama for travellers with disabilities.

Costs

Costs are higher than in countries such as Guatemala and Nicaragua, and have risen to Costa Rican levels in some areas. Staying in dorms, eating in inexpensive *fondas* and using public transport you can easily survive on $40–50 a day, less if camping, with anything from $40–160 on top for a day's guided excursion – snorkelling, surfing, fishing, horseriding or kayaking, for instance.

Staying in more comfortable accommodation and eating in more touristy restaurants can mean a daily food and lodgings budget of $120 with excursions and maybe car rental (minimum $35/day) on top, though a lot depends on whether you stay in Panama City and the Canal area, where prices are significantly higher, or make for the interior.

High-end accommodation – only really available in Panama City and at a handful of resorts across the rest of the country – will set you back more than $250 a night, with a three-course meal (without drinks) in one of the city's top restaurants averaging $80. Tipping should not add too much to any costs (see page 47).

Crime and personal safety

The presence of FARC guerrillas, paramilitaries, cocaine smugglers and people traffickers in the Darién jungle has helped promote the popular misconception that Panama is a dangerous country to visit. In fact, even though crime seems to be on the increase, especially in urban areas, Panama is still much safer than most other Central American states, with only a few areas to avoid or in which to take special care.

The eastern strip of the **Darién** and **Gunayala** that borders Colombia tops the danger list as a no-go area; it contains the fabled Darién Gap, which has long held a fascination for travellers seeking adventure by hacking through jungle to the border. While this was difficult but feasible, it is now very dangerous and prohibited; since the 1990s several travellers attempting the overland route have been kidnapped or killed. There are still ways of visiting the Darién safely both in an organized group and as an independent traveller, and for crossing to or from Colombia on the Caribbean side by boat (see box, page 25), all of which can provide excitement without putting your life in acute danger.

The second major trouble spot is **Colón**, where extreme caution needs to be exercised even during the day (see page 101). **Panama City** also has several areas to avoid, generally poor neighbourhoods with inadequate housing and high unemployment. **Violent crime** is on the increase, but ninety percent of this is estimated to be drug-related, often among rival gangs; petty crime too is on the rise in some areas, especially where there are significant economic disparities between the general population and those who are making decent money from tourism, such as in Bocas. That said, by far the vast majority of visitors enjoy their time in Panama without incident, with the main issues being theft of money and/or passport and the odd traffic accident. The usual common-sense guidelines apply.

The police

If you are a **victim of crime**, report to the Policía de Turismo (Tourist Police) in Panama City (see page 86) or the main police station in other towns. Even though your possessions are unlikely to be recovered, a police report (*denuncia*) will be required to make an insurance claim. At the police station, you will probably need to present your ID, which by law you should always carry with you, though it is acceptable to carry a photocopy of your passport details or show a copy on your phone.

Culture and etiquette

No society is homogenous but Panama is particularly diverse, and customs vary widely. Overall, though, people are very courteous – driving in Panama City aside – and quite formal. **Greetings** are customary before any exchange, such as asking for information, and the "usted" form of address is preferred to the "tu" form, which is reserved for close friends – although this is beginning to change among younger people or those who have spent significant periods of time out of the country. This formality is also reflected in **clothing**, particularly by the urban middle classes, who like to dress up to go out. Dress is also important on the beach; no nude sunbathing is permitted in Panama, except on one beach on Isla Contadora (see page 122), and beachwear should stay on the beach – cover your body in town.

ROUGH GUIDES TRAVEL INSURANCE

Looking for travel insurance? Rough Guides partners with top providers worldwide to offer you the best coverage. Policies are available to residents of anywhere in the world, with a range of options whether you are looking for single-trip, multi-country or long-stay insurance. There's coverage for a wide range of adventure sports, 24-hour emergency assistance, high levels of medical and evacuation cover and a stream of travel safety information. Even better, roughguides.com users can take advantage of these policies online 24/7, from anywhere in the world – even if you're already travelling. To make the most of your travels and ensure a smoother experience, it's always good to be prepared for when things don't go according to plan. For more information, go to Ⓦ roughguides.com/bookings/insurance.

Suitably modest attire (covered shoulders, no shorts) is appreciated in churches. When visiting **indigenous communities**, cultural sensitivity is particularly important as regards dress, alcohol and photography (see box, page 257).

Drugs

Drugs are widely available in Panama, **marijuana** and **cocaine** in particular, and you're quite likely to be offered something at some stage. However, possession of either is illegal and makes those caught liable for a prison sentence. While the police might – and only might – turn a blind eye to a joint being smoked discreetly on a deserted beach, being caught with weed trying to cross a border can have serious consequences. Possession of cocaine is punished very heavily, in part because Panama is a major trans-shipment hub for drugs heading from South America to the US and Europe

Electricity

The **voltage** in Panama is 110 volts and sockets take flat two- and occasionally three-pronged plugs. **Power cuts** and subsequent surges occur fairly frequently so if travelling with a laptop you may want to bring a surge protector. In many remote parts of the country, such as some islands of Gunayala and in much of the Darién, in national parks or in isolated villages, there is limited or no electricity at night, so a torch is essential.

Insurance

It would be unwise to head for Panama without **insurance** that covers theft, loss, illness, injury and flight cancellation. Before you take out a new policy, make sure that you aren't already covered: some all-risks home insurance policies may cover your possessions while abroad, and many private medical schemes also apply when overseas. In Canada, provincial health plans usually provide some cover for medical treatment when out of the country. Some student insurance packages also include vacation travel. When shopping around for a policy, bear in mind that what are termed **dangerous sports**, which usually include the likes of scuba diving and whitewater rafting, sometimes require an additional premium to be paid. Should you have to seek medical attention, keep all receipts, and if you lose something valuable, get a police report (*denuncia*). Whatever the situation you will still need to access sufficient funds to cover such emergencies (hence the usefulness of a credit card) while on your trip, and apply for reimbursement on your return home.

Internet

Where internet connectivity is available, almost all hostels and most hotels offer free **wi-fi**. There are also numerous government wi-fi hot spots (Ⓦ internetparatodos.gob.pa), though you have to register and the speed is very slow. However, internet access – along with mobile phone coverage – is more limited and unreliable in the **Darién** and **Gunayala**. In the former, wi-fi is restricted to a few places in the major settlements of Metetí, La Palma, Yaviza and Garachiné; in the latter it is only available in Puerto Obaldía, unless you manage to catch a signal outside a government office on one of the larger village-islands. We indicate in the Guide where wi-fi is available in these regions, though even then you should bear in mind that the service is often unreliable, especially in the rainy season (roughly May to mid-Dec).

In general, the exponential spread of smartphones has led to a decline in the number of internet cafés across the country, though there are several in Panama City (including in Albrook bus terminal) and in most towns the local **library** (where one exists), at the very least, usually has a couple of PCs. Note that the "@" sign is usually achieved by pressing ALT, "6" and "4" keys simultaneously.

Language

Spanish is the official language of Panama and the first language of more than two million of the population, though a recorded thirteen other first languages are spoken across the country. The latter are mainly indigenous but include Panamanian **Creole English**, preferred by around 10,000 Afro-Antillean Panamanians, primarily resident in Bocas, Colón and Panama City, and **Cantonese** or **Hakka**, spoken by around 150,000 Chinese-Panamanians. While many urban middle-class Panamanians speak **English**, some of whom are bilingual, the "everybody-speaks-English" myth is easily dispelled. Official estimates reckon around fourteen percent of the population can communicate in English but in small towns and rural areas you'll find many speak virtually no English and in a number of the remote indigenous communities some villagers, especially older women, do not even speak Spanish. Your travel experience in the country will be greatly enhanced by learning at least the basics of Spanish before you arrive. The Language section in the Contexts chapter of this Guide is a useful starting point (see page 319).

Learning Spanish in Panama

A good way of getting to grips with Spanish is to attend a **language school**. This also gives you an entrance into Panamanian life, especially if you take up the cultural immersion or homestay options and become involved in the volunteering projects on offer. Most schools run an extracurricular programme, which almost inevitably includes salsa classes and excursions, while some courses specialize in language learning combined with activities such as scuba diving or surfing.

Group, small-group (two to four people) and one-to-one tuition is usually available and sometimes a mix of online or in-person classes. Group classes, the cheapest option, generally comprise four hours of lessons per day at rates of around $225–250 per week, not including board and lodging. Weekly rates often decrease substantially, the more weeks you do. Make sure the institution is registered, that staff are qualified and that the teaching methodology is not just "chalk and talk" before committing any money. Ⓦ goabroad.com/language-study-abroad contains a list of recommended schools.

LANGUAGE SCHOOLS

EPA! Plaza Los Establos, Boquete 20–22, Ⓦ studyspanishinpanama.com; Centro Commercial Plaza Paitilla, 2nd floor, Av Balboa and Av Italia, Panama City.

Spanish by the River Entrada a Palmira, Alto Boquete, Ⓦ spanishatlocations.com.

Spanish by the Sea Calle 4, behind *Hotel Bahía*, Bocas del Toro, Isla Colón, Ⓦ spanishatlocations.com.

Spanish Panama Edif. Americana 1A, Vía Argentina, Panama City, Ⓦ spanishpanama.com.

Laundry

Most mid-range and top-end hotels offer a **laundry** service, while aparthotels (see page 77) and some hostels have their own washing machines for guest use. Otherwise you could find a *lavamático* (not as easy to locate in Panama City as in the provinces), an old-fashioned launderette where you bundle your clothes into a machine, and then a dryer, for no more than $5 per load, including detergent and conditioner. The more ubiquitous *lavanderías*, which more closely resemble dry cleaners, also usually cost around $6–7 for a bag of clothes to be washed in warm/hot water and then folded (*doblado*); it'll cost more if you want them ironed.

LGBTQ+ travellers

Homosexuality was finally decriminalized in Panama in 2008, which illustrates not only the country's prevailing social conservatism but also the fact that things are changing. The Asociación de Hombres y Mujeres Nuevos de Panamá (AHMN) (Ⓦ ahmnp.org) is active in campaigning for LGBTQ+ rights and low-key Pride marches have been held since 2005 in Panama City and now Las Tablas. Carnaval is also an unofficial celebration of LGBTQ+ self-expression. Otherwise, the LGBTQ scene is discreet; the clutch of nightclubs is not widely advertised but the list of "LGBTQ-friendly" accommodation listings, though small, is gradually increasing (see Ⓦ ellgeebe.com for listings in Panama City plus this page in PTY Life Ⓦ pty.life/panama-queer-guide). In general, hotels in Panama City and North American- and European-run establishments are likely to be more tolerant. Additionally, the Guna are particularly accepting, with their own "third gender" term, *omeggid*, to describe a boy/man who identifies as a girl/woman.

Mail

Since reopening after the Covid-19 pandemic, the government post office (*correos*) now only delivers international post to destinations in North America and the Caribbean, for reasons that are hard to fathom. Opening hours, though generally Monday to Friday 8am to 4pm and Saturday 8am to noon, do vary. For deliveries to Europe and elsewhere, or a speedier delivery to the Americas, use one of the more expensive private mailing or courier services widely available, such as Fedex (Ⓦ fedex.com/pa) or

PUBLIC HOLIDAYS

Jan 1 Año Nuevo. New Year's Day.
Jan 9 Día de los Mártires. Martyrs' Day, in remembrance of those killed by US troops in the 1964 flag riots.
Feb Carnaval. Five days up to and including Ash Wednesday.
March/April Viernes Santo. Good Friday.
May 1 Día del Trabajo. Labour Day.
Nov 3 Separación de Panamá de Colombia. Anniversary of the 1903 separation from Colombia and primary Independence Day.
Nov 4 Día de la Bandera. Flag Day.
Nov 5 Día de Colón. Celebrating Colón's separation from Colombia.
Nov 10 Primer Grito de la Independencia. "First Cry for Independence", marking the unilateral declaration of independence from Spain in La Villa de Los Santos.
Nov 28 4 Independencia de Panamá de España. Celebrating independence from Spain in 1821.
Dec 8 Día de la Madre. Mother's Day.
Dec 20 Día de los Caídos por la Invasión de Estados Unidos a Panamá in remembrance of those who were killed in the US invasion in 1989.
Dec 25 Día de Navidad. Christmas Day.

Mail Boxes Etc. (Ⓦ mbe.com). Panama's own Servientrega (Ⓦ servientrega.com.pa) also offers an international service.

Post offices also offer an *entrega general* (**poste restante**) service, keeping letters for up to a month. Passport ID needs to be shown when claiming post and you can't collect on behalf of another person. The sender should address items as follows: receiver's name, Entrega General, name of town, name of province, Republica de Panamá. If you are receiving post in Panama City then the postal zone also needs to be specified – enquire at the branch in question.

Maps

Country and city **maps** of Panama are increasing in number and quality though there's still some way to go. There are also some rudimentary trail maps for the parks in the former Canal Zone, usually available from the park offices. International Travel Maps (1:300,000; available online at Ⓦ itmb.ca and Ⓦ amazon.com) – updated in 2025 – and National Geographic (Ⓦ nationalgeographic.com) – updated in 2022 – both produce good maps of Panama. In Panama itself, large-scale maps are available in Panama City at the Instituto Geográfico Nacional Tommy Guardia (Mon–Fri 8am–4pm; Ⓦ ignpanama.anati.gob.pa) on Avenida Simón Bolívar, opposite the entrance to the university; that said, some are several years out of date and would really only be of use if you were planning some wilderness hiking. Alternatively you can download pdfs of their maps for free from their website.

Money

Panama adopted **US dollars** (referred to as *dólares* or *balboas*) as its currency in 1904, shortly after separation from Colombia. Apart from a seven-day print flurry in 1941, producing what is known as the "seven-day-dollar" (now a collector's item), the country has always used US paper currency, though it mints its own coinage: 1, 5, 10, 25 and 50 centavo pieces, and a dollar coin, which are used alongside US coins. Both $100 and $50 notes are often difficult to spend, so try to have $10 or $20 as the largest denominations you carry.

Most **banks** are open from 8am to 3.30pm Monday to Friday, and from 9am to noon on Saturday, though busier branches in the capital have extended hours; almost all branches have ATMs, as do many large supermarkets.

It is difficult to **change foreign currency** in Panama – convert any cash into US dollars as soon as you can. There are several RedPlus (Ⓦ grupored-plus.com) currency exchange counters in Tocumen International Airport, and branches in Albrook Mall and Multiplaza. Foreign banks will generally change their own currencies. Current **exchange rates** can be checked at Ⓦ xe.com.

Money transfers can easily be carried out through Western Union (Ⓦ westernunion.com), which has more than one hundred offices sprinkled around the isthmus, with a concentration in Panama City.

Cards and ATMs

With more than a thousand **ATMs** across the country, the most convenient way to access your money is by drawing out cash on a credit or debit card (you'll need your PIN). Most home banks charge a fee for credit and debit card withdrawal – check before departure – and almost all ATMs in Panama levy $6.80 per transaction, as well as limiting you to $250 per withdrawal, so using a travel card for which you don't pay extra fees for foreign transactions is worth seeking out. Make sure to inform your bank at home that you are travelling to Panama before you leave so that they don't block your credit or debit card when you try to use it.

Visa and MasterCard are the most widely accepted **credit cards** across the country, both at ATMs (recognizable by the red *Sistema Clave* sign outside) and to pay for services such as plane tickets, tourist hotels, restaurants, goods in shops and car rental. That said, some stores charge an extra 5 percent to use a credit card to offset their own costs for processing credit cards.

Many establishments in **Bocas del Toro**, **Gunayala** and the **Darién** only accept **cash**; denominations of $20 and below are preferred because of problems with counterfeit $50 and $100 notes. Note that there is only one ATM in the whole of Gunayala (in Narganá – though it doesn't allow cash withdrawal using a credit card), one in the archipelago of Bocas del Toro (in Bocas Town, Isla Colón), and just two in the Darién (in Metetí and La Palma).

Note also that heading into a major holiday weekend, ATMs at holiday destinations may run out of money, especially if there is only one machine in town.

Bargaining and tipping

Bargaining for goods is not the norm in Panama. If you're buying several items from a single stall in a craft market you can usually negotiate a slight discount (*descuento*), but it's rarely the lengthy social ritual it can be in some countries. Bear in mind too that while $40 for an intricate *mola* or $70 for a Panama hat may seem like a lot, they are likely to have taken several weeks to make.

Tipping is not universally expected and should be reserved for good service. While ten percent is customary in mid-range (or more expensive) restaurants, it should not be automatic. In local *fondas* you might round up a $.4.80 *almuerzo* to $5. Porters in hotels and at the airport are usually tipped $1 per bag; the going rate at Tocumen International Airport is $1–2 per bag. In hotels you might consider leaving a tip of $1–2 per day for the person who has cleaned your room, but it's not *de rigueur*. It's not usual to tip taxi drivers for a quick trip, or guides on short, organized tours. However, you might if you have a taxi driver for a whole-day tour, or a guide on multiday trips. If you hire the services of a park warden (*guardaparque*) to take you on a guided hike, you should ask what the going rate is; if there isn't one, $30 should be adequate for a full-day outing.

Overtipping is not helpful; it sets a precedent which other travellers may not be able to live up to, and can upset the micro-economy, particularly in small villages.

USEFUL PHONE NUMBERS

Ambulance: Red Cross T 315-1388; Seguro Social T 107 – both are free
Directory enquiries T 118
Medical emergency T 911
Tourism police T 506 7000

Opening hours and public holidays

Opening hours vary but generally businesses are open Monday to Saturday from 8/9am to 5/6pm. Government office hours are Monday to Friday 8am to 4pm. Shops usually open their doors Monday to Saturday from 9/10am to 7/8pm, though places selling souvenirs and crafts to tourists may open on Sundays too, and Chinese-Panamanian supermarkets often open early (6.30–7am) until late (10pm–midnight); some of the larger outlets of the major supermarket chains, e.g. Super 99, Extra and El Rey, are open 24 hours. Government-run museums tend to open Tuesday to Sunday (10am–6pm; check under *espacios culturales* on W sicultura.gob.pa).

Churches in Panama City's Casco Viejo are open 7am–7pm. Elsewhere, they rarely have official opening hours; most are open from around 8am until early evening, with the odd one closing for lunch.

Most government offices, businesses and shops close during the several national **public holidays**. When the public holidays fall on or near a weekend the government may grants a *puente* (bridge), at the last minute, usually for a Monday or a Friday, making a long weekend and prompting a mass exodus from the city to the beach or the countryside, with a scramble for plane tickets and accommodation – check W qppstudio.net/publicholidays.htm. Note that services shut down in Panama City on August 15 to celebrate the foundation of Panamá La Vieja, while other towns and cities have their own multiday festivities (*patronales*) during which most places close.

Over some public holidays, as well as during national elections, *ley seca* (literally dry law) is enacted, which means that alcohol can't be bought or consumed during that period, and nightclubs and other places of entertainment remain closed, although black market booze is fairly easy to get hold of and in remote areas, the law is less rigorously observed.

Phones

Apart from very remote villages, where the lone phone box – assuming it works – may be the community's only means of communication with the outside

CALLING HOME FROM PANAMA

To **make an international call from Panama**, dial the international access code (in Panama it's 00), then the destination's country code, before the rest of the number. Note that the initial zero is omitted from the area code when dialling the UK, Ireland, Australia and New Zealand from abroad.

Australia 0061 + area code minus initial zero
Ireland 00353 + area code minus initial zero
New Zealand 0064 + area code minus initial zero
South Africa 0027 + area code
UK 0044 + area code minus initial zero
US and Canada 001 + area code

world, **phone boxes** are now rare. Seven-digit phone numbers denote **landlines** – the first three digits comprise the area code – whereas eight-digit numbers are for **mobile phones**.

Making a call

To make a call **to Panama** you need to dial the international prefix (generally 00), followed by 507 – the country code for Panama – followed by the number. Local calls to landlines anywhere in Panama cost a pittance and are usually free from a hotel room. International calls are also relatively cheap provided you do not use a hotel phone. Some internet cafés (and Más Móvil offices) also have phone booths and offer decent rates for international calls as well as a degree of comfort, quiet and privacy. Off-peak time for international calls is between 6pm and 6am, and at weekends.

Mobile phones

Mobile phones have mushroomed in Panama, which now has many more numbers than people. Mobiles have transformed the lives of some indigenous communities that live far from the main population centres, and can be very useful for travellers too, especially in the more remote areas when wanting to confirm transport or a reservation from a dugout in the Darién. Coverage is much the same between the two service providers – Mas Móvil (from Cable & Wireless) and Tigo. If you have an unlocked mobile phone on an 850 GSM (the setting for much of the Americas), you can easily buy a SIM card on arrival for a few dollars, from numerous corner shops in Panama City, or from Albrook bus terminal. Only expensive phone packages (around $40) are available at Tocumen International Airport. Once the initial credit has expired, you can buy prepaid airtime cards from shops around the country. Alternatively, you might consider renting a mobile or satellite phone; the executive business hotels can usually procure one for you. Incoming calls are all free in Panama.

Photography

The dazzling sunlight of any tropical country, especially in the dry season (late Dec to April), can make it difficult to take decent **photographs**. The best times for the light are just after dawn and late afternoon to dusk, but since the sun rises and sets quickly it doesn't give you much time. If you need to purchase any photographic equipment in Panama City, try Digital Photo Supply in El Cangrejo (Ⓦdigital-photosupply.com); otherwise Panafoto (Ⓦpanafoto.com) has several outlets in Panama City, as well as shops in Colón's cruise ship terminal, Santiago and David.

People are fascinating subjects, but be sensitive. If you want to photograph one or more human beings, rather than a market scene with people in it, you should ask their permission. In indigenous villages in particular, ask the village chief or the head of the tourist committee what the protocol is – some villages do not permit photography at all. Tour groups to a village may be encouraged to snap away but you should still ask for permission from the individuals concerned. In Gunayala, in particular, each island has its own regulations (see page 257).

Senior travellers

Given that Panama is one of the world's top **retirement** destinations, especially for North Americans, Panamanians are well used to meeting older foreign travellers. Though senior Panamanian and resident foreign retirees are eligible for incredible **discounts** on everything from flights to cinema tickets, visitors generally are not.

Time

Panama is five hours behind **Greenwich Mean Time** throughout the year, the same as **Eastern Standard Time** in the US, though note US time changes for daylight-saving hours. Panama is one hour ahead of Costa Rica. If in doubt, consult Ⓦtimeanddate.com.

Toilets

Public toilets are thin on the ground in Panama but you will find them in airports, bus terminals and shopping malls. They usually require payment of c50 to an attendant, who in return will hand you an inadequate few sheets of paper – always travel with an emergency toilet roll. Other options are fast-food joints, *cafeterías* and petrol stations. Most places outside top-end or very modern hotels with their own septic system require you to throw used toilet paper into an adjacent basket. In Gunayala and parts of Bocas, a toilet cistern is no guarantee of a water treatment system; everything may still flush straight out to sea.

Tourist information

The official **tourist agency**, the Autoridad de Turismo Panamá (ATP; Ⓦatp.gob.pa), has a slowly improving website (in English too) at Ⓦtourismpanama.com, and the swanky air-conditioned tourist offices in the major towns and resort areas are finally gearing up to assisting passing tourists, and some now contain excellent interactive displays on local wildlife, history and culture. If you have a specific question, the employee will probably do their best to help you, but do not necessarily expect lists of local accommodation or tourist attractions, nor assume the person will speak English. **Reception staff** at a good hostel or hotel may be a better bet for reliable information.

The Visitor/El Visitante (Ⓦthevisitorpanama.info) lists attractions and upcoming events; there are a number of other sources, too (see page 83). Panama's **national parks** and other protected areas, which encompass many of the country's natural wonders, are administered by the Ministry for the Environment, or MiAmbiente (see box, page 42).

Travelling with children

Latin cultures are very family-oriented and Panama is no exception. While there is no pre-packaged entertainment for **children** such as theme parks, there's plenty to enjoy, including boat trips, snorkelling, horseriding, exploring the Canal and walking in the rainforest. Many **hotels** have extra beds or pull-outs in rooms for children and under-12s are often free, with older kids admitted at discount rates. The large resort hotels – the *Decameron* at Farallón on the Pacific coast (Ⓦdecameron.com), the *Hotel Meliá* on Lago Gatún (Ⓦmelia.com) and the *Gamboa Rainforest Resort* (see page 101) – have special activities laid on and child-minding services. Small B&Bs and ecolodges sometimes do not permit children or have a minimum age of 12 or 14.

Various tour operators in the UK and North America (check out Ⓦaudleytravel.com for the UK and US, and Ⓦresponsibletravel.com, for the UK, but with call offices in Ireland, North America, Australia and India) include **family-oriented itineraries**. Travelling to Gunayala and to the Darién, which can be challenging enough for adults, can be very hard work with kids in tow. Sticking to Panama City and the Canal area, the Pacific beach resorts, El Valle, Bocas and Boquete is much easier and more enjoyable all round, especially if you're on a modest budget.

Volunteering

It's possible to arrange **voluntary work**, which can be carried out on a tourist visa, in advance. Try one of the various reputable international agencies, such as Volunteer Abroad (Ⓦgoabroad.com/volunteer-abroad) or Volunteer World (Ⓦvolunteerworld.com), or arrange it via a Spanish language schools or directly through the websites of Panamanian organizations; alternatively, you may be able to show up on the spot. Key areas include conservation or social development projects, usually in poor, marginalized communities. Before you plunge into volunteering, do your homework to ensure that the programme is bona fide and sustainable and that you are sufficiently skilled and experienced for the job. If training is provided, ensure that there is adequate time devoted to it – often a problem if organizations are hard-stretched.

Volunteering in projects, particularly with marginalized or vulnerable groups, is fraught with ethical dilemmas, which usually have no easy or "right" solution and can have unexpected negative side effects. While a couple of weeks on a turtle or reef monitoring project may be fine, social development projects need long-term commitment since a constant rotation of volunteers can be unsettling for individuals and communities, especially for vulnerable groups such as young children. Moreover, as unemployment and underemployment rates are high in Panama, you should ask yourself whether you are taking away a job that a Panamanian could be paid to do.

That said, there are several well-established **programmes** in Panama, most notably with turtle conservation projects in Bocas del Toro (see box, page 237).

Panama City

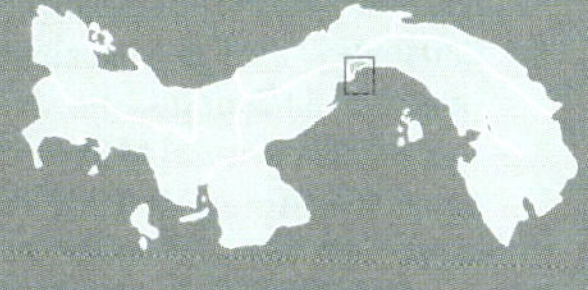

CASCO VIEJO AT DUSK

1

Panama City

Proudly positioned in the crook of land overlooking the Pacific, the soaring skyline of Panama City surveys the ocean before it. From its inception, the city has been situated on one of the world's great crossroads, and it has thrived on trade, attracting migrants from all over the world to a cosmopolitan melting pot bubbling with energy and ambition. Panama has long been considered a bridge between two continents and nowhere is this divided identity more apparent than in the capital, where glitzy skyscrapers, laser-lit nightclubs and chic restaurants more reminiscent of Miami than Latin America are juxtaposed with colonial churches, clamouring street vendors and chaotic traffic. Though it is the undisputed political, economic and social centre of Panama and home to 2 million in the metropolitan area – well over a third of the country's population – the city has very little in common with the rest of the country, which is often vaguely referred to as "el interior".

On the southwest end of the bay stands the old city centre of **Casco Viejo**, a jumble of immaculately restored colonial buildings, crumbling ruins and run-down housing on a rocky promontory, while a few kilometres to the northeast rise the shimmering skyscrapers of **El Cangrejo** and **Marbella**, the modern banking and commercial district, and the penthouse apartments of **Punta Paitilla** and **Punta Pacífica**. Further east, amid sprawling suburbs whose tentacles extend 30km along the coast, stand the ruins of **Panamá Viejo**, the first European city to be founded on the Pacific coast of the Americas, while west of the city centre the former US Canal Zone town of **Balboa**, with its clipped lawns and restrained utilitarian architecture, retains a distinctly North American character despite having been turned over to full Panamanian control in 1999. In the background, the Panamanian flag proudly flies on the summit of **Cerro Ancón**, a surprising oasis of greenery on what was once a major US military base.

For the vast majority of visitors to Panama, the capital provides their first point of contact. Many spend their entire stay here, since it makes a good base from which to explore many of the country's attractions while enjoying the material comforts of sophisticated city living – the Canal, a handful of national parks and the Caribbean coast as far as Portobelo can all be visited on **day-trips**. Other visitors, keen to leave behind the frenzied construction and thronging streets and escape into Panama's outstanding wilderness areas, still linger a couple of days to savour the colonial architecture of Casco Viejo and the vitality of the modern city, including its many bars and restaurants.

While it is easy to tire of Panama City's irrepressible energy, oppressive heat and relentless traffic, it's as simple to escape to nearby places of real tranquillity: the **Amador Causeway**, a breezy breakwater offering fabulous views of the Canal and the city skyline; **Isla Taboga**, the sleepy "Island of Flowers" an hour's boat ride off the coast; or the **Parque Natural Metropolitano**, the only natural tropical rainforest within the limits of a Latin American capital.

Brief history

Archeological finds demonstrate that the coastal area occupied by present-day Panama City was inhabited by fishing and agricultural communities over 1,500 years ago, long before the Spanish colonizers arrived on the scene. The latter established modern-day

COLONIAL ARCHITECTURE IN CASCO VIEJO

Highlights

❶ **Casco Viejo** Perched on a rocky promontory, the evocative old city has ancient churches, leafy plazas and grand buildings. See page 55

❷ **The Canal Museum** Fully renovated, bilingual (Spanish and English) and interactive, this unmissable museum explores the history of the canal and the country. See page 58

❸ **Cerro Ancón** Vantage point offering an unparalleled panorama of towering skyscrapers and the imposing Canal, plus a chance to spot toucans and sloths. See page 69

❹ **Parque Natural Metropolitano** A patch of tropical rainforest within the city limits – a must for birdwatching. See page 71

❺ **Panamá Viejo** Crumbling remains of the original Panama City, set in mud flats and mangroves on the edge of the metropolis. See page 71

❻ **Sundowner in a rooftop bar** Casco Viejo boasts some fabulous rooftop bars, perfect for sipping a cocktail on a balmy evening while watching the sun set, or admiring the glittering high-rises across the bay at night. See page 82

❼ **Isla Taboga** A delightful day-trip from the bustle of the city, offering a lovely boat trip across the mouth of the Canal, a laidback fishing village and pleasant scenic walks. See page 87

HIGHLIGHTS ARE MARKED ON THE MAP ON PAGE 54

PANAMA CITY AND AROUND
HIGHLIGHTS
1 Casco Viejo
2 The Canal Museum
3 Cerro Ancón
4 Parque Natural Metropolitano
5 Panamá Viejo
6 Sundowner in a rooftop bar
7 Isla Taboga
SHOPPING
Albrook Mall 2
Centro Artesanal Panamá para el Mundo 1
Multiplaza 3
Reprosa 3
ACCOMMODATION
Casa Mariposa 1
0 2
kilometres
Gamboa (20km) & Colón (75km)
Colón (73km)
Colón (73km)
Pedro Miguel Locks
Miraflores Locks
Cocolí Locks
Panama Canal
Ciudad de Saber (City of Knowledge)
AVENIDA GAILLARD
Estadio Nacional Rodney Carew
Bahá'í House of Worship
PARQUE NATURAL METROPOLITANO
Corozal Passenger Terminal (Panama Canal Railway Company)
COROZAL
Albrook Airport
AV DE LA AMISTAD
AV JUAN PABLO II
CORREDOR NORTE
AVENIDA RICARDO J. ALFARO (TUMBA MUERTO)
AVENIDA SIMÓN BOLÍVAR
TRANSISTMICA
EL DORADO
VÍA TOCUMEN (AV DOMINGO DÍAZ)
AV JOSÉ AGUSTÍN ARANGO
Estadio Rommel Fernández Gutiérrez
Arena Roberto Durán
Hipódromo Presidente Remón
PARQUE RECREATIVO OMAR TORRIJOS
EL CANGREJO
AV CENTRAL ESPAÑA
VÍA BRASIL
AVENIDA BELISARIO PORRAS
VÍA CINCUENTENARIO
SAN FRANCISCO
VÍA ISRAEL
Panamá Viejo
CORREDOR SUR
CORREDOR SUR
BALBOA
Cerro Ancón (199m)
BELLA VISTA
CALLE 50
PUNTA PAITILLA
Centro de Convenciones ATLAPA
SEE 'CERRO ANCÓN & BALBOA' MAP FOR DETAILS
BRIDGE OF THE AMERICAS (PUENTE DE LAS AMÉRICAS)
Bahía de Panamá
SEE 'CENTRAL PANAMA CITY' MAP FOR DETAILS
CASCO VIEJO
Balboa Yacht Club
Biomuseo
AMADOR CAUSEWAY (CALZADA DE AMADOR)
Isla Naos
Isla Perico
Punta Culebra Nature Centre
Isla Flamenco
Isla Taboga
PACIFIC OCEAN
Tocumen International Airport
N

Panama City, named **Panamá Nuevo**, in 1673, two years after the original settlement, **Panama Viejo**, had been sacked by the Welsh buccaneer Henry Morgan (see page 296). The new city developed in the area known today as **Casco Viejo**, on a rocky peninsula jutting out into the bay, 8km southwest of the old capital, and a more defendable and salubrious site than its swampy predecessor.

The Gold Rush and the railroad

Once the Spanish had rerouted their treasure fleet around Cape Horn in 1746, Panama City's commercial importance as a trade route slowly began to decline, only substantially picking up again in the mid-nineteenth century due to the isthmus's popularity as a transit point in the **California Gold Rush** and the completion of the **Panama Railroad** in 1855. The railroad, and subsequently the French and US canal construction efforts, brought immense prosperity and a wealth of new cultural influences that transformed the city and its inhabitants, who by 1920 totalled almost sixty thousand.

The Canal

Whereas the **Canal**, completed in 1914, confirmed Panama City's importance as a global trading centre, the outbreak of World War I, the waterway's official inauguration, opened the floodgates to large-scale **US military occupation** of the Panama Canal Zone, the 8km strip of land either side of the waterway under US jurisdiction. During World War II, defence installations proliferated and the predominantly US population topped one hundred thousand. Though other migrants continued to pour in, the lives of the city's population were regulated by the US military in the adjacent Canal Zone, who controlled everything from refuse collection and water supply to construction permits, and whose affluence and spending power inevitably shaped commercial development. No surprise then that Panama City found itself at the forefront of increasing nationalist sentiment that periodically erupted into violence, most notably in the flag riots of 1964 (see page 302). Only after the handover of the Canal had been assured, in the canal treaty of 1977, could the capital, and the country, start to plan its own path.

Modern times

The introduction of banking secrecy laws in the 1970s led to the rapid expansion of the financial services sector, including an influx of **narco-dollars**. Despite the tightening of banking regulations, the city's business district remains a hive of intrigue. Some of the luxury skyscrapers there and in Punta Paitilla, and further east in Punta Pacífica and Costa del Este, stand empty, the astronomical rents paid by their fictitious occupants providing a useful means of laundering money.

The handover of the last US bases to Panamanian control at the end of 1999 released huge amounts of real estate, enabling the city to expand further along the coast, though its spread inland is still checked by the backdrop of hills that form the protected Panama Canal Basin. This has resulted in ever increasing **traffic congestion**; in response, millions of dollars have been spent on two **metro** lines, with a third on the way – Central America's first metro system – and the Cinta Costera, a multi-lane highway around the Bahía de Panama, which includes a controversial ring road around Casco Viejo. Work has begun on another **bridge** over the Canal, and a tunnel is being made under the port of Balboa, to extend the metro westwards towards La Chorrera.

Casco Viejo and around

Most of Panama City's historical monuments and tourist attractions are concentrated in the colonial city centre of **San Felipe** – more commonly called **Casco Viejo** (sometimes Casco Antiguo) – which is the best place to start your explorations. For centuries the heart of Panama City's social and political life, and still home to the presidential palace, Casco Viejo, after decades of neglect, was declared a UNESCO World Heritage Site in 1997 and is gradually being restored to its former glory. The subsequent gentrification is not without its problems: while upmarket restaurants and cafés sit alongside chic offices and apartments in renovated colonial buildings, poor families are gradually being squeezed out and prices continue to rise. That said, Casco Viejo is an exceedingly pleasant place to visit – and the visible presence of the tourist police means it is safe to explore. **Caution** should still be exercised when walking around late at night, however; stick to the well-lit streets, and avoid straying into the adjacent neighbourhoods of El Chorillo and Santa Ana.

The best way to see Casco Viejo is to **walk** – you can get there by taxi or by taking any bus, or the metro, to Plaza Cinco de Mayo, from where there's a regular smaller shuttle bus that operates a circular route, passing the Mercado de Mariscos, along Eloy Alfaro, across to Plaza Herrera, down Avenida "A", then across past the National Theatre and back out along Avenida "B".

Avenida Central

From Plaza Cinco de Mayo you can walk up the rather dilapidated, pedestrianized **Avenida Central**, past Parque Santa Ana and the famous *Café Coca Cola* (see page 80), as it narrows into a cobbled street, passing through the now invisible city walls into the historic centre. On the left, the faded blue-and-white-striped Art Deco building was once one of the national lottery's two homes (the only one now in use lies

ACCOMMODATION
- AmazINN Places 7
- American Trade Hotel 5
- Las Clementinas 2
- Hotel La Compañía 6
- La Isabela Suites 3
- Magnolia Inn 4
- Oasis Hotel 1

EATING
- Al Alma 7
- Café Coca-Cola 5
- Caleta 10
- Calicanto 8
- Casa Sucre Coffee House 2
- Casablanca 3
- Grandclément 6
- Māhalō Cocina y Jardín 4
- Māhalō Snack Shak 12
- Saint Honoré 13
- Santa Rita 1
- Super Gourmet 11
- The Vegan Shack 9

DRINKING & NIGHTLIFE
- The Club 5
- Corcho 4
- La Rana Dorada 3
- Tántalo 1
- Teatro Amador 2

SHOPPING
- Casa Latina Panamá 2
- Galería de Arte Indígena 3
- Mia Mia 1
- La Ronda 4

on Avenida Perú). A little further along on the left is the gleaming white-and-cream Neoclassical **Casa de la Municipalidad**, seat of the city government. Opposite, a smarter charcoal grey-and-white Art Deco building once housed the central bank.

Iglesia de la Merced

C 10 at Av Central • Daily 9am–6.30pm • Free

Next door to the Casa de la Municipalidad stands the crumbling Baroque facade of the city's oldest church, **Iglesia de la Merced**, which in 1680 was reconstructed on its present site using the original stones from Panamá Viejo. The facade is the best-preserved section of the church, though the gilded wooden altar also retains some appeal.

Plaza de la Catedral

Midway down Avenida Central the street opens out into the old quarter's most impressive square, **Plaza de la Catedral** – also known as Plaza Mayor and Plaza de la Independencia, since the proclamations of independence from Spain and separation from Colombia were both made here (the restored *Central Hotel*, on the east side of the plaza, played a starring role in both events). Numerous busts of the nation's founding fathers are scattered beneath the shady trees surrounding the striking central gazebo, with the Republic's first president, Manuel Amador Guerrero, taking pride of place.

A **craft market** is held in the plaza on the last weekend of the month during summer, and the first non-bank-holiday Sunday of the month sees a **flea market** (10am–5pm). In addition, free evening **concerts** are frequently held on balmy summer nights.

Catedral Metropolitana

Plaza de la Catedral • Daily 10am–6.30pm • Free

Flanked by white towers sparkling with inlaid mother-of-pearl, the hybrid Neoclassical and Baroque olive-and-cream sandstone facade of the **Catedral Metropolitana** dominates the plaza. It was built between 1688 and 1796 using stone brought from the ruins of Panamá Viejo (see box, page 72). Three of its bells were also recovered from its ruined predecessor, and reputedly owe their distinctive tone to a gold ring thrown by Queen Isabella I of Spain into the molten metal from which they were cast. Fully renovated for the papal visit in 2019, the interior is now a dazzling white, with gleaming black-and-white chequered floor tiling. The large altarpiece carved from seven types of Italian marble is particularly imposing. To its right lies a trapdoor marking the entrance to tunnels – not open to visitors – designed as escape routes, connecting the cathedral to the churches of La Merced and San José. In the right-hand aisle, it's hard to miss the rather macabre waxwork effigy of a young canonized Mexican martyr that accompanies the reliquary of one of his bones. Thankfully, the other four reliquaries the cathedral received for the papal visit are buried inside the new marble altar, including a dose of Pope Juan Pablo II's blood.

Museo de Historia de Panamá

Palacio Municipal, Plaza de la Catedral • Tues–Sun 10am–6pm • Free

Southeast of the cathedral is the splendid Neoclassical **Palacio Municipal**, built in 1910 on the site of the former city hall. On the ground floor, the **Museo de Historia de Panamá** offers a cursory introduction to Panamanian history, focusing on symbols of independence such as the national flag, the national anthem and the coat of arms, alongside an eclectic mixture of maps and artefacts (explanations in Spanish). Despite some recent interactive additions, it will probably only appeal to history buffs. The languorous nude reclining in the entrance hall represents Panama bathing in the waters of the two oceans.

1

Museo del Canal Interoceánico

Plaza de la Catedral • Tues–Sun 9am–6pm • Charge; audio guides in English or Spanish or prebooked guided tours in English are extra; three people minimum • museodelcanal.com

Housed in a three-storey French colonial building, complete with mansard roof and shutters, the excellent **Museo del Canal Interoceánico** offers a comprehensive account of both the French and US endeavours to build a canal across the isthmus, and of the protracted handover of the Canal to Panama's control (see pages 298, 300 and 303). Yet the museum also offers a broader history of the country, highlighting the canal's centrality.

The highly polished marble entrance hall bears witness to the museum's former life as the city's grandest hotel. Take a sweater – the air conditioning is fierce.

The second floor

The bulk of the exhibition lies on the **second floor**, expounding the history of the transisthmian route, starting with the transoceanic trade between pre-Hispanic cultures, involved in interoceanic trading thousands of years before the invading Europeans landed. The exhibits then turn to the first attempt by the invading Spanish to find a passage to Asia, and the later construction of both the railroad and the canal.

Following a major overhaul that started in 2021, the exhibition rooms are now more creatively displayed, offering a well curated mix of artefacts, photographs, video and text, with plenty of interactive exhibits. The bilingual text also offers a slightly more postcolonial slant on events. That said, the brutality of colonialism is still underplayed and the video game for kids, which encourages them to escape across the isthmus with the stolen loot – dodging arrows, cannon balls, snakes and mosquitoes – is not exactly on message.

There are plenty of photographs, video montages, artefacts and maps offering striking comparisons between the different working conditions during the French and US canal eras which bring to life the huge scale of the achievements, especially by the 30,000-strong West Indian workforce, which primarily came from Barbados.

The third floor

The **third floor** displays address the apartheid living conditions of gold and silver roll employees (see page 301) during the canal's construction, including black resistance to the system. The exhibits include contemporary works of art and talking-head videos of descendants reading letters from their ancestors.

The **penultimate room** covers the period from World War II to the present-day, with a timeline of the deteriorating Panamanian–US relations that eventually led to the handover of the Canal. The US invasion of Panama is also covered (see page 303), accompanied by a soundtrack of bombs falling as residents recount their experiences. Resistance and activism during the country's two military dictatorships also feature and there is a particularly poignant **memory wall**, listing the names of those who were killed or disappeared during both the dictatorships and the US invasion.

Don't miss the **final display case** that summarizes the history of the canal in a dozen artefacts, from an ancient lithic tool to Spanish cannonballs, a signalling lantern from the Panama Railroad to a dynamite blaster used in the Culebra Cut.

The museum has a small **shop** selling modern and original Canal memorabilia.

Palacio Presidencial

Av Eloy Alfaro, between C 6 and C 5 • To join a free guided tour (Mon, Wed, Thurs & Fri 9am; 1hr), a letter suggesting possible dates needs to be emailed to the Oficina de Guías (527 9740, guiasdepalacio@presidencia.gob.pa) several days in advance, noting the names of those wanting to visit and the passport details

Built in 1673 as an opulent private mansion for a corrupt colonial judge, the present-day **Palacio Presidencial** went on to serve as a customs house, teacher training college and even a prison. In 1922 it was rebuilt as the presidential residence in grandiose neo-Mudéjar style under the orders of President Belisario Porras. It is commonly known as the "Palacio de las Garzas" after the white egrets given to Porras by his poet friend Ricardo Miró; white egrets have lived freely around the patio fountain ever since.

Unfortunately, it is no longer possible to take a peek at the palace from the outside though you can go on a free **guided tour**, which is well worth the hassle (see above) even though it only covers a few rooms. After admiring the marble floor and mother-of-pearl-encrusted columns of the Moorish vestibule, you are taken up to the first floor and the long **Salón Amarillo** (Yellow Hall), used for official ceremonies. From the presidential throne to the gilt mirrors and heavy drapes, the room is replete with shades of gold, amber and mustard, while striking murals by Roberto Lewis offer a selective romp through Panama's history. In the adjoining **Comedor del Palacio** (Dining Room), where state banquets are held, Lewis's distinctive murals are even more prominent, depicting idyllic country scenes. Secreted away at the far end of the dining room is the **Salón del Cabinete** (Cabinet Room), which contains portraits of all Panama's presidents.

Plaza Bolívar and around

A block back from the waterfront on Avenida B, elegant **Plaza Bolívar**, dotted with manicured trees, provides the perfect spot for a glass of wine or a meal at its pavement café-restaurants. At lunchtime the peace is periodically interrupted by the cries of primary-school children spilling out of class seeking out snow-cones (*raspados*) from the waiting vendors.

Simón Bolívar monument

Rebuilt after a fire in 1756, the plaza was dedicated in 1883 to **Simón Bolívar**, whose central **statue**, crowned by a condor, dominates the space. The monument was erected in 1926 to commemorate one hundred years since the Amphyctionic Congress – the first **Panamerican gathering**, organized by Bolívar, aimed at unifying the newly independent Latin American countries in their relations with Spain. Although "El Libertador" (The Liberator) failed to attend the congress, and his dreams of unity ultimately foundered, it was considered a historic event.

Palacio Bolívar and Salón Bolívar

Northeastern corner of Plaza Bolívar • Mon–Fri 10.30am • Free guided tour in Spanish; apply online with at least 48hrs notice Ⓦ mire.gob.pa/formulario-de-visitas-guiadas

The **Palacio Bolívar**, whose impressive peach-and-white facade extends along the eastern edge of the square, is well worth a peek. Having served as part of a convent, military barracks and a school, the building now houses the Ministry of Foreign Affairs, among other government offices. It has been beautifully restored, its courtyard – the **Plaza de los Libertadores** – boasting a magnificent translucent roof allowing in lots of natural light. From a raised platform at the far side a bronze bust of the visionary Liberator looks on. To the right as you enter is the **Salón Bolívar**, formerly the chapter house of a Franciscan monastery where the Amphyctionic Congress took place, and now a small museum. It contains a replica of the Liberator's gold ceremonial sword, encrusted with more than a thousand diamonds, and the congress's original documents.

Iglesia y Convento de San Francisco de Asís

Southeastern corner of Plaza Bolívar • **Church** daily 9am–6.30pm; free • **Belltower** Tues–Sun 9am–5.45pm; charge

On the southeastern corner of the plaza, next to the Palacio Bolívar (see above), stands the confectionery-coloured **Iglesia y Convento de San Francisco de Asís**. Established by the Franciscans in the seventeenth century, it was later taken over by the Jesuits, who were responsible for its present design, adding the imposing bell tower in 1918. The tower reopened in 2024, having been closed for sixteen years – its spiral staircase is punctuated with a couple of viewing platforms, including one offering a splendid aerial view down the nave. The panoramic view across the rooftops of Casco Viejo and the bay is well worth the effort. Get a welcome blast of cool air conditioning as you check out the church's restrained interior, which features delightful modern stained-glass windows laden with Franciscan symbolism, and, framing the main altar, a beautifully restored mural composed of Venetian mosaics.

Iglesia San Felipe de Neri

Plaza Bolívar at Av "B" and C 4 • Daily 9am–6.30pm • Free

Built in 1688, **Iglesia San Felipe de Neri** was one of Casco Viejo's earliest churches; it served as a shrine to the cathedral and then, much later, as a children's home and orphanage.

Teatro Nacional

Eastern end of Av "B" • Mon–Fri 8am–4pm • Charge • Ⓦ facebook.com/teatronacionalpanama

The handsome Teatro Nacional was one of the first grand national buildings to be commissioned by the newly independent Panamanian state. Built on the site of a former convent and designed by Italian architect Genaro Ruggieri, the magnificent Italianate Neoclassical edifice, with a splendid Baroque interior, opened its doors to the public in 1908. Despite initial success, the global depression of the 1930s brought a slump in the venue's fortunes, and it became a cinema for a while before falling into neglect. After substantial restoration work, the theatre reopened in 1974 with a performance by Margot Fonteyn, the British ballerina and long-term Panama resident, whose bronze bust adorns the foyer, alongside that of Roberto Lewis, whose allegorical frescoes depicting the birth of the nation can be seen on the vaulted ceiling. If you can't catch one of its occasional theatrical productions (see page 84), you can pop in for a daytime visit during the week for a small fee.

The ramparts

Two hundred metres southeast of the Teatro Nacional, steps lead up to **Paseo Esteban Huertas**, a delightful, breezy, bougainvillea-covered promenade that runs some 400m along the top of what were the ramparts. The walkway along the defensive seawall is a favourite haunt of smooching couples – earning it the nickname Paseo de los Inamorados – and Guna traders displaying their handicrafts to passing tourists. At the far end, before descending the steps into the Plaza de Francia, you get fine views across the bay. Peek over the wall and you can glimpse the windows of the dungeons, where prisoners were allegedly left at low tide to drown when the high tide flooded the cells.

Plaza de Francia

Plaza de Francia, at the southeastern tip of Casco Viejo, is an irregularly shaped space bounded by the seawall and the renovated arches of **Las Bóvedas** (vaults), Spanish dungeons that also functioned as storehouses, prison cells and barracks for the fort that occupied the plaza until the early twentieth century. Formerly the Plaza de Armas, the city's main square, the space is dominated by a substantial monument dedicated to the thousands of workers who died during the disastrous French attempt to build the Canal (see page 298). The central **obelisk** is topped by a proud Gallic cockerel and ringed by busts of the key figures involved, including Ferdinand de Lesseps, the French diplomat who first conceived of the canal yet whose ignorance and vanity were central to the project's ultimate failure (see page 298). Behind, vast marble tablets chronologically outline the bare bones of the dream to build a transisthmian waterway.

The Neoclassical **French Embassy** overlooks the square from the north, fronted by a huge statue of former Panamanian president Pablo Arosemena. The large building to the east is home to the **Ministerio de Cultura** (MiCultura). It was spruced up for the James Bond film *Quantum of Solace*, in which it featured as a Bolivian hotel. Adjacent is the intimate Teatro Anita Villalaz (see page 84).

Iglesia y Convento de Santo Domingo

Av "A" at C 3 • Irregular opening hours • Free

The ruined **Iglesia y Convento de Santo Domingo**, completed in 1678, is most famous for the **Arco Chato** (flat arch) over its main entrance – which remains open to the public. Just 10.6m high, but spanning some 15m with no keystone or external support, it was reputedly cited as evidence of Panama's seismic stability when the US Senate was debating where to build an interoceanic canal. Ironically, the arch inexplicably collapsed just after the centenary celebrations for Panama's independence in 2003, but has subsequently been restored.

Museo de Arte Religioso Colonial

Av "A" at C 3 • Tues–Sun 10am–6pm • Free

Tucked away in one of the convent's former chapels, the **Museo de Arte Religioso Colonial** has a small collection of religious paintings, silverwork and sculpture dating back to the colonial era. Realistically, the detailed information panels will only be of interest to colonial ecclesiastical history buffs who can read Spanish.

Iglesia de San José

Av "A" at C 8 • Daily 9am–6.30pm • Free

The **Iglesia de San José**, built in 1673 but subsequently remodelled, is exceptional only for being home to the legendary Baroque **Altar de Oro** (Golden Altar), which illuminates the otherwise gloomy interior. A carved mahogany extravaganza gilded with 22-carat gold leaf, it was one of the few treasures to survive Henry Morgan's ransacking of Panamá Viejo in 1671 thanks, apparently, to having been painted or covered in mud to disguise its true value. Legend has it that when Morgan demanded to see the gold, the priest explained its absence by pleading poverty, even persuading the buccaneer to make a donation to the church.

Museo de la Mola

C José de Obaldía at C 8 • Tues–Fri 10am–4.30pm, Sat & Sun 10am–5pm • Free • Ⓦ museodelamola.org

Making a welcome change from colonial history, the excellent **Museo de la Mola** showcases over two hundred magnificent *molas*, the emblematic multi-layered cloth panels that Guna women wear over their blouses. More importantly, the museum clearly explains (in Spanish and English) the symbolism of the various designs and how they relate to Guna cosmology. This is an essential stop for anyone intending to visit Gunayala (see page 253), or interested in Guna culture.

Plaza Herrera

At the western limit of Casco Viejo is **Plaza Herrera**, a pleasant square lined with elegant nineteenth-century houses, named in honour of General Tomás Herrera, the military leader of Panama's first short-lived independence attempt in 1840 (see page 297). His equestrian monument stands in the centre of the plaza. Just off Plaza Herrera to the west lies **Bastión Mano de Tigre** (Tiger Hand Bastion), a crumbling and indistinct pile of masonry that is the last remaining section of the city's original defensive walls on the landward side. To the north a gleaming white facade announces the restored *American Trade Hotel* (see page 77), which dates back to 1917.

1

Following Avenida "A" westwards out of the plaza, the road soon dissolves into the poor barrio and no-go area of **El Chorrillo**, which was devastated during the US invasion in 1989, leaving hundreds dead and thousands homeless. The neighbourhood has since been rebuilt, but the coloured concrete tenements that replaced the old wooden slum housing are already run-down. Despite a substantial increase in police presence, and investment in leisure facilities, it can still be a **dangerous** place, day or night.

Parque Santa Ana

Parque Santa Ana, the social hub of the impoverished neighbourhood of Santa Ana, marks the transition between the old colonial centre of Casco Viejo and the more commercial

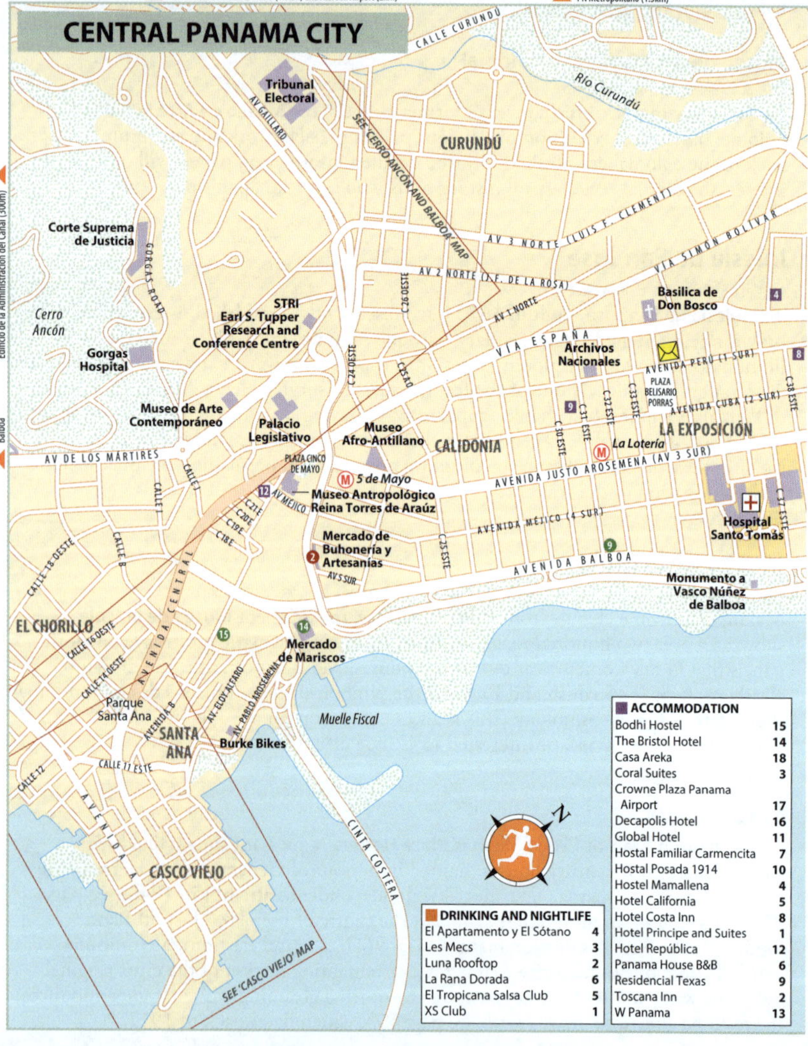

modern city. As the centre of activity outside the city walls in the early nineteenth century, it hosted colourful markets and bullfights and the central gazebo hosted the country's first national lottery; now it offers some respite from the swirling traffic, and is often populated by many of the locality's older residents, discussing the latest news. The pedestrianized section of Avenida Central starts on the park's northeastern side.

Central Panama City

In contrast to the relative calm of the city's historical centre and ancient remains, the **modern** streets of **central Panama City** reverberate with traffic noise and pavements

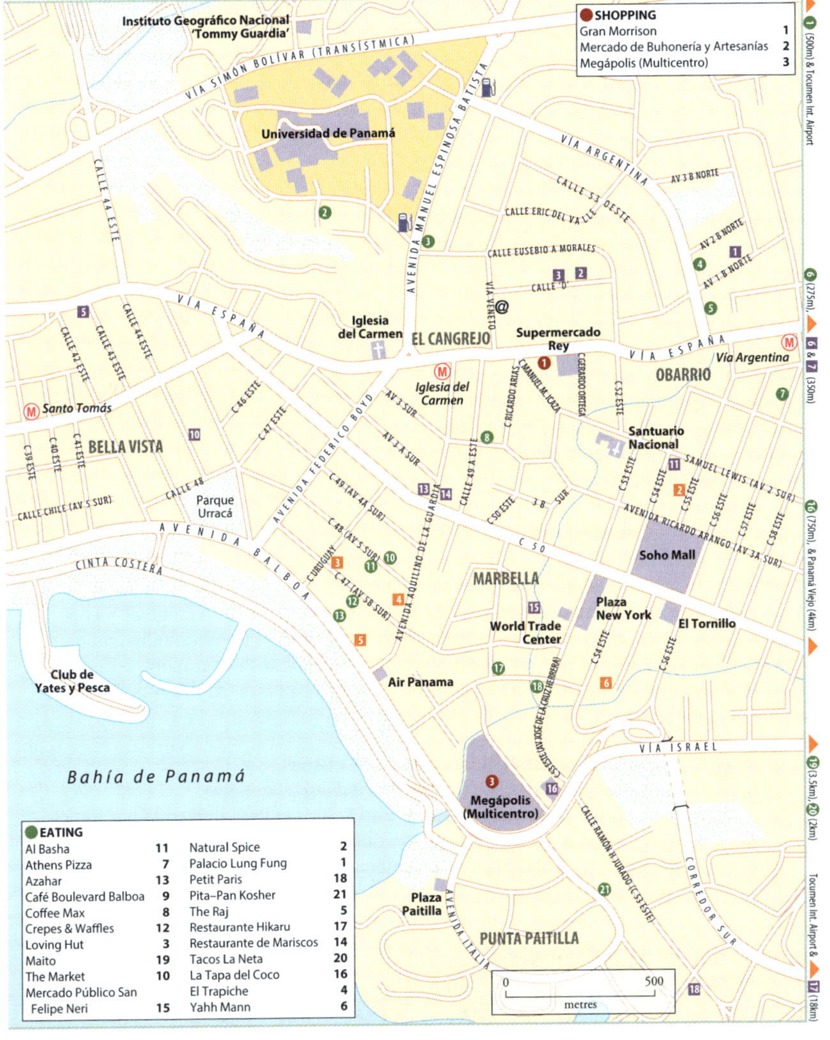

are packed with people squeezing in and out of the patchwork of shops, banks, hotels and restaurants or threading their way through street vendors, hawkers and other pedestrians. Wedge-shaped central Panama City stretches 3km around the Bahía de Panamá, from **Avenida Central** and **Plaza Cinco de Mayo** – home to the central government buildings – to **Punta Paitilla**, encompassing the older residential and commercial districts of **Calidonia** and **La Exposición** fanning out to include **Bella Vista** and the newer, plusher financial districts of **Marbella** and **El Cangrejo**.

Avenida Central

The pedestrianized stretch of **Avenida Central**, from Parque Santa Ana north as far as Plaza Cinco de Mayo, is one of the city's oldest shopping districts, now rather rundown. Air conditioning and loud music blast out from the huge, predominantly Hindu-owned superstores that sell cheap clothing, electronics and household goods, while hawkers flog pirate DVDs and cheap sunglasses, and vendors quench the thirst of shoppers with fruit or sugar cane juice. In the evening, in the pedestrianized area round Cinco de Mayo, extra food stalls pop up selling kebabs and sausages and as the night wears on, sex workers tout for custom. Exercise **caution** when walking around the streets either side of Avenida Central and north of Parque Santa Ana, and avoid wandering around the side streets at night.

Plaza Cinco de Mayo and around

The pedestrian zone of Avenida Central spills out into the busiest square in the city centre, **Plaza Cinco de Mayo**, where the traffic mayhem takes over again. To the east the square is bordered by the neglected Neoclassical building that was originally the proud Panama Railroad Pacific terminal; the government has been threatening to reopen the national anthropological museum here since 2010 but don't hold your breath.

On the northwestern side of the plaza is the rather uninspiring **Palacio Legislativo** (Legislative Palace), which stands in the raised **Parque José Antonio Remón Cantera**, named after a former president who was mysteriously gunned down at the hippodrome in 1955. Peer behind the towering black monolith at its centre and you are greeted by an enormous, rather unflattering head of the murdered president, protruding from the granite.

Museo de Arte Contemporáneo

Between Av de los Mártires and C San Blas • Tues–Sun 10am–5pm • Charge • macpanama.org • Cinco de Mayo

The privately owned **Museo de Arte Contemporáneo** houses a permanent collection of over 800 works by Panamanian (and some international) artists in a range of media. In 2022, the museum received a bequest of 400 art works from internationally renowned Panamanian artist Julio Zachrisson, who worked primarily with engravings and drawings. The museum periodically hosts interesting temporary exhibitions and has a small **café** and picnic area.

STRI Earl S. Tupper Research and Conference Centre

Av Roosevelt • Mon–Fri 9am–5pm; bookstore Tues & Thurs 1–2pm • Free • stri.si.edu • Cinco de Mayo

The Smithsonian Tropical Research Institute's **Earl S. Tupper Research and Conference Centre**, set in leafy grounds, hosts an impressive bookshop-cum-giftshop, a research library and a very pleasant, modestly priced cafeteria. You'll need to show your passport and register at the entrance.

Calidonia and La Exposición

Beyond Plaza Cinco de Mayo, Avenida Central continues north. The city's main thoroughfare runs through **CALIDONIA** and **LA EXPOSICIÓN**. Consisting of a dense

GETTING ACTIVE ON THE CINTA COSTERA

Sunday mornings on the Cinta Costera offer a spread of recreational activities, most of them free. **Cycling** is the main event; during **Ciclovía Panamá** (6am–noon) you can pedal 6km southwest from Punta Paitilla as far as the Estadio Maracaná, the other side of Casco Viejo. Plans are afoot to link this with the cycleway along the Calzada de Amador (see page 67). Sunday's *ciclovía* also offers round forty free bikes (for the first two hours), on a first-come-first-served basis; you'll find them opposite the *Hilton Hotel* at Calle Alquilino de la Guardia, in the middle of the Cinta Costera (you'll need to show your passport). Otherwise, you can rent a bike (see page 76). You're likely to need to navigate your way through joggers, skateboarders and assorted others while on your bike.

Alongside the Sunday cycling, there's plenty of **jogging**, plus early morning and evening **exercise classes**: choose from yoga, boxercise and Zumba. Search social media to locate the time and the place – often the Fuente Anayansi – and turn up suitably attired, then treat yourself to a *raspado* when you've finished.

grid of streets, these twin barrios are crammed with cheap hotels – many offering rooms by the hour – with a sprinkling of small parks and a couple of modest sights to provide welcome relief. This older section of the modern city dates back to the boom construction eras of the Panama Railroad and Canal in the mid- and late nineteenth century (see pages 297 and 298), when a large number of West Indian immigrants poured into the city. The area's population expanded yet further when non-US-Canal labourers and their families – again, primarily West Indian – were gradually forced out of the newly created Canal Zone (see page 300) in the early twentieth century. Both areas have become rather rundown in recent years, bearing the brunt of Panama's economic downturn since the Covid-19 pandemic, with increasing levels of petty crime, and while it's generally safe to wander around the main arteries during the day, provided you stay alert, the area is distinctly less salubrious at night.

Museo Afro-Antillano

Av Justo Arosemena (also known as Av 3 Sur) at C 24 • Tues–Sat 9.30am–3.30pm • Charge • ⓦ samaap.com • Ⓜ Cinco de Mayo

Housed in an unmarked wooden former church, and dwarfed by the surrounding high-rises, the **Museo Afro-Antillano** is dedicated to the history and culture of Panama's large West Indian population. The Church of the Christian Mission, as it was then, constituted the social centre of the barrio of El Marañon, once a thriving Afro-Antillean community dating back to the construction of the railroad (see page 297). As property prices escalated in the 1970s and developers moved in, residents were forced out to the suburbs. The community has maintained a precarious toehold in the centre of the city through this small but worthwhile museum, which highlights the pivotal role that Afro-Antilleans played in the construction of the railroad and the Canal. The photographs, tools and period furniture, with captioning in English, provide a sharp reminder of the harsh working and living conditions of black, "silver roll" Canal workers, which contrasted acutely with the privileges of white American "gold roll" employees, in the days of the Canal Zone. The museum also helps organize the annual **Afro-Antillean Fair** that takes place during Carnaval at the Centro de Convenciones ATLAPA (see page 84).

Plaza Belisario Porras

Av Perú, between C 33 and C 34 • Ⓜ La Lotería

Plaza Belisario Porras honours the country's three-time president and founding father. Amid the neatly trimmed flowerbeds rises a vast monument in which Porras cuts a dashing figure, overlooked by grand government buildings and the balustraded Spanish Embassy.

Basílica de Don Bosco

Daily 6am–6pm • Free • Ⓜ La Lotería

With your back to the Belisario Porras monument, looking up Calle Ecuador to Avenida Central, you can spy the rose window of the neo-Romanesque **Basílica de Don Bosco**, built in the 1950s. As well as being pleasantly airy with some lovely stained glass, the place is a glittering blue mass of modern mosaics, crafted in Italy and brought to Panama for the centennial celebrations.

Bella Vista

The district of **BELLA VISTA** contains the neighbourhoods of Bella Vista, Marbella, El Cangrejo and Obarrio, which form the financial and commercial core of Panama City – what is often nebulously referred to as the Área Bancaria (banking area). Either side of Calle 50, this was once a leafy district brimming with 1930s colonial mansions, which has all but been taken over by modern high-rise buildings. To the north on Vía España stands the incongruous twentieth-century neo-Gothic wedding cake of the **Iglesia del Carmen**. Particularly impressive when illuminated at night, the stained-glass windows along the aisles depict tropical flowers, while those higher up in the nave relate tales from the Old and New Testaments. The neo-Byzantine mosaic altarpiece also grabs your attention.

The church marks the beginning of **EL CANGREJO**, which melts into neighbouring **MARBELLA** and **OBARRIO,** home to many of Panama City's hotels and restaurants, as well as upmarket stores and shopping centres. These neighbourhoods are also among the city's nightlife zones.

Avenida Balboa and the Cinta Costera

The sweeping arc of **Avenida Balboa**, which connects the city's historic heartland, Casco Viejo, to its symbols of industrial progress, Punta Paitilla, now forms part of the **Cinta Costera**. The aim of this multimillion-dollar land reclamation project was to ease traffic congestion by constructing a parallel multi-lane highway alongside a promenade complete with trees, benches and leisure facilities. Although the project has delivered more concrete than the green spaces that were originally promised, it has marginally improved the traffic flow, and its jogging path and cycleway are well used by residents (see box, page 65). The Cinta Costera is also the focus of Panama City's Carnavales, which, outside the Azuero, are the country's most extravagant.

Mercado de Mariscos

Southern end of the Cinta Costera • Mon–Sat 6am–6pm; closed first Mon of the month for fumigation • Ⓜ Cinco de Mayo

The distinctive blue-roofed **Mercado de Mariscos** is a fabulous place to wander around. All shapes and sizes of seafood are on sale, some waving their antennae at you from tanks. You can observe the comings and goings from a table upstairs at the *Restaurante de Mariscos* (see page 81), or head around the back and catch the buzz of the *cevicherías* and fish stalls overlooking the busy public dock (*muelle fiscal*).

Monumento a Vasco Núñez de Balboa and around

The Cinta Costera's main sight, midway along, is the magnificent **Monumento a Vasco Núñez de Balboa**. Erected in 1913, it shows the sixteenth-century explorer in classical colonial pose, atop a globe, sword in one hand and flag in the other; once looking out in perpetual triumph on the southern ocean he "discovered", he now seems a tad lost in the traffic. Set back across Avenida Balboa is the grand Neoclassical facade of **Hospital Santo Tomás**, the largest public medical facility in the country.

Parque Urracá

A further 800m along the embankment from the Balboa monument, the pleasant **Parque Urracá** is named after the indigenous chief who famously defeated the Spaniards and later escaped from captivity (see box, page 295). Hemmed in by high-rises, this welcome green space comes alive in the late afternoons at weekends as locals congregate to play football and socialize.

Punta Paitilla, Punta Pacífica and San Francisco

Jutting out into the sea at the northeastern end of the bay, the artificial peninsula of **PUNTA PAITILLA**, packed with more than fifty shimmering skyscrapers, constitutes one of Panama City's most emblematic views. Built around 1970, the forty-storey high-rises and their luxury apartments, many of which lie empty due to absent or fictitious owners, became one of the city's most exclusive residential areas. It's also a major Jewish neighbourhood, with a synagogue and kosher food stores and restaurants in the vicinity.

Around the headland, the newer skyscrapers of **PUNTA PACÍFICA** house yet more opulent ocean-view residences, with the sail-shaped former Trump Ocean Club – currently housing a Marriot hotel – easily the most distinctive. Both exclusive enclaves form part of the broader district of **SAN FRANCISCO**, which is also gradually falling prey to Panama's skyscraper addiction. The area's two main landmarks are the **Centro de Convenciones ATLAPA**, one of the city's main convention centres (see page 84), and Parque Recreativo Omar Torrijos, generally shortened to **Parque Omar**, the city's second largest green space after the Parque Metropolitano. Hundreds of residents take their morning exercise here, or laze about at weekends, and there's a lovely outdoor swimming pool (see box, page 76).

Former Canal Zone

Established in 1903 to protect the Canal, the **former Canal Zone** ran the length of the waterway, extending approximately 8km either side of it but excluding Panama City and Colón. Under US military control until 1977, it was jointly administered by the US and Panamanian authorities until the eventual handover in 1999 (see page 303). Though gradually being swallowed up by Panama City's urban sprawl, **Balboa** – which was effectively the administrative capital of the "Zone" – still retains some of its pleasant leafy landscaping and original architecture, most notably the palatial **Canal Administration Building** and exclusive residential enclave of the Altos de Ancón (formerly Quarry Heights). Above, **Cerro Ancón** affords splendid views of the city and Canal, including south to the **Amador Causeway**, which marks the Pacific entrance to the Canal, and north to the forested **Parque Natural Metropolitano**.

Amador Causeway

Away from the deafening traffic, pollution and stultifying heat of downtown Panama City, the refreshing breezes of the **Amador Causeway** (Calzada de Amador, often shortened to "El Causeway") – the Canal's Pacific breakwater – make it an attractive weekend recreational area for many Panamanians as well as a draw for tourists. Over the years the causeway's popularity has waxed and waned. Currently, parts are on the up again, following a multimillion-dollar facelift that has seen a new dual carriageway, a regular bus service – including the hop-on-hop-off tourist bus (see page 75) – a cycleway, park benches and four viewpoints. Recovering after the latest knock caused by the Covid-19 pandemic, some bars and restaurants are beginning to fill once more; you can wine and dine while enjoying close-ups of transiting ships or more distant views of the Paitilla skyline. Nearer the mouth of the causeway stands the crumbling **Centro de Convenciones Figali** – peeking out from behind is the vast sleek, glass-fronted **Panama**

Convention Center, said to be the largest in the region. More practically, the causeway is the departure point for **ferries** to Taboga and the Archipiélago de las Perlas, as well as for Canal tours (see pages 89, 121 and 97). Consisting of four interconnecting islands – islas **Naos**, **Culebra**, **Perico** and **Flamenco** – the 5km causeway first came into existence in 1913, to help prevent crosscurrents silting up the entry to the Canal. Its strategic location, protruding out into the bay, resulted in Isla Flamenco becoming the site for a US military base. Flamenco also hosts the command centre for the Autoridad del Canal de Panamá (ACP), which controls all traffic transiting the Canal.

The best way to explore the area is on foot or by **bike**; you can rent cycles at several places (see page 76).

Biomuseo

Amador Causeway • Tues–Fri 10am–4pm, Sat & Sun 1am–5pm • Charge • biomuseopanama.com • Metrobuses run down the causeway from the back of Albrook Metro station (5.30am–10/11pm; every 20–30min); taxis and shared taxis also wait there

The unmissable, crumpled technicolour rooftop at the entrance to the causeway proper heralds the **Biomuseo** – designed by famed architect **Frank Gehry** – which, after almost fifteen years of political wrangling, finally opened in 2014, with a hefty price tag to match the hype.

Aimed at highlighting Panama's rich **biodiversity** due to its unique position as a land bridge between the two Americas, the Biomuseo also devotes space to Panama's **human history**. Although the permanent exhibition comprises just eight rooms, plus a couple of outdoor exhibits, its state-of-the-art interactive screens and large-scale audiovisual presentations are undeniably impressive. The **Panamarama** room is particularly striking, its ten-screen, surround-sound romp through Panama's ecosystems, accompanied by drumming and jungle noises, an assault on the senses. Other rooms focus on the geological formation of the isthmus, the ways in which the marine life in the two oceans evolved, and the interconnectedness of various ecosystems. Three new rooms were added in 2019, including two aquariums – one showcasing the country's Pacific marine life, the other its Caribbean counterparts, as well as information on how the emergence of the Panamanian isthmus three million years ago dramatically changed ocean ecology.

It's a good place to visit with kids, and should interest adults who don't have much prior knowledge of the topic. Inevitably, there is both a **gift shop** and **café** on site.

Outside, you can wander through a small **biodiversity park,** which features endemic and native plants, selected on aesthetic grounds or because of their significance to Panama's biodiversity.

Isla Naos and Punta Culebra

Isla Naos is the location of a marine research centre for the Smithsonian Tropical Research Institute (STRI), which maintains a small reserve on the adjoining peninsula, Punta Culebra. The **Punta Culebra Nature Centre** (Dec–Feb Tues–Sun 9am–5pm, March–Nov Wed–Fri 1–5pm, Sat & Sun 9am–5pm; charge; stri.org) is probably only worth popping into if you are travelling with young children. Set in a rare patch of tropical dry forest, the reserve offers a small visitors' centre, a couple of pools containing marine life and a short trail through the forest, where you should keep an eye out for green iguanas and two-toed sloths. Arguably, the biggest draw is the frog exhibit, which contains a number of Panama's emblematic and colourful amphibians. Next to the reserve entrance, at La Playita, is the departure point for Barcos Calypso ferries to Taboga (see page 89).

Isla Perico and Isla Flamenco

At the end of the causeway, the neglected strip mall of **Isla Perico** tends to be ignored in favour of **Isla Flamenco**, which features a cruise terminal and a flash marina sheltering sleek yachts and motorboats, surrounded by pricey bars and restaurants – a real tourist trap for unwary cruise-ship visitors, though its wonderful views make the island a choice spot for a sundowner.

Cerro Ancón

Visible from most of the surrounding area, the huge Panamanian flag fluttering in the breeze on the summit of **Cerro Ancón** (199m) is one of the city's most distinctive landmarks. The hill itself affords sweeping **vistas** of both the city and the Canal; what's more, it is topped with a protected area of secondary **forest** harbouring white-tailed deer, agoutis, sloths, toucans, Geoffroy's tamarin and white-faced capuchin monkeys, and is well worth climbing (see box, page 69).

By the mirador overlooking the city, and below the flagpole, sits the serene bronze figure of poet **Amelia Denis de Icaza**, who is remembered for *Al Cerro Ancón*; written in 1900, it served as a nationalist rallying cry.

Steps down the eastern side of hill, by a guardhouse that once marked the main gate, lead to the theme-park-style **Mi Pueblito** (Tues–Sun 10am–4pm; free), a set of four rather tacky replica villages recreating traditional architectural styles and flogging overpriced crafts. The main incentive is the café-restaurant on the pseudo-Spanish colonial square, whose fresh fruit juices aid recovery from any physical exertion on the hill.

Edificio de la Administración del Canal de Panamá

Western slope of Cerro Ancón • Mon–Fri 8am–4pm; tell the security guard that you want to see the "*murales*" – you may have to present ID

The stately **Edificio de la Administración del Canal de Panamá** (Canal Administration Building), which dominates the hill's western slope, houses four arresting **murals** that celebrate in graphic detail the Herculean achievement of building the Canal. Decorating an elegant domed marble rotunda, just inside the main entrance, they were painted by New York artist William Van Ingen, known for his work in the Library of Congress in Washington DC. A series of evocative lithographs adorn the outer walls of the rotunda.

Balboa

West of Cerro Ancón lies the district of **BALBOA**, whose centre, **El Prado**, is a palm-lined grassy rectangle measured to match the length and width of an original lock chamber. El Prado extends from the Goethals Monument at the foot of the administration building steps to Stevens Circle at the far end, by the main road. When George Goethals took over as chief engineer of the Canal in 1907, he surveyed all that his predecessor, John Stevens, had achieved and prophetically wrote to his

WALKING UP CERRO ANCÓN

One of the highlights of Panama City is undoubtedly a **walk up Cerro Ancón** in the early morning or late afternoon, when you're likely to encounter keel-billed toucans croaking from the treetops and a host of other wildlife.

To get there on foot, cross Avenida de los Mártires, behind the Palacio Legislativo on Plaza Cinco de Mayo, and cut through to the road that winds through the old Gorgas Hospital and Supreme Court. Skirting round the northern side of the hill, the road divides: to the right, it drops down to the Canal Administration Building, while ahead it climbs to **Quarry Heights**, the former US military command centre. These days it is an exclusive leafy residential area (renamed Altos de Ancón) and is worth a short detour for its unique Zonian wooden architecture. From the residential security gate, where taxis have to deposit their passengers, it's a twenty- to thirty-minute hike to the **summit**; take the first left, then immediate right. Only pedestrians and cyclists are admitted.

son, "Mr Stevens has done an amount of work for which he will never get any credit, or if he gets any, will not get enough". Nowhere is this more evident than in the monuments to their labours: while **Stevens Circle** consists of a small and rather neglected memorial down the far end of the Prado, the cream marble **Goethals Monument** monolith stands tall at the foot of the Canal Authority's seat of power, with water cascading over three stepped marble platforms – symbolizing the three sets of locks – into a pool below.

Centro de Capacitación Ascanio Arosemena

Edif. 704 • Mon–Fri 7.15am–4pm • Free • ⓣ 269 6426 • To reach the displays, enter the former school gates, taking the first right turn through a building, across a courtyard and into a second building. You'll need to present ID

Diagonally across from the Goethals Monument stands the former Balboa High School, site of the dramatic "flag riots" of 1964 (see page 302); the 21 Panamanians who died in the skirmish are honoured in a memorial near the back of the building. Today, the old school houses the **Centro de Capacitación Ascanio Arosemena**, which, in addition to providing technical training to Canal employees, contains a small but evocative Canal exhibition with bilingual labelling. Its **memorabilia** ranges from porcelain from the *Tivoli Hotel* – the grandest hotel of the Canal Zone era – to Goethals' hat rack, along with an excellent collection of **photographs** of the Canal construction.

Teatro Balboa and beyond

A stroll down the Prado takes you to Avenida Arnulfo Arias Madrid, across which stands the faded Art Deco **Teatro Balboa** (see page 84), worth peeking inside for its splendid mosaic floors. Turning left along the main road, you hit the main intersection with Calle la Boca, where you cannot fail to notice the vainglorious bronze **monument** to former president Arnulfo Arias Madrid (see page 302), standing on the end of what looks like a giant seesaw with citizens imploring his help crawling towards him.

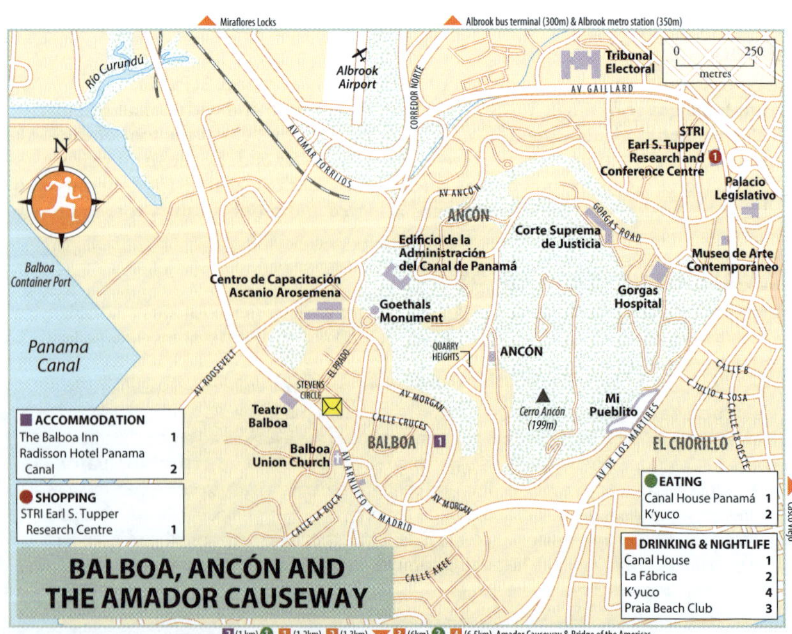

Parque Natural Metropolitano

The main entrance and park office are 200m along Av Juan Pablo II beyond the junction with Av Ascanio Villalaz • Daily 7am–4.30pm; office Mon–Fri 8am–4.30pm • Charge; 2hr guided tours available in English or Spanish; 24hr notice needed; contact via the WhatsApp number on the webpage • Ⓦ parquemetropolitano.org

Though it's not quite far enough from the city centre to escape the hum of traffic, the **Parque Natural Metropolitano** nevertheless offers genuine tranquillity. A hilly patch of semi-deciduous tropical forest, the park offers excellent **birdwatching** and glimpses of the city and Canal area from three lookouts and five short but well-marked **trails**. Arriving early in the morning enhances your chances of seeing sloths entwined around branches, agoutis or koatis snuffling in the undergrowth and colourful and abundant birdlife, including golden-collared mannakins, slaty-tailed trogons and red-lored Amazon parrots.

Park trails

The most interesting meander is the 1.7km **Camino del Mono Tití**, named after the Geoffroy's tamarin monkeys that can occasionally be sighted when making the moderate climb to the viewpoint. From the main park entrance, you'll need to walk 1km along the **Sendero El Roble**, so called because of the pink-flowering oak trees along the path. To make a circular route, walk the Mono Tití trail one way, returning via the steeper but shorter **Sendero La Cienaguita** ("little marsh" – only visible in the rainy season). You can pick up a free **map** at the main entrance, but it's hard to get lost since the park is only about two square kilometres and the trails are well signed.

Panamá Viejo

Vía Cincuentenario • Tues–Sun 8.30am–4.30pm • Charge; guided tours booked and paid for in advance – details on the website • Ⓦ patronatopanamaviejo.org • Metrobuses from the front of Albrook bus terminal run along the Cinta Costera and stop outside the ticket office (every 30min; 30min); return bus on Av Cincuentenario, across from the ticket office, or from the exit along Calle Santo Domingo

You'll need some imagination to reconstruct the neglected ruins of sixteenth-century Panamá La Vieja, or **PANAMÁ VIEJO**, as it's more often called, which was once the premier colonial city on the isthmus (see box, page 72). Yet while there's no comparison with the magnificent Maya sites elsewhere in Central America, the view from the **bell tower** and the excellent on-site **museum** make a half-day visit worthwhile.

Tickets are obtained from the Centro de Visitantes, around 800m west of the main site. Then, you can hop on the tourist train, which will transport you to the Plaza Mayor and the museum, or wander along the shoreline and visit the less well-preserved sites before reaching the main square. Note that there is a **craft market** in the large uninviting building close to the ticket office though stalls are not always staffed.

The convents

Outside the visitors' centre ticket office, you can backtrack 100m to peer over at the **Puente del Matadero** ("Bridge of the Slaughterhouse"), named after the neighbouring abattoir, which marked the western limit of the old city. Returning east along the shoreline, continue along the path a few hundred metres past extensive mud flats being probed by hundreds of migrating waders. Passing the scarcely visible or recognizable Iglesia y Convento de la Merced – which survived Morgan's assault and was relocated to Casco Viejo – and the Iglesia y Convento de San Francisco, cross the road and turn east down Calle de la Empedrada. To the left stands the well-preserved **Iglesia del Convento de la Concepción**, the city's only convent for women, built in 1597. Look over the nearby wall and you'll find the impressive remains of the convent's seventeenth-century reservoir. The tour continues past the skeletal remnants of the Jesuit Iglesia y Convento de la Compañia de Jesús before reaching the Plaza Mayor.

PANAMÁ VIEJO'S TREASURE TRAIL

Nuestra Señora de la Asunción de Panamá, to give Panamá Viejo its full name, was established in 1519 by the infamous Pedro Arias de Ávila. Despite the surprisingly swampy location, Panama City prospered as the Pacific terminal of the Spanish Crown's **treasure trail**, sending silks and spices from the East and plundered silver and gold from Peru to Europe via the isthmus. By the early seventeenth century, it boasted an impressive cathedral, seven convents, numerous churches, a hospital, two hundred warehouses and around five thousand houses. Being on the crucial trade route necessitated the construction of a huge customs house, a treasury and a mint; these were built in the most heavily fortified area of the Casas Reales (Royal Houses), the symbol of the Spanish Crown's might, originally separated from the rest of the city by a moat and wooden palisade.

Following the Welsh pirate Henry Morgan's sacking of the city in 1671 (see page 296), the place was razed to the ground. Little more than a pile of rubble now remains of these once impressive buildings – some of the original stones were quarried for construction of the new city, after which the site was largely neglected – but the **Iglesia del Convento de la Concepción** and the cathedral **bell tower** have been restored.

Museo de la Plaza Major

The excellent two-storey **Museo de la Plaza Mayor** should be your first port of call once reaching the main site. It is extremely informative, with many summaries in English, and contains **over 350 artefacts** from both the **pre-Hispanic** and **colonial** periods. Most of the ceramics and utensils originated from the site, which was first occupied over 1,500 years ago. The various displays give a sense of everyday life over the ages, for both the colonizers and the colonized, and a useful interactive **scale model** of the city in 1671 helps make sense of the ruins outside.

Plaza Mayor

The vast open space of the **Plaza Mayor** is overlooked by the imposing cathedral **bell tower**, one of Panama's most distinctive landmarks, which is increasingly dwarfed by the nearby skyscrapers of the Costa del Este, an upmarket residential and business district. The plaza was the social hub of the city, hosting events from political rallies to bullfights, and surrounded by the most prestigious buildings, including to the east the Cabildo (City Hall) and the cathedral – **La Catedral de la Nuestra Señora de la Asunción**. The stone edifice that replaced the original wooden structure was completed between 1619 and 1629. The magnificently restored belfry now has a modern staircase, which is worth climbing for the views. From here you can appreciate the city's former grandeur, as well as gazing out into the bay at container vessels waiting to transit the canal.

Leaving the cathedral by the vestibule, you can just make out the remains of the **Casa Alarcón**; formerly the domicile of the bishop, this nobleman's home dating back to the 1640s is the largest known and best-preserved private house on the site. Beyond lie the remains of the Dominican **Iglesia y Convento de Santo Domingo**. To the east, on a bluff overlooking the bay, stand the paltry remnants of the **Casas Reales.** Built out of wood and stone, and heavily fortified with a moat, this once vast complex was the seat of power, containing the governor's residence, customs house and treasury. It is here the loot from the empire was stored and counted before being transported across the isthmus.

The northern remains

A few hundred metres north along the Cincuentenario, little remains of the **Iglesia de San José**, which survived the fire of 1671 and contained the splendid golden altar that now sits in the church of the same name in Casco Viejo (see page 61). At the old northern city limit, a couple of hundred metres beyond, Panamá Viejo's famous **Puente del Rey** (King's Bridge) still spans the Río Gallinero, where it marked the gateway to the Camino Real, the conquistadors' mule trail across the isthmus. If you explore that far, exercise **caution**, since the surrounding Río Abajo neighbourhood is an impoverished barrio and tourist muggings are not unknown.

Bahá'í House of Worship

Apartado 143, Zona 15 • Daily 9am–6pm; Sun service 10am (30min) • Free • Ⓦ templo.panamabahai.net • Ⓜ San Isidro, almost the end of Line 1; follow the signs to the main exit, where a courtesy shuttle can take you up to the temple (see website for the timetable) – keep alert as you exit San Isidro metro, as muggings have been reported

In the foothills of the Cordillera Central, the **Bahá'í House of Worship** – the hilltop dome that resembles an alien spaceship – offers splendid vistas across the eastern suburbs to the Pacific. It's the focus of attention for an estimated sixty thousand Bahá'í followers in Panama and following the opening of the nearby metro station in 2015, it is attracting increasing numbers of tourists.

The Bahá'í faith, which developed in nineteenth-century Persia, is one of the world's youngest religions, and emphasizes equality and respect among religions and people. Panama was singled out for Latin America's first Bahá'í house of worship on account of a Bahá'í prophecy made in the early twentieth century that recognized the country's strategic location as a bridge between the Americas, and anticipated that the Canal would enhance its importance as a mean of accessing countries in other parts of the world.

Interested visitors can attend the Sunday service or simply wander through the delightful flower-filled gardens.

ARRIVAL AND DEPARTURE — PANAMA CITY

Panama City is the country's transport hub for both international and national traffic, with two international airports, one domestic airport, a port, a cruise ship terminal and a gigantic bus terminal. When it comes to moving on, most people use the country's efficient and extensive **bus system**; internal **flights** are available for a handful of places, with Bocas del Toro the most popular destination. **Car rental** is also easy (see page 28), but only worth it if you're heading off the beaten track.

BY PLANE

TOCUMEN INTERNATIONAL AIRPORT

Most visitors enter Panama through Tocumen International Airport (Aeropuerto Internacional de Tocumen; Ⓦ tocumenpanama.aereo), about 24km northeast of Panama City.

Facilities The airport has two adjacent terminals within walking distance of each other though there is a shuttle transfer. Most of the airlines and the services – a bank, money exchange, ATMs, a left luggage office, taxi stand and car-rental desks – are in Terminal 1.

Phone and internet Expensive mobile-phone packages are also for sale in the arrivals hall, but you can get a better deal in town (see page 47).

Taxis Most passengers take a private or *colectivo* taxi into the city. The official taxi service provider has a desk in the exit hall displaying the official rates, which you should consult if in doubt. At the time of writing, private taxis for one or two passengers cost around $30–40 for central Panama City. *Colectivos*, (which for obvious financial reasons are not heavily advertised) cost $20/person for three or more passengers – exit by the main terminal door, and cross the road to the *colectivo* taxi stand. Uber and Cabify exist but also have to pay airport fees so there's little difference in price.

Metro This is by far the cheapest way to get into the city (it's also safe to travel on), but there's no signage in the airport, apparently due to pressure from the powerful taxi drivers' union, which inevitably prefers visitors to use their services. Leave the departures hall, turn right and walk two hundred metres along the footpath until you reach the unmarked escalator and lift, which take you up to the metro station. Here you can buy the combined metro and bus transport card (*RapiPass*) for $2, then add some credit. There is an app, but it's not very reliable. You can reach the city centre (50min–1hr) for 0.85c. Take the airport link to Linea 2, at Corredor Sur, then head towards San Miguelito, where you change onto Linea 1 in the direction of Albrook.

PANAMÁ PACÍFICO INTERNATIONAL AIRPORT

Charter flights, and a couple of low-cost airlines, including Copa's sibling, Wingo (Ⓦ wingo.com), use the new Panamá Pacífico International Airport. Formerly the US Howard

1

Air Force base, in the Canal Zone, it lies 9km southwest of Balboa.

Taxis Taxis to central Panama City cost around $25.

Buses The bus to Veracruz from Albrook bus terminal (6am–9pm; every 20–30min; 20min) passes the airport entrance, from where it is a short walk to the terminal.

ALBROOK AIRPORT

Domestic flights from the main domestic carrier, Air Panama (☎ 316 9000, ⓦ airpanama.com), and the smaller FlyTrip (☎ 315 0478, ⓦ flytrip.com.pa) operate from low-key Albrook Airport (officially Aeropuerto International Marcos A. Gelabert; ☎ 5204 9406), 3km northwest of the city centre. Air Panama serves four domestic destinations whereas FlyTrip serves three. While in theory Air Panama accepts online credit-card bookings, the website doesn't always work. Nor is credit-card payment over the phone accepted. If online isn't an option, you need to buy a ticket in person at the airport (Mon–Sat 6am–6pm, Sun 8am–6pm). FlyTrip also has an office at Albrook (Mon–Fri 7am–5pm).

Facilities Several car rental firms have offices here; there's also an ATM.

Taxis Taxis to most places in the city should not top $4–5, although the more luxurious cabs waiting outside the terminal will charge you double the fare of a taxi flagged down on the road, which is easy and safe to do during the day.

BY BUS

All regional buses arrive at the upper level of Albrook bus terminal (officially Gran Terminal de Transportes de Panamá, more commonly referred to as "El Terminal"; ☎ 303 3030), the national bus terminal. It lies 3km northwest of the city centre, near Albrook Airport.

Getting into town Local buses (see page 74), leave from ground level at the front of the terminal. Taxis also stop here and can take you to your lodgings; this should cost no more than $5–6 for one or two passengers for a central area such as Casco Viejo or El Cangrejo, but they may try to charge more if you arrive late at night or don't seem to know what you're doing. The terminal is also at the end of Line 1 of the metro (see page 75), which can also get you to Plaza Cinco de Mayo – from where it's a 15min walk or a shuttle ride to Casco Viejo – or El Cangrejo and Obarrio.

Getting to the bus terminal To get to the bus terminal from the city centre, take a taxi, or a bus bound for Albrook on Vía España, along the Cinta Costera/Av Balboa, or at the side of the Palacio Legislativo off Plaza Cinco de Mayo. Alternatively, take the metro (see page 75).

Onward travel by bus Several major destinations are served by more than one company, some of which offer express and (cheaper) stopping buses – ticket prices charged by all companies to the same destination will be the same. To catch a bus out of town, first buy your ticket from the appropriate ticket office inside the terminal before passing through a turnstile to a numbered departure bay at the back. To do this you'll need a RapiPass, a rechargeable swipe card (*tarjeta magnética*) used on Metrobuses, the metro and the bus terminal turnstiles (10¢). You can buy the RapiPass for $2 (plus the credit you want to put on it) at kiosks in the bus terminal, or in any metro station.

Travelling to Costa Rica Ticabus (ⓦ tica-bus.com/destinos/panama) has daily departures to San José, Costa Rica (7am; 15–16hr) and an additional night bus on Saturdays. Tickets can be bought at their ticket office in the bus terminal several days in advance of travel, which is advisable. Alternatively, take a Panachif (☎ 314 6885) bus to Paso Canoas (see box, page 203) at the border via David, and transfer to Costa Rican transport there.

GETTING AROUND

Panama City's vast urban sprawl continues to expand at an alarming rate, and navigating your way around can at first seem daunting. However, places of interest to tourists are concentrated in a few areas easily accessible by **bus** or **taxi**, or, in the case of Casco Viejo, **on foot**. Avoid travelling at **rush hour** (Mon–Fri 7–9am & 4.30–7pm), when traffic grinds to a halt in horn-honking mayhem. The new **metro** so far has two lines (plus a link line to Tocumen airport) and it provides a quick way of travelling between El Cangrejo, Plaza Cinco de Mayo (with walking or shuttle bus access to Casco Viejo) and Albrook bus terminal. At the time of writing, a third line was under construction.

BY BUS

The orange Metrobuses operate on fixed routes without timetables, and use designated stops. The destination is indicated on the LED screen at the front of the bus. A handful of the old US school buses – *diablos rojos* (red devils) – still exist for some routes, and they stop and pick up passengers at will.

Fares and passes Travelling by bus is the cheapest way to get about, costing a mere 35¢ for any trip within the metropolitan boundary (except the buses that use Corredores – express toll roads – which cost $1.25). On the few *diablos rojos* that still exist, you pay 25¢ cash on exit. Metrobus journeys require a prepaid RapiPass swipe card (*tarjeta magnética*; $2, plus the credit you want to load onto it) available at Albrook bus terminal, metro stations and Tocumen International Airport.

Routes The city's main arteries and bus routes run vaguely southwest to northeast along Av Balboa and the Cinta Costera, Av Central (which becomes Av España) and Av Justo Arosemena (Av 3 Sur). All buses circulate every few minutes on the busiest routes, from 5.30/6am until 11pm/midnight; less frequently on Sun.

Getting to Casco Viejo Shuttle buses run to Casco Viejo from Plaza Cinco de Mayo (accessible by metro), or you can

MAJOR DOMESTIC BUS ROUTES

DESTINATION	FREQUENCY	DURATION
Antón	5.20am–8pm; every 30min	2hr
Bayano (via Chepo)	4am–4.40pm; every 40min	2hr
Bocas del Toro (take Changuinola bus)	7am, 6pm, 6.30pm & 7pm (8pm during busy periods)	10hr (via Almirante, for Bocas)
Chame	5.30am–9pm; every 20min	1hr 30min
Chitré	6am–10.30pm; every 50min.	4hr
Colón	express bus: 4.40am–10pm; approximately every 30min	1hr 30min
	regular bus: 4am–midnight; every 20–30min	2hr
David	4.30am–8.30pm; buses run hourly; express services at 10pm, 11pm & midnight	7hr
El Copé	6am–6.30pm; every 30min	3hr30min
El Valle (de Antón)	7am–7pm; every 25–30min	2hr30min
Gamboa	5am (7am Sat & Sun)–4.45pm; 4–5 buses daily	50min
Las Tablas	6am–7pm; hourly	4hr30min
Metetí	3am–5.20pm; hourly	5–6hr
Paso Canoas (border with Costa Rica)	6.30am–8.30pm; 9 daily plus express at 10pm, 11pm & midnight	8–9hr
Penonomé	4.50am–10.45pm; every 20min	2hr30min
San Carlos	6am–8.30pm; every 20min	1hr 30min
Santiago	6am–11pm; hourly (note that all buses for David also stop in Santiago)	3hr 30min
Soná (for Santa Catalina)	6.45am–5.30pm; five daily	5hr30min
Yaviza	Midnight express bus; and four more. Others bound for Metetí will continue to Yaviza if there is demand; otherwise change in Metetí to a local bus.	6–7hr

walk up the pedestrianized section of Av Central (15min). A taxi from the bus terminal should not cost more than $5–6.

Hop-on-hop-off sightseeing bus The red city sightseeing double-decker bus (Ⓦcity-sightseeing.com) is in many ways a disappointment thanks to a limited route and often unintelligible commentary. However, it might be of interest to solo travellers wanting to visit the Miraflores Locks, Casco Viejo (which it can't enter), the Biodiversity Museum and Amador Causeway in a short space of time. If you still fancy the idea, take the trip on a Sunday, when you'll spend less time sitting in traffic.

BY METRO

Route Panama City's new metro system – Central America's first – currently has two lines, with a third one underway. Line 1 runs from the Albrook bus terminal via Plaza Cinco de Mayo and northwards towards El Cangrejo and beyond, as far as the districts of Los Andes and San Isidro. Line 2 branches off eastwards at San Miguelito towards Nuevo Tocumen, a suburb which lies just beyond Tocumen International Airport. A two-stop link line branches off at Corredor Sur to take passengers to the airport. Trains run at frequent intervals (Mon–Sat 5am–10/11pm; Sun & public holidays 7am–10pm).

Fares Since the metro opened in 2014, the Line 1 fare has been 0.35c and the Line 2 fare 0.50c. To pay you will need a rechargeable metro or RapiPass swipe card (see page 73).

1

BY TAXI

Taxis are plentiful – around 28,000 in the city at the last count – and relatively cheap.

Fares Taxis are supposed to follow an overcomplicated zonal pricing schedule (see ⓦ transito.gob.pa) set by the transport authorities, but in practice the price is down to supply and demand, your negotiating skills in Spanish and whether they want to take you. For most destinations in the city you shouldn't pay more than $5–6 during normal working hours, the exception being to Panamá Viejo or the Amador Causeway, where prices may be inflated because the driver is concerned about finding a passenger for the return trip – that said, the arrival of Uber in the capital has curbed to some extent the tendency to overcharge tourists. If you're unsure, ask around for the current rates beforehand and agree a price before getting in. Note that the more comfortable a/c tourist taxis hovering outside the mid- to high-end hotels, recognizable by the SET licence plates, charge much higher rates.

Tours Taxi drivers often serve as chauffeurs and unofficial city tour guides; you may be charged from $15/hr. Higher rates are charged by taxi drivers that speak English.

BY BIKE

You would need to have a death wish to cycle in most of Panama City. The exceptions are along the Cinta Costera and the Amador Causeway, where the cycleways and the general lack of traffic and fumes make for a pleasant ride. There is even a popular Ciclovía (cycling festival) every Sun morning (see box, page 65). Other places include Cerro Ancón, which is steep (see box, page 69), and the Ciudad de Saber (see box, page 76), which is undulating.

Bike rental and repairs Bike rental is generally by the hour in Panama City, and expensive, but better long-term rates can be negotiated. Bicicletas Moses (ⓦ mosesbikerentals.com), by *Las Pencas* on the Amador Causeway, and at the Plaza Paitilla Inn, Punta Paitilla, rents regular bikes, plus tandems and pedal buggies for two or four. Burke Bikes (ⓦ burkebikepanama.com) has offices on C 1, Casco Viejo, and, further down the causeway on Isla Perico; they offer a similar variety for similar rates, which vary according to demand, so check in advance. Panama Bike Rental (ⓦ panamabikerental.com), in the RALI Business Center on Avenida Balboa, has a good range of top-quality bike and offers attractive weekly rates. You will need to present ID at all places.

BY CAR

Although rental cars are available at both airports and along Vía España near El Cangrejo, the city's cheap and plentiful buses and taxis mean there is no need to rent a car until you're ready to leave. Besides, the free-for-all attitude of many drivers makes driving a stressful experience.

RECREATIONAL ACTIVITIES

Many visitors to Panama are expressly here for the wealth of **outdoor activities**, all of which can be enjoyed on a day-trip from the capital, either independently or on a tour (see page 77). There are also options within the city itself, some of them free or costing very little. Head for the **Cinta Costera** (see box, page 65) or the following:

CIUDAD DE SABER (CITY OF KNOWLEDGE)

The **Ciudad de Saber (City of Knowledge)**, opposite the Miraflores Locks and accessible by bus (see page 97), contains some fabulous sports facilities open to the public. Set in a green recreational park, they provide a great escape from the city congestion and high-rises, and are open to all – though they can be busy at weekends. There is an Olympic-size open-air pool for lane swimming and a recreational pool (Tues–Fri 5.30am–8pm, Sat & Sun 8am–8pm; ⓦ comercial.ciudaddelsaber.org/parque-cds/piscina; charge; swimming caps obligatory). There are also **gym** and **tennis courts**, and plenty of picnic space. Piscina Adan Gordon (Tues–Sun 7am–2pm; ⓦ adangordon.xyz; charge; swimming caps obligatory) is a more central Olympic-size pool, though public swim times are limited due to classes and training slots.

PARQUE OMAR

Leafy **Parque Recreativo Omar Torrijos** (daily 4am–10pm), on Av Porras, San Francisco, has tennis courts, a jogging route, an outdoor pool (Tues–Sun 6am–6pm; charge) and lots of space to picnic. Though closer to the city centre than the Ciudad de Saber, and cheaper, the pool is not as easy to access: you'll need to present a current medical certificate, and two passport photos, which will get you a pass, valid for a couple of years (fee). Less hassle are the inexpensive weekday **exercise classes**, from yoga to Zumba, given in the park by qualified instructors (6–8am & 4–7pm; ⓦ parqueomar.gob.pa/clases). Just roll up and join in.

INFORMATION

Tourist information There are no tourist offices set up to deal with tourists, beyond the ATP kiosks at the airport – frequently left unstaffed. The hostels, tour operators and some of the more upmarket hotels are much better sources of information.

ACTIVITIES AND TOURS

Several excellent **tour operators** in Panama City offer bilingual guiding in English and Spanish on half-day- or day-trips from both Panama City and from the other main tourist destinations of Boquete and Bocas del Toro. They can also organize bespoke multiday excursions. Specialist tour operators for Gunayala and Darién have been listed in the relevant chapters (see pages 254 and 279). Day-tours, which usually require a minimum of four people, range from around U$150/person.

Ancon Expeditions ⓦ anconexpeditions.com. Very professional, expensive outfit, offering top-notch bilingual naturalist guiding services for single- and multiday adventures: birdwatching across Panama or exploring the cloud forests of Chiriquí. Their birding expertise may be worth the expense, but other tours are not.

Aventuras Panamá ⓦ aventuraspanama.com. Highly enjoyable soft adventure tours, chiefly hiking, kayaking and whitewater rafting along a variety of rivers, some within a couple of hours of Panama City in Panamá and Coclé provinces. The hike-and-rafting combination in the Chagres national park is a particularly favourite.

Ecocircuitos ⓦ ecocircuitos.com. Actively involved in promoting sustainable tourism and supporting community-based projects, this outfit offers a wide range of day-trips from the capital and elsewhere, including an exclusive behind-the-scenes tour of Miraflores Locks.

Emberá Tours ⓦ emberatourspanama.com. Run by Garceth Cunampio, an English-speaking Emberá guide who organizes day or overnight excursions to Emberá Puru on the Chagres, wildlife-viewing trips round Lago Gatún and longer expeditions to the Darién, on request.

Go Panama Bike Tours ⓦ gopanamabiketours.com. Offers 2–3hr historical-cultural tours by bike around Casco Viejo and the Causeway or the Cinta Costera. E-bikes also available.

Isthmian Adventures ⓦ iadventurespanama.com. Run by and working with excellent certified bilingual naturalist guides, at the upper end of the market, this company (formerly Sendero Panamá) offers a diverse range of acclaimed day-trips and multiday adventures.

Whalewatching Panama ⓦ whalewatchingpanama.com. Highly acclaimed, ethical seasonal tours given by the company owner and extremely knowledgeable cetacean specialist Joshua Hall. Best mid-July–end of Sept.

ACCOMMODATION

There are **accommodation** options to suit all tastes and all budgets in Panama City, but beds can be in short supply at busy times such as Carnaval or Christmas, when it is essential to **book in advance**. Some mid-range hotels offer special business rates (open to all) and most mid-range and high-end hotels offer substantial **discounts** for online bookings. Note that hotels located on a major bus route, such as Vía España or Av Perú, can get **noisy** from around 5.30–6.00am, when the traffic starts up and the horn honking begins, until late at night, so ask for a room at the back on one of the higher floors. As for **facilities**, hot water is standard in hotels (though not necessarily in hostels) and almost all have a/c (which may cost extra in the cheap hotels), cable TV and free wi-fi. Families or anyone staying a week or more might consider an **aparthotel** – these have kitchen/lounge/dining facilities and offer hotel services such as cleaning, laundry and breakfast. Long-term rentals and corporate rates are often negotiable.

CASCO VIEJO, SEE MAP PAGE 56

Budget accommodation is in short supply in Casco Viejo, the old colonial centre, which, since 2020 has lost its hostels and become home to several five-star hotels while experiencing an influx of chic bars and restaurants. The restoration of many of the historic buildings and limited traffic access make it a pleasant retreat from the congestion and the pollution of the rest of the city, though the increase in bars and construction noise where buildings are being restored mean that you still need to think carefully about where to stay if you want peace and quiet.

AmazINN Places ⓦ amazinnplaces.com/en/rentals/rentals-panama-p189. A collection of co-living properties with shared facilities (often including a plunge pool) dotted around Casco Viejo; rooms or whole flats are stylishly furnished in contemporary design and the business is run like Airbnb on a large scale, with additional cleaning charges and self-check-in. Some of the smaller rooms can be hit and miss, but you can't beat the locations. $$$–$$$$

★ **American Trade Hotel** Plaza Herrera ⓦ americantradehotel.com. Overlooking an elegant plaza, a gleaming white facade proudly announces Casco Viejo's first fully restored grand hotel. White and wood predominate in light airy rooms, many of which have their own balustraded balcony. Every detail has been considered, with modern comforts carefully blended into the historical structure. $$$$

★ **Las Clementinas** C 11 and Av "B" ⓦ lasclementinas.com. Half a dozen beautifully decorated suites (four studios and two flats – the latter with fully equipped kitchens), with hand-painted tiles, wooden floors and a combination of antiques and stylish modern furnishings. All have lofty ceilings and access to a fabulous rooftop terrace. Service is top-notch. $$$–$$$$

Hotel La Compañía Av "A" and C 8 hyatt.com/unbound-collection.com. Ignore the Hyatt tag (or how permission was given to convert a UNESCO World Heritage Site Jesuit convent into a five-star hotel). It's here now, unique and stunning, with contemporary design infused into the historical structures, reflected in chronologically themed Spanish, French and American wings. Sunset views from the rooftop pool and bar, too. $$$$

La Isabela Suites C 9, between Av Central and C Boquete laisabelapanama.com. Let yourself be pampered in this splendidly furnished and serviced luxury condo-hotel occupying a renovated nineteenth-century mansion. Set round an interior courtyard, and oozing style, are a handful of spacious one- and two-bedroom suites, catering to your every need, with an annexe that boasts an apartment with a glorious rooftop terrace overlooking Plaza Bolívar, although it can be noisier. $$$–$$$$

Magnolia Inn C 8 and Boquete, behind the cathedral magnoliapanama.com. This French colonial mansion is part boutique hotel, but mainly hostel – without the vibe, thanks to outsourced reception staff. Dorms (accommodating 4–10 beds) have a/c and in the smaller ones, beds have private reading lights. All have use of a comfortable chandelier-illuminated dining and lounge area, small corner balcony and well-equipped kitchen. The variously priced hotel rooms offer affordable comfort. Dorms $, doubles $$$

Oasis Hotel C 9 Este and Av "B" oasishotelpanama.com. A rare mid-range gem in a converted colonial mansion. A handful of individually designed, well-equipped suites of various shapes and sizes and eclectic decor; some also have balconies with bay views. Then there's a vibrant rooftop bar – the downside being thumping music at weekends and during holidays until 2am (earplugs provided). Discounted longer stays. $$–$$$

CALIDONIA AND LA EXPOSICIÓN, SEE MAP PAGE 62

Calidonia and La Exposición offer a wide selection of unexceptional but affordable modern hotels and *pensiones*. The streets off the main arteries are not very safe at night, however, and some of the hotels offer rooms by the hour – though usually on a separate floor. Also, places to eat are few and far between, though generally quite cheap.

Hostel Mamallena Primera C Perejil, off Vía España mamallena.com; Santo Tomás. One of the original backpacker places, where you can chill in the courtyard garden, bob in the (small) pool, or lounge in front of the TV. Dorms have a/c, quality mattresses and crisp cotton sheets while private rooms (also a/c) share bathrooms. The friendly, helpful staff have bags of info and deals on trips, and there are plenty of extras – complimentary tea, coffee; cheap airport transfers and a washing machine. Only the location could be improved. Dorms $, doubles $$

Hotel Costa Inn Av Perú at C 39 facebook.com/costainnpanama; Santo Tomás. Reliable budget option. Ask for one of the refurbished rooms, enlivened by cheerful tropical-themed wallpaper. The on-site restaurant is convenient, if not inspiring, but the rooftop pool offering stellar views is a real bonus though you may have to compete for space with petting couples at night. $$

Hotel República Plaza 5 de Mayo hotelrepublicapanama.com; Cinco de Mayo. Overlooking the action in the plaza, and with views across the bay, this multi-storey budget hotel is excellent value and has numerous rooms (or variable quality – so try several), featuring large beds, a fridge and plenty of furniture. The rooftop terrace is a bonus. $$

Residencial Texas C 31, between Av Perú and Cuba, beside the national lottery 225 0800; La Lotería. Friendly, secure family-owned place offering good-value rooms with spotless tiled bathrooms, decent hot showers and good mattresses, though the furniture is tired, and the street not very salubrious. $$

BELLA VISTA, SEE MAP PAGE 62

The district of Bella Vista contains the neighbourhood of the same name, plus Marbella El Cangrejo and Obarrio. These collectively form the hub of the modern city's nightlife and commercial activity and have the densest concentration of accommodation. Although hotel prices are generally high, the number of hostels in this area is steadily increasing too, and you're within striking distance of many restaurants, bars, clubs, shops and casinos. If you keep to the well-lit streets, it's safe to stroll around here at night.

★ **Bodhi Hostel** C 50D Este bodhihostels.com. This converted Bella Vista mansion makes for a great hostel: a delightful pot-plant-filled pool area, a well-equipped kitchen-dining area and plenty of chill-out spots. Add to that, sturdy wooden bunks in spacious dorms, light-filled doubles and friendly staff. Breakfast included. Dorms $, doubles $$

The Bristol Hotel Av Aquilino de la Guardia at C 50 thebristol.com; Iglesia del Carmen. From the moment you glide across its gleaming marble foyer, this classically designed luxury boutique hotel exudes exclusivity. Carpeted rooms are elegant and sumptuously furnished, with vast marble bathrooms and 24hr butler service. Spa services and an award-winning restaurant, too. $$$$

Coral Suites C Eusebio A. Morales, coralsuites.com; Iglesia del Carmen. Comfortable aparthotel aimed at the business market, in a convenient location. Nicely furnished spacious suites have fully equipped kitchens and living/dining areas. Enjoy an American breakfast (included in the rates) after a few lengths in the rooftop pool or a session in the gym. Discounts for longer stays $$–$$$

Decapolis Hotel Av Balboa, Megápolis (formerly Multicentro) decapolishotel.com. Brash or stylish (depending on your viewpoint), this thirty-floor glass-and-steel edifice, with touches of modern art, leads into the Megapolís Mall and Majestic Casino. The big, tasteful guestrooms have all the frills – go for an upper-floor room with an ocean view. There's an on-site restaurant (excellent breakfast buffet included in rates), sushi bar and pool. $$$

Global Hotel Twist Tower C 54 Este and Av Samuel Lewis, Obarrio globalpanamahotel.com; Vía Argentina. Occupying the ground floor and various upper floors of a quirkily designed skyscraper, this luxurious place exudes urban chic. The airy rooms have floor-to-ceiling windows, understated colours – with the odd flash of royal blue – and glitzy bathrooms; amenities include a gym, spa, outdoor rooftop plunge pool and jacuzzi, and a fine-dining restaurant. Excellent online rates. $$$–$$$$

Hostal Familiar Carmencita C Ricardo Miró, El Carmen hostalfamiliarcarmencita.com; Fernández de Córdoba. A handful of simple but comfortable doubles and a couple of larger rooms in this congenial converted family home, with use of small kitchen and patio, walled garden and laundry service. $$

Hostal Posada 1914 C 44 Este and C Colombia posada1914.com; Santo Tomás. Convivial hostel with bags of character and welcoming staff. Accommodation is in small single-sex dorms and a few doubles (with shared or private bath), but the brightly painted plant-filled terrace and semi-open spacious kitchen are a treat, though the star feature is the climbing wall. Dorms $, doubles $$

Hotel California C 43 Este and Vía España, La Cresta hotelcaliforniapanama.com; Santo Tomás. Set on a noisy main road – so choose your room carefully – in an uninspiring part of the city, this long-standing budget traveller favourite is four short blocks from a Metro station and offers good value for money. Clean, tidy but basically furnished with flat-screen TV, its star attraction is the small pool-cum-jacuzzi on the rooftop terrace. $$

★ **Hotel Principe and Suites** C 1A Norte principehotelandsuites.com; Vía Argentina. Offering frequent discounts, this modern four-star hotel is excellent value: rooms are spacious with comfortable beds piled high with pillows, a large TV and spacious bathrooms; suites boast kitchenettes and/or a living area. Reception is 24hr, and there are two on-site restaurants, a small pool area, and a 24hr convenience store next door. Doubles $$, suites $$$

★ **Toscana Inn** C "D" at C Eusebio A. Morales toscanainnhotel.com; Iglesia del Carmen. Good-value mid-range hotel in an excellent location, with warmly decorated en-suite rooms crammed with heavy wooden furniture and all modern amenities, topped with efficient, friendly service. $$

W Panama C 50 at Aquilino de la Guardia marriott.com/en-us/hotels/ptywh-w-panama; Iglesia del Carmen. A Marriot with a difference: rooms exude a sleek, contemporary feel with excellent service plus full business amenities, gym, pool and spa treatments – located bang in the middle of the financial district. $$$$

FORMER CANAL ZONE, SEE MAPS PAGES 54 AND 70

There is a handful of lodgings scattered round the former Canal Zone, an area that includes the Amador Causeway, Balboa and Cerro Ancón, stretching to Albrook, Clayton and Miraflores Locks. These often offer greater tranquillity than the city-centre hotels and, in some cases, superb views, though they are some distance from the main watering holes which means you may need to spend more on taxis.

The Balboa Inn Las Cruces 2311a, Balboa balboainnpanama.com. In the quiet residential area of Balboa, yet close to bus and taxi routes, this established B&B offers simple, nicely furnished rooms with excellent beds and plenty of light. The delightful garden breakfast terrace allows you to birdwatch while you enjoy your full American breakfast. $$

★ **Casa Mariposa** C Guanábano 637, Clayton cascocapital.com/casamariposa. A delightful escape from the city bustle: four large three-bedroom apartments with patios or balconies, plus two studio apartments, with hot plate, microwave and kettle – but washing up is in the wash basin. By no means "luxury" as billed, but serviced and supremely comfortable, in a relaxing setting, surrounded by nature and birdlife. Buses from Albrook are frequent, though it's a stiff 10min walk from the bus stop. Minimum four-night stay. $$–$$$

Radisson Hotel Panama Canal Amador Causeway choicehotels.com/en-uk/panama/amador/radisson-hotels. A standard motel in a stunning location, right by the Canal entrance. Pay the extra to watch the ships from your balcony – otherwise you may get a view of the car park. The large, bright rooms are equipped with all conveniences. There's an on-site *TGI Friday's* and a couple of pools. $$$

OTHER AREAS, SEE MAP PAGE 62

★ **Casa Areka** C Ramón H Jurado at C56 Este Punta Pacífica, Casa 16 hostalcasaareka.com. Unlikely swish location for a small, super-friendly hostel, with the cosy pool and patio area the main draw, attracting a young backpacker crowd. Dorms are small but with good beds and double en-suite rooms are good value with cable TV. The supermarket over the road is convenient for self-caterers. Dorm $, doubles $$

Crowne Plaza Panama Airport Av Domingo Díaz, Tocumen ihg.com/crowneplaza/hotels; Aeropuerto or ITSE. Convenient, modern four-star chain hotel only a few hundred metres from the terminal but still with complimentary 24hr shuttle service every

1

hour. Rooms have all the standard business amenities, plus there's a large pool and a grill restaurant open long hours. $$$

Panama House B&B C Primera 32, El Carmen panamahousebb.com; Fernández de Córdoba. A hostel-type B&B with an attractive restful patio and garden, shared kitchen, helpful travel advice and free breakfast and laundry. It's popular, so usually full; book well ahead. Dorms are better value than the doubles. Breakfast included. Dorms $, doubles $$

EATING

Panama City's **cosmopolitan** nature is reflected in its restaurants: anything from US fast food to Greek, Italian, Chinese, Peruvian, Japanese and French cuisine can be found, along with traditional and Panamanian fusion dishes as well as excellent seafood. **Bookings** are advisable at weekends, if there's live music or a show, and during holiday periods. Outside the five-star hotels, **Casco Viejo** is the place for fine dining, with very few budget choices, whereas Bella Vista, Marbella and El Cangrejo have a greater range of restaurants both high-end and more moderately priced. New places are opening in Obarrio and San Francisco, with a handful of restaurants sprinkled along the **Amador Causeway**. Cheap hot and cold **takeaway** meals are available from the Rey supermarket (6am–10.30pm) on Vía España, while the **food courts** in the numerous shopping malls (see page 85) are popular at weekends.

CASCO VIEJO, SEE MAP PAGE 56

In the evenings the city's smart set jam the streets of Casco Viejo with their 4WDs, heading for the neighbourhood's many chic restaurants in converted colonial houses. There are also a few open-air dining locations, where you can soak up the historic surroundings.

Al Alma Plaza de la Independencia alalmacafe.com/cafe-restaurante. Boasting cheerful eclectic decor including bountiful artwork, basketry and toucan-filled wallpaper, this Colombian chain outlet is a go-to daytime venue for a snack, breakfast, brunch or lunch. Note there's an appealing weekday *menú ejecutivo*. Plenty of North American favourites, such as eggs Benedict and waffles laden with syrup, but also more regional mains, such as *ropa vieja* and shrimp in coconut milk. $$–$$$

Café Coca-Cola Plaza Santa Ana, C 12 at Av Central 228 7687. The self-proclaimed "oldest café in Panama" and something of an institution among the city's older residents, who gather to drink good coffee, read the paper and discuss the news. Affordable, filling Panamanian staples – fish with *patacones* or chicken with rice – plus generously portioned breakfasts cooked to order. $$

Caleta Sofitel Legend Casco Viejo, C 1 Oeste. Evoking French colonial elegance, with leather chairs, mahogany panelling and ambient lighting, the city's top restaurant is a five-star gastronomic treat. A carefully curated menu specializing in seafood ensures inventive Panamanian twists on international classics – try yuca gnocchi in octopus sauce. Vegetarians too are well served, and the desserts are veritable works of art. $$$$

Calicanto C José de Obaldía and C 8 Oeste 390 3385, facebook.com/calicantopty. The corner-café appearance of this small, unassuming Italian restaurant belies the quality of its cuisine – and its espresso. The usual pastas and pizzas are joined by *arancini*, home-made bread and fresh salads. But the signature dish is a plateful of stuffed pyramidal pizza parcels spread over a sumptuous salad topped with a huge blob of home-made *burrat*a. It's enough for two, but leave room for the tiramisu. $$$

Casa Sucre Coffee House Av "B" and C 8 Este casasucrecoffeehouse.com. Laidback, arty café decked out with eclectic antiques and a similarly eclectic spread of coffee-table books. They serve gourmet coffees, deli sandwiches, all-day breakfasts, *tamales* and *empanadas*, and a filling soup served in a bread bowl. $$

Casablanca Plaza Bolívar instagram.com/casablancacasco. A perennial favourite for romantic outdoor dining in Casco Viejo's most scenic plaza (with a/c seating inside). Pick from standard international fare (pastas, salads, burgers, steaks) or more local flavours (ceviche or *cazuela de mariscos* (seafood stew). The cocktails too are knock-out, but pricier than most. $$$

Granclément C 9 Este at Av "B" granclement.com.pa. A fabulous indulgence after tramping the streets of Casco Viejo, this French-style artisanal ice-cream parlour offers an array of creamy flavours – including chocolate every which way – and mouthwatering sorbets, though at a price. $$

Mähalō Cocina y Jardín Las Clementinas, Av "B" at C 11 mahalopanama.com. Beautifully presented dishes in a relaxed environment under fairy lights in a lush tropical garden patio, or inside with the a/c. Many just come to enjoy a drink – wine, beer, cocktails and mocktails – but there's plenty on the menu to delight vegans, vegetarians and carnivores alike, including cauliflower tempura, falafel, Thai shrimp curry and bruschetta-type mini pizzas. $$$

★ **Mähalō Snack Shak** Av "A" at C 5 mahalopanama.com. This delightful, trendy courtyard café is the perfect spot to linger over Sunday brunch, chat over a glass of wine and eat healthily; quinoa, beetroot and avocado feature strongly in burgers, exotic salads, poke bowls, soups and sandwiches. Lots of vegan options. $$$

Saint Honoré Av "A", between C 1 & 2 Oeste sainthonorepty.com. A choice spot for breakfast – croissants, pancakes or eggs royale – a light lunch, or afternoon indulgence: a café au lait and some exquisitely presented patisserie. Bag one of the tables tucked away in the back patio. Has larger outlets boasting outside tables in

Bella Vista and San Francisco. $$

Santa Rita Hotel Casa Panama, Av Eloy Alfaro at C 11 Este restaurantesantaritapanama. Earthy tones, wooden tables and intimate pendant lighting create a warm atmosphere for a special evening meal. The menu is Spanish and Argentinian, so expect plenty of beef cuts and Spanish omelettes, though the black rice seafood mix is a speciality, and the deserts are a worthwhile indulgence. $$

★Super Gourmet Av "A" at C 6 supergourmetcascoviejo.com. Longstanding informal café serving delicious deli sandwiches and inexpensive light lunches, including soups and salads. Set yourself up for the day with a full breakfast. $$

★The Vegan Shack instagram.com/theveganshack. Tucked away down a narrow street, it's easy to miss the narrow entrance of this homely vegan café, offering all-day breakfast. Dishes are inventive and tasty: almond labneh, lentil patties and chickpea omelette feature among the Buddha bowls and smoothies. Time your visit outside regular mealtimes as tables are in short supply. $$

CALIDONIA AND LA EXPOSICIÓN, SEE MAP PAGE 62

Café Boulevard Balboa Av Balboa at C 31 Este facebook.com/boulevardbalboa; La Lotería. This city institution provides an a/c oasis of calm midst the brutal traffic and heat outside – though there's also a raised outside terrace. Lively with a smart lunchtime business crowd, the place specializes in toasted sandwiches, though also offers more filling Panamanian dishes and a good-value three-course *menú del día*. $$–$$$

★Mercado Público San Felipe Neri Av "B" and Av Balboa. A dozen *fondas* serving heaps of tasty hot food – noodles or rice with fried vegetables and strips of meat or chicken – for a few dollars, with communal seating. Breakfasts and lunches. $

Restaurante de Mariscos Av Balboa, above the Mercado de Mariscos; Cinco de Mayo. The catch couldn't be any fresher, landing straight from the boat onto your plate. Crab, conch, octopus, lobster, langoustines, shrimp, snapper, dorado – it's all there, to eat with coconut rice, fried yuca or *patacones*; just don't expect too many vegetables. Other seafood restaurants are downstairs, around the back, at the row of *cevicherías*, but you'll run into some hard sell. $$–$$$

BELLA VISTA, SEE MAP PAGE 62

From the converted colonial mansions of Bella Vista to the neon lights of El Cangrejo and high-rises of Marbella this area offers by far the greatest variety of dining and drinking venues, mainly at the mid to high end of the price scale.

Al Basha C 49 Este at C Uruguay albashapty.com; Iglesia del Carmen. A cavernous, contemporary interior, with nods to Islamic architecture, plus an ample terrace provide the setting for Lebanese appetizers and better-value, large mezze platters to share, plus the usual pizzas and spaghetti for lunchtime specials. Hookah rental and belly-dancing at weekends. $$–$$$

Athens Pizza C 57 Este at Vía España athenspizzapanama.com; Vía Argentina. The original restaurant of a now extensive chain, where you can tuck into tasty filling meals surrounded by images of Greece. Greek dishes, including salads and gyros abound, and the pizza provides great comfort food. $$–$$$

Azahar Edif. PH Yoo, 7th floor, Av Balboa azaharpanama.com. This place screams sophistication and originality, from the boutique florist's that marks the hidden entrance to the decor to the exquisitely presented (small) dishes. Choose from an array of sushi and sashimi or a fusion menu: goat's cheese and artichoke risotto, or chicken confit in cashew sauce. The outdoor terrace affords splendid bay views. Reservations a must. $$$$

Coffee Max C Elvira Méndez and C 52 Este facebook.com/coffeemax507; Iglesia del Carmen. Bamboo and palm trees provide a taste of the tropical in the very untropical surroundings of the banking district's skyscrapers. Delightful frappés and superb hot chocolate as well as toasted sandwiches, bagels, freshly made salads, pasta and cake – all produced in a food truck – make this place a popular pitstop. $$–$$$

Crepes & Waffles C 47, No. 22 fe.crepesywaffles.com/ubicaciones/marbella. Part of a Colombian chain, this longstanding family favourite in Bellavista offers crepes and waffles laden with savoury fillings, such as bolognese or chicken curry or sweet treats – mounds of ice-cream topped with a dollop of Chantilly. $$$

Loving Hut C Manuel Espinosa Batista, Edif. Cali lovinghut.com/pa; Iglesia del Carmen. Part of a global vegetarian and vegan chain, this no-nonsense *cafetería* dishes up delicious, inexpensive food. The ambience is a little antiseptic, but you can "pick and mix" a healthy plateful for a few dollars $–$$

The Market C 48, between C Uruguay and Aquilino de la Guardia lafapa.com/market-restaurant; Iglesia del Carmen. This trendy US-style joint, its walls bedecked with wine bottles, is the place to come for a juicy steak and sweet potato fries or a deli burger. Save space for a key lime pie or cheesecake. Weekend brunch too. $$$–$$$$

Natural Spice C José de Fábrega, Edificio El Pilar 6516 1799; Iglesia del Carmen. Tucked away down a leafy cul-de-sac, this friendly, inexpensive vegetarian restaurant is a popular lunchtime haunt for students of the nearby university, though it's also open in the early evening some days. The vegan burrito is a solid hit and there's a changing menu of daily specials. $$

Petit Paris C Anastacio Ruíz, opposite Felipe Motta petitparispty.com. A genuine French-run patisserie-boulangerie-bistro serving beautifully prepared food at Parisian prices. Forget the delicious bread and quiches, and indulge in the exquisitely crafted cakes and chocolates, to be enjoyed with great coffee or a hot chocolate. $$$–$$$$

★ **The Raj** Av Argentina at Vía España Ⓦtherajpanama.com; Ⓜ Vía Argentina. Eschew the tacky neon-and-chrome nightclub decor inside and seat yourself on the patio to savour the city's best Indian food. This is veggie heaven, with subtle flavours and textures infusing all the dishes. A main with all the trimmings – roti, dahl, basmati rice – washed down with a mango lassi, will leave you smiling with satisfaction. $$$

★ **Restaurante Hikaru** C Anastacio Ruíz, at C de Vallarino Ⓦhikaru.restaurant. *The* place to come for Japanese food: beautifully presented fresh sashimi, sushi and hot mains in a minimalist space. At weekday lunchtimes choose from one of three menus – each includes miso soup, salad and a main. $$–$$$

El Trapiche Vía Argentina, between C Guatemala and Av 2B Norte Ⓦeltrapicherestaurante.com; Ⓜ Vía Argentina. *The* place where tourists are directed to try traditional food, such as *mondongo* (tripe and chorizo stew) and *tamal de olla* (local *tamale* without the leaf wrapping), though it attracts Panamanians too. Prices are moderate and there's a lively atmosphere on the terrace, but the quality is variable, and there's plenty on the menu to be avoided if you're worried about your cholesterol. Other outlets across the city. $$–$$$

Yahh Mann Edificio PH Rainbow, C 1, El Carmen Ⓦinstagram.com/yahhman2024; Ⓜ Fernández de Córdoba. Faux greenery, national flags and the inevitable portrait of Bob Marley ensure you know you're in a Jamaican restaurant. The place to come for authentic jerk chicken, rice and peas, plantain, curried goat, escovitch fish, and all your island favourites, washed down with a glass of sorrel. $$–$$$

BALBOA, ANCÓN AND THE AMADOR CAUSEWAY, SEE MAP PAGE 70

Canal House Panamá Old Balboa Yacht Club, Amador Ⓦcanalhousepanama.net. A lofty, lantern-lit, thatched *rancho* opens onto a vast deck overlooking the canal entrance. The vibe is chilled and rustic, and dishes are marine-focused – fish, ceviche and lobster, with the odd vegetarian poke bowl, burger and flatbread pizza. Service is variable. Live music on Fridays and Saturdays. $$$

K'yuco Isla Flamenco, Amador Ⓦinstagram.com/kyucoislaflamenco. With outdoor tables overlooking the marina, this longstanding, moderately priced venue is still the liveliest spot in the area. Sip a cocktail at sunset while savouring sizzling grilled seafood, including vast platters to share, accompanied by *patacones*, yuca fries or regular chips. $$

OTHER AREAS, SEE MAP PAGE 62

Maito End of Calle 60, Coco del Mar Ⓦmaitopanama.com. Light, airy and unpretentious, with plantation-style wicker furniture, this is Panama's most decorated restaurant – the only place to have broken into Latin America's top 50. Exponent of *nueva cocina Panameña*, chef Mario Castrellón uses local ingredients from Darién and Bocas del Toro in particular, resulting in inventive starters such as octopus and coconut dumplings. The tasting menu between two is a treat to savour. $$$$

Palacio Lung Fung Transístmica and C 62 Oeste, Los Ángeles Ⓦpalaciolungfung.com. It's some way from the action, but every taxi driver knows this vast Chinese-style palace, whose thousand-seater upstairs ballroom with its glittering chandeliers is packed at weekends with Panamanians enjoying the *dim sum* breakfast (until 11.30am). The food is average, but the social experience makes it well worthwhile. $$

Pita-Pan Kosher Bal Harbour, Punta Paitilla Ⓦpitapankosher.com. This casual, slightly chaotic *cafetería* is popular with Jewish families. Serves appetizing, moderately priced dishes, with lots of veggie options – hummus, *baba ghanoush* and falafel – alongside the ubiquitous pasta and pizza, and even kosher sushi. $$

Tacos La Neta C 70 San Francisco Ⓦtacoslaneta.com. You can't beat the ambience at this verdant venue, with hanging plants, lanterns and a tree-shaded terrace, where the tequila flows. Pick up a quartet of tacos from shrimp, mushrooms and cauliflower, pork belly or beef, or choose your burrito, quesadilla, or fajita, with veggie versions too. And catch the mariachi band on a Friday evening. $$–$$$

La Tapa del Coco C 68 Este, San Francisco Ⓦlatapadelcocopanama.com. Close to Parque Omar, this highly acclaimed upscale Afro-Panamanian diner is immensely popular. Here, it's the food and service that count. Try the one-pot Colonense, a full plate of coconut rice, pork ribs, beans, shrimps, crispy plantains and a lot more besides – or the vegan equivalent. Reservations recommended at weekends. $$$

DRINKING AND NIGHTLIFE

Panama City arguably has the best **clubbing** in Central America, although many places feel like imitations of Miami nightspots. In addition, there are plenty of **bars**, plus live music **venues** putting on rock concerts. **Casco Viejo** is the nightlife hub that attracts the smart set. Rooftop bars are very much in vogue. Elsewhere, nightlife is more dispersed, with venues dotted around the Causeway, parts of El Cangrejo and San Francisco.

ESSENTIALS

Clubs and bars Clubs are called *discotecas* – ask for a club and you'll end up at a strip joint. Bars and *discotecas* open, close and reinvent themselves at an alarming rate. As regards music, you'll hear everything from techno to reggae and salsa to reggaeton – especially reggaeton. In the smarter bars and clubs you'll need to dress up – no shorts or sandals.

Costs Local beers cost around $4–6, with imports, spirits and cocktails at $8–10. If you're in a group, buying a bottle of spirits between you (which can sometimes get the entry charge waived) or a *cubetazo* (bucket of beer) will help keep costs down. *Discoteca* entry, generally $10–20, may include an open bar up until a certain time and the usual "Ladies' Night" enticements.

What's on To find out what's on, pick up a copy of *La Prensa* (Ⓦprensa.com) or the free weekly The Visitor/ El Visitante (Ⓦthevisitorpanama.info); also the major ticketing websites: Ⓦticketpluspty.com, Ⓦeventbrite.com/d/panama--panamá/events and Ⓦpanatickets.boletosenlinea.events. You'll find gig listings in Ⓦbandsintown.com/c/panama-panama.

CASCO VIEJO, SEE MAP PAGE 56

BARS

Corcho C 9 Este at Boquete. The perfectly named Corcho (meaning "cork" in Spanish) is a cosy wine bar with mellow music and dimmed lighting, and – best of all – hundreds of wines to be savoured by the glass or the bottle, including from some unlikely countries. Enjoy with Mediterranean-style tapas: bruschettas, arancini, croquettes, olives and Serrano ham ($$$).

★**Tántalo** Tántalo Hotel, Av "B", between C 8 and C 9 Ⓣ262 4030, Ⓦtantalo.com/roofbar. The original Casco Viejo rooftop bar has stellar views – get here early to bag your high stool. Watch the city skyline light up while sipping one of their signature cocktails – try the passionfruit mojito – then join in the dancing. Wednesday night offers a chance to show off your salsa moves alongside professional dancers. Food served until 9pm.

CLUB

Teatro Amador Av Central, between C 11 and C 13 Ⓦteatroamador.com. This converted theatre, complete with scintillating chandelier and large dancefloor, failed to recover its weekend mojo after the Covid-19 hiatus, but still hosts occasional events (check the website for details).

LIVE MUSIC

The Club American Trade Hotel, Plaza Herrera Ⓦamericantradehotel.com/the-club. An intimate 60-seater venue hosting occasional events by international and local artists (you can pay for tickets online). Jazz predominates but you can also catch the occasional Latin, soul or blues performers too, to be enjoyed with a cocktail in hand.

BELLA VISTA, EL CANGREJO AND MARBELLA, SEE MAP PAGE 62

BARS

Les Mecs C Uruguay at C 47. A collage of artwork, Persian carpets, chandeliers, faux-antique furniture and plants inside and out make for a super cool retro Parisian vibe. The perfect place to unwind with a glass (or bottle) of wine and listen to jazz on Tuesday and Thursday evenings, with a DJ at weekends. Only the no-cash, self-service ordering system is likely to tax the brain.

★**Luna Rooftop** Edificio PH Downtown, C 55, between Av Ricardo Arango and Samuel Lewis; ⓂVía Argentina. Perch on your bar stool on the 31st floor and survey the city skyline, including the iconic neighbouring El Tornillo (the screw) skyscraper. A great place for cocktails served by friendly staff. The food's decent too. Get here early to bag a table at the balcony edge.

La Rana Dorada C 54 Este at Anastacio Ruíz Ⓦlaranadorada.com; ⓂVía Argentina. One of several golden frog (*rana dorada*) brasserie-bars popular with

SALSA LESSONS

For many, a night out in Latin America is synonymous with **salsa**, though with reggaeton ruling the roost these days, salsa nights – and salsa classes for the uninitiated – are harder to find than you might think in Panama City. Several of the large casinos, conveniently located near or in the high-end hotels, have live salsa bands at weekends, and offer classes for a few dollars on another evening. *El Tropicana* (Ⓦinstagram.com/eltropicanapanama) in the Starbay Casino, below *The Hilton*, on Avenida Balboa, is the current top pick, with a live orchestra Friday nights, Latin DJ Thursdays, dance shows and classes at 5pm Saturday. The *Royal Casino* (Ⓦroyalcasino.com.pa) in El Cangrejo is another favourite; classes take place on Wednesdays at 6.30pm and you can return to try out your moves on Fridays with the live entertainment. *Hotel Torres de Alba*, in Vía Veneto, hold salsa and bachata classes Thursday nights 7–10pm (Ⓦfacebook.com/talleresdesalsa/relax). Finally, *Salsa Safari* (Ⓦsalsasafari.com) in Casco Viejo offers a range of salsa experiences, with something for everyone: lessons, one-on-one, or for couples or groups, catering to novices or old hands. Alternatively, a class followed by a night out in a club, or even a choreographed routine leading to a video on their studio rooftop.

1

young expats, tourists and Panamanians, serving craft beer – try the sampler flight – cocktails, pizza and mounds of nachos. Nice location with a/c inside and tree-shaded picnic tables on the pavement outside. Catch the extended happy hours (noon–6pm for beer only). Its sibling bar in Casco Viejo (C 9 at C Boquete) is equally popular.

CLUB

El Tropicana in the Starbay Casino below The Hilton, Av Balboa ⓦ instagram.com/eltropicanapanama. Billed as a salsa club, it bursts with other tropical rhythms too, with live orchestras and sequined dancers, Fri & Sat nights are best. Check their social media for what's on.

LIVE MUSIC

El Apartamento y El Sótano Féderico Boyd at Av Balboa ⓦ instagram.com/aptsotano; Ⓜ Iglesia del Carmen. Unmissable yellow two-storey villa in Bella Vista offering an alternative, Bohemian vibe aided by good food, drink and indie music. Rock bands tend to play downstairs and singers and smaller groups upstairs. But also features DJs, drag shows and other entertainment.

BALBOA, ANCÓN AND THE AMADOR CAUSEWAY, SEE MAP PAGE 70

BARS

Canal House Panamá Old Balboa Yacht Club, Amador Causeway ⓦ canal-house-panama.cluvi.co. With a pleasant waterside location this is the perfect spot for a sundowner, watching the ships exiting the Canal and the yachts bobbing at their moorings. Live music Fri & Sat.

La Fábrica Amador Causeway ⓦ lafabricapty.com. Breezy hangar on the causeway serving craft beer (but also wine and spirits) to a soundtrack of classic rock. Burgers (including vegan) and hummus are their gastro specialities. Live band at weekends.

K'yuco Isla Flamenco, Amador Causeway ⓣ 314 1998. With outdoor tables overlooking the marina, fringed with pot plants, this is by far the liveliest spot in the area to enjoy inexpensive cocktails accompanied by sizzling grilled seafood.

Praia Beach Club Isla Perico, Amador Causeway ⓦ praiaamador.com. Two-storey venue offering a relaxing rustic beach vibe, complete with hammocks, imported sand, pool and jacuzzi – the latter only for champagne drinkers! – and lots of music, both live and DJ. Splendid sea views and breeze. Food and service variable but the dragon fruit mojito is knock out. Cover charge for some events.

OTHER AREAS, SEE MAP PAGE 62

CLUB

XS Club Av Juan Pablo II at Tumba Muerto, La Locería ⓦ instagram.com/xsclubpty. The city's biggest gay club, featuring laser lights, foam parties, dancing boys and drag acts. Cover charge for events.

ENTERTAINMENT

While there's no shortage of places to go drinking, dancing or clubbing in Panama City, other more "high-brow" entertainment is harder to come by. **Theatre** (mainly in Spanish) is doing relatively well, with a number of small theatres and companies. In contrast, **classical concerts** (see the Filarmónica de Panamá's website: ⓦ facebook.com/orquestafilamonicapanama) are infrequent and **opera** (ⓦ operapanama.com) or ballet (ⓦ facebook.com/panamaballetfestival) are extremely rare. **Cinema**, on the other hand, is very popular, with multiplexes including 3-D, IMAX and VIP screens dotted around the city's malls. Screenings predominantly consist of the latest Hollywood offerings, generally in English with subtitles (*subtitulada*), though sometimes dubbed (*doblada*); check out ⓦ cinespanama.com. There are also several **bowling alleys**, including one in Albrook Mall.

Ateneo Ciudad de Saber, Edif. 182, Clayton, Ancón ⓦ ciudaddelsaber.org/ateneo. Seven-hundred-seat auditorium with a small stage and cinema screen for theatrical, musical and movie presentations.

Centro de Convenciones ATLAPA Vía Israel, San Francisco ⓦ atlapa.gob.pa. The centre has two auditoriums: Teatro Anayansi, seating almost three thousand, hosts pop, jazz, classical, ballet, circus acts and even ice-skating, with plays and beauty pageants in the smaller Teatro La Huaca.

Teatro Anita Villalaz Plaza de Francia, Casco Viejo ⓦ facebook.com/pages/Teatro-Anita-Villalaz. Once part of the Supreme Court, this intimate 250-seater hosts a range of cultural activities, from poetry readings, theatre to reggae nights.

Teatro Balboa Av Arnulfo Arias Madrid, Balboa ⓦ facebook.com/pages/Teatro-Balboa/133429593385051. Spacious Art Deco theatre, staging all kinds of events, including concerts by the resident National Symphony Orchestra (ⓦ osnpanama.com).

Teatro En Círculo Av 6C Norte, El Carmen ⓦ teatroencirculo.org. One of the premier venues for plays (in Spanish), staged a few times a year.

Teatro Nacional Av "B" between C 3 and C 4, Casco Viejo ⓦ facebook.com/TeatroNacionalPanama. Occasional classical concerts, ballets and operas staged in the sumptuous Rococo interior of the capital's premier artistic venue (see page 60).

Teatro de la Plaza C Abel Bravo at Av Samuel Lewis, Obarrio ⓦ laplazapty.com. Intimate theatrical space putting on drama, comedy, musicals and screening independent films.

SPECTATOR SPORTS

Catching a **baseball** game at the Estadio Nacional Rod Carew (about 8km northeast of the city centre on Vía Ricardo J. Alfaro, off the Corredor Norte) is a real treat and worth the taxi fare. **Horse racing** has a rich tradition in Panama; you can see races at the Hipódromo Presidente Remón (races Thurs 5.30pm, Sat & Sun 2pm; ⓦhipodromo.com), 10km east of the centre on the way to Tocumen International Airport. Panama's resurgence as a global **boxing** powerhouse has encouraged an increased number of bouts in the capital, above all in the slick new Arena Roberto Durán, named after Panama's former megastar. Check the press for details. **Football** matches occur at the Estadio Rommel Fernández and tickets from very modest prices are available online at ⓦfepafut.com.

Theatre Guild of Ancón Foot of Cerro Ancón, by the police station ⓦanconguild.com. Community theatre established to entertain Zonians and still putting on English-speaking productions but with more diverse casts.

SHOPPING

Despite the hype about duty-free **shopping** in Panama City, there's actually very little around and though the streets are bulging with malls and shops, you're unlikely to be overly impressed by either the selection or the prices – indigenous **crafts** and other **souvenirs** aside. However, there is an ever-expanding multitude of malls dotted round the city.

MALLS

Albrook Mall By Albrook bus terminal ⓦalbrookmall.com; see map page 54. Arguably, the largest mall in Latin America: a two-storey kilometre of retail therapy with discount stores, a handful of more upmarket boutiques and a vast food court. Also banks, ATMs, an Apple Store, a cinema and Super 99 – the nearest supermarket for anyone staying in Balboa or Cerro Ancón.

Megápolis (formerly Multicentro) Av Balboa, Paitilla ⓦmegapolisoutlets.com; see map page 62. Convenient shopping centre for Marbella, with a cinema and a good kosher supermarket in the basement (ⓦdelimarket.net).

Multiplaza Vía Israel, Punta Pacífica; see map page 62. More than 350 shops, with many upmarket boutiques, such as Paul Smith, Carolina Herrera, Gucci and Tiffany, plus a cinema.

ARTS AND CRAFTS

If a *mola* is on the shopping list, you'll probably get the best prices from the Guna craftspeople who spread out their wares on the pavements around Casco Viejo and Vía Veneto; they can often organize you a trip to Gunayala too. You'll also find high-quality *molas*, along with good basketry and woodcarvings, in shops dotted round Casco Viejo, though the prices are higher than elsewhere in the city; Vía Veneto (in El Cangrejo) is another good area to look. Craft markets are another option; the stalls are generally run by members of the community who made the goods, and more of the money you spend is likely to trickle down to the actual artisans.

Casa Latina Panamá Av "A" at C 5, Casco Viejo ⓦfacebook.com/casalatina.pty; see map page 56. Very pricey offerings, of exquisite quality: the absolute very best of Panamanian handicrafts as well as beautiful Peruvian alpaca knitwear and Mexican silver jewellery.

Centro Artesanal Panamá para el Mundo Plaza Cárdenas Center, Av Omar Torrijos (opposite the Ministry of Education); see map page 54. An easy stop on the way to or from the Miraflores Locks (see page 97), it is the pick of the craft markets, albeit in rather antiseptic surroundings, selling hammocks, *molas*, basketry, jewellery and the like, as well as offerings from other Latin American countries.

Galería de Arte Indígena C 1, Casco Viejo ⓦinstagram.com/galeriadearteindigena; see map page 56. The best selection of Wounaan and Emberá basketry in the capital at suitably elevated prices, alongside high-quality tagua and *cocobolo* carvings, mounds of *molas*, and a host of other gift ideas.

Mercado de Buhonería y Artesanías C 24 Este, just off Plaza Cinco de Mayo; see map page 62. A series of dirty shipping containers housing craft stalls selling Panama hats, Guna *molas*, tagua carvings and the like at more modest prices.

Mia Mia Av Central at C 10 ⓦinstagram.com/miamiacentroartesanal; see map page 56. Fine collection of indigenous craft work where the artisans themselves decide what price to charge and the shop takes a percentage.

Reprosa Multiplaza ⓦreprosa.com; see map page 62. Beautifully crafted gold and silver reproduction pre-Columbian and Spanish colonial jewellery. There's another branch on the Costa del Este (just beyond Panamá Viejo).

La Ronda C 1, Casco Viejo ⓣ264 5035; see map page 56. Excellent selection of arts and crafts at Casco Viejo prices.

1

BUYING OUTDOOR GEAR

If you're considering **hiking** or **camping** in Panama, you'd be wise to bring all the necessary **equipment** and clothing with you – there's limited availability here and prices are high. However, if you find yourself short of a few essentials, the following sellers are worth checking out:

Decathlon Ⓦ decathlon.com.pa. Inexpensive French chain with its own Quechua brand sells tents, hiking and other sports gear. In Multiplaza (see page 85) and Metromall (towards the airport).

Do It Center Ⓦ doitcenter.com.pa. General hardware store that also stocks camping and outdoor gear, such as camping stoves and fishing tackle. Outlets in Albrook Mall and Multiplaza (see page 85), and across the country.

Novey Ⓦ novey.com.pa. Amid the hardware, agricultural and household goods of this nationwide chain, Novey also offers outdoor equipment from cheap tents and sleeping bags to snorkel masks. The most convenient outlets are in Albrook Mall (see page 85) and opposite Multicentro on Av Balboa in Paitilla.

Outdoor Adventure Ⓦ tiendasoutdoor.com. Located in several malls in the capital – Albrook, Megápolis (Multicentro) and Multiplaza (see page 85) – this place supplies general camping and hiking equipment and clothing, including tents, sleeping mats and bags, solar-powered battery chargers and headlamps.

BOOKS

Gran Morrison Vía España, next to El Rey supermarket, El Cangrejo Ⓦ granmorrison.com; see map page 62. This small department store has a small selection of English-language books on Panama.

STRI Earl S. Tupper Research Centre Av Roosevelt Ⓣ 2212 8029, Ⓦ stri.si.edu; see map page 70. The Smithsonian bookshop stocks an excellent selection on wildlife, ecology and environmental issues in Spanish and English though opening hours are limited.

DIRECTORY

Embassies and consulates Australian Honorary Consul, Edif. Midtown, 10th floor, no.10–4 (Ⓣ 6325 3852); Canada, Torres de las Américas, Tower A, 11th floor, C 53 Este, Punta Pacífica (Ⓦ canadainternational.gc.ca/country-pays/panama); Colombia, Condo Posada del Rey, Planta Baja, Vía Italia, Punta Paitilla (Ⓦ panama.consulado.gov.co); Costa Rica, Galerías Balboa, Pimer alto, Av Balboa at Aquilino de la Guardia (Ⓦ embajadacostaricaenpanama.com); Ireland, Honorary Consul, Torre Delta, 14th floor, Vía España (Ⓔ juancarlos.rosasdonnell@honoraryconsul.ie); South Africa, Av 18C Norte, No. 25H, Bethania, (Ⓔ juliomantovani07@gmail.com); UK, Humboldt Tower, 4th floor, C 53, Marbella (Ⓦ gov.uk/world/organisations/british-embassy-panama-city); US, Edif. 783, Av Demetrio Basilio Lakas, Clayton (Ⓦ pa.usembassy.gov).

Health Excellent care is available in the public and private sectors, with many US-trained and English-speaking staff. Recommended public hospitals include Hospital Santo Tomás, C 34 Este at Av Balboa (Ⓣ 507 5600, Ⓦ hospitalsantotomas.gob.pa) and Hospital Santa Fé, Vía Simón Bolívar at Av Frangipani (Ⓣ 227 4733, Ⓦ hospitalsantafepanama.com). Good private options include Clínica Hospital San Fernando, Vía España, Las Sabanas, next to *McDonald's* (Ⓣ 305 6300, Ⓦ hospitalsanfernando.com) and Centro Médico Paitilla, Av Balboa at C 53 (Ⓣ 208 8400, Ⓦ cmpaitilla.com). The Centro de Medicina Natural, Edif. Guadalupe on C 42 Este at Av Mejico, (Ⓣ 225 0867) offers natural and traditional treatments. For a dentist, try Clínica Dental Fábregas (Ⓣ 399 4251) in Hospital Punta Pacífica or the Eisenmann Dental Clinic (Ⓦ en.dentalpanama.com), C 53 at Av Samuel Lewis. Staff at both speak English.

Immigration The immigration office (*migracíon*) is at Av Ricardo J. Alfaro, Tumba Muerto (Mon–Fri 7am–3pm; Ⓦ migracion.gob.pa).

Internet Many public places are free wi-fi hot spots, provided you register your laptop. All hotels and hostels also offer free wi-fi, at least in the foyer; larger hotels also often have a PC or laptop for guest use. The city also has a sprinkling of internet cafés, notably along Vía Veneto in El Cangrejo and in Albrook bus terminal (usually $1/hr).

Money If you need to change currency, head for Panacambios (Mon–Fri 8am–5pm; Ⓣ 223 1800, Ⓦ panacambios.com) on the ground floor of Edif. Plaza Regency on Vía España; alternatively RedPlus (Ⓦ gruporedplus) has branches in the Albrook and Multiplaza shopping malls, as well as in Avenida Italia and at Tocumen International Airport.

Pharmacies Farmacias Arrocha (Ⓦ arrocha.com) is the largest chain, often open 24hr, with huge branches in Albrook Mall and in front of the *Hotel El Panamá* on Vía España. The large 24hr supermarkets also have pharmacy counters.

Phones The main Cable & Wireless office (Mon–Fri 8am–6pm, Sat 8am–4pm) is on Vía España, next to the National Bank and Plaza Concordia.

Police The Policía de Turismo are on Av Central at C 3, Casco Viejo (Ⓣ 511 9261).

Isla Taboga

Just 20km off the coast and a short boat-ride away, the lush hills of **Isla Taboga** have provided a popular weekend escape for Panama City residents since the capital's sixteenth-century foundation. After the frenetic energy of the capital, the island's relaxed atmosphere makes for a welcome break and the views from its vantage points are well worth seeking out. Packed on summer weekends and holidays, at other times the place can feel gloriously deserted. Most visitors are day-trippers who spend their time lounging on the indifferent **Restinga beach**, bathing in the shallow waters and strolling the traffic-free streets of **San Pedro** fishing village, where most of the island's thousand-odd inhabitants live. However, it's definitely worth summoning up the energy to do one of the island's two **walks**; other popular diversions include **boat trips**, which, in the nesting months of January to June, allow close-ups of pelicans thrusting fish down the gullets of their squawking chicks. There is also reasonable **snorkelling** on the far side of Taboga and Isla El Morro and around a wreck off Isla Urabá, though currents can be strong.

Much of the island, together with neighbouring Isla Urabá, comprises a wildlife refuge for a large colony of brown **pelicans** – check with MiAmbiente (see page 42) if you want to visit. Elsewhere, hibiscus, bougainvillea and sweet-smelling jasmine are in evidence, but the succulent pineapples for which the island is traditionally famous are now a rarity.

Brief history

Taboga's present-day tranquillity belies a turbulent past. The Spanish arrived in 1515, and wasted no time in enslaving and removing the native Cueva Indians before populating the island with freed enslaved people from elsewhere and constructing a fort on the adjoining **Isla El Morro** – its cannons are sprinkled round the island. Taboga's excellent natural harbour has crucially shaped the island's history, forming the base for Francisco Pizarro's expeditions against the Incas, as well as for pirates including Morgan and Drake. After an English steamship company established its headquarters on Isla El Morro, Taboga became a buzzing port for supplies and repairs and, though the island's maritime importance has dwindled, many contemporary Taboganos still live off the sea, either through small-scale fishing or unloading tuna from fishing boats to larger trans-shippers.

The beaches

Approaching Isla Taboga's floating pier, you are greeted by the sight of the whitewashed buildings and red rooftops of San Pedro, strung out to the left behind **Playa Honda**, a shingly strip dotted with small fishing boats, which extends to a swathe of tan sand at low tide. Turning right after leaving the pier takes you to Taboga's main beach, **Playa Restinga**, a golden crescent, half of which forms a sand bar reaching to Isla El Morro; at high tide the sandbar becomes submerged. The beach's appeal is somewhat diminished by the piles of overgrown rubble from the demolished *Hotel Taboga* at the back, and by the rubbish that can wash up on the shore after heavy rains. Even so, crowds of Panamanians happily swim from here, and from Playa Honda. Beach umbrellas and deckchairs are available for rent.

San Pedro

Heading back towards **San Pedro**, along the jasmine-scented Calle Abajo, a steep path to the right leads up to the **plaza**, the social hub of the island – where villagers of all ages gather to watch or play football or volleyball, dance or simply hang out. At one end, steps lead up to the gleaming white stucco walls of the **Iglesia San Pedro**, built in 1550 and reputedly the second oldest church in the western hemisphere. Leaving the square via Calle Arriba at the opposite end, and turning left, you come across a shrine to the Virgen del Carmen and the house where Pizarro apparently lived, while a brightly tiled plaque nearby commemorates the French painter Paul Gauguin, who had a short stint working on the Canal before heading off for the South Seas.

Cerro de la Cruz

The shorter of the island's two hikes, to **Cerro de la Cruz**, takes an easy thirty minutes. Leaving town along Calle Abajo, you pass the delightful **casa de la concha** on the right, decorated by its former owner, a one-time pearl fisher, with scallop and pearl shells. Further on is the site of an old French canal-era **sanitorium**, which the Americans converted into a rest and recuperation centre for "gold roll" Canal employees (see page 301) before upgrading it to a hotel. Beyond the weed-strewn **cemetery**, take the dirt road down to the left, then a path up an embankment to the right 100m later, after which it's an easy walk to the gigantic sixteenth-century cross, where you can soak up the sweeping sea view.

Cerro Vigía

The panorama is truly spectacular from the mirador at the top of **Cerro Vigía** (370m), Taboga's highest point, making the hour-long hike a rewarding experience. Heading along the main path out of the village, you pass the turn to Cerro de la Cruz, before arriving at a junction. Straight ahead lie the MiAmbiente offices (signposted but not open to the public), the island's desalination plant and the refuse dump; to the right, the widening dirt road meanders slowly up the hill. The more direct route to the summit, up the **Sendero de las Tres Cruces**, presents a shorter but more challenging

climb through lush forest, not least because of poor signposting. After heavy rain, the path becomes a mudslide, but the rewards are almost-guaranteed sightings of green and black poison dart frogs and tarantulas. The route is indicated from the plaza; after the housing ends, turn sharp right and keep to the right of the stream until, ten minutes into the forest, the route bears left across a stream, which the path crisscrosses several times before arriving, forty-five minutes later, at three well-tended crosses – the burial sites of a trio of buccaneers who foolishly tangled with some Taboganos. Bearing left again, the trail soon emerges from the undergrowth onto the dirt road to the summit, which is marked by the remains of US World War II bunkers.

ARRIVAL AND INFORMATION — ISLA TABOGA

By boat Two companies run boats to Taboga. The traditional way to travel is on the *Calypso Queen* (facebook.com/CalypsoBarcos), which offers great views from the open top deck and affords close-ups of the ships waiting to transit the Canal. There are usually two daily departures from La Playita on the Amador Causeway, near the entrance to the Punta Culebra Nature Centre (50min), with extra crossings at weekends and on public holidays, when you'll need to get there 1hr beforehand to be sure of a seat, or even buy a ticket a day in advance. There are fewer departures in the rainy season; call to confirm. *Taboga Ferry Express* (T 6234 8989, tabogaexpress.com) runs a more frequent, faster and more expensive daily service from Isla Flamenco, at the bottom of the causeway (30min).

Tourist information The Panama Tourist Authority website (tourismpanama.com/places-to-visit/taboga-island/places-to-stay) and a private website (tabogapanama.com) are useful references.

ACTIVITIES AND TOURS

Kayaking One- or two-person kayaks are available for rent at Playa Restinga.

Taboga Tour Centre 30m to the right of the jetty, as you leave the ferry tabogatourcenter.com. This little outfit can fix you up with SUP and beach towel rental, a couple of hours in a *panga*, including snorkelling, a guided walking tour of San Pedro, or truck ride up to the summit of Cerro Vigía.

Taboga Express The ferry company (see above) also offers day passes (including transport, beach umbrellas, bilingual walking tour and a meal) and can even organize a hotel pickup.

ACCOMMODATION — SEE MAP PAGE 88

Accommodation on the island is limited and generally overpriced. Some locals rent out **rooms** informally for around $40; they'll often meet the morning ferry to drum up custom, otherwise ask at *Restaurante Mundi* by the jetty.

Cerrito Tropical Ecolodge Up the hill from the village centre tabogaislandhotel.com. This friendly place surrounded by greenery offers a handful of simple, but nicely decorated rooms and mini-self-catering suites, with shared or private balcony, plus a communal wooden deck and plunge pool. Good breakfast available. $$$

Taboga Palace Spa Hotel Calle Francisco Pizarro tabogapalace.com. Gleaming white edifice offering spacious, airy well-appointed rooms opening onto ocean-facing balconies (in most rooms). The decor may be a little florid for some – balustrades, pillars and flowery bedding – but there's no denying the excellent service, comfort or the allure of the infinity pool $$$

EATING — SEE MAP PAGE 88

The island's **eating** options are restricted, overpriced and service is slow, so if you join the summer weekend crowds it's probably worth bringing a picnic, or heading for the beach food shacks that line the back of Playa Honda. In the rainy season, hours are shorter and less reliable.

★ **Calaloo** Main path, 50m to the left when leaving the jetty T 6000 5172, facebook.com/CalalooPanama. Cheery, breezy café-restaurant looking across the main path to Playa Honda – great for people-watching. The tasty, varied menu ranges from hummus and roast vegetables to fresh fish with *patacones* and salad, plus fresh fruit juices and ice-cold cocktails. $$$

Sabor Isleño Restaurante 50m to the right when leaving the jetty T 6390 3997. Small restaurant with an agreeable prow-shaped deck over the water and rustic wooden furniture, serving fried breakfasts and tasty seafood with rice or *patacones* at tourist prices. Caters to day-trippers. $$$

DIRECTORY

Money Take sufficient cash with you; although there is one ATM on Taboga, in peak season it may not always have money. You will have to pay a small municipal fee on arrival.

The Panama Canal and central isthmus

SHIP TRANSITING THE PANAMA CANAL

The Panama Canal and central isthmus

Running 80km across the isthmus between the Pacific and Atlantic oceans, straddling the provinces of Panama and Colón, the Panama Canal remains a colossus among engineering achievements, a truly awe-inspiring sight and justifiably the country's prime tourist attraction. What's more, it can easily be explored on an excursion from Panama City, with the Centro de Visitantes de Miraflores offering the best location from which to view the action. Though the corridor that flanks this vital thoroughfare is home to almost two-thirds of Panama's population, for much of its length the waterway cleaves through pristine rainforest, large tracts of which are protected within national parks.

Parque Nacional Soberanía is one of the most accessible tropical rainforest preserves in Latin America, while **Isla Barro Colorado** is home to the world-renowned Smithsonian Institute. Both support an exceptional degree of biodiversity and are easy day-trips from the capital. The quiet town of **Gamboa** is the embarkation point for excursions to Barro Colorado and for most tours offering partial transits of the Canal; it is also the starting point for rainforest hikes and birdwatching outings along the famous **Camino del Oleoducto** (Pipeline Road). Three of the area's national parks – Soberanía, the smaller adjacent **Parque Nacional Camino de Cruces** and the larger, less accessible **Parque Nacional Chagres** – also offer the opportunity to walk along the remnants of the historic, partially cobbled **Camino de Cruces** and the **Camino Real**. These paths were carved by mule trains across the forested spine of the isthmus in colonial times to transport Spain's plundered treasures from Panama City to the Caribbean coast.

The Canal reaches the Atlantic at **Colón**, Panama's second city, synonymous with poverty and crime in the minds of many Panamanians, yet rich in history, with a strong Afro-Antillean and Afro-Colonial heritage. Either side of Colón stretch kilometres of Caribbean coastline, peppered with small communities and limited tourist development. To the west, along the **Costa Abajo**, the formidable remains of the **Fuerte San Lorenzo** are the country's most impressive colonial ruins, still guarding the mouth of the Río Chagres amid untouched tropical rainforest. To the northeast lies the **Costa Arriba**, an isolated region of rich coral reefs and laidback fishing villages, much of which is nominally protected by **Parque Nacional Portobelo**, set around the ruins and beautiful natural harbour of the old Spanish port of **Portobelo**.

At the Pacific end of the Canal, an hour and a half by boat from Panama City, lies the **Archipiélago de las Perlas**. A former hideout of privateers and pirates and a long-standing weekend refuge for the capital's social elite, the archipelago's translucent waters and powdered beaches offer a pricey slice of tranquillity.

The Panama Canal

The **PANAMA CANAL**, which runs between Panama City on the Pacific coast and Colón on the Caribbean, or Atlantic side, is the country's most recognizable landmark, crucial to its economy and inextricably entwined with its historical and cultural development. One of the world's most important waterways, it has seen around fourteen thousand vessels and more than three hundred million tonnes of cargo passing through its locks every year, a figure which has the potential to double following the Canal's recent ambitious expansion, which was inaugurated in 2016 (see box, page 306).

WOMAN IN EMBERÁ PURU

Highlights

❶ **Canal transit** Experience the great, iconic waterway on a boat and marvel at the tropical scenery. See page 95

❷ **Canal locks** Get a close look at the precision manoeuvring of gargantuan container vessels as they squeeze through the lock chambers at Miraflores or Agua Clara. See pages 97 and 109

❸ **Rainforest exploration** Hike along the conquistadors' old booty trails of the Camino de Cruces or kayak down the Chagres, through tangled, lush rainforest. See pages 98 and 102

❹ **Birdwatching in Soberanía** More than five hundred bird species have been recorded here: grab your binoculars and scan the canopy at dawn. See page 98

❺ **Stay in an Emberá village** Overnight in a traditional thatched home, experiencing Emberá culture and learning about the surrounding rainforest. See page 104

❻ **Spanish colonial forts** Step back in time at the desolate, evocative ruins of Fuerte San Lorenzo or the well-preserved forts of Portobelo. See pages 110 and 114

❼ **Archipiélago de las Perlas** Picturesque islands offering near-deserted beaches, fine snorkelling and diving, and great whale-watching opportunities. See page 121

HIGHLIGHTS ARE MARKED ON THE MAP ON PAGE 94

THE PANAMA CANAL AND CENTRAL ISTHMUS
HIGHLIGHTS
1 Canal transit
2 Canal locks
3 Rainforest exploration
4 Birdwatching in Soberanía
5 Stay in an Emberá village
6 Spanish colonial forts
7 Archipiélago de las Perlas
N
CARIBBEAN SEA
PACIFIC OCEAN
COLÓN
PANAMÁ
COCLÉ
GUNAYALA
Isla Grande
Isla Mamey
La Guaira
Cacique
Puerto Lindo
Nombre de Dios
Costa Arriba
Viento Frío
Palenque
Miramar
Cuango
Nuevo Tonosí
Portobelo
Río Nombre de Dios
Cerro Brujo (979m)
PARQUE NACIONAL PORTOBELO
Río Boquerón
Río Pequení
Cerro Hope (702m)
María Chiquita
Río Piedra
Isla Galeta
Isla Galeta Marine Research & Education Centre
Boquerón
PARQUE NACIONAL CHAGRES
Fuerte Sherman
Colón
Cristóbal
Sabanitas
Río Gatún
Fuerte San Lorenzo
Río Chagres
Gatún Locks
Puente Atlántico
Centro de Visitantes de Agua Clara
Transisthmian Highway (Transístmica)
Autopista Panamá-Colón
Piña
Gatún Dam
Agua Clara Locks
Nuevo Vigía
Lago Alajuela
Cerro Jefe (1007m)
Achiote
Islas Brujas
Isla Tigre
Panama Canal Railway
PARQUE NACIONAL SOBERANÍA
PN Chagres HQ
PN Chagres office
Costa Abajo
Panama Canal
Rainforest Discovery Centre
Cerro Azul
Chepo
Darién
Boca del Río Indio
Isla Barro Colorado
Gamboa Rainforest Resort
Chilibre
Miguel de la Borda
Escobal
Lago Gatún
Gamboa
Canopy Tower Ecolodge
PARQUE NACIONAL CAMINO DE CRUCES
Darién Highway (Interamericana)
Coclé del Norte (30km)
Río Miguel de la Borda
Río Indio
Río Lagarto
Cuipo
PN Soberanía HQ
Senafront HQ
Culebra Cut
Paraíso
PN Camino de Cruces HQ
PANAMA CITY
Tocumen International Airport
Puente Centenario
Pedro Miguel Locks
Miraflores Locks
Corozal Passenger Terminal (Panama Canal Railway Company)
Cocolí Locks
Balboa
Arraiján
Bridge of the Americas
Amador Causeway
Panamá Pacífico International Airport
Western Panama
Archipiélago de las Perlas (see inset)
0 25 kilometres
Isla Saboga
Isla Contadora
0 10 kilometres
Archipiélago de las Perlas
San Miguel
Isla del Rey
Isla Pedro González
Isla San José

A gargantuan feat of engineering, the original Panama Canal, completed in 1914, set the standards for twentieth-century engineering. At $352 million it was the most expensive project ever undertaken, with the world's largest earthen dam creating the world's largest artificial lake. The most enormous locks ever built contained the greatest amount of concrete ever used – just over three million cubic metres, the equivalent of sixty Empire State Buildings – and possessed the largest-ever swing doors. Statistics notwithstanding, it is the combination of the scale and ingenuity of the achievement with its ruggedly beautiful tropical setting that makes the Canal so special.

There are several ways to appreciate what the Canal has to offer, all of them within easy striking distance of the capital. Most people take a trip to **Miraflores Locks** – a convenient bus ride out of Panama City – which has a well-situated visitors' centre

TRANSITING THE CANAL

To fully appreciate the Canal, you need to see it up close. Things may not be quite as you'd expect – the gargantuan Panamax vessels (the biggest ships the original locks could hold), and the even larger Neopanamax, are manoeuvred with surprising delicacy, while the banks of this vast commercial enterprise are lined with jungle and spotted with unspoilt islands. In a **partial transit**, from the tip of the Amador Causeway in Panama City to Gamboa (or vice versa), you get to experience the excitement of passing under the impressive Bridge of the Americas, through the narrow Culebra Cut and being raised and lowered in the lock chambers of both Miraflores and Pedro Miguel locks. The **full transit** from Panama City to Colón takes in the most breathtaking scenery, crossing Lago Gatún and weaving among tiny forested islands. You'll glide past a silent stream of giant ships, before passing through the enormous Gatún Locks, slipping under the magnificent new Puente Atlántico, and terminating in Colón. From here it can be up to a two-hour bus journey back to the capital.

Although completing a full transit ($210) might hold a certain cachet, the advertised eight to nine hours can often be a lot longer if you get caught up in one of the frequent log jams in Gatún Locks. A partial transit ($145–155) provides enough excitement and interest for most people, and if you take a northbound trip, docking at around 1pm in Gamboa, you can skip the bus transfer back to the Amador Causeway and enjoy a drink at the *Gamboa Rainforest Resort* (see page 101) before catching the public bus, or a taxi, back to Panama City.

The cheapest way to see the Canal is to get a job as a **line-handler** – a person who helps keep the boat positioned in the locks; it's a requirement for all transiting cruising vessels to have four line-handlers. If you're interested, contact Shelter Bay Marina (ⓦ shelterbaymarina.com) or Linton Bay Marina (ⓦ lintonbaymarina.com) about advertising your services.

INFORMATION AND TOURS

The two companies listed below offer similar trips but charge different prices: rates include the boat, bilingual guided commentary, soft drinks, meals and snacks, and coach transfer to or from the original meeting point. Departures are early morning (usually between 6–9am) but exact times are confirmed the day before and depend on other canal traffic. In the tourist season (Dec–April) there are frequent transits and boats can be very crowded, especially with cruise ship groups; out of season there are fewer transits, with a full crossing often only once a month. Various other tour operators offer Canal transits, though they are all obliged to use boats from the two companies listed below.

Canal and Bay Tours ⓦ canalandbaytours.com. The cheaper, though slightly less reliable of the two companies, has two larger craft for full transits. All tours leave from La Playita, Isla Naos, and most are northbound; contact the office for dates of the occasional southbound partial transit.

Panama Canal Tours ⓦ panamacanaltrips.com. The pricier Panama Canal Tours caters predominantly to foreign tourists. Transits usually leave from one of the Flamenco marinas but can also leave from La Playita. Southbound transits start with a bus journey to Gamboa. An "alternative tour" combines time in a small boat on the Río Chagres and Lago Gatún before returning on land via the Miraflores Locks.

with a museum and viewing platform, offering a fine view of ships as they pass through. The Canal's other main observation point, across the isthmus at the new **Agua Clara Visitor Centre** takes longer to reach, and looks down from a hilltop, offering a more panoramic and holistic view of the Canal expansion programme in particular (see box, page 306). Different perspectives again are offered by fishing or boating trips on **Lago Gatún**, and by speeding across the isthmus and alongside the Canal by **train**. But by far the best way to get your head around the technical brilliance, natural beauty and sheer magnitude of the feat is to travel along the Canal ("transit") by **boat**.

The Canal by train: Panama Canal Railway

Corozal Passenger Terminal, Corozal West, Panama City • Mon–Fri departs 7.15am (1hr), returning from Colón at 5.15pm; reservations are advisable and it's worth getting there early (6.30am) to secure your vantage point • Charge • Ⓦ panarail.com • Taxi or bus from Albrook bound for the Miraflores Locks

The Corozal Passenger Terminal of the **Panama Canal Railway** is the departure point for the scenic transisthmian train journey. The original Panama Railroad, built in the 1850s during the California Gold Rush (see page 298), transported more than $700 million in gold before the completion of the Union Pacific Railroad across the US in 1869 made it obsolete, forcing it into bankruptcy. Following a short revival during the Canal's construction, the railway fell into disrepair until 1998 when the government agreed to privatize it. Though the railway company predominantly ferries freight to and from the Atlantic and Pacific container ports, it offers a commuter passenger service to

THE BIG DITCH

Erroneously nicknamed the **Big Ditch**, the 77km Canal eschews straight lines as it weaves its way from the Pacific to the Caribbean or Atlantic entrance, which is actually 42km to the west, on account of Panama's eel-like shape. British politician and historian James Bryce dubbed the waterway "the greatest liberty Man has ever taken with nature", though ironically it has resulted in a symbiotic relationship between the two: the Canal's constant thirst for water to feed the locks is highly dependent on the preservation of the adjacent national parks to protect the water catchment area. This is even more true since the Canal's recent expansion; despite the new locks' ingenious basins, which can recover sixty percent of the water used, the overall water loss from the Canal has increased.

The original **lock chambers** measure 304.8m by 33.53m, affording colossal Panamax vessels a mere 0.6m of leeway either side, yet they function in much the same way as they did when they were first used. Once the gates are closed, these vast vessels are kept aligned by cables attached to pairs of electric locomotives known as mules (*mulas*). The huge tunnel-like culverts then kick in with phenomenal efficiency, taking only eight minutes to fill the giant chamber with the equivalent of 43 Olympic swimming pools. The new locks, which are more than half as big again, demand an arguably even trickier operation, since the mules have been abandoned in favour of tugboats, which are attached to the bow and stern of the ships, and squeezed into the same lock chamber as the towering metal behemoths they're guiding.

Tolls for ships are calculated depending on type of vessel, and size and type of cargo. The average toll for Panamax vessels is around $250,000 for the 8–10hr journey, including almost $12,000 each for up to three tugboats required for the more difficult stages of the transit, as well as fees for the obligatory Canal pilot. For Neopanamax vessels, which can carry up to fourteen thousand containers, costs are over a million dollars.

It is no wonder then that the Canal's annual revenue in 2024 was almost $5 billion. For the ships, despite the eye-watering costs, the Canal still represents a major saving in time and money, as it avoids them having to make the difficult 15,000km-journey around the treacherous seas of Cape Horn.

The **history** of the Canal is covered in more detail in the Contexts chapter (see page 300).

Colón that is very popular with tourists. During high season (publicized on the railway's Instagram site) the company offers an occasional Saturday tourist excursion that leaves at 9.30am and returns around 12.30pm. A supremely comfortable way to enjoy the Canal, the train serves up old-world elegance in wood-panelled, carpeted carriages with large windows. In fine weather, make sure you also get out onto the open viewing deck.

Miraflores Locks and around

A mere fifteen minutes from downtown Panama City, along Avenida Omar Torrijos, the **MIRAFLORES LOCKS (Esclusas de Miraflores)** are home to the four-storey **Centro de Visitantes de Miraflores**, which provides a prime location for observing the Canal in action. Marking the Pacific entrance to the waterway, the locks raise or lower vessels 16.5m between sea level and the artificial Lago Miraflores in two stages, a process best appreciated from the visitor centre's observation deck.

Southwest of Miraflores, action in the new three-chambered **Cocolí Locks** can be enjoyed from a small concrete **mirador** along the road that skirts the western flank of the new channel, leading to the Puente Centenario (see page 98), while just over 3km beyond Miraflores lie the smaller **Pedro Miguel Locks**. These are closed to the public, but if you park in the small layby (or get off the bus), you can peer through the chainlink fence and watch the ships manoeuvring, saving yourself the hefty Miraflores entry fee in the process. Any bus bound for Gamboa or Chilibre (see page 100) can drop you off or pick you up at Pedro Miguel.

Centro de Visitantes Miraflores

Daily 8am–6pm (5.15pm last entry), including holidays • Charge • Ⓦ visitcanaldepanama.com; online booking preferred • Direct Metrobuses leave from stand A, at the front of Panama City's Albrook terminal (see page 74) to the visitors' centre (5am–5pm; every 30min; hourly on Sundays); or take a taxi

The **Centro de Visitantes Miraflores** houses an informative introductory museum on the Canal's history and workings as well as a three-tier **observation deck** just metres from the locks. Optimum viewing times for vessels transiting are before 9– 9.30am, when ships are usually entering the Canal from the Pacific, and after 3pm, when they are exiting. It's advisable to get there early in high season as the viewing platforms can get very crowded.

The **museum** serves to promote the Autoridad del Canal de Panamá (ACP) – particularly though a 45-minute Imax film – as much as to inform you about the Canal. At the time of writing, the visitors' centre was undergoing renovations, both to increase capacity with a new viewing deck, but also a complete overhaul of the museum, featuring seven rooms with state-of-the-art, interactive exhibits. Canal memorabilia is on sale at the **gift shop**.

ACCOMMODATION **MIRAFLORES**

Holiday Inn Ciudad de Saber (City of Knowledge), Clayton Ⓦ ihg.com/holidayinn. Bang opposite the Miraflores Locks (to which there's a free shuttle); from upper-floor rooms you can watch the action night and day. The well-appointed, spacious rooms have giant plasma-screen TVs, crisp white sheets, sparkling bathrooms and the usual business amenities. Although you are outside the city, there's free shuttle to Albrook (from where you can easily access the rest of the city), and it's only a five-minute walk next door to the plaza at the City of Knowledge (Ciudad de Saber) for places to eat. $$$

The road to Gamboa

Once beyond the Miraflores and Pedro Miguel locks, the road to the somnolent Canal-era town of **Gamboa** (Carretera Gaillard) skirts the emerald rainforest of the contiguous **Parque Nacional Camino de Cruces** and **Parque Nacional Soberanía**, both of which have trails to suit hikers, bird-lovers and anyone interested in the

Spanish conquest. It then ascends to the continental divide at the **Parque Municipal Summit**, before swooping down to the bridge across the Río Chagres, which marks the entrance to Gamboa. Unfortunately, buses to Gamboa are infrequent, so visiting several sites in one day is tricky unless you have your own transport. A saloon car will do for all the sights.

Corte Culebra

Beyond the Miraflores Locks, the Canal narrows into the infamous **Corte Culebra** (formerly the Gaillard Cut), where more than two-thirds of all the original Canal excavation occurred and many workers lost their lives. Its 13km stretch posed the most persistent technical headache for engineers, and severe landslides continued long after the eventual opening of the Canal. On the left, a little beyond Paraíso, the Canal's former dredging headquarters, rows of small white crosses mark the **French Cemetery**, which sits on the continental divide, a poignant reminder of the doomed French attempt to build a canal in the 1880s (see page 298).

The road then climbs, passing a turn-off to the elegant, cable-stayed **Puente Centenario**, opened in 2004 to celebrate Panama's hundred years of independence. After 3km of dense rainforest the road forks: to the right it cuts through Parque Nacional Soberanía to the Transístmica and the new motorway, both of which link Panama City with Colón, while to the left it continues to Gamboa.

Parque Nacional Camino de Cruces

Vía Centenario near Merca Panamá • Daily 8am–3pm • Charge • 500 6326 • Take bus C970 or C974 from Bay D at the front of Albrook bus terminal bound for Merca Panamá

Despite bearing the name of the conquistadors' famous trade route across the isthmus (named after the now-submerged settlement of Cruces), **Parque Nacional Camino de Cruces** is often overlooked as a tourist destination. Yet, while it is hard to escape the sound of nearby traffic, this ever-shrinking reserve is a prime location for spotting **sloths** and provides important traces of colonial history.

At the time of writing, two short **trails** had been cleared: the **Sendero El Camarón** provides an easy 2km stroll from the park office through tropical forest, while the even shorter **Sendero Pescador** (1.4km) takes you to a small lake. Two more trails await rehabilitation. For the much longer **Sendero Camino de Cruces**, which finishes in Soberanía, you need to go with a certified guide. However, you don't need to venture far along the route before coming across some of the original cobblestones.

Camping is permitted near the park office, though there are no facilities beyond toilets and running water.

Parque Nacional Soberanía

Providing the most accessible substantial body of tropical rainforest from Panama City, a mere thirty-minute drive away, **PARQUE NACIONAL SOBERANÍA** is one of the country's most visited national parks and well worth exploring. Stretching north and west from the **park office**, it hugs the Canal and encircles Gamboa, covering more than 190 square kilometres. It encompasses a stretch of the majestic **Río Chagres**, the Canal's lifeblood, which you can explore by boat; there are also several well-maintained **trails** either side of Gamboa, including a stretch of the historic **Camino de Cruces** and a world-renowned birding hot spot, the **Camino del Oleoducto**. The trails are not particularly close to each other or the park office, however, arguably making the area best enjoyed with a car, parking at the various trailheads or – especially if you want to walk the Camino de Cruces, which you are advised to do with a guide – on a **tour**. Several Panama City operators offer trips to the caminos de Cruces and Oleoducto, or

WILDLIFE IN PARQUE NACIONAL SOBERANÍA

With 525 recorded bird species, 105 mammals, 79 reptiles and 55 amphibians, Parque Nacional Soberanía offers good opportunities for wildlife-spotting. White-tailed deer, agoutis, coatis, pacas, howler monkeys and Geoffroy's tamarins are fairly commonplace, but you'll need a good guide to locate the rarer, more elusive nocturnal kinkajous or **silky anteaters**. Following an extensive breeding programme, a number of **harpy eagles** have been released into the park in recent years, so there is even a (slim) chance of catching sight of these endangered birds (see box, page 288). Other **birds** to look out for include crested eagles, red-lored amazons, great jacamars and trogons – the park's symbol.

you can **hire a ranger** from the park office as a guide – a much cheaper option, though they are unlikely to speak English.

The trails

Although most of Soberanía's trails are easy and safe enough to walk on your own, you're strongly advised to hike the **Camino de Cruces** on a tour or with a **guide**. The trail is overgrown and difficult to follow in places – and the occasional robbery has been known. Independent travellers can pick up a **map** and should enquire about the current security situation at the office or at the entry barrier to the **Camino del Oleoducto**, if there is someone there when you arrive.

Camino del Oleoducto

By far the most tramped trail in Soberanía is the unpromising-sounding **Camino del Oleoducto** (Pipeline Road), so named because it was originally built to service an oil pipeline constructed across the isthmus by the US in World War II. The pipeline was never used but the 17.5km dirt-road service track, which lies 1km beyond Gamboa, draws birding enthusiasts from around the world. Though it's visually unremarkable – this is no wilderness trail – the likely wildlife sightings more than compensate. Even if you can't tell a white-whiskered puffbird from a band-tailed barbthroat, you cannot fail to be impressed by the array of brightly coloured birds; you'll see a great deal more if you go with a good guide (see pages 37 and 77).

Camino de Cruces and Sendero de la Plantación

A 10km section of the isthmus-crossing **Camino de Cruces** traverses the park's dense vegetation from the borders of Parque Nacional Camino de Cruces (see page 98). The trail begins 6km up the road that forks right at the park office, ending up at the shores of the Río Chagres, site of the barely distinguishable remains of the Ruinas de Venta de Cruces, which served as a resting post for weary, booty-laden mules and conquistadors. You don't have to venture that far to get a flavour of the history – after a ten-minute hike your guide should be able to point out a restored section of the original sixteenth-century paving stones.

If you decide to walk the whole trail – preferably with a guide (see above) – you can avoid returning along the same route (in an exhausting eight-hour trek) by hopping across the Chagres to the *Gamboa Rainforest Resort* (see page 101) and reviving yourself with a drink before catching a bus back. You would need to organize a boat to meet you in advance (at a cost); the park wardens can arrange this for a few dollars. Alternatively, hike half of the Camino de Cruces in a westerly direction, breaking off down the 5km **Sendero de la Plantación (Plantation Trail)**. This is the gravelly remnants of a paved thoroughfare that once led to the largest private agricultural venture in the old Canal Zone, harvesting rubber, coffee and cocoa, which you can still occasionally spot growing wild amid the rainforest. It eventually disgorges you onto the road to Gamboa, where you should time your arrival to coincide with one of the Gamboa–Panama City buses.

Canopy Tower Ecolodge

Semaphore Hill, on the main road to Gamboa, 6km south of Gamboa and around 20km from Panama City • Half-day visits include a meal, park fee and guided walk • canopytower.com • It's a steep 1km to the lodge from the drive entrance

For serious nature lovers who can't afford the overnight rates (see page 100), it's still worth considering a half-day trip to the **Canopy Tower Ecolodge**, which has to be organized in advance, and includes a guided walk on which you're likely to spot manakins, antbirds, tinamous, sloths, coatis and agoutis, as well as an abundance of butterflies and insects. You also get time on the truly special canopy-level **observation deck**, which is equipped with a telescope and sun loungers, allowing you to indulge in some spectacular armchair birdwatching.

2

Rainforest Discovery Centre

2km along the Camino de Oleoducto from central Gamboa • Daily 7am–5pm • Maximum 25 people on the observation deck at one time • Charge; advance booking is advisable • pipelineroad.org

The **Rainforest Discovery Centre**, on the park boundary, boasts an impressive **canopy observation tower** with multilevel viewing platforms, a series of short trails and an interpretive centre, whose main draw is the observation deck, where bird feeders attract scores of **hummingbirds**. The drawback is the hefty entrance fee, though it's definitely worth the outlay if you're keen on birds or you make a day of it with a picnic. Profits go towards environmental education, research and conservation projects.

ARRIVAL AND INFORMATION — PARQUE NACIONAL SOBERANÍA

Park entrance and fees See page 42 for more information on fees. You might also want to drop by the park headquarters to check on security along the trails (Mon–Fri 8am–4pm, though there is always a warden on site out of office hours; 232 4192), 15km northwest of Panama City on the road to Gamboa where the road forks.

By bus Gamboa-and Chilibre-bound buses from Panama City's Albrook terminal can drop you off at the park HQ, several kilometres away from the main trails, and the Gamboa bus can also drop you 2.5km further along the road, at the entrance to the Sendero de la Plantación – also the turn-off for the *Canopy Tower Ecolodge*. For the Camino del Oleoducto, get off the bus at the park in Gamboa, walk 1km along the road parallel to the railway and Canal, then follow the signs up a dirt road to the right to the entrance barrier.

By car There are car parks at the trailheads.

By taxi A taxi from central Panama City will cost around $30–40 depending on where in the park you want to go.

Tours Panama City tour operators (see page 77) run a variety of day-trips to the park, which can involve birdwatching, hiking, kayaking or even mountain biking.

ACCOMMODATION

Canopy Tower Ecolodge Semaphore Hill, Parque Nacional Soberanía canopytower.com. US radar tower converted into a four-storey, twelve-room ecolodge with a genuine commitment to conservation. Simple, functional single rooms with shared bathroom are offered alongside more comfortable en-suite doubles and suites; all have screens, fans and hot water. Guests get a free guided walk each day, with excursions available that also cater to non-birders. Multiday packages include full board, with tasty meals served from the panoramic dining lounge. Minimum two-night all-inclusive package; rates include transfers and guiding. $$$$

MIA camping It is possible to camp at the park headquarters (where they have an ablutions block) or, if you prefer, you can arrange to camp wild along the Camino del Oleoducto; though there are no facilities, several of the available spots are near running water. Per tent $

Gamboa

Surrounded by the luxuriant vegetation of Parque Nacional Soberanía and bordered by the impressive Río Chagres and Lago Gatún, into which the river spills, the sleepy former Canal Zone town of **GAMBOA** is the portal to many attractions on and off the water, most of which are organized as day-trips from Panama City. For nature lovers and birding enthusiasts in particular, Gamboa provides access to the legendary **Camino del Oleoducto** and the adjacent Rainforest Discovery Centre (see page 100).

It is also the departure point for excursions to the scientific research station on **Isla Barro Colorado** (see page 102), for boats offering Pacific-bound partial Canal transits (see box, page 95), fishing trips or wildlife viewing on **Lago Gatún** (see page 102), and for cultural excursions to indigenous **Emberá communities** upriver (see box, page 104). The town is easily accessed by bus and though some activities need organizing in advance, others can be arranged on the spot.

Beyond the activities hosed by the *Gamboa Rainforest Resort* (see page 101), there's little to do in town but soak up the tranquil yesteryear feel, taking in the attractive (and often empty) Canal-era architecture, indulging in a little birdwatching around the wooded fringes or strolling along the Chagres, looking out for iguanas and turtles sunning themselves along the riverbanks and marvelling at the constant procession of container ships. It's a pleasant place to bring a picnic, or you can stock up with some supplies in the Gamboa Store, next to *El Encanto* restaurant.

Brief history

Isolated Gamboa – its only road access via an old single-track bridge shared with the Panama Railroad – was built in 1911 as a settlement for around seven hundred "silver roll" employees and families (see page 301), its population did not increase significantly until the Canal's dredging division relocated here from Paraíso in 1936. By 1942, Gamboa's residents exceeded 3800, much more than the current population, and the community boasted a cinema and golf course. But once the Panama Canal Authority started to transfer operations to Panama City following the 1977 treaties, services began to close and the town dwindled.

ARRIVAL AND INFORMATION — GAMBOA

By bus Gamboa is a 50min bus ride from Panama City. Buses (Mon–Fri, five daily, 5am–4.45pm, Sat & Sun four daily from 7am/8am; last bus back to Panama City Mon–Fri 5.20pm; Sat & Sun 4.50/5.10pm) depart from the front of Albrook terminal. After crossing the bridge into Gamboa, the bus circles the tree-filled park, where you alight for the Sendero del Oleoducto or Rainforest Discovery Centre, before it heads up towards the *Gamboa Rainforest Resort*, where it turns, taking the same route back. Catch it back to Panama City outside the entrance to the dredging division, at the park corner.

By taxi A taxi from Panama City costs around $40 (30min).

ATMs There is an ATM at the *Gamboa Rainforest Resort*, but note that outside the resort, cash is preferred for most businesses in Gamboa.

ACCOMMODATION AND EATING

Canopy B&B 114a Jadwin Ave Ⓦ wildlife-lodges.com/lodge/canopybandb.com. This beautifully restored two-storey Canal-era house provides five tasteful, airy rooms with a/c, fan and private bathrooms. Common areas are comfortable, and they offer reductions on day passes to the Canopy Tower (see page 100). A set dinner can be pre-ordered. $$$

★ **Encanto de Gamboa** Av Omar Torrijos Herrera, by the park. Inexpensive, casual restaurant offering simple but well-cooked cafeteria-style and a la carte local dishes. Being Chinese-Panamanian, the place ensures vegetables feature too. Opens early to catch birdwatchers and workers for breakfast. Closed Sundays. $–$$

Fonda Mary Gaby Av Omar Torrijos Herrera, by the park Ⓣ 677 6728. Open weekdays, serving fixed-price traditional breakfasts and lunches to workers from the canal's dredging division. $

Gamboa Rainforest Resort Ⓦ gamboaresort.com. This all-inclusive luxury resort offers several dining experiences, though you'll be paying tourist prices and the quality of food and service is variable. The location, however, is hard to beat. A lunch buffet is available at the main *Corotú* restaurant, while snacks and cocktails are served at the *Monkey Bar* terrace, a breezy spot with fabulous views across the Chagres. The riverside *Don Caimán*, whose specialities include fish and jerk chicken, offers splendid opportunities for wildlife viewing. Accommodation is in spacious rooms and suites, some with balconies and stunning rainforest and river views. $$$

Treehouse Pizza Gamboa 185b Harding Ave Ⓣ 6061 1374. Not actually a treehouse, sadly, but the simple wooden tables, enclosed by tropical trees illuminated by hanging lights, make for a congenial setting nonetheless. Only open in the evening, when reservations are required. $$–$$$

2

Lago Gatún

Following the damming of the Río Chagres in 1910, the waters took three years to rise, culminating in the formation of **LAGO GATÚN**, at the time the largest artificial lake in the world, covering 425 square kilometres. The lake now provides 33km of the waterway's total 77km length – with the ships following the original course of the Río Chagres, where the lake is at its deepest – and collects and releases the 43 million gallons of water necessary for each vessel to transit the Canal.

The undulating topography ensured that this impressive body of water developed into a place of great beauty, with dozens of peninsulas and tree-topped islands, and a myriad of inlets easing their tentacles into the lush rainforest, all of which are best explored by boat. Favourite destinations are **Isla Barro Colorado** and the archipelago of **Isla Tigre** and **Islas Brujas**. You can't land on the seventeen or so islands, but with a good pair of binoculars you can usually observe from your boat the islands' monkeys cavorting in the trees. Several tour operators include the islands on their wildlife-viewing trips (see page 77) though some, unfortunately, can't resist the urge to feed the monkeys.

Other **wildlife** to look out for, which can easily be spotted while on a fishing trip, includes crocodiles and caimans slithering in the muddy shallows, as well as sloths and snakes entwined round branches. The lake is famous for its prolific peacock bass, and fishermen hanging out at the public dock, before the bridge, will happily take you out for a few hours **angling** or wildlife viewing for around $60–70 for the boat.

Isla Barro Colorado

Tours depart from the Smithsonian Tropical Research Institute (STRI) jetty, 1km beyond Gamboa • Tours Tues, Wed & Fri–Sun 7am–4pm, Sat & Sun 8am–3pm • Rates include boat transfer from Gamboa and lunch • Book through the STRI (stri.si.edu/visit/barro-colorado) or via a tour operator

Isla Barro Colorado (BCI), whose name derives from the dominant reddish clay (*barro colorado*), is home to the most studied patch of tropical forest in the New World. Administered by the Smithsonian Tropical Research Institute (STRI), it draws scientists from all over the world to pore over the sixteen square kilometres of flora and fauna, but can also be visited on a day-long **tour**, which makes for a diverting outing.

After a short **talk**, you set out on a **guided walk**, during which you'll learn about some of the island's 1300-plus plant species and 110-odd species of mammal, more than half of which are bats. A favourite route leads to the "Big Tree", an enormous 500-year-old kapok with a 25m diameter, laden with epiphytes. Although the small island is home to both ocelots and pumas, you're unlikely to see more than their prints in the mud. Much more visible are the vast colonies of leafcutter ants, estimated to chew fifteen percent of all leaves produced in the forest to feed the fungus they eat in their subterranean nests. After **lunch** in the cafeteria, you can watch for wildlife in the immediate vicinity of the research station, where you're likely to see howler monkeys, but you are not allowed back in the forest unaccompanied.

Parque Nacional Chagres

North of Panama City, encompassing large tracts of Colón and Panama provinces, the vast, sprawling rainforest wilderness of **PARQUE NACIONAL CHAGRES** stretches from the northern rain-soaked mountains overlooking the Caribbean to the park's highest peak, **Cerro Jefe**, in the south. The tropical vegetation harbours large but elusive populations of tapirs, endemic salamanders and an abundance of birdlife, including harpy eagles and the rare Tacarcuna bush tanager, and is laced with waterfalls and rivers rich in fish as well as otters, caimans and crocodiles. Hikers are also drawn to the area, particularly by the prospect of following in the steps of the conquistadors along the **Camino Real**, which slices across the western edge of the reserve.

At the heart of the park, the powerful **Río Chagres** and its tributaries – home to several **Emberá and Wounaan villages** that welcome visitors (see box, page 104) – carve their way through rugged terrain. They spill into the elongated **Lago Alajuela** reservoir at the park's southwest corner, built to help regulate the water level in Lago Gatún further downriver.

Supplying 45 percent of the water necessary for the Canal to function and providing all the water for domestic and industrial consumption – as well as electricity through **hydroelectric power** – in Panama City and Colón, the Río Chagres is of vital importance to the country. In order to protect the river and its catchment area, the national park was formed in 1985, its 1296 square kilometres making it one of the country's largest reserves.

Río Chagres and around

Most tourist activities rely on the area's main artery, the **Río Chagres**, be it **whitewater rafting** the cascading torrents of the upper river or more leisurely **kayaking** along the slower, lower stretches, both of which are generally organized as day-trips from Panama City (see page 77). One of the best ways to explore the park is by visiting one of the numerous **Emberá** communities sprinkled along the banks of the Chagres and its tributaries (see box, page 104). The Emberá, together with the closely related Wounaan, have been relocating from the Darién since the late 1960s. Since their traditional means of livelihood – seminomadic subsistence agriculture and hunting – are now largely denied to them thanks to the restrictions of living within a national park, they are being encouraged to make a living from tourism.

As with the neighbouring parks of Camino de Cruces and Soberanía, Parque Nacional Chagres also includes important traces of the country's colonial past, containing a lengthy portion of the **Camino Real**, one of the conquistador mule routes across the isthmus, which skirts the eastern shores of Lago Alajuela. There is currently no clearly marked route but several tour companies offer day- or multiday guided hikes along this historic trail (see page 77).

Cerro Azul

On the southern edge of Parque Nacional Chagres, 40km northeast of Panama City, the area known as **Cerro Azul** is one of two entry points to the park – the other being at Lago Alajuela (see page 103). It's very popular with affluent Panamanians – and increasingly with foreign retirees – attracted by the fresh mountain air and great views (when the mists clear); many have second homes peppered along the fringes of the park boundary. It's not particularly wild, but its highest point, the antenna-covered **Cerro Jefe** (1007m) has an impressive **mirador** and a couple of overgrown **birdwatching trails** near the summit, which is a 4.5km hike from the park office – the warden can give you directions.

ARRIVAL AND GETTING AROUND — PARQUE NACIONAL CHAGRES

Despite its proximity to Panama City, the reserve's vastness and the lack of tourist development make **access** difficult if you're reliant on public transport. Most tourists visit with a tour operator (see page 77), generally bound for the western end, round **Lago Alajuela**, around 35km north of the capital by road. There, several jetties serve as departure points for kayaking, fishing or rafting excursions, or for visiting an Emberá village or hiking along the Camino Real. Other than die-hard birdwatchers, few tourists head for the **Cerro Azul** entrance.

LAGO ALAJUELA

By bus Take a Colón bus from Albrook bus terminal, getting off at Mini Super Mario along the Transístmica, and walk the remaining 3km.

By boat The jetties at Madden Dam, Nuevo Vigía and Victoriano Lorenzo, further round the lake from the park headquarters, are the embarcation points for visits upriver to Emberá communities (see box, page 104).

By car The headquarters at Campo Chagres are about a 40min drive from Panama City, possible in an ordinary car.

2

VISITING AN EMBERÁ COMMUNITY

Just a couple of hours' travel away from Panama City and Colón, the **Emberá village tour** is an established favourite with cruise ships and tour operators (see page 77). Brochures glibly talk about the Emberá "living much as their ancestors did centuries ago" although you don't need to look further than the use of outboard motors, mobile phones and Spanish – not to mention the jeans and T-shirts often donned once the tourists have evaporated – to see that the Emberá are undergoing radical change. Staying **overnight**, or preferably for several nights, affords a better opportunity to interact with villagers and venture deeper into the forest. That said, the day-tours can still offer a fascinating snapshot of traditional Emberá life, and there are obvious benefits to communities: income that will afford them greater self-determination, and a revival of ancestral skills and traditions. For a less touristy scene, visit an Emberá or Wounaan community in the **Darién** (see box, page 277), where it's easier to learn about village life without disrupting it.

THE TOUR ITINERARY

Although villages vary in setting and character, excursions are similar. **Prices** ($120–200) and tour-group sizes vary; even travelling in a small party is no guarantee you won't be cheek by jowl with other tourists once you're in the village, especially during the cruise ship season (Oct–April). Morning pickup (8am–8.30am) is followed by an hour's bus journey to Lago Alajuela, where life-jacketed tourists fan out towards different villages in motorized dugouts. The **boat trip** (30–60min depending on the village location and river water levels) is itself a highlight, gliding through vine-laden forest with raptors wheeling overhead and metallic kingfishers flashing past. At the **villages**, traditional wood-and-thatch buildings sit on stilts, and you'll be greeted by enthusiastic kids and women who form a dazzling collage of fluorescent sarong-like skirts (*uhua*) and multicoloured bead-and-silver-coin necklaces, their hair often adorned with hibiscus flowers.

Activities generally include a talk about the traditional Emberá way of life (see box, page 277) and a demonstration of basketry or woodcarving, as well as a short walk into the rainforest with a village elder to learn about medicinal plants or a trip to a waterfall. A simple lunch precedes traditional dances (when visitors are often encouraged to join in) accompanied by drums, bamboo flutes and maracas, after which tourists can get their bodies painted with *jagua* dye and peruse the finely made crafts on display. Unlike the Guna, the Emberá are fairly comfortable being photographed and general shots of the village (though not inside homes) and dances are allowed, though permission should always be sought from individuals. Most tours pile back into the dugouts at 2.30–3pm for the return trip.

VISITING INDEPENDENTLY

It is possible and cheaper to visit **independently from Panama City** – several of the communities have their own website with mobile phone contact numbers (listed below). They generally charge around $75 per person (for up to two people, less for larger groups) for the day, which is approximately what they receive per tourist from the tour operators. But you'll still need to call in advance to ensure a boat ride. Getting **from Panama City to Puerto de Corotú**, the departure point for most villages on Lago Alajuela, can be time-consuming on public transport (1hr–2hr 30min) and may require some waiting around. Take the Metro to San Isidro then change onto a bus bound for La Cabima, or take a Corredor Norte bus that goes that way; walk back to the 99 supermarket for the minivan transfer to the port.

CONTACTS FOR INDEPENDENT TRAVELLERS

Comunidad Drua ⓣ6709 1233, ⓦtrail2.com/embera. Scenic location and great river trip. Overnight stays possible.

Comunidad Emberá Quera ⓣ6703 9475, ⓦemberaquera.com. This almost too perfectly maintained thatched village sits on Río Gatún, so departure is from Puente Río Gatun – a short taxi ride from Sabanitas. Overnight stays possible.

Comunidad Tusipono Emberá Contact Regu ⓣ6702 5078 or Tamara ⓣ6324 2898. Day-tours only, which can include the community's butterfly breeding conservation project, and a visit to a waterfall.

CERRO AZUL

By bus Take any transport bound for 24 de Diciembre or Chepo from Albrook terminal, getting off at La Doña Super 99 (just before Xtra); cross the road to the bus terminal at the back of the shopping centre, where minibuses wind their way up to Cerro Azul (6am–6pm; every 30–45min; 30min).

By metro Take the metro to 24 de Diciembre (Line 2); cross the road to the bus terminal at the back of the shopping centre.

By car Head east along the Corredor Sur from Panama City; 6km past the airport turn-off, you enter the nondescript district of 24 de Diciembre, where Cerro Azul is signposted off to the left, just before Supermercado Xtra. The park office – not the headquarters – is at the end of the main road.

INFORMATION

The **park headquarters** is at Campo Chagres (Mon–Fri 8am–4pm; no phone), a small headland jutting into Lago Alajuela; there's also a **visitors' centre** at nearby Nuevo Caimitillo and a **park office** (Mon–Fri 8am–4pm; no phone) at the end of the main road that winds up from the Interamericana, in Cerro Azul.

Colón

Situated at the Atlantic entrance to the Panama Canal, with a population of around 42,000, **COLÓN** makes it into few holiday brochures; for most Panamanians its name is a byword for poverty, violence and urban decay. Sadly, most visitors come here solely to shop at the **Zona Libre**, or **Free Zone**, a walled enclave on the eastern edge of the city where goods from all over the world can be bought at very low prices – it's the world's second largest duty-free zone after Hong Kong. Vestiges of the city's former grandeur do remain, however, and it's worth exploring (by taxi, for **safety** reasons) for an hour or so before heading out to several tourist destinations within striking distance. The people of Colón, mostly descendants of West Indians who came here to build the Canal, are as warm and friendly as anywhere in the country and just as fond of partying.

Brief history

As work began on the construction of the Panama Railroad in 1850, the settlement now known as Colón began to mushroom on a low-lying lump of coral known as Isla Manzanillo. Surrounded by mosquito- and sandfly-infested mangrove swamps and lacking a source of fresh water, the location was so unfavourable that the workers initially lived on a brig anchored in the bay rather than on the island itself. American historian H.H. Bancroft, on his arrival in 1851, summed up the general view: "The very ground on which one trod was pregnant with disease, and death was distilled in every breath of air".

Nonetheless the Americans in charge of the railway bewilderingly insisted on establishing the Atlantic terminal here, and in 1852 unilaterally named the place Aspinwall after one of the railway's owners. This upset the New Grenadan (present-day Colombia and Panama) authorities, who insisted that it be called Colón, after Cristóbal Colón (Christopher Columbus), leading to a long-running dispute that the Colombians finally won by ingeniously instructing the postal services not to deliver letters from the US if addressed to Aspinwall.

The railway brought many immigrants and a degree of prosperity to the town despite the constant threat of yellow fever, malaria and cholera. Since then, wealth – via Canal construction, a spell as a fashionable cruise-ship destination in the 1950s and the success of the Free Zone, founded in 1949 – has come and gone, and Panama's main port predominantly remains a slum city.

In the face of extreme **poverty** and soaring unemployment levels, it is little surprise that many have turned to crime, particularly drug and arms trafficking, as a way to survive. Successive governments have promised to renovate the city centre and rejuvenate the economy, but there's little to show for their efforts.

The city centre

At the entrance to Colón, opposite the train station, is the rather dull **Aspinwall monument**, honouring the American founders of the city and owners of the Panama Railroad. A left turn takes you past the bus terminal, behind which lies the port enclave of **Cristóbal**, then north up dilapidated **Avenida del Frente** until you reach the **New Washington Hotel** (newwashingtonhotel.com), which overlooks the Caribbean. Initially constructed in wood around 1870 to house railway engineers, the current concrete and cement-block edifice dates from 1913. It's worth stopping to have a peek at the entrance hall, with its chandeliers and ornate double marble staircase – poignant reminders of Colón's former splendour. To the right of the hotel as you face the sea is the dark-stone Episcopalian **Christ Church by the Sea** (daily 8am–noon), the first Protestant church in Central America, built in the mid-1860s for the railroad workers; it has some delightful stained-glass windows, so is worth popping inside.

Four blocks east along the seafront, a statue of Christ the Redeemer, arms outstretched, faces down Avenida Central, the city's main street, which is lined with

SAFETY IN COLÓN

Although sometimes exaggerated, Colón's reputation throughout the rest of the country for **violent crime** is not undeserved, and if you come here you should exercise extreme caution – mugging, even on the main streets in broad daylight, does happen. Don't carry anything you can't afford to lose, try and stay in sight of the police on the main streets, and consider hiring a taxi driver (your hotel will recommend one) to take you around, both as a guide and for protection.

monuments. The **Catedral de la Inmaculada Concepción de María**, built between 1929 and 1934 with high, neo-Gothic arches and some attractive stained-glass windows, can be found three blocks west of Avenida Central on Calle 5.

Along the waterfront of the Bahía de Manzanillo, on the eastern side of the city, **Colón 2000**, the cruise-ship terminal, holds a collection of shops (including a 99 supermarket) and restaurants primarily catering to cruise-ship passengers. In 2020, a larger, swankier extension opened: Colón 2000 Duty Free (colon2000dutyfree.com) contains duty free shopping, but at elevated prices, and 30 food outlets.

ARRIVAL AND INFORMATION — COLÓN

By train The most comfortable way to reach Colón is on the fabulous, but expensive, Panama Canal Railway train (see page 96) to the Atlantic terminus, from where it's a short taxi ride or 10min walk to the bus terminal. If you walk, keep to the left-hand side of the road, hugging the fence, otherwise you are likely to get mugged.

By bus Take the express coaches (every 30min; 1hr 15min). The bus terminal (on the corner of Av del Frente and C 13) is fairly safe during the day, but avoid arriving after dark.

Destinations Achiote (6.30am–3.20pm; every 45min; 45min–1hr); Cacique (daily 3.30pm; 1hr 40min); Escobal (6.30am & 8am, then every 40min until noon & hourly until 7.30pm; 45min–1hr); La Guaira, for Isla Grande (9.30am–5.30pm; five buses; 1hr 40min); Portobelo (Mon–Sat 6am–8pm, Sun 6am–6.30pm; every 30min–1hr; 1hr).

GETTING AROUND

By taxi Though the city centre is compact, you are strongly advised not to wander around but to use licensed yellow taxis or the fancier, pricier tourist taxis (white with a yellow band) wherever possible. Consult your hotel about hiring a reliable driver to do your sightseeing; hourly rates (approximately $15–20) depend on where you go and the number of passengers.

By car Budget (budgetpanama.com), Hertz (321 8312) and Thrifty (panamathrifty.com) have car rental offices in Colón; all are closed on Sun.

ACCOMMODATION — SEE MAP PAGE 106

You are very unlikely to want to spend the night in Colón, but if you do, the following recommendations have good security and on-site restaurants so that you do not need to go out at night.

Hotel Sotelo C 11 & Av Amador Guerrero facebook.com/hotelsotelo. Recently refurbished, this secure place is a top budget choice, with modern if minimal furnishings and faux parquet floors. Also with an on-site restaurant. $$

Marina Hotel Shelter Bay, 28km south marinahotelatshelterbay.com. Though aimed at yachties wanting on-shore pampering, these new, simple and nicely appointed rooms above a restaurant (see below) provide a comfortable (though overpriced) base from which to explore Fuerte San Lorenzo and the Atlantic side of the Canal. Two-night minimum stay. Room only. $$$

New Washington Hotel C 1, Paseo Washington newwashingtonhotel.com. Superbly situated on the waterfront, the hotel's ornate facade and impressive marble foyer hark back to its illustrious history. Its three-star present is far more modest, but having completely overhauled their large rooms – which afford amazing views of container vessels waiting to enter the canal – and the pool, the hotel offers good value for money. $$

Radisson Colón 2000 Paseo Gorgas, C 13, Colón 2000 radisson.com. Probably the best in town, this hotel offers unremarkable business-standard rooms with the usual amenities, plus a spa and casino on site. It's in the cruise-ship terminal, Colón 2000, so be prepared for cruise passengers to be peering over you when you're lounging by the pool. There's a varied buffet spread for breakfast. $$$

EATING — SEE MAP PAGE 106

For **safety** reasons you should eat in or near your hotel in the evening. If you have to go out, take a taxi for all but the

BUILDING THE PANAMA RAILROAD

So often overshadowed by the building of the Panama Canal, the **Panama Railroad** was the world's first transcontinental railway and a phenomenal engineering feat in its own right. Anticipating the Gold Rush, wealthy American businessman William Aspinwall constructed a 76km track linking the Atlantic and Pacific oceans to facilitate trade between New York and the East Coast and rapidly developing California. At a total cost of almost $8 million (six times the original estimate), it became the most expensive track per mile in the world, though the hefty first-class transit fee, $25 in gold, also made it one of the most profitable.

The **human costs** were brutal. During the five years of construction an estimated six thousand to ten thousand workers died, though appallingly records were only kept of the white employees, who constituted a fraction of the workforce. The high death toll enabled the railroad to sustain a grisly sideline in pickling bodies in barrels to sell to hospitals worldwide. Although most of the labourers came from the Caribbean, others migrated from as far as India, Malaysia and Ireland. Despite the constant influx, work occasionally stalled since at any one time only a third of the men, who spent long days up to their waists in swamp, attacked by mosquitoes and disease, were fit enough to wield a shovel.

Little sign of the dreadful human cost remained when the inaugural transit was made in 1855 amid much pomp. As one passenger wrote, "It affords the observant traveller an opportunity of an easy enjoyment and acquaintance with intertropical nature unsurpassed in any part of the world". The same is still true today (see page 96).

shortest journeys. During the day, stick to the main streets and exercise caution.

Colón 2000 Duty Free Mall food court The escalator in the mall leads up to a long breezy balcony-cum-food court, which offers a variety of chain restaurants, offering Panamanian, Korean, Greek and Peruvian food – to name but a few. The dining area affords super views across the bay. $$–$$$

The Dock Shelter Bay Marina, 28km south ⓣ 433 0471, ⓦ shelterbaymarina.com. Lovely bayside setting for sipping a cocktail or enjoying a leisurely lunch on your way back from San Lorenzo (see page 110). The food's nicely presented and freshly prepared – soups and salads, gourmet sandwiches and burgers and succulent flame-grilled seafood options. $$$

Nuevo Dos Mares C 5, between Av Central and Arosemena ⓣ 439 8180. Behind an unpromising frontage, this place specializes in Caribbean cuisine, with a spread of tasty fish and seafood with coconut rice, fried yuca or *patacones*. Take a taxi and organize a pickup time, or get a takeaway. $$–$$$

Santizo Afro-Kitchen Av Central and C 4 ⓦ instagram.com/santizoafrokitchen. Friendly service from a food truck with streetside seating (under shade). Order a polystyrene tray full of monster shrimps dripping in garlic (and a fair bit of oil, it has to be said) or chicken, with coconut rice, salad and plantain. $

Around Colón

Southwest of Colón, a road runs through to the enormous **Gatún Locks**, where you can get up close to gigantic container ships being raised and lowered between sea level and Lago Gatún. Once across the Canal, the road divides: to the right it meanders 22km through dense forest to the evocative ruins of the colonial **Fuerte San Lorenzo**, standing guard at the mouth of the Río Chagres; to the left, it rises above the shoreline of Lago Gatún, offering splendid views across the water and its sprinkling of tree-topped islands before undulating through agricultural land to the rarely visited coastal communities of the **Costa Abajo**. Meanwhile, anyone interested in marine ecology should consider heading to the coast northeast of Colón to visit **Isla Galeta**, where the Smithsonian has a research centre.

Isla Galeta marine research and education centre

Isla Galeta • Tues–Sun 9am–3pm, with prior reservation • Charge for guided tour • ⓦ stri.si.edu • No public transport

About 12km northeast of Colón lies **Isla Galeta**, which is actually a headland and home to the Smithsonian's **marine research and education centre**. A far lesser known attraction than Isla Barro Colorado, the centre is more on the scale of Punta Culebra (see page 68), its main attraction a modest boardwalk through the **mangroves**, where crabs and tree snakes can be spotted. There's also an **interpretive centre** and a handful of exhibits, including touch pools and the 15m skeleton of a Bride's whale. Given the cost of a taxi here, it's only worthwhile if you have your own transport.

The Atlantic locks and around

Eight kilometres southwest of Colón, accessible by bus (and a walk) or taxi, are the Canal's Atlantic locks. First up are the new mammoth three-chambered **Agua Clara Locks** for the Neopanamax ships, overlooked by a visitors' centre. Beyond lie the famous **Gatún Locks**, the largest and most impressive of the original locks; comprising three sets of double lock chambers, they stretch for 3km – if you include the approach walls – which made them the greatest concrete structure in the world until the Hoover Dam's completion in 1930. A new viewing platform is planned, but in the meantime, the only way to get a close-up of the tremendous studded steel plate breastplates of the lock's mitre gates is by transiting the canal on a boat (see box, page 95). The impressive cable-stayed bridge, which spans the Atlantic entrance to the canal, was opened in 2019. To your left, a couple of kilometres west along the road after crossing the bridge below the locks, is Gatún Dam.

Centro de Visitantes de Agua Clara

Lago Gatún, on the eastern side of the new locks • Daily 8am–4pm; last entry 3.15pm • Charge • Ⓦ visitcanaldepanama.com

The **Centro de Visitantes de Agua Clara** overlooks the three new larger lock chambers and the adjacent water-saving basins, with the original Gatún Locks in the background – bring your binoculars. Although you're further from the action than at Miraflores, the elevated position on the side of a hill affords a **panoramic view** of both the locks and Lago Gatún, which you don't get at the other sites. For the steep entry fee, you also get a twelve-minute video (in English or Spanish) and access to a very short **interpretive trail** through a patch of rainforest. There's also a snack bar, a tourist-priced restaurant, and lots of shade and seating for picnics.

Puente Atlántico

In 2019 the impressive **Puente Atlántico** was inaugurated, finally allowing uninterrupted road traffic between the two sections of Colón province, which up until then had been reliant on ferries, or crossing Gatún Locks's swing gates when a ship was not in transit.

Gatún Dam

Despite being the longest dam in the world when it was built, at 2.3km, and a brilliant technical achievement, the earthen **Gatún Dam** is not as visually impressive as it should be. That said, the curved concrete **spillway** at its centre can be an awe-inspiring sight when the floodgates are opened following heavy rains. Since the Puente Atlántico opened in 2019 and the road across the Gatún Locks was closed, the dam is only accessible with private transport.

ARRIVAL AND DEPARTURE — THE ATLANTIC LOCKS AND AROUND

By bus Catch any Costa Abajo bus from Colón (see page 107). For the Centro de Visitantes de Agua Clara, ask the driver to let you off before you head onto the bridge to cross the Canal and walk 2.5km up the access road to your left.

By taxi A taxi from Colón will take you to the Agua Clara visitors' centre (around $20, including wait time. Taxis waiting around the cruise terminal are always more expensive.

Fuerte San Lorenzo

Mouth of the Río Chagres, 13km northwest of Gatún Locks • Daily 8am–4pm; last entry 3.15pm • Charge • ppysl.org/sanlorenzo

Perched high on a rocky promontory, standing guard over the mouth of the Río Chagres, the well-preserved ruins of **FUERTE SAN LORENZO** bear witness to its importance during Spanish colonial times. Its spectacular location, commanding views of both the brooding river and the glistening Caribbean, coupled with its isolation and forest surroundings, make it a far more evocative place than the more accessible and more visited Portobelo (see page 112). Along with the forts at Portobelo, the place was declared a UNESCO World Heritage Site in 1980 and is now a popular destination on the cruise-ship circuit, but if you get there early (or visit during the rainy season) you can often have the place to yourself.

2

The fort is set within the 120-square-kilometre **Área Protegida San Lorenzo**, amid a swathe of secondary forest and swampland, which provide excellent **birdwatching**. Though the only developed trail lies close to the village of Achiote (see page 111), a wander down any of the tracks off the road to the fort with your binoculars is likely to be productive. Some areas are still out of bounds on account of unexploded mines that the US military left behind after deciding it was too expensive to clear – there are warning signs about the dangers but they are not everywhere, so stick to the paths.

Brief history

Construction of the original sea-level earth-and-wood fort began in 1595 to protect loot-laden Spanish boats sailing down the Chagres to Portobelo from attack by foreign vessels. Though Francis Drake failed to take the place in 1596, it fell to one of **Henry Morgan**'s privateers in 1670, enabling Morgan and his band to pass unhindered up the river and destroy Panama City. The fort was rebuilt in coral stone in the 1680s in its present cliff-top location, where it was eventually ruined in 1740 by the British. Although San Lorenzo was rebuilt and further strengthened, the fortifications were never really tested again, though they were used as part of the US military defences in World War II – note the still visible antiaircraft platform next to the tower.

Exploring the fort

As you cross over the **drawbridge** (not the original one) and through the smart, squat stone-and-brick **guardhouse**, the main entrance to the fort, you come out onto the **esplanade**, which offers the best view of the fort and served to collect rainwater that was channelled off into a **water tank** over the parapet in front of you. The vast grassy area below is the **parade ground**, containing the ruined troops' and officers' quarters. Taking the ramp down, follow the wall along to the ruins of the **powder magazine** and the **tower** built into the side of the hill, now scarcely more than a deep hole filled with litter. Though the adjacent wall parapets and cannons have now gone, the view is as it always was, and it's easy to picture watchmen anxiously gazing out towards the horizon for enemy ships. Before climbing back up towards the guardhouse, peer inside some of the many remarkably preserved **vaults** underneath the esplanade, used to store equipment and food and, much later, prisoners. Crossing the drawbridge once more you'll find yourself on the **exterior platform**, with the one surviving sentry box to the left. Here the parapet is still intact, as are the nine **cannons** pointing out towards the putative enemy.

ARRIVAL AND DEPARTURE — FUERTE SAN LORENZO

On a tour With no public transport to San Lorenzo, unless you have your own transport, your best bet is to go on a tour. Several Panama City tour operators (see page 77) include San Lorenzo as stop on one of their day-trips itineraries, which also usually include the train journey across the isthmus (see page 96) and/or a visit to Agua Clara Locks (see page 109).

By taxi A taxi (including waiting time at the fort) from Colón will cost about $70.

By car Renting a car allows you to stop off at the Agua Clara Locks and Gatún Dam on the way, enjoy a bite to eat at the *Shelter Bay Marina* (see page 108), or explore more of the protected area. Once you've driven across the new Puente Atlántico that spans the Canal, take the well-signposted road straight ahead towards Shelter Bay (formerly the US base Fort Sherman). After crossing the remains of excavations made for the French canal, the road continues for 12km, reaching a checkpoint at the entry to the former fort, where you may need to show ID. The road to San Lorenzo bends off to the left, continuing for another 10km along a tarred road to the fort. You'll come across the park office after a couple of kilometres, where there may be someone to relieve you of your park fee.

Costa Abajo

The area to the west of the Canal is known as the **COSTA ABAJO**, which includes a number of inland communities sandwiched between Lago Gatún and the Caribbean coast as well as a handful of coastal villages. A hinterland in tourist terms, the area will really only appeal to avid birdwatchers and those who want to get off the beaten track.

Two villages here earn a trickle of visitors. **Escobal**, attractively situated on Lago Gatún, is a pleasant spot to engage in a little kayaking, fishing or horseriding while **Achiote**, further inland, is a prime location for birdwatching. The other settlements strung out along the wild, windswept coastline rarely see tourists.

Escobal

The road to the sprawling lakeside fishing village of **ESCOBAL** (and Cuipo beyond) periodically offers glimpses of sparkling Lago Gatún and its many wooded islands through the trees and prolific elephant grass. After about 10km the road divides: to the right it heads back up towards the coast via Achiote; ahead it continues to ethnically diverse Escobal, primarily populated by descendants of Canal labourers and communities displaced by the damming of the Río Chagres. It's an attractive spot to relax; you can engage a boatman to explore the tiny islands and secret inlets on the vast reservoir, or go horseriding or hiking in the forest.

ARRIVAL AND DEPARTURE — ESCOBAL

By bus Buses from Colón marked "Costa Abajo Cuipo" pass through Escobal (6.30am & 8am, then every 40min until noon & hourly until 7.30pm; 45min).

ACCOMMODATION AND EATING

Restaurante Doña Nelly Main road by main bus stop ⓣ434 6029. Simple local restaurant with outside seating dishing up decent fried chicken or fish with rice or *patacones* and beans.

Campamento Punta Macú Take a left turn in the centre of the village before Restaurante Kastillo's ⓣ6336 2435. If you have a tent, head for this lovely camping spot on a headland down by the lakeside. Facilities are sparse (but there's electricity, water and toilets and *bohíos* when you need to escape the sun. With 24hr notice you can arrange for a boat trip on the lake. Avoid weekends and holiday periods when the place can be overrun with partying campers. They also have two basic rooms to rent out. $/person

Achiote

Located in a flat-bottomed valley just outside the Área Protegida San Lorenzo – its five hundred inhabitants primarily survive on livestock rearing and subsistence agriculture, with coffee the main crop – the hamlet of **ACHIOTE** provides a good base for exploring the area. Strung along the main road, backing onto a flower-filled and forested hillside and surrounded by bucolic countryside, it is also home to a community-based ecotourism project in the **Centro El Tucán**, which focuses on **birdwatching** and **hiking** as well as offering a tour of a local **coffee** farm and a **boat trip** on Río Lagarto.

Some 435 recorded bird species are spread across the **Área Protegida San Lorenzo**, which encompasses tracts of mangrove, cativo and palm swamps and vast swathes of other secondary forest types, including some deciduous growth.

Sendero El Trogón

Charge for combined entry to trails and the Área Protegida San Lorenzo

The main **birdwatching trail** is the **Sendero El Trogón**, which lies 4km before Achiote, within the park boundary, and was so named on account of the three types of trogon that frequent the area. Although it's a pleasant walk, the birding is often easier (and free) along the more open areas of the main road. If you're willing to dodge the occasional speeding bus or truck, you'll get a chance to see brilliant chestnut-mandibled and keel-billed toucans, blue-headed parrots and beautiful blue cotingas.

ARRIVAL AND DEPARTURE — ACHIOTE

By bus From Colón, take the bus bound for Miguel de la Borda (6.30am–3.20pm, approximately every 45min; 45min–1hr to Achiote; 2hr 30min to Miguel de la Borda) or, more commonly, Río Indio, also confusingly marked "Costa Abajo". The last bus back to Colón passes through Achiote from Miguel de la Borda at around 4pm.

Tours To visit the reserve, you can arrange a guide for hiking or birdwatching; contact Centro El Tucán (see below), which can also organize homestays and a visit to the local coffee farm in the harvesting season (Dec–Jan).

ACCOMMODATION AND EATING

La Cascá Main road, towards the far end of the village. Only open for breakfast and lunch (unless you make an advance reservations), this inexpensive community restaurant serves up tasty, filling food – though it's often a case of being offered whatever's in the pot that day. $

Centro El Tucán Main road at the village entrance facebook.com/centroeltucan. The centre has camping space plus two basic dorms (fans and mosquito screens) with shared cold-water showers and kitchen. They also have a *cabaña* that sleeps up to six people, sharing the communal kitchen. Mobile coverage is intermittent; if you fail to make contact in advance you can usually find someone to let you in if you arrive before nightfall. Camping $/person, dorms $$, *cabaña* $$

Piña to Miguel de la Borda

There are regular buses from Colón to Miguel de la Borda, passing through Piña (6.30am–3.20pm; every 45min; 2hr 30min); boats to Coclé del Norte

Beyond Achiote the road rises, twists and turns through pleasantly undulating pastures before reaching the coast at the village of **PIÑA**. Here bracing winds and waves batter the rugged coastline while treacherous currents throw up driftwood and fishing debris on the black-streaked beaches. The coastal road meanders a further 40km through a string of settlements to the village and river of **MIGUEL DE LA BORDA**. Here, the truly adventurous can negotiate passage by boat to the small community of **Coclé del Norte**, which maintains links with the rest of the country via motorized dugout up the river of the same name to Coclecito, followed by a *colectivo* to Penonomé (see page 140). The boats leave infrequently, particularly when the sea is rough (Nov–Feb).

There are currently no **places to stay** along this stretch of coast though, with a little Spanish and perseverance, you can probably find a very basic bunk or hammock for the night, or pay to pitch a tent.

Portobelo

In colonial times the scenically situated town of **PORTOBELO** was the most important settlement on the isthmus after Panama City, since all the plunder from South America passed through here en route to Spain. The main tourist sites are the **ruined fortresses**, remnants of the conquistadors' attempts to safeguard the treasure from the envious grasp of pirates and privateers. A soldier's-eye view across the turquoise bay from the forts' rusting Spanish cannons is one of the most popular postcard images in Panama, conveying the impression of a remote military outpost surrounded by dense vegetation – it therefore comes as a shock to find the forts smack in the middle of an economically deprived modern town, with dilapidated houses propped up against the historical ruins and kids playing football in what was once a parade ground. The town itself is mostly squeezed along a thin strip of land between the main road and the bay, which spills into the Caribbean, and is easily walkable. A half-day provides ample time to explore the colonial relics, leaving you the afternoon to enjoy a nearby beach, a spot of **snorkelling** or **diving**, a **kayaking** session or a **boat trip** around the bay (see box, page 117). Before setting out to explore, it's well worth visiting the town's excellent **Centro de Visitantes**, which provides an overview of the area's historical, cultural and natural attractions.

Portobelo gets busy during two famous **festivals** (see box, page 115): the Festival del Nazareño in October and the hugely enjoyable Afro-Colonial Festival de los Diablos y Congos, held biannually in March. Smaller annual celebrations take place along the coast in the weeks leading up to Carnaval.

There is an intermittently functioning ATM just outside Portobelo (opposite the police station) though none in any of the villages further along the coast; nor is there any reliable place to get **petrol**. The last reliable ATM and petrol station are by the supermarket in Sabanitas (see page 116).

2

Brief history

Archeological evidence points to sparsely populated itinerant settlements along the coast from 800 BC–750 AD until the Spanish arrived and all but wiped out the indigenous population. Cue the arrival of **Christopher Columbus**, who, believing himself to be at death's door after days on a storm-tossed sea, spotted a beautiful sheltered bay surrounded by forested hills and gratefully exclaimed, "Che porto bello". While the name stuck, the strategic importance of the natural harbour was not truly appreciated until 1585, when it became clear that Nombre de Dios – then the principal Spanish port on the Panama's Caribbean coast – was too exposed and should be relocated to Portobelo. As if to reinforce the point, Sir Francis Drake destroyed Nombre de Dios in 1595 before dying of dysentery – his coffin supposedly lies at the bottom of the ocean at the entrance to the bay, near an islet which bears his name.

In 1597 **San Felipe de Portobelo** was officially founded, prompting further fortification and providing a new target for spoil-hungry **pirates** and privateers, including notorious buccaneer Henry Morgan, who pounced at night in 1668, and squeezed one hundred thousand pesos from the Spanish authorities in exchange for not levelling the place. British naval commander **Sir Edward Vernon**, attacking seventy years later, made no such concession and destroyed the two fortresses. Though new forts were built in the mid-eighteenth century – those still visible today – they were smaller, since Portobelo's commercial importance was already waning as the Spanish had rerouted their ships round Cape Horn. When the Spanish garrison finally abandoned the town in 1821, its 150 years of strategic significance came to an end.

2

Fuerte Santiago and around

Main road • Open access • Free

Fuerte Santiago is the first fort you encounter from the west before entering the town proper, built in the mid-eighteenth century following the destruction of the original fortifications by the British. The main entrance takes you through a vestibule protected by gun ports to the grassy **parade grounds**, where the ruined walls of the officers' quarters, barracks, kitchen and artillery emplacement are visible. More impressive are the lower and upper **batteries**, their cannons pointing out across the bay.

Mirador El Perú

If you've time, it's worth crossing over the road from Fuerte Santiago for the steep five-minute climb to the **Mirador El Perú**. The mirador is on the site of a watchtower of the former **Fortaleza Santiago de la Gloria**, whose scarcely visible overgrown ruins are now bisected by the main road below.

Fuerte San Fernando

Across the bay from Fuerte Santiago • Open access • Free • Take a water-taxi from the jetty by Fuerte Santiago

Across the bay from Fuerte Santiago you can make out what little remains of **Fuerte San Fernando** peeking through dense foliage. As with the other forts, many of the original stones were plundered for construction of the Canal. Though smaller than its sibling fort, the scenic spot gives a different perspective on the town.

Casa Real de la Aduana

Plaza Central • Tues–Sun 8am–4pm • Free

The small **Plaza Central** in the town centre is dominated by the two-storey coral stone and brick **Casa Real de la Aduana**, built in 1638 to replace an earlier wooden structure. A third of the world's gold, alongside copious other treasures, passed through this customs house for more than a century; there was only one entrance and one exit to reduce fraud and theft and to ensure the Crown got its full royal cut of the spoils. Destroyed in an earthquake in 1882, it underwent restoration in 1997, gradually slipping back into disrepair until a multi-million-dollar makeover resulted in the excellent Museo de la Memoria Afropanameña, which opened in 2023.

Gone are the piles of rusting cannon balls and colonial military memorabilia as the area's fascinating history and culture are now viewed through a postcolonial lens. Exhibits are bilingual, interactive and highly informative. Room One presents a nuanced view of Afro-Panamanian history, which moves beyond enslavement and resistance to describe the lives of their descendants, who, by the second half of the eighteenth century, made up over half the Isthmian population. Room Two focuses on culture, specifically gastronomy, and the origins and significance of the town's two big festivals – the Cristo Negro and the Congos (see box, page 115). There's plenty of photos and video footage and an opportunity to hone your African drumming skills.

Fuerte San Jerónimo

Behind the Casa Real de la Aduana • Open access • Free

Down by the waterside and hemmed in by housing lies **Fuerte San Jerónimo**, the town's largest and most impressive ruin. The former **parade ground** stretches along the eighteen-gun emplacements of the lower battery, with nearly all the original rusting cannons intact. It's worth walking along to the high battery, where you can still see the rainwater reservoir, storage rooms for gunpowder and the latrines, and get a great view of the entrance of the bay.

PORTOBELO FESTIVALS

Two very different **festivals** bring this otherwise lethargic town to life, causing traffic to grind to a halt well before the first fort, and streets to heave with people, as you find yourself knee-deep in discarded polystyrene containers, beer cans and chicken bones.

EL FESTIVAL DEL NAZAREÑO

In mid-October, Portobelo bursts into a frenzy of religious fervour and wild partying at the Festival del Nazareño – more commonly dubbed the **Festival del Cristo Negro** (Black Christ Festival) after Panama's most revered religious icon, a striking, dark-skinned Christ with a penetrating gaze and bearing the Cross, which resides in the Iglesia de San Felipe. The effigy's iconic status was cemented in 1821 when it apparently spared the townsfolk from an epidemic that was sweeping the isthmus.

Though the main **procession** occurs on October 21, the build-up begins days before as up to forty thousand pilgrims, including general party-goers and a small number of criminals wanting to atone for their crimes, march into town. Thousands walk the 35km from Sabanitas and a handful hoof it from further afield, many in ankle-length purple robes. Some crawl the last stretch on their hands and knees, urged on by faithful companions wafting incense, rocking miniature shrines in front of their eyes or even pouring hot wax on their backs. To compound the suffering, the pilgrims are frequently overdosing on carbon monoxide from the festival traffic, which weaves in and out of the bodies struggling along the scorching asphalt. Shelters, food stalls and medical posts are set up along the route while the town itself is jam-packed with makeshift casinos, stalls selling religious paraphernalia and food outlets dishing out chicken and rice.

At 8pm an ever-changing cohort of robed men begin to parade the icon, bedecked in a claret robe, round the packed town in a rhythmical swaying, to the accompaniment of brass and drum, followed by the penitents. Once the candlelit litter has been returned to the church around midnight, the pilgrims discard their robes at the entrance as an explosion of fireworks marks the start of a hedonistic feast of drinking, gambling and dancing that continues through the night. **"El Naza"**, as the statue is affectionately known, gets another celebratory town outing on the Wednesday of Holy Week, this time clothed in purple, though the festivities are not quite as grand.

CONGOS AND DEVILS

In the weekends leading up to **Carnaval**, **Congo** societies along the Costa Arriba erupt in colourful explosions of traditional song, dance and satirical play-acting that originated in the sixteenth century among outlawed communities of escaped slaves, known as *cimarrones*. Congregating in mock palaces, each with its king (*Juan de Dios*) and queen (*Mecé*) togged out in extravagant costumes and ludicrously large crowns, they communicate in their own dialect. The general view is that the characters represent a **parody** of the Spanish court, though a more recent interpretation maintains that they refer back to the Kingdom of Konga in Central Africa. The men sport painted faces, conical hats and outlandish tattered clothes, worn inside-out and decorated with everything from empty beer cans to teddy bears; the women wear multicoloured *polleras*, their hair garlanded with flowers, and dance to beating drums and choral chants. In the many comic rituals, "prisoners", including the odd unsuspecting tourist, are taken and released for ransom – a few coins or an offer of a beer will usually do. The celebrations reach their climax on Ash Wednesday with the **Festival de los Diablos**. The ferocious scarlet-and-black devils (representing the evil spirits of the Spanish colonials), who have been previously running amok in frightening masks, brandishing whips, are captured by a posse of angels, who drag them off to be baptized.

A more formalized biennial **Festival de los Diablos y Congos** takes place in April or May which is well worth seeing, alternating with a more recently instituted **Festival de la Pollera Congo**, which still features a number of devils and plenty of drumming and dancing.

2

Iglesia de San Felipe

Main road • Daily 6am–6pm • Free

One of the town's major landmarks, and focus of the annual Festival del Nazareño (see box, page 115), is the **Iglesia de San Felipe**, which overlooks a bare square. Although construction started in 1606, the church was only completed in 1814, making it the conquistadors' last religious building in Panama, with the bell tower added in 1945. Inside you'll find white walls and a large, carved gilt mahogany altarpiece, though the focus inevitably is on the object of so much devotion, the so-called **Cristo Negro**, a dark-skinned, lifelike statue of Jesus bearing the Cross that peers out from behind a glass casement. The **museum** at the back of the church is supposed to showcase the splendid collection of luxurious velvet robes donated by wealthy devotees over the years for the Nazareño to wear. However, funds have been lacking for the building's restoration; in the meantime, some of the garments have been squeezed into a tiny one-room municipal museum in the street opposite, and can be viewed on request.

Casa Congo

Waterfront, west of the Casa Real de la Aduana • Daily 8am–4pm • Free • casacongo.com

Well worth a visit is the **Casa Congo**. It houses an informative display on the origin and meaning of the Congos (see box, page 115), featuring some fine photographs of the major festival characters. The centre also hosts an excellent exhibition of high-quality associated **arts and crafts** made by local artisans.

ARRIVAL AND INFORMATION — PORTOBELO

Most people visit Portobelo as a **day-trip** from Panama City, though there is an increasing number of places to stay.

By bus Take any Colón-bound express bus from Panama City, getting off at the El Rey supermarket at the Sabanitas junction (the last sure chance to get money from an ATM). Here you can hop on a Portobelo-bound bus from Colón (daily 6am–8pm; every 30min–1hr; 1hr). At busy festival or holiday times, it's worth going into Colón itself to make sure of a seat. Return buses to Colón leave from the square in front of the Iglesia de San Felipe (every 30min–1hr); the last bus is at 6pm.

Tourist information The new Centro de Visitantes is in a beautifully restored old merchant's house where the road forks coming into town (Mon–Fri 7.30am–4.30pm, Sat & Sun 9am–5pm). It boasts informative and visually appealing displays (in Spanish and English) on the town's history, Afro-Panamanian culture and the biodiversity of the surrounding national park. Staff can also provide contact details of certified guides.

ACCOMMODATION — SEE MAP PAGE 113

If you're hitting town for a festival, you will need to make a **reservation** well in advance, or book a homestay through the tourist office (see above). There's nowhere safe to **camp** around the town itself but you could pitch a tent on one of the beaches if you get a boat out there.

Casa Congo Waterfront, 80m west of the Casa Real de la Aduana casacongo.com. Four light, modern en-suite rooms filled with local Congo art, plus a/c and fan and a mini-fridge. It's worth splashing out the extra for a room with a private balcony overlooking the bay. The income helps to support the cultural foundation – hence the elevated prices. Five slightly cheaper, less fancy rooms occupy an annexe (Casa del Rayo Verde), sharing a porch and BBQ facilities. Both include breakfast at *El Palenque* (see below). $$$–$$$$

El Castillo 2km west of Portobelo on the main road elcastilloportobelo.com. This delightful over-the-water restaurant offers a small dorm and single private room, which share a rudimentary cold-water shower and are fan-ventilated. But the view from the deck makes up for any discomfort. Dorm $, double $

Hostel Portobelo 200m up the hill from the main road in the town centre 6155 3145, facebook.com/hostelportobelo. Back-to-basics hostel with one rather cramped, hot, mixed dorm ventilated with small fans, though beds have good mattresses, hosting travellers arriving from, or waiting for, a boat to Colombia. The bar-restaurant serves a mix of affordable Panamanian and international staple on a breezy veranda, which offers nice views of the church and bay. Dorm $, doubles $$

★ **La Morada de la Bruja** Waterfront west of the Casa Real de la Aduana lamoradadelabrujaportobelo.com. Striking Congo-themed murals invite you to this welcoming spot, which runs art workshops, rents kayaks and offers boat tours. *La Morada* offer various artistically decorated rooms, studios and houses. All have a/c, most are self-catering, variously accommodating two, four and eight people, and sharing a grassy lawn by the water's edge. $$$

ACTIVITIES AROUND PORTOBELO

Portobelo may be famed for its forts and festivals, but there are plenty of outdoor activities to keep you occupied.

DIVING AND SNORKELLING

With numerous reefs and scuttled ships in the waters round Portobelo, this is one of the country's top **diving** and **snorkelling** destinations – though you won't get the diversity and quantity of fish that you can find in the Pacific. **Popular dive spots** include a B-45 plane wreck by Drake's Island, where some still hold out hope of uncovering the privateer's sunken lead coffin amid the encrusted coral; the varied marine flora and fauna of the Three Sister Islands; and the labyrinth of canyons off Isla Grande. Two reliable **scuba companies** are on the main road on the left shortly before you reach Portobelo from the west; both are PADI-certified with good reputations. **Panama Dive Adventure** (Ⓦdivepty.com) whereas the pricier **Scuba Panama** (Ⓦscubapanama.com), a little further out from Portobelo has its own lodgings.

KAYAKING, HIKING AND BIRDWATCHING

For **kayaking** in the mangroves or **hiking**, **camping** or **birdwatching** in the rainforest, contact Jason (English- and Spanish-speaking) of the acclaimed **Portobelo Adventures** (Ⓣ6954 7847, Ⓦgoldenfrogscuba.com/portobelo-adventures2.html). Panamore Tours (Ⓦportobelotour.com) offers similar activities as well as nature photography and **horseriding**, and is based at *Restaurante Casa Vela*. Otherwise, ask at the Centro de Visitantes for details of local guides whom you can contact directly. Both *Casa Congo* and *Casa Vela* rent out kayaks.

BOAT TRIPS

You can also contract boatmen hanging round the main **jetty** by Fuerte Santiago for a two-hour trip around the bay and up the mouth of the Río Congo or request a drop-off and pickup at **Playa Blanca**, Portobelo's prettiest beach, reachable only by boat. The current favourite destination is the heavily marketed **Venas Azules** (Blue Veins) – so popular it now has its own website (Ⓦvenasazules.com) – an area of crystalline, turquoise waterways that weave between clumps of mangroves, which lie a thiry-minute boat ride from Portobelo, en route to Playa Blanca. Boat trips, which usually need a minimum of four to run, cost $30–60/person depending on the destination(s) and what's included.

★ **El Otro Lado** Across the bay by Fuerto San Fernando Ⓦelotrolado.com.pa. Occupying a stunning waterside location, across the bay from Portobelo, this boutique luxury retreat is full of style and character with original Congos art work decorating all the rooms, suites and common areas. Supremely relaxing, the place is surrounded by jungle, and has its own lake and waterfall. All-inclusive rates also available. B&B $$$$

EATING

SEE MAP PAGE 113

El Castillo 2km west of Portobelo on the main road Ⓦelcastilloportobelo.com. A mellow, rustic over-the-water bar-restaurant, where you can gaze out across the bay while lolling in a hammock and sipping a cocktail – all reasonably priced. Food is tasty, and portions are generous, and there are some good-value daily specials among the more expensive dishes; try a Thai or Vietnamese speciality. $$$

Don Quijote Main road, 6km east of Portobelo at Nuevo Tonosí Ⓣ6738 5852. A large roadside restaurant serving delicious, moderately priced French/Italian cuisine, including home-made pasta and tasty thin-crust pizzas along with an assortment of *parilladas* and Panamanian favourites. Open Fri–Sun. $$$

El Palenque Casa Congo, waterfront, west of the Casa Real de la Aduana Ⓦcasacongo.com. A cheerfully painted Congo-themed interior and an excellent terrace right by the water's edge, offering a small but varied menu, from wraps to substantial seafood dishes with coconut rice. Service can be hit and miss. Part of the Fundación Bahía de Portobelo's local development programme. $$$

Panadería On the main street Ⓣ6957 7088. This bargain bakery is open Thurs–Sun. In addition to pastries, baguette sandwiches, *empanadas* and fresh bread, it sells inexpensive fresh juices, coffee and tea. $$

Restaurante Pizzería Roma On the main street opposite the Iglesia San Felipe Ⓣ6805 1355. Italian restaurants abound in Portobelo but this unmissable red-and-white painted terrace offers more budget-friendly prices. Dining is casual (and sometimes slow) featuring the ubiquitous (but excellent) pizzas and pasta, but also popular Panamanian dishes such as Chow Mein and shrimps in garlic. $–$$

Parque Nacional Portobelo

2

Bordering Parque Nacional Chagres, **PARQUE NACIONAL PORTOBELO** covers 360 square kilometres of varied landscape around Portobelo. From Cerro Bruja (979m), the carpet of **rainforest** sweeps down to a 70km wriggle of **coastline**, taking in coral reefs, mangroves – home to crab-eating raccoons – and golden beaches, where four species of **turtle** come to lay their eggs. There are also significant populations of green iguana. Deforestation was already a major concern before the area was declared a park in 1976, but continued surreptitious tree-felling is putting even greater strain on the scarcely protected and highly fragmented natural resources. As yet, no self-guided trails or accommodation have been developed, though the tour operators in Portobelo (see box, page 117), and the lodgings in and around the town and nearby Puerto Lindo, usually offer **guided walks** of some description.

Puerto Lindo

PUERTO LINDO, a small fishing village en route to Isla Grande, consists of little more than a clutch of simple dwellings strung out along a sheltered, palm-fringed bay, where fishing vessels and yachts bob nonchalantly in the natural harbour. It's become a popular transit point for travellers heading to or from Colombia by sailboat (see box, page 25). The village has a shop selling basic supplies and a reasonable **restaurant** and bar. It's also a short hop to the popular island beach of **Isla Mamey** and within easy reach of **Isla Grande**.

ARRIVAL AND DEPARTURE — PARQUE NACIONAL PORTOBELO

By bus The La Guaira bus that passes through Puerto Lindo (5km before La Guaira) leaves Colón (see page 107) five times a day (9.30am–5.30pm; approximately every 2hr; 1hr 15min), passing through Portobelo after about an hour and Puerto Lindo 15mins later; weekdays, the last bus back to Colón passes at around 12.45pm). If there is sufficient demand, the bus may detour via Cacique, which has a daily bus to Colón at 11am.

By taxi It's worth taking the number of a taxi driver in Portobelo in case you miss the last bus back.

ACCOMMODATION AND EATING

Casa X Water's edge, by the yacht club, Puerto Lindo. Informal restaurant serving delicious, freshly prepared seafood with a side of salad, *patacones* or rice, to be washed down with a chilled beer. $$

Hostal Wunderbar On the left, main road, just after the turn-off to Cacique, Puerto Lindo hostelwunderbar.de. This former backpackers' hostel offers a handful of small en-suite doubles with a/c (some with TV) of varying prices in a modern building, with a semi-open shared kitchen, patio and hammock-strewn wraparound balcony. A basic grocery, restaurant and bar are nearby. Activities can be organized with local guides. Water outages can be a problem. $$

★ **Ranchos de Chalia** On the right, main road, just before Puerto Lindo facebook.com/ranchosdechalia. Stacked up the hillside and surrounded by rainforest, this place exudes charm, with rooms overlooking an attractive infinity pool, each with balcony – perfect for armchair wildlife-watching. Decor is simple and rustic but stylish. The raised lounge-deck offers great views of the bay. Superior breakfast included and restaurant on site. $$$–$$$$

Isla Mamey

The nearest island offering a decent sandy beach topped with wafting palms is tiny **ISLA MAMEY**, which is just offshore from Puerto Lindo is a short boat ride away. Provided you avoid busy summer weekends and holiday periods, you can have the tropical paradise to yourself. Accommodation in Puerto Lindo can organize kayak rental, allowing the energetic to paddle out here. Though there are no facilities on the island beyond a few thatched palm shelters and a couple of toilets, it's a top spot to take a picnic and chill for the day. For a few dollars extra, the boat can take you through the nearby **mangroves**, known as the "Tunnel of Love."

Isla Grande

With a larger, hyperbolic reputation, **ISLA GRANDE** has long been a day or weekend beach getaway for Panamanian urbanites. In truth, it doesn't measure up to the stunning islands of Gunayala or Bocas del Toro, but if you're in the area and want a quick shot of Caribbean vibe, a dose of fresh air and a splash in the sea before tucking into Creole cuisine, then Isla Grande will do very nicely. As there is no **ATM** on the island you'll need to bring cash, although most of the accommodation options take credit cards.

At just 3km long and under 1km wide, with only a couple of paths and no roads, it's easy to orient yourself on the island. Most of its four hundred residents of predominantly Afro-Antillean descent live off fishing and tourism and reside in the **main village**, which is strung out along a coastal footpath running the length of the island. At weekends in the dry season and peak holiday times, when the island bulges with up to a thousand fun-loving Panamanians, the place is throbbing, often with music blaring from portable stereos (despite the island's attempts to ban them) and the one decent stretch of sand at **La Punta**, on the southwestern tip, is inevitably packed. Since the public beach has more or less been eroded, sun-lovers will have to pay the **Hotel Isla Grande**; a day pass grants access to the gorgeous soft-sand beach and sheltered bay and allows you to use the facilities, including showers, toilets, sun loungers, picnic tables and a volleyball court.

El Faro

The island's highest point is crowned by an 85m steel **lighthouse** designed by Gustav Eiffel, and built by the French in 1894. The original lens from the top sits in the Panama Canal Museum in Panama City (see page 58). After being renovated in 2020, the historic lighthouse is now safe to climb, and the panorama from the top makes it well worth the 112 steps. Access is via a steep path at the eastern end of the island.

ARRIVAL AND DEPARTURE — ISLA GRANDE

Access to the island is generally from the fishing village of **La Guaira**. Alternatively, boat transport from Puerto Lindo costs $10–15 return.

TO LA GUAIRA

By bus Five buses make the journey from Colón to La Guaira (Mon–Sat 9.30am–5.30pm; approximately every 2hr; 1hr 20min) via Sabanitas and Portobelo. The last bus back to Colón usually departs at 1pm, but check with the bus driver that these times still hold. On Sundays, anything can happen (or not).

By car Cars can be left by La Guaira dock for free, or in the more secure partially fenced area nearby. Either way, don't leave valuables in the vehicle.

FROM LA GUAIRA TO ISLA GRANDE

By water-taxi At La Guaira a water-taxi takes you 200m across the water to the main jetty by *Jackson's* shop, which is the unofficial information point – for a little extra you can be taken further afield.

ACCOMMODATION AND EATING

There's a reasonable range of basic **accommodation** on the island; much of it is overpriced for what you get, though

EXCURSIONS FROM ISLA GRANDE

A popular **boat trip** from Isla Grande leads you through a mangrove "tunnel of love" to the best local white-sand beach and **snorkelling** destination, **Isla Mamey**. A half-day excursion (about $60 for up to ten people) can be arranged through your hotel or directly with one of the boatmen hanging out at the main jetty – note though, that it's a shorter, cheaper boat ride from Puerto Lindo. **Surfers** should head for Playa Grande on the mainland, towards Nombre de Dios.

midweek in low season you can usually bargain for better rates. The island's **restaurants** predominantly serve fresh seafood almost straight from the boats, often accompanied by coconut rice or plantain, though you'll be lucky to get anyone to serve you a meal midweek during the rainy season.

El Bucanero Close to La Punta ⓣ6964 8114. Relaxed beach bar-restaurant, where you can lounge on the shaded sea-facing deck at a handful of tables. Fairly inexpensive seafood dishes are served – try the *patacones* stuffed with octopus. $$–$$$

Cabañas Blue 400m east of the main jetty ⓦlinktr.ee/cabanasbluepanama. Painted in marine blue and white, a collection of cool, simply furnished cement cabins (en suite, with a/c, fans and porch space) are set round a pool in a lawn dotted with coconut palms. It all makes for a relaxing setting. There's also a house with an over-the-water balcony, a small on-site bar-restaurant and a table-tennis table. $$$

Candy Rose Next to the main jetty ⓦinstagram.com/hotelcandyrose. It's all about the location – an over-the-water gazebo at the end of a jetty provides a delightful dining or drinking area, and with sofas to sink into. But the walk from the kitchen can slow things down (even more) and chill your spicy seafood soup. $$–$$$

★ **Macondo Hostel** 50m from main jetty ⓦmacondohostel.my.canva.site. The bright artwork makes this friendly hostel unmissable. You've the choice of simple but cheerily decorated rooms of various configurations, set amidst lush greenery, with shared or private bathroom, a/c or fan. There's plenty of chill-out space where you can play board games or pool, or simply mull over tour options. The communal, well-equipped kitchen is spotless. $$

The eastern Costa Arriba to Cuango

For most people the Costa Arriba stops at Portobelo; very few venture much further along the windswept coastline, though bearing right at the fork after Nuevo Tonosí takes you through a string of **surfing beaches** and sparsely populated **villages** – Viento Frío, Palenque and **Miramar** – before terminating at Cuango.

Nombre de Dios

The most compelling of the coastal settlements, **NOMBRE DE DIOS** is famed as the Atlantic terminus for the Camino Real, where in colonial times treasure was transferred from exhausted mules to ships bound for Spain. Apocryphally, the village derived its name from the words of its founder, Diego de Nicuesa, who, desperate to land his starving crew, espied the spot and cried out, "Paremos aquí en el nombre de Dios!" ("Let's stop here in the name of God!"). Sadly no trace remains of the town's historical past, largely thanks to Sir Francis Drake, who razed the place to the ground in 1595, thus persuading the Spanish to move their operation to Portobelo.

Nevertheless, Nombre de Dios is a scenic place to stroll through, situated on the palm-fringed Río Fato, and with a pleasant five-minute meander up to a **mirador** offering a view of the village and the turquoise sea beyond. **Playa Damas**, a short hop away by boat, is the best local beach and there are a couple of local *fondas* in town for when you fancy a bite to eat.

Miramar and around

There's little reason to stop off in **Viento Frío** and **Palenque**, but the forlorn cargo port of **MIRAMAR**, the next village along – and the only place you can (sometimes) get **petrol** – supports a small beachside hotel and a couple of restaurants. At the end of the tarred road lies **Cuango**, with a tangible end-of-the-road feel, especially now the bus no longer goes that far, though the vast new *Decameron* resort planned on the other side of the river may change all that.

ARRIVAL AND DEPARTURE — THE EASTERN COSTA ARRIBA TO CUANGO

By bus Buses from Colón go as far as Nombre de Dios (nine daily, last bus 5.45pm; 1hr 10min) and are marked "Costa Arriba–Nombre de Dios"; the last return bus departs at 3pm. Fewer buses reach Viento Frío, Palenque, Miramar and Cuango.

ACCOMMODATION

★ **Casita Río Indio** 5min along the Nombre de Dios road from Portobelo after the fork to La Guaira ⓦ panamacasitarioindio.wordpress.com. Set well back from the road in verdant surroundings by a stream is a simple wooden *cabaña* with two very rustic rooms at bargain rates, joined more recently by two cosy modern cabins with kitchenettes that are lightly more expensive, and a family cabin. The friendly French owners can provide inexpensive breakfast and dinner but you'll need to venture out to the kiosk down the road, or bring supplies, for lunch. Activities such as horseriding, jungle hikes or night outings to look for caimans can be organized. Ask the Nombre de Dios bus to drop you off, or catch a taxi from Portobelo. $$

Archipiélago de las Perlas

Set in coral-rich crystalline waters in the Golfo de Panamá just a twenty-minute flight southeast of Panama City, the 220 islands and islets that comprise the **ARCHIPIÉLAGO DE LAS PERLAS (Pearl Islands)** were named by Vasco Nuñez de Balboa in 1513 after their once prolific black-lipped pearl oysters. Yet the islands had been inhabited since around 200 BC by the Cueva and Coclé people who had regular contact with the mainland and used the pearls for trading.

Sprinkled over an area of around 1700 square kilometres, only a handful of islands are inhabited and many remain under-explored.

The attractive **Isla Contadora** has the most developed tourist infrastructure, though the golden beaches of nearby **Isla Saboga** and the cream-coloured sands of **Isla Viveros** – close to the archipelago's largest island, **Isla del Rey** – are beginning to draw visitors, particularly on good-value day-trips from Panama City (see box, page 121).

In addition to the lure of countless deserted sugar-sand **beaches** and **reefs** teeming with multicoloured fish, a visit to the archipelago between June and October can be rewarded with sightings of humpback **whales** that come to breed. As elsewhere in Panama, high season coincides with the dry season but since the archipelago receives far less rainfall than the mainland, it's worth considering a visit at other times when prices are lower and beaches less crowded.

Fly Trip has **flights** to and from Isla Contadora on Fridays and Mondays (from around $80 one way). In addition to various day-trips (see box, page 121), Sea Las Perlas (ⓦ ferrypearlislands.com) also provides a **ferry service** from Panama City to Isla del Rey, predominantly for the island's inhabitants (see page 110).

DAY-TRIPS TO THE PEARL ISLANDS

The advent of faster and more frequent ferries from Panama City has helped increase the demand for **day-trips** to the Pearl Islands; while you can just book a return ferry passage (from $98 return to Contadora) and pack a picnic, the full-day packages are good value, especially when on special offer (approximately $120–160). These **all-inclusive** rates include the return trip by ferry, a welcome drink, use of hotel or beach club facilities, including towels and umbrellas, and lunch – usually a main dish and a dessert.

The main day-trip **destinations** include: Isla **Contadora,** either Playa Cacique or Playa Larga; the beach club at Playa Encanto on **Isla Saboga**, which additionally includes use of sea-kayaks and stand-up paddleboards; at the Sonny Island Resort on smaller **Isla Bolaños**, which is another half-hour boat ride away but has a beach club and overnight accommodation too (ⓦ sonnyislandresort.com).

Ferries (see page 123) set off around 7.30am, arriving back in Panama City at around 5.30pm. Day-trips with **Sea Las Perlas** (ⓦ ferrypearlislands.com), which offers daily tours to Contadora and Saboga are the cheaper option, giving a good view of the Canal and causeway. Red Cat megacatamaran (up to 120 people) does day-trips to Contadora too, leaving from the Balboa Yacht Club, but expect loud music, an open bar and a party spirit (ⓦ panamsailingtours.com).

2

Isla Contadora

Home to the main public airstrip, **ISLA CONTADORA** is by far the most developed and most popular destination in the archipelago. It derives its name from the counting house the conquistadors established on the island to tot up their riches from the pearl trade before shipping them off to Europe. As well as possessing its own fine selection of lovely soft-sand **beaches**, Contadora provides a sound base for **snorkelling** and **diving** trips to the corals and crystalline waters of neighbouring islands, visits to **seabird colonies** and **whale watching**. Away from the shoreline, the wooded areas provide shelter and food for a surprising array of **wildlife** – deer, agoutis and iguanas can all be spotted here.

Only a handful of families are permanently resident, while workers from nearby Isla Saboga commute daily to service the 180 luxury villas, which remain empty for much of the year. **Inland**, the centre of the island is occupied by a football pitch, which comes alive in late afternoon. South of the pitch there's a small whitewashed church, while the road up the eastern side of the pitch passes one of the island's two **ponds**, on the left. Both ponds are magnets for thirsty wildlife such as magnificent frigatebirds that skim the surface scooping up water at dusk.

2

The beaches

Playa Larga, on the island's eastern side, provides the longest stretch of sand and the most sheltered swimming in the warmest water; it is also the place where the ferries dock. A rusting abandoned ferry is the only eyesore. South round the headland, **Playa de las Suecas** ("Swedish Women's Beach"), Panama's only public nudist beach, is suitably secluded and also offers the island's best snorkelling round the headland towards Playa Larga, where sharks, stingrays and turtles can often be seen. Another few minutes' stroll, skirting the end of the runway, brings you to the island's loveliest swathe of soft, sugary sand, **Playa Cacique**. Backed by lush vegetation, it looks across turquoise waters to Isla Chapera.

On the northern side of the island the charming, sheltered cove of **Playa Ejecutiva** stands out, backed by manicured grass dotted with shady trees. Further east, at the northern end of the airstrip, *Hotel La Isla* surveys **Playa Galeón**, where the ferries arrive and depart, and fishermen can take you to Isla Saboga or further afield.

ARRIVAL AND DEPARTURE — ISLA CONTADORA

By ferry Sea Las Perlas (ferrypearlislands.com) operates daily departures to Contadora (and Saboga) from the marina on Isla Flamenco at the end of the Amador Causeway (7.30am, returning 3.30pm from Playa Cacique; 1hr 30–40min; around $100 return). Tickets are sold online and at their offices in Albrook Mall (8am–7pm).

By plane Fly Trip flies from Albrook Airport (1 daily Fri & Mon, with extra flights over holiday periods; 20min; $150 return).

GETTING AROUND

By golf cart Most hotels and the kiosk at the back of Playa Galeón do a thriving trade in golf cart and mule rental. Prices vary (starting around $75/24hr), with lodgings generally offering better rates to their guests.

By taxi Golf cart taxis can also take you to your destination for a few dollars.

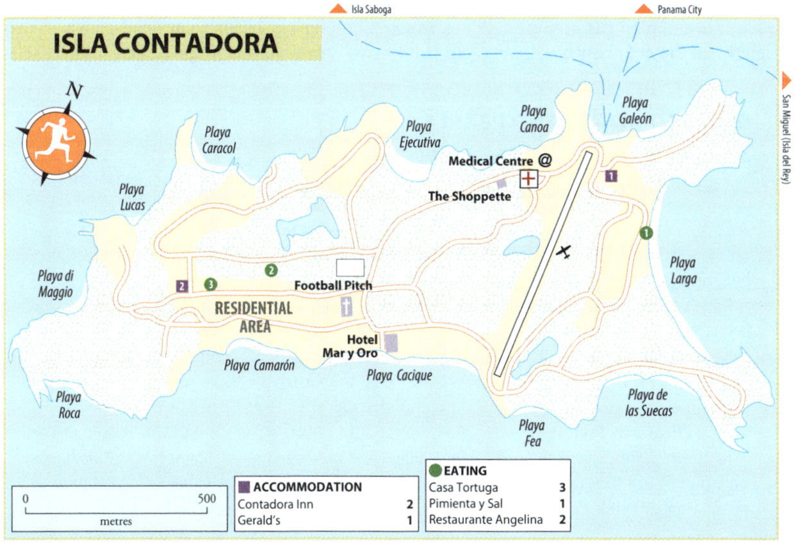

2

ACCOMMODATION

SEE MAP PAGE 123

There's no such thing as budget **accommodation** on Contadora and most lodgings are overpriced for what they offer. All places listed below have a/c. Off-season midweek rates drop considerably and are often negotiable. **Camping** is frowned upon, though you can easily arrange transport to camp on one of the nearby, uninhabited islands.

Contadora Inn Paseo Urraca ⓦcontadoraislandinn.com. This place offers excellent service and five comfortably furnished, if slightly dated, en-suite rooms spread across two houses. Guests share a kitchen and spacious lounge that opens out onto a large balcony, backed by luscious forest, with books and games. Breakfast extra. $$$

Gerald's Above the airstrip ⓦfacebook.com/bbgeraldpanama. Ten neat and cool tiled rooms with flatscreen TV, fridge and spacious bathroom. The breezy rooftop deck with plunge pool has sea views, but could offer more comfort. Excellent breakfast with tasty home-made bread included. $$$

EATING

SEE MAP PAGE 123

As with accommodation, **eating** options are limited and supply problems from the capital can mean some dishes are not always available – though the vast stocks of Möet & Chandon in the village shop on the main square look unlikely to run out. Be aware that the island's few main restaurants are involved with day-pass visitors, so at weekends and during holiday periods, places can be jammed and service even slower than usual.

Casa Tortuga Paseo Urraca ⓣ6715 2223. Authentic Italian restaurant in a family environment (which may mean sharing a table with other guests). Fixed price, tasty set three-course menus, with wine on top. With only eight tables, reservations are a must. $$$$

Pimienta y Sal Back of Playa Larga. Don't be put off by the plastic picnic tables, pub benches and faux-grass carpet squares – the food's decent enough, if simple: though chicken, beef and pork are on the menu, the fresh seafood is the real draw, with coconut rice, beans and sauteed mixed veg. Cocktails hit the spot and the sea view is delightful. $$$

Restaurante Angelina Paseo Anayansi ⓣ6510 5542. Casual local restaurant with half a dozen tables on a covered deck backed by tropical foliage. The small menu offers simple, moderately priced dishes for breakfast, lunch or dinner: chicken and pork chops, burgers and sandwiches, fish and seafood – the ceviche is a good choice – with the usual choice of carbs plus a smidgen of salad. $$–$$$

Isla Saboga

Just across from Contadora lies the slightly larger **Isla Saboga**, whose four hundred inhabitants populate the main village, **Puerto Nuevo**, perched on the hilltop above the main pink-shell beach, spilling off a central paved path. Many villagers commute to Contadora to work; others fish and ferry tourists in their boats or carry out subsistence agriculture. The island's eighteenth-century hilltop **church** – a rare trace of Spanish occupation left in the archipelago – is worth a quick peek before you head across to the delightful **Playa Encanto**, where a handful of two-storey handsome wooden holiday lets

SLAVES, PIRATES AND PEARLS

Little is known about the **indigenous population** of the archipelago, which was wiped out in the sixteenth century after news of the abundance of **pearls** reached the conquistadors' greedy ears. Needing labour to harvest them, the Spanish brought over African slaves, the ancestors of most of the current population. Over the next few centuries, the maze of islands provided hideouts for pirates plundering Spanish galleons en route from Peru, often with the help of local bands of *cimarrones* (escaped slaves).

The end of Spanish rule did not spell the end of the pearl trade, which thrived until the oyster beds became diseased in the 1930s. Though they have recovered to an extent – pearl fishers still operate from Isla Casaya – there's little chance of a new pearl rivalling the archipelago's most famous find, the pear-shaped Peregrina ("pilgrim"). Plucked in the sixteenth century, the plundered pearl belonged to Spanish and English royalty before ending up with Hollywood legend **Elizabeth Taylor**. Following her death in 2011, it fetched a record $11 million at auction.

Tourism in the islands took off in the 1970s when businessman and diplomat Gabriel Lewis Galindo bought the island for a bargain $30,000. By constructing roads and selling off plots to other wealthy Panamanians, he established Panama's first resort island.

ACTIVITIES ON CONTADORA AND SABOGA

Most organized **activities** on both islands involve getting on or in water, which your hotel can usually arrange for you. If you're on a day-trip some activities may be included – such as use of kayaks on Saboga – but other activities will need to be booked separately with the operator in advance. Although there's reasonable **snorkelling** off some of Contadora's beaches, there is more to see a little further afield. Snorkelling and **diving** excursions usually take in the islands of **Chapera**, **Mogo Mogo** and the sandy cay of **Boyarena**, which lie in a cluster south of Contadora, but trips sometimes also chug round **Isla Pacheca**, to the north, to see the seabird colonies. Alternatively, you could simply arrange to be dropped at one of the nearby islands, with a tent (or sheet sleeping bag and mosquito net) and supplies, and ask to be picked up a day or two later. On a clear night the stars are truly scintillating.

ACTIVITY OPERATORS

Coral Dreams No office, Contadora ⓦ scubalasperlas.com. PADI-certified outfit offering good-value half-day snorkelling (rates include equipment and soft drinks; minimum four people, maximum sixteen) and diving for both beginners and certified divers. Whalewatching in season (July–Oct); sightings are almost guaranteed. Tourists can be packed rather sardine-like in the boat in the busy summer months, so check on numbers in advance.

Sailing Club Panama Playa del Pueblo, Saboga ⓦ sailingclubpanama.com. Outings with this sailing school are highly recommended; fun and experienced sailing instructors provide sailing or windsurfing lessons, half-day trips sailing or combining SUP and snorkelling, and equipment rental, including sailboats to those who have some experience.

Pearl Island Paddle Playa Ejecutiva, Contadora ⓦ pearlislandpaddlepanama.com. Stand-up paddle lessons (individual or in a group) and guided tours, with SUP board rental for more experienced paddlers.

peek out through the foliage at the glorious soft-sand strand. It's a wonderful spot to loll in a hammock and watch the pelicans gliding and diving.

At low tide, it's an exciting two-hour scramble south over rocks and past the pre-Columbian stone remains of a marine trap on **Playa El Coral** to the soft salt-and-pepper expanse of the island's premier beach, **Playa Larga**, from where you can hike down a dirt road back to the village in less than thirty minutes.

ARRIVAL AND DEPARTURE — ISLA SABOGA

By boat The daily ferries from Panama City to Isla Contadora (see page 123) will drop off/pick up passengers at Saboga at the new jetty just north of the village. At other times, you can usually get a ride in a fishing boat between the two islands for $5–10. Boats usually leave from Playa Galeón on Contadora and Playa del Pueblo, below the village on Isla Saboga.

ACCOMMODATION AND EATING

Beyond the expensive, high-quality cuisine available at **Playa Encanto**, there are a couple of village *fondas* on Saboga; value for money, service and quality are all highly variable.

La Choza Playa Encanto ⓣ 6934 8501. Catering mainly to day-trippers from Panama City and chalet residents, this sophisticated raised-deck *rancho* at the back of the beach offers a small selection of delicious mains with a French twist, succulent seafood, burgers and pizza, as well as expensive cocktails and superlative sea views and sunsets.

Community house At the top of the steps from the beach, by the police checkpoint. Ask around for whoever's in charge. With a superb hilltop location, this community house has four small, basic en-suite rooms, beds with decent mattresses and a shared balcony overlooking the bay. Great value, provided someone has been taking care of the rooms. Check before you commit. $

★ **El Remanso Villa** 30 El Encanto, Playa Encanto ⓣ 6575 2447, ⓦ sabogavacations.com. Part of the exclusive *El Encanto* development, above a secluded spot on the beach, peering through trees to the sea. Two lovely studio apartments with fully equipped kitchens and two spacious rooms, tastefully designed and rich in wood, with all mod cons as well as expansive balconies and easy beach access. The owners also manage other property owners' house lets. Minimum two-night stay. $$$$

Señora Mare's Puerto Nuevo, main street ⓣ 6641 0452. The warm Sra Mare offers a handful of clean double and single rooms in the heart of the village, with ceiling fan. $$

Central Panama

PARQUE NACIONAL ALTOS DE CAMPANA

Central Panama

Speeding west along the Interamericana, in a hurry to reach the loftier peaks of Chiriquí or the golden beaches of Bocas, foreign tourists often ignore Central Panama. It might be better known for the arable and cattle farmland that extends over its denuded Pacific lowland slopes, and its peasant farmers who claim varying mixtures of indigenous, African and Hispanic ancestry, but central Panama does possess its own swathes of sand. What's more, strung out along the Pacific coast across the provinces of Panamá and Coclé, the region's beaches are within easy access of Panama City. Central Panama also boasts some impressive mountain scenery harbouring a wealth of wildlife, and a couple of the country's most important archeological sites.

After grinding through the urban sprawl of **La Chorerra**, 40km southwest of Panama City, the **Interamericana** crests at Loma Campana, where you've scarcely time to gasp at the views across the sparkling Golfo de Panamá and the brooding peaks of the Cordillera Central – assuming you dare risk taking your eye off the hair-raising traffic – before it swoops down like a roller coaster onto a narrow alluvial plain hemmed in between the mountains and the Pacific. Fringing these lowlands is a string of **beaches** that lure surf- and sand-loving urbanites in equal measure. While ill-conceived developments have reduced their charm in recent years the accessibility of these beaches – most are less than a ninety-minute bus journey from the capital – is still a draw. Further west lie the towns of **Aguadulce** and **Penonomé**, which have little intrinsic appeal but they provide access to some of the country's main historical attractions, such as the old colonial church at **Natá**, which contains wonderful wooden carvings, and the pre-Columbian remains of **El Caño**, an important ancient ceremonial and burial site.

Yet it is the **mountains** that hold the greatest allure in central Panama, offering a splendid array of hiking and birdwatching opportunities. The volcanic tors of **Parque Nacional Altos de Campana** afford sweeping vistas of the coastline, while the scenic crater town of **El Valle** makes a good base for a range of outdoor activities. Further west, **Parque Nacional Omar Torrijos** offers mist-shrouded peaks and a chance to explore the little-visited rainforested Caribbean slopes north of the continental divide.

Parque Nacional Altos de Campana

Established in 1966 as part of the protection for the canal basin, **PARQUE NACIONAL ALTOS DE CAMPANA** is Panama's oldest national park, and at only 55km from the capital, just off the Interamericana, one of the most accessible. It's often overlooked by tourists, visited only at weekends by enthusiastic birdwatchers or fleeing urbanites in search of cool fresh air and exercise. But the stellar views from the park's summits – the highest, **Cerro Campana**, tops 1000m – make Altos de Campana a worthwhile hiking day-trip, and its dramatic and singular landscape of craggy tors and lava fields hosts a surprising range of species.

Although the denuded lower western and southern slopes have suffered from deforestation, elsewhere peaks are cloaked in pre-montane and tropical forest. Of the park's 39 **mammal** species, the black-eared opossum is the most numerous, though it'll be tucked up in its den during the day. More likely sightings include two- and three-toed sloths, coatis and Geoffroy's tamarin monkeys. Colourful **birds** also abound, including the striking orange-bellied trogon, rufous motmot and collared aracari.

THE BASÍLICA MENOR SANTIAGO APÓSTOL IN NATÁ

Highlights

❶ **Parque Nacional Altos de Campana** Spectacular views greet hikers in this rugged landscape, just an hour from Panama City. See page 128

❷ **Punta Chame** This spit, much loved by kitesurfers and birdwatchers, offers vast stretches of sand on both sides. Perfect for long beach walks, with fabulous views inland and out to sea. See page 132

❸ **El Valle** Lovely crater town filled with flowers and fruit trees, its surroundings home to horseriding, hiking, zip lines and fabled golden frogs. See page 134

❹ **Parque Nacional Omar Torrijos** Hire a local guide to scale the rainforested peaks of this little-explored park or get the binoculars out for a spot of birdwatching. See page 145

❺ **El Caño** While many of the recent finds are still being analyzed, the two open burial chambers still make poignant viewing in this significant pre-Columbian site. See page 148

❻ **Natá** This small town boasts one of the oldest churches in the Americas, with a dazzling white exterior and intricate wooden carvings inside. See page 148

HIGHLIGHTS ARE MARKED ON THE MAP ON PAGE 130

Above all, though, the fifty square kilometres of park is renowned for its 62 **amphibian** and 86 **reptile** species, including the near-extinct golden frog (see box, page 136) in the area's western fringes.

If you've time after exploring the park, head for the village of **CHICÁ**, a few kilometres along the road at the end of the bus route. It makes a pleasant postscript, with bougainvillea-filled gardens and several *fondas* serving traditional **food**.

The trails

The park's network of five interconnecting **trails** is concentrated in the southeastern section. Easily accessible and relatively well demarcated, most are shady strolls, with one a moderately strenuous hike through scenic forest.

Sendero Panamá

The main trail, the flattish **Sendero Panamá** (1.5km), leads to the other trails: first to the moderately strenuous Sendero La Cruz, then *senderos* **Rana Dorada** and **Zamora** – both

are only a few hundred metres long. The slightly longer **Sendero Podocarpus** is the next turn-off and worth a detour (see below). The trail eventually peters out; either return the way you came, or turn right to descend a disintegrating asphalt road down to the main road, where you can flag down a bus, or walk back down to the park entrance.

Sendero La Cruz

About 800m along the Sendero Panamá, the **Sendero La Cruz** climbs steeply to the right, through trees dripping with epiphytes. Twenty minutes later the path

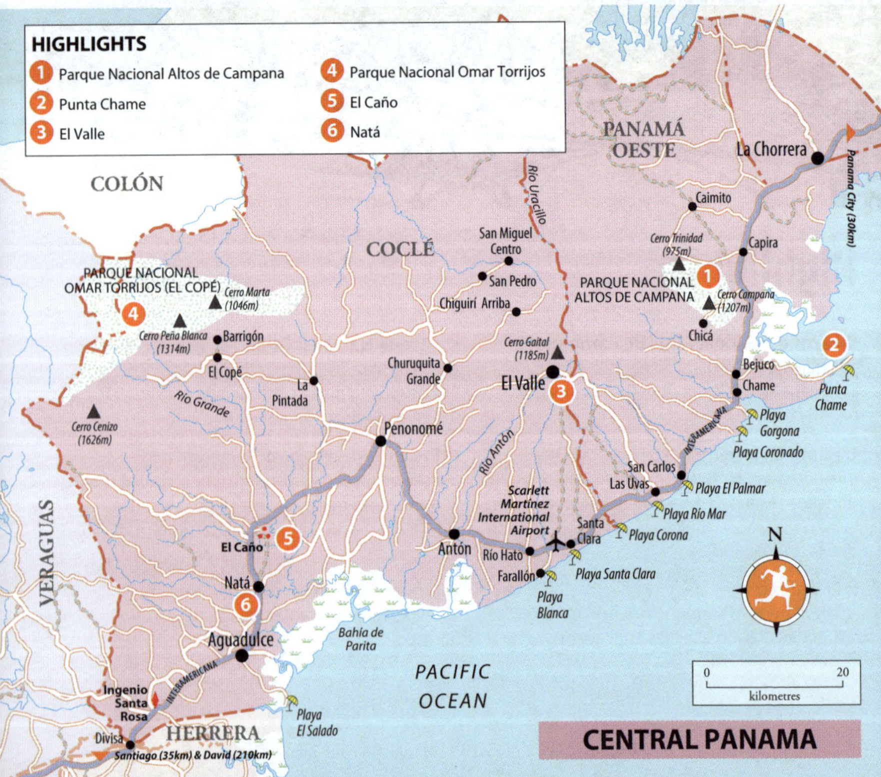

forks: to the left it climbs to the 1000m domed peak of **Cerro Campana**, the park's highest point, while to the right it descends and then climbs again for another forty minutes, culminating in a giant boulder topped with an enormous cross. Unless you're a proficient rock-climber, follow the trail under the boulder for an easier clamber to the other side. Although at 860m **Cerro La Cruz** is lower than Campana, it affords a slightly better panorama, taking in the meandering Río Chame and the distant Pacific beach resorts, with the rugged ridge of the Cordillera Central disappearing into the distance.

Sendero Podocarpus

The **Sendero Podocarpus** (600m), a loop trail off the Sendero Panamá, takes you through some of Panama's only native conifers of the same name, ending up in the park's campsite at *Refugio Los Pinos*. To return to the Sendero Panamá, turn left at the T-junction below the campsite, then left again once you reach the main path to return the way you came, or right at the second junction to reach the main road.

ARRIVAL AND DEPARTURE — PARQUE NACIONAL ALTOS DE CAMPANA

By bus Take any San Carlos, Capira or Chame bus from the Albrook bus terminal to the town of Capira, about 50km west of Panama City. Ask to be dropped off on the Interamericana a few hundred metres after the Puma garage, at *Lily's* restaurant, where minibuses bound for the mountain village of Chicá, via the park, depart (hourly 7am–8pm, returning on the hour; 40min).

By car The park is signposted off the Interamericana to the right 5km beyond Capira. You can leave the car at the park entrance. Follow the path up beside the large house, where a sign marks the trailhead.

INFORMATION AND FEES

MIA office The park office (daily 8am–4pm; ⓣ254 2848 in Panama City), is on the left-hand side of the road, 4km from the Interamericana turn-off. Unless you want to take a photo of the map on the wall, or you're camping, there's no need to stop there since it's more than 3km further up the mountainside to the park itself. The entrance is on the right-hand side, after a sign declaring "No Estoy", but you are likely to be asked by the park warden to sign the register and show that you've paid your park entry fee online (see page 42).

ACCOMMODATION AND EATING

Cabanas Gavilán Guardián Chicá ⓣ63156624, ⓦcabanasgavilanguardian.com. Affording magnificent views down to the coast, these eight stone-and-wood *cabañas* set in flower-filled gardens make the perfect weekend getaway from Panama City and are within a stone's throw of the national park. Variously accommodating 2–6 guests, the cabins also range in their facilities, from a private terrace and barbecue area or full kitchen to a simple room, though most offer great views. Breakfast is included at the on-site restaurant and there's a restful communal terrace with splash pool. Much cheaper rates during the week $$$

★ **Quesos Chela** Interamericana, on the right-hand side, heading west out of Capira ⓣ248 5457, ⓦfacebook.com/quesoschela. Stock up with supplies in Capira at one of Panama's gastronomic gems, which makes fresh yoghurt, croissants, *empanadas* and fancy breads, as well as renowned cheeses.

Refugio Los Pinos In the park. A pleasant camping spot surrounded by pine trees, about a 30min hike from the trailhead. Facilities are limited to toilets, water and space to make a campfire. Make sure at the MIA office (see above) that the ablutions block is unlocked. $/person

The Pacific beaches

Once the Interamericana hits the coastal plain at the western edge of Panama province, roads start to branch off the main artery like blood vessels, feeding the various **beaches** along the Pacific coast. With locations to suit surfers, swimmers and sunbathers, and sand ranging from charcoal grey through tan to pale cream, these beaches have become increasingly **built up** over recent years. The developments – beyond the odd surf spot – primarily cater to weekending capital-dwellers, a few expat communities and Latin Americans on package holidays. Travellers looking for less developed beaches will find offerings in the Azuero, Chiriquí and Bocas with greater appeal. That said, provided you avoid weekends, public holidays and the holiday season, the beaches are perfectly pleasant to spend a day or two.

Punta Chame

The least built up of the Pacific beaches is **Punta Chame**, which you access by taking the first beach exit as you travel west along the Interamericana. The road travels the length of a 12km sandy spit to a low-key fishing village, where the vast flat beach, strong winds and choppy waters have transformed this otherwise deserted swathe into Panama's **kitesurfing** centre (season Dec–May) – though beware the stingrays at low tide. **Birdwatching** is also good here as the tidal pools and mud flats attract a variety of waders. Looking northwards across the more sheltered **Bay of Chame**, you get lovely views of the mainland.

Playa Gorgona to Playa Río Mar

Playas Gorgona and **Coronado** were once the most fashionable weekend destinations for middle-class residents of Panama City, with beachfront properties overlooking the marbled charcoal sand; Coronado now has a sizeable expat community. There are two good **surfing spots** here – Playa Malibu in Gorgona and Punta Teta (predictably dubbed "Tits" by surfing gringos), 3km down a dirt road not long after the Coronado exit. The only substantial settlement in the area, 12km on from El Rey, just off the Interamericana, is **SAN CARLOS**, worth noting mainly as a place to buy provisions and catch a bus. The other surfing hot spots in the area lie down two asphalt roads a few kilometres west of San Carlos at **Playa El Palmar** and **Playa Río Mar**. Playa El Palmar hosts one of Panama's longest-established **surf schools**, which specializes in courses for beginners (Ⓦ panamasurfschool.com). Non-surfers should continue a further 20km to hit the best beaches on this stretch of coast.

Playa Santa Clara

Although large concrete developments are beginning to encroach, and quad bikes and jet skis roar about the place at weekends, **Playa Santa Clara**, 30km east of Penonomé, is probably the loveliest beach in the area, and you can have it all to yourself midweek. A seemingly endless belt of pale sand lapped by calm waters, it features a number of pleasantly informal bars and restaurants.

Farallón

A few kilometres further along the coast from Playa Santa Clara, at the equally impressive beige swathe of **Farallón (Playa Blanca)**, things are even busier, and the local fishing village is becoming increasingly hemmed in among greedy resorts, condominium complexes and gated retirement communities. Most accommodation can fix up some gentle **horseriding** along the beach or a **boat trip** with one of the local fishermen.

ARRIVAL AND DEPARTURE — THE PACIFIC BEACHES

BY BUS

Buses generally only drop off passengers at the "entrada" (exit) on the Interamericana, from where a 10min stroll or a sweaty 8km hike – depending on the destination – will get you to the beach; occasional local buses or taxis are sometimes available.

FROM PANAMA CITY

For Punta Chame Take a Chame-bound bus as far as the Plaza Imperial, Bejuco, just east of the turn-off to Punta Chame (5.30am–9pm; every 20min; 1hr 10min), and transfer to the hourly bus (20min) or take a taxi for the 12km journey.

For Gorgona Take a San Carlos bus (6am–8.30pm; every 20min; 1hr 20min) alighting at the Gorgona exit, 8km further west of the Punta Chame junction; the beach is within walking distance.

For Coronado Take a San Carlos bus – at the Coronado exit minibuses and taxis will shuttle you to the sand. The highly visible El Rey supermarket, which contains an ATM and is next to a petrol station, marks the turn-off.

For Playa El Palmar and Playa Río Mar Take an Antón or Penonomé bus (5.20am–8pm; every 20min; 1hr 30min); you will probably need to hike the 2km down the road from the Interamericana stop to the beach.

For Santa Clara To get to Santa Clara, 13km west of Playa Corona, take an Antón or Penonomé bus (5.20am–7.30pm; every 20min; 1hr 40min); taxis are likely to be hanging round the turn-off from the highway and there is the occasional minibus.

For Farallón (Playa Blanca) To get to Farallón, 3km west of the Santa Clara exit, take an Antón or Penonomé bus and get off at the turn-off. Walk the 2km, or flag down the occasional bus from Río Hato, or a taxi.

ACCOMMODATION

The **accommodation** is as varied as the sand along this stretch of coastline; you can take your pick from a thousand-room all-inclusive resort to a boutique B&B. Our list below runs from the surf-happy eastern stretch, where Playa Coronado offers the best options, westwards towards Santa Clara, which boasts a mega-resort and a hammock and tent spot.

PUNTA CHAME

★ **Hotel Casa Amarilla** hotelcasaamarilla.com. Charming place set in lush gardens, with a sparkling pool, offering a range of accommodation, all beautifully decorated and immaculately maintained, from simple wooden cabins (with shared bathrooms) to larger, more comfortable en-suite lodgings in the main house. Delicious, moderately priced French cuisine tops off the experience. Closed June–Oct. Cabins $$, doubles $$$

Ocean Souls Beach House & Happy Corner By the beach on the north side puntachametours.com. Run by two German sisters, this small kite school, tour agency, beach house and bar-restaurant occupies a choice spot, overlooking the sand. Upcycled pallets and soft cushions make comfortable sofas to chill and dine on moderately priced dishes ($$), from healthy feta and rosemary omelettes to acai bowls, wraps and salads or local fried fish, burgers and the *menu del día*. A small beach house has rooms to rent. Beach house: dorm $$, doubles $$

PLAYA GORGONA TO PLAYA RÍO MAR

Coronado Golf & Country Club Av Punta Preita, Playa Coronado coronadogolfandcountryclub.com. A sprawling, hacienda-style place 1km off the beach in extensive, landscaped grounds. There's plenty to entertain guests beyond the eighteen-hole golf course, namely: an Olympic-size pool, tennis courts, stables and chocolate massage at the spa, and that's before you've even thought about the sea. Very busy at weekends. Two-night minimum stay $$$

El Littoral Av Punta Prieta, Playa Coronado litoralpanama.com. Classy health-centre-cum-B&B offering yoga, Pilates, acupuncture and massage, and with a swimming pool and comfy common areas. Use of a kitchen possible for an additional fee. Breakfast included. $$$

PLAYA SANTA CLARA

Las Sirenas facebook.com/lasirenasdesantaclara. Undoubtedly with the best location, either over the hilltop among the bougainvillea or right on the beach, these tranquil one- or two-bedroom self-catering cottages (sleeping four or six) provide a relaxing getaway. Though each has a large patio, hammock and BBQ, the price is still on the high side. Midweek reductions. $$$

Villa Botero By Casa Mojito C Aviación at C Arroyo casamojitopanama.com. A short hop from the beach, this charming lodging offers a handful of nicely furnished rooms in a colonial-style tiled-roof cottage with all mod cons – flatscreen cable TV, fridge, coffee-maker – overlooking a pool and surrounding garden. Use of a shared stove and BBQ. Excellent breakfast available. $$$

FARALLÓN

★ **Casa Guardia** C La Venta casaguardia.com. A relaxing and welcoming stay is guaranteed at this family-owned hotel which has eight spacious rooms or suites with lots of natural light – some with balconies – set in a pleasant leafy garden. There's an on-site restaurant, pool and table-tennis tables but it's fabulous beach-side pool area and hammock-strewn *rancho* that really make this place. Excellent breakfast included. $$$

★ **Togo B&B** C La Venta togopanama.com. Thoughtfully designed and exquisitely appointed rooms (one with kitchenette) in an airy house within a verdant, tree-filled garden. Living space is shared with the owners though there are plenty of hammocks and shady patio spots for privacy. Additional meals can be ordered. Breakfast included. $$

EATING

The large **resorts** take care of the catering and evening entertainment for their guests. Otherwise, there is a sprinkling of local bars and *fondas* amid a handful of restaurants aimed exclusively at tourists and expats, where prices are high. The **opening hours** we quote in our listings are for high season; in the rainy season, hours depend a lot on the weather and some places may shut down completely for a few weeks.

3

PLAYA GORGONA TO PLAYA RÍO MAR

Los Camisones La Ermita, Km 104 off the Interamericana to the right between San Carlos and Santa Clara facebook.com/camisones.com. Its reputation for serving the best seafood in the country (including paella) has pushed the prices up in recent years, though this Spanish-Panamanian restaurant rarely disappoints. A changing menu using fresh produce is enjoyed in a relaxed large *rancho* in a pleasant garden. $$$

PLAYA SANTA CLARA

Tortugas Beach Bar and Grill Playa Santa Clara facebook.com/tortugasbeachbar. Two-storey, open-sided, breezy bar-restaurant at the back of the beach, with a small beer garden in front, and sun loungers, *ranchos* and umbrellas for rent. They also rent SUP boards, and have showers. Fresh, succulent seafood. $$–$$$

Xoko Interamericana, entrance to Santa Clara facebook.com/people/restaurante-xoko/100062945276077. It won't win any architectural awards, and the highway location is hardly conducive to intimate dining, but the cuisine at this highly acclaimed Basque restaurant more than compensates. Specializing in tapas, paella (between two) and other seafood dishes, they also do a fine portion of *papas bravas*. Don't be in a hurry to be served, though. $$$

FARÁLLON

La Fogata C Central Arriba lafogatapanama.com. Cosy *rancho* in a garden setting, specializing in Caribbean-Panamanian cooking, with plenty of coconut rice. Try the signature mixed seafood platter, a veritable seafood orgy of prawn cocktail, lobster and jumbo shrimp. Reservations essential at weekends. $$$

★ **Pipa's Beach Bar** instagram.com/pipasbeachpanama. At the end of the sandy road, past the landmark *Decameron* hotel, this bar-restaurant has a two-tiered terrace smack on the sand. The excellent lobster and trimmings will set you back but you can tuck into other fresh seafood dishes for around half the price. Also rents out *ranchos*, sun loungers and umbrellas. Daytime hours only. $$$

El Valle

About 100km southwest of Panama City, just beyond San Carlos, a winding road ascends 600m into the cordillera to **EL VALLE**, a small town of around seven thousand inhabitants nestled in the crater of a now-extinct volcano. Undulating hills rise to the south and west, ascending to more dramatic, forested peaks to the north, often shrouded in mist.

The picturesque location, cool climate and relative proximity to the capital (90min away by car) have made El Valle the holiday-home location of choice for Panama City's elite – a fact which becomes immediately obvious after a quick peek at the immaculately kept gardens and luxury residences down the aptly named **Calle de los Millonarios** (Millionaires' Road). Pleasantly quiet during the week, the place comes alive at weekends and on public holidays as a stream of 4WDs arrives from the city and the otherwise still roads resound with the sound of clopping hooves or revving quad bikes.

The huge explosion that blew the top off the volcano three million years ago left a vast caldera that over time filled with rainwater. When the crater-lake drained, it left behind a flat layer of rich volcanic soil. Perfect for agricultural production, the fertile earth also nourishes the expanses of trimmed lawn, abundant fruit and flower-laden trees, and attendant hummingbirds tucked away down El Valle's side streets, which are central to the place's charm.

The surroundings are instantly impressive. Spectacular stream-filled cloud forests envelop the elevated mountain reserve of **Monumento Natural Cerro Gaital**, which provides first-rate birdwatching, and visitors can also explore the puzzling petroglyphs of **La Piedra Pintada** and the spectacular falls of **Chorro El Macho**. If you enjoy fresh mountain air, there are enough decent **hiking**, **horseriding** and **cycling** opportunities to keep you in El Valle for several days.

EL VALLE
ACCOMMODATION
Blasina El Valle 7
Bodhi Hostel 5
Cabañas Potosí 4
Canopy Lodge 1
Casa di Pietra 3
Golden Frog Inn (Villa Rana Dorada) 2
Hotel Residencial El Valle 6
EATING
L'Italiano 6
Panadería y Dulcería Cano 3
Restaurante Dos Hermanos 5
Restaurante Las Nubes 1
Restaurante Massiel 4
Volcancito 2
1 (1km), Chorro El Macho (2km), 1 (3.5km), La Mesa (8km) & Cerro Gaital (9km)
Hotel Campestre (100m) & EVACC (200m)
La Piedra Pintada (600m)
4 (500m), Chorro Las Mozas (1km) & La India Dormida (5km)
2 & 2 (200m)
Interamericana (26km)
Kiosk
El Nispero
Stables
Supermarket
Iglesia San José
Library
Museum
Bank & ATM
ATM
Medical Centre
Avenida Central
Police
Market
Butterfly Haven
Laundry
Calle Coronado
Calle del Macho
Calle del Mercado
Calle Los Millonarios
Calle Los Guayacanes
Calle de los Sauces
Calle El Ciclo
Calle El Hato
Calle Ranita de Oro
Calle El Valle
Calle Espavé
Centro de Visitantes
E-Valley Bikes
APROVACA Orchid Nursery
MIA office
Río Guayabo
Río Antón
Thermal Baths
N
0
250
metres

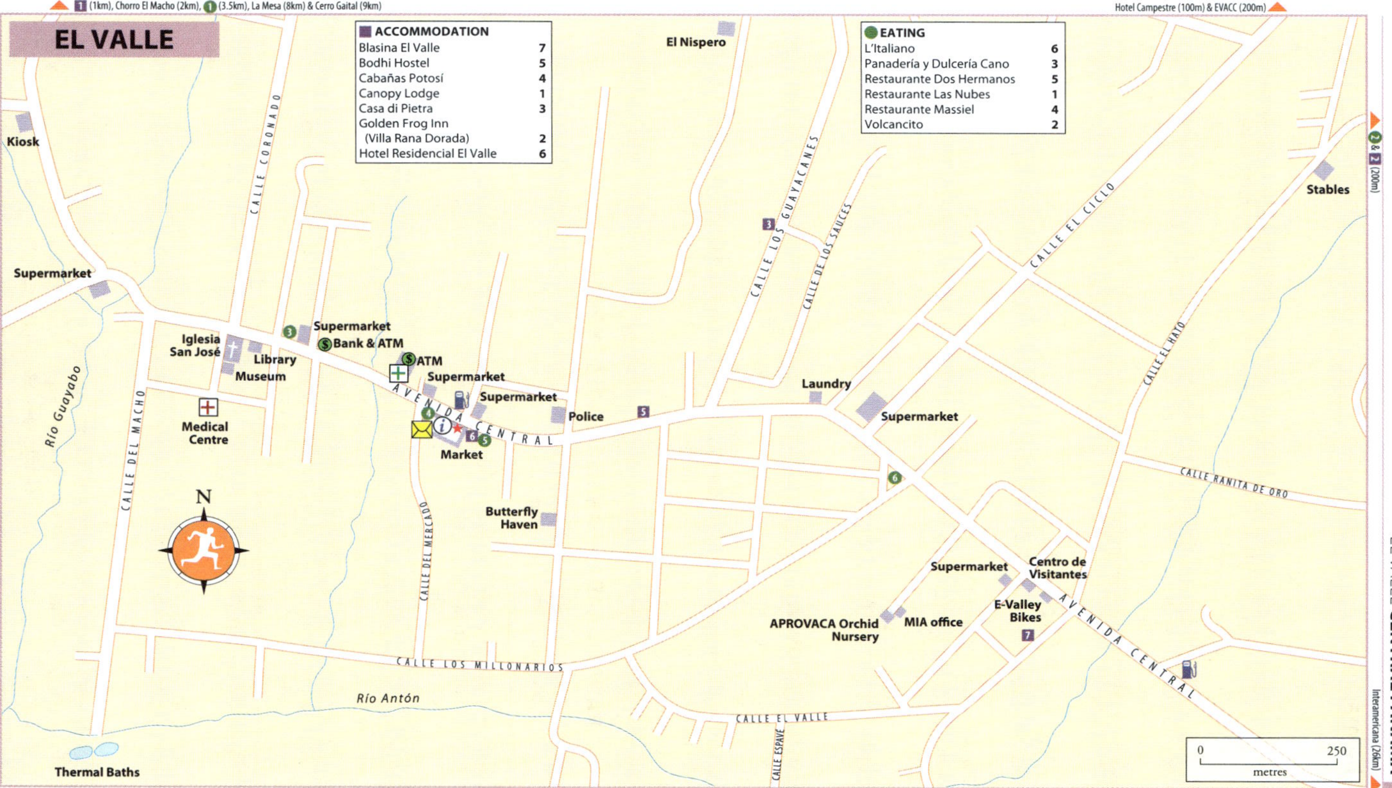

3

The market

Av Central • Daily 7am–6pm

Town life revolves round the daily **market**, which draws the largest crowds at weekends, especially on Sundays, when farmers and artisans pour in to sell fruit, vegetables, flowers and handicrafts. Though small, it's Panama's best-known **craft market** outside the capital; as well as straw hats you'll find a decent range of ceramic figurines, painted wooden trays (*bateas*) and soapstone carvings (mostly by Ngäbe or Buglé artists) alongside Guna *molas* and Emberá or Wounaan basketry. That said, the *artesanía* sold in the shops attached to the two central lodgings of *Don Pepe* and *Residencial El Valle* is more varied and often of higher quality.

APROVACA Orchid Nursery

Signposted to the left on the way into town from the Interamericana, next to the MIA office • Tues–Sun 8am–4pm • Charge • Ⓦ sites.google.com/view/aprovacapanama

The **APROVACA Orchid Nursery** nurtures around five hundred of Panama's twelve hundred orchid species, including the country's rare endemic national flower, the delicate *flor del espíritu santo* – named for the centre of each bloom, which resembles a white dove. The centre aims to reintroduce many of the endemic species – threatened by poaching – back into the wild.

Butterfly Haven

Signposted left off Av Central, just before the police station • 9.30am–3.30pm; closed Tues • Charge • Ⓣ 6062 3131

The **Butterfly Haven** has a butterfly house with around 250 multicoloured butterflies, including the magnificent blue morpho, flitting around and feeding on carefully selected host plants. There's also a nursery where you can learn all about the life cycle of lepidoptera, a garden café and a gift shop.

LA RANA DORADA – PANAMA'S GOLDEN FROG

Decorating everything from pre-Columbian talismans to tacky T-shirts and lottery tickets, Panama's **golden frog** (*rana dorada, atelopus zeteki*) is one of the country's most enduring cultural icons, associated above all with El Valle since the surrounding cloud forest provides its only known habitat.

In **ancient times** the Guaymí (or Ngäbe) revered the frog, carving ceramic and golden likenesses for jewellery and *huacas* – precious objects buried with chiefs and other prominent citizens – of this symbol of fertility and prosperity. Indeed, legend had it that possessing one of these "true toads" in life would ensure good fortune in the afterlife as it would transform into a golden *huaca*. Even today it is believed that a glimpse of this tiny dazzling amphibian in the wild will bring good luck, though a sighting is highly improbable thanks to the deadly **chytrid fungus**, which decimated amphibian populations worldwide and wrought devastation in the area in 2006. The waterborne fungus, which attacks the skin and suffocates the animal, was at one stage thought to have wiped out the wild population. Since there have been no confirmed sightings since 2009, the frog is considered to be extinct in the wild. Thankfully, successful breeding in captivity through the Amphibian Conservation and Rescue Project (Ⓦ amphibianrescue.org) in the Smithsonian's amphibian centre in Gamboa and numerous zoos and other institutions in the US and Canada has resulted in an adult population of around 1000 in captivity, which gives hope for their eventual return to the wild. You can catch a glimpse of golden frogs, alongside other amphibians, in the El Valle Amphibian Conservation Center (EVACC), which is strangely located in some shipping container laboratories behind the *Hotel Campestre* (Jan–April daily 9am–4pm; May–Dec closed Wed; charge; Ⓦ evaccfoundation.org).

Museo Padre José Noto

Av Central, behind Iglesia San José • 8am–4pm, closed Wed • Charge

On the south side of the main street, west of the market, protrude the whitewashed twin towers of the small **Iglesia de San José**, behind which is a modest one-room **museum**. Many of the displays – lumps of volcanic rock, household objects and contemporary crafts – are forgettable, but there are some striking polychromatic pre-Columbian ceramics and interesting carved faces.

Thermal baths

End of C del Macho • Daily 8am–5pm • Charge • T 6808 7927

In the south of town, the low-key **thermal baths** (*pozos termales*) by Río Antón allegedly have medicinal powers. The weekends are hectic, but the warm cement pool can be a pleasant experience midweek – take your swimming costume. A mud facepack is included in the entry price; an extra few dollars gets you a pot of exfoliating, mineral-rich mud (*barro*), which is fun to slather all over your body before rinsing off and taking to the pool.

La Piedra Pintada and Chorro Las Mozas

After crossing the bridge over the Río Guayabo at the west end of Avenida Central, the road forks: a fifteen-minute walk along the central prong leads to a massive petroglyph known as **La Piedra Pintada** (community fee), where there's no shortage of kids offering to guide you to the giant rock face and attempt to explain the mysterious pre-Columbian carved spirals and anthropomorphic and zoomorphic figures. You can continue up the path that follows the stream, which becomes more of a scramble as it forges through the forest, passing three pretty waterfalls. Ten minutes beyond the third one, to the right, stands the smaller petroglyph of **Piedra El Sapo**, named after the toad-like shape of one of its hieroglyphs, before the path continues up to the mythical ridge of **La India Dormida** (see box, page 138).

The left fork from the bridge leads to the **Chorro Las Mozas** falls (community fee) – more a series of tumbling rapids; fifteen minutes' stroll from town, it's a popular place for the local youth to splash around, especially at weekends.

Chorro El Macho

Road to Cerro Gaital, 2km northwest of the town centre • Daily 8am–5pm • Charge • W canopyadventurepanama.com • Cross the bridge over the Río Guayabo at the west end of Av Central, then take the right-hand fork; alternatively, take the bus to La Mesa from the market (hourly 5am–7pm), which passes the entrance

One of El Valle's most popular excursions is to **Chorro El Macho**, a picturesque 35m **waterfall** set in a private ecological reserve. A short circular path leads to a viewing platform at the base of the falls, where lizards bask on the rocks and hummingbirds dart through the foliage. Though you can't take the plunge here, near the entrance there is a delightful **natural swimming pool** in the river, or you might prefer a guided nature walk with a bilingual guide.

Canopy Adventure

Chorro El Macho • Daily 8am–4pm • Charge • W canopyadventurepanama.com

The **Canopy Adventure**, accessed via the park entrance, adds adrenaline to the delightful flora and fauna and its five cables – one taking you across the face of the falls – forms one of El Valle's major attractions. If you're heading for Chiriquí you might want to save your cash to do the more impressive Boquete Tree Trek (see page 187). But here the adventure has the potential to combine thrills with a guided (uphill) hike through the rainforest (around 30min).

LA INDIA DORMIDA

The undulating hilltop at the western end of El Valle, known as **La India Dormida**, is believed to be the slumbering silhouette of Flor del Aire, beautiful daughter of Urracá, the Guaymí chief famed for his fierce resistance to Spanish colonization. The story goes that while battles were raging, Flor fell in love with one of the conquistadors, unaware that she was admired by Yaraví, Urracá's most courageous warrior. Failing to get Flor's attention, Yaraví took the drastic measure of hurling himself off a mountain in front of the whole village. Understandably distraught, Flor renounced her love for the Spaniard and wandered off into the forested hills, where she eventually died of grief. Her body, it is said, is immortalized in the shape of a mountain. With a great deal of imagination and a little prompting from a local resident, you can usually make out her recumbent form, denuded of trees except for the distinct forested section to the right-hand side, which more clearly resembles the tresses of her hair.

ARRIVAL AND GETTING AROUND — EL VALLE

By bus Buses pull in across from the market on Av Central (also known as Av or C Principal), which acts as the town's unofficial bus terminal. Among them are regular services to and from Panama City (7.30am–7pm; every 20min; 2hr30min); the last return bus is 4.30pm. To travel west from El Valle, take a San Carlos minibus (6.30am–6pm; every 30min; 20min) and get off at the "entrada" at Las Uvas, on the Interamericana; here you have to flag down a westbound bus coming from Panama City. The large ones to Santiago or David are almost always full and rarely stop; your best bet is to get a smaller bus to Penonomé (see page 141) and change, though on Fri afternoons or at the start of a public holiday you could be in for a long wait for any bus to have space. There are also around eight buses a day that go to Penonomé via a cross-country route; ask around at the market.

By bike Though most places can be reached on foot, cycling is convenient; bikes can be rented at the central *Hotel Don Pepe*, by the market, or at several other lodgings in the town.

By taxi Taxi rides should not cost more than a couple of dollars to most places, though finding one available is about as easy as locating one of El Valle's fabled golden frogs.

By local minibus During the day, occasional blue minibuses circulate the town and will drop you off wherever you want, while yellow school buses shuttle back and forth from Capirita, at the eastern end of the town to La Pintada to the west (every 30min). Minibuses also head from outside the market up the mountain to La Mesa (5am–7pm; hourly), the access point for Cerro Gaital.

INFORMATION

Tourist information The small tourist kiosk (daily 8am–4pm; ☎983 6474) next to the market is very helpful while the owners of Artesanías Don Pepe (below *Hotel Don Pepe* on Av Central near the market), or the adjacent Davi's Gift Shop, are also excellent sources of local information. The privately-owned Centro de Visitantes at the entrance to the town (Mon, Wed–Sun 9am–5pm; charge) covers a lot of wall space with relatively little content.

MIA office Signposted to the left off Av Central on the way into town from the Interamericana (Mon–Fri 8am–4pm; ☎983 6411).

ACTIVITIES AND GUIDES

ACTIVITIES

Birdwatching Enthusiasts can join one of the tours offered by the *Canopy Lodge* (see below) or contract one of the guides listed below.

Cycling Rent a bike from *Hotel Residencial El Valle* either to travel the roads or explore the mountain trails; or rent out a more expensive electric bike from E-Valley Bikes (🌐evalleybikes.com), which also offers guided bike tours.

Horseriding The long-established stable at El Hato, south of *Hotel Campestre* (☎6646 5813), offers horseriding (hourly rates); it's worth paying a few extra dollars for a guide (Spanish-speaking) to accompany you. A popular guided route, lasting around 4hr, takes you round Cerro Gaital.

GUIDES

There is a list of certified local guides with contact numbers on thee Ven Valle tourism website (🌐venalvalle.com). Note that many of the hotels also have their own local guides whom they regularly call on.

Mario Bernal ☎231 3811 or ☎6693 8213, ✉mariobernal@gmail.com. An internationally renowned naturalist from El Valle; he is in great demand, so often away on tour. English and Spanish spoken.

Mario Urriola ☎6569 2676, ✉info@panamabirdguide.

com. A professional biologist and enthusiastic ornithologist, who also runs the serpentarium. English and Spanish spoken.

ACCOMMODATION

SEE MAP PAGE 135

Most of El Valle's accommodation can be found within walking distance of Av Central. **Prices** can be higher than elsewhere in the interior and are often higher at weekends than during the week. Holiday weekends are busy, when a minimum two- or three-night booking may be required.

Blasina El Valle Av Los Millionarios 80 ⓣ6275 6961. Small, friendly hostel in a converted house, with two dorms containing comfortable private pods (with curtains), and a handful of good-value private rooms with TV and shared bathroom. It's perfect for self-catering, with a large kitchen and supermarket across the road. You won't get bored in the evening, with a TV-lounge, table tennis and pool tables, plus hammocks. Dorms $, doubles $$

Bodhi Hostel Av Central, by Melo ⓦbodhihostels.com. This friendly hostel makes the most of its small space: plant-filled patio, with comfy chairs and hammocks; coffee bar; tidy shared kitchen; bikes for rent; and an upstairs cine-lounge for a rainy afternoon. Sleep in a three-tiered bunk on a quality mattress – each with curtain, reading light, fan and charger – or in one of the small (overpriced) private rooms. Dorm $, doubles $$

★ **Cabañas Potosí** On the road to Chorro Las Mozas, 1km west of town centre ⓦcabanaspotosi.com. Surrounded by trees and flowers, with a shared gazebo for relaxation and armchair birdwatching, this welcoming place has four simple, spotless rooms (with double and single bed). Two have a semi-open kitchen attached, and all share a long patio facing La India Dormida (see page 138). Birdwatching tours offered with one of Panama's finest guides. $$

★ **Canopy Lodge** On the road to Chorro El Macho ⓦcanopytower.com. Though not in the canopy, unlike its Gamboa cousin (see page 101), this lodge overlooking the Río Guayabo is superbly situated in a private nature reserve. It's aimed at birders, but the fine surroundings, tasteful furnishings and comfortable common areas make it a fine spot for anyone to unwind. Various all-inclusive packages including guiding. $$$$

Casa di Pietra 46 C Los Guayacanes ⓦcasadipietra.net. Surrounded by greenery and birdlife, this large house boasts a pebbled exterior with more stones than a cobbled street, and contains six suites, each with private balcony. A delightful place to unwind, offering splendid breakfasts (included) and a restaurant supported by an extensive wine cellar. $$$

Golden Frog Inn (Villa Rana Dorada) C Las Veraneras ⓦgoldenfroginn.com. You get satisfying views across the crater valley floor from this superior hillside inn, a 20min walk from the town centre. A handful of rooms some with private verandas and some with fully equipped kitchen, are set in a nicely landscaped garden with a decent-sized pool, shared kitchen and hammock deck for enjoying the daily

3

HIKING AROUND EL VALLE

Though not as lofty as the peaks of Chiriquí, the mountains encircling El Valle still offer a wealth of **hiking** opportunities. For most hikes you'll need a **guide**, since trails are not well marked and if the mist descends it's easy to lose your way, though on a clear day you can manage **La India Dormida** (see box, page 138) without being accompanied. There are several routes up the legendary hill, the most direct being to follow the path up past the Piedra Pintada, hugging the stream until you reach the top. A better circular route heads out past the baseball stadium, bearing left at the next fork. When the road ends, a path off to the right brings you out on the lower part of what is presumed to be Flor's body. Walking north along the deforested ridge, you can enjoy the splendid views across the crater before taking the path down from the "head" that eventually passes the refreshing waterfalls and natural swimming pools near La Piedra Pintada, where you can cool off.

A more challenging hike scales the area's highest peak, the forbidding forest-clad **Cerro Gaital** (1185m), for which you should be charged a few dollars but there's often nobody at the entry booth. The most direct route involves a steep climb from a path behind *Hotel La Compañía del Valle*, for which you'd need a guide. Alternatively, you can labour 7–8km up the road to La Mesa (or take the bus), bearing right at the fork after the village and arriving, a few hundred metres later, at the entrance to the reserve. The orchid-rich area is a haven for **birdwatchers** as well as hikers, harbouring a rainbow of hummingbirds, honeycreepers, toucanets, tanagers and trogons, as well as the elusive black guan. A 2.5km loop trail, Sendero El Convento, winds through cloud forest, circling the summit, with a turn-off to a mirador, which on a clear day affords stellar views down to the coast.

happy hour. Bountiful breakfast included. $$$

Hotel Residencial El Valle Av Central, by the market hotelresidencialelvalle.com. The unpromising motel-like exterior belies light, clean en-suite rooms (for 2–6 people) with sizeable windows and cable TV. A great open-sided hammock deck provides views across to the hills. Other benefits include bike rental and laundry service. $$

EATING SEE MAP PAGE 135

There are a number of places to eat in El Valle, particularly Italian and mainly on the main road, but the quality is uneven. At **summer weekends**, it pays to eat early before the crowds gather and the kitchens struggle to cope with the influx of people and quality and service can suffer.

L'Italiano Av Central 6682 9398. The town's favourite Italian restaurant has wooden chairs and tables both inside and on a covered patio. The two amiable Italian owners make their own pasta and buffalo mozzarella, and the topping-laden thick-crust pizzas are cooked in a wood-fired oven. Try the pumpkin ravioli in a pink sauce, accompanied by some wine from their fine cellar. $$–$$$

Panadería y Dulcería Cano Av Central 983 6420. Just the place to stock up on sticky buns, cakes and bread to keep you going on a hike. The sugary *orejas* (elephant ears or palmiers) are especially popular. $

Restaurante Dos Hermanos Av Central 983 6201. This great, cheerful café-restaurant is a favourite lunchtime stop for Panamanian families. Tasty traditional mains (with a few veggie options) include top-quality *patacones* with a few Peruvian additions – try the fried ceviche – washed down with delicious home-made juices and *batidos*. $$–$$$

Restaurante Las Nubes Off the road to La Mesa, 4km uphill from El Valle instagram.com/rest_lasnubes. A spectacular mountaintop location, where you're paying as much for the view (and possibly the taxi) as for the food – so reserve a window table. The dishes rarely disappoint but expect a mix of the mundane – deli-burgers and mushroom risotto – and the creative: lamb chops in plum sauce with pureed yam and goat's cheese. $$$–$$$$

Restaurante Massiel Av Central, beyond the market 6214 4480. The town's best budget option is a friendly, efficient *fonda* serving *comida típica* and fast food – chicken with salad, rice and beans for only a few dollars, and hamburger combos go for much the same. It's also a good choice for a breakfast fry-up. $–$$

Volcancito's Golden Frog Inn C las Veraneras. Ample portions of Tex-Mex tacos every which way, enchiladas, quesadillas and nachos share the menu with Panamanian staples such as *ropa vieja* and *sancocho*. Dine on a pleasant terrace facing flowers and mountains. $$–$$$

Penonomé and eastern Coclé

The capital of the province of Coclé, **PENONOMÉ** was founded by Spanish colonizers in 1581 and briefly served as capital of the isthmus after the destruction of Panamá Viejo. Standing at the geographical centre of Panama (a plaque marks the fact), this bustling market town remains important both as a transit point and for the surrounding land, which is used for fruit, vegetables, rice and maize as well as for pig, poultry and cattle farming. The seventeen thousand inhabitants are predominantly *mestizo*, while some have Arab and Chinese origins. Fittingly for a town that served as a *reducción de Indios* – a place where conquered indigenous groups were forcibly resettled – Penonomé was named after Nomé, a local chieftain cruelly betrayed and executed.

Though a provincial capital and major agricultural centre, Penonomé is surprisingly small, with a very rural feel, with just a couple of modest sights and a pretty river within walking distance. Its aquatic celebrations for **Carnaval** are a real crowd-puller (see page 141), and it makes a decent base for visiting places of interest nearby. Chief among them are the tranquil village of **La Pintada**, famed for its finely woven **sombreros**, and the scenic mountains to the north, including **Chiguirí Arriba**, with its hiking trails and spectacular views and the vibrant Cucuá community of San Miguel Centro. Topping the mist-swathed peaks to the northwest, **Parque Nacional Omar Torrijos** is a treat for birdwatchers and hikers.

Plaza Bolívar and around

The town's main drag, Avenida J.D. Arosemena (also known as Vía Central), runs a few hundred metres from the Interamericana to the pleasant **Plaza Bolívar** (also known

as Plaza 8 de Diciembre). Featuring a statue of Simón Bolívar, the square is flanked by government buildings and the **Catedral de San Juan Bautista**, where the early morning or evening light projects dancing rainbows of colours through the new stained-glass windows. East of the cathedral, a small *plazuela* features monuments to Penonomé's glitterati, including a bust of **Victoriano Lorenzo**, a local nationalist hero who was eventually tricked into capture and executed by firing squad (see page 299).

Museo de Historia y Tradición Penonomeña

C San Antonio • Tues–Sat 9am–4pm, Sun until 1pm • Charge • ☎ 997 8490

Located in quiet San Antonio, the oldest part of town, the **Museo de Historia y Tradición Penonomeña** occupies a tiled blue-and-white *quincha* (wattle and daub) building and contains a modest collection of pre-Columbian ceramics, colonial religious art and period furniture.

Balneario Las Mendozas

If the heat gets too much, take a five-minute walk northeast out of town to the **Balneario Las Mendozas**, a popular swimming area in the Río Zaratí – this is the location of the aquatic parade at Carnaval, when the floats literally float down the river. Though it's a party place at weekends and during holidays, you can enjoy a quieter dip here at other times, or upstream at **Las Tres Peñas**, a more attractive pool.

ARRIVAL AND INFORMATION — PENONOMÉ

BY BUS

Buses arrive and leave from the new bus terminal, 2km southwest of the city centre on the Interamericana by the new Boulevard shopping mall. Given its inconvenient location, many buses still pass through the town centre and the market en route to or from the bus terminal.

Destinations Aguadulce (5.25am–10pm; every 30–45min; 30min); Chiguirí Arriba (6am, 9am then every 15min until

FESTIVAL DEL TORO GUAPO

The small agricultural town of **Antón**, just off the Interamericana almost midway between Farallón and Penonomé, really only registers on the tourist radar once a year, during the festival of **Toro Guapo** ("Fierce Bull") in mid-October, when the pleasant colonial square and whitewashed church are transformed by hordes of visitors.

The fun-filled five-day extravaganza takes its name and much of its action from the cattle farming that has defined the area for centuries and is well worth sampling. Alongside the usual array of folkloric dancing, colourful street parades, beauty pageants and progressively more drunken revelry are **toros** – men who cavort around the streets, charging at all and sundry. They dress in fantastical costumes draped over wooden or bamboo frames, topped with a bull's head adorned with ribbons and mirrors.

3

Many of the surrounding villages produce such a beast, with the creativity of the costume and acrobatic skills of the wearer a source of local pride, to be displayed during the parade on the final morning. After being blessed in the church, the bulls are led round the town as they playfully harass the *pollera*-swishing dancers, accompanied by bands of drummers. Listen out among the beats for the distinctive chime of the *almirez* – a bell-shaped bronze mortar of Afro-Colonial origin that pharmacists once used to grind their medicinal herbs, and is now a musical instrument unique to Antón.

Other festival highlights include **water fights** (*mojaderas*), competitions testing traditional **rural skills** such as carrying firewood, peeling coconuts and milking a cow, and dancing by extravagantly dressed **diablos limpios**, or "clean devils" (see box, page 159). Strangest of all is the **cutarras**, when a poor cow is wrestled to the ground by several farmers, often the worse for wear, who then struggle to fix sandals (*cutarras*) over the hooves, recalling an old trick of cattle rustlers attempting to hide the telltale hoof prints.

ARRIVAL AND ACCOMMODATION

By bus Antón is well served by bus from Panama City (5.20am–8pm; every 20min; 2hr), especially as additional buses are laid on during the festival.

Hostal Las Catalinas Av 2da, just off the central park ☎6427 6822. Panamanian hospitality at its best offering good value for money. A handful of perfectly comfortable simple double and family rooms surround a delightful central courtyard-cum-garden area overflowing with plants and local art or craftwork, with plenty of places to lounge about. There's also a shared kitchen. Cold-water showers $$

6.30pm; 1hr); Chitré (8am–9.10pm; hourly; 1hr 20min), El Copé (6am–7pm; every 20min; 1hr); Panama City (4.45am–10.45pm; every 20–30min; 2hr); La Pintada (6am–8pm; every 10min; 20min); Las Tablas (8am–7pm; hourly; 1hr 50min), San Miguel Centro (infrequently; 1hr 30min).

INFORMATION

MIA office The regional MIA office (Mon–Fri 8am–4pm; ☎997 9805) is on the Interamericana at the junction with C San Agustín. Call in if you need information (in Spanish) on Parque Nacional Omar Torrijos.

ACCOMMODATION SEE MAP PAGE 141

It's unlikely you'd want to stay in Penonomé, but in case you get stuck here, the two accommodation options reviewed here are motel-like, with midweek **reductions**.

Hotel Coclé Interamericana, Iguana Mall, west of Av J.D. Arosemena facebook.com/HotelCocle. Bland but good-value business hotel offering modern rooms with large beds, bedside lights, a desk, room service, safe, large flatscreen TV and laundry service. Plus there's a business centre, gym, pool and bar-restaurant. $$$

Hotel Guacamaya Interamericana, at the junction with Av J.D. Arosemena ☎6448 7976. Unmissable large mustard-coloured edifice, with serviceable spacious rooms with tiled floors and dark wooden furniture. Since there is only a bar at the hotel, you'll need to eat elsewhere. $$

EATING SEE MAP PAGE 141

★ **Gambrinus Pub & Grill** Hallinus Mall. A stone's throw from the Interamericana, this popular, convivial semi-open grill offers weekly specials, burgers with crunchy fries, and other international fare – filet mignon with a deliciously creamy mushroom sauce is a good bet – and a few German specialities, such as currywurst and Jägerschnitzel. The craft beer selection is substantial. $$–$$$

Hotel Dos Continentes Interamericana, at the junction with Av J.D. Arosemena 997 9325. The glass-fronted hotel restaurant is justifiably popular, serving a good range of international dishes and Panamanian staples. Breakfasts are excellent. $–$$

La Pintada Café Plaza Casa Carles, Simon Quiroz instagram.com/lapintadacafe. Across from the museum, this charming café occupies a leafy courtyard of an old stone house in the San Antonio district. All kinds of breakfasts are on offer, from Panamanian fry-ups to eggs and all-day waffles. At lunchtime, choose from sandwiches made with artisanal bread or *empanadas* accompanied by a smoothie or a cappuccino. $$

Restaurante Gallo Pinto Plaza Esmeralda, Interamericana instagram.com/restaurantegallopinto. With its handy location on the highway and plenty of parking, this diner-style *cafetería* serving *comida criolla* is a popular pitstop for travelling families as well as a favourite with the town's residents. $$

La Pintada

Aficionados of **Panama's hats** – as opposed to Panama hats, which are made in Ecuador – should consider making a detour out to the village of **LA PINTADA**, 15km northwest of Penonomé in the foothills of the cordillera, which is famed for its high-quality palm-woven *sombrero pintado* or "*pintao*" (see box). It has been a major business in the village and surrounding area, once involving several thousand individuals, and there is a hat festival here in late October. The **Mercado de Artesanías La Pintada** (daily 8am–4pm), which these days displays the crafts of only a handful of local families, selling hats in addition to decorated gourds, soapstone carvings and a few pots, is struggling, as few international tourists pass by these days. As a result, finding the place open can be tricky, especially in the rainy season. Master hat-maker Señor Quirós, next door, lives at the back of his shop, **Artesanías Reinaldo Quirós** (daily 8am–5pm; 6963 0945). He is usually easier to locate and has a good collection. Both places are easy to spot, on the left-hand side of the football pitch.

3

ARRIVAL AND DEPARTURE — LA PINTADA

By minibus Minibuses leave Penonomé for La Pintada (6am–8pm; every 10–15min; 20min) from the bus terminal on the Interamericana. Return buses run to a similar timetable.

ACCOMMODATION AND EATING

La Pintada River Inn 4km north of La Pintada lapintadainn.com. If you'd like a restful base up in the

PANAMA'S HAT – THE SOMBRERO PINTADO

Though not as famous nor as sought after as its Ecuadorian cousins, Panama's own straw hats are growing in reputation. Ubiquitous in rural Panama, worn by men and women, both as everyday work attire and a luxury accessory, they vary in style according to province and function. But while the hats have their origins in indigenous societies, Coclé's **sombrero pintado** or *pintao* ("painted hat"), which takes its name from the black and white design, has become the most popular and emblematic; in 2018 it was even accorded intangible world heritage status by UNESCO.

Quality (and therefore price) is principally determined by the number of **rings** (*vueltas*), but takes into consideration the consistency and fineness of the weave. A coarse seven-ring weave takes a week to make and costs around $20–30 whereas a 22-ring *fino* usually requires four to six weeks and can sell for more than $1000. The cost may seem high, but immense and skilled labour is involved. Once cut, the fibres are stripped from the leaves and cooked to be made pliable before being dried and bleached in the sun. For a high-quality *sombrero pintado*, the finest fibres are culled from bellota alongside coarser junco fibres, naturally dyed by being boiled with *chisná* leaves and buried in earth for several days, to form the distinctive black rings, while fine threads of sisal (*pita*) are used to stitch everything together.

hills, head for this eight-room B&B in a lovely location beyond La Pintada and accessible by bus. It has a sparkling pool and pleasant woodland walk down to a river, where you can bathe; you could also cross the river and hike further into the forest. With advance notice you can order the *cena del día* to enjoy in the lovely *bohío*. $$

Chiguirí Arriba and Churuquita Grande

From the market area in Penonomé, *chivas* head off through the surrounding cultivated fields to villages scattered in the folds of the cool, forested mountains that rise to the north. **CHIGUIRÍ ARRIBA**, 30km to the northeast, makes an easy day-trip, with plenty of good hiking trails, spectacular views across forested limestone hummocks and a 30m waterfall, **Cascada Tavida** ($5 charge) within *Villa Tavida*'s private reserve (see page 145). More adventurous trips can be organized across the mountains to El Valle, or over to the Caribbean rainforests; contact *Villa Tavida* for the name of a reliable local guide.

3

If you're in the area in late January, it's worth dropping by the village of **CHURUQUITA GRANDE**, halfway between Penonomé and Chiguirí Arriba, for the citrus-filled **Festival de la Naranja**, to marvel at the elaborate and inventive wood-and-thatch displays overflowing with local produce, all vying for the prize of best stall.

ARRIVAL AND DEPARTURE — CHIGUIRÍ ARRIBA AND CHURUQUITA GRANDE

By bus Buses leave Penonomé by the market (6am, 9am then every 60–90min until 6.30pm; 1hr 15min) for Chiguirí Arriba, via Churuquita Grande.

By car An ordinary saloon car is fine as far as Chiguirí Arriba, and will reach *Villa Tavida* (a 15min hike from the main road) unless it's very wet.

ACCOMMODATION

Hostal Don Mene On the road to Chiguirí Arriba, 24km northeast of Penonomé ⊤ 6456 4043, Ⓦ facebook.com/hostaldonmene. By the roadside, 1.5km before the main village, this charming simple place is set in flower-filled gardens, with three simple tiled rooms (Room 1 is the nicest) and a dorm loft (with outside toilet) and shared kitchen.

LOS CUCUÁS DE SAN MIGUEL CENTRO

San Miguel Centro, 35km northeast of Penonomé, is home to the **Cucuá** community, who are famed for their devil dance conducted in elaborate, cream-coloured, pyjama-like costumes made from cucuá bark, painted with geometric shapes using natural dyes and topped with a fanciful deer mask complete with real antlers and a peccary's jawbone. As with other devil dances, it was originally associated with Corpus Christi celebrations; at one time in danger of dying out, it is now regularly performed at folk festivals across Panama. The dance is the central attraction of the annual **Festival de los Cucuás**, which takes place in March in San Miguel Centro. The bark "material" used for the costumes is beaten against a tree until smooth, then washed in soap and hot water before being laid out to dry. Such has been the demand for the costumes in recent years (they can sell for around $500) that the cucuá tree has become endangered, prompting a recent reforestation programme.

Descended from the Guaymí, like the Ngäbe and Buglé, and originally from Veraguas, the Cucuás fled the Spanish colonizers centuries ago to settle in the mountains of Coclé. These days they make a living primarily from coffee cultivation and the sale of *artesanías*; the latter, along with the devil dance, forms a major part of a community-based **ecotourism** project aimed at preserving and promoting Cucuá culture.

ARRIVAL AND ACCOMMODATION

By bus Transport for San Miguel Centro (1hr 30min) leaves infrequently from Penonomé bus terminal (see page 141).

San Miguel Centro homestays Simple lodging is offered with families by the eco-community project for a modest fee; extra is charged for a performance by the dance troupe. To organize a visit, ask about transport at the bus station, or around the market in town.

The on-site *fonda* serves traditional, inexpensive fare on the terrace, which offers fabulous mountain views. $$

★ **Villa Tavida Lodge & Spa** Chiguirí Arriba, 28km northeast of Penonomé ⓣ6485 0505, ⓦinstagram.com/villa_tavida. Set in the Reserva Privada Tavida, this delightful lodge offers six spacious, light double and family rooms (sleeping two to six). All have cable TV and a/c; four have private balconies with a hammock to admire the wonderful mountain views. Day-visitors are welcome to enjoy the birdwatching trails and dine at the moderately priced restaurant. There's a spa with sauna, offering massages and other treatments. You can also organize a local guide here (with advance notice) if you want to hike further afield. Breakfast included. Restaurant open daily for visitors and residents. $$$

Parque Nacional Omar Torrijos

PARQUE NACIONAL OMAR TORRIJOS may be tricky to get to, but this little-visited, 250-square-kilometre protected carpet of lush forest astride the continental divide is well worth the trip. Its full name, **Parque Nacional General de División Omar Torrijos Herrera**, was given on its formation in 1986 in remembrance of Panama's flamboyant populist leader, whose plane mysteriously crashed into one of the area's highest peaks, Cerro Marta, in 1981. The 13km, 8hr trek to the summit, plus a ghoulish peer at the remnants of the plane, makes this hike one of the most popular.

These days the park is more usually referred to as "Parque Omar Torrijos" or "El Copé" after the nearby village. Averaging 20°C in the cloud-forested peaks of the Cordillera Central, the canopy cascades down to the more moist vegetation of the Caribbean side, where temperatures average 25°C and the area receives 4m of rainfall annually.

There's some fine **wildlife**: tapirs, peccaries and all five of Panama's species of large cat roam the undergrowth, while red-fronted parrotlets, orange-bellied trogons and the extraordinary bare-necked umbrella bird draw bird-lovers. You're more likely to hear than see the three-wattled bellbird, which has one of the loudest birdcalls in the world – a bizarre metallic "dong" that carries for almost 1km.

Around the visitors' centre

A few hundred metres beyond the park entrance, an informative **visitors' centre**, with a rear balcony offering splendid views, marks the start of a couple of fairly short, well-kept circular routes (2km and 4km) and an interpretive loop, aimed at enhancing visitors' appreciation of the abundant and diverse flora. For **longer hikes**, to Cerro Peña Blanca, Cerro Marta or La Rica for example, you will need to arrange a **guide** (see page 142).

Cerro Peña Blanca

With a guide, **hikers** should consider aiming for **Cerro Peña Blanca** (1314m), which occasionally peeks out from the mist to the west of the park entrance. The moderately strenuous four-hour trail ascends west from the village of **BARRIGÓN** and on a rare clear day you are rewarded at the summit with spectacular views of both oceans.

La Rica

The other popular route heads over the continental divide from the park entrance down to the community of **LA RICA**, a good four-hour hike away. Set in verdant surroundings laced with waterfalls and natural swimming pools and within reach of giant guayacán, cuipo and cedar trees, La Rica is the perfect spot to appreciate the park's natural beauty, though getting there can be a very muddy affair for much of the year – a guide is essential.

ARRIVAL AND DEPARTURE — PARQUE NACIONAL OMAR TORRIJOS

By bus First, take a bus to the mountain village of El Copé. There are direct buses from Panama City (6am–6.30pm; hourly; 3hr30min); minibuses from Penonomé are even more frequent (6am–7pm; every 20min; 1hr). There are also services from Aguadulce (6am–6pm; every 1hr 30min; 1hr). Occasional minibuses from El Copé make the journey

LA CASCADA LAS YAYAS

A worthwhile diversion on the way to Parque Nacional Omar Torrijos from Barrigón is **La Cascada Las Yayas** (daily 8am–6pm; charge; ☎6809 6372). A shady 300m trail offers several viewpoints from which to appreciate the series of three falls, the highest of which is 25m. The falls, inevitably, are at their most impressive in the rainy season, though in the dry season there's the pleasure of taking a dip in the pool at the base of the main cascade. The surrounding rainforest is excellent for spotting hummingbirds and amphibians, especially in the late afternoon. A couple of very rudimentary wooden **rooms** with shared kitchen are available at the entrance ($/person).

3

to the even smaller village of Barrigón (7am–7pm), after which only a 4WD can crawl the remaining steep 4km to the park entrance – on foot that hike will take well over an hour. For the return, the last bus back from Barrigón to El Copé is around 6.30pm, and from El Copé to Penonomé it is at 7pm, slightly earlier for Aguadulce. Buses heading west along the Interamericana will pick up/drop off passengers at the junction.

By 4WD taxi Enquire at *Hostal Buena Esperanza* in El Copé, or ask your guide, for a contact to arrange 4WD transport in advance. Costs are approximately $20 from El Copé to the park entrance, $8 from Barrigón.

INFORMATION

Park entrance The park entrance is 4km beyond Barrigón, which is 3km northwest of El Copé. At the time of writing there was no entry fee to the park.

Hiking guides Macedonia Pérez (☎6549 7321) is an experienced certified local hiking guide who lives in Barrigón, and can guide you (in Spanish) to any of the surrounding peaks. He can also offer simple lodgings in his home. Samuel Lorenzo is another guide (☎6913 9718). Both are members of the local community-based tourism committee.

Centro de Visitantes The visitors' centre, a few hundred metres from the park entrance, provides information on the park's flora and fauna.

ACCOMMODATION

MIA cabin Park entrance; contact the MIA regional office in Penonomé (☎997 7538). A spacious solar-powered self-catering cabin near the entrance affords sweeping vistas, though conditions are often misty, and comprises a large lounge, a dorm with four bunks and a kitchen with a stove, fridge and basic utensils. Bring a sleeping bag, as it's chilly at night. Camping is possible, but there is no electricity and it is likely to be very wet. Camping $/person, dorms $

Glamping El Copé 1km before the park entrance on the road from Barrigón facebook.com/p/Glamping-El-Cope-100088525651229. Bring your own tent or rent a safari tent carpeted with artificial turf and containing two sturdy double wooden beds – bring warm clothing as it can gets cold at night. Kitchens are under thatch and there's a small pool. Own tent $–$$; safari tent $$

Western Coclé

West along the Interamericana from Penonomé, past the new windfarm – Panama's first and Central America's largest – across the flatlands of Coclé, the terrain becomes duller and drier. Skirting endless fields of sugar cane and cattle, you enter the crescent known as the **Arco Seco** (Dry Arc), which sweeps round the Bahía de Parita west of the Pacific beaches to the eastern section of the Azuero Peninsula (see page 152). Plum in the middle of what transforms into an unpleasant dust bowl in the dry season stands the important agroindustrial town of **Aguadulce**, synonymous with sugar, salt and – more recently – shrimp. Though the town itself is unremarkable, at the right time of year you can observe its agricultural processes first-hand, while avid birdwatchers head for the saltpans of **Playa El Salado** to the southeast. East of Aguadulce lie two of Panama's major historical attractions, the intriguing pre-Columbian site **Parque Arqueológico El Caño** and the fine colonial church at **Natá**.

Aguadulce and around

As ever, town life in **AGUADULCE** centres on the main square, **Plaza 19 de Octubre**, where the **Iglesia de San Juan Bautista** exhibits a mishmash of styles, the original altar frescoes having disappeared beneath an expensive pile of red brick – the current altarpiece.

El Museo de la Sal y el Azúcar

Plaza 19 de Octubre • Tues–Sat 8am–4pm • Free • 997 4280

The charming two-storey nineteenth-century building – in need of repair – that was once the post office now houses the **Museo Regional Stella Sierra** (named after a local poet, whose work is on display), much better known by its previous title, **El Museo de la Sal y el Azúcar**. You'll see a modest assortment of pre-Columbian relics, photos and instruments from the early days of the salt and sugar industries, plus weaponry and uniforms from the civil war, during which two major battles were fought in the town. Space is also devoted to Aguadulce's two most famous citizens – the aforementioned poet, Stella Sierra, and Rodolfo Chiari, one of Panama's former presidents.

3

Ingenio Santa Rosa

14km west of Aguadulce, north of the Interamericana • Jan–March Tues–Fri 8am–noon; 24hr notice needed to book a tour (in Spanish); to see the cane-processing, you need to wear long sleeves, trousers and closed shoes; otherwise you can only visit the museum • Free • 987 8101, azunal.com • Take a taxi from the bus terminal at Aguadulce, or any bus heading along the Interamericana, which can drop you off at the factory entrance, from where it's a 2.5km hike north

Of greater interest than Aguadulce's sugar museum is a tour around Panama's oldest and most important sugar mill, the **Ingenio Santa Rosa.** Here, during the harvesting season, you learn about the fascinating process of production, following the action from the cane fields to the bags of sugar. A small on-site museum, inside the reproduction wooden house of the pioneering DelValle family, is stuffed with period furniture and memorabilia. Outside, the grounds are sprinkled with early mill machinery, including old sugar cane presses. At the time of writing, the *casa-museo* was being renovated but hoped to re-open in 2026.

ARRIVAL AND DEPARTURE — AGUADULCE AND AROUND

By bus Buses arrive at the main bus terminal behind the OnDGo shopping mall west of the city centre on the Interamericana. Local buses tend to do a round of the city centre too to pick up/drop off passengers. Through buses between the Azuero Peninsula, David and Panama City, buses may stop by the *Hotel Interamericana* if they have space and/or inclination to take on more passengers.

Destinations Chitré (8.40am–9.40pm; every 20min; 50min); El Copé (6am–6pm; every 1hr30min; 1hr); Panama City (3.20am–11.25pm; frequent; 3hr); Penonomé (3.20am–11.25pm; every 30–45min; 30min); Santiago (5.55am–11.55pm; every 30–50min; 1hr10min).

ACCOMMODATION AND EATING

Hotel La Central Av Aberlardo Herrera, 100m north of the main plaza 6260 5566. Bland, functional business hotel with the odd bit of Chinese decor lies plum in the centre of town – as the name suggests – conveniently opposite the most reliable restaurant (see below). As it's new, everything is at least clean and the basics (modern a/c, flat-screen TV and decent hot-water shower) are all working, though the place was obviously completed in a hurry. Room only. $$

Los Faroles Av Rodolfo Chiari, one block north of the main plaza instagram.com/losfarolesaguadulce. For years, the town's most consistent restaurant – though steer clear of the pizzas – serving standard Panamanian fare. It has two entrances: the main, sterile, air-conditioned diner-style room at the front, and a pleasant old-fashioned fan-ventilated, semi-open dining room (open only for lunch and dinner) accessed via Av Aberlardo Herrera. $$

★ **Inkas Restaurant** Aguadulce. One of a small Peruvian chain – with restaurants in Santiago (see page 208) and Antón. Ignore the lack of ambience and tacky decor (awful paintings of Machu Picchu and the life-size alpaca) and focus on the high quality of the food. Peruvian classics – *lomo saltado* (stir-fried strips of steak, with onions, tomatoes and fries) and *papa a la Huancaina* (potatoes in white cheese sauce with yellow pepper) are done well, and the seafood platter to share is another highlight. $$$

Parque Arqueológico El Caño

18km north of Aguadulce, just off the Interamericana • Tues–Sat 8am–4pm; last entry 3.30pm • Free • T 228 3317, W fundacionelcano.org • Buses between Aguadulce and Penonomé can drop you on the Interamericana at the entrance to the village of El Caño, from where it's a further 3km walk to the site – a taxi from Natá might be easier

Parque Arqueológico El Caño is one of Panama's most significant pre-Columbian archeological sites, which narrowly escaped bulldozing in the 1970s. Sadly, a combination of plunder, vandalism and neglect means there is relatively little for the lay visitor to appreciate, while the park's floodplain location makes it a mosquito-infested quagmire in the rainy season. Even so, the well-preserved skeletons are quite impressive and definitely worth a look if you're in the area.

3

An important **ceremonial site** (or necropolis for the social elite) from 700 to just after 1000 AD, El Caño later became a regular cemetery, and was still in use as such after the Conquest. One of the most fascinating finds was a set of more than a hundred basalt statues that formed what was described as the "Temple of the Thousand Idols". These were illegally decapitated and plundered by an American Indiana Jones-style adventurer in the early twentieth century, and the best of their zoomorphic and anthropomorphic heads are now scattered in museums in the US, with a few in Panama City's anthropological museum (which has been closed to the public for years). Only the **stone pedestals** remain.

In 2005 new electronic survey techniques indicated the presence of **funeral mounds**, two of which were excavated in 2008, revealing fairly complete skeletons. One, presumed to be a chief's burial mound, threw up a number of **gold and emerald** items, which are currently being examined by archeologists, though replicas are on display in the museum. In 2024 another high-status tomb was uncovered, laden with gold and other precious artefacts, and other funerary mounds are thought to lie under the nearby sugar cane fields.

The small **museum** is well worth a peek, though explanations are all in Spanish. Some fine ceramics, figurines and reproductions of gold pieces found at El Caño are on display. More generally, the museum contextualizes the site, relating what the findings can tell us about society in the Gran Coclé region at that time: its hierarchies, funerary rites and cosmovision.

Natá

It's hard to picture **NATÁ**, a quiet backwater 11km north of Aguadulce, as the major Spanish settlement it once was, until you arrive at the plaza to be confronted with the dazzling white Baroque facade of the expansive **Basílica Menor Santiago Apóstol**. Possibly the oldest church in the Americas still in use, and recently fully restored to its former glory, the church bears testament to the town's historical importance.

Founded in 1522 by Gaspar de Espinosa (whose bust surveys the church from the square) and named after the local indigenous chief, the town supposedly gained its subsequent full name, **Santiago de Natá de los Caballeros**, from a hundred knights (*caballeros*) – hand-picked by King Charles V of Spain – who were sent to subjugate the local population and spread the Catholic Word. The surrounding fertile plains made Natá a perfect base for confronting the main indigenous resistance forces under Cacique Urracá, who relentlessly attacked the site (see box, page 295), and for providing supplies to the now long-abandoned gold mines on the Caribbean coast.

Basílica Menor Santiago Apóstol

Plaza 19 de Octubre • Daily 8am–6pm • Free

Apart from the splendid belltower, the main attractions of the **Basílica Menor Santiago Apóstol** are the ornately **carved wooden altars** framed by exquisite columns laden with vines, flowers and angels, which adorn an otherwise simple wooden interior. Though the least elaborate, the main altar importantly contains images of the patron saint,

Santiago el Menor (James the Lesser), and the co-patron, San Juan de Díos, who are removed from their niches and paraded round the town on their saint days of July 25 and March 8, respectively.

ARRIVAL AND DEPARTURE — NATÁ

By bus Regional buses westbound to Aguadulce or eastbound to Penonomé drop and pick up passengers at the entrance to Natá on the Interamericana (every 15–20min), a 10min walk from the village. Local shuttles between Aguadulce and Penonomé may even enter for a quick sweep of the plaza.

Playa El Salado

Heading southeast out of Aguadulce, a tarred road navigates 8km between mud and salt flats and shrimp farms to the mangrove-lined coast at **Playa El Salado**. In the dry season, salt is heaped like snow by the evaporation pools while September and October are the best months to catch flocks of migrating **waders**; among the numerous sandpipers and plovers, look out for striking black-necked stilts probing the mud for crustaceans and lovely roseate spoonbills filtering the tidal pools.

At weekends, many Aguadulceños head this way to escape the heat of the town and to stroll along the pleasant **beach.** The biggest attraction for many, though, are the **jumbo shrimp** for which the fishing village is famous, and which you can sample at one of the restaurants dotted along the road.

ARRIVAL AND DEPARTURE — PLAYA EL SALADO

By minibus The only scheduled bus leaves Aguadulce's main square at 7am (15min) with the return bus leaving Playa El Salado at 8am. Theoretically, it runs back and forth hourly (with a break for the driver's lunch) but it very much depends on demand.

By taxi Taxis from Aguadulce are not too expensive.

EATING AND DRINKING

Bicho's Restaurant 100m beyond the village mirador 6205 0379, facebook.com/bichosrestaurant. Bright, cheerful and justifiably extremely popular with families on account of producing tasty seafood at accessible prices – a plateful of *patacones* stuffed full of shrimps washed down with an ice-cold beer for very little. Plus there's a kids' play area, hammocks, and volleyball court. $–$$

Restaurante Reina del Mar Main road, almost at the end of the village 6030 3159. Boasting a pleasant view across the scrub, this friendly restaurant dishes up moderately priced, freshly prepared seafood, including Ngäbe clams, shrimps, ceviche and fish. $$

The Azuero Peninsula

CELEBRATIONS IN LOS SANTOS

The Azuero Peninsula

Mention the Azuero Peninsula, the box-shaped land mass that protrudes into the Pacific, and clichéd images abound of smiling women dancing in *polleras*, cowboys lassoing cattle and quaint village squares with whitewashed colonial churches. And the peninsula still sometimes delivers on such images: peasant farmers stride off to the fields at the crack of dawn, *sombrero* on head and machete slung across shoulder; some hamlets still contain the occasional tile-topped adobe houses, adorned with bougainvillea; and small villages celebrate their saint's day with bands of accordionists and fiddlers playing foot-tapping folk melodies. That said, the pace of development is increasing: trucks rattle along tarred rather than dirt roads; unprepossessing cement-block mini-supers with zinc roofs and garish shop signages unfortunately now dot the townscapes; and vast tracts of land are being gobbled up by mushrooming real-estate agents and mining companies, looking to force rapid and irrevocable social change. For the moment, though, cattle farming and agriculture still prevail in the interior while coastal communities continue to derive their livelihood from fishing – supplemented by tourism in places.

The peninsula, which covers a substantial 7616 square kilometres, is sometimes referred to as Eastern and Western Azuero; there is no connecting road across the dividing mountainous spine that runs down the western flank. The former comprises the vast bulk of the terrain and the small provinces of Herrera and Los Santos, clustered around their respective provincial capitals of **Chitré** and **Las Tablas**, which make good bases for exploring the region. The Western Azuero, on the other hand, is an oft-forgotten sliver of Veraguas province that trickles down the western seaboard. Dotted with small ranching and fishing communities – with a few developments sprouting up – it ends in one of Panama's least explored wilderness areas, Parque Nacional **Cerro Hoya**, with its sparkling waterfalls and several endemic species of animals and plants. That and the little-visited **Reserva Forestal El Montuoso** contrast acutely with the rest of the peninsula, which more than anywhere else in the country has been stripped of forest due to excessive logging and slash-and-burn agriculture. The desert-like **Parque Nacional Sarigua**, at the heart of the **Arco Seco** (Dry Arc) – Panama's driest, hottest region, which curves around the eastern shore of the Azuero – is a compelling reminder of the consequences of such practices. For a visitor, this means choosing your time to visit carefully; when fed by the rains (roughly May to mid-Dec), the verdant rolling pastures punctuated by villages ablaze with flowers and fruit trees create a picturesque landscape, but when the clouds dry up, they lose much of their natural beauty, becoming parched and dusty as temperatures soar.

Panama's Spanish **colonial heritage** is also at its most visible and vibrant in the Azuero, from the cattle ranching, bullfighting and Baroque churches to the elaborate costumes – the best examples of which are crafted on the peninsula – and distinctive music that enliven the numerous religious festivals. This has led to the region being fondly dubbed the *cuña* (cradle) of national culture and traditions by many Panamanians – a statement that takes little account of the cultural affinities or contributions of the country's non-*mestizo* populations and conveniently ignores the existence of much earlier cultures. Vestiges of **pre-Columbian** communities, the most ancient of which was an 11,000-year-old fishing village at Sarigua – currently the oldest known settlement on the isthmus –

BLACK IGUANA ON ISLA IGUANA

Highlights

❶ **Azueran artesanía** Catch artisans at work in village workshops, crafting exquisite ceramics, devil masks and straw hats, as well as embroidered *polleras* and *montunos*. See page 159

❷ **Festivals** The peninsula excels in fiestas: devil dances for Corpus Christi in La Villa; the nation's biggest folkloric jamboree, the Festival de la Mejorana, in Guararé; and the glitz of Carnaval at Las Tablas. See pages 163, 164 and 167

❸ **Isla Iguana** A wildlife retreat of black and green iguanas, chest-puffing frigatebirds and shoals of rainbow-coloured fish. See page 170

❹ **Playa Venao** A lovely swathe of beach best appreciated by surfing the waves or horseriding along the sands. See page 171

❺ **Isla de Cañas** Camp out among the turtles that arrive in their thousands to nest along glorious sand each year. See page 173

❻ **The Western Azuero** Explore the undulating hillsides and rugged coastline of the peninsula's western flank, whose near-deserted beaches offer spectacular sunsets. See page 176

HIGHLIGHTS ARE MARKED ON THE MAP ON PAGE 154

provide evidence both of an earlier history and of the conquistadors' brutal efficiency in wiping it out. Still today you'll notice the region's lack of indigenous inhabitants.

The Azuero's greatest appeal may lie in its many **festivals** (see box, page 155), but there's more to the peninsula than partying. For nature lovers, **Isla Iguana** and **Isla de Cañas** offer very different but fascinating wildlife experiences; the former is a major nesting site for the chest-puffing frigatebirds, boasting coral beaches and rich snorkelling, while the latter affords a rare opportunity to witness the mass breeding of olive ridley **turtles**. On the eastern seaboard, **La Ciénega de las Macanas** is an important **wetland**, teeming with birdlife; while deserted **beaches** – broad tan, chocolate and black stretches of sand – welcome top-notch **surfing** waves and world-class **sport fishing** takes place off the legendary "Tuna Coast". Although some enthusiasts still use understated **Pedasí** as a base, more are finding the tourist scene at **Playa Venao** to be a greater draw. In contrast, the more undulating, and slightly greener western flank of the peninsula offers a chance to get off the beaten track and explore a more rugged coastline, boasting more **surfing** hot spots and glorious **sunsets**.

Chitré and around

CHITRÉ, the provincial capital of Herrera province and the main urban centre in the Azuero Peninsula, makes an ideal base for exploring the surrounding area and for attending the

FESTIVALS IN THE AZUERO

The Azuero's **festivals** reel in thousands of Panamanians from all over the country, particularly for the major parties of **Carnaval** in Las Tablas and Chitré, **Corpus Christi** in La Villa de Los Santos and the **Festival de la Mejorana** in Guararé. Despite being championed as fine examples of the country's Spanish heritage, the festivities actually illustrate its hybridity: solemn religious ceremonies combine with pagan rituals and hedonistic excess; traditional folk groups are followed by DJs blasting out reggaeton, bachata and salsa; and stylized Andalusian-inspired dances such as the *tamborito* (Panama's national dance) and *punto* are imbued with African and pre-Columbian rhythms using drums, gourds and seed pods. More than five hundred festivals are held annually in the region, so you could spend a whole year here in a permanent alcoholic haze drifting from one celebration to the next, soaking up (literally and metaphorically) the legendary Azueran hospitality.

MAIN EVENTS

Jan 6 Fiesta de los Reyes Magos and Encuentro del Canajagua, Macaracas.
Jan (second Sat) Desfile de las Mil Polleras, Las Tablas (see box, page 167).
Late Jan (date varies) Feria de San Sebastián, Ocú (see box, page 161).
Feb (date varies) The country's biggest Carnaval celebration, Las Tablas (see box, page 167).
March/April (date varies) Semana Santa, celebrated most colourfully in La Villa de Los Santos, Pesé and Guararé.
Late April Feria Internacional de Azuero, La Villa de Los Santos.
late May/June (date varies) Festival de Corpus Christi, La Villa de Los Santos (see box, page 163).
June 24 Patronales de San Juan, Chitré.
July (third week) Festival de La Santa Librada and Festival de la Pollera, Las Tablas (see box, page 167).
Aug (second week) Festival del Manito, Ocú (see box, page 161).
Late Sept Festival de la Mejorana, Guararé (see box, page 164).
Nov 10 The "First Cry for Independence", La Villa de Los Santos.

region's numerous festivals. A laidback commercial town with an attractive colonial centre, Chitré was founded in 1848, though indications are that conquistadors had been there since the mid-1500s. Life centres on the bustling streets around **Calle Manuel María Correa** (where you'll find the interesting regional **museum**) and the well-manicured **Parque Unión** with its splendid **cathedral**, notable for its wooden interior. The compact colonial quarter of Chitré can easily be explored in a couple of hours, leaving time to make an afternoon excursion to the coast. Nature lovers will also be drawn to the nearby mud flats of **Playa El Agallito** and the wetlands of **Cenegón del Mangle** and **La Ciénega de las Macanas**, which attract prolific birdlife, particularly migratory waders. Of more general interest is the picturesque village of **Parita**, possessing a delightful church and, further afield, the surreal desert-like **Parque Nacional Sarigua**. Some of these destinations are not easily accessible without your own transport, especially in the rainy season.

Catedral de San Juan Bautista

Parque Unión • Daily 6am–8pm • Free

The imposing **Catedral de San Juan Bautista**, built between 1896 and 1910, underwent a major restoration in the late 1980s, which took the unusual step of exposing some of the exterior stone walls to provide a striking contrast with the snow-white facade and bell towers. The restrained, polished wooden interior also makes a refreshing change from the ornate decor in many Catholic churches, especially the gilded mahogany altar, which is complemented by bright stained-glass windows.

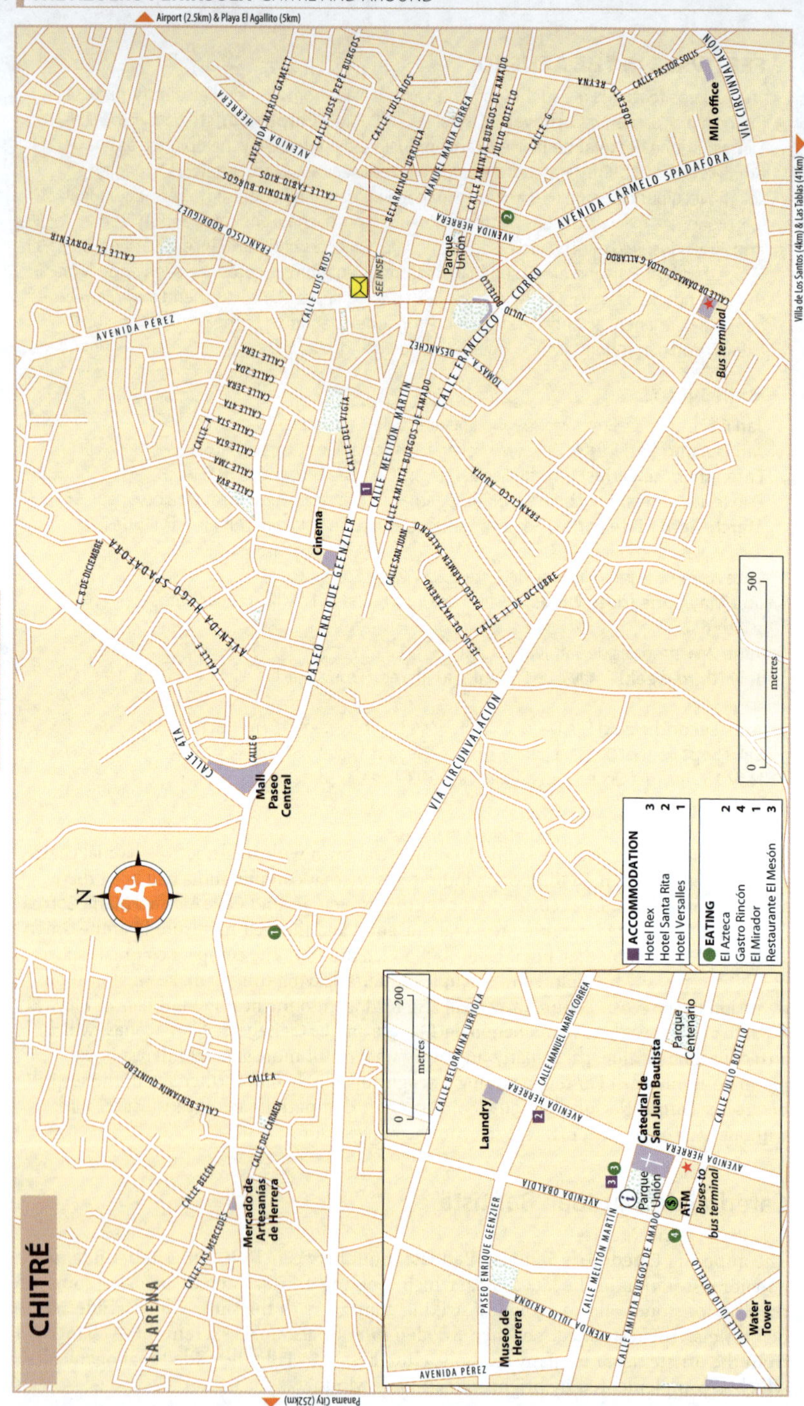

CHITRÉ
Airport (2.5km) & Playa El Agallito (5km)
Villa de Los Santos (4km) & Las Tablas (41km)
Panama City (252km)
ACCOMMODATION
Hotel Rex 3
Hotel Santa Rita 2
Hotel Versalles 1
EATING
El Azteca 2
Gastro Rincón 4
El Mirador 1
Restaurante El Mesón 3
0 500 metres
0 200 metres
N
LA ARENA
Mall Paseo Central
Cinema
Bus terminal
MIA office
Mercado de Artesanías de Herrera
Parque Unión
SEE INSET
Catedral de San Juan Bautista
Parque Centenario
Laundry
ATM
Buses to bus terminal
Museo de Herrera
Water Tower
AVENIDA PÉREZ
PASEO ENRIQUE GEENZIER
VIA CIRCUNVALACIÓN
AVENIDA HUGO SPADAFORA
AVENIDA CARMELO SPADAFORA
CALLE FRANCISCO CORRO
CALLE MELITÓN MARTÍN
CALLE AMINTA BURGOS DE AMADO
AVENIDA HERRERA
AVENIDA OBALDÍA
AVENIDA JULIO ARIONA
CALLE JULIO BOTELLO
CALLE BELORMINA URRIOLA
CALLE MANUEL MARÍA CORREA
CALLE LUIS RÍOS
CALLE JOSE PEPE BURGOS
AVENIDA MARIO GAMETT
CALLE FABIO RÍOS
ANTONIO BURGOS
FRANCISCO RODRÍGUEZ
CALLE EL PORVENIR
CALLE DEL VIGÍA
CALLE SAN JUAN
CALLE 11 DE OCTUBRE
FRANCISCO AUDIA
TOMAS A DESANCHEZ
CALLE DR DAMASO ULLOA G ALLARDO
CALLE PASTOR SOLIS
ROBERTO REYNA
CALLE G
CALLE 4TA
CALLE 6
CALLE A
C. 8 DE DICIEMBRE
CALLE BENJAMÍN QUINTERO
CALLE DEL CARMEN
CALLE BELÉN
CALLE LAS MERCEDES

Parque Unión and around

The cathedral is flanked by the formal gardens of **Parque Unión**. Neatly clipped flowerbeds and swaying palm trees around a stately bandstand provide the backdrop for a melding of modernity and tradition: young, suited executives hold forth on their mobile phones while elderly *campesinos* in *montunos* and *sombreros de junco* – the traditional embroidered shirts and workday straw hats – discuss the local news. A one-block stroll east brings you to **Parque Centenario**, a more low-key affair, dominated by a majestic guachapalí tree, and surrounded by squat red-tiled houses with wrought-iron grillwork.

Museo de Herrera

Parque Bandera, C Manuel María Correa • Mon–Sat 8am–4pm • Charge

Though quite modest (with some captions in English), the **Museo de Herrera**, in an elegant converted colonial mansion and former post office, is probably the best museum outside Panama City. Downstairs focuses on the pre-Columbian era: a couple of fine ceremonial **metates** stand out, as well as the impressive collection of **ceramics**. A reproduction **burial chamber** shows a life-size model *cacique* decked out in his gold arm- and leg bands, while replicas of gold **huacas** from the anthropological museum in Panama City line the walls. Upstairs, fast-forward several hundred years to the colonial and post-colonial periods, with displays of **traditional musical instruments** and **costumes**, including elaborate *polleras* and devil outfits, and various **tools** from rural life. Back downstairs, don't miss the pouch made from a bull's scrotum used to carry staples for mending fences. The museum also offers Spanish-language **cultural tours** of the area.

4

ARRIVAL AND DEPARTURE — CHITRÉ

By bus Chitré's bus terminal (T 996 6426) is 1km south of the town centre on the bypass, Vía Circunvalación. Frequent minibuses shuttle to Parque Unión, where you can catch the return bus to the terminal. Taxis from the bus terminal cost around $2 to most places in town. Getting to Chitré from Panama City involves taking a bus from Albrook bus terminal (6am–7pm; hourly; 3hr 30min). The last bus bound back to the capital leaves at 4.45pm.

Destinations Aguadulce (4am–6pm; every 20min; 1hr); La Arena (6am–9pm; every 10–15min; 10min); La Villa de Los Santos (6am–9.30pm, with a last bus at 10.30pm; every 10–15min; 15min); Las Minas (6am–6pm; every 30min; 45min); Las Tablas – change for Pedasí and Tonosí (6am–9.30pm; every 20min; 40min); Macaracas (6am–6pm; every 30–45min; 1hr); Ocú (6.30am–7pm; every 30min; 1hr); Panama City (2.30am, 4.30am, 6.30am, then hourly 8am–4.45pm; 3hr 30min); Pesé (6.30am–6.30pm; every 15–20min; 30min); Playa El Agallito (6am–6pm; every 30min; 20min); Santiago – change for David (5am–6.30pm; every 30min; 1hr 10min).

By plane Air Panama (W airpanama.com) offers daily flights to Chitré from Panama City's Albrook Airport (30min).

By car It might be worth renting a car for a couple of days, especially to get to the less accessible protected areas or to explore the area further inland. Avis (T 996 0233, W avis.com/en/locations/pa/chitre), Hertz (T 996 6219, W panamahertz.com), Sixt (T 918 0933, W sixt.com/car-rental/panama/chitre) and Thrifty (T 996 9565, W panamathrifty.com), for example, all have offices in central Chitré. Alternatively, hire a taxi driver for the day; rates are usually $15/hr, but around $80–100 for the whole day. The tourist office or your lodgings can recommend a driver; however, they are unlikely to speak English.

INFORMATION AND TOURS

Tourist information There is an ATP kiosk in the northwestern corner of Parque Unión (Mon–Fri 8am–4pm; T 974 4532, W atp.gob.pa).

MIA office The regional MIA office is on C Pastor Solis, just north of Vía Circunvalación on the southeastern side of town (Mon–Fri 8am–4pm; T 913 0793); get in touch for permission to stay in La Reserva Forestal El Montuoso (see page 161) or for information on Parque Nacional Sarigua (see page 159).

ACCOMMODATION — SEE MAP PAGE 156

Hotel Rex Parque Unión, C Melitón Martín W hotelrexchitre.com. You're paying for the prime location on the plaza so it's worth splashing out for the French windows, wooden panelling and a view over the park. Slightly faded furnishings and brick walls for most rooms, though the comfy beds make it a reasonable option if you're not too fussy. Upstairs terrace with views across the park. $$

Hotel Santa Rita C Manuel María Correa, at Av Herrera

996 4610. Offering good value in a prime location, this ageing but well-maintained hotel has dark, simple en-suite rooms (fan or a/c, cable TV, good bed and hot water) off long corridors. Mattresses are variable so check out several rooms. Weekdays are much cheaper. Wi-fi only at reception. $$

Hotel Versalles Paseo Enrique Geenzier hotelversalles.com. Don't delude yourself with visions of regal French splendour; that said, rooms in this functional business hotel on the main approach road are comfortable and well equipped (a/c, phone, cable TV, room service and hot water), if lacking in character. Small pool and bar-restaurant. $$–$$$

EATING

SEE MAP PAGE 156

★ **El Azteca** Av Centenario at C Pablo Ríos B facebook.com/elaztecaazuero. The liveliest place in town transports you to Mexico on its cosy back patio – the hats, music videos, colourful tablecloths, plus the bar is awash with tequila and Mexican beer. Tuck into tasty tacos or kebabs, with guacamole and refried beans as sides, or share mounds of nachos over cocktails. The gargantuan Festín Azteca is a substantial treat for two: soup followed by a large mixed platter. $$–$$$

Gastro Rincón Corner of Av Obladía and C Aminta Burgos 978 8289. A pleasant restaurant mercifully devoid of soap operas on TV, serving nicely presented fish and seafood – red snapper, *corvina*, shrimps – with a variety of sauces and a choice of a choice of starchy sides. It's a good-value mid-priced place with better than average service. $$

El Mirador Up the hill off the Carretera Nacional between Chitré and La Arena instagram.com/restauranteelmiradorchitre. Atmospheric open-air hilltop spot (well signposted) to enjoy a cheap beer while admiring the sunset or the twinkling night lights of Chitré. Specializes in whole fried fish and seafood. $$

Restaurante El Mesón Downstairs at Hotel Rex, Parque Unión 996 2408. Eschew the a/c dining room for the open-air café overlooking the park – great for people-watching. In the morning it serves inexpensive breakfasts and well-prepared snacks (toasted sandwiches, burritos). Lunch and dinner items include the usual Panamanian and international staples and Spanish specialities such as paella, chorizo and tongue. Don't miss the weekday *menú ejecutivo*. $$

4

Parita

11km northwest of Chitré, a few hundred metres off the Carretera Nacional; take any bus bound for Santiago or Aguadulce from Chitré (4.30am, 5.30am, 6am–8pm; every 30min; 15min)

Named after an indigenous leader famed for his resistance to the Spanish conquest, **PARITA** is one of the oldest – founded in 1556 – best-preserved and most picturesque villages on the peninsula. That said, it's not immune to bland modern constructions. Particularly attractive is the sparkling white eighteenth-century **Iglesia Santo Domingo de Guzmán**, with its attractive clay-tiled roof; peek inside and you'll see some ornately carved wooden altarpieces and an elaborate pulpit. Surrounding the plaza, terraces of pastel-coloured traditional adobe (*quincha*) cottages with tiled roofs take you back in time, though a line of telegraph poles remind you that the village was not totally bypassed by the twentieth century. The days leading up to August 8, the anniversary of the village's foundation, mark a big **fiesta** in Parita.

La Casa del Folklore

C 3 de Noviembre at C2, 50m south of the church • Hours • Free; donations appreciated

A labour of love curated by retired schoolteacher Rafael Medina, the **Casa del Folklore** is stuffed full of cultural artefacts, especially **masks** and costumes from the area's Corpus Christi celebrations (see box, page 163) and historical *polleras* from around the country – including one from 1905.

Playa El Agallito

5km northeast of Chitré • Buses run from Chitré, via Av Herrera (6am–6pm; every 30min; 15–20min); inexpensive taxis are also available

Despite the continued clearing of mangroves to make way for shrimp farms, the silty mud and salt flats of **Playa El Agallito** still provide sustenance for thousands of **shore**

MASK-MAKERS

Ghoulish **devil masks**, which form the centrepiece of Corpus Christi celebrations (see box, page 163) across the country and feature in other festivals throughout the year, make great souvenirs. They are made predominantly from papier-mâché coated onto a greased clay or earthen mould; their horns, wooden teeth and eyes – usually ping-pong balls or marbles – are added later. They're available in various craft centres and agricultural fairs, and you can also visit some of the mask-makers in their workshops. Expect to pay around $10–15 for a small mask and up to $150 for a larger and more elaborate one. The most renowned artist, with almost fifty years' experience, who makes both *diablicos sucios* and *limpios* (see box, page 163), is **Darío López** (instagram.com/artesaniasdariolopez), who is now passing on his skills to his children and grandchildren; his hard-to-miss home-based workshop is on the Carretera Nacional, just north of **Parita**, beyond the petrol station, on the eastern side of the road. Another well-known artisan is **José González** (instagram.com/mascarasjoseoficial) taxi drivers should be able to find his workshop in **Llano Bonito**, on the outskirts of Chitré, or ask at the Museo de Hererra for directions (see page 157).

birds and **waders**, many migratory, who return to the same spot to feed each year. It's one of the country's top spots for sighting the splendid roseate spoonbill as well as American oystercatchers and wood storks, amid a potpourri of terns, egrets, herons and sandpipers. The best time to visit – bring the binoculars – is at high tide, when birds feed close to shore.

4

Parque Nacional Sarigua

A little further up the coast from Playa El Agallito, and 25km north of Chitré, the eighty-square-kilometre **Parque Nacional Sarigua** is squeezed between ríos Santa María and Parita on land, and stretches out into the Bahía de Parita. **Birdlife** is restricted to a coastal sliver of threatened mangrove; further inland lie vast salt flats and tracts of dry forest, and bleak saline-streaked gullies dotted with cactus, acacia and snowy blobs of wild cotton. Less a tourist attraction, as it is often heralded, than a cautionary tale, this desert-like wasteland is testament to the devastating consequences of a century of slash-and-burn agriculture and overgrazing. Covered with a layer of surreal bronze-coloured dust and home to a vast solar farm, it is the country's hottest and driest area.

The silver lining in this sad tale of environmental degradation is that the resulting erosion helped uncover important **archeological remains**, including evidence of an 11,000-year-old fishing village, the oldest known settlement on the isthmus, and more recent traces (between fifteen hundred and five thousand years ago) of an ancient farming community. When walking around the park it's easy to stumble on shards of ancient ceramics or discarded shells, just as the sparse vegetation makes it easier to spot boas curled around parched branches, armadillos digging in the undergrowth or lizards and iguanas sunning themselves. The landscape is best appreciated from the top of the **mirador** by the ranger station, from where you can also make out distant shrimp farms. Rangers offer guided walks for a tip, but note that the park is rather undeveloped, with only a couple of short trails.

ARRIVAL AND INFORMATION — PARQUE NACIONAL SARIGUA

Park entrance and fees The park entrance is signposted off the Carretera Nacional just north of Parita (daily 8am–4pm). Entrance fees are payable online in advance (see page 42).

By bus and taxi Either catch a bus to Parita and pick up a taxi there, or take a taxi from Chitré.

By car The turn-off is well signposted off the Carretera Nacional.

La Ciénaga de las Macanas

4km east of El Rincón, which is 32km northwest of Chitré • Daily 8.30am–3.30pm • Charge • Take a bus to El Rincón from Chitré; you can then walk the 4km to the marsh (right at the church, then right at the fork); the local environmental organization GEMA (T 976 1040 or Hector Escudero T 6021 4919) offers guiding services (in Spanish) and boat trips, and can arrange transport for you

Set on Río Santa María's floodplains, **La Ciénaga de las Macanas** is the region's largest freshwater wetland area. It attracts an abundance of resident and migratory **birdlife** – over 120 species have been recorded. In addition to waders and ducks, you might see Brahman cattle chomping through the greenery; they help regulate the invasive water hyacinth, though conservationists are keen to reduce the number of grazing livestock.

Amenities are in desperate need of restoration though at the time of writing plans were afoot to renovate the facilities. Until that time, there's a short interpretive path and a rickety jetty protruding over the water. If you fancy **boating** on the water to get closer to wildlife or throw a fishing line, contact one of the ecotourism groups in the nearby village of **El Rincón** (de Santa María). Alternatively, get in touch with René Chang Marin (T 6434 4727, E renechangmarin@gmail.com), who owns Finca Agroturística Las Macanas, which abuts the reserve, and has constructed a slightly raised viewing platform across the wetland.

The central peninsula

4

The best way to get a feel for rural life in the Azuero is to head west of the Carretera Nacional into the **agricultural heartland** of the peninsula. Here you pass rolling hills of pastureland sprinkled with giant hardwoods, fields of sugar cane and flower-filled towns and villages where the unhurried pace of life is infectious. There is precious little accommodation in these places, but the main population centres, such as **Ocú** and **Pesé**, are well connected by public transport on decent roads and two or three can easily be combined into a day-trip.

Pesé

One of the prettiest towns within reach of Chitré, lying 24km southeast and surrounded by a carpet of sugar cane, **PESÉ** is known for its liquor and its Good Friday re-enactment of the Passion of Christ. The ironic juxtaposition of faith and booze is evident the moment you set eyes on the church, which looks disapprovingly across the road at the Varela Hermanos **distillery**.

Varela Hermanos distillery

Hacienda San Isidro • Tours in English or Spanish, including rum tasting and lunch • T 974 9401 or 6550 4498, E reservaciones@varelahermanos.com

Founded in 1908 by Spanish émigré José Varela – ancestor of Panama's recent president Juan Carlos Varela – as a sugar mill and refinery, **Varela Hermanos** became a **distillery** in 1936 and has never looked back. Today it supplies ninety percent of Panama's spirits, including the country's top **rum**, Ron Abuelo, and the national knockout tipple, seco (35 percent). A million cases of spirit a year are produced here, much of which ends up down the throats of revellers at the Azuero's many celebrations, including the **Festival de la Caña de Azúcar** held in Pesé at the end of March to mark the end of the harvest.

ARRIVAL AND DEPARTURE — PESÉ

Regular **buses** leave Chitré bus terminal for Pesé (6.30am–7pm; every 30min; 30min).

EATING

Restaurante Marithel C José Varela Blanco, 50m from the church T 6648 9901. This friendly restaurant, with a shady patio draped with foliage and hibiscus flowers, serves a decent beef stew and the like for a few dollars. $–$$

Ocú

Twenty kilometres west of Pesé, the larger village of **OCÚ** makes up for its lack of quaint charm with its **festivals** (see box, page 161) and its **hat-making** – above all the distinctive white sombrero Ocueño, with a thin black trim, which is still produced in home-based **workshops**. Try **Artesanías Oceuñas** (Mon–Sat 8am–6pm, Sun 10am–3.30pm; ☎6458 4529), a women's cooperative in the centre of town, on Plaza Sebastian Ocú, which also produces fine *polleras*, *montunos* and other embroidered items.

ARRIVAL AND DEPARTURE — OCÚ

By bus Buses leave Chitré bus terminal for Ocú via Pesé (6.30am–7pm; every 30min; 1hr) with the last bus back to Chitré at 7pm. Buses from Santiago terminal also run to Ocú (6am–6pm; every 20min; 1hr); the last return bus is at 6pm.

ACCOMMODATION AND EATING

Hotel Casa Pueblo 200m west of the church ☎6615 6791. The best of the limited options. Simple air-conditioned en-suite rooms lined along a shady shared patio. Each has two beds and a TV. There's a pool (the main plus) and a children's playground but the whole place seems to have been put together in a hurry. Overpriced, but rates negotiable. $$

El Punto Ocueño Main plaza opposite the church ⓦinstagram.com/restaurante_punto_ocueno. Busy *cafetería* dishing up an inexpensive *menú del día* or *cena* for a few dollars or plates of roast chicken or chow mein for a little more. $–$$

Las Minas, Los Pozos and Macaracas

Though Pesé and Ocú are the more common day-trip destinations in the central peninsula, it is a pleasant drive, by car, to cover the further 30km through **LAS MINAS** and **LOS POZOS** before returning to Chitré or continuing southeast to **MACARACAS** – by bus you'd probably need to return to Chitré and take another bus back out into the countryside. There's nothing particular to see or do in any of these places, except chill out and watch rural life unfold. The party most likely to attract outsiders occurs in Macaracas; celebrated in the church plaza every January 6 for almost two hundred years, the **Fiesta de los Reyes Magos** (Three Wise Men) features a two-hour dramatization of the Adoration of the Magi.

ARRIVAL AND DEPARTURE — LAS MINAS, LOS POZOS AND MACARACAS

By bus Buses leave Chitré for Las Minas (6am–6pm; every 30min; 1hr); Los Pozos, via Pesé (6am–7.25pm; every 25min; 40min) and Macaracas (6am–7pm; hourly; 40min) en route to Tonosí (1hr 30min).

Reserva Forestal El Montuoso

Up the valley from Las Minas, the seriously denuded peaks of the optimistically named **RESERVA FORESTAL EL MONTUOSO** pale in comparison with the richly forested mountain ranges in Chiriquí, Bocas or the Darién, so if you're heading for one of those

OCÚ'S FESTIVALS

The **Festival del Manito** (second week of Aug) is Ocú's premier event. Apart from the usual parades, there are two stand-out elements: the **tamarind duel** (*duelo del tamarindo*) and the **peasant wedding** (*matrimonio campesino*). The latter is a wonderful sight: following a mock church wedding, the bride, decked out in an all-white *pollera*, is paraded on horseback through the streets while the groom holds an umbrella above her head to protect her from the sun (or rain). In contrast, the tamarind duel harks back to the bygone days of testosterone-fuelled fights to the death over women, family honour or simply from overdoing the liquor; such fights are re-enacted with swords and sabres in the centre of the plaza. The town's other five-day extravaganza, **La Feria de San Sebastián** (late Jan), is an agricultural fair honouring the patron saint.

locations, El Montuoso can easily be skipped. But if you're lingering in the Azuero and aching to get into the hills, this is the best place to come, until the rugged wilderness of Parque Nacional Cerro Hoya (see page 175) becomes more accessible.

The 120-square-kilometre reserve, dubbed the "*pulmón*" ("lung") of Herrera, was created in 1977 to safeguard the four rivers that rise in the mountainous region and to protect the rapidly vanishing tracts of forest being eaten away by illegal farming and timber extraction. In response, several reforestation projects have been initiated. Though only twenty percent of the reserve is now forested, what remains is concentrated around the reserve's highest point, Cerro Alto Higo (953m). Steep-sided mountains cleaved by river-eroded ravines harbour plenty of wildlife, such as red brocket and white-tailed deer, howler monkeys, white-faced capuchins and collared peccaries. This is also one of the easiest places to spot the endemic brown-backed dove while other specialities include violet sabrewings and blue-throated goldentails – both hummingbirds – and the ever-acrobatic orange-collared manakin.

Exploring the reserve

The park office is set in a lovely orchard, where a short, pretty **trail** crisscrosses the nascent Río La Villa up to a cascading pool. One of the main trails, **Sendero Alto Higo**, leads up the mountain of the same name, heading off to the left after Chepo, at a place known as the Caras Pintadas (Painted Faces), an imaginative reference to the petroglyph near the start of the path, where rare sundews are in evidence in winter. A moderately strenuous hike of just over an hour brings you out at a peak by a radio mast, which offers a tantalizing restricted view – thanks to some unfortunately located trees – towards the Golfo de Montijo.

ARRIVAL AND ACCOMMODATION — RESERVA FORESTAL EL MONTUOSO

Park entrance and fees The entrance (daily 8am–4pm) is at Tres Puntas, 4km before the village of Chepo. Remember to pay the park fees online in advance (see page 42).

By bus Buses run from Chitré bus terminal to Las Minas (6am–6pm; every 30min; 1hr) – take one of the infrequent *chivas* bound for Chepo, alighting at Tres Puntas (30min).

MIA bunkhouse 5min walk from the road at Tres Puntas. The reserve bunkhouse has two comfortable dorms, a shared kitchen and a camping area. You'll need to stock up with food before you reach the limited shopping options of Las Minas; note that alcohol is prohibited in the reserve. Camping $/person, dorms $

The road to Las Tablas

Just south of Chitré, the Carretera Nacional crosses the Río La Villa, the peninsula's longest river, which marks the provincial boundary between Herrera and Los Santos, and continues southeast, running parallel to the coast. After skirting the diminutive yet historically important town of **La Villa de Los Santos**, whose small museum and impressive church interior merit a detour, the road bypasses tiny **Guararé**, host to the country's largest folkloric festival, before arriving in the provincial capital, **Las Tablas**, about halfway down the peninsula.

La Villa de Los Santos

LA VILLA DE LOS SANTOS is famous for the vibrant costume-clad celebrations of **Corpus Christi**, a historic rebellion against Spanish colonial rule, and the Feria Internacional de Azuero, the peninsula's annual ten-day agricultural jamboree in April. If you arrive outside party time, though, it's easy to be disappointed. "Los Santos", or "La Villa" as the town is usually called, is much smaller and quieter than neighbouring Chitré, and not as spruced up or as vibrant as Las Tablas.

You'll need little more than an hour to check out La Villa's two main attractions, the **church** and **museum**, both on the **central plaza**. The plaza is named after the great Latin

American liberator **Simón Bolívar**, to whom the town's influential citizens addressed a letter on November 10, 1821, asking to join his revolutionary movement against Spain. This unilateral declaration, called the *Primer Grito de la Independencia* (**First Cry for Independence**), started the domino effect that led to national independence from Spain eighteen days later; it is celebrated annually with the customary flag-waving parades of marching bands, traditional folk costumes, speeches and fireworks.

Museo de la Nacionalidad

North side of Parque Simón Bolívar • Tues–Sun 8am–4pm • Charge • ☎ 966 8192

The room in which the townspeople's famous letter to Simón Bolívar was penned, complete with original furniture, forms part of the beautifully restored – and moderately interesting – **Museo de la Nacionalidad**. Much of the museum, which was formerly a school and a prison (though not at the same time), overflows with details (in Spanish) of leading figures in the independence movement though there is a room dedicated to the area's pre-Columbian heritage.

Iglesia San Atanasio

Northeastern side of Parque Simón Bolívar • Daily 8am–6pm • Free

LA VILLA'S FESTIVAL DE CORPUS CHRISTI

By far the most fascinating and famous of La Villa's celebrations is the **Festival de Corpus Christi**, a heady mix of **Christian** and **pagan** imagery in an exciting narrative of dance, drama and dialogue. It features a cast of larger-than-life characters and dancers decked out in extravagant costumes, interwoven with a series of religious ceremonies. Corpus Christi became an important tool in Spanish colonization across Latin America, as the invaders attempted to woo the indigenous population to the Christian faith by incorporating elements of their traditions and rituals into the ecclesiastical ceremonies. Though there is plenty of local variation, the basic good-versus-evil plot is the same.

The action starts on the Saturday before Corpus Christi when church bells at noon bring hordes of *diablicos sucios* (dirty devils) rampaging onto the streets. Clad in crimson-and-black-striped jumpsuits, wearing ferocious devil masks with flame-coloured headdresses and letting off firecrackers at will, they terrify all and sundry to the beat of drums and whistles. Fast forward to Wednesday, several Masses later, when at 11.30am on the Eve of Corpus Christi, the Diabla or Diablesa (though as with all roles, performed by a male) also races around the town announcing the arrival of her husband, the Diablo Mayor, who convenes with three other devils in the central plaza. Joking and knocking back the booze, they carve up the globe in a bid for world domination.

Before dawn on Corpus Christi, Santeños roam around town, on foot and on horseback, in search of the Torito Santeño – a man in a bull's costume – who is causing havoc, but is eventually rounded up in the **Danza del Torito** as the party proceeds through the streets to a large communal breakfast. The centrepiece of the drama unfolds mid-morning before the church, on a magnificent carpet of petals, as the Archangel Michael and the *diablicos limpios* (clean devils), distinguishable from the bad guys by their white sleeves and a rainbow of handkerchiefs attached to the waist, vanquish the villains in the Danza del Gran Diablo or Diablicos Limpios before allowing them in to the service. All the dance troupes – including an assortment of dwarves, roosters, vultures, Mexican conquistadors and escaped African slaves – attend the Mass, which then relocates outside as Holy Communion is offered to the townsfolk before the serious partying begins.

Further merrymaking takes place a week later, culminating in Saturday's **Día del Turismo**, which provides a highlights show on stage in the plaza, and Sunday's **Día de la Mujer**, offering Santeñas, whom tradition has prohibited from participating thus far, the chance to dust off their *polleras* and join in the fun.

FESTIVAL DE LA MEJORANA

Panama's largest and best folk festival is Guararé's **Festival de la Mejorana** (ⓦfestivalnacionaldelamejorana.com), named after Panama's five-stringed guitar, the *mejoranera*. The five-day jamboree, which coincides with the *patronales* for the Virgen de la Mercedes in late September, is for lovers of Hispanic traditions; there's not a techno-beat in earshot and although, just as at most Panamanian festivals, the booze flows, it's a less hedonistic affair than many. The plaza resounds with folk music day and night, with dancers and musicians from around the country converging to entertain and compete. Adults and children vie for medals in playing violin, accordion or *mejoranera*, and drumming, singing or dancing. There are even competitions for traditional work clothes – a kind of beauty pageant for both men and women. Bullfights are also on the agenda, usually dominated by seco-sodden guys staggering around a muddy field waving a filthy rag at a tired bull, cheered on by supporters – a far cry from the celebrity matadors of Spain. The festival highlight on Sunday morning is the **Gran Desfile de Carretas**, when superbly decorated ox-carts parade through the town, accompanied by *tunas* (African-inspired bands of call-and-response singers and drummers).

Inevitably all eyes are on the float carrying the **Reina del Festival de la Mejorana**, decked out in her *pollera de gala* finery and wearing a gold crown. It's an incredibly prestigious position, a national honour that lasts beyond the queen's year-long reign. Families are prepared to shell out $15,000 for the privilege, and that's just for starters. For decades, if there was more than one candidate at the pre-fiesta deadline, a run-off was held over three rounds (*escrutinios*) lasting several months, during which the candidates' families had to outdo each other in fundraising – a prospect that had the organizing committee rubbing its hands in glee, since it means more cash for the festival coffers. The belle with the most financial backing at the end got to wear the crown; her rivals had to settle for being princesses. When the promised sum offered to secure festival glory reached almost $113,000, in 2018, it was decided the rules should change. Now, theoretically, any woman can apply for the post provided they can pay a deposit of $2,000 and they have the requisite historical knowledge. Once the candidates have passed this initial screening, it's a case of submitting a bid in a sealed envelope and the highest bid and winner is revealed when the envelopes are opened at a public event ("and the Oscar goes to…"). The queen-elect (or her family) must then pay the promised sum in instalments.

Some of the money the *reina* gets to spend on her regalia – the elaborately embroidered *polleras de gala* cost several thousand dollars – and on other necessities such as dancing lessons and float decoration.

The central attraction in the main plaza is the gleaming white **Iglesia San Atanasio**, which contains a series of magnificent carved altars – a profusion of spiralling columns adorned with vine leaves, winged cherubs and flowers, all dripping with gold. Most splendid of all is the main altar, framed by an even more opulent archway that predates the completion of the church. Though the first stones were laid some time between 1556 and 1559, the edifice was not completed until 1782. Note also the painted wooden tracery above the nave and the life-size entombed Christ figure in the glass sepulchre, which is paraded around the streets on Good Friday in a candlelit procession. The church is also the focal point for the town's famous **Festival de Corpus Christi** (see box, page 163). Although it is celebrated throughout Panama, the festivities in La Villa stand head and shoulders above the rest.

Parque Rufina Alfaro

Av 10 de Noviembre, three blocks southeast of Parque Simón Bolívar

At the southeastern end of town, **Parque Rufina Alfaro** celebrates the possibly apocryphal local heroine of the independence movement, **Rufina Alfaro**. A monument to the plucky Santeña has her seemingly emerging from a swamp. The story goes that she exploited the local Spanish commander's affections and secured crucial intelligence about when to attack the army barracks, and that she then headed the march there that cemented the bloodless coup.

ARRIVAL AND DEPARTURE — LA VILLA DE LOS SANTOS

By bus Local buses shuttle between Chitré and La Villa (6am–9.30pm; every 10–15min; 15min) and can drop you off at Parque Simón Bolívar. Direct buses leave Panama City for La Villa (6am–7pm; hourly; 3hr 30min); for the return to Panama City, or other major destinations, board a Chitré-bound minibus and change there.

ACCOMMODATION AND EATING

Hotel La Villa A few hundred metres off the Carretera Nacional ⓦ hotellavillapanama.com. The more charming of the town's two hotels – though service can be indifferent – is a low-key place with overpriced and rather characterless tiled rooms with firm beds, ranging from doubles with various sized beds to suites. The garden setting is the main plus, with a pool and moderately priced restaurant. $$

Rancho Kevin Hotel Just south of the bus terminal ⓦ instagram.com/hotelkevinlavilla. Set back from the main road, offering compact, clean, functional rooms set round a grassy area, with a shared hammock-strewn porch. Filling *comida criolla* is served at the adjacent restaurant. $$

Restaurante Los Cuates Main road, close to the fairgrounds ⓦ instagram.com/hotelkevinlavilla. Texmex joint under a breezy *rancho* sells tacos, burritos and the like plus a *menú ejecutivo* on weekday lunchtimes and well-priced barbecued chicken and yuca. It's a good place for a drink, too. $$

Guararé

The somnolent town of **GUARARÉ**, 6km north of La Tablas, springs to life once a year when enthusiastic crowds arrive in droves to enjoy the famous **Festival de la Mejorana** (see box, page 164). That aside, Guararé's other claim to fame is as the birthplace of Panama's greatest sporting legend and one of the all-time greats of world boxing, **Roberto Durán**, better known as Manos de Piedra ("Hands of Stone").

4

Casa Museo Manuel Fernando Zárate

Five blocks north of the main square • Tues–Sun 8.30am–3.30pm • Free • ⓣ 6808 0247

The Festival de la Mejorana, first held in 1949, was the brainchild of a local teacher, Manuel Zárate, whose nostalgia for Panama while studying abroad made him realize the need to promote and preserve the country's cultural traditions. The **Casa Museo Manuel Fernando Zárate** chronicles Zárate's life and the festival's history. Walls are plastered with photos, including portraits of previous *reinas*, some antique *polleras* and menacing devil costumes.

ARRIVAL AND ACCOMMODATION — GUARARÉ

By bus Any Chitré–Las Tablas bus (see page 167) can drop you off on the Carretera Nacional at Guararé.

Bienvenidos a Guararé Main road and Paseo Ricardo Fábrega. Welcoming hosts providing excellent value for money. Tidy, clean, basic rooms with comfortable beds, modern bathrooms and outdoor patio areas, but you'll have to head out for breakfast. Book through Booking.com $$

Las Tablas

Famed for hosting Panama's wildest **Carnaval** (see box, page 167), the provincial capital of **LAS TABLAS** moves at a much more sedate pace for the rest of the year. In comparison with neighbouring Chitré, Las Tablas is a modest town, but it possesses a sprinkling of tourist amenities, as well as an attractive **church** and a small **museum** dedicated to Belisario Porras, three-time president and Las Tablas's most famous citizen. Besides these, the only other building of note is the **Escuela Presidente Porras**, with a smart maroon-and-cream exterior, and a distinctive clock tower and majestic portal. Built in 1924, this immaculately kept state school possesses high ceilings, large windows and beautiful louvred shutters.

Most business in Las Tablas is conducted along the two main streets, Avenida 8 de Noviembre (also Av Carlos López) and Avenida Belisario Porras, which converge in the undistinguished main plaza, Parque Belisario Porras. The vortex of the maelstrom that is Carnaval, at any other time **Parque Porras** is a tranquil spot to enjoy a snow-cone or ice cream. Midweek evenings are quiet unless there's a baseball match on at the **Estadio Olmedo Solé** (Jan–May; fedebeis.com) – a highly entertaining party atmosphere to be savoured even if you don't know a home plate from a dinner plate.

At weekends, many Tableños head for the nearest beach at **Playa El Uverito**, a broad belt of chocolate-covered sand 10km east of town, and reachable by bus; here families tuck into platefuls of **fresh fish** at the beachside restaurants, or picnic on the sand.

Brief history

Spanish nobles apparently founded the town in 1671; having fled Panamá Viejo after its sacking by pirate Henry Morgan, they were swept by fierce winds onto the shores of the Azuero. Here – so the story goes – an image of the **Virgen de Santa Librada** appeared before them as a statue, which they interpreted as a sign that their new settlement should be established on that very spot. Santa Librada, unsurprisingly, was adopted as the patron saint. The name Las Tablas is thought to have derived from the planks (*tablas*) salvaged from the ships and used to construct the initial houses.

Iglesia Santa Librada

Parque Porras

Iglesia Santa Librada features a figurine of the patron saint set at the facade's apex. The magnificent golden altar, which suffers from an overdose of pale-faced cherubs, illuminates the otherwise pedestrian interior – look out for the reliquary said to contain a segment of the saint's leg. Although originally built in 1789, a lot of the church structure visible today dates from the late 1950s.

4

Museo Belisario Porras

Parque Porras • Tues–Sat 8am–4pm • Charge • 994 6326

Diagonally across the square from the church the neat, red-tiled **Museo Belisario Porras** celebrates the life of Panama's most illustrious president in the house of his birth. Ironically its most striking exhibit is the Napoleonic-size tomb intended to house Porras's remains,

CARNAVAL AND OTHER LAS TABLAS FESTIVALS

For many people Las Tablas is synonymous with **Carnaval**, the nation's wildest party, which sees an estimated eighty thousand people squeeze into the narrow streets and central plaza for the five-day bacchanal. Though scaffolding is erected and bodies cram every window and balcony ledge, it is still a crush, so it's not for the claustrophobic or faint-hearted. The festivities revolve around a Montagues-versus-Capulets-style feud that divides the town down the middle in their loyal support for either **Calle Arriba** (Ⓦ carnavalescallearriba.com) or **Calle Abajo** (Ⓦ calleabajolastablas.com), during which water pistols are substituted for swords and the calles shell out at least $500,000 each year to compete for the best music, supporters, fireworks, costumes, floats and queen.

The proceedings start on the Friday night in a blaze of fireworks with the coronation of the new queens, followed by dancing until dawn in a swirl of seco and sweat. Mornings kick-start around 10am with *culecos* or *mojaderos*, which essentially entail being doused by hosepipes from large water tankers as you dance in the street. The queens parade around the square enthroned on gigantic themed floats followed by percussion and brass *murga* bands, who work themselves up into a frenzy to inspire the *tunas* – the all-singing all-dancing support groups – to pump up the volume and outdo the opponents with insulting lyrics. The glam factor is ratcheted up a few notches at night, both on the streets and on the even more extravagant and glitzy floats, and general hedonism takes off until people flake out, often in cars or in the park, before starting all over again the next day. The good times are formally ended when a sardine is symbolically buried in the sand at dawn on Ash Wednesday to mark the start of Lent.

OTHER FESTIVALS

The **Festival de Santa Librada** is commemorated annually in the third week of July. This event is less frenetic and a shade less hedonistic than Carnaval, though there is no shortage of boozing and carousing, plus all the usual attractions of traditional costumes, dancing and music, street food, bullfighting, fireworks and, of course, religious devotions. These start as the pilgrims file into town, bearing an effigy of the saint, who is dripping in gold jewellery given by devotees. For tourists the most interesting aspect is the **Festival de la Pollera**, which offers a chance to see streams of women in Panama's glorious national dress sashaying through the streets. A more recently established dusting off of the *polleras* occurs at the end of the second week of January in the **Desfile de las Mil Polleras**. Thousands of women from all over the country converge on Las Tablas to show off regional variations of the national dress, accompanied by *tuna* bands.

which lies empty as family members wrangled over whether the bones should be moved from the prestigious Cementerio Amador in Panama City, where they are interred. Walls in the single display room are plastered with faded photos, certificates and memorabilia, which only partly succeed in conveying (in Spanish) the extent of his many achievements (see pages 299 and 302). On one famous occasion the statesman's bust, which stands outside the museum, was stolen and discarded in a latrine. On hearing the news, Porras wryly remarked: "*Mis enemigos, no pudiendo llegar hasta mí, mi han hecho descender hasta ellos*" ("Since my enemies cannot reach me, they have dragged me down to their level").

ARRIVAL AND INFORMATION — LAS TABLAS

By bus Buses from Panama City arrive at a separate terminal, four blocks north of Parque Porras down Av 8 de Noviembre. Most other buses depart from the bus terminal on the north side of Av Belisario Porras, just over 1km east of the central park, though the Chitré buses still have their own terminal a couple of blocks closer to the main square, and the one daily bus to Cañas (via Playa Venao) leaves from just off the main square.

Destinations Cañas via Pedasí and Playa Venao (1–2 daily, 12.30–1pm & 2.30pm, sometimes; 2hr); Chitré (4am, 6am–9pm; every 20min; 45min); Panama City (2am, 4am, 6am–4.15pm; hourly; 4hr); Pedasí (6am–6.45pm; every 45min; 45min); Tonosí (8am, 9.30am, then every 45min until 5pm (4pm on Sun); 1hr 20min).

MIA office The regional office for Los Santos province lies along the main road to Pedasí, around 1.7km east of Parque Porras (Mon–Fri 8am–4pm; 500 0921). Stop here if you want more information on Isla Iguana, Isla de Cañas or La Reserva Forestal El Montuoso.

ACCOMMODATION

SEE MAP PAGE 166

Casa Juliana C Agustín Cano Castillero at C de Estudiante 6860 0625. Nine cheerful rooms, of varying sizes and rates, in a homely environment – some sharing a bathroom and others en-suite, and with a fridge. There's also a shared kitchen and a pleasant shady patio at the back for eating, drinking and relaxing. B&B $$

Hotel Pacheco Av Belisario Porras, opposite Super Carnes 923 2544, facebook.com/hotelpacheco. Reliable modern hotel with a busy bar-restaurant offering inexpensive dishes (including a daily changing *menú ejecutivo*) and cheap beer. Rooms $10 cheaper Sun–Thurs. $$

★ **Hotel Presidente** C Pablo Arosemena, half a block east of Parque Porras hotelpresidente.com.pa. An attractive three-storey building boasting 34 rooms, with pale stone-tiled floors, set around an interior courtyard. Standard business-style decor is offset by the stylish bathroom with decorative floor tiles, and some rooms have a balcony. Other pluses are the rooftop pool and bar, a decent restaurant and welcoming staff. Cheaper midweek rates. Breakfast and welcome cocktail included. $$–$$$

EATING

SEE MAP PAGE 166

Decent restaurants are in short supply in Las Tablas. You are often better off dining in a hotel.

La Molienda Hotel Presidente C Pablo Arosemena hotelpresidente.com.pa. The air-conditioned dining room and cool interior courtyard are both pleasant. Choose from Panamanian perennials – *sancocho,* various ceviches or pork chops in tamarind sauce – or consider salads, pastas, steaks, burgers or pizzas. All nicely prepared. Also boasts an extensive and inexpensive list of spirits and beers. $$–$$$

★ **La Paulina Café** Joaquín Pablo Franco and Av Belisario Porras instagram.com/lapaulinacafe. Pop into this cosy café tucked down a side-street with pavement tables for lunch – deli-sandwiches in home-made baguette with chips or salad, or the dish of the day – or for cakes and coffee or an ice cream. $

Restaurante Hotel Piamonte Av Belisario Porras, between C 12 de Octubre and Joaquín Pablo Franco instagram.com/rest.piamontelt. Nicely prepared Panamanian dishes at reasonable rates ensuring that the restaurant attracts more than just the hotel guests. $$

The southern coast

At the flat southeastern tip of the peninsula, the tiny, quaint colonial town of **Pedasí**, 40km south of Las Tablas, is the centre of an unlikely development boom, attracting tourists and luxury real-estate agents in equal measure; as yet, though, its character remains relatively intact. The nearby wildlife refuges of **Isla Iguana** and **Isla de Cañas** draw wildlife enthusiasts, while the waves that batter the headland and southern coastline act as magnets for **surfers**. Though the best conditions are encountered between March and November, the coastline is surfable all year round. As the main road turns southwest, beyond Pedasí, skirting the golden arc of Playa Venao and the mangrove-lined bay encircling Isla de Cañas, the farmland becomes hillier and more rugged, eventually arriving in **Tonosí**, the peninsula's last main town, nestled in a valley. Heading south from there, a tarred road heads south to the remote coastal community of **Cambutal** – another surfing destination – halfway along the coast. To the west, the Azuero's western massif looms, containing its highest peaks, which top 1500m and crown the little-explored **Parque Nacional Cerro Hoya**.

Pedasí and around

The town of **PEDASÍ** lies near the southeastern corner of the peninsula. A former small fishing village, it was catapulted into the national consciousness in 1999 as the birthplace of Panama's first female president, **Mireya Moscoso** (see page 306), whose picture greets you on arrival. If you are in any doubt about the significance (or at least political clout) of the Moscoso family, then head for the **main square**, where the front room of the former president's childhood home has been turned into a quasi-museum, which is little more than a collection of photos and a couple of rather spooky waxworks of her parents sitting in rocking chairs. Note also a monument to the family's fallen standing by the church.

There's nothing much to do here once you've visited the **visitors' centre** (see below) and glanced around the plaza, but it is a tranquil place to hang out, and provides a base for trips to Isla Iguana and Isla de Cañas, as well as being within easy reach of a string of great **surfing beaches**. Other **activities** that can be organized, depending on the season, include snorkelling, kayaking, whale watching, horseriding and turtle watching. There is some basic **accommodation** and a couple of decent **restaurants**, though as much of the action has moved down to Playa Venao (see page 171), places tend to come and go.

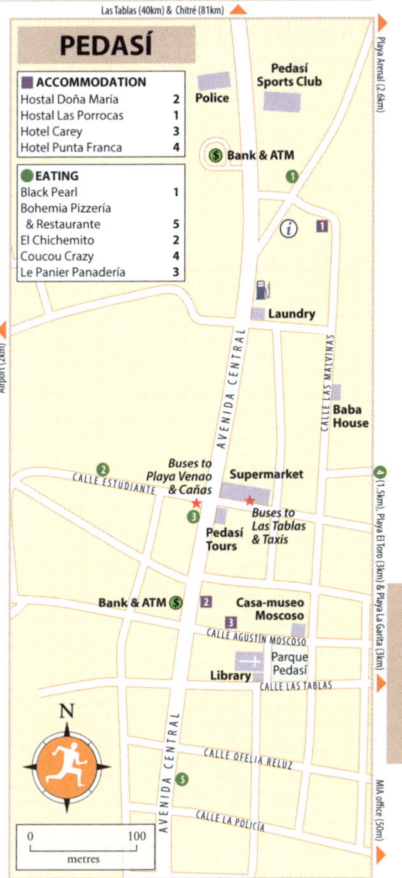

Centro de Visitantes

50m off the main road, on the road to Playa Arenal • Mon–Fri 8am–4pm, Sat & Sun 9am –5pm • Free • ☎ 926 0703

A new **visitors' centre** was opened in 2024, which is well worth visiting. More a mini-museum, it is full of informative visual and auditory interactive displays (in Spanish and English) on the peninsula's history, customs and traditions, and biodiversity, and includes video-interviews with local Azuerenses. Staff can also provide information on tourist activities and contacts for guides.

Surfing beaches

Playa El Toro and Playa La Garita are a walkable 3km or short taxi ride from Pedasí; follow the road out of the main square until the fork, heading left to El Toro and right to La Garita. Three kilometres south of Pedasí at the village of El Limón, a road leads off 7km to the band of chocolate sand and rocks at Playa Los Destiladeros (bear right at the fork), which offers point and beach breaks as well as fabulous views across the ocean

ARRIVAL AND DEPARTURE — PEDASÍ

By bus Minibuses run from Las Tablas to Pedasí (6am–6.45pm; every 45min; 45min). Heading back to Las Tablas, buses leave from outside the supermarket at similar intervals, with the last service at 6.45pm. The elusive buses bound for Cañas via Playa Venao (see page 171) leave at 7am and noon, and the 12.30–1pm bus from Las Tablas stops outside the bakery on Av Central, theoretically at 1.15–1.45pm and 3.15pm, though timings are vague.

INFORMATION

Tourist information The Centro de Visitantes (see above) can provide tourist information.

MIA office On a backstreet southeast of the main square (Mon–Fri 8am–4pm; no phone); note that, despite the official opening hours, it is often closed.

4

TOURS AND ACTIVITIES

Pedasí Sports Club Av Central on the way into town ☎995 2894, 🌐pedasisportsclub.com. Pedasí's longest established tour operator offers snorkelling trips to Isla Iguana, horseriding in the hills, whale watching (seasonal), and nocturnal turtle tours to Isla de Cañas.

Bike rental Baba House, one block east of Av Central, behind the supermarket, rents out bicycles (🌐babahousepedasi.wixsite.com/baba-house).

ACCOMMODATION

SEE MAP PAGE 169

IN PEDASÍ

Hostal Doña María Av Central at C Agustín Moscoso. A homely two-storey B&B surrounded by greenery, with six bright, simply furnished old-style en-suite rooms (electric showers) with large windows, fans and a/c. Sink into the sofas on the shared balcony terrace or doze in a hammock under shade in the back yard. Your welcoming hostess has all the contacts to arrange excursions and activities. $$

★ **Hostal Las Porrocas** C Las Malvinas at Vía a Playa Arenal 🌐facebook.com/lasporrocaspedasi. Small, welcoming hostel in a shady, tree-filled garden decked out with wooden pallet furniture, cushions and hammocks, plus a well-equipped semi-open kitchen. The single eight-bed dorm has solid wooden bunks, thick mattresses and privacy curtains. Staff can organize tours. Breakfast included. Dorms $

Hotel Carey C Agustín Moscoso 🌐instagram.com/hotelcarey. Rooms are varied in this central hostel turned hotel. Most are cheerily painted but sparsely furnished, with good-quality bedding; some are en-suite, with TV and patio; cheaper, more cell-like, rooms share bathrooms. The main draw is the garden pool area, with places to lounge and a pool table. Helpful staff. Breakfast available. $$–$$$

OUTSIDE PEDASÍ

★ **Hotel Punta Franca** Above Playa Destiladeros, 10km south of Pedasí 🌐hotelpuntafranca.com. Set on a splendid bluff above one of the peninsula's top surfing beaches, and affording stunning vistas, this is a spot to disconnect and soak up the sea breezes. The attractive painted stone villas with terracotta tiled roof are simple but spacious, though service can be hit and miss. But the isolated setting is lovely and the clifftop restaurant serves decent food. It's worth paying extra for an ocean view. Breakfast included. $$$

4

EATING

SEE MAP PAGE 169

Black Pearl Road to Playa Arenal at C Las Malvinas 🌐theblackpearl-pan.com. A friendly family-run restaurant serving up a small menu of Peruvian fusion cuisine at tourist prices. Beyond a couple of beef dishes, it's all about the super-fresh seafood delivered in ceviches, Chaufa rice and poke bowls. Highly recommended. $$$

★ **Bohemia Pizzería & Restaurante** Av Central ☎995 2950 or 6905 2330, 🌐facebook.com/bohemiapedasi. The cosy, rustic interior creates a mellow ambiance to enjoy varied pasta dishes – try the ricotta and artichoke ravioli – but the deli-pizzas top the bill: super-fresh ingredients piled onto a crispy base. Cash only. $$

El Chichemito C Estudiante 🌐facebook.com/chichemito. This semi-open bamboo-lined spot is the pick of the restaurants serving local cuisine. You can tuck into inexpensive a la carte Panamanian favourites, such as roast chicken, with rice, beans and plantain, or the *menú del día* for even less. $–$$

Coucou Crazy Just off the road to Playa del Toro 🌐coucoucrazy.wordpress.com. Longstanding institution (a shipping container and shady gravel garden) with a mellow vibe, hosted by multi-talented Belgian Dennis, whose home-roasted and freshly ground coffee is renowned, as is his craft beer and kombucha. There are indulgent cakes and simple savoury dishes to enjoy, plus inexpensive rooms to rent out back among the chickens, goats and pigs. $$

Le Panier Panadería Av Central by the bus stop 🌐instagram.com/lepanierpedasi. The small patio is the ideal spot to grab an espresso and a croissant or a slice of pizza for breakfast or while waiting to flag down one of the elusive buses bound for Playa Venao.

DIRECTORY

Money and supplies Pedasí's three banks lie on Av Central; all have ATMs, though they sometimes run out of money. Note that after Pedasí there is no cash (and petrol) until Playa Venao.

Refugio de Vida Silvestre Isla Iguana

Undoubtedly the best day-trip from Pedasí is to **Isla Iguana**, 4km offshore. This tiny lump of basalt, covered in dry scrub and grass, forms the centrepiece of the **REFUGIO DE VIDA SILVESTRE ISLA IGUANA**, created in 1981 to protect one of the largest and oldest coral reefs in the Golfo de Panamá. Home to more than two hundred species of colourful fish, the coral itself is not in great condition since a large chunk of the reef was blown off in the 1990s when two large bombs – relics of US training during World War II – had to be detonated; two more were located in 2018.

Avoid travelling to the island during **major holiday periods**, when tourist numbers can top six hundred in a day, which puts huge pressure on the island's natural resources. Isla Iguana is a far better destination between May and December, when the calmer conditions mean crossings are smoother and snorkelling more rewarding; the sea can be so rough between January and March that it's sometimes too dangerous to set out. In the migratory season (June–Dec, especially Sept & Oct) **humpback whales** are visible, sometimes in the company of **dolphins**.

Playa El Cirial

The rugged coastline of guano- and cactus-covered basalt is interrupted by two coral-sand beaches: the larger **Playa El Cirial**, where all boats pull up, accommodates the park office and dilapidated visitors' centre. Playa El Cirial's small crescent of silky sand backs a sheltered cove of translucent water barely covering coral formations inhabited by a rainbow of reef fish, making it a superb spot for **swimming** and **snorkelling**.

Playita del Faro

From Playa El Cirial, a 200m **path** across the island through iguana-favoured scrub takes you to **Playita del Faro**. Strong offshore currents mean swimming and snorkelling are sometimes prohibited here, but at low tide rock pools offer plenty to explore. The basalt outcrop to the left as you reach the beach provides a vantage point for one of the island's main attractions: Panama's largest colony of **magnificent frigatebirds**, estimated to be around five thousand. January to April offers the best chance of seeing males puffing out their extraordinary inflatable scarlet pouches, but nesting goes on all year. Return from the south end of the beach via the **Sendero Árbol Panamá,** which takes its name from a particularly tall specimen of the Panamá tree.

4

ARRIVAL AND INFORMATION — ISLA IGUANA

Refuge entrance and fees Park fees need to be paid for in advance online (see page 42).

On a tour Pedasí Sports Club arranges snorkelling trips to the island, as do most of the hotels. Organized trips usually provide drinks and snacks for lunch; they may provide snorkel gear, and can help sort the park fee payment.

By taxi and boat Most Pedasí lodgings, or the tourist office, should be able to give you contact details of a fisherman with a boat at Playa Arenal – the nearest beach to the island, 3km from Pedasí – and a taxi driver to get there. There are no buses. Arrange a pickup time with the taxi. An average price is $80 for a small boat (for up to six people) for a half-day trip; the crossing can take upwards of 40min depending on conditions, which can be rough. Take a picnic, but note alcohol is not permitted, and you should bring your litter back with you.

Playa Venao

The imposing 3km swathe of charcoal-coloured sand that is **Playa Venao** (or Venado), 30km southwest of Pedasí, is the region's best-known surfing spot, providing waves suitable for beginners and more experienced surfers alike. A glorious arc, Playa Venao's beauty has been somewhat diminished in recent years by ill-considered hotel developments at the eastern end of the beach, where the weekend party scene takes hold. In contrast, at the western end of the strand, a couple of more environmentally sensitive lodgings offer a more chilled vibe, and a chance to unwind and enjoy the sand, sea and the sunsets in peace and quiet.

A few kilometres out from the bay, the guano-flecked rocky stacks of **Islas Frailes** are at times covered in thousands of nesting sooty terns and other passing seabirds; you'll need a good pair of binoculars to get a decent view from the boat, since landing is impossible.

ARRIVAL AND DEPARTURE — PLAYA VENAO AND ISLAS FRAILES

By bus Buses from Las Tablas (see page 167) and Pedasí (see page 169) bound for Cañas pass through Playa Venao

(1hr). Return buses from Cañas, 15–20min from Playa Venao, leave at 7am for Las Tablas, and at 9am and 3pm for Pedasí. Note that these timetables are only approximate and do not apply on Sunday.

By shuttle Venao Tours (Ⓦ venaotours.com) offers private and shared shuttle services to and from Panama City and between Playa Venao and Bocas del Toro. My Pink Bus (Ⓦ mypinkbus.com) is another option.

By taxi A taxi from Pedasí to Playa Venao costs around $30.

By car There is a petrol station at Playa Venao.

ACTIVITIES

Surfing Numerous surf schools give lessons, run camps and rent out boards; try Kahuna Venao (Ⓦ instagram.com/kahunavenao) at the *El Sitio* lighthouse at the east end, and Dojosurf (Ⓦ surfdojo.com) at the west end. Shokogi (Ⓦ shokogi.com) also offers stand-up paddle, kitesurfing and foil surfing.

Yoga Classes and retreats are widespread; check the Venao Guide for dates and timings (Ⓦ venaoguide.com).

Other activities Horseriding – generally a sedate stroll along the sand – and kayaking are also popular, as are excursions to Isla Iguana (see page 170) and Isla de Cañas (see page 173). Ask at your lodgings for recommended operators or check out the Venao Guide.

Turtle conservation Based at *Eco Venao*, where you can help with beach patrols (Ⓦ tortugasplayavenao.com).

ACCOMMODATION

Prices are often much higher for **weekends**. If you're **self-catering**, you can stock up on fresh fruit and veg in Al Natural Market, and get most other items at the Super Venao supermarket.

La Choza 200m from the beach break Ⓣ 6299 3044, Ⓦ facebook.com/la chozapv. Old-style basic hostel, offering compact, budget air-conditioned rooms, a breezy balcony and intimate garden-*rancho* kitchen facilities – all at the back of the beach, in a shady spot. Dorms $, doubles $$

★ Eco Venao 1km west of the beach entrance Ⓦ ecovenao.com. Arguably the country's most genuine eco-retreat, practising sustainable tourism to support its reforestation project (over 25,000 trees so far), composting and carbon capture. Wake to howler monkeys and birdsong. A range of accommodation is spread across the forested hillside overlooking the bay: from the eight-bunk restored original wooden farmhouse to moderately priced riverside *cabañas* with shared ablutions and private decks, fancier, self-catering stone cottages, plus four new beachside *cabañas*. Campers share the lodge facilities, including the numerous hammocks, a volleyball court, yoga deck and short trail to a viewpoint. Boat trips can be arranged, or you can explore the bay on horseback. Don't miss *La Barca*, their vibey boat-shaped beach bar. Camping $, dorms $, doubles $$, cabins $$–$$$

Tiny Homes West end of the beach Ⓦ inaterrahomes.com. Compact units among the trees at the back of the sand. Chic minimalist design using lots of wood and floor-to-ceiling glass that allows an uninterrupted view of the waves. All have private patio and hammock, but the cheaper suites share a kitchen whereas the two-storey homes have their own. Suites $$, houses $$$–$$$$

Villa Marina East end of the beach Ⓦ villamarina.com.pa Tucked away at the back of the sand, this spacious hacienda-style boutique hotel is set in lush grounds surrounded by tropical forest with a stone infinity pool overlooking the beach. Tastefully designed with all mod cons. Continental breakfast included. $$$

TURTLE WATCHING AT ISLA DE CAÑAS

Five species of turtle nest on Isla de Cañas, the most numerous being the world's tiniest sea turtle, the olive ridley. Their extraordinary mass **nesting**, or *arribada* (arrival), when thousands storm the beach over several nights, is a sight to behold. Pacific green turtles also nest in large quantities alongside significantly smaller numbers of loggerhead, leatherback and hawksbill. Nesting primarily takes place between May and November, with September to November considered the peak months, though timing your visit to coincide with an **arribada** – generally several days either side of a full moon – is tricky. The island was designated a protected area in 1994 and a number of the eight-hundred-strong population are involved in protecting the turtles – for which they are permitted to harvest a percentage of the eggs for consumption and sale. Villagers also act as turtle-watching guides (see page 173), an offer worth taking up if only to increase the likelihood of more eggs hatching rather than being sold on the black market. Since female turtles are easily spooked by bright lights, it's better not to bring cameras, or torches, unless infrared; rely on the guide and let your eyes adjust to the light (see box, page 237).

EATING AND DRINKING

Coleos 100m east of the main beach entrance ⓦinstagram.com/coleosvenao. Small café, with a handful of tables on a shaded patio offering hummus every which way, wraps, and tasty salads enlivened with nuts and seeds. Popular, more substantial dishes include chicken curry or pad Thai, washed down by inexpensive beer or a home-made juice. $$

La Hummuseria 50m east of the supermarket, by the eastern beach entrance ⓦfacebook.com/lahummuseriavenao2019. There's plenty to please vegetarian and vegans in this friendly, informal hummus-focused venue. Choose from six varieties, or share a platter of Middle Eastern tapas-cum-dips with a pile of soft pita bread to stuff or dip. Round it off with a glass of refreshing home-made lemonade. $$

★ **La Quincha** 50m east of the main beach entrance ⓦla-quincha-playa-venao.cluvi.co. The terrace of this popular Spanish-Panamanian fusion restaurant has a real buzz about it most nights. The menu is small but inventive, and dishes are bursting with flavour, complemented by great cocktails, a decent wine list and attentive service. *Carimañolas* stuffed with *ropa vieja* (yuca fritters filled with spicey shredded beef) is the starter of choice. $$$

★ **La Barca Eco Venao** 1km west of the beach entrance ⓦecovenao.com/food-drink. Shady boat-bar-restaurant, at the back of the beach, illuminated by fairy lights at night. Listen to the surf through the music, with your toes in the sand, and enjoy a cocktail or a coffee, or even a tasty bite to eat. $$

Pizzería Gavilán Beach Break Surf Camp, east end of the beach ⓦbeachbreaksurfcamp.com/playa-venao-pizza-gavilan. Excellent artisanal pizzas and a fabulous location bang on the beach – no wonder it's a popular hangout. Thin-crust pizzas, burgers, substantial salads and inexpensive beer. $$–$$$

Refugio de Vida Silvestre Isla de Cañas

In the bay to the west of Playa Venao, nestled among the mangroves and a stone's throw from the swampy shoreline, lies the long sliver of land that is **REFUGIO DE VIDA SILVESTRE ISLA DE CAÑAS**. The island is synonymous with **turtles**, which arrive annually in their thousands, availing themselves of a glorious 14km band of sand to lay their eggs.

Turtles are not the only attraction, however. The reserve extends into a muddy tangle of mangroves both on the island's shore-side and along the mainland, providing roosting and nesting sites for **waterbirds**, which can be seen close up on a round-the-island **boat tour**, which also takes in a pre-Columbian archeological site (with little to see) and a strangely formed cave dubbed the "*casa de piedra*". You can also enjoy a couple of hours' gentle **fishing** or a ride in a **horse and cart** around the island's beaches and cultivations – rice, maize, banana and cocoa are all grown alongside vast quantities of juicy watermelons, which should definitely be sampled.

ARRIVAL AND DEPARTURE — ISLA DE CAÑAS

TO THE JETTY

By bus Take the bus from Las Tablas (1–1.30pm; 2hr) or Pedasí (7am & noon; 1hr) to Cañas village; you may be able to persuade the driver to take you to the island dock (El Encerrao) for a few extra dollars. A battered minibus shuttles between Tonosí and Cañas four times a day (8.30am, 10.30am, 12.30pm & 2.30pm; 30min) and will pass via the island dock if requested. The early-morning bus leaves Cañas at 6.45am.

By car The turn-off to the jetty is 6km west of Cañas village, from where it's another 2.5km down a tarred road to the dock.

By taxi A taxi from Pedasí costs around $40.

TO THE ISLAND

By boat The island is only about 50m across the water, so shout across if you haven't arranged transport in advance, or ring ⓣ6716 4095 to call for a boat to be sent over.

DAY-TRIPS AND PACKAGES

Isla Cañas Tours (ⓣ6718 0032, ⓔislac2010@hotmail.com), a local operation run by Daniel Pérez, offers all-inclusive day or overnight packages to the island.

INFORMATION

Park entrance and fees There is a small MIA office on the island, but there is rarely anyone there.

Guides Trained community guides are assigned to visitors to lead the turtle watch. Fernando Dominguez (ⓣ6716 4095) is a reliable local guide with a couple of boats who can take you to explore the mangroves and nearby river estuary, on the lookout for crocodiles, or on fishing trips.

4

ACCOMMODATION

Community accommodation The village has very rudimentary cabins with fans or a/c for an extra $10; alternatively you can pitch a tent, or stay with a family. There are also a couple of small inexpensive *fondas*. Camping $, cabins $–$$

Pachamama 1.5km east of the main village facebook.com/pachamama.islacanas. Disconnect from the modern world (solar-powered electricity, w-fi etc.) and fall asleep to the sound of breaking waves. Accommodation is *very* basic in dome tents and private or shared thatched wooden huts – a simple bed and very necessary mosquito net (bring plenty of repellent) – with outside shared toilet and showers. There's ample hammock space to curl up with a book midst the coconut palms, while there's kayak and SUP rental for the more active, and boat tours – not to mention turtle watching. Unless you self-cater, you're reliant on their bar-restaurant. Dorms $, tents (with mattress) $, cabins $$

Cambutal and around

For most people Playa Venao is remote enough, but die-hard surfers may want to try the even more out-of-the-way spots around **CAMBUTAL**, a small fishing village 60km west. The journey takes you through undulating cattle country – spectacularly lush in the rainy season, desperately barren once the moisture has been sucked out of it. Picturesque, charcoal **Playa Cambutal** and some of the surfing beaches further west get serious 3m waves. Non-surfers, meanwhile, can explore the caves, blowholes and crevices of this impressively rugged coastline. Boat trips, birdwatching and hiking into Cerro Hoya national park (see page 175) are also possible.

4

Fifteen kilometres east, around Punto Morro, the less publicized **Guánico Abajo** enjoys a fabulously scenic location. There are a couple of surf camps here, plus good waves at **Playa Guánico Abajo** and mangroves to explore; at the nearby **Playa Marinera,** where cream-coloured sands are hemmed in by cliffs, more than thirty thousand olive ridley turtles lay their eggs each year. To reach both Cambutal and Guánico Abajo, you first have to head inland and pass through **Tonosí**, which is little more than a glorified regional crossroads surrounded by hilly cattle ranches; it does, however, offer all the basic amenities around the main square, including an ATM and the local **MiAmbiente office**.

ARRIVAL AND DEPARTURE — CAMBUTAL AND AROUND

By bus To reach Playa Cambutal or Playa Guánico Abajo you first need to take a bus to Tonosí from Las Tablas (8am, 9.30am, then every 45min–1hr until 5pm; last bus back to Las Tablas at 4pm; 1hr 20min). From Playa Venao, take the first bus to Cañas, and catch the 9.30am or 12.30pm minivan to Tonosí. From Tonosí local buses depart from outside the two supermarkets in the town centre, near the main square. Cambutal departures are at approximately 6am and 10.30, returning to Tonosí at 7am and 11.30am, though there is a one direct bus from Las Tablas that leaves at 1pm, passing through Tonosí at around 2.20pm; Guánico Abajo departures are at 10am and 2pm, returning to Tonosí at 11am and 3pm.

By car The roads to Cambutal and Guánico Abajo are tarred, but sections of the road can be very pot-holed at times; seek advice before driving a saloon car there in the rainy season.

By taxi Taxi prices from Tonosí to Playa Cambutal or Playa Guánico Abajo partly depend on the state of the road.

INFORMATION AND TOURS

MIA office On the left-hand side of the road as you enter Cambutal (Mon–Fri 8am–4pm; 995 8180). Incumbent Armadio Ortega (6215 7408) can provide information on accessing Parque Nacional Cerro Hoya (see page 175).

Bank The only bank (with ATM) in the area is on the main square in Tonosí.

Turtle patrols Tortuagro (6264 9124, facebook.com/agrotortugasc), Cambutal's local turtle conservation group, welcomes visitors on nightly beach patrols and for hatchling releases (July–Dec), for a small donation.

Tours Azuero Tours (azueroadventures.com) works with community guides and experts in Cambutal to provide sustainable tours exploring the coastline and national park: hiking, horseriding, birdwatching and boat tours.

ACCOMMODATION AND EATING

PLAYA CAMBUTAL

★**La Finca Cambutal** Three stylish, individually designed cabins surrounded by greenery, featuring lots of attractive hardwood and light. Each with mini-fridge, private patio, hammock and rain showers – the Treehouse has the ocean view. All share a kitchen. Minimum two-night stay. $$$

★ **Hotel Kambutaleko** hotelkambutaleko.com. Breezy hilltop spot with charming hosts, boasting six simple fan-ventilated doubles and one family room all sharing a wraparound, ocean-view terrace. All have a private bathroom and some have a/c and a fridge. No kitchen, but there's an affordable patio restaurant. $$

Hotel Playa Cambutal hotelplayacambutal.net. This colonial-style hotel at the back of the beach offers ten spacious rooms with ocean views. The grassy palm-studded grounds melt into the sand, and there's a pool and an excellent bar-restaurant offering happy hour and pizza night. $$$

PLAYA GUÁNICO ABAJO

Surf House On the beach surfhousepanama.com. Three smart, identical mini-apartments tastefully decorated, from matching tiles, bathmats and patio furniture, to bed linen and curtains. Though aimed at surfers, the oceanfront private patio and large hammock should entice anyone keen to get away from it all. $$$

TONOSÍ

Hotel Mi Valle Main square 6616 4076. The only option if you get stuck here, a modern, functional hotel facing the park in the centre of town, offering 24 bland but clean en-suite rooms with the usual amenities (a/c, satellite TV, wi-fi); some have fridges. The on-site restaurant serves inexpensive Panamanian food. $–$$

Parque Nacional Cerro Hoya

Tucked away in the southwest corner of the Azuero Peninsula, **PARQUE NACIONAL CERRO HOYA** covers 325 square kilometres of the isthmus's most ancient volcanic rocks, and contains more than thirty species of endemic plant. This is one of the country's most inaccessible parks; transport is tricky, and formal trails and accommodation are lacking. But the rewards are plenty: giant mahogany, cedar, cuipo and ceiba trees soar above the forest canopy, and carpets of moist **forest** rise up from the sea to lofty Cerros Hoya (1559m), Moya (1478m) and Soya (1326m). A few scarlet and great green **macaws** maintain a fragile foothold in the forest, as does the endemic Azuero **parakeet**; other critically endangered species include the **Azuero spider** and **howler monkeys**, while substantial populations of **white-tailed deer** pick their way through the forest floor, shared with agoutis, collared peccaries and coatis. As the park's name suggests (*hoya* means river bed), the massif nourishes more than ten major rivers, home to caimans and otters, and hundreds of streams that tumble down to the coast, leaving natural **swimming pools** and **waterfalls** in their wake. The protected area extends out into the sea, including precious mangroves and secluded coves enclosed by sheer cliffs, providing sheltered sands for hawksbill, olive ridley and even some leatherback turtles to lay their eggs.

Created in 1985, in a desperate attempt to stop the Azuero's haemorrhaging of forest through destructive agricultural practices, the national park and its protecting agencies are helping the population of about two thousand – scattered around 25 communities – to make a livelihood from sustainable agroforestry, ecotourism, animal husbandry and fishing projects. The best time to visit is early in the **dry season** when the views are more spectacular, the mud less overwhelming and the hiking more pleasurable, yet the waterfalls and rivers – two of the major attractions – still hold sufficient water to impress.

ARRIVAL AND DEPARTURE — PARQUE NACIONAL CERRO HOYA

FROM THE WEST

The park is most accessible from the Western Azuero, via the community of Flores, close to the northern park boundary, or via the coastal hamlet of Restingue, which marks the southwestern park boundary. The latter is closer to the park itself though less easy to reach.

To Flores A tarred road leaves the Interamericana just east of Santiago, skirting the coast for more than 90km down to the village of Arenas, where it heads east the last 6km to Flores. There are infrequent buses from Santiago to Arenas and Flores (see page 176).

To Restingue Getting to Restingue means travelling south from Arenas along an 18km dirt road (high-clearance 4WD necessary) and crossing two major rivers. This is only possible in the dry season, when the occasional *chiva* also makes the journey; once the rains start, horses may be able to pass, or you have to travel by boat.

Guides In Flores seek out Miguel Moreno (6597 0280), who runs a small shop opposite the primary school, and can guide in the park, or Juancho Velásquez (see page 176).

4

FROM THE EAST

To El Cobachón To get to Cerro Hoya from the east, take the dirt road west from Cambutal for 22km to the hamlet of El Cobachón, close to the park boundary. Whether on horseback, in a 4WD or on foot (which entails shortcuts along the beach at low tide, so a tide timetable is essential), the road from Cambutal is only accessible in the dry season, since several rivers need to be forded. Alternatively, take a boat from Cambutal or neighbouring Los Buzos to El Cobachón. Marcelino Rodríguez usually accepts campers in El Cobachón.

Guides Daniel Sáenz, based in El Cobachón, comes highly recommended for birding or hiking, and can arrange horses (T 6789 9528 – but note signal can be sporadic).

INFORMATION AND TOURS

The park entry fee should be paid online in advance (see page 42).

Organized tours You can explore the west side of the park with Tanager Tourism, run by the owners of *Hotel Heliconia* south of Mariato (see page 177). In Flores, Juancho Velásquez in is also recommended (W yeylinvelasquez7.wixsite.com/fincajuanchovelsqu-2; T 6306 2114). In Arena, contact Cerro Hoya Tours (see below). Further south, Morillo Beach Eco Resort (W morillobeachresort.com) provides guided excursions. From the east side, contact Azuero Tours (W azueroadventures.com) in Cambutal.

The Western Azuero

4

The little-explored coastline of the **Western Azuero** has a very different feel to the dry, flat stretches of sand that line the eastern seaboard. Receiving much more rain, the countryside is greener and lusher, despite the cattle ranching and occasional rice cultivation. As the sole access road threads its way more than 100km south from the Interamericana through an increasingly undulating landscape, it offers tantalizing glimpses of rocky coastline, hidden coves and foaming surf. Best of all, since the beaches face west, they witness glorious **sunsets**, which has given rise to the marketing sobriquet of the Sunset Coast. Sprinkled along said coast some delightful lodgings offer perfect places to unwind for a few days.

Settlements are few and far between in the Western Azuero, and transport is sporadic: the first place of note, some 50km south of the turn-off from the Interamericana, is **Mariato**, with a broad central boulevard dotted with *fondas*. Its main feature is its temple-like bank and ATM, and with a couple of small supermarkets and a petrol station, it's a good place to stock up with essentials if you're travelling in your own vehicle or self-catering. Three kilometres southwest of Mariato, the pebble-and-sand **Playa Reina** stretches south to the mouth of the Río Negro, where you can find transport to Isla Cébaco (see box, page 212).

Fifteen kilometres south of Mariato on the main road, the tiny hilltop hamlet of **Torio**, and its surrounding area, is the unlikely centre of the area's nascent tourism scene, offering several places to stay and eat. The increasingly roller-coaster road then bypasses **Punta Duarte** and the surfing hot spot of **Playa Morillo** before arriving in **Arenas** and **Flores**, where the tarred road comes to a halt before the massif of Parque Nacional Cerro Hoya.

ARRIVAL AND INFORMATION — THE WESTERN AZUERO

MARIATO AND TORIO

By bus Buses run from Santiago to Mariato (Mon–Fri 5.30–7am every 30min, then hourly until 6pm; 1hr 15min), with some buses continuing to Torio (1hr 40min). The last return bus from Torio to Santiago leaves at 5.30pm. At weekends, and Sunday in particular, transport is far less frequent, and less reliable.

ARENAS AND FLORES

By bus Two buses a day from Santiago are scheduled to go as far as Arenas and Flores (Mon–Fri 9am & 1.30pm; 2hr 30min–3hr), and other Mariato and Torio buses from Santiago may go that far depending on demand; if there are no local passengers, you'll have to pay extra for the driver to take you the full way. On weekdays buses leave Flores for Santiago at 5am & 7.30am; other, infrequent buses tend to leave Arenas, though you should be prepared to hitch a ride.

By car The road is tarred all the way to Flores but note that the last petrol station is in Malena – and it is often closed, so fill up in Santiago or Atalaya (see page 205).

ACCOMMODATION AND EATING

If you are without your own transport, you may be reliant on your lodgings for lunch and dinner too, so it's worth finding out approximate meal prices and the type of food offered before making a reservation.

MARIATO

La Fondita Mariato behind the centro de salud facebook.com/FonditaMariato. Run by two Italian couples, this place makes its own pasta and serves crispy pizzas amid brightly painted wooden furniture. $$

Hotel Heliconia Main road, Palmilla, 8km south of Mariato hotelheliconiapanama.com. Spotless four-room B&B with a porch offering comfortable seating and surrounded by a lush tropical garden. The Dutch biologist owners operate Tanager Tourism: the most popular trip is a three-day tour to Isla Coiba but outings to Isla Cébaco and Cerro Hoya are also possible, as well as whale watching (Aug–Sept). Other meals on request. $$$

★ **Hotel Playa Reina** Playa Reina, 3km south of Mariato hotelplayareina.com. A relaxing place set in shady surroundings on the beach, this hotel has a/c rooms to suit all wallets – from superior dorm bunks with lockers to standard doubles and ocean-facing suites (with fridge, kitchenette and various trimmings). Curl up in a hammock with a book, splash in the infinity pool, surf the waves or explore with the free kayaks, SUPs or bicycles; snorkelling excursions to Isla Cébaco are available at extra cost. You can eat nicely prepared fresh food at the restaurant – or find cheaper eats nearby. Midweek reductions. Dorms $, doubles $$–$$$, suites $$$

TORIO

Brisas del Mar Main road at the beach road turn-off instagram.com/cabanasbrisasdelmar. The wooden tables of this no-frills bar-restaurant are packed with locals, expats and tourists during the summer, especially on Fri and Sat nights, reeled in by inexpensive fresh fish, langoustines and lobster, good-value *comida corriente* and cheap beer. $$

★ **El Sol** 8km south of Torio 6616 1632, ecoelsol.com. This exclusive, design-conscious retreat makes the most of its hillside location, offering stunning ocean views. The dazzling yellow exteriors, reflecting the hotel's name, give way to more sophisticated colour schemes and works of art in the seven guestrooms. It's a place to indulge, relaxing in a hammock or in the pool, or being pampered with massage and spa treatments. The gourmet meals, prepared by the owner-chef, draw on fresh local ingredients. Breakfast included. $$

MORRILLO

Morrillo Beach Eco-resort Playa Morillo morillobeachresort.com. Perched on the hillside, peering out through the surrounding forest at the ocean and neighbouring river, this boutique hotel boasts six comfortable but simple rooms, with private balcony, and personalized service. There are activities galore – though rates are high – from surfing the waves, to kayaking through mangroves or hiking in the national park. Changing fixed menu each day $$$

ARENAS

Cerro Hoya Hostal y Tours instagram.com/cerrohoya_hosttours. Two comfortable en-suite rooms available in the scenically located home of two welcoming Azuerenses. They also offer fairly priced hiking to Cerro Hoya and boat tours. Breakfast included. $$

4

TURTLE CONSERVATION IN THE WESTERN AZUERO

The tranquil soft sands of the Western Azuero coastline provide prime nesting sites for **turtles**: the vast majority are olive ridley, with the occasional leatherback, green or hawksbill turtles also laying their eggs here. Two established **turtle conservation groups** run nightly beach patrols during the nesting season (July–Nov), monitoring and protecting turtle nest sites: on **Playa Malena** in the hamlet of the same name, 11km south of Mariato, and in the small settlement of **Quebro**, midway between Torio and Arenas. In the latter, the community Asociación de Agropesca Ecoturística Quebro (AAPEQ), which also works on mangrove reforestation, collaborates with the Fundación de Agua y Tierra (aguaytierra.wixsite.com/fundat) on turtle conservation on nearby Playa Mata Oscura. You can accompany either organization on a beach patrol for a small donation, or could even offer your services as a volunteer, if you can speak some Spanish. Both offer cheap **accommodation**, and some volunteers camp on Playa Mata Oscura.

ACCOMMODATION

Centro AAPEQ Quebro 6418 3932, playamataoscura.blogspot.com. Bunks in roadside accommodation. Breakfast available. $

Hostal Iguana Verde Malena 6865 8908. Ana González, chair of the local turtle association, rents out a few simple rooms with fan or a/c, as dorm beds or privates. Shared kitchen. Dorms $, doubles $$

Chiriquí and Veraguas

PARQUE NACIONAL COIBA

Chiriquí and Veraguas

From the raging torrents of the Río Chiriquí Viejo and the verdant peaks of the Cordillera Central to the marine-rich coral, swampy mangroves and empty sands of the Golfo de Chiriquí, the diverse scenery of Chiriquí and Veraguas offers some of Panama's top natural attractions. Magnificent in their own right, they also provide the setting for a range of exhilarating outdoor adventure activities, including whitewater rafting, kayaking, diving, surfing, hiking and zip lining. Though Veraguas is the only province in the country to border both the Atlantic and Pacific oceans, Chiriquí gets most of the headlines since – as Chiricanos will proudly remind you – the province is the *granero* (granary) or *canasta de pan* (breadbasket) of Panama. As well as growing most of the country's agricultural produce – everything from rice to strawberries – it also boasts the country's second city, David, and its best-known mountain resort town, Boquete.

The **Tierras Altas** (Highlands) at the western end of Panama, north of David, attract the most attention and the most tourists, with the cool, sunny climate and spectacular scenery of **Boquete** drawing North American and European retirees. The town makes a great base for exploring the cloud forests or ascending Panama's highest peak, **Volcán Barú**, which can also be approached from the less touristy settlements of **Volcán** and **Cerro Punta** on its western flanks. The latter provides a convenient springboard for the rugged, little-explored peaks of the **Parque Internacional La Amistad**.

A large area of the forested slopes of eastern Chiriquí forms part of the **Comarca Ngäbe-Buglé**, which includes some of western Veraguas on both sides of the continental divide and extends into much of Bocas del Toro province (see page 218). South of the central cordillera lie the **Tierras Bajas** (Lowlands), home to the tranquil provincial capitals of **David** and **Santiago**, the former coming alive during its annual international agricultural fair in March (see box, page 199); the region's other main festival, celebrating flowers and coffee, takes place in Boquete every January.

South of David lies the **Golfo de Chiriquí**, a vast body of water with beautiful coastal fringes and deserted islands, which stretches from the Costa Rican border to the Veraguas side of the Azuero Peninsula in the east. Surrounded by nutrient-rich waters that attract dazzling aquatic life, including humpback whales, the gulf contains the mangroves and coral of **Parque Nacional Marino Golfo de Chiriquí** and the former penitentiary of **Isla Coiba**, which is renowned for its scuba diving and pristine rainforest. It is most easily accessed from **Santa Catalina**, a mellow fishing village and the country's top surfing venue, tucked away in the southwestern corner of Veraguas. To reach here you pass through the provincial capital, **Santiago**, a bustling commercial and agricultural centre that is also the gateway to the **central highlands** to the north. The standout destination in this region is the delightful unspoilt mountain village of **Santa Fé**, which is renowned for its orchids and waterfalls, and provides access to a little-explored national park.

Brief history

The **Ngäbe** and closely related **Buglé** – both recognizable by the women's brightly coloured cotton dresses – were collectively referred to as Guaymí in colonial accounts, featuring prominently as fierce warriors. Their populations, alongside many others that never survived the colonial struggle, were pushed up into the mountains by the **Spanish**, who moved into the region in the late sixteenth century. Founding major centres in

STRIPE-TAILED HUMMINGBIRD

Highlights

❶ **Coffee** Learn to tell a "buttery" from a "chocolatey" aroma on some of the world's finest gourmet coffee estates. See page 187

❷ **Birdwatching** Seek out the resplendent quetzal and rare hummingbirds in the eerie cloud forests of the Chiriquí Highlands. See page 187

❸ **Hiking in the Chiriquí Highlands** From the glorious cloud forests of the Sendero de los Quetzales to the breathtaking panorama at the summit of Volcán Barú, the region provides some of Panama's most spectacular trails. See page 192

❹ **Parque Nacional Marino Golfo de Chiriquí** Head out in a boat to explore swathes of mangrove and idyllic tropical islands, with abundant marine life. See page 203

❺ **Santa Fé** This tranquil mountain town makes a good base for exploring the surrounding waterfalls and hills, with strenuous hiking on offer in the nearby national park. See page 208

❻ **Santa Catalina** The country's capital of surf boasts first-class waves and a laidback ambience. See page 211

❼ **Parque Nacional Coiba** You can enjoy outstanding diving, snorkelling, whale watching and pristine rainforests in this penitentiary turned wildlife reserve. See page 213

HIGHLIGHTS ARE MARKED ON THE MAP ON PAGE 182

5

Remedios (1589) and Alanje (1591), the colonizers also established numerous mission towns such as San Félix, San Lorenzo and Tolé. Though some Guaymí succumbed to their evangelizing efforts, others formed alliances among themselves and with passing pirates, and the towns were regularly raided and sometimes destroyed.

Following the separation from Colombia, the province of Chiriquí, which had been established in 1849, gained its own railway (which folded around 1980) in recognition of its agricultural importance; soon the United Fruit Company began banana production round Puerto Armuelles in 1927 and coffee plantations started to thrive. It is on such plantations that the Ngäbe and Buglé now work, travelling great distances

throughout the provinces of Chiriquí and Bocas del Toro – frequently exploited migrant wage labourers on rich lands that once belonged to their ancestors.

The Chiriquí Highlands

North of David rise the slopes of the eastern limits of the Cordillera de Talamanca, home to Volcán Barú (3475m), the country's highest point. These are the **Chiriquí Highlands**, or Tierras Altas, a region of forested peaks, fertile valleys and mountain

villages. The cool, temperate climate and stark scenery give the highlands a distinctly Alpine feel, an impression reinforced by the influence of the many European migrants who have settled here since the nineteenth century. Sadly, their agricultural success poses a threat to the survival of the region's spectacular **cloud forests**, which have been cleared at a devastating rate over the past forty years, while Chiriquí's picturesque rivers have attracted major hydroelectric projects, which are beginning to cause serious environmental damage, as well as posing a major threat to the livelihoods and cultural heritage of the indigenous communities.

More positively, large tracts of forest are now protected by **Parque Nacional Volcán Barú** and **Parque Internacional La Amistad**, whose flanks are home to wildlife including jaguars, pumas, tapirs and resplendent quetzals, and whose trails offer some of the best hiking in Panama.

Two roads wind up into the highlands on either side of Volcán Barú. The first climbs due north to **Boquete**, an idyllic coffee-growing town cradled in a picturesque valley, which has become popular among foreign retirees and tourists and is the easiest place from which to climb **Volcán Barú**. The second runs north from the town of La Concepción, 25km west of David, snaking 32km through countless dairy farms to the smaller settlement of **Volcán**, before threading its way through a steep-sided valley to **Cerro Punta**, the highest village in Panama and the best base for visiting the cloud forests and Amistad.

Boquete

Set in a scenic valley on the banks of the Río Caldera, 37km north of David and 1000m above sea level, **BOQUETE** is the largest town in the Chiriquí Highlands, with a population of more than 23,000. It is to gourmet **coffee** what Bordeaux is to fine wine, with an array of informative *finca* tours to choose from (see page 187). It's also a popular weekend resort, offering some of the country's best **hiking**, **birdwatching** and **adventure sports** in a delightfully refreshing climate. Life in the laidback town revolves around the small Parque Central and the main street, Avenida Central, dotted with souvenir shops, and at weekends, the town's riverside **park** attracts families with its duck ponds and picnic-tables. There's plenty to occupy you for several days – longer if you take a **Spanish course** at one of the town's acclaimed language schools (Ⓦstudyspanishinpanama.com, Ⓦspanishatlocations.com).

Technically, Boquete, spread out along the west bank of the Río Caldera and set against a mountainous backdrop, is separated into **Alto Boquete**, on the lip of the escarpment leading into the valley, and **Bajo Boquete**, considered to be Boquete proper. The surrounding slopes are dotted with shady coffee plantations, lush gardens and orange groves, and rise to rugged peaks. The thick cloud that envelops them often descends on the town as a veil-like fine mist known as *bajareque*, producing spectacular rainbows when the sun emerges. Only when the sky clears, most often in the early morning, can you see the imperious peak of **Volcán Barú**, which dominates the town to the northwest.

Brief history

Though the **Guaymí** were the first inhabitants of this remote valley, seeking refuge from the conquistadors, formal settlement only started in 1911, when **European and North Americans migrants** joined the existing population. Drawn to Panama during the canal construction eras, these pioneering settlers started up the various coffee estates and hotels as Boquete continued to develop, especially when, in 1916, the (now defunct) national railway improved connections with David and other lowland centres.

In recent decades, the increase in **foreign retirees** and associated **real estate boom**, driven by the government's attempts to increase foreign investment, has resulted in considerable deforestation and has forced major changes on the tranquil mountain community. Many Guaymí descendants (present-day Ngäbe and Buglé) are only resident for the duration of the coffee harvest (Oct–March, depending on the estate), when families migrate from across the province for the tiring, and often badly paid, work of picking the "cherries", the earnings from which have to support many for the rest of the year.

Centro de Visitantes

Alto Boquete • Mon–Fri 8am–4pm, Sat & Sun 9am–5pm • Free • Take any bus bound for David

Inconveniently, if splendidly, located on a bluff overlooking the town at Alto Boquete this state-of-the-art **Centro de Visitantes**, which opened in 2025, is worth the detour. Occupying two floors of the tourist office, it gives a good introduction to Boquete

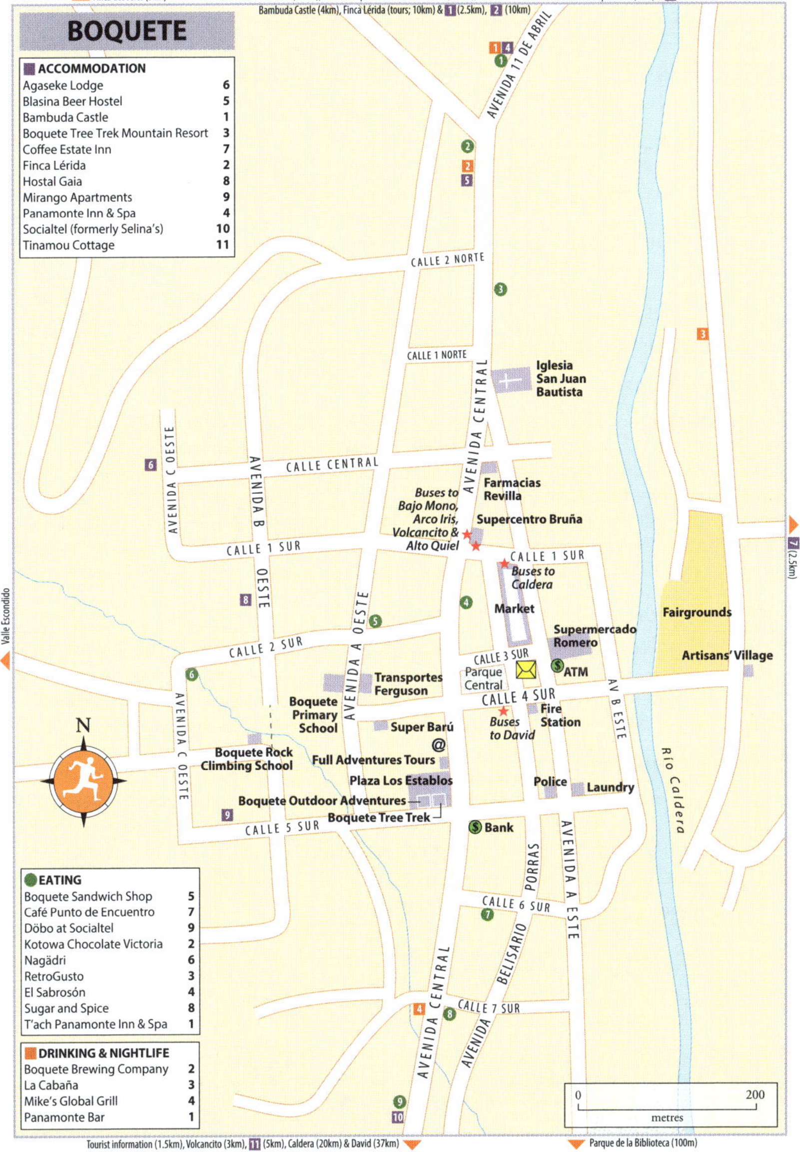

5

in both Spanish and English. On the ground floor, interactive displays focus on the area's biodiversity; upstairs the two-part exhibition turns to the region's early history, showcasing some ancient ceramics, and the history of coffee-growing. A **café** is planned.

Parque Biblioteca Boquete

Main entrance on • Daily 6am–6pm • Free

Financed by the town's library foundation – hence the name – the **Parque Biblioteca Boquete** comprises an area of recovered farmland on the western banks of the Río Caldera. Both an environmental and social project, it is still a work in progress as it only opened in 2022. So far, over 2500 trees have been planted – both native and introduced – and three stream-fed duck ponds have been created. The raised riverside footpath affords magnificent views up the valley and the shaded benches and tables make the park an ideal spot for a **picnic**.

Jardín El Explorador

Jaramillo Arriba, 2km north of Boquete • Daily 9am–6pm (in low season closed Mon and reduced hours) • Charge • ⓦ facebook.com/ElExploradorBQT • A 40min uphill walk; cross the bridge in Boquete and follow the road north; turn right at the fork and walk uphill to Jaramillo Arriba

If you've time to spare, and don't mind the high admission charge, the quirky **Jardín El Explorador** northeast of Boquete is worth the uphill hike. Its steep gardens are decorated with tin men and scarecrows, with plants protruding from Wellington boots and old TV sets, plus scattered homilies in Spanish. On a clear day the views of the Caldera Valley and Volcán Barú from the rose garden are fabulous, as are the strawberry juices at their café.

ARRIVAL AND INFORMATION — BOQUETE

By bus The only way to reach Boquete by bus is from David's bus terminal (4.50am–7.10pm; every 20min; returning at similar intervals 5.45am–7.45pm; 45min); buses drop passengers on the west side of the Parque Central, and depart just off its southeast corner.

By shuttle Hello Travel Panama (ⓦ hellotravelpanama.com) operates shuttle services to and from Bocas del Toro (rates include the water taxi) and Santa Catalina.

Tourist information The best advice and information is to be gained from the hotels or tour operators. The tourist office (Mon–Fri 8am–4pm, Sat & Sun 9am–5pm; no phone), is in the new Centro de Visitantes, in Alto Boquete, on the road to David. Few of the staff speak English and their knowledge is limited.

GETTING AROUND

On foot or by taxi Getting around the centre of Boquete is easy on foot, while a $2–3 taxi ride will get you to most places on the fringes of town.

By minibus Local minibuses from outside Supercentro Bruña, close to the Parque Central, head up to the surrounding hillside hamlets such as Volcancito and Alto Quiel (Mon–Sat 6.30/7am–5/6pm; every 15–40min, depending on demand; less frequent on Sun).

ACTIVITIES AND TOURS

You will need a **guide** for some of the hikes; inevitably, however, in a tourist-boom area everyone wants a piece of the cake, and some "guides" and operators lack the skills and equipment (first-aid kits for mountain guides, for example) for the job. If in doubt, seek **advice** from your accommodation. Half-day activities or excursions cost from around $35.

BOQUETE'S FESTIVALS

Boquete's main festival, **Feria de Flores y Café** (ⓦ instagram.com/feriadeboquete), takes place midway through the coffee harvest in January. Its ten-day riot of craft stalls, flowers, stage shows and throbbing late-night music centres on the fairgrounds bordering the eastern banks of the Río Caldera. Around $20,000 is spent annually on a vibrant floral carpet – which you can still admire once the fair has ended. The fairgrounds burst into colour again for the annual **Feria de las Orquídeas** in April, while the **Boquete Jazz and Blues Festival** (ⓦ instagram.com/boquetejazzandbluesfestival) reels in visitors in February/March.

GEISHA COFFEE

In most of the world, the word "**geisha**" evokes elaborately made-up Japanese entertainers. Mention the word in Boquete and you'll be naming a deluxe beverage that took the speciality coffee world by storm in 2004, prompting ecstatic experts to exhaust their thesauruses. As with fine wine, the world of gourmet coffee tasting or **cupping** is full of hype, jargon and poetry. Geisha – a variety of bean named after its village of origin in Ethiopia – has variously been characterized as spicy, honeyish, chocolatey and citrusy, with one critic likening the experience to "diving head first into a swimming pool of mixed fruits". The fuss started when the small Hacienda Esmeralda began sampling individual cups of beans from different parts of the farm – usually combined in blends – and discovered an extraordinary Ethiopian variety that had been growing neglected for some years. After being declared the world's best coffee on several occasions by the prestigious Specialty Coffee Association of America, the estate's "Esmeralda Especial" was soon very much in demand, setting auction records and prompting everyone else to start planting geisha. In 2024, the Elida Estate's geisha fetched a record price of over $10,000 per kilo. Since most of Boquete's quality beans are for export, you stand a better chance of locating them at Fortnum & Mason than anywhere in Panama. You certainly won't get to sample the best beans on a Boquete coffee tour (see page 187), but you will at least learn what goes into making a great coffee.

COFFEE TOURS

Coffee tours, offered in English or Spanish, range from 45min introductions to 4hr interactive marathons, involving a lesson on how to hone your cupping (tasting) skills and a tour of the estate and roasting facilities. For the 2–3hr tours that most visitors do, prices range from $35–45. Remember not to wear scent, repellent or any strong-smelling lotion. Tours need to be prebooked.

Elida Estate Alto Quiel Ⓦ lamastusfamilyestates.com. Popular tour of the award-winning estate (2hr 30min) comprising an informative stroll round the plantations a visit to the mill and a cupping session. Also offers longer, more in-depth tours. Transfer included.

Finca Casanga Palmira Ⓦ buypanamacoffee.com. Extremely popular tour as you get to try your hand at everything here, form picking the "cherries" (in season) to roasting the beans, which you can then take home with you. Transfer from their shop in town at 9am and 1pm.

Finca Dos Jefes El Salto Ⓦ boquetecoffeetour.com. Enjoyable hands-on tour (9am & 2pm; 2hr 30min–3hr; cash only) – including a roasting session – of a small organic farm where coffee is cultivated in accordance with the lunar calendar. The US owners practise Direct Trade and support a school feeding programme for Ngäbe children. Hotel transfer included.

Finca Lérida Alto Quiel Ⓦ hotelfincalerida.com. Spectacular setting for a comprehensive estate tour (most days morning and afternoon; 3hr), which includes watching the action in the original 1922 processing plant. Take the Alto Quiel bus from Boquete or a taxi – transfers are not included.

HIKING, RIDING AND BIRDWATCHING

Feliciano González Ⓣ 6624 9940, Ⓔ felicianogonzalez255@hotmail.com. Though Feliciano has retired from taking people up and down Volcán Barú, Boquete's most experienced mountain guide still has plenty of energy and enthusiasm (as well as improving English and Dutch) to take people hiking round the more scenic trails in the area.

Franklin Rovetto Ⓣ 6588 5054. Two-hour horseback excursions across the open countryside in the foothills of the cordillera round Caldera (including Boquete transfer; English spoken). It's cheaper to deal directly with Franklin than through the tour operators.

Jason Lara Ⓦ jasonlaratours.com. Trained English teacher turned renowned birding guide, Jason Lara is *the* person to take you birdwatching (with his telescope) for a morning. Birdwatching can also be booked through Boquete Tree Trek.

CANOPY TOURS

Boquete Tree Trek Office in Plaza Los Establos, zip line in Palo Alto Ⓦ boquetetreetrek.com. Soar across the valleys along an impressive 3km zip line tour high above Boquete (1600m) in a series of adrenaline surges that scarcely give you time to admire the breathtaking scenery. Alternative activities include a guided walk through the canopy along eight swing bridges; a half-day birdwatching in the cloudforest; or a combination of activities. After your outdoor exertions, you can chill at their pleasant terrace café-cum-bar-restaurant – you can even stay overnight in spacious cabins (see below). Transport included from Los Etablos (daily departures).

Finca El Oasis Ⓦ finca-oasis.com. For a more local experience (in Spanish) visit this family-run farm in the folds of Volcán Barú (but avoid weekends in high season); they have an eight-cable zip line and offer other outdoor activities.

5

WHITEWATER RAFTING FROM BOQUETE

Until the completion of a controversial dam in 2012, the tumbling waters of the 128km-long **Chiriquí Viejo**, hugging the border of Costa Rica, constituted one of the world's great **whitewater rafting** rivers. It's still a great route to raft, providing an exhilarating descent with mostly category III rapids carving their way through stunning scenery. There are, however, other equally picturesque and enjoyable rivers within closer striking distance of Boquete, such as the **Fonseca**, **Gariché** and **Majagua**, with category II and III rapids. The rafting **season** predictably dovetails with the rains (May to Dec).

Although the rafting outfits are located in Boquete, by the time all the passengers have been picked up and you've crawled up the spectacularly sinuous road to the drop-off point, Chiriquí Viejo is almost two hours' drive away, whatever the operators may claim. If you are staying in **David**, you can arrange a pickup there (which operators regularly do) or, if you're in **Volcán**, a rendezvous on the Interamericana at the turn-off in Concepción. The descent ends at the Interamericana bridge near Paso Canoas.

The rafting companies in Boquete are professional outfits, but the sport is not without risk. Bring sun block, trainers and a change of clothes (you will get wet and possibly thrown out of the raft); don't be afraid to ask for clarification on safety issues, and know your limits.

RAFTING AND KAYAKING OPERATORS

Boquete Outdoor Adventures Plaza Los Establos ⓦ boqueteoutdooradventures.com. Known for rafting, but also offers the usual hiking, birdwatching, coffee and adventure day-tours as well as multiday, multi-activity adventures – including kayaking and snorkelling in the Golfo de Chiriquí (see page 203) – with optional accommodation add-ons.

Full Adventures Tours Rafting, canyoning, bouldering, visiting the thermal pools in Caldera or the Cangilones in Gualaca.

CYCLING

Soul Planet Cycles ⓦ soulplanetcycles.com. Popular 2hr or 4hr e-bike tours of Boquete's natural surroundings. The more leisurely 4hr tour includes stops to sample local food and beverages.

U-Rides ⓦ u-rides. Mountain or e-bike rental, plus a map of suggested self-guided routes.

BEES AND BUTTERFLIES

Boquete Bees and Butterflies ⓦ natureboquete.com. offers a fascinating, though pricey, tour of their apiary, which can be combined with honey tastings and a peek at their small butterfly house. Good honey-focused gift shop.

ROCK CLIMBING AND RAPPELING

Boquete Rock Climbing School C 4 Sur ⓦ instagram.com/boqueterockclimbing. Offers rock climbing for all ages and levels of experience, plus slacklining, highlining and abseiling (rappelling). The favoured rock-climbing destination is El Gunko, at Los Ladrillos, a fascinating lump of basalt that was spewed out of Volcán Barú when it last erupted, a 10min drive north of Boquete.

ACCOMMODATION

SEE MAP PAGE 185

There's a decent range of **accommodation**, all with hot water, in a burgeoning mid-range market. Since most places only have a handful of rooms, everywhere fills up during holiday and festival periods – when prices are hiked – so book ahead.

IN TOWN

Agaseke Lodge Av "C" Oeste at C Central ⓣ 6005 1136, ⓔ agasekelodge@gmail.com. More a hybrid hostel-hostal than a lodge set in delightful flower-filled gardens. There are a handful of private rooms and one spacious six-bed dorm (the better deal) that share a porch laden with comfortable furniture and a homely semi-open kitchen-dining area at the back (which could be chilly on a winter night). Breakfast is available. Dorm $, doubles $$

Blasina Beer Hostel Av Central, 200m north of the church ⓦ blasina-beer-hostel.panamahotel24.com/en. Attached to the brewery – hence the name, which means loud (and sometimes live) music most nights. But great rooftop terrace and lawn with awesome mountain views. Good kitchen too though cleanliness here, and in the bathrooms, can be variable. Institutional-looking 14-bed dorm, but with privacy curtains, reading lights and sockets, plus several private rooms. Dorm $, doubles $$

Hostal Gaia Av "B" Oeste ⓣ 720 1952. Good-value hostel with helpful staff in a quiet residential street spread over two small houses. Each has its own kitchen, but they share the main house's living-dining area and balcony, which overlooks a shady garden with a bubbling stream at the far end. $$

Mirango Apartments C 5 Sur mirango-apartments.panamahotel24.com. Compact, modern city-style studios and two-bedroom apartments in a quiet street, a 5min walk from town. All possible amenities are fitted into the space, including more drawers and cupboards than you'll ever need, with knick-knacks and pictures on the wall to give a more homely feel. $$$

Panamonte Inn & Spa Av 11 de Abril, off the top end of Av Central panamonte.com. This historic 1914 hotel (with modern extensions) has hosted the likes of Roosevelt and Ingrid Bergman, and offers refined elegance in flower-filled surroundings. When the chill nights close in, huddle next to the cosy log fires while you sip your wine. Breakfast included in some rates. $$$$

Socialtel (formerly Selina's) Av Central, between Av Centenario and C 8 Sur socialtel.com/properties/Boquete. Part of an international chain explicitly aimed at Millennials, Gen Z and digital nomads – so plenty of co-working space and fast internet. Accommodation of all types: smart spacious rooms, concrete barrel-pods, dorms and more. Airy and light common areas with lots of polished and painted wood, plus a garden and stream running through the building and restaurant (no kitchen). Dorms $–$$, doubles $$–$$$

OUTSIDE TOWN

★ Bambuda Castle El Santuario, Los Naranjos, 5km north of town bambuda.com. Straight out of Disneyland, this castle – complete with moat! – has a backpacker vibe. It boasts a stunning setting and deluxe facilities, including an indoor pool, jacuzzi and grassy areas for sunning yourself and soaking up the views. Dorm bunks are high quality, while couples can share delightful Hobbit-hole doubles as well as romantic rooms in the tower. There's an on-site restaurant but buses to Boquete pass nearby if you prefer to eat out. Dorms $, doubles $$$

Boquete Tree Trek Mountain Resort Palo Alto, 8km northeast of Boquete boquetetreetrek.com. Home to Panama's longest and best zip line, you're high in the mountains here. Accommodations are in snug log cabins or wood-panelled rooms with warm duvets and heavy drapes to keep you warm at night, and a log fire in the main lodge. Views are spectacular and the on-site restaurant is fine, plus there's plenty to do in the surrounding forests. $$$

★ Coffee Estate Inn Jaramillo Arriba coffeeestateinn.com. A deluxe retreat in lush gardens, which enjoys an unparalleled reputation. It has studio rooms and larger bungalows, each with kitchenette. Each bungalow possesses a lounge, dining room and a terrace affording spectacular vistas across to Volcán Barú. A nearby mountain chalet is also available for rent. Light suppers and gourmet candlelit dinners are on offer and a coffee tour is included. Advance reservations essential. $$$–$$$$

Finca Lérida Alto Quiel, 10km up the valley hotelfincalerida.com. This is less about ambience and all about location: plum in the middle of a historic coffee estate, with cloud-forested slopes and birding trails above. The deluxe rooms have vast windows and private patios with quality hammocks affording stellar views down the valley on clear days. In the evenings, snuggle up by the fire in the cosy common room. Pricier rooms with old-world charm are available in the original family home. Breakfast included. $$$–$$$$

Tinamou Cottage Finca Habbus de Kwie, Jaramillo de Abajo coffeeadventures.net. Three snug self-catering cottages (variously accommodating 2–4 people) tucked away in a small Dutch-owned hillside coffee estate a 10min drive from Boquete; a choice retreat for birdwatchers who don't want to have to stay in town. Meals can be ordered. Reduced rates for online booking and stays of two nights or more. $$$

EATING

SEE MAP PAGE 185

Most restaurants are clustered round the main street, and charge tourist prices. If you're self-catering, or needing to buy food for a picnic in the hills, you've no worries. A vast El Rey supermarket sits on the main road into town, by Calle 11 Sur, while Super Baru, on C 4 Sur, stocks more imported deli-products.

Boquete Sandwich Shop C 2 Sur at Av "A" Oeste 730 9527, instagram.com/boquetesanwichshop. All-day breakfast, plus sandwiches, salads, wraps and burgers, in this popular ex-pat pit stop. All kinds of sandwiches, including US favourites pulled pork and BLTs, with fries. Inexpensive tea, coffee and soup. Service can be slow. $$

Café Punto de Encuentro C 6 Sur off Av Central 730 9340. Otherwise known as *Olga's*, this pleasant terrace overlooking a garden specializes in brunch, attracting Panamanians and foreigners alike, who feast on a varied menu of eggs – with great crispy bacon, French toast, *hojaldres*, *tortillas*, pancakes or waffles. Coffee refills allowed. Service is glacially slow when it's busy. Cash only. $$

Döbo at Socialtel Av Central, between Av Centenario and C 8 Sur dobo.cluvi.co. Part of celebrity chef Mario Castrellón's Grupo Maito, this casual-chic gastro pub does not disappoint. The wood-fired chicken and yam *sancocho* is a favourite or there are tacos and burgers. But save space for the delicious desserts: baked cheesecake in blackberry coulis or the banana geisha cake with coffee caramel. $$–$$$

Kotowa Chocolate Victoria Av Central at Av 11 de Abril instagram.com/kotowachocolate. You know a café is serious about its hot chocolate (as it is about its coffee – they serve geisha) when you choose the percentage of cacao to have in your cup. You can also pair a glass of wine with a selection of artisanal chocolates that are temptingly on display. Total indulgence. $$

★ **Ngädri** C 2 Sur ⓦ facebook.com/restngadriboquete. Imaginative menu of contemporary Latin dishes beautifully presented, using locally sourced ingredients. Try the tuna in lemongrass sauce, or the vegan broccoli and cauliflower curry in coconut sauce. All mouthwateringly good. $$$–$$$$

RetroGusto Av Central, between C 1 & 2 Norte ⓦ facebook.com/retrogustopanama. Fine dining provided by an award-winning Italian owner-chef in a convivial environment. Beyond the traditional artisanal Neopolitan pizzas, there's plenty of gourmet fare, such as risotto with black truffles and beef in red wine. $$$–$$$$

El Sabrosón Av Central, between C 1 Sur and C Central ⓣ 720 2147. Probably the most reliable of the local *cafeterías* – hence the long but swift-moving lunchtime queues – serving hot, freshly made rice, plantain, beans, salads and a range of meat dishes, plus usually some fish, all for a few dollars. $–$$

★ **Sugar and Spice** Av Central at C 7 Sur ⓦ sugarandspiceboquete.com. This bakery-café is a major expat meeting place, serving a vast array of great cooked breakfasts, salads, soups and deli-sandwiches using their posh breads, such as sourdough, nine-grain and rye. Sweet snacks include a dizzying array of muffins. Efficient service. $$

T'ach Panamonte Inn & Spa Av 11 de Abril ⓦ panamonte.com. Hands-down the most sumptuous dining in Boquete, laid on by celebrity chef Charlie Collins. Inventive gourmet dishes, such as salmon smoked on cedar with cilantro aioli, can be savoured at candlelit damask-covered tables in the formal dining room or more casually in the fireside lounge or on the terrace. Try the tasting menu. $$$$

DRINKING AND NIGHTLIFE

SEE MAP PAGE 185

Boquete Brewing Company Av Central, 200m north of the church ⓣ 6403 7576, ⓦ boquetebrewingcompany.com. The place to quench your thirst after a hike, and a favourite expat hangout, offering a changing menu of craft beers (and a three-beer tasting tray) and ciders – some packing a punch – along with a bar food menu. Occasional live music at the weekend.

La Cabaña Left after the bridge, 200m north of the fairground. For a loud blast of a variety of sounds (especially reggaeton) and blinking plasma screens, try dancing or drinking in this joint's dark recesses. Fri & Sat only.

Mike's Global Grill C 7 Sur, at Av Central ⓦ mikesglobalgrill.com. Hit the happy hour (3–6pm) then stay on for the live music (usually good), or the popular Friday night fried chicken and open mic (more hit and miss).

Panamonte Bar Panamonte Inn, Av 11 de Abril ⓦ panamonte.com. For a refined cocktail or an elegant glass of wine, this is the spot, especially on the intimate back patio, where you can sink into the sofas with your martini, and still enjoy the benefits of a blazing hearth.

Short hikes round Boquete

There are a number of attractive half-day **hikes** within a short bus or taxi ride of Boquete, promising panoramic **views**, sparkling **waterfalls** or prime **birdwatching**, often on or around private land that abuts the two main national parks.

Trails around Finca Lérida

Alto Quiel • Daily 7am–4.30pm • Guided birdwatching last about 4hr, including lunch; day-visitors can pay to walk the trails with a map • Take an Alto Quiel bus from Boquete and get off at the entrance (20–25min)

The **Finca Lérida** ecolodge (see page 187) offers good-value hikes through 10km of trails on its estate; **birdwatching**, you may see quetzals, highland hummingbirds such as the white-throated mountain gem, sulphur-winged parakeets, silver-throated tanagers and the impressive black guan. Much of the trail network actually lies within the **Parque Internacional La Amistad** (see page 197), next to Parque Nacional Volcán Barú.

Sendero de las Tres Cascadas

North of Boquete on the Bajo Mono loop • Daily 7am–3pm • Charge • ⓦ instagram.com/thelostwaterfalls • Driving, turn right at the T-junction 8.5–9km north of Boquete, in the direction of the Sendero de los Quetzales, and park at the sign 1.2km along the road (from where it's a 10min hike to the entrance); otherwise, catch a Bajo Mono bus, get off at the T-junction and walk the rest of the way, or take a taxi

Also known as the Lost Waterfalls – a somewhat ironic name given the trail's popularity – the **Sendero de las Tres Cascadas** is a delightfully scenic cloud-forest trail that takes in three waterfalls, each of which tumbles into a (cold) natural swimming pool. The first two are the most accessible, though still involve some moderately strenuous patches, especially when muddy. The last cascade involves more boulder clambering. Inevitably the trail is at its wettest when the falls are at their most impressive, but even in the dry season, be prepared for some mud. Give yourself two or three hours to visit all three waterfalls at a leisurely pace, and at weekends in the dry season, get there early before the crowds.

Sendero Pipa de Agua

8km northwest of Boquete • Daily 8am–3pm • Charge • Take a Bajo Mono bus from Boquete and ask to be dropped off at the trailhead at the T-junction with the road that leads to the Sendero de los Quetzales

An easy 4km trail, **Sendero Pipa de Agua** – also known as the Cascada Escondida (Hidden Waterfall) – is a birdwatchers' favourite, following a water pipeline up a relatively gentle incline in a dead-end valley to an impressive waterfall. Beware of a scam by the occasional unscrupulous taxi driver who, in order to save petrol, leaves hikers here claiming it's the start of the Sendero de los Quetzales (see page 191). That said, quetzals can occasionally be spotted on this trail too, which will take a couple of hours to the end and back.

Piedra de Lino and Piedra del Musgo

Two increasingly popular short trails are the **Piedra de Lino** and the **Piedra del Musgo.** Favoured by rock climbers (see page 188), their main attraction for the casual hiker are the superb panoramic views from the large boulders (*piedras*) that mark their summits. The Piedra de Lino is the easier of the two, an hour-long steep slog mainly through farmland and a little secondary forest. You can hike from town, or take the Arco Iris minibus, getting off at the trailhead, marked with an official sign. It offers a great overview of Boquete and Volcán Barú. The Piedra del Musgo, off the road to Jaramillo Arriba, is a longer climb (1hr 30min) with a moss-covered sugar-loaf stone at the trail end.

Parque Nacional Volcán Barú

Jade-coloured cloud forests sit in the mist high above Boquete, many of them within the boundaries of **PARQUE NACIONAL VOLCÁN BARÚ**, which stretches west towards the town of Volcán. This is prime **birdwatching** territory, and the favoured habitat of the metallic green **resplendent quetzal**, the Holy Grail of Boquete birding. The male in particular, with its ruby breastplate and lengthy trailing iridescent tail, which it only dons for the breeding season, is a dazzling sight. These otherwise elusive birds are at their most visible from the end of December to April, just after first light, when breeding pairs can sometimes be seen on the path.

Sendero de los Quetzales

A far more beautiful, rugged hike than the slog up the brooding volcano it skirts, the 8km **Sendero de los Quetzales** offers the additional thrill of a possible glimpse of a male quetzal in full regalia (Dec–April). The trail reopened in 2025 after being closed for several years for maintenance following serious landslides, so the route should now be easy to navigate. Nevertheless, hiring a guide (see page 187) will substantially enhance your chances of spotting a quetzal as well as allowing you to learn more about other

SAFETY IN THE MOUNTAINS

Although you can enjoy the shorter trails round Boquete on your own, it is advisable to engage a **guide** (see page 187) to hike the longer ones. The guide should be experienced and have a first-aid kit and emergency equipment with them. That said, many tourists still hike on their own, which in fine weather isn't usually too hazardous. Yet every year someone gets seriously lost when bad weather closes in since there are no trail maps and virtually no signage. Most notably in 2014, two young Dutch backpackers set off on the Il Pianista trail and never returned. Whichever trail you take, don't hike alone and make sure you tell your lodgings where you are going. In recent years, the authorities have tended to close the national park trails altogether when the weather is bad.

5

fauna and flora. If you go on an **organized tour**, which is strongly advised, transport to/from Boquete will be provided; if you decide to walk the trail on your own towards Cerro Punta, you can get your luggage transferred for you (see page 193).

The trail can be hiked in both directions, though conventional wisdom has it that it's easier to start from the Cerro Punta side (over 2400m) because of the drop in altitude between there and the eastern trailhead at Alto Chiquero (over 1800m). A moderately fit person soaking up the scenery and making occasional stops to spot the odd shy bird in the undergrowth should count on five to six hours to complete the trail, including the extra few kilometres to get to/from the official trailhead on the Cerro Punta side.

Climbing Volcán Barú

The unremarkable haul up **Volcán Barú** (3474m), Panama's highest point, is rewarded at the summit, which on a good day boasts a truly breathtaking panorama of the Pacific and Caribbean, both dotted with a myriad of islands. The **dry season** (roughly mid-Dec to April) is the best time to attempt the ascent but even then clouds and rain can close in quickly. To maximize your chance of a clear view, you should attempt some, or all, of the climb at night – for which you'll need a torch – in order to arrive at dawn. At the time of writing, this should mean camping overnight at the rather inadequate camping spot, Los Fogones, an hour from the summit, since the park office only opens to register entrants at 4am. In practice, many hikers still set off in the dark, without registering and without paying the park fee, in order to do the climb in one day.

Going with a **guide** (see page 187) is highly recommended in case you injure yourself or the weather turns bad. If you set off from the trailhead, at 11pm or midnight, the 13.5km ascent takes four to six hours, getting you to the peak in time to enjoy a sunrise picnic – you'll need to turn a blind eye to the radio masts and graffiti-covered rocks on one side – before descending. No rock-climbing skills are necessary, just the grit to plod up a boulder-strewn track (dodging the clouds of dust from passing 4WD vehicles shortly before sunrise) and endure a little rock-scrambling. You'll need warm, waterproof clothing, as it's cold on the summit, along with plenty of water and the usual hiking essentials.

ACTIVITIES AROUND VOLCÁN

Hiking and **birdwatching** are very much the order of the day, in particular on the forested slopes of the volcano within the protected boundaries of **Parque Nacional Volcán Barú**, which lies between Volcán and Boquete. The **Sendero de los Quetzales** (see page 191) is by far the most popular destination for hikers and birding enthusiasts, offering a wonderful twisting trail through verdant forest round the northern flanks of the volcano. Accessing the **summit** of Volcán Barú itself (see page 192) from this western side (from near Paso Ancho) is a much more daunting though potentially satisfying prospect, clambering across overgrown lava flows and navigating round precipitous tors, where you should look out for the spectacular black and white hawk eagle soaring above. It's either an overnight trek, for which you'll need to bring (or rent) and carry your own equipment, or an exhausting day-long slog up and down, which only the super-fit should attempt. Rates are around $180–200. Less energetic targets include the **Pozos Termales de Tisingal**, a collection of thermal pools, or the breathtaking 80m cascade of the **Salto de Tigre**, both in a lovely setting off the Río Sereno road.

TOUR OPERATORS AND GUIDES

Baru Expedition baruexpedition.com. Nationally and internationally certified bilingual wilderness guide Jorge López runs this outfit, which specializes in leading expeditions up the eponymous volcano, but offers other tours, and can rent out equipment too.

Tamandúa Guadalupe tamanduaphoto.com. Top-notch birding and naturalist guides running high-end multiday birding trips (including up Volcán Barú) but they can put you in touch with someone to guide shorter hikes or more casual birdwatching.

Climbing Volcán Barú from the **western side** (see box, page 192) is more physically demanding, and takes longer, but is much more rewarding as you are taken up a path, albeit very indistinct in places, rather than a road, and across more varied terrain. A guide is obligatory (and even more necessary) this side.

ARRIVAL AND DEPARTURE — PARQUE NACIONAL VOLCÁN BARÚ

MIA STATIONS AND FEES

If you are on a tour or with a guide (see page 187), the park (and camping) fee may be included in the tour price. Independent hikers should pay the park fee(s) online (see page 42) and register at the MIA stations at either end of the Sendero de los Quetzales, about 8km apart: the Alto Chiquero ranger station and refuge is at the Boquete side of the trek, while the El Respingo ranger station is at the Cerro Punta end. There are also two MIA offices at the start of the trail that climbs Volcán Barú, on both the Boquete and Cerro Punta sides, where you are supposed to sign in and may have to show proof of payment. These places are not always staffed. If you are not accompanied by a guide, remember to tell your lodgings where you're going.

ALTO CHIQUERO RANGER STATION

By taxi The Alto Chiquero park office, accessible by 2WD (but better in 4WD) is a steep, almost completely tarred 11km up from Boquete, reachable by taxi.

By bus You can take a bus as far as the T-junction, followed by a 3km hike.

EL RESPINGO RANGER STATION

By taxi You can hire a 4WD taxi from Cerro Punta to the park office a 40min hike below the trailhead or go right up to the refuge.

By bus You can get dropped off any Cerro Punta-bound bus from Volcán and walk the rough 5km road to the office.

THE VOLCÁN BARÚ TRAILHEAD

You'll need a 4WD taxi to take you to the trailhead at Los Llanos from Boquete; you can arrange a pickup time, or simply walk down to the main road and flag down a taxi or bus there.

INFORMATION

Park information The Centro de Visitantes in Alto Boquete may be able to provide you with up-to-date information. Failing that, Boquete's MIA office (Mon–Fri 8am–4pm) is at C 21 Suroeste, Alto Boquete, several kilometres south of the town centre.

Luggage transport service If you want to hike the Sendero de los Quetzales to Cerro Punta without returning and without carrying your rucksack, go to Transportes Ferguson (Boquete ☎720 1454, Volcán ☎771 4566; both Mon–Fri 8.30am–4pm, Sat 8.30am–noon). They have an office at Av "A" Oeste at C 4a Sur in Boquete, and another behind the Romero's in Volcán, on C 3a Este, and can courier your rucksack to the other location within 24hr.

ACCOMMODATION

In addition to the **camping** detailed below there is also a small camping spot (Los Fogones) about two-thirds of the way up Volcán Barú. It's on an inconvenient slope, with no facilities, though at the time of writing, funds had been allocated to make improvements.

MIA bunkhouses/camping You can arrange to sleep in the bunkhouse at the ranger stations at either end of the Sendero de los Quetzales, though you'll need to take warm bedding and food, and be prepared for cold-water showers. Payment needs to be made online in advance. Camping also available. Camping $, dorms $$

Mirador la Roca Halfway along the Sendero de los Quetzales. The nicest camping location, at a picnic spot with tables, but with no other facilities. $

Volcán

Spreadeagled on the lower western slopes of Volcán Barú, at an altitude of 1700m, the twelve-thousand-strong town of **VOLCÁN** (formally known as El Hato de Volcán) is little more than a glorified road junction en route to the more appealing fertile valleys of Cerro Punta and the cloud forests of the Parque International La Amistad, or the little-used Costa Rica border crossing at Río Sereno. That said, it does offer the most impressive views of the volcano, and a rejuvenated main street – with a wide pavement lit with retro street lamps, punctuated with benches and the odd shrub, plus a sprinkling of restaurants – has encouraged folk to promenade on summer evenings. There are also a few diverting excursions, not least to scale **Volcán Barú** (see page 192),

5

and you could easily spend a couple of enjoyable days exploring the area, but if you're short of time it's probably best to push on to Cerro Punta and Guadalupe. Even if you don't overnight here, it's a convenient place to stock up on supplies for self-catering in the mountains (leave the fruit and vegetables to Cerro Punta) and visit a bank.

ARRIVAL AND GETTING AROUND — VOLCÁN

By bus Buses between David and Cerro Punto and Guadalupe pass through Volcán (5am–8pm; every 15min; 1hr 20min; last return bus from Guadalupe 8pm). Buses from David also pass through Volcán en route to and from the Costa Rica border at Río Sereno (6.20am–6.20pm; every 45min–1hr; 1hr 10min).

By taxi Taxis hover near the main junction, charging a couple of dollars for a short hop round town.

ACCOMMODATION

Hostal Victoria Volcán C 4a Norte, between C5s and 6a Oeste ⓦ victoriahostelpa.com. Converted family home a few blocks from the main street, with simple, spotless rooms. Advertised rates are ridiculously overpriced but seem to be permanently on special offer. Tours on offer. $$

★ **Los Brezos** C 3 Norte ⓦ losbrezosvolcan.com. This surprisingly upscale hotel – for Volcán – has six stylish, modern rooms, with plenty of polished hardwood, lots of light and balconies from which to admire the mountain views, plus all the amenities you'd expect in a business hotel: desk, minibar, laptop safe, coffee-maker etc. Staff are welcoming and professional. Rates include breakfast. $$$

Las Plumas Paso Ancho, 2km north of Volcán ⓦ yourpanama.com/panama-las-plumas-holiday-homes. Excellent value for groups or families with their own vehicle, comprising four fully equipped (laundry, cable TV, wi-fi and phone) two- or three-bedroom modern self-catering bungalows set in manicured wooded grounds, bordered by the Chiriquí Viejo. Three-night minimum stay; good long-term rates. $

EATING

Burrico's Av Central ⓦ facebook.com/burricosvolcan. Bright tables and cheery Mexican decorations make this an inviting spot, even before you see the food: a mix of Panamanian – a superior yet moderately priced *menú del día* with a choice of beef, chicken and pork – and Tex-Mex favourites. $–$$

Cerro Brujo Gourmet Restaurant Brisas del Norte, 500m up a dirt road signed off east of Av Central ⓦ facebook.com/cerrobrujo. Overlooking a garden, the delightful, Mediterranean-style stone-and-tile interior is laden with artwork. An eclectic changing daily menu lists a couple of locally sourced, organic gourmet dishes, such as dorado fillet in sesame seeds and mushrooms, and doesn't disappoint; leave room for dessert. Regular musical, artistic and gourmet evenings. Reservations preferred.

Fanny's Terrace Bistro 1.8km up the road to Cerro Punta on the right-hand side ⓦ facebook.com/fannybistroterrace. In addition to the regular Italian-focused American comfort food (pizza, pastas and grills, including vegan options), this unassuming roadside diner provides excellent daily specials chalked up on the board, to enjoy on the eponymous terrace. All is freshly prepared and served with enthusiasm. $$–$$$

Restaurante Aquí Va la Niña Av Central at C 1 Oeste ⓦ instagram.com/aquivalanina. A popular restaurant sharing a relaxed semi-outdoor food court with several other food outlets. It serves burgers and nice crispy fries with craft bear. Elsewhere there's *comida criolla* at *El Tamalito* and the *Mama Chila* café sells coffee, *empanadas* and cakes. With swings for the kids to play on while you wait, it's an altogether relaxed place. $$

★ **Restaurante Los Brezos** C 3 Norte, Brisas del Norte ⓦ losbrezosvolcan.com. Ignore the elevator music and bland hotel dining room, the food is seriously tasty here, and surprisingly modestly priced, given this is the top place in town. The eclectic menu of international and Panamanian dishes has plenty to offer, such as *paella Panameña*, quinoa Mediterranean salad and pad Thai. $$–$$$

Around Volcán

A few kilometres west of Volcán lie several modest attractions – a couple of **lakes**, a **coffee estate** and an **archeological site** – which will appeal to enthusiasts or may be worth swinging by if you've a free couple of hours and your own transport. South of the town, the **waterfall** of Cañon Macho de Monte is a spectacular sight in season.

Lagunas de Volcán and Janson Coffee Farm

3–4km west of Volcán • **Farm** Tues–Sun 10am–6pm • Charge, includes guided tours • ⓦ jansoncoffee.com • 4WD needed for the lagunas, 4km west of Volcán along C 6a Oeste, crossing the disused airstrip. For the coffee estate, travel 3km west along C 5a Oeste

The **Lagunas de Volcán** (1300m), Panama's highest wetlands and an important sojourn for migrating **birds**, will appeal to birders keen to spot northern jacanas, masked ducks and, in the forested fringes, the rare rose-throated becard. The lakes are on the land of the **Janson Coffee Farm**, which offers several estate tours and has a delightful **coffee shop** that provides magnificent views of Volcán Barú as well as excellent coffee and cake.

Sitio Barriles

5km west of Volcán, on the road to Caisán • Daily 7am–5pm • Charge, includes guided tours in English or Spanish • ⓣ 771 4281 or 6575 1828 • A taxi from Volcán will cost a few dollars

The private *finca* of the Landau family harbours one of Panama's most important archeological sites, **Sitio Barriles**, named after the barrel-shaped stones unearthed in 1947 that provided the first modern-day evidence of what is presumed to be the country's oldest pre-Columbian culture, which was prominent around 500 AD. The most interesting artefacts have been carted away to Panama City, but the farm possesses a couple of **petroglyphs** – the *pièce de résistance* is a silky smooth slab of basalt, which when doused with water reveals yet more squiggles. There's also an unconvincing re-creation of an archeological dig chamber and a small, rather chaotic display of ceramics.

Cañon Macho de Monte

Roughly 13km south of Volcán, east of the Concepción–Volcán road • No fixed hours • Free • Any David–Cerro Punta bus can let you off at the hamlet of Cuesta de Piedra; take the turn east at the mini-super and hike 2.5km along the tarred road, crossing two bridges, to the canyon – if travelling by car, park at the hydroelectric project, where a path leads to the precipice above the fall

A worthwhile detour is **Cañon Macho de Monte**, a dramatic (less so in the dry season) waterfall that tumbles into a gorge. It's also a good **birdwatching** site, where orange-collared manakins and fiery-billed aracaris are the stars of the show.

EATING — CAÑON MACHO DE MONTE

Mirador Alan-Her Road to Volcán, 2.5km south of Cuesta de Piedra. A good pit stop for tea or coffee, this place is also a top spot to pick up regional delicacies, from local mozzarella and ricotta to *bienmesabe* – a slow-cooked dessert of rice, milk and *panela* – and *sopa borracha* ("drunken soup"), sponge cake soaked in cinnamon-flavoured rum.

The road to Río Sereno

From Volcán, a well-paved road snakes its way 42km to the small border town of **Río Sereno** (see box, page 196), swooping round tight bends, across cascading rivers and through coffee and banana plantations. Unless you're bound for Costa Rica, the only reason to make this spectacular drive is to visit a couple of places favoured by nature lovers. **Mount Totumas**, which abuts Parque Internacional La Amistad, is a private reserve tucked away in cloud forest, 7km north of the Río Sereno road, some 10km west of Volcán; it boasts a range of lodgings and trails that make the most of the spectacular natural surroundings. A further 17km west lies **Finca Hartmann**, a birding hot spot and charming coffee estate, which also offers delightful back-to-nature lodgings.

Finca Hartmann

Santa Clara • Coffee tours, in Spanish or English (1hr 15min); Charge for trail access for day-visitors • ⓦ facebook.com/fincahartmann • Any David–Río Sereno bus (via Volcán) can drop you at the entrance, which is signposted – if you are driving, the 1km drive up a dirt track from the entrance is best undertaken in a high-clearance vehicle, or 4WD

A family-run, ecofriendly coffee estate, **Finca Hartmann** has recorded more than 280 species of **bird** – it's the best place in Panama to see the dazzling turquoise cotinga and fiery-billed aracari – as well as 62 different mammals. Birds are most easily spotted round the main farm at Palo Verde, where the coffee roasting and other operations take place. Taking a **coffee tour** (best during harvesting season, Oct–March) also allows you to stroll the five **trails** on the estate, one of which leads up to Amistad park (see page 197).

5

ACCOMMODATION **THE ROAD TO RÍO SERENO**

★ **Mount Totumas** 18km northwest of Volcán ⊕6963 5069, ⓦmounttotumas.com. A special place in a fabulous setting, surrounded by cloud forest, with several glorious mid-priced lodgings, made predominantly of wood. The four rooms in the *Coffee House* share a long porch – perfect for birdwatching – and have direct access to the coffee-roasting facilities; the self-catering two-storey *Cabin* sleeps up to seven; and the *Bellbird Lodge* boasts three rooms, two suites – all with vast windows and skylights – and a fine-dining restaurant open to all guests. The *Howler Tree Cabin,* a more rustic but delightful proposition is hidden away in the forest. All the rest have plenty of deck and hammock space from which to admire the breathtaking views and the iridescent hummingbirds; a vast network of trails to waterfalls, thermal springs and mountains await the more active. Access via high-clearance 4WD, or from Volcán a $60 transfer (one way), or local bus to Los Pozos (followed by a 2hr 30min hike). Two-night minimum stay. Breakfast included in most. Set-menu meals in the restaurant or use the shared kitchen in the *Coffee House*. Rooms & suites $$$, cabins $$$$

★ **Ojo de Agua Cabañas** Finca Hartmann, Santa Clara ⊕6450 1853, ⓦluis-miranda-rekr.squarespace.com/cabins-rental. The *finca's* two rustic cabins are tucked away in the forest. The smaller one-bedroom *cabaña* is cosier, with a kitchenette, whereas the larger six-bedroom two-storey cabin with full kitchen and fireplace is more of a bunkhouse, accommodating up to ten people. Both have hot-water showers (though neither has electricity – gas lamps and candles are used) and are regularly visited by howler and white-faced capuchin monkeys. A sturdy 4WD is necessary for access, or you can arrange transfers. Cabin $$, bunkhouse $$$

Cerro Punta and around

Shortly after leaving Volcán, the road to **Cerro Punta** starts to twist and turn, threading its way up a mist-filled ravine. The **Río Chiriquí Viejo** gushes through, flanked by almost vertical pine-clad slopes dotted with alpine chalets, some established by early European settlers. Roadside stalls overflow with locally produced vegetables; stop off and gorge on a heaped bowl of strawberries or blackberries and *natilla* (a local creamy custard) or pick up a pot of home-made jam.

Cerro Punta

Set almost 2000m above sea level in a fertile basin-shaped valley – the scarcely recognizable crater of an extinct volcano – and surrounded by densely forested, rugged mountains, **CERRO PUNTA** is the highest village in Panama. In the ninety or so years since it was formally settled, partly by Europeans, agriculture has expanded so rapidly that the area now supplies over sixty percent of all the vegetables consumed in Panama, with fields forming a tapestry of produce from lettuce, onions and carrots to commercial flowers and strawberries. This agricultural boom has come at the expense of the surrounding

CROSSING THE BORDER AT RÍO SERENO

A 35km drive west from Volcán along a spectacular winding mountain road brings you to the somnolent frontier town of **RÍO SERENO** and the least-used **border crossing** with Costa Rica. It is easily reached by bus from David, via Volcán (5am–5pm; every 45min–1hr 30min; 2hr 30min). The last return bus to David leaves Río Sereno at 4.15–5pm, passing through Volcán after 1hr 10min. Buses leave Río Sereno from close to the T-junction at the entrance to the town. **Panamanian immigration** (daily 8am–5pm; ⊕722 8054) is 400m from the bus stop, by the police station (look for the flag); the **Costa Rican immigration** office (same hours, though note that Costa Rica is one hour behind Panama) is next door. Don't forget that whether entering Panama or Costa Rica you'll need to get an exit stamp from immigration in the country you are leaving and an entry stamp from immigration in the country you are entering; you will also need to show proof of onward travel and financial solvency. Should you get stranded in Río Sereno for the night, the town's lone **accommodation**, the *Posada Los Andes* (⊕6845 7078; $) on the main square can provide you with a rudimentary room wood-panelled room in a fairly rickety building, though Finca Agroturística Doña Rufa (ⓦinstagram.com/fincadonarufa; $$), 2km north of town, on a coffee estate, is likely to hold greater appeal.

forests, but the village, frequently swathed in cloud, and the surrounding fields are still undeniably beautiful, filled with abundant flowers and buzzing with hummingbirds.

The spectacular scenery, together with the cool, crisp mountain air (temperatures drop to well below 10°C at night), makes Cerro Punta a superlative base for **hiking**, and the pristine cloud forests of La Amistad (see page 197) and Volcán Barú (see page 192) national parks are both within easy reach.

Guadalupe

From Cerro Punta, the bus heads off in a loop, turning left and downhill, passing the turn-off to Las Nubes and Amistad to the left. It then climbs steadily uphill to **GUADALUPE**, an enchanting flower-filled hamlet of around four hundred inhabitants, dominated by the rustic *Los Quetzales Lodge and Spa*. From here, the road (and bus) sweeps round to the right, heading back downhill to Cerro Punta. Orchid fanatics may fancy dropping in at nearby **Finca Dracula** (ⓦ fincadracula.com; charge) – a ten-minute walk from *Los Quetzales* – while horse lovers can arrange a visit to a nearby **stud farm** (ⓦ harascerropunta.com).

ARRIVAL AND DEPARTURE — CERRO PUNTA AND AROUND

By bus Buses from David via Volcán pull up on Cerro Punta's one main street before heading up to Guadalupe (5am–8pm; every 30min; 2hr), though sometimes a change of bus is necessary. The last return bus to David leaves Guadalupe at 7.45pm, passing through Cerro Punta 10min later.

ACCOMMODATION AND EATING

CERRO PUNTA

★ **Hostal Cielito Sur** Nueva Suiza, main road 5km south of Cerro Punta, 10km north of Volcán ⓦ cielitosur.com. This outstanding B&B is run by genial hosts, who provide a perfect blend of knowledgeable warm hospitality and privacy. Set amid beautiful grounds, five vast, immaculate rooms, some with kitchens, are decorated with traditional Panamanian artwork and share a homely living room. Rates include a substantial breakfast with plenty of home-made goodies. Two-night minimum stay in high season. $$$

GUADALUPE

Hostal Chumbaga ⓦ instagram.com/chumbagahostal. This friendly family-run operation is a sound budget choice, offering comfortable warm beds and hot-water showers, plus cable TV to entertain you on a chilly misty night. The preferred upstairs rooms share a wraparound balcony. Dine at their local restaurant next door, or splash out on more refined fare at *Los Quetzales*. $$

★ **Los Quetzales Lodge and Spa** ⓦ losquetzales.com. The lodge offers standard doubles, suites and glorious cloud-forest cabins that sleep five to six people. All guests have access to the comfy lounge and games room, full of books and sofas, warmed by a log fire, and with table tennis. Activities include spa treatments, cycling, horseriding, birdwatching and cloud-forest walks. The restaurant caters to a range of budgets, offering delicious soups with home-made bread, pizza and pasta, alongside pricier, fancier mains accompanied by more vegetables than you are likely to see in a month elsewhere in Panama. Doubles $$, cabins $$$

Parque Internacional La Amistad

Just 6km from Cerro Punta or Guadalupe, the hamlet of **Las Nubes** provides access to **Parque Internacional La Amistad** (International Friendship Park), often abbreviated to PILA or Amistad. Covering 4000 square kilometres of precipitous forested mountains straddling Panama and Costa Rica, the park forms a crucial link in the "biological corridor" of protected areas running the length of Central America. Given its varied topography, Amistad is the most ecologically diverse park in the region, including more than four hundred different **bird** species (see page 310), making it the most important protected area in Panama after the Darién. Although almost all of the Panamanian section lies in Bocas del Toro, it is far more accessible from the Pacific side of the country. There are three short **trails** with *miradores* offering excellent views of some of the highest mountains in Panama (at least before the cloud descends) and a 50m **waterfall**. At the time of writing, longer, steeper trails were reportedly being renovated, including the less distinct trail (8km round trip) through virgin cloud forest to the summit of Cerro Picacho (2986m), but you'll need to go with a guide for this hike and stay overnight.

ARRIVAL AND INFORMATION — PARQUE INTERNACIONAL LA AMISTAD

On foot or by taxi From Cerro Punta or Guadalupe, walk the 6km – or take a taxi – to the entrance.

By car The road is tarred up until the park entrance; thereafter, you need 4WD. If driving a saloon car, you'll probably need to park at the gate and walk from there to the office.

MIA office and fees You should pay the park fee (and accommodation) online in advance and but you can still pay for a camping spot or bunk bed (see below) at the permanently staffed MIA office, a 10min walk uphill from the entrance.

ACCOMMODATION AND EATING

Finca Galán To the left of the park entrance fincagalan.com. Abutting the national park, this buffer reserve currently offers three large well-equipped cabins for large groups (6, 10 & 14) and a raised concrete camping area under a large aluminium roof, aimed at even larger groups. The aesthetics are sadly lacking in the lodgings but hopefully the nascent botanical gardens (which will need a few years to develop) will make up for it. Trails which will meet up with the trails in national park, are also being cleared. $$$$

Mama Chila to the left of the park entrance instagram.com/mamachilacafe. Quirky café in a converted shipping container displaying local artwork. The terrace offers great mountain view when the mist lifts. You can't guarantee all the menu items will be available, but there's usually toasted sandwiches with fries, coffee and cake, and local strawberries with cream – better without the marshmallows. $$

MIA refuge One of the larger, better-equipped bunkhouses, with kitchen facilities but cold water only. Bring your own food – though you could pop down to *Mama Chila* (see above) – and a warm sleeping bag, as it gets cold at night. Camping $, dorm $

Along the La Fortuna road

The serpentine road that traverses the continental divide to the Caribbean coast is Panama's most spectacular drive. On a clear day you get **breathtaking views**; conversely, if you find yourself peering through thick fog to see the edge of the asphalt, it can be one of the scariest journeys you ever make. During the October and November rains, landslides are frequent, sometimes blocking the route for days. Midway across the cordillera, before descending into Bocas del Toro province, you cross the dam wall of **Lago Fortuna**, Panama's main source of hydroelectric power.

Los Cangilones de Gualaca

1km north of Gualaca, which lies 17km north along the La Fortuna road from the Interamericana • Dec–April daily • Charge • Buses run from David to Gualaca (every 40min; 35min); get off at the junction by the baseball stadium, from where it is a 1km walk

Just north of the village of **Gualaca** the sparkling waters of Río Este squeeze through a narrow, shallow canyon, known as **Los Cangilones de Gualaca**, creating a refreshing **natural swimming pool** – an ideal place to cool off in the summer, though it's packed at weekends. The flat slabs of volcanic rock either side of the canyon are thought to have come from lava slides from Volcán Barú, through which the river has eroded its path over time. There are no facilities beyond toilets and changing rooms, but it makes a delightfully tranquil **picnic** spot provided you avoid the weekend crowds. Several of Boquete's tour operators run trips here.

ACCOMMODATION — ALONG THE LA FORTUNA ROAD

Lost and Found Hostel Km 42 on the La Fortuna road thelostandfoundhostel.com. This one-of-a-kind hostel with shared kitchen or food provided is worth visiting for the views alone (on a clear day). Perched at well over 1300m, on the edge of the Reserva Forestal La Fortuna – established to protect the Fortuna reservoir's catchment basin – it boasts numerous cloud-forest trails, offers a range of modestly priced tours and puts on free fun activities, including treasure hunts. Accommodation is in four dorms, offering both single and double beds, bunks, pod-style or standard beds, and in five relatively expensive private doubles with shared ablutions. To get here by bus, alight at the Km 42 marker, at the hamlet of Valle de la Mina, where a sign directs you up a lengthy flight of steps to the right. Very popular, so book in advance. Cash preferred. Dorms $$, doubles $$

David and the Chiriquí Lowlands

In contrast to the Highlands – the destination for the vast majority of visitors to the province – the oppressive heat of the **Chiriquí Lowlands** does little to attract the punters. Nor do endless fields of maize, rice, bananas, sugar cane and cattle. Still it's hard to avoid **David**, or at least the city's vast bus terminal, since virtually all the province's public transport passes through here. What's more, Chiriquí's capital is growing in appeal as a place to chill out for a couple of days and enjoy a few city comforts as well as a couple of local attractions. West of David, the Interamericana speeds along 47km of flattish terrain to the frontier with Costa Rica. Just before the border post, the road veers off left down the narrow **Península Burica**, weaving through plantations and passing the former banana boom town of **Puerto Armuelles**, before an undulating road eventually peters out close to the southern tip, where the handful of travellers who make it this far can stroll along deserted beaches and watch the waves.

David and around

The only one of three Spanish settlements founded in the area in 1602 to survive repeated attacks from displaced indigenous groups, **DAVID** developed slowly as a remote outpost of the Spanish Empire, only beginning to thrive when Chiriquí's population swelled in the nineteenth century. Today, despite being a busy commercial city of more than 140,000 people – the second largest in Panama – and the focus of Chiriquí's strong regional identity, it retains a sedate provincial atmosphere.

Oppressively hot and either humid or dusty, its unexceptional modern architecture spread out on a grid that derives from colonial days, David has few attractions *per se*, but its very ordinariness holds a certain appeal for a couple of days. It's also a good place to stock up before a trip to the highlands or break a journey between Panama City and Costa Rica or Bocas del Toro. Several **day-trips** – chiefly the mangroves at **Pedregal**, the natural pool at **Balneário Barranca** and the **wildlife reserve** at **Playa Barqueta** – are all possible on public transport, and popular with Davideños at weekends as they attempt to escape the city heat.

City centre

David's heart is vibrant **Parque Cervantes**, where snow-cone sellers, shoe-shiners and hawkers peddling sugar cane and fresh fruit juice all vie for business, overlooked by the nondescript **Iglesia de la Sagrada Familia**. The park's curved stone seating maximizes the leafy shade, making it a prime spot for watching urban life unfold. Just southeast of the park lies **Barrio Bolívar**; the former colonial hub has more or less lost the battle against encroaching modern architecture, with a crumbling **bell tower** next to the nineteenth-century cathedral its most salient feature.

Pedregal

10km south of David • Buses leave from Av 2 Este, between C Central and C "A" Norte (6am–10.50pm; every 10–15min; 15min)

Beyond the airport, the road fizzles out at **Pedregal**, David's small port and marina, which provides entry by **boat** into the morass of mangroves and islands in the **Golfo de**

THE INTERNATIONAL AGRICULTURAL FAIR

David's annual highlight is its international agricultural fair, **Feria Internacional de San José de David** (@feriadedavid.com), whose ten days of festivities coincide with the patron saint day for San José on March 19. Although principally a trade show, there's plenty to entertain, with rodeo and lasso competitions, music and dancing, not to mention the annual *cabalgata*, a colourful horseback parade through the city streets.

Chiriquí. There's a pleasant restaurant, El Pescador (ⓦfacebook.com/elpescadorchiriqui; $$–$$$), overlooking the marina – just the place for a leisurely lunch serving all manner of super-fresh seafood with fried yuca, *patacones* or sautéed potatoes. Get in touch with Maribel Victoria Tours (ⓦinstagram.com/serviciosturisticosmaribel) to rent a kayak or join an afternoon boat tour through the mangroves, where you'll spot a wealth of wading birds. It's to be hoped that the planned mega port is relocated to Puerto.

Refugio de Vida Silvestre de Playa Barqueta Agricola

25km southwest of David • Daily 8am–4pm • Charge • Park warden ⓣ 6602 5770 • Buses leave David at 6am, 8am & 11.20am (40min), returning at 2.30pm & 5pm, or take a bus to Guarumal, then a taxi to the beach

Unremarkable, grainy **Playa Barqueta** is the nearest spot to dip in the sea, and has a couple of informal places to eat and enjoy a beer. A large portion of the beach lies within the boundaries of the low-key **Refugio de Vida Silvestre de Playa Barqueta Agricola** whose 14km stretch of sand, scrub and mangrove protects nesting sites for olive ridley turtles, above all, but also hawksbill, leatherback, loggerhead and green sea **turtles**. Visits to check out the night-time nesting (late May–Nov is best) can be arranged with the park warden or at the MiAmbiente office outside David (see page 201). The reserve entrance lies east of *Las Olas Resort* (ⓦlasolasresort.com), where the bus stops; alternatively, the warden will come and pick you up. Visitors in their own vehicle (with a permit from MIA) will need a 4WD.

ARRIVAL AND DEPARTURE — DAVID

BY PLANE

Airport Flights from Panama City arrive at Aeropuerto Enrique Malek (ⓣ6679 1136), about 4km south of town, a short taxi ride away.

Flights Air Panama (ⓦairpanama.com) offers two to three daily flights to and from Panama City's Albrook Airport (40min). Copa Airlines (ⓦcopaair.com) also has code-share connecting flights to/from North American and European destinations via Tocumen International Airport in Panama City.

Airline offices Air Panama has an office at the airport (ⓣ721 0841) and in *Hotel Hilton by Hampton* in Calle "F", opposite Super 99 (Mon–Fri 8am–5pm; ⓣ6378 0217). Copa Airlines also has an office at the airport and in town on Av Central at C "B" Norte (Mon–Fri 8am–5pm, Sat 8am–noon; ⓣ6482 2075).

BY BUS

Bus terminal The main bus terminal, for local services and long-distance routes, including to Costa Rica (see box, page 202), is on Paseo Estudiante, a 15min walk north of the town centre. It has good facilities, including a self-service restaurant, toilets, ATMs, a left-luggage office (daily 6am–8pm) and internet café.

Buses to Panama City Terminales David-Panama (ⓣ775 2974), with its own a/c waiting room at the far end of the terminal, has numerous departures daily (6am–1pm hourly, then every 1hr 30min–2hr until 8pm; then several overnight express buses; 6hr30min–7hr). Panachif (ⓣ777 4217) has nine daily departures (7.30am–10pm) from its own terminal on Av Francisco Clark, a 5min walk from the main bus station.

Other destinations Boquete (4.50am–7.10pm; every 20min; 50min); Caldera (hourly 7.25am–7.30pm; 1hr); Cerro Punta (5am–8pm; every 15min; 1hr 50min); Las Lajas (frequent 6.35am–11pm; 1hr 30min); Puerto Armuelles (via the Costa Rican border at Paso Canoas; 5am–9pm; every 15min; 1hr 30min); Río Sereno (5/5.45am–4.15/5pm; every 45min–1hr; 2hr 30min); Santiago – from a terminal across the road from the main bus terminal (5am–7.30pm; approx every 45min; 3hr) or take one of the faster buses to Panama City; Soloy (7am–7pm; approx every 30min when full; 1hr 30min); Volcán (5am–8pm; every 15min; 1hr 20min).

GETTING AROUND

By taxi Taxis are plentiful and should not cost more than $2–3 for a ride in town.

By car Several rental chains have offices at the airport; a good local operator is Arrendadora Económica (ⓦarrendadoraeconomica.com).

INFORMATION

Tourist information The tourist office (Mon–Fri 8am–4pm; ⓣ775 2839) is at the airport.

MIA office For the latest information on Chiriquí's several national parks, contact the MIA office, on the road to the airport (Mon–Fri 8am–4pm; ⓣ500 0922).

ACCOMMODATION — SEE MAP PAGE 200

A broad range of good-value **accommodation** exists in David, most of it near the city centre. Even so, it's difficult to get a room during the Feria Internacional de San José de David (see box, page 199) and the festival periods in Boquete (see box, page 186). The places reviewed below all have hot water and a/c.

Chambres en Ville Av 5 Este, between C "A" Sur and C "B" Sur ⓦchambresenville.info. The town's best hostel with cosy, if dark, en-suite private rooms enlivened by colourful murals. The large open-air kitchen leads to a fruit-filled garden, with hammocks and a decent-sized swimming pool. Dorms $, doubles $$

Hotel Gran Nacional C Central and Av 1 Este ⓦfacebook.com/GranHotelNacionalDavid. Once the top hotel in town with marble lobby to match but with stately refurbished rooms, furnished with flatscreen cable TV and other mod cons. There's also a bar, pool, 24hr casino, gym and restaurant. Plenty of special deals. Buffet breakfast included. $$$

Hotel Puerto del Sol Av Bolívar at C Central ⓦhotelpuertadelsol.com. Conveniently central three-star hotel offering moderately priced en-suite rooms with comfortably furnished beds, and some with other welcome pieces of furniture. $$

Hotel Toledo Av 1 Este, between C "D" Norte and C "E" Norte ⓣ774 6732. Furnishings may be dated, but it's handy for the bus terminal, and offers good value clean rooms with firm beds, and friendly service. There's an on-site bar-restaurant. $$

★ **Patampa** C El Varital, Las Acacias ⓣ6981 0195, ⓦpatampa.net. This welcoming guesthouse in a quiet neighbourhood has half a dozen warmly furnished rooms in tropical hardwoods, with supremely comfortable beds. A decent breakfast spread is available, served on the poolside terrace. Accommodating hosts. $$$

5

BUSES TO COSTA RICA

Tracopa (tracopacr.com) operates two daily services to San José, Costa Rica, at 7.30am and 8.30am (8–9hr). Buses leave from the main bus terminal on Paseo Estudiante, where the company has an office (daily 7am–3pm). Tickets should be prebooked for peak holiday periods.

It is often quicker, though, to take one of the frequent **minibuses** from the bus terminal to the border at **Paso Canoas** (see box, page 203) and walk across, getting exit and entry stamps at Panama and Costa Rica immigration respectively, before hopping on one of the regular shuttles to Ciudad Neily, the first sizeable population centre over the border 18km away, where there are connections with San José.

EATING

SEE MAP PAGE 200

★ Café Rincón Libanés C "F" Sur, between Av Central and Av 1 Este facebook.com/caferinconlibaness. A deservedly popular spot, with an outside terrace – often full of men smoking hookahs in the evening – and an icy air-conditioned interior, where you can enjoy a range of well-prepared Lebanese and Panamanian fare. Highly recommendable is a mezze platter – falafel, baba ghanoush, shawarma and the like – though costs can add up. $$$

El Chalan Chiriquí Av 4 Oeste, off Av "F" Sur by the Crowne Casino instagram.com/el_chalanch. Despite the colourful tablecloths, the atmosphere is a little bland but the food more than compensates: lots of Peruvian favourites (to be accompanied by pisco sours), including mountainous platters of succulent seafood to share between two or four. $$–$$$

Multi-Café No. 2 C "A" Norte, between Av 2 Este and Av 3 Este facebook.com/multicafechiriqui. Modern self-service restaurant with a/c and parking that attracts a busy weekend crowd. There's a vast array of local and international staples on offer, with omelettes for breakfast. $$

Restaurante Bar El Fogón Av 2 Oeste, between C "C" Norte and C "D" Norte instagram.com/elfogondavid. Spacious and airy restaurant, painted in warm colours, which is a real favourite with Davideños though it doesn't always live up to the hype. But the atmosphere is friendly, and the menu is extensive: choose from grilled meat, poultry and seafood mains – try the *pescado parmesano* – or a selection of burgers and sandwiches. The quality can suffer when it gets busy. $$–$$$

Restaurante Bocachica C "A" Sur, between Av 4 and Av 5 Este instagram.com/bocachicarest. Favoured by university students drawn by the cheap beer, the pleasant elevated patio here is a prime spot to tuck into tasty, good-value dishes, with seafood a speciality. $$

Restaurante Puerto del Sol Hotel Puerto del Sol, Av Bolívar at C Central hotelpuertadelsol.com/restaurant. This hotel restaurant is one of the few reliable choices in the town centre for breakfast, lunch or dinner. Mon–Sat it does a good-value three-course *menú ejecutivo* popular with city workers. Otherwise you've an a la carte menu of regional staples. $$

Restaurante La Típica Av 3 Este and C "F" Sur 777 1078. Busy, no-nonsense Chinese-Panamanian semi-open *cafetería* serving mounds of palatable food around the clock (almost). A reliable budget choice. $$

Península Burica

Aside from a handful of die-hard surfers and fishing enthusiasts, few tourists venture down to the distant tip of the **Península Burica**, resembling an upside-down skittle straddling the Costa Rican border. Here, 50km southwest of David, the remoteness is tangible and the sunsets spectacular. The gateway to the peninsula is **Puerto Armuelles**, for more than seventy years Panama's thriving Pacific hub of the infamous United Fruit Company (now Chiquita Brands) until it pulled the plug in 2003 (see page 218). The rotting pier and abandoned wooden houses serve as poignant reminders of the town's former importance.

ARRIVAL AND ACCOMMODATION

PENÍNSULA BURICA

By bus Frequent minibuses run from David's main bus terminal to Puerto Armuelles (5am–9pm; 2hr 30min). A daily *chiva* (1hr 30min–2hr) makes the 30km trip down the peninsula from the town's waterside transport depot to the community of Bella Vista; timing depends on the tides, since much of the "road" is on the beach, only accessible at low tide – make sure you arrive before noon and bring your passport.

Paso Canoas and the Costa Rican border

It's a short hop from David along the Interamericana to Panama's main border crossing with Costa Rica at **Paso Canoas** (see box, page 203). Others are at Río Sereno, west of Volcán (see box, page 196) and Guabito (see page 244), over the cordillera in Bocas province. The busy frontier town exudes an edgy tackiness, with stalls, money changers and taxi drivers all competing for business.

Parque Nacional Marino Golfo de Chiriquí

There's not much to the laidback fishing village of **BOCA CHICA** – 30km southeast of David as the vulture flies – beyond a small supermarket, an upmarket fishing lodge, and a handful of places to eat. It does, however, provide the gateway to one of the province's most prized natural treasures: **Parque Nacional Marino Golfo de Chiriquí**, a nirvana for **scuba-diving**, **snorkelling** and **sport-fishing** enthusiasts. Created in 1994 to protect almost 150 square kilometres of terrestrial and marine wildlife, the park comprises 25 islands – some with places to stay – and nineteen coral reefs, teeming with hundreds of fish in a rainbow of colours. The coastline to the west of Boca Chica, meanwhile, is thick with **mangroves** – which means you'll have to venture to the more distant islands to find white sand or crystalline waters. Note that when the wind drops in the rainy season, sandflies can be a nuisance, so bring repellent.

Islas Parita and Paridita

Isla Parita, by far the largest land mass, together with the much smaller **Isla Paridita**, are the only two inhabited islands on account of their fresh water sources; the rest are generally small, low-lying sedimentary outcrops that enjoy a tropical savannah climate, with beaches backed by coconut palms and manchineel trees, where the only visitors to disturb the hermit crabs and iguanas are nesting hawksbill and leatherback turtles.

Boca Brava and beyond

Across the narrow water channel in front of Boca Chica's jetty is **Boca Brava**, an island hosting several lodgings aimed at contrasting budgets, while on the mainland several upmarket fishing lodges and small guesthouses do little to disturb the tranquillity of the place. Snorkelling trips head out into the national park, to the gorgeous white-sand coves of **islas Bolaños and Gámez**, but there is even better snorkelling and diving to be

THE BORDER WITH COSTA RICA

The **border at Paso Canoas** is by far the busiest of the three border crossings Panama shares with **Costa Rica**; in recognition of this, **immigration** is open longer hours (7am–10pm Panamanian time). Don't forget that whether entering Panama or Costa Rica you need to get an exit stamp from immigration in the country you are leaving and an entry stamp from immigration in the country you are entering; proof of onward travel and financial solvency is also required.

Paso Canoas is reached by frequent **minibuses** from David, with regular **onward transport** to San José and other destinations in Costa Rica (see box, page 202). If you are arriving from Costa Rica, you can find transport to both Panama City and David 100m down the Interamericana from the border. The Panachif (Ⓦ instagram.com/transportespanachif) office here sells tickets for buses to Panama City via David (9 daily; 7am–9pm; 8–9hr). Small minibuses also scoot off down the highway to David (4am–9pm; every 10–15min; 40min), from where onward transport is easy (see page 201).

had around the more remote (and pricier) **Islas Secas**, **Islas Ladrones** and **Isla Montuoso**. The marine life is breathtaking, from sea horses and starfish to giant manta and eagle rays, pods of dolphins, turtles, sharks and vast schools of fish swirling round volcanic pinnacles, with humpback whales arriving to calve from June.

ARRIVAL AND DEPARTURE PARQUE NACIONAL MARINO GOLFO DE CHIRIQUÍ

BOCA CHICA

By bus and taxi There are no direct buses from David to Boca Chica. Five buses leave David for Horconcitos, 36km to the east (five daily 11am–5pm; 45min), 5km south of the Interamericana on the road to Boca Chica. From there, you could catch the occasional (and unreliable) Boca Chica bus (12.30pm, 2.30pm & 4.30pm; driver Rommel ⓣ6189 2638), take a taxi – Chago Moreno is reliable and lives in Horconcitos (ⓣ6575 8500) – or hitch a ride, paying the *colectivo* rate. Returning, the bus may leave Boca Chica in the morning, and can drop you at the Interamericana. In the not entirely unexpected event of a no-show, you'll need to negotiate a ride.

By car Boca Chica is down a paved road, accessible in a saloon car; turn off from the Interamericana to Horconcitos, 36km east of David, and then take the middle road at the three-way fork in the village, coming to a halt at the Boca Chica jetty 16km later. There are a couple of places where you can leave your car safely overnight for a small fee.

TO THE ISLANDS

By boat Transfer to *Hotel Boca Brava* from Boca Chica is $3. The other island lodgings charge around $60 return fare, which may be included in some package fares.

ACCOMMODATION

Boca Brava Lodge Isla Boca Brava ⓦbocabravalodge.com. Possessing simple tiled rooms with fan or a/c, and private or shared bathroom (for less) – many in need of some TLC, this long-standing retreat offers an affordable rub with nature. Awake to the cries of howler monkeys, and stroll along to the modest beach. The cliff-top bar-restaurant serves decent food at reasonable rates and inexpensive drinks. $$

Bocas del Mar Boca Chica, signposted to the left 2km before entering the village ⓦbocasdelmar.com. Gaze out at the wooded landscape and glistening sea through the vast French windows in your spacious bungalow, or from your private porch or your luxurious bathroom. Stylish rooms have a contemporary feel, and include all the comforts (a/c, satellite TV, minibar); some even have a private outdoor hot tub, and others a kitchenette. The pleasant open-air restaurant is set round an infinity pool and there are a variety of inland or water-based activities to choose from. Breakfast included. Promotions and low-season discounts are substantial. $$$$

Isla Palenque Isla Palenque ⓦislapalenque.com. An idyllic island retreat with eight romantic bungalows set off the back of the beach amidst tropical foliage – the perfect blend of modern sophistication and rustic chic, with a semi-outdoor bathroom and supremely comfortable outdoor furnishings, with room service at the tap of an Ipad. It's the ideal place to do nothing, but there are island trails, kayaks and SUPs for the more active. All-inclusive rates. $$$$

Pacific Bay Resort Punta Bejuco ⓦpacificbayresort.org. There's an unequalled panorama of the bay from the hilltop bar-dining area, though you'll earn your food hiking up there from the four well-spaced, solar-powered, wood-furnished duplex cabins. Set on an extensive forested headland with three beaches, and coves to explore by kayak, this is a wonderfully relaxing place and is only open June–Feb to minimize the environmental impact. Meals are included in the rates (but take some snacks); horseriding and moderately priced boat excursions are also on offer. The resort is only accessible by boat and you'll need to arrange transport in advance ($35 per trip; see website for details). $$$

Selva Tierra Isla Boca Brava ⓦselvatierraresort.com. A sophisticated all-inclusive retreat comprising a/c bungalows, each with a gorgeous private *rancho* looking out to sea, as well as a beach house and villa, affording even

PARQUE NACIONAL MARINO GOLFO DE CHIRIQUÍ ACTIVITIES

Snorkelling outings in the park can easily be arranged through the hotels, or you can hire the services of one of the local boatmen. Trips usually visit islas Bolaños, Parida (where there's a beach restaurant) and Gámez and costs from around $150 per boat for two to six people – bring a picnic. You can usually join a tour for around $35/person. Contact reliable boatmen Marcelo Rios (ⓣ6209 6420) or "Jaye" (ⓣ6214 6883) in Boca Chica.

Alternatively, you can explore the area's islands, inlets, caves and mangroves in a **kayak**; most of the accommodation options that we review have kayaks available for guests.

greater luxury and seclusion. The lovely bar-restaurant deck serves gourmet fusion (international-Panamanian) cuisine using local produce. Boat rides, horseriding, diving – they have their own dive shop – hiking, birdwatching and even day-trips to the highlands can all be laid on (additional fee). Breakfast and use of kayaks, surf boards and SUPs are included, as well as the transfer from David. Themed retreats also available. $$$$

Playa Las Lajas and around

The impressive broad belt of flat tan-coloured sand of **Playa Las Lajas** is by far the most popular weekend beach destination for urbanites from David (81km) and even Santiago (124km) in need of sand, sea and surf. However, since the beach, backed by wafting palms, stretches for kilometres both ways, there's plenty of space to escape the crowds – except over the weekends leading up to Carnaval, when you can expect all-night partying on the sands. The benign waves are more suited to body surfing and playing around in the waves than serious surfing.

If you are interested in **Ngäbe** or **Buglé** culture, you should take time to visit the major communities of San Félix and Tolé north of the Interamericana; the latter, which lies east close to the border with Veraguas, is noted for its **handicrafts** – the versatile *kra* (string bag, or *chácara* in Spanish) made of plant fibres, or beaded *ngüñunkua* (necklace, or *chaquira* in Spanish) – many sold at stalls along the Interamericana close to the turn-off. For a homestay experience, head for **Soloy** (see box, page 206).

ARRIVAL AND DEPARTURE — PLAYA LAS LAJAS AND AROUND

By bus and taxi If you arrive too late for a direct bus to La Lajas village from David (6.30am–6.30pm; every 30min; 1hr 30min), you can take a bus bound for Tolé or San Félix (every 20–30min) and get off at the busy intersection, El Cruce de San Félix, 68km east of David (1hr). You are likely to find a taxi at the petrol station at the junction that can take you the 12km to the beach; make sure to get a contact number for your return trip.

ACCOMMODATION AND EATING

Johnny Fiestas Just off the beach; turn left at the T-junction ⓣ6240 4728, ⓦfacebook.com/johnnyfiestaslaslajas. Small hostel with a garden. Stay in a dorm bunk, private room with shared amenities, or a dome tent kitted out with electricity, fan and camp beds. The vibe is relaxed, with hammocks galore and sport on TV, plus board games to play and surfboards to rent. Fast wi-fi. Cash only. Camping $, dorm $, double $–$$

Las Lajas Beach Resort On the beach; turn right at the T-junction ⓣ6790 1972, ⓦlaslajasbeachresort.com. Set back from the beach, a dozen expansive, tiled, minimally furnished rooms (one with wheelchair access) look onto the lawn through floor-to-ceiling windows. The two upstairs suites have spectacular sea views from the balcony and there's a large pool and bar-restaurant serving moderately priced American-style food. Substantial online discounts often available. $$$

Santiago and the central highlands

The administrative, economic and cultural capital of Veraguas province, **SANTIAGO** is a bustling centre of around forty thousand inhabitants. Founded in its present location in 1637, and previously of great agricultural importance, it is now a thriving commercial hub – evidenced by the proliferation of banks and a state-of-the-art baseball stadium. Situated almost halfway between Panama City and David, Santiago is a **major transit point** as well as a marketing centre for the livestock, rice, maize and sugar from the surrounding farmlands. If you're travelling round Panama by public transport, it's highly likely that at some stage you will, at the very least, spend time in the bus terminal or stranded on the Interamericana here, though there's little incentive to venture further into town unless you happen to coincide with the **patronales** around July 25, which draw in the crowds for some serious partying.

5

Of greater tourist interest is the city's status as the gateway to various tourist destinations: the undulating **Península de Soná**, at the tip of which lies Santa Catalina, Panama's surfing capital (see page 211); the cooler mountain slopes of the **central highlands**, including the charming hilltop village of **Santa Fé** (see page 208); and the western seaboard of the Península de Azuero (see page 152). Closer to town, a few kilometres outside Santiago, are a couple of delightful **village churches** worth a detour, both accessible by bus.

The town centre

Most of the businesses are strung along the Interamericana and Avenida Central, which branches west off the highway heading into the town centre, coming to an abrupt halt in front of the impressive exterior of the **Catedral Santiago Apóstol**, stunningly illuminated at night. Adjacent is **Parque Juan Demóstenes Arosemena**, the city's main plaza; it takes its name from the former president, revered here for choosing the town as the site for Panama's first teacher-training institution. The college, **Escuela Normal Juan Demóstenes Arosemena**, lies several blocks northeast of the plaza on Calle 8A Norte and is the architectural jewel of Santiago, with a majestic Baroque frontispiece.

Across the leafy plaza from the cathedral stands the rather uninspiring – save for a few pre-Columbian ceramics – **Museo Regional de Veraguas** (Tues–Sun 8am–4pm; free), housed in the former prison where three-time president Belisario Porras was incarcerated during the civil war. More surprisingly, the city hosts the country's first **Centro Interactivo del Canal de Panamá** (Tues–Sun 9am–5pm; free). Aimed at educating

STAYING WITH THE NGÄBE IN SOLOY

Though the **Ngäbe** are Panama's most numerous indigenous citizens by far, they see considerably fewer tourists than the Guna or Emberá, and are understandably wary of outsiders given the recent history of conflict – sometimes violent – with both the Panamanian authorities and international mining and hydroelectric power corporations. Arranging a **homestay** in the mountain community of Soloy, in the southwest corner of the Comarca Ngäbe-Buglé provides a unique opportunity to begin to learn about the Ngäbe, their traditions and their present-day challenges, though you'll need some Spanish to make the most of it, and be prepared for very rudimentary lodgings and simple food. The village itself has no nucleus, but rather is strung out several kilometres along the main road and the Río Soloy. The river, and the even more powerful Río Fonseca into which it flows, are crucial to community life and are also the basis for **tourist activities**, such as waterfall visits – Cascada Kiki is much visited – rafting and kayaking; visitors can also go hiking (40min–6hr) or horseriding and learn the processes of extracting plant fibres and mixing natural dyes to make a traditional *kri* (string bag). You may need to rent a 4WD in Soloy if venturing further into the *comarca*. Costs are inexpensive in the *comarca* but as there is no ATM, you'll need to bring sufficient cash.

ARRIVAL AND INFORMATION

By bus Buses leave David's main bus terminal for Soloy approximately hourly (7am–7pm; 1hr 30min; last return bus 4pm); alternatively take a bus bound for Horconcitos and get off at the turn-off south to Horconcitos from the Intermericana, where you can hop on a pickup truck (*chiva*) heading north for Soloy (approximately every 30min). Where you get off in the village depends on where you have agreed to meet your guide.

ACCOMMODATION AND EATING

Homestays Homestays are currently only arranged by a handful of families as many in the community remain suspicious of tourists and tourism. The following contacts should help:

Destino Soloy (destinosoloy.com). Community-based tourism organization. Wilfredo Mitre (6431 6089) is the coordinator. They organize tours and have a community restaurant, Mrö Café, which serves traditional food.

Juan Carlos Bejerano (6638 0944) is an experienced Ngäbe whitewater rafting guide and tour leader.

children about the canal, it offers state-of-the-art exhibits; you can even pilot a ship through the locks, which is just as much fun for adults.

Iglesia Atalaya

Atalaya, 8km southeast of Santiago • Buses from Santiago every 15min (30min)

From the outside, the **Iglesia Atalaya** resembles an inauspicious two-tier wedding cake; inside, its lofty vaulted ceilings covered in splendid frescoes and lovely stained-glass windows more than compensate. Tucked away in a side altar, the Cristo de Atalaya, said to date back to before 1730, is one of Panama's most venerated icons, a magnet for thousands of pilgrims every first Sunday in Lent.

Iglesia San Francisco de la Montaña

San Francisco de la Montaña, 16km north of Santiago on the Santa Fé road • Irregular hours • Take a Santa Fé-bound bus from Santiago (see below); hop off at the fork by the police post and bear right a few hundred metres

The **Iglesia San Francisco de la Montaña** lies on the road to Santa Fé, north of Santiago, in a village of the same name. The simplicity of the small stone church, believed to have been built around 1727, belies the wonderfully elaborate wooden interior, with nine intricately carved Baroque altarpieces betraying both Spanish and indigenous influences. You are likely to have to ask around to get someone to open up.

ARRIVAL AND DEPARTURE — SANTIAGO

Panama City–David buses The more luxurious buses running between Panama City and David and the border with Costa Rica (see page 203) stop at one of three service areas: at the more popular Centro Los Tucanes or the Centro Piramidal, at Santiago's northeastern and eastern exits to the Interamericana respectively, or at a smaller office in between. If they have space, they'll pick up extra passengers but at peak times (Fri afternoons and holidays) you're better off taking the slower services from the main terminal.

Bus terminal All other transport leaves from the bus terminal on C 10 Norte, a 10min walk or short taxi ride from Los Tucanes or the Centro Piramidal. The terminal has a left-luggage office and public toilets.

Destinations Aguadulce (Mon–Fri 5.30am–8pm, Sat & Sun 5.30am–9pm; every 15min); Chitré (5.30am–9pm; every 30min; 1hr 30min); David (6am–6pm; every 30min; 3hr); Panama City (3.15am–9.15pm; hourly, plus through buses from David and Paso Canoas; 4hr); Santa Fé (5am–7pm; every 30min; 1hr); Soná – change for Santa Catalina (6am–9.40pm; every 20min; 50min).

5

GETTING AROUND AND INFORMATION

By taxi Taxis are abundant and will ferry you to most places within town for a couple of dollars.

Tourist information The tourist office (Mon–Fri 8am–4pm; ⓣ 998 3929) is behind the cathedral between calles 1 and 2.

MIA office On the Interamericana, north of the Av Central exit (Mon–Fri 8am–4pm; ⓣ 998 4387).

ACCOMMODATION SEE MAP PAGE 207

Hostal Travellers Paso Las Tablas, by the polyclinic ⓦ facebook.com/travelerhostal. Out in a quiet suburb, this friendly hostel in a converted family home comprises a dorm and a handful of private air-conditioned rooms, decorated with murals. The leafy back patio provides a relaxing kitchen-lounge area complete with hammocks. Inexpensive meals can be prepared. Dorm $, doubles $$

Hotel Corotú Plaza Corotú, just off the Interamericana ⓦ instagram.com/hotelplazacorotu. Well soundproofed, business-grade rooms, including gleaming, spacious bathrooms with rain showers, at affordable rates. $$

★ **Hotel Mykonos** Interamericana, opposite the airfield, 2.5km east of Av Central ⓦ hotelmykonos.com. To capture the allure of Greece, spacious contemporary rooms are decked out in cerulean blue, turquoise and gleaming white with marble-topped bathrooms and full business amenities. Arranged in two blocks facing a large inviting pool, rooms boast private balconies and patios. Buffet breakfast included $$$

EATING SEE MAP PAGE 207

★ **Anawa's** Interamericana 100m east of Av Central ⓦ facebook.com/anawaspanama. Sophisticated roadside café serving healthy or full American breakfasts, Mediterranean-style deli-snacks such as sourdough toasts and paninis, and all kinds of tea and coffee, including expressos and chai lattes. A real find. $$

★ **Annisa** C 14B Sur ⓦ instagram.com/annisapanama. This cosy café with a mellow vibe serves superb coffee and croissants, first-rate deli-sandwiches in home-made bread in addition to an eclectic changing menu of mouthwatering, treats ranging from lasagne or chicken wings, to clams in cream and coriander, sushi, poke bowls, and even dim sum at weekends. $$

Inkas Interamericana, at Av Central ⓣ 6416 8544. Highly recommended restaurant serving genuine Peruvian ceviche and other national favourites, including *lomo saltado* (stir-fry beef with rice and chips) albeit in an uninspiring setting. It even sells Inca Kola – Peru's favourite soft drink, and pisco sour– the country's famous national tipple. $$$

Santa Fé

A hilltop village about 60km north of Santiago, **SANTA FÉ** is a jewel of a mountain retreat that has been a well-kept secret for years. Surrounded by a stunning necklace of verdant mountains sprinkled with sparkling cascades and serene stretches of river, with easy access to a forested swathe of national park, it is a hikers' and birdwatchers' dream. Thanks to its 500m altitude, Santa Fé de Veraguas – to give it its full name – enjoys a pleasant, fresh climate, and is famous for its flowers, boasting more than three hundred species of **orchid**; the annual three-day orchid festival in August, when most are in bloom, attracts aficionados from around the country – contact the tourist office in Santiago (see page 207) for dates. The annual **agricultural fair** (late Jan–early Feb) also pulls in the crowds. Only time will tell whether the new tarred road over the cordillera to Calovébora (see box, page 210) will threaten the tranquillity of the place.

The village

Daily activity centres on the small covered **market** area, where fresh local produce is on display alongside a smattering of predominantly Ngäbe craft stalls. Across the road stands a monument to Santa Fé's most famous resident, **Padre Héctor Gallego** (see box, page 209), whose kidnap and murder has left the village emotionally scarred. A nonprofit foundation that bears his name continues his community development work, offering support and skills training to local farmers and artisans. More visibly, the priest's legacy resides in the continued success of the cooperative he helped found; it includes a couple of supermarkets, several grocery stores, a restaurant, bus and taxi services, and the jewel in the crown, the local organic coffee mill, **Café El Tute**. Tours (in Spanish) of the processing plant, where you can buy some of the delicious product, and to a nearby organic coffee farm, can be organized via the Fundación Héctor Gallego (see page 209) in the village.

Around Santa Fé

The area's natural beauty makes it perfect for **hiking**, **birdwatching** and **bathing** in clear streams and rivers – provided the weather holds – though the mountainous topography means there'll be steep inclines wherever you wander. A good start is to head down to the river, near the entrance to the village, below the *Hotel de Santa Fé*, or follow the road up towards Alto de Piedra and the Santa Fé national park.

If you intend to tackle the area's loftiest peaks, Cerro Tute (930m) and Cerro Mariposa (1200m), cloaked in montane forest, or want to penetrate the wilderness areas of the park, then hiring a **guide** is a must (see page 209). More accessible hiking destinations include the impressive Salto Alto de Piedra and Salto El Bermejo, as well as the 30m cascade of El Salto, slightly further afield. Your accommodation should be able to provide directions and/or a sketch map, or put you in contact with a guide. For the hardcore, it's possible to organize a multiday hike over the cordillera to the Caribbean coast.

Two of the most pleasurable activities in the area, given the magnificent scenery, are **horseriding** and **tubing**, floating down the nearby river for more than an hour, gliding past kingfishers, herons and egrets.

ARRIVAL AND DEPARTURE — SANTA FÉ

By bus Santa Fé is served by buses from the main terminal in Santiago (5am–6.40pm; every 30min; 1hr). For the return trip they leave from outside the village bus terminal; last bus 6pm.

TOUR OPERATORS, ACTIVITIES AND GUIDES

Coffee tour The community organization Fundación Héctor Gallego (Mon–Sat 8am–4pm; ⓣ954 0737) can fix up a tour of the coffee cooperative (in Spanish).

Farm tour At Finca María y Chong (ⓦinstagram.com/mariaychonorganicfarm), the engaging María can happily show you round their small-scale organic operation – growing citrus fruits, prize-winning orchids, green vegetables and producing artisanal coffee – before serving a farmhouse lunch. Camping is also available.

Hiking and birdwatching The experienced and extremely knowledgeable Edgar Toribio (ⓦinstagram.com/santafewildlife) guides hiking and wildlife trips. Fit, adventurous travellers should enquire about the four-day trek to the Caribbean – though you'll need to take a tent or hammock to sleep in. Maritza de Naturitza (ⓣ6414 1274) is another certified guide recommended for birdwatching and hiking.

Horseriding Horseback Panama (ⓦhorsebackpanama.

HÉCTOR GALLEGO AND THE SANTA FÉ COOPERATIVE

In the middle of the night of June 9, 1971, **Padre Héctor Gallego**, the 33-year-old priest of Santa Fé, was **abducted** by two uniformed men of Omar Torrijos's National Guard (see page 303) and was never seen again. In 2002, the Truth Commission set up by President Moscoso to examine crimes committed during Panama's two dictatorships found what they believed to be the tortured remains of the revered priest. It is generally presumed that Manuel Noriega, then head of the secret service, gave the orders, though it seems likely that Torrijos, even if unaware of events at the time, was complicit in the cover-up.

Gallego had arrived in Santa Fé from Colombia in 1967 as the town's first parish priest. Appalled at the exploitation of the local farmers by the wealthy merchant elite, the energetic priest set about educating and organizing the peasant population into becoming self-reliant, helping them to establish a **cooperative** so their products could be sold directly to the market, bypassing the merchants. Perceived as a threat to the authorities, Gallego was subjected to a campaign of intimidation, which started with insults and threats, escalating into arson, and culminated in the priest's final "disappearance". Foreseeing his own death, Gallego had earlier announced: "If I disappear, don't look for me. Continue the struggle." His prophetic words now figure on the monument dedicated to him in the village.

5

com) is a professional stables, charging professional rates, offering short, full-day or – for more experienced riders – multiday tours.

Tubing William Abrega (T 6583 5944; life jacket provided); you can pay extra for him to guide you on the river, to show you the best line into the occasional rapids.

ACCOMMODATION

★ **Coffee Mountain Inn** 500m downhill on the right-hand turn before the bus terminal W coffeemountaininn.com. Set in pleasant grounds, this beautifully appointed lodge offers six options, ranging from a simple compact double with shared terrace, via more luxurious doubles with cable TV and private terrace, to an apartment with kitchenette and wraparound balcony. Breakfast, included in the price, is served on your private terrace. $$$

Hostal La Qhia 50m from the bus terminal W facebook.com/laqhiaecoretreatPA. Set in a lush garden, this is the village's original tourist accommodation: a rustic stone-and-bamboo style main house (the location of the two small dorms) with a lovely balcony, and hammock-filled *rancho*, now with an expanding number of private rooms and more modern chalets – some with kitchenettes. The yoga deck and on-site restaurant complete the tranquil scene – the early-morning dog-barking and cockerels less so. Dorm $–$$, doubles $$

Rainforest Yasmín Hotel 250m downhill on the right-hand turn before the bus station W facebook.com/rainforestyasminhotel. The best-value accommodation in Santa Fé boasting cool, tiled rooms with hot showers and porch space overlooking a leafy central area and pool. A spacious kitchen is available for all to self-cater. $$

EATING AND DRINKING

Anachoreo Left after the bus station and first right down a dirt road T 6911 4848. The rather unatmospheric, cavernous dining room is more than compensated for by the delicious (if pricey) Cambodian cuisine – stir-fried vegetables, chicken ginger and fish *amok*, for example – using fresh green veg and herbs from the garden. All dishes come with steamed rice. Only open Wed–Sun in high season (Nov 1– April 30) $$$

Café Dorado On the main road when entering the village T 6686 4237. You can't beat the mountain views here – a lovely south-facing deck provides an ideal spot to enjoy breakfast, lunch or dinner – soups, seafood and chicken dishes or burgers – or to just chill with a drink. $$

Casita del Sazón Main street, across from the park. Small family restaurant serving traditional fried breakfasts and nicely presented *almuerzos* – take you pick of protein: chicken, beef, fish or pork with rice, a small bowl of beans in sauce and a smidgen of salad – all for under $5. A few basic a la carte offerings too. $–$$

DIRECTORY

Money There is no ATM in Sant Fé, and although some places take credit cards, the machines don't always work, so it's wise to bring cash.

Península de Soná and Isla Coiba

Though dwarfed by the Azuero Peninsula to the west, the hilly **Península de Soná** does attract its own share of tourists. Small cattle farms cover the interior and fishing communities dot the rocky coastline, which protrudes into the Golfo de Chiriquí;

CALOVÉBORA

Now that the tarred road across the cordillera to **Calovébora** on the Caribbean coast has been completed, minibuses heading in that direction leave from Santa Fé (the bus stop just up from the market) several times a day. They go as far as the tiny one-street community of Río Luis, where you can transfer to a *chiva* to reach the Buglé coastal community of Calovébora. At the moment, the main attraction is the **spectacular scenery** on the way there – as the road snakes through the glorious forested Parque Nacional Santa Fé, before cascading over the continental divide down to Río Calovébora; it then skirts the eastern edge of the Comarca Ngäbe-Buglé before coming to an abrupt halt at the wild, wind-lashed beach at the river mouth. At the time of writing, there was only one rudimentary lodging, plus a *fonda* or two. However, further development had already started since the road is now the main route for traffic out of the eastern side of the *comarca*, and it's only a matter of time before the area's tourism potential is exploited.

meanwhile, Panama's surfing capital, **Santa Catalina**, is expanding. More and more visitors are using the mellow fishing village as a launch pad for excursions to the rainforests and coral reefs of **Isla Coiba**, which offers some of the world's finest scuba diving, snorkelling and sport fishing.

Santa Catalina

At the southern end of the peninsula, the sleepy fishing village of **SANTA CATALINA** reels in visitors for its internationally renowned **surf** spots and as a jumping-off point for **Isla Coiba**. As a result, the village has developed into a pleasantly bohemian tourist centre, with mostly foreign-owned small-scale operations scattered along the main road in, or spilling off the paved road that leads to the main beach, **Playa El Estero**.

ARRIVAL AND DEPARTURE — SANTA CATALINA

By bus There are direct buses from Panama City to Soná (6 daily; 5hr), an unendearing town 47km southwest of Santiago, and 63km north of Santa Catalina; most visitors, however, use the more frequent buses to Santiago (see page 205), where they change onto Soná-bound services (daily 6am–9.40pm; every 20min; 50min). Buses from Soná to Santa Catalina are sporadic (Mon–Sat 7 daily; 5am–4.30/5pm, returning 7am–5pm; Sun four daily). Note that the last bus from Santa Catalina sometimes does not run, or may only go as far as Guarumal, where there are other bus connections with Soná.

By taxi Taxis, found hanging round Soná bus terminal can take you there for around $40 if you miss the last bus.

By shuttle Hello Travel (hellotravelpanama.com) runs a daily shuttle service between Boquete and Santa Catalina.

By car Whether you come from the east via Santiago, or from the west, turning south off the Interamericana at Guabalá, the road is tarred all the way to Santa Catalina. Note that there is no petrol station in Santa Catalina – fill up in Soná or Guarumal. Detailed driving instructions are given on various accommodation websites.

GETTING AROUND AND INFORMATION

On foot Once in Santa Catalina, you'll be on foot unless you've your own transport, but nowhere is further than a 20min hike from the bus stop.

Tourist information There is no tourist office in the village. You'll have to ask your lodgings for advice, but also shop around online and on foot.

TOUR OPERATORS

For specialized trips you're best off going with one of the **tour operators** listed below, whose offices are spread along the 200m of main road from the junction to Playa Santa Catalina. For general snorkelling, surfing, fishing or trips to Isla Cébaco or Coiba you may pay less by organizing things through your accommodation or by negotiating directly with the **fishermen** hanging out on the beach by their *pangas* (small flat-bottomed metal boats) or advertising outside their houses. Make sure you agree on exactly what the fee will cover. For Coiba, expect to pay from around $65–70 for a full day of snorkelling, surfing or fishing, possibly including food and drinks. Note that park fees ($20/day) are not usually included (see page 215).

BIRDWATCHING AND HIKING

Javier Elizondo 6544 1804. Bilingual (English/Spanish) bird guide who can take serious birders to seek out Coiba endemics or take novices or casual birdwatchers on a morning birdwatching tour near Santa Catalina – has extra binoculars for those without their own.

DIVING AND SNORKELLING

There are several dive shops in Santa Catalina; while the operators are generally of high quality and the diving can be superb, there have been occasional complaints of failing to satisfy all clients when mixing day-trippers with those on overnight excursions, combining novices with experienced divers, and mixing divers with snorkellers (with divers prioritized). Make sure your needs are likely to be fully met when making enquiries. Two-tank dives in Coiba typically cost $140–160, less if diving outside the park.

Discover Coiba Panama Main road into the village, opposite Bodhi Hostel discovercoibapanama.com. Snorkelling and camping trips.

Panama Dive Centre Main street, by the junction panamadivecenter.com. The first five-star PADI resort in Santa Catalina, offering courses from three-day regular Open Water to Divemaster, as well as the regular Coiba trips.

Scuba Coiba Playa Santa Catalina scubacoiba.com. Pioneering dive centre run by Austrian Herbie Sunk. Specializes in multiday trips to Coiba.

SURFING AND KAYAKING

Fluid Adventures Playa Santa Catalina fluidadventurespanama.com. Acclaimed Canadian outfit specializing in surfing and kayaking tours and rental.

5

SANTA CATALINA ACTIVITIES AND TOURS

The most popular day-tour from Santa Catalina is to **Parque Nacional Coiba** (see page 213), noted for its sparkling clear waters, good coral and rich marine life; you'll be sharing the sea with colourful schools of snappers, jacks, tunas, butterfly, angel and puffer fish alongside moray eels, turtles and white-tip reef sharks. At certain times of year, you're likely to have the company of even more impressive sea creatures such as whales, sharks and rays. Most day-trips (specialist dive trips aside) to Coiba involve a look around the bilingual interpretive centre at the MiAmbiente ranger station followed by a short rainforest walk, a picnic lunch and two or three snorkelling stops. **Isla Cébaco,** which also offers powdery beaches and crystalline fish-filled water is also becoming a more popular destination. Closer still is **Isla Santa Catalina** – the small island in sight of the town beach – which has a delightful white-sand beach, with offshore snorkelling and a 2.8km trail round the island, offering several viewpoints. It's the perfect picnic destination. Get dropped off by boat or rent a kayak to paddle out there.

Experienced surfers should head for Santa Catalina's most famous surf break, **La Punta**, which boasts an international reputation, with waves often topping 5–6m in the season (April–Aug); novice surfers will be happier at **Playa El Estero**. *Oasis*, *Sol y Mar*, *Rancho Estero* and Fluid Adventures, among others, all offer beach-based lessons for beginners at varying rates ($20–35 for a 1–1hr 30min class, including board rental). In addition to the above, various other places rent out surfboards, and some lodgings offer accommodation and surf packages.

While the Santa Catalina website mantra of "surf, dive, fish and chill" just about sums up what the village is about, it doesn't do justice to an array of other **activities** that includes yoga and massage, horseriding, kayaking and birdwatching (see page 211).

Tours range from an easy paddle and snorkel round Isla Santa Catalina, or the coastal mangroves, to three- or six-day kayak and camping adventures in Coiba with wonderful access to wildlife. *Rolo's* offers inexpensive kayak rental.

ACCOMMODATION

Bambuda Off C a Playa del Estero, 1km from the village bambuda.com/santa-catalina. Striking, gleaming-white boutique hotel-cum-hostel on a bluff overlooking the ocean. Contemporary design – warm earthy tones, lots of wood and natural light – aiming to please a wide range of guests: backpackers (upmarket dorms, but no kitchen), surfers (glass-fronted sea-facing wooden cabins), digital nomads, families, couples. All get to share the same stunning pool and expansive bar-restaurant area. Look for offers on their website. Dorms $$, rooms and cabins $$$

Bodhi Hostel Main road into the village bodhihostels.com/santa-catalina. Small friendly hostel comprising two dorms in a cool stone building, plus a handful of tiny, Hobbit-hole-style thatched cabins (with bedroom, bathroom and porch), set round a garden. Space is tight in the well-equipped kitchen, and on the hammock-hung terrace. Breakfast included. Dorms $, cabins $$

Hotel Santa Catalina C Kenny and C a Playa del Estero 6571 4387, hotelsantacatalinapanama.com. Some of the nicest lodgings overlook the village's most famous surf break, which can you admire while lolling in the infinity pool, or in a hammock, drink in hand. Rooms have whitewashed walls, and a tasteful mix of stone and reforested teak, with fridge, safe, TV and even a hair dryer. Free use of kayaks, SUPs and bicycles. Breakfast included. $$$

Oasis Surf Camp Playa El Estero oasissurfcamp.com. With a great beach location among the palms (which can make it party central in holiday periods), this place offers a combination of no-nonsense stone or thatch cabins (fan and a/c), and camping. Italian dinners in the restaurant *rancho* are a highlight. Watch out for the river – you'll need to wade across at high tide. Dorm $, camping $, doubles $$

★ **Rolo's Family Hostel** Main road, by the beach hostelrolocatalina.com. A Santa Catalina institution, *Rolo's* is one of the few locally owned operations, and is the top choice for travellers who want a relaxed hostel vibe without the dorm. Its brightly painted, neat en-suite rooms sleep two to four, with comfy beds, fan or a/c. There's a kitchen for guest use, and a pleasant dining and social area. Neat pine-furnished doubles with a/c, cable TV and fridge also available at *Mi Serena* next to *Pizzería Jammin'*. Cheap kayak and board rental. $$–$$$

EATING

If you are headed for the islands and need to take **food** supplies or a picnic, the mini-super at the junction by the ATM has a good selection of dry products for its size and Frutería G will satisfy all your fruit and veg needs.

Los Pibes Off the beach road instagram.com/losplbessantacatalina. Pleasant Argentinian-run open-air bar-restaurant (with TV and pool table) dishing up *empanadas*, home-made burgers, fish and other meats chargrilled to perfection, complemented by fresh salads, and lathered in home-made *chimichurri* sauce. $$–$$$

Mama Inés Beach road just before Playa del Estero mamaineshotel.com/restaurante Perched on a bluff with a great sea view – an ideal location for lunch or a relaxing drink, while fairy lights and music create a good evening vibe. Tuck into tasty tacos or burgers or something more substantial; try chicken curry with coconut rice. $$–$$$

★ **Panawok** 250m along the beach road panawok.vercel.app. Part of a lively tree-shaded food enclave (also with a bar, pizza, souvenir shop) that comes to life at night, with live music or DJ. Wok stir-fry cooked to order: choose your carbs (rice or noodles), protein (chicken, shrimps or tofu) followed by a pick of veggies, sauce, seasoning and toppings and level of spiciness. $$

Pizzería Jammin' Off the beach road 6447 1373. It may no longer be owned by an Italian, but the pizzas are just as good as they ever were: crispy, clay-oven-fired pizzas under thatch or in the garden, accompanied by a steady dose of reggae. $$

★ **Restaurante Iguanito** 50m up the beach road 6549 7464. This pleasant raised patio is a prime spot to sip a cocktail or linger over an intimate dinner. Mouthwatering Mediterranean mains chalked up on the board include the likes of passion fruit couscous with jumbo prawns; or you could sample some tapas – the *surtido de tapas* (ten items) is a treat. $$$

Restaurante El Pacífico Just before the village beach on the main road. Local restaurant at affordable prices, serving filling Panamanian favourites – fish and chicken with beans, rice and salad, and a fry-up breakfast before you head off for Coiba. Can fix up boat trips too. $$

DIRECTORY

Communications Internet and mobile phone connections have improved significantly over the last few years; however, power cuts still occur, which can delay responses to enquiries.

Money There is one ATM in the village, but it may run out of money at weekends; the closest ATMs are in Soná, so pick up sufficient cash there, or in Santiago, since not all places in the village take credit cards.

Parque Nacional Coiba

Some say "Panama" means "abundance of fish", and nowhere is this more apparent than in the crystalline waters of **Parque Nacional Coiba**. The 2700 square kilometres of reserve encompass Panama's largest island, **Isla Coiba**, plus eight smaller islands and forty islets, but the vast majority consists of ocean brimming with spectacular sea life, including the second largest coral reef along the eastern Pacific. As part of the nutrient-rich Central Pacific Marine Corridor, the park is on the migration route of humpbacks (June–Sept), orcas, pilot and sperm **whales**. Diving conditions are good year-round, but for land-based activities, it's better to visit the island in the **dry season** since the trails are less boggy and there's a better chance of spotting mammals.

The island possesses large tracts of **virgin forest**, most of it still unexplored, home to numerous mammal and bird species. Of the estimated two thousand different types of plant, under half have so far been formally classified. The surrounding **oceans** contain countless varieties of fish, ranging from delicate sea horses to vast manta rays, with 33 species of shark – including tiger, hammerhead and whale sharks, though most are harmless reef varieties.

For years, the island's gruesome history as a penal colony (see box, page 215) helped protect its forests and waters, but the colony's animals (cattle, buffalo and dogs) are now roaming free, threatening the **ecological balance**. Incursions by large fishing vessels (limited artesanal fishing is permitted), illegal timber extraction and resort development could also damage the reserve, and ongoing negotiations between the government, environmental pressure groups and interested businesses will have a critical impact on Coiba's future.

The standard day-trip tends to involve 2–3 snorkelling stops at a couple of the small islands – usually **Isla Ranchería** (Coibita) and the favoured **Granito de Oro** ("the little grain of gold"), a speck of soft sand surrounded by translucent water, plentiful coral and prolific fish, including the occasional nurse shark and turtle. However, smaller cruise ships (Dec–April) periodically stop off at the latter and smother the sand with

5

deckchairs and assorted aquatic paraphernalia, causing the fish to scarper. The park rangers can advise you on timing. The tour inevitably involves stopping off at Isla Coiba itself, for lunch, and to pay park fees. The trip may also involve a walk around Sendero de los Monos (see page 214).

Isla Coiba

All visitors to **Isla Coiba** report first to the MIA station at Playa Gambute, on the northern tip of the island, to register and show proof of payment. There's an interpretive centre, moderate snorkelling in the sandy cove and a couple of easy short **walks** affording pleasant views and tranquil birdwatching. Iguanas and agoutis are frequent dawn visitors to the lawn-cum-part-time-football-pitch fronting the main beach, and spider monkeys are often sighted swinging through the surrounding vegetation.

The trails

Beyond climbing the steps to the impressive **viewpoint** above the MIA ranger station, the most popular trail – a short boat ride away – is the 1km interpretive **Sendero de los Monos**. You'll need to be here early, though, to encounter the elusive white-faced capuchins or the island's unique variety of howler monkey. For serious hikers, a more rewarding outing is the **Sendero de Santa Cruz**, which leads from the ranger station through primeval rainforest, crossing crocodile-infested rivers to the island's west coast at Santa Cruz. You may want to engage one of the park wardens as a guide (see page 215); if you have your own boat, you can hike the trail one way (2–3hr) and arrange a pickup time to be ferried back to the MIA station – but factor in the extra fuel (and cost) needed for this.

South to Bahía Damas and beyond

Just south of Punta Damas is the main camp of the former **penal colony** (see box, page 215), whose crumbling, eerie buildings are slowly being reclaimed by nature – though some parts have recently been "cleaned up" for the tourists. Further south, across **Bahía Damas**, the aquamarine reef-filled shallows of the eastern coast provide many of the prime diving and snorkelling sites. Panama's last remaining nesting site of the spectacular **scarlet macaw** is at the south of the island, near Barco Quebrado, though

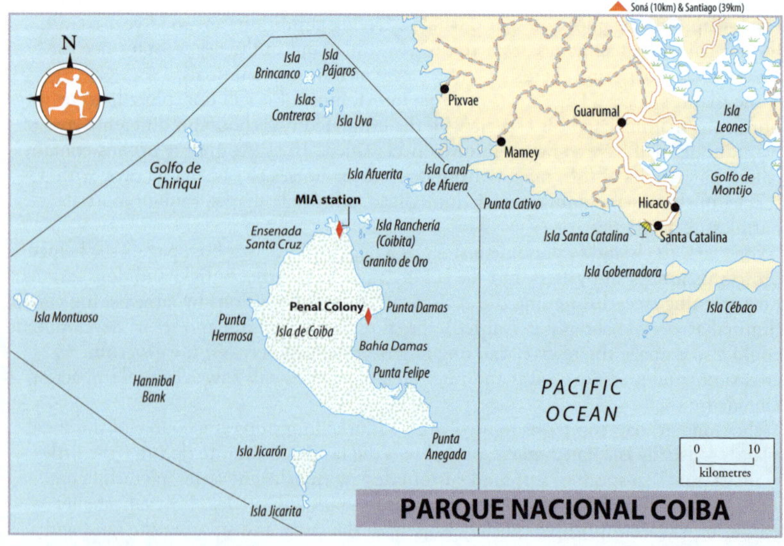

THE PENAL COLONY ON COIBA

For almost eighty years Coiba was synonymous with fear and brutality, as horror stories of forced labour and torture, political assassinations and gang warfare leaked from the island. Designated as a **penal colony** in 1919, it was intended to be an open prison, staffed by civilians and aimed at reforming serious offenders – hence the inclusion at the main camp of a school, rehabilitation centre and church. But with up to three thousand prisoners on the island at one stage, scattered around sixteen different camps, most offenders were unable to access these resources, and the planned civilian custodians never materialized. Instead, prisoners worked twelve-hour shifts on farmland and forest on only one meal a day, suffering violence from gangs and guards, malnutrition, poor sanitation and scant medical care. A peek inside the decaying **high-security block** is sobering. Here ten to twenty people used to share a humid, windowless cell no more than 3m across, with nine bare concrete "beds" and a hole for a toilet, incarcerated for 24 hours a day, with no exercise, no visitors and little chance of release. Unsurprisingly, **escape attempts** were frequent but usually failed as those who managed to get through the island's dense undergrowth, avoiding the crocodiles and snakes, generally came to grief in the shark-infested waters and strong sea currents.

Far from the public gaze, the island also gained notoriety during the **military dictatorships** of Omar Torrijos and Manuel Noriega as a prime location for "losing" political opponents, some of whose tortured bodies were unearthed in around 180 graves discovered during President Moscoso's Truth Commission investigations. The penitentiary finally closed in 2004; the only former convict still remaining on the island is "Mali-Mali", now the park's most famous ranger and much-sought-after tourist guide.

these magnificent birds are more easily heard than seen in the forest canopy. Some tours take a plunge in the invigorating **thermal springs** at Punta Felipe or venture into tangled mangroves at **Boca Brava**, or at **Punta Hermosa**, on the less-explored west coast.

ARRIVAL AND DEPARTURE — PARQUE NACIONAL COIBA

Day-trips from Santa Catalina Day-trips from Santa Catalina can be both costly and a little disappointing if you want to do more than snorkel, since the lengthy journey plus the unavoidable *tramites* (bureaucracy) at the ranger station mean that by the time you actually venture into the rainforest any animal or bird with sense will be hiding from the heat and humidity. Organization is straightforward enough – fishermen on the beaches will probably do the return trip for around $60–70/person (assuming a group of six), or a great deal more if you want them to take you round the island to some of the sights, which are inconveniently spaced out along the eastern coastline (see page 214). The journey to Coiba from Santa Catalina usually takes around 90min, depending on the weather conditions and the boat.

Multiday tours Because of the limitations of day-trips, it pays to spend at least one night on Coiba with a boat and guide willing to take you out at first light. It's therefore worth splashing out the extra for a hassle-free multiday deal with a tour operator; particularly rewarding are those that include some beach camping away from the ranger station (see page 211).

INFORMATION

Park permits At the time of writing, you have to pay the park fees ($20/day) and any camping fees in advance online (see page 42) unless the tour operator does it on your behalf. Tour prices do not usually include park fees.

Ranger guides You can sometimes engage a park ranger to accompany you on trips around the island if you want to do one of the trails and don't have a guide with you.

When to visit As there are no limits on visitor numbers to the national park, holiday periods and summer weekends should be avoided at all costs.

ACCOMMODATION AND EATING

MIA cabins At the time of writing, "renovations" to the accommodation had been ongoing for five years. There was no indication of when or whether they would reopen, future pricing or arrangements for catering. Camping is permitted at the ranger station and in several other locations within the park, with permission from MIA. Thus, unless you go with a tour operator, which already has the permits, you should enquire in advance at the MIA office in Santiago.

Bocas del Toro

MANGROVES, BOCAS DEL TORO

Bocas del Toro

Isolated on the Costa Rican border between the Caribbean and the forested slopes of the Cordillera de Talamanca, Bocas del Toro ("Mouths of the Bull") is one of the most beautiful areas in Panama. It's also one of the most remote – the mainland portion of the province is connected to the rest of Panama by a single spectacular road that carves its way over the continental divide, often blocked by landslides during the heaviest rains, while the island chain offshore requires a boat ride to reach.

For most people, Bocas – confusingly, the abbreviation for the province, archipelago, provincial capital and even sometimes Isla Colón – means the **tropical islands**, which attract more visitors than anywhere else outside Panama City, offering opportunities for relaxing on pristine **beaches** and snorkelling and diving among **coral reefs** in a maze of tangled **mangroves** and undisturbed **rainforest**. The archipelago's unique history has made it the most ethnically diverse region in Panama outside the capital, its Afro-Caribbean, Panamanian-Chinese, *mestizo* and indigenous Ngäbe residents recently joined by North American retirees and US and European hotel owners. English is the dominant language, though Spanish is still widespread. That said, however cosmopolitan Bocas has become, it is the languid pace of the dominant **Afro-Caribbean culture** and its distinctive vernacular wooden architecture that most clearly defines the place.

The archipelago only constitutes a small percentage of the province, much of which is taken up by the **Comarca Ngäbe-Buglé** in the east and the inaccessible but spectacular Talamanca mountain range to the southwest, whose lofty peaks form the backbone of the vast **Parque Internacional La Amistad**, which boasts an awe-inspiring array of wildlife. The lowlands of the mainland, often dismissed as an endless stream of banana plantations, also offer a couple of notable attractions. Panama's banana capital and the province's main commercial centre, **Changuinola**, provides access to the magical **Parque Nacional Humedales de San San Pond Sak**, the country's main refuge for the manatee and an important beach for nesting marine turtles. Inland, on the banks of the picturesque Río Teribe, a stay with the **Naso**, one of the less-well-known indigenous peoples, provides a unique opportunity for intercultural exchange in a stunning natural setting.

Brief history

Archeological evidence suggests that **indigenous peoples** inhabited the islands and mainland of present-day Bocas del Toro two thousand years ago, long before an ailing Christopher Columbus limped into the bay on his final voyage in 1502 in search of a route to Asia. Later, during the colonial era, the calm waters of the archipelago provided shelter for European pirates and by the early nineteenth century the islands were becoming the ethnic melting pot that they are today. British and US trading **merchants** came with their West African slave workforce, founding the town of Bocas del Toro in 1826. Following construction of the **Panama Railroad** and the French canal effort, West Indian migrants continued to drift into the area.

The banana trade

For the last two centuries, the ebb and flow of the **banana trade** has most clearly defined the province. By 1895 bananas from Bocas accounted for more than half of Panama's export earnings, and Bocas Town boasted five foreign consulates and three English-language newspapers. Around 6500 were employed by the United Fruit Company in its heyday, and the company was responsible for building the now-defunct mainland railroad system and constructing canals, hospitals, telegraph networks and entire towns.

STRAWBERRY POISON DART FROG, ISLA BASTIMENTOS

Highlights

❶ **Tour an organic cocoa farm** Learn how the Ngäbe make chocolate and experience village life on the Bocas mainland. See page 229

❷ **Relax in a secluded eco-retreat** Disconnect from the modern world in an island retreat, set in fabulous tropical surroundings. See pages 229 and 235

❸ **Cocktails in Bocas** After a hard day at the beach, enjoy an iced cocktail at one of Bocas Town's many waterside bars. See page 232

❹ **Isla Bastimentos** Explore the Caribbean community of Old Bank, Ngäbe villages and windswept surfing beaches while looking out for the famous red frogs. See page 233

❺ **Cayo Crawl** Snorkel among gorgeous soft corals before tucking into a seafood platter at a restaurant over the water. See page 234

❻ **Parque Nacional Humedales de San San Pond Sak** This wetland manatee refuge also provides nesting sites for marine turtles and hosts an array of birdlife. See page 242

❼ **Stay in a Naso village** Learn about Panama's only monarchy and explore the surrounding rainforest. See page 243

❽ **Isla Escudo de Veraguas** Alluring desert island fringed with mangroves, hidden coves and crystalline waters – home to the endemic pygmy three-toed sloth. See page 238

HIGHLIGHTS ARE MARKED ON THE MAP ON PAGE 220

BOCAS DEL TORO
HIGHLIGHTS
1 Tour an organic cocoa farm
2 Relax in a secluded eco-retreat
3 Cocktails in Bocas
4 Isla Bastimentos
5 Cayo Crawl
6 Parque Nacional Humedales de San San Pond Sak
7 Stay in a Naso village
8 Isla Escudo de Veraguas
N
CARIBBEAN SEA
Golfo de los Mosquitos
Archipiélago de Bocas del Toro
Puerto Limón
Río Sixaola
Las Tablas
Sixaola
Guabito
Humedales de San San Pond Sak
Río San San
Changuinola
El Silencio
Finca 60
Canal de Soropta
Swan Cay (Isla Pájaros)
Isla Colón
Bocas Town
Old Bank (Bastimentos Town)
Isla Bastimentos
PARQUE NACIONAL MARINO ISLA BASTIMENTOS
Isla San Cristóbal
Isla Solarte
Cayo Crawl
Cayos Zapatillas
Isla Popa
Cayo de Agua
Almirante
Silico Creek
Río Teribe
PARQUE INTERNACIONAL LA AMISTAD
BOSQUE PROTECTOR DE PALO SECO
Río Changuinola
Cerro Fábrega (3336m)
Cerro Itamut (3279m)
Cerro Echandi (3163m)
CORDILLERA DE TALAMANCA
COSTA RICA
Kusapin
Península Valiente
Río Caña
Isla Escudo de Veraguas
Laguna de Chiriquí
Chiriquí Grande
BOCAS DEL TORO
Río Manatí
Río Criamola
Río Chucará
Calovébora
VERAGUAS
CORDILLERA CENTRAL
Río Sereno
PARQUE NACIONAL VOLCÁN BARÚ
Cerro Punta
Volcán
Volcán Barú (3475m)
Boquete
Lago Fortuna
CHIRIQUÍ
Río Piedra
Río Majagua
Gualaca
San José
INTERAMERICANA
Paso Canoas
David
Interamericana, David & Panama City
0
25
kilometres

But following repeated devastation by disease early in the twentieth century, the banana harvests failed, causing the archipelago's economy to languish. When the banana trade started up again in the 1950s and 1960s, Guna and Guaymí workers were also integrated into the workforce, many suffering serious ill-health from noxious pesticides. Now, with the trade in "*oro verde*" (green gold) flagging, the business is confined to the plantations round Changuinola, the headquarters of Bocas Fruit Company, the current incarnation of "the company" and part of Chiquita Brands International. With over five thousand direct and indirect employees it is still the most important employer in the province. Workers earn pitifully low wages though in 2024, after months of unrest, a four-year agreement was signed that promised a wage increase and incentives for female workers.

Tourism and real estate

In recent years, **tourism** and **real-estate speculation** have soared, generating employment and income for some residents while leaving others behind to struggle with the inevitable rise in the cost of living, increased pressure on services and the threat of being thrown off their land. Foreign investors have been allowed to purchase huge portions of the archipelago for luxury resorts and holiday homes, despite local opposition. Given the complex ecosystems involved and the lack of infrastructure on the islands due to years of government neglect, much concern exists over the sustainability of such developments.

Archipiélago de Bocas del Toro

Most tourists make a beeline for the **Archipiélago de Bocas del Toro**, scarcely setting foot on the mainland except to catch a bus or a boat. Despite the existence of several

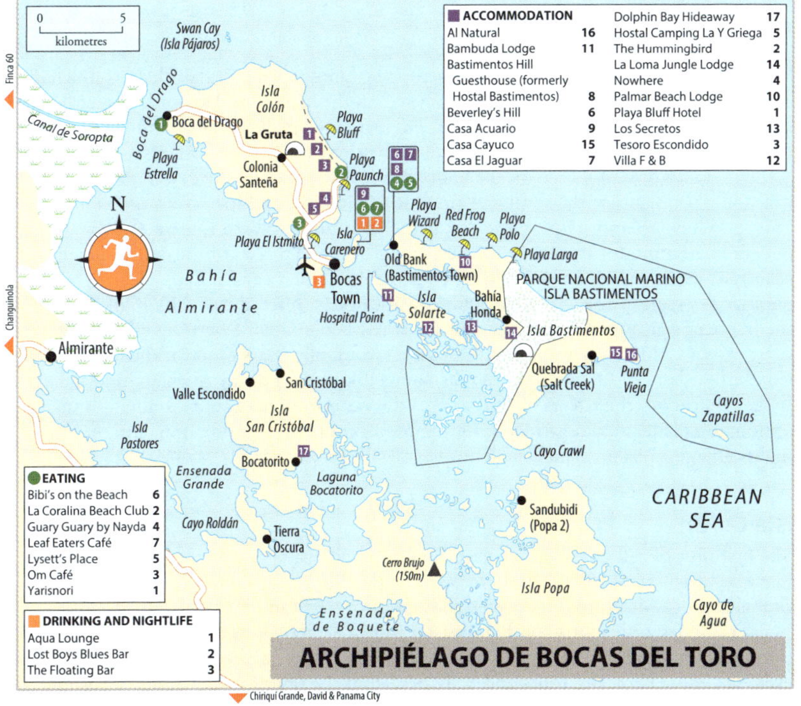

THE NGÄBE AND BUGLÉ

The province's highest-profile indigenous peoples are the **Ngäbe** (pronounced "No-bay") and the **Buglé**. These two related groups speak mutually unintelligible languages, and are probably the oldest surviving ethnic groups on the isthmus, descended from the great Guaymí warrior people, whose best-known chief, Urracá (see box, page 295), graces the 1¢ coin. Forced into remote and mountainous lands by the Spanish, where many have remained, the majority live within the Comarca Ngäbe-Buglé, a semi-autonomous area established in 1997, covering almost 7000 square kilometres in the eastern half of the province and pockets of Veraguas and Chiriquí. With poor access to potable water, health care and education, the *comarca* suffers Panama's highest levels of poverty.

Most Ngäbe and Buglé practise **subsistence agriculture**, supplemented by hunting, fishing and limited cash crop cultivation. Struggling to survive in an increasingly cash-based economy, some make seasonal migrations to the banana, coffee or sugar plantations, where they do the harshest jobs for the worst wages. A few produce traditional handicrafts – the distinctive colourful cotton dresses (*nagua*), necklaces (*nguñunkua*) and woven bags (*kra*) – to sell to tourists; others have abandoned the rural areas altogether.

Traditionally, both groups have lived in small kinship groupings – half a dozen thatched huts with dirt or wooden floors, though coastal communities prefer rectangular lodgings built on stilts – which control access to land and work in cooperation. These, and other cultural practices, such as the Ngäbe custom of polygamy (the Buglé have always espoused monogamy), have been eroded by missionary and other outside influences. One of the traditions that clings on in some places within the *comarca*, despite attempts to outlaw it, is the **krün** (*balsería* in Spanish), a violent "sport" in which members of two teams take turns to try and knock their opponent off-balance by hurling a wooden pole at their calves. The contest is a core part of the four-day **chichería**, which involves plenty of its namesake, the potent maize-based *chicha fuerte* brew, alongside dancing and music.

hundred atolls, islets and cays scattered across the bite-shaped gulf that shelters much of the archipelago, most tourist activity is centred on the handful of larger islands, covered in rainforest and fringed with mangroves, populated by small **Ngäbe** communities or, in the cases of islas Colón and Bastimentos, largely **Afro-Antillean** settlements.

The majority of visitors stay in the laidback provincial capital **Bocas del Toro**, which spills off a peninsula at the southeast tip of **Isla Colón**, the archipelago's largest and most developed island. During the day, launches brimming with tourists scatter outwards, heading for the reefs, beaches, mangroves and forests of the neighbouring islands of **Bastimentos**, **Solarte** and **Carenero** or the distant cays of **Zapatillas**. Other popular destinations include the **Laguna de Bocatorito**, often dubbed Dolphin Bay for the frequent sightings of dolphins, and the seabird colonies of **Swan Cay** off the north coast of Isla Colón. When sea conditions are favourable, boats head for the remote and wonderful island of **Escudo de Veraguas,** some 40km adrift of the main archipelago. In late afternoon, the streets of Bocas fill as the **waterfront bars** come to life. Dining options are plentiful and varied, reflecting the cosmopolitan population, and on most nights energetic visitors can usually find somewhere to dance till dawn.

Isla Colón

The first port of call in the archipelago for almost all visitors – whether arriving by plane or boat – is **ISLA COLÓN**, or, to be more precise, **Bocas Town**, the provincial capital of Bocas del Toro. Connected to the rest of the island by a slender isthmus, Bocas explodes with tourists in high season (mid-Dec to April), and is the easiest base from which to explore the islands, beaches and reefs of the archipelago. It also offers an ever expanding choice of tours and activities, from the traditional pursuits of **surfing**,

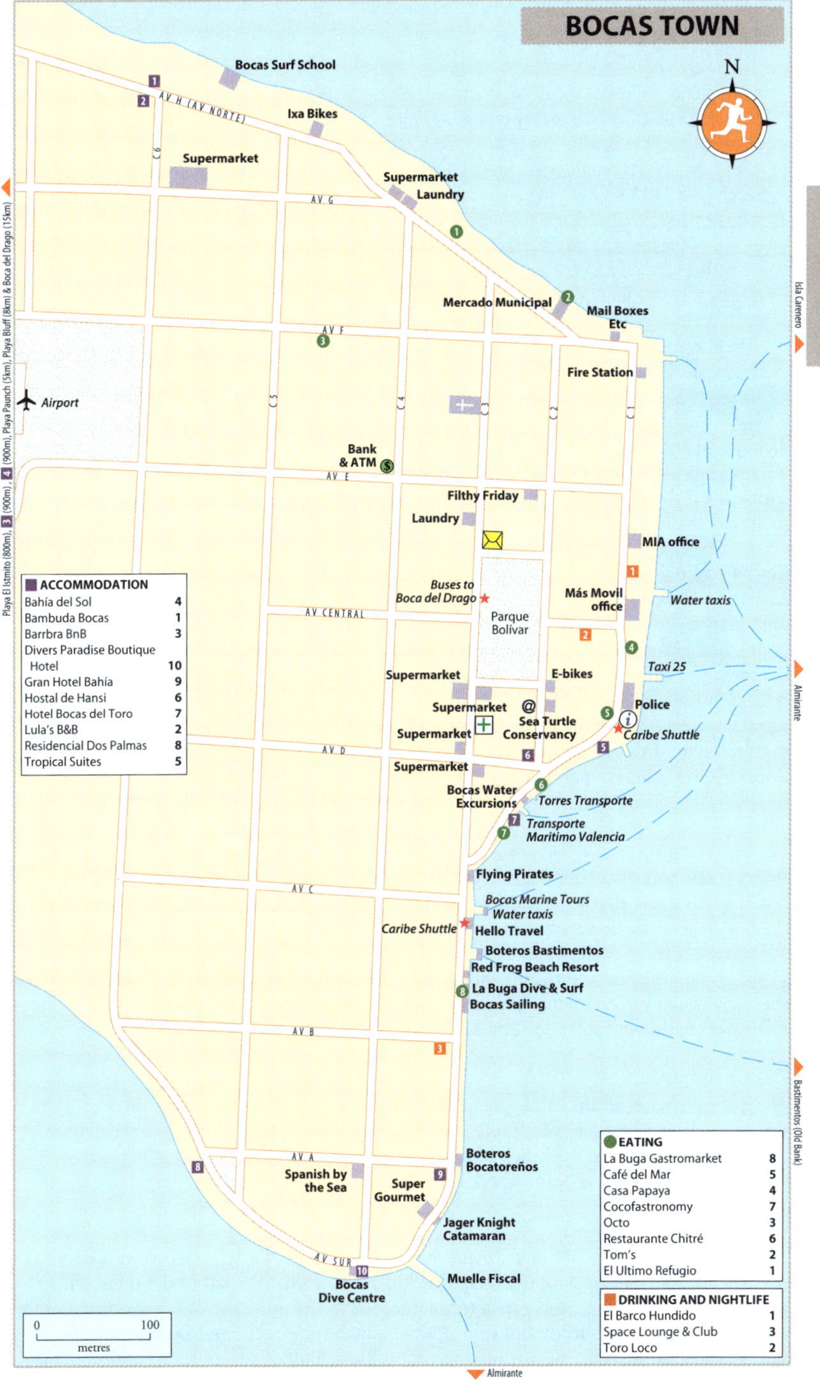
BOCAS TOWN
N
6
Bocas Surf School
Ixa Bikes
AV H (AV NORTE)
Supermarket
Supermarket
Laundry
AV G
Mercado Municipal
Mail Boxes Etc
AV F
Fire Station
Airport
Bank & ATM
AV E
Filthy Friday
Laundry
MIA office
Buses to Boca del Drago
Parque Bolívar
Más Movil office
Water taxis
AV CENTRAL
Taxi 25
E-bikes
Supermarket
Supermarket
Supermarket
Sea Turtle Conservancy
Police
Caribe Shuttle
AV D
Supermarket
Bocas Water Excursions
Torres Transporte
Transporte Maritimo Valencia
AV C
Flying Pirates
Bocas Marine Tours
Water taxis
Caribe Shuttle
Hello Travel
Boteros Bastimentos
Red Frog Beach Resort
La Buga Dive & Surf
Bocas Sailing
AV B
AV A
Boteros Bocatoreños
Spanish by the Sea
Super Gourmet
Jager Knight Catamaran
AV SUR
Muelle Fiscal
Bocas Dive Centre
0 100 metres
Isla Carenero
Almirante
Bastimentos (Old Bank)
Almirante
Playa El Istmito (800m), 3 (900m), 4 (900m), Playa Paunch (5km), Playa Bluff (8km) & Boca del Drago (15km)
ACCOMMODATION
Bahía del Sol 4
Bambuda Bocas 1
Barrbra BnB 3
Divers Paradise Boutique Hotel 10
Gran Hotel Bahía 9
Hostal de Hansi 6
Hotel Bocas del Toro 7
Lula's B&B 2
Residencial Dos Palmas 8
Tropical Suites 5
EATING
La Buga Gastromarket 8
Café del Mar 5
Casa Papaya 4
Cocofastronomy 7
Octo 3
Restaurante Chitré 6
Tom's 2
El Ultimo Refugio 1
DRINKING AND NIGHTLIFE
El Barco Hundido 1
Space Lounge & Club 3
Toro Loco 2

6

SAFETY IN BOCAS

The collapse of the banana trade and the social inequalities exacerbated by the mushrooming tourism and real-estate industries, compounded by the fallout from the Covid-19 pandemic, have led to an increase in **petty crime**. Valuables can go missing from even the most apparently empty beach, especially on islas Colón and Bastimentos, despite police patrols. Even in daylight there are periodic robberies on Isla Bastimentos, on the path across to Wizard Beach from Old Bank, with the occasional report of guys threatening with knives. If you hike this path, seek local advice and ensure that you are in a group. However tempting, **camping** on any of the beaches on the main islands outside an official campsite is very unwise.

Another safety issue concerns **boats**. Serious, even fatal collisions have occurred in the bay, usually at night, generally involving an unlicensed or inebriated boatman and/or a lack of lights on the vessel. Don't get into a boat until you've assessed the level of risk. And finally, take note of **riptides**, which are prevalent in the archipelago. Ask locals about currents, riptides and rogue waves before swimming, especially on Bastimentos. Every year, someone drowns.

diving and **snorkelling** to options such as forest walks, kayaking and wildlife viewing, as well as yoga and massage. Despite the lush rainforest on the island, most tourist activity happens on the wild and relatively deserted **beaches** of the east coast or the more sheltered shallows of **Boca del Drago**, on the western point close to the mainland.

Bocas Town

Arriving in **BOCAS TOWN**, you are welcomed to the island's casual melee by a spread of rickety, wooden, pastel-painted buildings and a laidback, often English-speaking, population. After falling into decline with the collapse of the banana trade (see page 218), the town was catapulted into another era by a steady trickle of backpackers and American retirees in the 1990s, followed by a country-wide real estate boom. Around twenty years ago there were only three hotels here; now there are more than seventy, though tourist numbers have dropped off in recent times. There's no sightseeing as such – experiencing Bocas is more about hanging out in the waterfront bars and restaurants, soaking up the relaxed vibe, getting out on the water or on the bike during the day and partying at night.

The town centre

Bocas is laid out on a simple grid system with most activity centred on **Calle 3**, the broad main street that runs north–south, spilling into Calle 1, which bulges out into the bay, where the decks of attractive wooden hotels, bars and restaurants stretch over the water on stilts. Halfway up the main drag, lined with a less appealing architectural blend of supermarkets, souvenir shops and stalls, hotels and hostels, sits **Parque Bolívar**, the social heart of the town, shaded by coconut palms and fig trees, with a bust of the Liberator, the town's sole monument.

Playa El Istmito

The nearest stretch of sand and general town beach is tatty **Playa El Istmito**, on the eastern side of the causeway that links Bocas with the rest of Isla Colón. Although a cycle route and footpath parallel to the beach has encouraged late afternoon exercise, the place only really comes alive during September's Feria del Mar festivities (see box, page 226).

Playa Bluff and around

Three kilometres north of Bocas Town, the road divides at "La Ye"; a left turn takes you over the hilly terrain to Boca del Drago, 12km away, while the road to the right, which eventually becomes sand and gravel (4WD needed in the rainy season), hugs the coastline for another 5km past **surfing** hot spots **Playa Paunch** (or Punch) and **Dumpers**, until the start of the glorious 4km swathe of sand that is **Playa Bluff**. An important nesting site for leatherback and green **turtles**, Bluff can be visited at night during the nesting season (May–Sept) by arrangement (see box, page 237). None of these beaches is suitable for swimming, with powerful waves and strong currents, but the thundering breakers on Bluff beach are a sight to behold and the golden sands provide a lengthy, scenic promenade. Besides, several great beach bars are dotted along this stretch of coast, where you can recline, cocktail in hand, and watch the surf. At the far end of Playa Bluff, a trail heads towards the blissfully deserted northeastern area of the island known as Mimitimbi. The **natural pools** and sheltered sands round the river mouth are well worth the extra hike or cycle.

WATER IN BOCAS

Tap water is not safe to drink throughout the province; meanwhile, used plastic bottles are a major environmental headache, especially on the islands. Where possible, try to buy the large gallon containers and refill a smaller bottle from them, rather then purchase a succession of small bottles. Better still, try to fill up from the eco-aware establishments that provide filtered water.

6

La Gruta

Colonia Santeña, 7km along the road to Boca del Drago • No fixed hours • Charge • Take the Boca del Drago bus from Bocas Town; La Gruta is signposted to the right off the main road, from where it is a short walk

Halfway across the island on the bumpy, tarred Boca del Drago road, past the eyesore that is the plastic bottle "village" (plasticbottlevillage-theline.com), lies the small settlement of **Colonia Santeña**. The main reason to stop here is to visit a sacred cave, often referred to simply as **La Gruta**, a place of pilgrimage on July 16 for the Festival de la Virgen del Carmen. Push the fronds of greenery aside and, depending on the time of year and the amount of rain, you'll be wading in a delightful freshwater creek or a stream of guano. The shrine to the Virgin is near the entrance; flash a torch around and you'll see hundreds of bats clinging to the rock.

Boca del Drago

Northwest tip of Isla Colón, 16km from Bocas Town • Visit on a boat tour (see box, page 228), take the Boca del Drago bus (see page 227), or rent a bicycle: take the left fork at "La Ye" at the north end of Playa El Istmito, and turn left at the T-junction at the north end of the island

One of the most popular day-trips from Bocas Town is to take the bus to the Ngäbe community of **Boca del Drago**, at the northern end of the island. Supposedly the first place in Panama that Christopher Columbus set foot on, Boca del Drago can be a pleasant place to spend a relaxing day, outside holiday weekends. The beach, though slight, consists of lovely white palm-fringed sand, but the real appeal is the sheltered translucent water, perfect for safe bathing and snorkelling while you wait for your seafood order at the beachfront restaurant (see page 231).

Playa Estrella

A fifteen-minute walk along the shoreline from Boca del Drago takes you to **Playa Estrella**, whose shallows were once dotted with an amazing number of orange cushioned starfish. Sadly, thanks to a combination of increasing numbers of water-taxis and thoughtless actions by some tourists, touching or picking up the starfish for photos, numbers have dwindled. Here the beach is backed by a string of informal seafood restaurants and bars, which are packed at weekends and during the holiday season, with music blasting out across the sand. However, if you visit midweek, you'll encounter a more tranquil scene (though fewer options for eating) and by snorkelling a little further out from the beach, you might spot a few more starfish.

Swan Cay

2km off the north coast of Isla Colón • Visit on a boat tour (see box, page 228) or negotiate a rate with a fisherman in Boca del Drago

Swan Cay, a fifteen-minute boat ride off the north coast (accessible only in good weather conditions), is one of the area's main attractions. Known locally as **Isla Pájaros**

(Bird Island), this impressive 50m stack, topped with cascading vegetation, is a **bird sanctuary**. Seabirds wheel above, with star billing going to the elegant white **red-billed tropicbird**, which shares this nesting spot with a colony of brown boobies.

ARRIVAL AND DEPARTURE — ISLA COLÓN

6

BY PLANE

Airport All flights arrive at, and depart from, Bocas Airport, three blocks west of the main street, C 3.

Airlines and flights Air Panama (757 9841 in Bocas; 316 9000 for general reservations; airpanama.com) offers four daily flights from and to Panama City, which get booked up early over long weekends and holiday periods. Flytrip (flytrip.com.pa), a charter airline with much smaller planes, also operates one scheduled flight a day. The Costa Rican domestic airline Sansa (flysansa.com) provides direct flights between San José and Bocas (Tues, Thurs & Sun; 50min; from $240 one way). All three airlines have a desk at the airport in Bocas.

Luggage allowance Air Panama and Sansa flights allow 14kg of checked baggage, plus hand luggage. Both airlines charge supplements for surfboards, which can be pre-booked, provided there is space on the plane.

BY BUS

Almirante, a port on the Caribbean mainland, is the departure point for almost all boats to Isla Colón, the gateway to the Bocas del Toro archipelago, although a few now leave from Chiriquí Grande, further east (see panabocas.com; five daily; 45min). At Almirante, whether you're coming from or heading to Costa Rica, Panama City or David by bus, you will be dropped off/picked up at "La Ye" de Almirante (see page 224), the junction between the main coastal road and the entrance to Almirante. Shared taxis shuttle back and forth between here and the water-taxi terminals ($1/person), where boats depart for/arrive from Bocas Town on Isla Colón.

From Costa Rica After crossing the Costa Rican border at Sixaola/Guabito (see page 244), take the bus to Changuinola, the first main town, 17km from the border (5.30am–7pm; every 25min; 30min), and transfer to a bus bound for Almirante (see page 240); alternatively, take a private or *colectivo* taxi to Almirante (50min). A shuttle service also runs between Puerto Viejo, in Costa Rica, and Bocas del Toro (see below).

From/to Panama City Tranceibosa (facebook.com/p/Tranceibosa-Bocas-del-toro-Bus-Company-100063564141610) operates buses between Panama City and Changuinola, dropping off/picking up passengers at Almirante, and Santiago, en route, if space. Buses from Panama City leave at 7am (11hr) 6pm, 6.30pm and sometimes 7pm, depending on demand (10hr); departures from Almirante to Panama City leave at 8am and 6pm daily. Tickets can be bought at Albrook bus terminal in Panama City, and at the Tranceibosa office by Taxi 25 in Bocas Town (754 9493) up to two days in advance – buying ahead is advisable in high season. You'll need warm clothes to combat the invariably glacial a/c on the overnight buses.

From/to David Buses run frequently between Changuinola and David, stopping at Almirante (5am–7pm; every 25min; 4hr).

Shuttles The Caribe Shuttle (C 1 Bocas 757 7048; Puerto Viejo, Costa Rica 2750 0626, caribeshuttle.com) offers a hassle-free, daily door-to-door a/c service to Bocas from Puerto Viejo (6am, 8am & noon; 4hr; fare includes water taxi) or San José (8am; 10hr) in Costa Rica. Departures from Bocas to Puerto Viejo also leave at 6am, 8am and noon, while for San José the shuttle leaves at 8am. Hello Travel (757 7004, hellotravelpanama.com), which has an office on C 1, Bocas Town, operates a daily shuttle between Boquete and Bocas Town, leaving Boquete at 9am (4hr) and Bocas at noon. All shuttle prices include water-taxi fares.

BY BOAT

Water-taxis The number of water-taxi companies providing transfer across the bay between Almirante

BOCAS FESTIVALS

Bocas Town's main festival is the **Feria del Mar**, held on Playa El Istmito in late September; endless rows of exhibition stands, craft stalls, mountainous fry-ups and late-night partying on the sands draw visitors in their thousands. Other dates for the diary include November 16, when Bocas' main street becomes the focus of multiday celebrations for the **foundation of Bocas del Toro** province, marked by daytime parades with marching bands and *pollera*-garbed women, and nighttime drinking and dancing to DJs and live music. **Carnavales**, though less wild than in the Azuero, involve a fair amount of partying nonetheless – the strong Afro-Panamanian influence ensures regular street outings of Congo bands and *diablitos* brandishing whips (see box, page 163).

DIVING, SNORKELLING AND SURFING IN BOCAS

Diving and **snorkelling** are the most established diversions around Bocas Town. The area offers the healthiest **coral** on the Caribbean coast, covered in sponges and anemones, fed on by colourful reef fish and frequented by turtles and nurse sharks, while moray eels, lobsters and crabs hide in the crevices. The main problem with snorkelling and diving in Bocas is drastically reduced **visibility** caused by run-off from the mainland following heavy rains, which are frequent, even in the dry season. Strong winds and rough seas limit accessibility to more remote dive sites too.

Bocas also has a growing reputation for **surfing**, and while it can't match Santa Catalina (see page 212) for consistency of waves, it offers some excellent rides when conditions are right, generally between December and March.

DIVING AND SNORKELLING

Snorkelling highlights include the distant **Cayos Zapatillas** in the national marine park, though currents are strong, and, off the southern tip of Bastimentos, the magical soft coral gardens of **Cayo Crawl**. Closer to base, the shallows by Hospital Point off **Isla Solarte** are favoured by both snorkellers and divers, who can explore the impressive wall and rocky outcrop sheltering schools of fish. The best diving is undeniably **Tiger Rock**, a group of beautiful pinnacles visited by schools of large fish, which lies 40km offshore and requires a full day-trip and calm seas.

SURFING

Most surf spots are for **experienced** or **intermediate** surfers, though everyone will need reef booties for the sharp reef breaks and to protect against sea urchins. On the east coast of Isla Colón, top billing goes to **Playa Bluff**, which can produce huge tubes when the swell is in and is only for experienced practitioners. **Dumpers** – nearer Bocas Town – provides a tricky reef-bottom left break, whereas the reef break at nearby **Paunch** is usually the place to take **beginners**. Over on Isla Bastimentos the left and right beach breaks of **Playa Wizard** and **Red Frog Beach** are also usually accessible to novice and intermediate surfers. Other hot spots for experts include the reef break that lies off **Isla Carenero** and along the northern coast of Bastimentos; and, between the two islands, the giant waves of **Silverbacks**.

Numerous places rent out boards in various states of repair ($15–25/day), and several places offer lessons ($50–60/half-day), transfers to surf spots and even guided surf tours (see page 229).

and Bocas ebbs and flows. At the time of writing three companies were active: each has a separate jetty along the same 100m of road in Almirante with departures every 30min (6am–6pm, occasionally 6.30pm; 30min; $6 one way but $10 return if you use the same company). The most established company is Taxi 25, which has a smart dock next to the police station in Bocas Town; newer companies Transporte Maritimo Valencia and Torres Tours have jetties on C 1 and offer cheaper rates when business is slack.

Ferries The inexpensive Palanga car ferry (ferrybocas.com) leaves Almirante at 6am, 11am and 3.30pm Mon–Sat, 7am and noon on Sun (1hr 30min) and will transport a bicycle or a motorbike for a small fee. The ferry docks at the southern end of Bocas Town's main street, returning to Almirante at 8.30, 1.15pm and 6pm Mon–Sat, and 10am and 3pm Sun.

GETTING AROUND

There are currently two minibus services (see below); otherwise, beyond the town centre – which is easily navigable on foot – you're reliant on taxis.

By taxi Though generally unnecessary in town, *colectivo* and private taxis are readily available. Travelling further afield, a 4WD taxi to Playa Bluff will set you back from $20 depending on how far up the beach you are going, and the condition of the road.

By bus There are two bus routes across the island. Transporte Boca del Drago (774 9065) operates the more regular and reliable service, to and from Boca del Drago. It leaves from Parque Bolívar hourly (7am–6pm; 30min) and departs from outside *Yarisnori* in Boca del Drago (see page 231) at similar intervals for the return trip. There is also a

TOURS FROM BOCAS TOWN

Generally, you get what you pay for in a **tour**, in that the pricier operators tend to use better and safer boats, take fewer people and show greater customer service and respect for the environment and the indigenous communities, though this is not universally the case. Make sure you establish the itinerary and what's included in the price. If you get a group of about six together, you can usually negotiate a deal for your own itinerary with one of the boatmen hanging out around the dock.

The standard day-trip excursions combine snorkelling with other activities, and cater predominantly to budget travellers ($30–35/person for a minimum of four to six people), depending on the destination and boat quality. Most leave at around 9.30am, returning about 4–4.30pm and stopping off for a seafood meal (not included in price) at a local restaurant along the way, though some trips include a picnic lunch. Bad **weather** can result in a change of itinerary or cancellation and the seas further out can get very rough. We offer a selection of the town's best **tour operators** in Bocas' listings section (see page 229).

THE ITINERARIES

There are three longstanding itineraries offered by most operators and two relative newcomers. The first takes you to **Laguna Bocatorito** (Dolphin Bay), where you have a chance of seeing the rather shy **bottle-nosed dolphins** that live there year-round. This should be boycotted in high season when the place is overrun with boats, many engaging in potentially harmful practices. The next stop is the gorgeous, rainbow-coloured soft coral of **Cayo Crawl**, where lunch is at one of the three over-the-water restaurants (extra – cash only), before returning to lounge on **Red Frog Beach** (charge), sometimes with an additional spot of snorkelling nearer home.

Another similar but pricier option takes you on from Cayo Crawl to the national marine park and **Cayos Zapatillas** (park fee) for further snorkelling and beach lounging, stopping off at another snorkelling spot, such as **Hospital Point**, on the way back. Alternatively, boats head round Isla Colón to the easy shallows of **Boca del Drago**, with lunch at a restaurant on the beach, a visit to **Playa Estrella** and a trip out to see the seabirds at **Swan Cay** before snorkel masks are donned once more at **Punta Manglar** on the way back. In an attempt to avoid the crowds or offer some variation, some operators are now offering a visit to a Ngäbe village, such as Bocatorito or Bahía Honda.

A relatively new addition to the tour menu is a night tour to seek out **bioluminescence**, and swim (or kayak) among glowing plankton – more impressive under a new moon, when the night sky is really dark.

The longest, most expensive and most adventurous tour travels east around the Península Valiente to the remote **Isla de Escudo de Veraguas** (see box, page 238). Reaching this magical island involves at least four hours journey by boat there and back, plus the time to circumnavigate the island – longer if conditions are rough. The tour sometimes includes other stops en route. Some operators offer overnight camping.

less regular bus service to Playa Bluff, when the road is dry, which also leaves from Parque Bolívar (7am–5.30–6pm; roughly every 1hr–1hr 30min; 20–30min); the last bus returns around 5.30–6pm. Schedules are dependent on weather and demand.

By water-taxi Water-taxis regularly ferry people back and forth from Bocas to Isla Carenero ($1 to the near shore; $2 anywhere else) and to Old Bank on Bastimentos ($3) at fixed rates, from around dawn to dusk. Taxis leave once they've gathered a few passengers, every 10–15min or so, and the rates go up at night. The main water-taxi dock for Carenero is by *El Barco Hundido* on C 1, while for Old Bank, Bastimentos, you should head for the Boteros Bastimentos water-taxi dock, on the main street, opposite Av "C". On C 1, opposite Av "D". That said, you should be able to grab a water-taxi from any dock.

By bike The main cycling destinations are Playa Bluff and Boca del Drago. Several places in Bocas Town rent out bicycles (around $12–15/day; $50/week) in varying states of repair. Ixa Bikes (facebook.com/bicicletasixa), on Av "H' and C 5, is a good choice as they also do bike repairs. Bocas E-bikes C 2, by the park (bocasebikes.com) takes the slog out of cycling and will easily get you to the end of the island and back without your breaking out in too much of a sweat though you'll pay a great deal more. A bike lock, helmet and map can also be provided. Flying Pirates (flyingpiratesbocas.com) also offers quad-bike rental.

INFORMATION

Tourist information The tourist office (daily 8am–4pm; 757 9642) on C 1 has toilets, and may be able to provide a map, but is otherwise of limited help. The free monthly *Bocas Breeze* (bocasbreeze.com) advertises local events. The sustainable tourism group, Alianza de Turismo Sostenible de Bocas del Toro runs a useful website (redtucombo.bocasdeltoro.org) containing information and contact details for some of the local community-based tourism projects.

6

ACTIVITIES AND TOURS

Birdwatching Biologist Stacey Hollis is very knowledgeable about birds, other wildlife and ecosystems, and is committed to genuine ethical ecotourism. She can take you walking or kayaking to seek out birdlife, and can lend you binoculars if necessary.

Cocoa farm Río Oeste Arriba (oreba.bocasdeltoro.org; rates include lunch and transport from Almirante; minimum two people) offer fascinating tours in Spanish and English of their organic cocoa farms, with plenty of tasting along the way.

Horseriding At Playa Bluff, you can arrange horseriding at *Bluff Beach Retreat* (bluffbeachretreat.com).

Kayak and SUP rental Several places, such as *Bambuda Lodge, Bibi's* and *La Buga* rent out kayaks and SUP boards. Bocas Divers rents out both and offers tours.

Turtle watching See box, page 237.

TOUR OPERATORS

There are many tour operators in Bocas Town, and at the budget end of the market, service can be variable. Many of the more upmarket and secluded lodgings run their own tours.

Bocas Dive Centre Av Sur at C 4 bocasdiversparadise.com. Highly regarded dive shop emphasizing safety while having fun. Two-tank dives from $110 at various locations and dive instructor training on offer. Discounts offered at their boutique hotel and restaurant (see below).

Bocas Surf School Av Norte, between C 5 and 6 bocassurfschool.com. Professional private lessons with qualified instructors offering two-hour classes (including board rental) at all levels and three-day surf packages; the same people run a small, quiet on-site hostel.

Bocas Water Excursions C 1 near Hotel Bocas del Toro facebook.com/BocasWaterExcursions. Reliable general tour operator

Boteros Unidos Bocatoreños C 3 at Av "A" boterosunidosbocas.com. An association of local boatmen formed to try and compete against some of the slicker foreign tour operators, offering the usual tour favourites, as well as trips further afield to the mainland and the remote island of Escudo de Veraguas often at slightly lower prices, and with bags of local tales to tell.

La Buga Dive & Surf C 3, at Av "B" labugapanama.com. Highly recommended, this dive centre, offering PADI certification as well as surfing, snorkelling and fishing trips, plus SUP, kayak and surfboard rental. They also have lovely cabins out of town.

Crossing with Sugar instagram.com/crossingwithsugar. One-of-a kind personalized and flexible tours led by Bocatoreño "Sugar"and his crew.

Jager Knights Tours C 3 at Av "A", opposite Super Gourmet bocasdeltorocatamaran.com. Excellent-value catamaran trips either to Dolphin Bay and Cayo Crawl (including picnic lunch) or Boca del Drago, plus snorkelling off Isla Solarte on the way back. Private charter also possible (minimum eight people).

ACCOMMODATION

There's a good range of **accommodation** in Bocas, including several hostels, though very little for those on a tight budget. Prices are particularly high and rooms are scarce during high season and holiday periods. **Advance booking** is a good idea, though some backpacker lodgings don't accept reservations, so if you intend to stay in a hostel or budget hotel try to arrive before 11am. More luxurious foreign-owned lodges and guesthouses occupy the more remote corners of Isla Colón; staying in these you are close to nature but generally reliant on their amenities – so check out their restaurant prices and menus before booking – since public transport is scarce and costly. Out of high season you can often get good deals by booking through the hotel websites. And it pays to remember that water shortages, power cuts and floods often affect Isla Colón – and other areas in the archipelago – however much you're paying.

BOCAS TOWN, SEE MAP PAGE 223

Bahía del Sol Saigon Bay villabahiadelsol.com. Situated in a local community, a 15min walk from town, this cosy over-the-water guesthouse offers a range of rooms and prices from affordable rustic comfort to rustic luxury. The most sought-after suite boasts an ocean veranda with open-air jacuzzi and shower (no a/c). A well-equipped shared kitchen, gracious hosts and wonderful sunsets make this place a treat. Two-night minimum stay. $$$

★ **Bambuda Bocas** Av "H" at C 6 bambuda.com/bocastown. More hotel than hostel though with a hostel vibe. The stunning open-sided lounge-bar-chillout area that melts into an over-the-water sundeck makes this place special. Relax in a deckchair, play board games, or sprawl on a sofa amid the pot plants, and soak up the sea views. Light airy rooms with lots of wood and pastel shades at standard hotel rates. You pay premium hostel rates for pod-like dorms with privacy curtains and more for an ocean-view dorm. There's a shared kitchen, bar-restaurant and lots of activities, such as SUP, live music and yoga. Dorms $, doubles $$–$$$

Barrbra BnB Saigon Bay barrbrabnb.com. Exceptional bed and breakfast, in a traditional over-the-sea wooden house with four individually decorated rooms (with a/c). Upstairs are en-suite; downstairs guests share an outdoor shower with a sea view. It's worth splashing out on the suite with its private balcony overlooking the bay. Fabulous well-equipped shared kitchen and deck from which to watch the sunsets and fabulous breakfasts too. Two-night minimum stay. $$

Divers Paradise Boutique Hotel Av Sur at C 4 diversparadise.com. For those who find rustic Bocas lodgings *too* rustic, this is the place. Located in the quieter end of town, this new hotel offers modern comforts 24 spacious, light rooms, with a/c, ceiling fan, downlighters, minibar, safe and a balcony – some affording a sea view. The on-site dive centre and restaurant are top-notch. Reduced rates often available. $$$

Gran Hotel Bahía C 3 at Av "A" ghbahia.com. You're definitely paying more for the history than facilities or service (though refurbished rooms have a/c and cable TV) – the impressive former headquarters of the United Fruit Company (1905) is steeped in it. Hang out on the fabulous first-floor wooden veranda and splash out the extra $20 plus for the larger, brighter rooms upstairs. Breakfast extra. $$$

★ **Hostal de Hansi** C 2 at Av "D" hostalhansibocas.com. Immaculately clean and tidy, catering to couples and single travellers on a budget who want to avoid the dorm party scene. Fan-ventilated singles with small desk, shelving, and shared or en-suite bathroom have use of a communal kitchen and terrace. Often full so book in advance. $$

Hotel Bocas del Toro C 1, between Av "C" and Av "D" 757 9018, hotelbocasdeltoro.com. Attractive polished wood abounds here and the eleven rooms (with a/c, cable TV and coffee-maker) are elegantly furnished, some with stunning ocean-view balconies. The restaurant deck overlooks the water. They also organize tours, rent kayaks and offer massage. Breakfast included. $$$

Lula's B&B Av "H" at C 6 lulabb.com. Professional B&B offering six spotless rooms with private hot-water bathroom, a/c or fan, plus a spacious communal balcony, homely, nicely furnished living room, an honesty bar and shared kitchenette. More for credit-card payments. $$$

Residencial Dos Palmas Av Sur at C 5 757 9906, residencialdospalmas@yahoo.com. On the quieter southern tip of town in a residential area, this local lodging offers the best budget over-the-water deal, with a handful of faded but tidy rooms (a/c, cable TV and hot water) plus a terrace with hammocks and chairs from which to watch the sun set. $$

★ **Tropical Suites** C 1 at Av "D" bocastropical.com. Stylish aparthotel with helpful English-speaking staff and sixteen well-equipped design-conscious suites with lots of natural light; particularly good value for families, these comprise a kitchenette, large double beds and pull-out double sofa beds, with patio or balcony; you'll pay more for a sea view. Expansive pool deck and bar area overlooking the sea. Cheaper weekly rates. $$$$

REST OF THE ISLAND, SEE MAP PAGE 221

Hostal Camping La Y Griega At "La Ye" hostalcampinglay.my.canva.site/isla-colon. If you're not prepared to rough it a bit – even in one of the four basic rooms (with fan or a/c) – then this place is not for you. Small dome tents furnished with mattresses, pillows and sheets and a fan (at extra cost). The shared ablutions and basic kitchen are not the cleanest, but the vibe is mellow and the place is cheap. $

★ **The Hummingbird** Playa Bluff thehummingbirdpanama.com. Six-room boutique eco-B&B – solar power and rainwater harvesting – in tropical gardens replete with butterflies and hummingbirds. Book a room in one of the raised wooden bungalows with screened louvred windows and folding doors that open onto a fabulous balcony to maximize the breeze and keep out the bugs. There's also a pool and gourmet bar-restaurant (open to non-residents; booking preferred) serving varied breakfasts – included in the rates. Minimum two-night stay. $$$$

Nowhere Big Creek nowhere-remote.com. Ignore the pretentious website (aimed squarely at digital nomads) and appreciate the originality of the accommodation: Jules Verne-style concrete domes (king-size or twin beds) with porthole-windows through which to gaze at the rainforest while you work. Alas, the desk and chair are not designed for spending hours on a laptop – so head for the pool, watch the birds, do some yoga or cycle to the beach. Shared kitchen area. Breakfast included. $$$

Playa Bluff Hotel Playa Bluff playabluffhotel.com. Set back in forest midway along the beach road, this place has 20 spacious, cool fan-ventilated rooms with private or shared bathroom, most with terraces or patios, in verdant surroundings brimming with wildlife just a stone's throw from the beach. Breakfast included. $$$

★ **Tesoro Escondido** Playa Bluff Ⓦ tesoro-escondido.com. Delightful, genuine ecofriendly resort offering rustic rooms, a couple of cottages and a small apartment (sleeping two to four) – all set amid lush tropical forest up on the cliff or down near the beach with plenty of terrace and porch space. Solar-powered rooms and cabins are simply yet quirkily furnished with recycled artwork; mosquito nets are provided. Self-cater in the communal kitchens or enjoy home cooking at reasonable rates. Good weekly or monthly discounts in low season. $$$

EATING

Bocas has an excellent range of **restaurants**, with vegetarians enjoying a decent selection. Lobster, conch and other local seasonal specialities taste particularly delicious in local coconut milk and Caribbean spice preparations. Yet, **quality** can be variable, especially in high season, as small kitchens and wait staff struggle to deal with the numbers and you're often paying for the venue and the vibe – a charming over-the-water deck – more than for the food. **Opening hours** can be erratic, especially in low season, and service seriously soporific. Note that **tap water** is not safe to drink (see box, page 225).

BOCAS TOWN, SEE MAP PAGE 223

La Buga Gastromarket C 1, between Av "B" and Av "C" Ⓦ instagram.com/labugagastromarket. Vibey repurposed dive deck, with frequent live music and a natural swimming pool cut into the floor. Happy hour drinks flow as friendly, efficient staff help you decide what to eat – tricky as five kitchens with five menus serve this place (Hawaiian, with Japanese influence; Mexican; Italian; pizza; burgers). $$–$$$

★ **Café del Mar** C 1, opposite the tourist office Ⓦ instagram.com/cafedelmarpanama. Cosy café with arty decor and half a dozen tables. Breakfasts and well-priced light meals are freshly prepared and a change from the norm: spinach and feta omelette with coconut bread, say, *gallo pinto* burrito, or tuna steak burger. $$–$$$

Casa Papaya C 1 at Av Central Ⓦ instagram.com/casapapayapty. The place for Sunday brunch but arrive early for a table on the shadeless back deck before the sun gets too strong, or it rains. Martina's menu offers eggs Benedict and the like – beautifully presented but a little pricey. There are also Peruvian and sushi and wok-based menus. $$$

Cocofastronomy C 1, at the junction with C 3 Ⓦ cocofastronomy.com. Serves nicely presented dishes – the jerk chicken in the half-pineapple bowl takes the prize – with *patacones* or coconut rice. The stuffed *bapés* (crispy rolls with fluffy insides) are another feature, crammed with all manner of tasty filling, including Cajun chicken and Thai curry – which can result in a soggy bun. Cocktails hit the spot. $$–$$$

Octo Av "F", between C 4 and 5 Ⓦ instagram.com/octo_bocas. Don't be fooled by the simple food truck and a handful of wooden tables set out on gravel under a sheet of aluminium – the food and the ambiance is what it's about, though portions are on the small side. Grilled on a barbecue to perfection are delicious Caribbean treats such as jerk chicken or fish *escobeche*, served with coconut rice and plantain. $$$

Restaurante Chitré C 2, between Av Central and Av "D" Ⓦ instagram.com/restaurantechitre. One of the few local restaurants in town, serving probably the best hot sauce and fried chicken. There's a cafeteria-style breakfast and lunch, but also a la carte. Tuck into traditional staples for around $5 on their waterside deck. $–$$

Tom's Av "H" at C 4, upstairs, behind the municipal market Ⓦ instagram.com/rest.tom. Local Caribbean food for under $10 (more for seafood mains). Expect sides of coconut rice, plantain and *escobeche* with hot pepper sauce and watch the boats bobbing in the careenage. $$

★ **El Último Refugio** Av "G", between C 3 and 4 Ⓦ ultimorefugio.com. A high-quality dining experience is guaranteed in a convivial, cheerily lit over-the-water deck. The ever-changing, mouthwatering fine-dining menu includes the likes of grilled shrimp on polenta with bacon and chili oil, or Asian-style pulled pork, and great cocktails. Occasional live music too. $$$

REST OF THE ISLAND, SEE MAP PAGE 221

La Coralina Beach Club Playa Paunch Ⓦ instagram.com/lacoralinabeachclubs. A casual yet sophisticated beachside spot with a raised deck for dining and sun-loungers nearer the waves for unwinding, cocktail in hand while watching the surfers. Poke bowls, salads and sandwiches are freshly prepared but pricey; the delicious catch of the day with guacamole and coconut rice offers better value. $$$

Om Café La "Ye" Ⓦ facebook.com/OmCafePanama. The new out-of-town venue should be open by the time you read this. This perennial tourist favourite burnt down in 2024, but the Canadian-Indian owner is starting again, and will continue to draw on traditional family recipes, dishing up excellent curries, as well as juices and *lassis*. For breakfast the eggs vindaloo *roti* wrap will set your day off with a blast, or choose from bagels and bowls of fruit, granola and yoghurt. $$–$$$

Yarisnori On the beach, Boca del Drago Ⓣ 6615 5580. This mellow open-air restaurant on the beach is the longest established of the casual seafood places along this stretch of coastline. Enjoy succulent snapper, mahi-mahi or grouper in garlic or Creole sauce, or tackle some fresh lobster with a slice of lime. $$$

6

6

DRINKING AND NIGHTLIFE

Bocas is famed for its nightlife, but truth be told, it has struggled to regain its mojo after the pandemic. That said, the little that is available can provide plenty of fun. For a start, the popularity of Filthy Friday (filthyfriday.rocks) – an endurance island-hopping bar crawl – has not waned. For $40 you get nine hours of non-stop boozing, partying and even some fire-eating, on Isla Colón (Barco Hundido), then Solarte (Blue Coconut; thebluecoconut.com), finishing off at the Aqua Lounge on Carenero. Take a flask of water, a hat, plenty of sunscreen and repellent, and some money to buy food, to soak up the booze.

BOCAS TOWN, SEE MAP PAGE 223

El Barco Hundido C 1, beside Mas Móvil. Known as the "Wreck Deck" both for the illuminated shipwreck by the dancefloor and the late-night state of its clientele, this legendary hangout has DJs most nights, playing everything from Latin to reggae though reggaeton rules these days. It gets lively after 10pm. Serves cheap beer and shots, and slabs of pizza to soak up the booze.

Space Lounge & Club This two-storey semi-outdoor place is the current hot spot for locals and tourists alike to socialize and party. Food trucks provide *empanadas* and inexpensive grub, while the beer is cheap and cocktails well priced. All kinds of music is played (including live artists and DJs).

Toro Loco Av Central, between C 1 and 2 instagram.com/torolocosportsbar. Beyond NFL and baseball fixtures on the TV screens, this sports bar offers friendly, efficient service, moderately priced drinks (including an extended happy hour) and US comfort food – wings, mozzarella sticks, burgers and pasta – to a soundtrack of classic rock. Plus live rock music on Sat nights.

REST OF THE ISLAND, SEE MAP PAGE 221

★ **The Floating Bar** 500m southwest of Bocas Marina bocasfloatingbar.com. It doesn't get much more decadent than this two-storey wooden floating bar and sun deck, a short water-taxi ride from town. Though it can get overcrowded at weekends in high season, at other dry times it's idyllic, lounging on the deck, sipping margaritas to mellow music, munching tacos, then sliding (or diving) into the sea to cool off. Bring repellent for the sandflies at sundown.

DIRECTORY

Learning Spanish Spanish by the Sea (spanishatlocations.com) is a well respected language school. Weekly rates for small group classes start from around $240.

Massage In keeping with the boho vibe of Bocas, there's no shortage of people willing to knead your aching post-surf limbs; check the Bocas Breeze (bocasbreeze.com) notice boards and posters throughout town.

Money The one bank in town, with two ATMs, is on the corner of Av "E" and C 4. It can run out of cash before major parties such as New Year or Carnaval.

Isla Carenero

A short water-taxi ride from Bocas Town, **Isla Carenero** presents a 2km sliver of low-lying land surrounded by shallow waters and a thin necklace of beach that periodically dissolves into mud, tangled roots and, around the northeastern end, jagged rocks, where one of the archipelago's best **surf breaks** pounds the reef. Most of the four hundred occupants are squeezed onto the southwestern tip, in makeshift wooden housing on littered and boggy ground. Though the settlement is quieter than Bocas Town, which could be a plus, the island has a reputation for vicious sandflies; moreover, there's not much to do or see. Most visitors hop across for a drink, a bite to eat or just a change of scene.

ARRIVAL AND DEPARTURE — ISLA CARENERO

By water-taxi Isla Carenero is a short hop by water-taxi from the dock beside *El Barco Hundido* in Bocas Town ($1 to the nearest, unnamed, bit of land, or the *Aqua Lounge*).

ACCOMMODATION — SEE MAP PAGE 221

★ **Casa Acuario** Southwest side of the island casaacuario.com. This delightful wooden structure, built over the water, has five spacious rooms (fan, a/c and cable TV) with vast windows, some with hammock and deckchairs. Plus, there's a wraparound deck and communal kitchen-dining area. $$$

EATING — SEE MAP PAGE 221

Bibi's on the Beach Buccaneer Resort, southeast side of the island bibisonthebeach.com. Popular tourist and expat over-the-water watering hole with great Caribbean views. It serves fresh seafood – try the ceviche with passion fruit, including whole fish and locally caught lobster as well as soups, salads and sandwiches. The cocktails are refreshing too; catch happy hour 4–7pm. $$–$$$

★ **Leaf Eaters Café** Southwest side of the island leafeaterscafe.com. A gem of a vegetarian and vegan café, in a breezy over-the-water setting, whose warm decor has Indian and Caribbean touches. Try the specials: a nutty veggie burger or a tripartite salad bowl of the day, or go for the smoothies, cakes and coffee. Healthy eating *par excellence*. $$

DRINKING AND NIGHTLIFE **SEE MAP PAGE 221**

Aqua Lounge Southwest side of the island bocasaqualounge.com. A legendary over-the-water party venue boasting a swimming pool carved out of the deck, swings, a water trampoline – and plenty of cheap booze. All-night parties are wild, but there's something happening every night, from "beer pong" games evening to live music. Don't expect much sleep if you book a room.

Lost Boys Blues Bar West of the island, 500m north of the Cosmic Crab Resort lost-boys-blues-bar.com. At the time of writing, the final touches were being put to the renovations of this large wooden, over-the-water music events venue, with rock the preferred genre.

6

Isla Bastimentos

The sprawling and beautiful 52 square kilometres of **ISLA BASTIMENTOS** boasts the mellow, Afro-Antillean fishing community of **Old Bank**, marble-sand **surfing beaches** and lush inland **forest** inhabited by strawberry poison dart frogs. Most visitors are day-trippers: some come independently to tuck into tasty Creole seafood in Old Bank or to hike across the island to the surfing beaches; others visit with organized tours, which generally cut across the western arm of the island to the much vaunted Red Frog Beach. If you want to escape the tourist scene in Bocas, Bastimentos is a good place to hang out and the place where you're most likely to hear "Guari-Guari", English patois embellished with Spanish and Ngäbere.

The island's two Ngäbe communities of **Bahía Honda**, in the crook of the bay of the same name on the island's south side, and **Quebrada Sal** (Salt Creek), over towards the eastern end by Punta Vieja, both welcome visitors.

STRAWBERRY POISON DART FROGS

Probably Bastimentos' most famous residents, the dazzling **strawberry poison dart frogs** (*oophaga pumilio*), no larger than a thumbnail, are actually widespread along the Caribbean lowlands from Nicaragua to western Panama. But nowhere is their colouration and size – "morphs" as they are termed – as varied as here. That said, the place you're least likely to spot these amphibians, ironically, is on **Red Frog Beach**, where local kids have captured many of them to impress tourists and charge for photos – or they've simply scarpered.

The most commonly sighted poison dart frog is the smart **"blue-jeans"** morph, whose brilliant scarlet torso fades into cobalt blue or purple legs; on Bastimentos these seductive amphibians span red, orange, gold, green or even white, and are often speckled with black. The "poison dart" title given to the family derived from the likes of the Colombian golden poison frog (*phyllobates terriblis*) that secretes a particularly lethal toxin – sufficient to kill up to twenty people – and which has traditionally been used by the Chocó (ancestors of the present-day Emberá) to coat darts and arrows for hunting.

While the dazzling colouration aimed at alerting would-be predators to the poison beneath their skin is what most attracts tourists to these fluorescent creatures, their **behaviour** is equally striking. Extremely territorial, male dart frogs can be seen locked in combat among the leaf-litter like miniature wrestlers, comically teetering on their hind legs trying to pin their opponent down in submission with the front legs. Mating occurs at any time of year and after the small clutch of eggs has been laid and fertilized, the male periodically pees on them to keep them moist. Once hatched, the female gives each tadpole a piggy-back ride, one by one, up to the canopy, depositing them in separate water-filled bromeliads. Over the next few weeks, she returns frequently to deposit unfertilized eggs in the water for the tadpoles to eat as they mature.

Old Bank (Bastimentos Town)

OLD BANK – affectionately referred to as **Basti** – the island's main settlement, with a population of around nine hundred, sits on the westernmost point, a short jaunt by water-taxi from Bocas. An undulating, cracked concrete path acts as its main thoroughfare, snaking its way between tightly packed houses built out over the water on stilts, passing reggaeton beats, discarded bikes and old men slamming down dominoes, and winding up to a steep, green hillside dotted with precariously built wooden homes. Check out the information boards that line the footpath, explaining more about the history and culture of the place. A jungle **path**, occasionally impassable after heavy rains, leads to several glorious **beaches** twenty minutes away on the other side of the island.

The beaches

Renowned for riptides that claim lives every year, the sea that pounds the northern surfing **beaches** of Bastimentos is often too dangerous to swim in, but there is lots of good walking to be had along these curved broad belts of creamy sand backed by palms and thick vegetation. Heading along the overland path from Old Bank (see box, page 224), you pass **Playa Wizard** (Playa Primera) after fifteen to twenty minutes, and, further east, Playa Segunda, and then **Red Frog Beach**, though you won't find its namesake waving to you from a beach towel (see box). A short hike further east brings you to **Playa Polo**, a smaller, sheltered cove protected by a reef; it's good for snorkelling, though it can get busy, and the eponymous Polo, who lives there, happily cooks up the catch of the day with coconut rice for visitors. Even further east lies another surfing stretch of sand, **Playa Larga** (see page 236).

If you're planning a whole day at the beach, take enough water with you; there are a couple of restaurants on Red Frog Beach.

Bahía Honda

6km southeast of Old Bank • A minimum of two people needed; the fee includes transport, guiding and lunch; one day's notice needed • Community tourism project ☎ 6726 0968 (ask for Rutilio Milton), Ⓦ timorogo.bocasdeltoro.org • Pick up from the dock by the *mercado municipal*, Bocas Town

The 25 or so thatched homes of the dispersed Ngäbe community of **BAHÍA HONDA** are hidden among a dense tangle of mangroves at the eastern end of the bay of the same name, with a few across the water on Isla Solarte. In addition to a chapel and primary school, they have a restaurant, the heart of a **community tourism project** whose star attraction is a guided excursion up the **Sendero del Peresoso** (Trail of the Sloth) to the Cueva Nivida. You'll be paddled up a nearby creek, where you can often see the trail's namesake furled round a branch and crabs and caimans in the shallows, before heading off on foot through forest that was once a cocoa plantation, to wade through a series of caves thick with stalagmites and coated with several species of Bastimentos bats. A harder hike to the Bastimentos **lagoon** is another option for the more adventurous. If you ring a day in advance, you can stop off at the community restaurant on the way back and sample traditional dishes such as *morongodo*, a green plantain pancake.

Cayo Crawl

At the southern tip of Bastimentos amid a myriad of mangrove islets lies tiny **Cayo Crawl**, where three thatched restaurants do a roaring trade in seafood lunches. After rounding the point, you come to the gorgeous soft coral fields of the same name, which feature on many day-trips. In order to protect the coral, fins are not allowed when snorkelling.

Quebrada Sal

Near Punta Vieja • Community fee in addition to the fee for the excursion • ☎ 6142 1476, Ⓦ aliatur.bocasdeltoro.org

On Bastimentos' southeast coast, close to Punta Vieja, the Ngäbe community of **QUEBRADA SAL** (Salt Creek) is seeing an increasing number of day-trippers, generally from

CULTURAL ECOTOURISM IN BOCAS DEL TORO

Several **Ngäbe communities** in the province have initiated cultural **ecotourism** projects to supplement their subsistence livelihood: Bahía Honda and Quebrada Sal (Salt Creek) on Bastimentos, Sandubidi on Isla Popa and Silico Creek and Río Oeste Arriba on the mainland are all trying to attract visitors. The less well-known and less numerous **Naso**, too, are also active in community-based tourism (see box, page 243). While several day-tours from Bocas Town include communities in some of their itineraries, you learn and experience much more by staying overnight (see pages 229 and 235). In addition to the obvious interest of being able to interact with the Ngäbe (or Naso) and learn about their culture, the communities often offer traditional dishes, crafts for sale and guided walks into the rainforest, with good wildlife-spotting opportunities and the chance to learn about medicinal plants. With some of the mainland communities, you can undertake more strenuous hiking.

Details of how to contact the communities directly, and therefore ensure that all your money goes directly to them, are to be found in English and Spanish on the Red de Turismo Comunitario Bocas del Toro **website** redtucombo.bocasdeltoro.org.

6

the lodges around that end of the island; they also offer basic accommodation in the village itself. The surrounding wetlands and nearby Playa Larga – part of the marine park that occupies a swathe of the island (see page 236) – can be explored via several trails, which also provides a chance to learn about medicinal plants and other aspects of Ngäbe culture.

ARRIVAL AND GETTING AROUND — ISLA BASTIMENTOS

BY WATER-TAXI

To Old Bank Boteros Bastimentos, from their jetty on C 3 at Av "C", Bocas Town, offers the most frequent trips to Old Bank (10min; $3).

To Red Frog Beach Bocas Water Excursions on C 1 runs a 10am ferry service (and every 30min-1hr, depending on demand) from the jetty behind their office to their marina on the south side of Bastimentos ($15 return; $8 one way), though if you can get a group together other boats may charge less. From the marina dock it's a 10min walk (or 3min shuttle) across the island to the beach. A $5 landing fee (included in the day-pass) imposed by the developers ostensibly goes towards maintaining the path across the island. To avoid the fee, hike the beach path from Old Bank, though be mindful of security issues (see box, page 224).

REACHING THE NGÄBE COMMUNITIES

If you want to visit a Ngäbe community and are struggling to make your own arrangements, contact the Bocas del Toro Community Tourism Network (redtucombo.bocasdeltoro.org).

ACTIVITIES AND TOURS

Red Frog Zipline Red Frog Beach facebook.com/bastimentosskyzipline. Daily tours (2hr) take you along seven rainforest zip lines and a swing bridge. Transfer from Bocas Town included. Book at the Red Frog office in Bocas Town on Calle 3.

Other tours Most of the accommodation, especially the more remote, all-inclusive lodgings provide SUP or kayaks for use, organize their own boat tours, to Cayos Zapatillas for example, or visits to neighbouring Ngäbe communities. Some also provide daily transfers to Bocas Town.

ACCOMMODATION — SEE MAP PAGE 221

The handful of lodgings in Old Bank are mainly **budget-oriented** and attract people wanting to experience the "real" Bocas; be prepared to be lulled to sleep by ear-splitting music on occasions. They are found along, or just off, the cement path that winds through the village. The all-inclusive **ecolodges** elsewhere on the island offer a more back-to-nature, yet luxurious experience.

OLD BANK

★ **Bastimentos Hill Guesthouse (formerly Hostal Bastimentos)** Turn right from the main dock 6474 2222. A rambling hostal spread over the hillside behind town, offering basic en-suite doubles and family rooms with fan or a/c, hot water, fridge and private balcony, plus great views. Two communal kitchens (which have seen better days), plenty of hammock space and lovely views of the bay. Good value. $$

Beverly's Hill Turn left from the main dock ⓦfacebook.com/beverlyshillguesthouse. A gem on the hillside, this friendly family-owned place offers very basic, rustic wooden *cabañas* (shared or private bathroom and shared kitchen) in a lush tropical garden that's home to the elusive red frog (see box, page 233), and brimming with birdlife. The pricier room at the top has stunning Caribbean views. $$

Casa El Jaguar 50m to the right of the main dock ⓦhostaleljaguar.com. Owned by local Arnulfo Archibald, who is happy to share his knowledge of the islands, this *hostal* is good value; the spacious over-the-water hammock deck and shared kitchen provide the main appeal. Basic, painted wooden rooms have fans, with private or shared bathroom. Free kayak use for a day if you book on their website. $$

THE REST OF THE ISLAND

★Al Natural Punta Vieja ⓦalnaturalresort.com. Beautiful, isolated spot with single- or double-decker Ngäbe-style palm-thatched huts that open onto the sea. Rustically decorated with hewn driftwood, with solar-powered fans and showers and comfy beds with netting. Three loft-style apartments with a more contemporary feel comprise a new wooden "villa" constructed nearby. Delicious meals are served communally in the bar-restaurant *rancho*, with a games and reading room plus an observation deck upstairs. Rates include transfer from Bocas, meals, use of kayaks and snorkel gear, but tours and diving are extra. The two-storey superior bungalow is worth the extra. Two-night minimum stay. $$$$

Casa Cayuco Punta Vieja ⓦcasacayuco.com. A three-storey lodge and five lovely raised wooden cabins (for two to eight people) with private balconies, most tucked away in the rainforest just off the beach. Rates include transport, communal (plant-focused) fine dining and use of kayaks, SUPs, boogie boards and a village tour. Three-night minimum stay. $$$$

La Loma Jungle Lodge Bahía Honda ⓦthejunglelodge.com. On a hilltop surrounded by rainforest, this working cocoa farm offers five wooden *ranchos, some with super views*, and rooms with a shared common areas in the cacao farm, further downhill. Rates include transfer, meals and some activities, including a tour of the farm and yoga classes, with other excursions for a fee. Gourmet cuisine, with ingredients from the lodge's organic garden, makes this very popular, so book ahead. Some costs go to the Bahía Honda community development fund. Two-night minimum stay. $$$$

Palmar Beach Lodge Red Frog Beach ⓦpalmarbocas.com. Set in rainforest at the back of the beach, this expanding resort offers wood-cabin dorms, simple, delightful, private safari tents and incongruous wooden bungalows with kitchenette and LED TV (two with a/c). Facilities include solar-powered fans, lamps and showers plus a bar-restaurant, beach volleyball, kayaking, daily yoga, massage and snorkel rental. Dorms $$, double tents $$$, cabins & bungalows $$$–$$$$

Los Secretos Bahía Honda ⓦlossecretosguesthouse.wordpress.com. Enjoying a commanding view overlooking the channel between Bastimentos and Solarte, this well-established wooden guesthouse provides a friendly and efficient service. Half a dozen homely, quaint rooms have semi-private balconies affording both sunrise and sunset views, and share a lounge balcony and pool, while kayaking, fishing or rainforest hikes await the more active. Two-night minimum stay. Rates are for half-board. $$$–$$$$

EATING

SEE MAP PAGE 221

Most **eating** options in Bastimentos are low-key, with local flavours at locally affordable prices. You're likely to find traditional **Caribbean dishes** such as *rondón*, a fish and vegetable stew in coconut milk, or *pescado escabeche*, a spicy marinated fish dish, and plenty of dishes served with coconut rice and plantain.

OLD BANK AND AROUND

Guary Guary by Nayda 250m east of the main dock. This is simple restaurant – a handful of wooden tables down by the waterside – with many inexpensive menu options. The lengthy wait for the food is worth it for fresh, succulent lobster tails or a monster mixed seafood platter, with a choice of sauce. Pasta and burgers are also available. $$–$$$

Lysett's Place Next to the main dock. Great deck (ignoring the faux grass flooring) high above the jetty, where you can gaze across to Isla Solarte while tucking into some fresh seafood. Fishburgers are a sound choice, especially doused in hot pepper sauce. Expect friendly staff, good cocktails and tourist prices (though not as high as in Bocas Town). $$–$$$

Parque Nacional Marino Isla Bastimentos

PARQUE NACIONAL MARINO ISLA BASTIMENTOS is one of the archipelago's major attractions. The 130 square kilometres of boomerang-shaped reserve sweep across a central swathe of Isla Bastimentos and include a chunk of the northern coastline, dominated by the 6km **Playa Larga**, an important nesting site for hawksbill, leatherback and green **turtles** (March–Sept).

MARINE TURTLE CONSERVATION

One of the most poignant scenes in the natural world is the laborious nesting process of the female **turtle** as she drags herself up the beach beyond the high tide mark, excavating a hole with her flippers, before depositing fifty to two hundred eggs, their sex later determined by the temperature of the sand. After around sixty days, usually under cover of darkness, the hatchlings break out from their shells en masse and scuttle down to the sea, unless they become disoriented by lights or emerge in daylight and are picked off by seabirds. Each egg has less than a one in a thousand chance of reaching maturity.

Of the five species of turtle found in the country, four are known to nest along the beaches of Bocas del Toro. Historically the **hawksbill** (*eretmochelys imbricata*) and **green turtle** (*chelonia mydas*) reproduced prolifically on the province's sands but over the last seventy years, as eggs were overharvested and adults killed for their meat and shells, among other threats, the populations were decimated – though significant numbers of hawksbill still nest on Islas Zapatillas (May–Sept). The 29km expanse of Playa Chiriquí, which lines the Golfo de los Mosquitos, east of the Península Valiente, is the most important rookery in all Central America for gigantic **leatherbacks** (*dermochelys coriacea*). Measuring around 1.5m on average and weighing half a tonne, these leviathans dig seven thousand nests annually (March–June). In contrast, there are fewer records of **loggerheads** (*caretta caretta*) nesting in Bocas, though they occasionally deposit their eggs on Playa Bluff.

VOLUNTEERING

If you're interested in volunteering (five nights; March–July), **monitoring and tagging** turtles and patrolling beaches – most likely leatherbacks on Playa Soropta on the mainland – contact the Sea Turtle Conservancy in Bocas Town on C 2 by E-bikes (ⓦ conserveturtles.org/project/bocas-del-toro). Note that volunteering is not free: $700 covers five nights of (very basic) accommodation, meals and training. More qualified individuals can apply to be a research assistant for three months (March–June or June–Sept).

TURTLE-WATCHING TOURS

ANABOCA (ⓦ anaboca.bocasdeltoro.org), a community tourism organization on Playa Bluff leads **turtle watches** (2hr) in the breeding season (April–Aug). Transport from Bocas is not included, so it's a good idea to get a group together to pay for a taxi, including wait time. The community run an information kiosk in Parque Bolívar during the season.

While turtle watching can be a captivating experience, bear in mind that female turtles can easily be spooked into not depositing their eggs. Avoid bright clothes and try to go when there is a good moon, so as not to be tempted to use a torch (unless it's infrared). Leave your camera behind and maintain a respectful distance from the turtle.

Cayos Zapatillas

Southeast of Isla Bastimentos, but still within the park boundary, are the **Cayos Zapatillas** (Little Shoes), so named because they resemble a pair of footprints in the sea. The two dreamy, coral-fringed islands, encircled by powdery white sand, offer **snorkelling** off the beach, where you'll find more and larger fish than in Cayo Crawl. The main reef is exposed to the ocean, often with strong currents and choppy water. On the prettier northern island, there is a short trail.

ARRIVAL AND ACCOMMODATION — PARQUE NACIONAL ISLA BASTIMENTOS

By tour or boat The easiest way to visit the Parque Nacional Isla Bastimentos is with a tour operator on a day-trip. Alternatively, consider contracting a boat yourself, in which case it's best to arrange for an early start so that your visit doesn't coincide with the tour groups at Laguna Bocatorito and Cayo Crawl.

Park entry fees Park fees should be paid for online in advance (see page 42). They are always additional to the tour cost.

6

Isla Solarte

Sheltered in the leeward crook of Isla Bastimentos, thin, hilly **Isla Solarte** – also known as Cayo Nancy, a corruption of "nance", the cherry-sized yellow fruit much in evidence on the island – is surrounded by tranquil waters. Its most famous feature, **Hospital Point**, at its northwestern tip, was the location of a hospital built by the United Fruit Company in 1900 during the banana boom to quarantine malaria and yellow-fever sufferers. The point is now one of the most popular **dive** and **snorkel** spots, at the end of many day-trip itineraries, with a healthy reef of cauliflower and brain coral and an impressive wall full of tropical fish, shelving off a pencil-thin strip of beach.

Solarte is home to a **Ngäbe village** of around 250, which has a school and even a football field. Most of the villagers live from fishing and subsistence agriculture.

ARRIVAL AND ACCOMMODATION — ISLA SOLARTE, SEE MAP PAGE 221

By water-taxi A 10min ride from Bocas will get you to anywhere on Isla Solarte.

★Bambuda Lodge 1.3km southwest of Hospital Point bambuda.com/es/lodge. Wooden lodge – part luxury hostel, part hotel – with a fabulous rainforest location and great sea views, a large pool (with daytime music and waterslide) and kayak rental. Wraparound balconies, sofas and hammocks make it a great place to chill – with board games and ping-pong for rainy days. There's no kitchen, but the family-style restaurant serves delicious food. Fan-ventilated rooms have shared or private bathroom; no mosquito nets. Dorms $$, doubles $$$

Villa F & B 5km southeast of Hospital Point villafbhotelbocasdeltoro.com. Set above mangroves just off Solarte, this outstandingly stylish yet welcoming boutique B&B is run by a charming French couple. The handful of rooms are spacious with a contemporary feel, each with its own stellar sea view from a private patio. Keep cool in the small sparkling pool, or swim and snorkel off the jetty, working up an appetite for some of the owner-chef's gourmet fare. $$$$

ISLA ESCUDO DE VERAGUAS – A BIODIVERSITY HOTSPOT

Marooned in the Caribbean east of the main archipelago and some distance from the mainland, lies the magical tiny island of **Isla Escudo de Veraguas**. Known as "Dekö" in Ngäbere, it is largely uninhabited except for a few Ngäbe families. Pristine rainforest covers the island's four square kilometres, cascading over sandy bluffs that have eroded to leave curved cliffs and spectacular caves and arches. Surrounded by mangroves, coral reefs and fringed with powdery beaches, the island is a haven for biodiversity, with high levels of **endemism**, including the pygmy three-toed sloth and its own species of Thomas' fruit-eating bat. With all these natural riches, it's no surprise that the island is becoming an increasingly popular day-trip destination from Bocas (see page 228) and, especially, Calovébora (see box, page 210), with some visitors camping overnight on the beaches. Given that there are no facilities, and the beaches are important nesting sites for hawksbill and leatherback **turtles**, tourism needs to be carefully managed in order to preserve the island's unique ecology.

VISITING THE ISLAND

The best time to visit is during March, and September to October, when it usually rains less and the sea tends to be calmer. In high season (Dec–Feb) the sea can be very rough. Boat trips are organized by Bocas tour operators (see page 229), involving at least two hours by boat, one way, and on a more ad-hoc basis from Calovébora (see box, page 210), which takes 1hr 30min. A more rewarding experience all round (provided you speak some Spanish) is to go with Ngäbe guides from the mainland community of Río Caña (sostur.org/rio-cana), which involves a boat pick-up from Chiriquí Grande (see page 239) and overnight stay in the thatched cabins of their community tourism project. From there, the island is only 30min away by boat. Consider also contacting Felipe Baker (6881 7915, felipebaker@gmail.com), biologist with the Turtle Conservancy in Bocas (see page 237), who comes from Río Caña, and is involved in both turtle conservation and a culture-focused women's cookery initiative (ariuguenrien.org).

Isla San Cristóbal

A large mangrove-fringed island, nestled in the Bahía de Almirante facing the mainland peninsula of Cerro Brujo, **Isla San Cristóbal** is home to three **Ngäbe** communities: **Bocatorito**, in the south, which overlooks a bite-shaped lagoon populated by dolphins, much visited on day-trips from Bocas Town; and **Valle Escondido** and **San Cristóbal** to the north. While cacao, yuca and rice cultivation provides much of their diet, fishing is still the mainstay of these villages. Look out for the navigation lights on the north side of the island, used to guide the banana cargo boats into Almirante.

6

ARRIVAL AND ACCOMMODATION — ISLA SAN CRISTÓBAL, SEE MAP PAGE 221

By water-taxi Bocatorito is a 20–30min journey by water-taxi from Bocas Town.

Dolphin Bay Hideaway Bocatorito dolphinbayhideaway. Intimate eco-focused retreat among the mangroves, with five individually designed wooden rooms (that come with fans and mosquito nets), decorated in tropical colours, affording nice views of the bay and their gardens. Offers organic food and healthy activities – SUP, kayaks, yoga – are on hand, as well as tours (extra cost). Half-board, use of water toys and transfer from Bocas included. $$$$

Isla Popa

Just off the southern tip of Isla Bastimentos lies the archipelago's second largest land mass, **Isla Popa**, home to five Ngäbe fishing communities and the only island where you can spot toucans. The northern village of **Sandubidi** (Popa 2) has a community-based tourism project that offers walks along a trail with a local guide, and a **community homestay** (meringobe.bocasdeltoro.org). Nearby, on the island's northeastern tip, you'll find several thin, sandy **beaches** leading off into coral-filled shallows and acres of **rainforest**.

Mainland Bocas

Mainland Bocas covers the vast majority of the province, yet its imperious jagged peaks clad in virgin forest, its boggy wetlands and its powerful rivers are ignored by most visitors. That said, while the three mainland towns of **Chiriquí Grande**, **Almirante** and **Changuinola** have little for tourists, the **Parque Nacional Humedales de San San Pond Sak**, home to countless aquatic birds and the endangered manatee, and the spectacular wilderness **Parque Internacional La Amistad** are definitely worth the effort to reach. The two main obstacles to exploring the region – poor accessibility and lack of infrastructure – have helped preserve the province's natural heritage; today, however, the indigenous Bri-Bri, Naso and Bokota populations' livelihoods are under threat from hydroelectric projects (see box, page 242).

Chiriquí Grande to Almirante

From the village of Chiriquí, 14km east of David on the Interamericana, a spectacular road heads over the Fortuna hydroelectric dam, cresting the continental divide that marks the entry into Bocas del Toro, before descending to the small town of **Chiriquí Grande**, the Atlantic terminus of the Trans-Panama Oil Pipeline. The road then hugs the crinkled coastline for 60km to the port of **Almirante**, before continuing to Changuinola (see page 241). Few visitors venture east of Chiriquí Grande into the increasingly deforested **Comarca Ngäbe-Buglé**, where rivers cut through the Caribbean slopes of the Cordillera Central, flowing into the Golfo de los Mosquitos. The 29km Playa Chiriquí here is home to a major turtle conservation programme (see box, page 237).

6

THE WEST INDIAN MANATEE

Occasionally called a "sea cow", the **West Indian manatee** (*trichechus manatus*) resembles a cross between a sea lion, a hippo and an elephant, its barrel-like greyish-brown body propelled by two flippers and a spatula tail, its large snout equipped with a prehensile upper lip that helps it feed. Adults average 3m in length though can reach 4.5m, including tail, and weigh in at 200–600kg; to sustain such a size, they have to spend six to eight hours a day munching floating or submerged greenery. When not feeding, they often rest, floating like large logs on or below the surface, frequently surfacing to breathe. Moving easily between freshwater and marine environments, the shy yet playful mammals are surprisingly agile, and can exceed 25km/hr for short bursts. In Panama, the vast majority of these aquatic behemoths inhabit the wetlands of Bocas del Toro, though in 1964 a small number were relocated to Lago Gatún by the Americans in a failed attempt to tackle the rampant spread of water hyacinth in the Canal. Though lacking natural predators, manatees are threatened by **human activity**, experiencing collisions with motorboats and getting tangled up in fishing nets or canal locks, while suffering from loss or pollution of habitat. What's more, since they only give birth to a single calf every three to five years, it takes a long time to boost numbers.

Silico Creek

Km 25, Punta Peña • Community tourism Ⓦ urari.bocasdeltoro.org • David–Changuinola buses pass through Silico Creek (2hr 30min–3hr from David; 30–40min from Almirante)

Between Chiriquí Grande and Almirante, on the border of the Comarca Ngäbe-Buglé, lies the Ngäbe community of **SILICO CREEK**, a dynamic village that has successfully retained traditional values while adapting to the modern economy. Tours usually involve learning about their organic permaculture projects in coffee, plantains, banana, yuca and, most successfully, cocoa. Sometimes, you get to venture further into the rainforest. At the time of writing community tours were temporarily suspended.

Almirante

The ramshackle town of **ALMIRANTE**, its rusting tin-roofed wooden houses propped up on stilts over the Caribbean, is the departure point for **water-taxis** to the Bocas del Toro archipelago. Like Bocas, the port is a product of the banana boom, and suffered a similar decline. Unlike Bocas, there is no tourism-fuelled renaissance on the horizon. Basic services are lacking, unemployment and its associated ills are a major concern, and most visitors pass through as quickly as possible. If you miss the last water-taxi, try the *Hotel 888* (ⓣ758 3318), between the port and the bus terminal – it's very basic but clean and safe.

ARRIVAL AND DEPARTURE — ALMIRANTE

By bus Through buses from/to Panama City, David or Changuinola will drop you/pick up at the intersection ("La Ye"), on the main road (see page 224).

By minibus Minibuses career between Almirante – the main bus station close to the water-taxi terminal – and Changuinola (6am–10pm; every 20–25min; 30min), where you can get connections for the border. Other local destinations have their own bus stops in town.

By water-taxi There are water-taxis to Bocas Town from Almirante (see page 226).

By car, bike or motorbike If you're coming by car to Almirante, it's advisable to leave it in a secure compound at Leiza's near the water-taxi terminal. Anyone wanting to take a bike or motorcycle across should take the car ferry (see page 227).

Changuinola

The hot, dusty town of **CHANGUINOLA**, Panama's most important banana centre, lies 29km west of Almirante and just 17km from the Costa Rica border.

Surrounded by flat, drained wetlands, a patchwork of plantations and pastureland, this bustling, unattractive town of around fifty thousand possesses little of interest for visitors but does provide a launch pad for trips to the **Parque Nacional Humedales de San San Pond Sak** or **Parque Internacional La Amistad**. It is also the best place to stay if you are too late to make it to the Costa Rican border.

Most of the action occurs along the congested **Avenida 17 de Abril**, whose crowded central pavements overflow with cheap goods. Cut through east to the parallel street, Avenida Omar Torrijos, and you can glimpse rusting carriages in railway sidings and disused tracks, the last vestiges of what was once an impressive rail network built by the United Fruit Company extending along the coast back to Almirante and well into Costa Rica.

6

ARRIVAL — CHANGUINOLA

BY PLANE

The airport lies just northeast of the town centre. Air Panama (☎316 9000, Ⓦairpanama.com) operates daily flights to and from Panama City (1hr).

BY BUS

Urracá terminal On the northern end of Av 17 de Abril, this terminal serves long-distance buses between Panama City and David. Tranceibosa (☎758 8455) has daily departures for Panama City, leaving at 7am and 6pm, and at 11am if there are sufficient passengers (11hr). They fill up fast, so buy tickets as early as possible. Buses to and from David are much more frequent (5.30am–7pm; every 25min; 5hr).

SINCOTAVECOP terminal Set back from the main street, this is the main bus terminal, serving all local destinations. Destinations Almirante (6am–10pm; every 20–25min; 30min); El Silencio, Río Teribe (6.30am–8pm; every 20min; 25min); Guabito and the Costa Rican border (take the Las Tablas bus; 5.30am–7.30pm; every 20min; 30min).

BY COLECTIVO OR TAXI

Colectivos and private taxis run to and from the Costa Rican border at Guabito (see page 244).

ACCOMMODATION SEE MAP PAGE 241

Hotel Plaza Changuinola Av 14 de Abril ☎758 6168. Only come here if the *Semiramis* is full. Its redeeming feature is a huge outdoor pool and its convenient location by some shops, including Romero's supermarket. En-suite rooms have the essentials (a/c, cable TV, hot water), but cleanliness is not a given, so check out several before committing. $$

Hotel Semiramis Av 17 de Abril ☎758 6006. Probably the pick of an uninspiring bunch in Changuinola, this place has two floors of dated, dark but clean rooms (a/c, cable TV, good hot-water showers). Service is friendly. Room only $$

EATING SEE MAP PAGE 241

Restaurante Ebony Av 17 de Abril Ⓦinstagram.com/restebony. Chock-full of Bob Marley memorabilia, inflatable sharks and balsa-wood birds, this popular Afro-Antillean restaurant delivers authentic Caribbean cuisine:

6

THE NASO KINGDOM

When the Spanish arrived in what is now Bocas del Toro (and southeast Costa Rica), the **Naso** (or Teribe) were both numerous and widespread, but centuries of conflict with the conquistadors and other tribes decimated their numbers, which declined further in the early twentieth century due to tuberculosis. Of the remaining 3500 Naso in Panama, around a third have been assimilated into the dominant Latin culture, living and working in Changuinola, while the rest mostly inhabit sixteen settlements along the Río San San and Río Teribe. Teribe is believed to be a corruption of "Tjër Di", meaning water of Tjër, the grandmotherly guardian spirit of the Naso, one of the more tangible traces of a sorely eroded culture. Since the Naso language is not taught at school, only an estimated twenty percent still know how to speak it, with Spanish often the preferred language even in the villages, though Naso legends are still widely recited.

The more immediate threat to the Naso lies in the form of the recently completed hydroelectric dam upstream on the Río Bonyik, a tributary of the Teribe, which has ripped the kingdom apart. In 2004, the reigning monarch, **Tito Santana**, approved the project without proper consultation, for which he was deposed and chased into exile. His uncle, **Valentín Santana**, who took over, garnered the support of national and international environmentalists and human rights groups in a battle to stop the dam and safeguard their ancestral lands and livelihood. However, as the Panamanian government refused to recognize his authority, the Naso were forced to elect a new king – Alexis – from the Santana dynasty in 2011. In 2018, the National Assembly finally approved the Naso's long-standing demand for their own *comarca*. Despite a veto by Varela, the president at the time, the Supreme Court ruled in favour of the Naso and thus, in 2020, the Comarca Tjër-Di was finally confirmed

salt fish, ackee, rice and peas, spicy shrimp in coconut milk. Prices are high for Changuinola. $$–$$$

Restaurante La Fortuna Av 17 de Abril ☎ 758 9395. Very popular Chinese restaurant, offering friendly, efficient service and good value in a/c comfort. The wide-ranging menu has several veggie options and set menus. Choose a sizzling hotplate dish with first-rate chips. $$

Parque Nacional Humedales de San San Pond Sak

One of the premier natural attractions of mainland Bocas is the **PARQUE NACIONAL HUMEDALES DE SAN SAN POND SAK** (with numerous variant spellings), which encompasses more than 160 square kilometres of coastal wetlands stretching from the Costa Rican border, past Changuinola, to the Bahía de Almirante. In response to the multiple threats from agriculture and development, the reserve was upgraded to the status of national park in 2025, to help give it better protection. Only a small section of the reserve is accessible to visitors but its mix of seasonally flooded swampy forests, dense mangroves and peat bogs makes for a magical boat trip, especially at first light when the prolific **birdlife** – 160 species at the current tally – is at its most active.

As you glide along the river, keep an eye out for caimans and river otters lurking in the waters. A dawn visit will also heighten your chances of spotting the wetlands' most celebrated inhabitant, the shy, endangered **manatee** (see box, page 240). Though there are now an estimated 150–200 in the area, they remain fairly elusive except when banana leaves are provided at the viewing platforms when tour boats enter the reserve. The river eventually fills out into a coastal lagoon before emptying into the sea, its progress blocked by a sandbank on which there is a poorly maintained **refuge**. Behind the hut lies a long stretch of **beach** where hawksbill, leatherback and green **turtles** nest (see box, page 237).

ARRIVAL AND INFORMATION — PN HUMEDALES DE SAN SAN POND SAK

By bus or taxi To reach the reserve from Changuinola, take the Guabito–Las Tablas bus (see page 244) to the Río San

San bridge, or take a taxi.

Reserve fees The admission charge, payable to MIA, needs to be made online in advance (see page 42).

AAMVECONA Activities in the reserve are managed by AAMVECONA (T 6480 7238, W aamvecona.bocasdeltoro.org); the office is by the road bridge on the Río San San, 6km northwest of Changuinola, on the road to the Costa Rica border.

TOURS

The following tours (in Spanish) are offered by **AAMVECONA**, from their office (by prior arrangement). Note that turtle and manatee tours can be combined. Tours are also offered (for guests only) by one or two of the pricier lodgings in Bocas, but these will be more expensive.

Manatee tours The most popular excursion is the manatee tour ($60/person; less for more than two people), which gives you several hours gliding through the wetlands by boat, with great birdwatching opportunities, and likely manatee sightings. Go early in the morning, cover up well and/or douse yourself with repellent as the sandflies on the viewing platform are vicious.

Turtle tours In the season (March–July) evening excursions (8pm) are organized to watch leatherback turtles nesting on Playa San San. This means staying overnight in the rudimentary and rather unappealing bunkhouse at the far end of the lagoon, where turtle conservation volunteers lodge. Take your own food, or ask for meals to be prepared.

6

Parque Internacional La Amistad

Divided equally between Panama and Costa Rica, the remote **PARQUE INTERNACIONAL LA AMISTAD** (International Friendship Park), often abbreviated to PILA or Amistad, covers a vast 4000 square kilometres of the rugged Talamanca massif, with a topography and biodiversity unmatched in Central America. Precipitous volcanic tors clad in prolific cloud forest, containing the greatest density of **quetzals** in the world, plunge into deep ravines in Panama's most dramatic mountain scenery.

From the treeless *páramo* of **Cerro Fábrega** (3336m), the park's highest peak, to the Caribbean rainforests only 40m above sea level, Amistad encompasses an incredible range of **flora** and **fauna**, including many endemics and endangered species. All five of Panama's resident cat species prowl the forests while the soaring canopy is pierced by impressive specimens of ceiba, almendro and cedar, home to endangered harpy and crested eagles and great green macaws. A crucial link in the "biological corridor" of protected areas running the length of Central America, it is now under threat from agricultural incursions, illicit timber extraction and poaching, but most of all from the ill-considered hydroelectric projects under way. As well as imperilling

STAYING IN A NASO VILLAGE

Lodgings are **basic**: rudimentary wooden beds with mosquito nets and sporadic water. You'll need a torch, as there's no electricity. **Meals** consist of simple traditional dishes made from local organic produce. Note also that price details quoted online are not necessarily up to date, so enquire before you go.

OCEN Bonyik W ocen.bocasdeltoro.org. Reachable by road. Guests are lodged in several traditional balconied wooden houses. Guided hikes are on offer (4–12hr); bring snacks and make sure you have a water bottle (preferably with purification tablets). Costs are separate for accommodation/person, three daily meals, return boat from Bonyik to Seiyik, and rainforest hikes. Ask for costs in advance and bring sufficient cash.

OMUB (Organizacíon de Mujeres Indígenas Unidas Naso Bonyik) W sostur.org/bonllik. The group provides basic dorm accommodation with shared facilities in a wooden two-storey structure (*Posada Media Luna*) and offers inexpensive classes in bread or chocolate making and guided walks over the river in WEKSO.

Soposo Rainforest Adventures Soposo W soposo.bocasdeltoro.org. The best advertised and most patronized project was set up by a US-Naso couple. They offer pleasant wooden cabins with porches, lit by solar lanterns, and have pricier all-inclusive rates for a one-, two- or three-day tour, including lodging, meals, transport from Changuinola and a range of excursions. If travelling from Bocas, you can be met at Almirante provided you meet the additional transport costs.

the area's unique biodiversity, the projects are threatening numerous indigenous communities.

Given the park's remoteness and the ruggedness of the terrain, any **visit to Amistad** proper is a major undertaking, to be made with a good guide, suitable hiking and camping gear, a readiness for rain (more than 5m tips down annually in places) and mud, plus a spirit of adventure. Climbing Cerro Fábrega (Panama's second highest peak) is a major undertaking, which starts off in Costa Rica. Most visitors content themselves with a trip organized through one of the Naso communities dotted along the banks of the Río Teribe (see box, page 242), in the buffer zone of the **Reserva Forestal de Palo Seco**, a haven for colourful butterflies, dazzling birdlife, and a host of other wildlife.

The Naso villages

The **Naso**, boasting Central America's last remaining monarch, are one of the country's least numerous indigenous groups, whose recent history has been particularly troubled (see box, page 242). As well as inhabiting the park, they also live on the San San and Yorkin rivers and around Changuinola, where, seeking further schooling and employment, many have abandoned their traditional lifestyles. Those that have remained generally inhabit wooden houses built on stilts covered in thatch or occasionally zinc, practising animal husbandry and subsistence agriculture supplemented by fishing and hunting. Though the spiritual heart of the Naso lies in their ancestral lands high up the headlands of the Teribe, the present-day capital is **SEIYIK**, the largest Naso community. Around ninety minutes upriver from Changuinola, the five hundred inhabitants are dispersed over a pleasant hillside overlooking the river. In the grassy clearing at the centre of the village stand a medical centre, primary school and the unremarkable **royal palace**.

Three communities are involved in **ecotourism** projects, which give visitors the chance to learn about medicinal plants, Naso history and culture, hike in the rainforest, make and travel on a traditional bamboo raft (*balsa*), and visit the capital. The Naso are warm and welcoming and the potential for spectacular **river trips** set against the brooding backdrop of the Talamanca range alone make a visit worthwhile, though to do the place and the people justice you should plan at least a two-night stay. Among the many pernicious effects of the controversial hydroelectric dam (see box, page 242) is the daytime traffic noise on the access road. However, once you're on the WEKSO trail or up in Seiyik, traffic disturbance is thankfully absent, as it is at night in the communities.

ARRIVAL AND INFORMATION — THE NASO VILLAGES

By bus Take the regular bus to El Silencio from the main bus station in Changuinola (6.30am–8pm; every 20min; 25min). From El Silencio, infrequent *chivas* go as far as Bonyik, from where you can travel by boat up the Río Teribe (30min) to Seiyik.

Contact details Contact details for all three communities are on the Bocas del Toro community tourism website (ⓦ redtucombo.bocasdeltoro.org).

Guabito and the Costa Rica border

From Changuinola, the road runs 17km to the border with Costa Rica at **Guabito–Sixaola**, where, on the Panamanian side, there is little more than a handful of shops. It's a short walk from **immigration** across the old railway bridge to Costa Rica (an hour behind Panama time), where you can change currency in the town of Sixaola. At the time of writing, a new wider bridge and access road were being constructed.

ARRIVAL AND INFORMATION — GUABITO AND THE COSTA RICA BORDER

Getting to the border To reach the border from Changuinola, take one of the *colectivos* or private taxis hanging around the bus terminal, or, if you're in no hurry, the bus marked for the village of Las Tablas (5.30am–7pm;

every 25min; 30min).

Onward travel in Costa Rica After getting an exit stamp at Panamanian immigration (8am–5.45pm; ⓣ 759 7019), cross the border bridge to Costa Rican immigration (same hours, though Costa Rica is an hour behind Panama time) in Sixaola. There you can catch a through-bus to San José (2am, 4.30am, 8am, 11am & 3pm) or to Puerto Viejo in southeastern Costa Rica (daily every 1–2hr; 2hr; 90min).

Arriving from Costa Rica After getting your exit stamp from Costa Rican immigration and paying your exit fee, cross the bridge to Panamanian immigration – where you may have to show proof of onward travel (a return bus ticket will suffice) and the ability to support yourself financially. Beware of the scam that occasionally operates of being directed to a hut to pay a bogus "municipal tax". Once through immigration, walk 400m down to the main road for the bus to Changuinola (5.30am–7.30pm; every 25min; 30min), from where there are frequent connections to other destinations in Panama (see page 241). Alternatively, hop into a *colectivo* or private taxi to Changuinola (20min). Note that some taxi drivers are not beyond spinning yarns about buses not running or taking longer than they actually do in order to secure clients. Since there is no bank or ATM in Guabito, make sure you are carrying sufficient US dollars for you to reach your next destination.

Immigration office The immigration office (daily 8am–5.45pm, ⓣ 759 7019) is on the east side of the bridge.

Gunayala

DUGOUT CANOES, ACHUERDUB

Gunayala

A Guna woman in traditional attire – hair bound in a scarlet headscarf (*muswe*), embroidered blouse (*mola*) tucked into a sarong-like patterned skirt (*saburet*), her forearms and calves bound with intricate beadwork (*wini*) and her nose pierced with a golden ring (*olasu*) – is a sight that has launched a thousand travel brochures. Yet the Guna's relationship with tourism remains ambivalent, and their suspicion of outsiders (*uagmala*) and determination to ensure that tourism is conducted on their terms has been born of bitter experience. This can make a trip to Gunayala – frequently referred to by the colonial name of San Blas (after a Catholic saint) – fairly challenging, though the benefits can far outweigh any frustrations or inconveniences. A visit is an opportunity to engage with an evolving, unique, indigenous culture, to experience village life first-hand, to loll on heavenly white-sand islands and to explore the little-visited, rainforested mainland.

The Guna (pronounced "Guna" or "Kuna" depending upon the dialect) – or the Dule (pronounced "Dule" or "Tule"), as they call themselves – are Panama's highest-profile indigenous people. They inhabit a vast semiautonomous region (or **comarca**) along the eastern Caribbean coast, which stretches some 375km from the Golfo de San Blas to Puerto Obaldía and comprises almost four hundred islands and a swathe of land whose limits extend to the peaks of the *serranías* de San Blas and the Darién. Around 50,000 Guna are estimated to live within the Comarca de Gunayala, with a further 47,000 predominantly spread among two smaller inland *comarcas* in eastern Panama (see page 280) and Panama City, though populations are fluid given the constant toing and froing between the capital and the *comarcas*.

In Gunayala, for the most part, people are packed onto a chain of 38 low-lying coral outcrops close to the shore, with eleven communities established on the coast and two further inland. These days, overpopulation, compounded by the threat of rising sea levels, has encouraged some island-based families to relocate to the mainland. Plans are afoot for entire communities to move to the mainland over the coming years, as it becomes increasingly likely that their homes will become permanently submerged.

The waters of the western archipelago, in particular, are sprinkled with near-deserted **cays** covered in coconut palms, surrounded by dazzling **beaches** that shelve into turquoise waters, whose coral reefs provide great opportunities for **snorkelling** (diving is prohibited across the *comarca*). Trips to the luxuriantly rainforested mainland are equally magical, whether gliding upriver in a dugout, visiting a Guna burial ground or seeking out the spectacular birdlife. These attributes make Gunayala a wonderfully idyllic location for a holiday, but to appreciate its unique nature, engaging with **Guna culture** in all its variations, complexities and contradictions is essential.

There are basically two types of islands of interest to tourists. The palm-topped **deserted islands**, surrounded by white-sand beaches, are predominantly distinguished by their accommodation, ranging from simple cane *cabañas* to more comfortable lodges, all owned by families or communities from the more densely populated **village-islands**. These latter – overcrowded coral outcrops chock-full of cane-and-thatch buildings interspersed with cement structures, schools, medical centres and the occasional shop – generally lack beaches. To the casual visitor, the village-islands are very much alike: jetties hold tethered dugouts and fibre-glass boats and traditional over-the-water toilets, with litter often floating among the pilings, while sandy streets

CHILDREN ON DIGIR DUBBU (ISLA TIGRE)

Highlights

❶ **Village-islands** Experience a compelling mix of tradition and modernity in crowded communities such as Agligandi, taking in the meeting and *chicha* houses and museums. See page 269

❷ **Blissful near-deserted islands** Camp out in a thatched *cabaña*, laze in a hammock or float in the turquoise shallows of the palm-topped white-sand islands of western Gunayala – choose from Misdub, Wailidub or Naranjo Chico. See pages 261, 260 and 263

❸ **Cayos Holandeses and Coco-Bandero** The archipelago's best snorkelling; marvel at a marine wonderland of corals and tropical fish. See page 264

❹ **Digir Dubbu (Isla Tigre)** The fascinating home of the Guna dance and one of the few remaining places that practises community-based traditions. See page 265

❺ **Armila** A very different Guna village on the forested mainland at the far southeastern end of the *comarca*, where you can explore the jungle by dugout and watch leatherback turtles nesting. See page 271

HIGHLIGHTS ARE MARKED ON THE MAP ON PAGE 250

gravitate towards the centre, where meeting and *chicha* houses (see box, page 267) and the basketball court stand out. Only by spending a couple of nights in different places will you begin to appreciate the subtle variations between communities.

There are more than 365 islands to choose from, most with two names (one in Dulegaya, one in Spanish) and a handful with the same name. However, the fact that only around 38 of them support villages, and that many are conveniently arranged in identifiable **clusters**, simplifies planning. During one visit most visitors are satisfied to explore just one cluster.

The islands in the **western area** of the archipelago, such as those in the **cayos Limones or Holandeses**, or north of **Río Sidra**, are by far the most visited, possessing the greatest

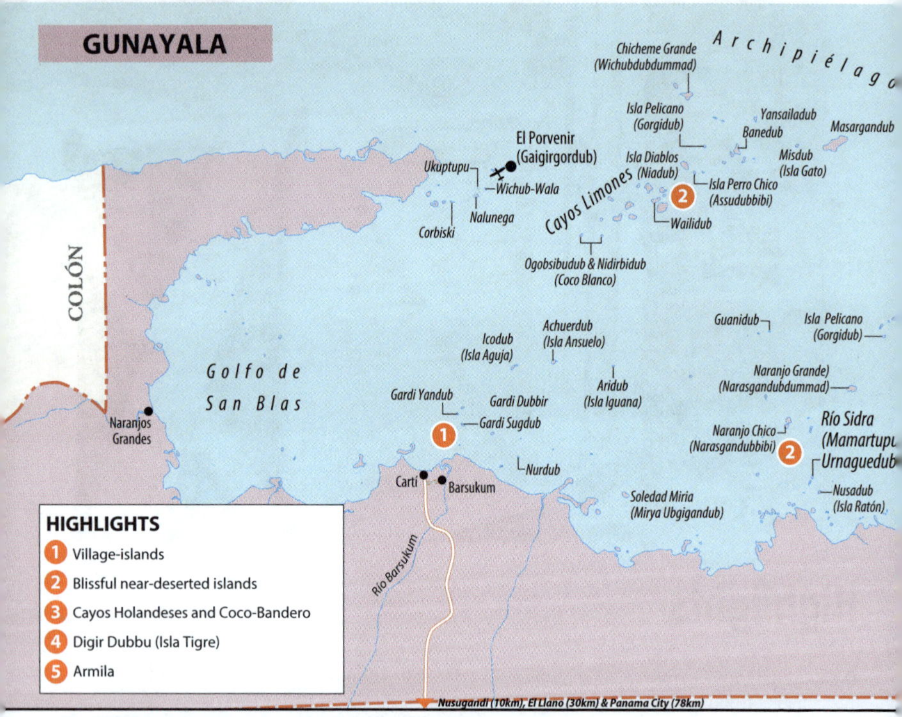

GUNAYALA
Archipiélago
Chicheme Grande
(Wichubdubdummad)
Isla Pelicano
(Gorgidub)
Yansailadub
Banedub
Masargandub
El Porvenir
(Gaigirgordub)
Isla Diablos
(Niadub)
Misdub
(Isla Gato)
Ukuptupu
Wichub-Wala
Cayos Limones
Isla Perro Chico
(Assudubbibi)
Wailidub
Corbiski
Nalunega
Ogobsibudub & Nidirbidub
(Coco Blanco)
COLÓN
Guanidub
Isla Pelicano
(Gorgidub)
Achuerdub
(Isla Ansuelo)
Icodub
(Isla Aguja)
Golfo de
San Blas
Aridub
(Isla Iguana)
Naranjo Grande)
(Narasgandubdummad)
Gardi Yandub
Gardi Dubbir
Gardi Sugdub
Naranjos
Grandes
Naranjo Chico
(Narasgandubbibi)
Río Sidra
(Mamartupu
Urnaguedub
Nurdub
Cartí
Barsukum
Soledad Miria
(Mirya Ubgigandub)
Nusadub
(Isla Ratón)
HIGHLIGHTS
1 Village-islands
2 Blissful near-deserted islands
3 Cayos Holandeses and Coco-Bandero
4 Digir Dubbu (Isla Tigre)
5 Armila
Río Barsukum
Nusugandi (10km), El Llano (30km) & Panama City (78km)

GUNAYALA (CONTINUED)
0
5
kilometres
San Ignacio de Tupile
(Dadnaggwe Dubbir)
Agligandi
Achutupu
(Assudub)
Mamitupu
(Mammidub)
Usdub
Ogobsucum
Playón Chico
(Uggubseni)
Yandub
Playón Grande
(Uggubba)
Niadub
Punta Niamulo
Irgandí
Río Masargandi

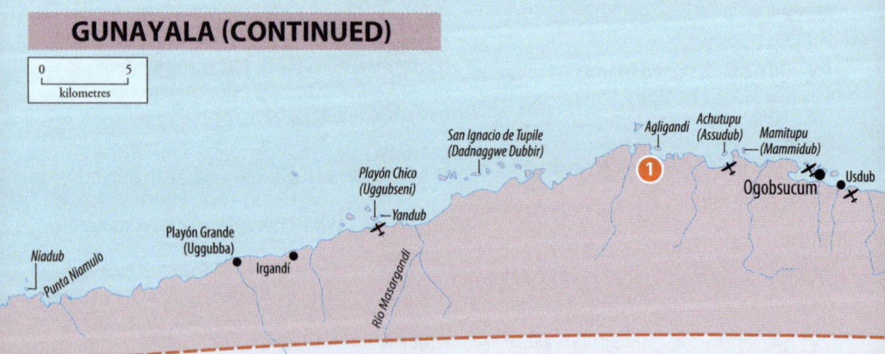

sprinkling of tiny Robinson Crusoe-style beaches and the best snorkelling, and plenty of accommodation options. Moreover, they – together with a handful of islands in the **central region** – are generally the most geared up for tourism. For these reasons, along with improvements in the only road link with the *comarca*, which makes it just a three-hour drive from Panama City at most, have led to a great increase in visitor numbers. This in turn has inevitably put great strain on the natural resources, and sometimes on Guna–tourist relations, and has undoubtedly diminished the appeal of this particular group in high season. Visiting the more isolated **eastern islands**, such as **Agligandi** or **Mamitupu**, you'll experience greater cultural engagement with the Guna – provided you can speak Spanish – since you may well be the only outsider there. Even on islands

GUNAYALA ESSENTIALS

WHEN TO GO

Peak tourist season in Gunayala, as elsewhere in Panama, is the **dry season** (roughly mid-Dec to April) though for some of the period, you'll suffer from the trade winds (Dec–Feb/March), which whip up the waters into large waves, making travel uncomfortable – and scary at times – impairing snorkelling and leaving the outer islands inaccessible. Late March and April are more appealing times to visit, although water levels can be low on the mainland, restricting river trips.

If possible, avoid the popular palm-topped islets of **western** Gunayala – islas Perro Chico and Diablos above all – at weekends or **public holidays** during the dry season. At this time hundreds of weekenders and day-trippers flock here from Panama City, saturating the beaches with deckchairs, vast cooler boxes and sound systems, making it almost impossible to hear the waves and see the sand, never mind sit on it.

The **wet season** lasts from May to mid-December; in the early months, from May to July, the unbearable humidity and lack of breeze is balanced by a sea that can be millpond-still – perfect for snorkelling, except during the afternoon downpours, when run-off muddies the waters. June to October spells the season for *chocosanos*, terrifying electric tempests that generate monstrous waves capable of flooding an island and dashing a ship onto a reef in an instant.

WHAT TO TAKE

A **mosquito net** may be a good idea, depending on the season (though some places provide them), together with lashings of **repellent**, **sun cream**, a basic **first-aid kit** and a **torch** and/or candles (there is limited or no electricity on some islands), plus a **sheet sleeping bag** in high season – if water is short, or the weather bad, sheets may not get a full wash. Some kind of **waterproof protection**, such as a plastic bin liner, is desirable to protect your gear from getting soaked in the boat, and you may want a breathable waterproof for yourself. In **budget accommodation** it's recommended to take snacks with you, as meal portions are often small, plus a toilet roll. It's not advisable to drink **tap water** in Gunayala. Some hotels provide purified water for guests at meals; most charge. Bottled water is on sale in most islands, but is expensive and its disposal an environmental headache; it's far better to use a water filter or purifying tablets (see box, page 86). If that's not possible, buy a gallon container of purified water to take with you (and take back out). Use of **snorkelling equipment** is sometimes included in package deals, or the *cabañas* may rent out masks. In either case, masks are often not in good condition, so if you intend to spend some time in the area, consider buying a cheap snorkel in Panama City (see box, page 86).

TAXES AND MONEY

At the road entrance to the *comarca* at **Nusugandi**, around 20km before you reach the coast, all non-Guna have to pay a **tourist tax** ($20), which is not included in transport costs. There is also a $2 fee to use the docks at Cartí, Barsukum or Tupile (see page 253). Visitors generally also have to pay a **community tax** ($3–10 for the village-islands, around $3 on near-deserted beach islands); these costs are usually not included in tour packages (see box, page 254). You have to take all the cash you might need with you, in small denominations – the *comarca*'s only bank, in Narganá, does not permit credit-card withdrawals. Some of the more expensive lodges and tour operators accept online payments for a basic package, but extras, such as drinks, community taxes, extra tours, and snorkel rental, usually need to be paid for in cash.

COMMUNICATION

Mobile coverage has now reached most parts of the *comarca* through Más Móvil and Tigo networks, though the signal may be weak and the system is often down when the weather is bad. **Wi-fi** access is slowly improving across the region (though in more remote islands you may manage to use a signal from a government building by lurking outside).

unused to seeing tourists, you are likely to be able to negotiate a hammock for the night in someone's home for a few dollars.

Brief history

Guna **oral history** traces their origins to the Sierra Nevada de Santa Marta of present-day Colombia. Fleeing from people such as the Emberá, in the fifteenth or sixteenth century, they took refuge in the mountainous areas of the **Darién**, including Mount Tacarcuna – the highest peak in eastern Panama (1874m), lying just outside the *comarca* – which became a sacred place in folklore. Violent conflict ensued against the Spanish, with the Guna often forming unlikely alliances with English and French pirates, and gradually being forced towards the Caribbean. Though Guna had visited the coast for many years, colonization of the **islands** they inhabit today did not start until the mid-nineteenth century as they sought greater access to passing traders and escape from disease-carrying insects on the mainland.

Panamanian independence

Geographical isolation ensured the Guna were pretty much left alone until **Panamanian independence** in 1903, when the new state refused to recognize the **Comarca Dulenega**, which had been established by Colombia in 1870. It covered Guna territories straddling the two countries and had guaranteed a certain measure of independence.

The Revolución Dule

Tension between the **Guna Congress** and Panamanian authorities escalated as the latter granted concessions to outsiders to plunder resources in Guna territory and persistently attempted to suppress Guna culture – banning women's traditional attire or forcing missionaries and colonial schooling onto the communities. Matters came to a head in 1925, when a gathering of Guna leaders on Ailigandi – today's Agligandi – resolved to declare independence and rose up in what is proudly commemorated as the **Revolución Dule** (Guna Revolution), which marked its bicentenary in 2025 with wild celebrations. Around forty people lost their lives in the uprising, and only the intervention of the US – concerned for the safety of the Canal – prevented further government reprisals. A settlement was finally reached in 1938, when the Guna agreed to recognize Panamanian sovereignty in exchange for a clearly defined *comarca* and a high degree of political autonomy.

ARRIVAL AND DEPARTURE GUNAYALA

Most visitors, and the Guna themselves, bound for the western or even some of the central islands, travel from Panama City by road, which connects with one of two dock areas at the western end of the *comarca*. The main departure area is by the disused **Cartí** airstrip, which in turn has three jetties: Sugdub, Dubbin and Carti Tupile. A 15min walk away, close to the mouth of the Río Barsukum, is the much smaller riverside **Barsukum** dock. Cartí is often used as shorthand to refer to both places. From the docks speedboats and motorized dugouts fan out to the various islands; there are few scheduled services, however, so access is limited and unpredictable. You can also reach some destinations by **light aircraft** from Albrook Airport.

BY ROAD

By car It takes 2hr 30min–3hr by road (4WD only) from Panama City to the dock at Cartí or Barsukum. Head east out of Panama City on the Interamericana; the turn-off for Gunayala is just east of Chepo, where the 40km El Llano–Cartí road crosses the peaks of the Serranía de San Blas to the Caribbean coast. Though completely repaved in 2024, the road is still treacherous as it's incredibly steep, winding and narrow; only 4WD vehicles are granted entry. The vehicle fee is $10, payable at Nusugandi (see box), in addition to the entry fee, and there's a charge of around $3–5 for parking.

Hostel/hotel transfers Hostels and hotels in Panama City can arrange a pickup in a Guna-approved 4WD vehicle – $25 one way to the Cartí/Barsukum docks, plus taxes (see box, page 252). Vehicles should only take four or six passengers, though they may try to squeeze in more – check in advance – and will collect you from your accommodation at around 5am. Try and negotiate the front seat if you're prone to motion sickness. Drivers generally stop at the supermarket and *cafetería* at El Llano to allow passengers to have breakfast and stock up on supplies.

PACKAGE STAYS IN GUNAYALA

Given the complexities of travelling independently around the archipelago, the easiest way to visit the region is on a **package tour**. In fact most hotels only offer package deals – the Guna prefer this as it affords them greater control over tourist activities. The majority of hotels are aimed at budget travellers; there's little mid-range **accommodation** and no luxury lodgings. Panama City hostels and hotels can help organize a multiday trip, or you can make arrangements yourself for the same price – a **minimum stay** of three days and two nights is recommended.

Itineraries may change depending on sea conditions. Most packages in the western region include: return **transport** by boat from the Cartí docks (ordinarily $30–50 for the return transfer, depending on the distance to be travelled; some also include transport from Panama City); three basic **meals**; rustic accommodation; and a daily **excursion**. The excursion usually entails a trip to a near-deserted palm-fringed island (there's usually someone living there to look after the place), or a cultural visit to a village-island or to the mainland to visit a cemetery (see box, page 264) or a waterfall. The *comarca* taxes and the 4WD transport fees may be additional; check in advance exactly what's included. There is often a fuel supplement to visit the Cayos Holandeses, which offer the best snorkelling in the *comarca* but are sometimes inaccessible due to rough seas (Dec–Feb).

On the **sandy atolls**, all of which are privately owned, accommodation is usually in simple white-cane *cabañas* or wooden cabins, with a mattress and perhaps somewhere to keep your belongings out of the sand. Increasingly, some islands are offering camping, with a tent and airbed/mattress provided, though for less visited isles you'll need to provide your own tent and possibly food for the resident Guna family to cook if there's no restaurant. Whichever option you choose, the often-basic **toilets** (which may have to be flushed with sea water from a bucket) are usually shared, and **electricity** is not a given; you may have to wash under overhead cold **showers**, or use a barrel of water and a jug or *calabash* (gourd). At weekends in peak season, fresh water for washing may run out on islands that have to transport it from the mainland.

For more **comfort**, a couple of islands such as *Akwa Reef Lodge* (see page 269) and *Cabañas Wailidup* (see page 262), fit the bill, offering cabins with private bathrooms (flush toilets, hand basins and cold-water showers), often with private balconies, fancier cuisine and English-speaking guides.

At the budget backpacker end, you will pay from $35 per person per night for dorm accommodation, three meals a day and a daily outing to a couple of beaches, but you'll pay more than $100 each for more comfortable options. Prices depend heavily on the cost of fuel, and may be negotiable in low season. Accommodation and package rates in Gunayala – be they for private or shared/dorm *cabañas* or tents – are almost always quoted per person. We have therefore quoted accommodation rates per person for a package staying in a double room, dorm or camping (lodging plus the three meals and tours) without including the transport to and from Panama City and the transfer from Cartí.

7

Independent booking If you've make arrangements for somewhere to stay, they can sort transport for you. But if you intend to pitch up at the dock and see what your options are, contact the recognized Guna transport service Nicanor Transporte (☎ 6948 7665) to arrange a ride.

Onward travel – packages On arrival at the docks, visitors who have arranged their trip via their hotel or hostel pile into a collection of motorized dugouts waiting to transport them to their island lodgings; this cost is usually included in the overall deal.

Onward travel – independent travellers It's worth asking the waiting boatmen about vacancies on their *lancha*, though bear in mind that transport to popular backpacker islands, such as islas Diablos, Perro Chico or Senidub, is often booked up. Transfer fees vary, starting from around $30 return to one of the islands near Cartí and Río Sidra. Many communities in the western and central isles have daily early-morning departures (5–6am) for Cartí, which can then transport you back to their island, leaving Cartí between 8–9am. For the eastern isles, departures are less frequent, and when sea conditions are rough, boats will be cancelled. For likely departure times, contact the island transport company or one of the lodgings on the island you are heading for.

BY PLANE

Most of the airstrips are on the mainland a few hundred

Day-trips (from around $100/person, including transport) and **overnight trips,** offering two days (leaving around 3pm the second day) either in *cabañas* or camping (from around $160) from Panama City are increasingly popular in high season, though the former are rarely worth the time and expense, given the six hours needed to get to and from the dock, plus the boat travel time. For the overnight trips you can often extend your stay, if you fancy, once there.

TOUR OPERATORS

In theory only **Guna-owned companies** are entitled to operate within the *comarca*, though several others do, including backpacker boats to and from Colombia (see box, page 24). The overnight stays organized by the tour companies tend to be more expensive than tours arranged directly with the accommodation concerned, though in some cases you're paying the extra for smoother transfers and an English-speaking guide. Recommendations are difficult since booking with one Guna company can result in actually being handed over to another 'sibling' company, usually operated by a relative.

Expediciones Tropicales (Xtrop) ⓦ xtrop.net. Excellent sea-kayak tours working with trained Guna guides and communities, and with plenty of beach-lounging and snorkelling opportunities. They've also branched out into doing day tours in the canal basin, including down the Río Chagres to Fuerte San Lorenzo. The longer excursion often starts from Digir. Two people minimum.

Kuna Yala Adventure ⓦ kunayalaadventure.com. All-Guna family operation organizing everything from all-inclusive day-trips from to multi-night stays on islands in Cayos Limones.

Kuna Yala Expeditions ⓦ kunayalaexpedition.com. Run by experienced and knowledgeable guide Elias Pérez (owner of *Cabañas Corbiski*; see page 258), who speaks English and is committed to sustainable tourism. Offering tours focused on Guna culture, including Guna culinary traditions, though he can find you a beach too if you prefer.

San Blas Amazing Tour ⓣ 6075 2305, ⓦ facebook.com/sanblasamazingtour. Guna company run by operatives experienced in hospitality, providing inexpensive day or overnight camping trips to Cayos Limones. Some English spoken.

San Blas Dreams ⓦ sanblasdreams.com. Well-organized and recommended Guna company offering package-tours to 16 islands in the western region and island-hopping tours that including cultural visits too.

San Blas Sailing ⓦ sanblassailing.com. Professional and pricey but providing an idyllic way to see the archipelago, offering catamaran tours (in French, Spanish and English; three to six days), generally in Western Gunayala, including kayak or dingy forays to the mainland. Prices depend on the boat capacity and cabin occupation, the degree of luxury and the season – in high season it's easier and cheaper to share; from $250/day for a catamaran). Private charters are more expensive. Transport to/from the *comarca* – they have a charter flight deal with Aero Albrook – and Guna taxes are not included. Catamaran Adventures (ⓦ catamaranadventreus.net) is also highly acclaimed and approved by the Guna Congress.

Viajes San Blas ⓦ viajessanblas.com. Efficient Guna outfit offering (almost) all-inclusive day- and multiday trips from Panama City to a wide range of islands at slightly higher rates than the island lodgings themselves charge (4WD transfer from Panama City and *comarca* tax extra).

metres from the islands themselves. However, since the Covid-19 pandemic, the main domestic airline, Air Panama, has not resumed scheduled flights to any of the destinations within Gunayala, though it is offering spaces in charter flights to Achutupu (see page 269), Ogobsucum (see page 270), Mulatupu, Playón Chico (Uggubseni) (see page 266) and Puerto Obaldía (see page 270). Other charter companies with smaller planes also offer flights. All operate out of Albrook Airport. So if you're short on time, but have an ample budget and you want to explore the central or eastern end of the *comarca*, it is worth considering charter flights. Aero Albrook (ⓦ aeroalbrook.com), for example, has negotiated fly+sail or fly+stay shared charter flight deals with a couple of the more upmarket island operators: to Corazón de Jesús with San Blas Sailing (see below) and to El Porvenir for *Cabañas Wailidub* (see page 262). Air Panama (ⓦ airpanama.com) has a well-priced charter deal with *Cabañas Ibedi* in Armila (see page 271). Blue Skies Panama (ⓦ blueskiespanama.com) offers private charter flights (for up to three or five people) to Achutupu (see page 269), Corazón de Jesús (see page 265), Playón Chico (Uggubseni) (see page 266), Mulatupu and Puerto Obaldía (see page 270), by the border with Colombia. One-way tickets for a full five-seater plane work out at around $240–300/person, depending on the destination. If you have a choice of time, book an early morning flight which should guarantee a smoother journey. Flight times range from 20min to 1 hr.

Transfer to your hotel If you have arranged a package, there will be a boat from your accommodation at the airstrip to take you to your destination. This transfer may or may not be included in the tour cost. Independent travellers may be able to catch a ride (for a fee); otherwise, other boatmen are usually hanging around with whom you can negotiate a deal.

BY BOAT

The main entry point by sea is Puerto Obaldía in the southeastern corner, where you'll almost inevitably be arriving from Colombia (see page 270). Backpackers travelling to and from Cartagena, Capurganá or Sapzurro, Colombia, by sailboat from Puerto Lindo or Portobelo usually spend a couple of days in Gunayala en route (see box, page 25).

7

From Puerto Obaldía Smallish fibreglass motorboats (*lanchas*) head up the coast from Puerto Obaldía to Cartí (approximately $110/person) several times a week, depending on demand (see page 270), and can drop you off at other islands en route. Note that the sea can be very rough and dangerous between Puerto Obaldía and Achutupu (especially Dec–March), and the experience is likely to be extremely wet and uncomfortable. Make sure the boat has two engines and life jackets as a minimum, is robust enough to withstand the waves, and preferably has a roof and satellite phone.

Island-hopping transfer A compromise between the sailboat and the *lancha* transfer is the four-day island-hopping, partying speedboat venture offered by San Blas Adventures (sanblasadventures.com), which runs between Cartí and Sapzurro in Colombia ($545), hugging the coastline and so avoiding the two-day open ocean crossing involved in sailing to/from Cartagena. Andutu (andutu.com) offers a similar trip between Cartí and Capurganá in Colombia.

GETTING AROUND

ORGANIZED TOURS

If you are on an organized tour (see box, page 254), inter-island transport will be arranged by your hosts. Included in the package will be one or two tours per day to another beach or village-island, or to the mainland. Some lodgings also offer optional excursions for set prices. Generally though, if you want to visit somewhere not on the schedule you will need to pay for another boat and pilot. Cost will depend on the distance, the boat's engine size and quality (see page 256) and the number of people wanting to do the trip. However, this may not be possible at weekends in high season, when there's often a shortage of boats due to multiple transfers to and from Cartí. That said, sometimes they manage to stagger timings for pickups and drop-offs. If you stay on a populated village-island such as Playón Chico, you have more options for additional boat rental.

INDEPENDENT TRAVEL

Inter-island transport Since there are few fixed itineraries or schedules for boats, you need to ask around about transport heading the way you want to go. This is relatively easy in the populated western region of the *comarca*, and not too difficult if you are heading westwards in the general direction of Cartí from other parts of the region, since most islands have early-morning boats carrying Guna bound for Panama City. Transport in such cases is inevitably cheaper than renting a boat privately. The best places to enquire are the main dock or fuel depot.

Private boat rental The further east you travel, the less frequent and more expensive inter-island transport becomes – in part because fuel costs are higher. You are more likely to need to rent a private boat, which is fairly easy (with some Spanish) but you will probably need to cover the fuel costs for the boatman's return trip.

Cartí–Puerto Obaldía Fairly regular speedboat services between Cartí and Puerto Obaldía (around $110) leave when they have enough passengers to cover the fuel costs. Contact, for example, Andutu andutu.com).

Types of boat Travel around the *comarca* is usually in a fibreglass *panga,* or *lancha*, generally with a roof to shade you from the sun. On your travels, though, keep an eye out for the traditional dugout (*ulu* in Guna, *cayuco* in Spanish), sometimes used for short distances, or even a traditional canoe sailboat with a cotton-sheet sail attached to a rough-hewn mast and boom.

Western Gunayala

Most visitors to Gunayala stay at the **western end** of the *comarca*. It's more accessible than the rest of the region, with a good number of idyllic islets and white-sand beaches – especially in the **cayos Limones** and **Holandeses** – better snorkelling and more accommodation (most of it at the budget end). For independent travellers, there is also more inter-island transport available (see above) and more shops for supplies – in **Gardi Sugdub** and **Río Sidra** – though choice is limited and prices high. The downside,

ETIQUETTE WHEN VISITING GUNAYALA

In Gunayala, particularly in the more remote areas, it is important to remember that you are a guest of the Guna, irrespective of how much you have paid for the privilege, and should abide by their laws. On islands less frequented by visitors it is customary to ask **permission** from the local *saila* when you visit a particular community or wish to stay on an island, as indeed the Guna themselves do – and they often still seek permission to leave their island too. **Photography** is another contentious area: on some islands it is forbidden, on others it is governed by strict regulations. Never photograph anyone without asking. Traditional beliefs still held by some of the older generation maintain that a photograph takes away a part of the soul, which is why you should resist the temptation to surreptitiously snap away. Generally, $1–2 is charged to take a single photograph, more for group shots, whereas filming, if permitted, can cost around $15 (use of drones is forbidden). Women selling *molas* – the distinctive brightly coloured, embroidered cloth panels – will usually allow you to photograph them if you purchase an item, but do not presume that the cost includes the photo charge.

Beachwear is fine when you're lazing in a hammock on one of the coconut islands, but you should **dress** more modestly in villages – no bikini tops or bare chests. Villagers may not say anything, but it doesn't mean you haven't caused offence. The Guna are particularly sensitive about the *onmagged nega* (meeting house) and the cemeteries on the mainland – never enter or photograph these without permission. **Alcohol** too is a thorny issue. Traditionally during ceremonies large clay pots of *chicha* (see box, page 267) would be prepared for the whole village; once the jars were exhausted, the drinking spree was over. Though this is sometimes still the case, outside the ceremonies communities now vary in their regulations on alcohol: in western Gunayala, drinking is unregulated, but people may be fined if found drunk; some communities allow seco and beer to supplement the *chicha* at celebrations but not at other times; some have licensing hours; and others ban alcohol completely, though may allow its sale to tourists. Always enquire first, and drink discreetly if alcohol is available to tourists but not to villagers.

7

of course, is that with greater exposure to tourism, especially in communities that have put up with more than their fair share of insensitive visitors, some Guna are understandably jaded with outsiders.

El Porvenir and around

The diminutive, scarcely inhabited island of **EL PORVENIR (Gaigirgordub)** belies its status as administrative **capital** of Gunayala. A sliver of bare land, it barely manages to squeeze on an airstrip (only used for charter flights) alongside a handful of buildings, including a police post, hotel and craft shop, plus a clump of palm trees. Though this is not one of the more popular destinations, the water off El Porvenir's thin strip of sand is cleaner than at the more heavily populated neighbouring islands.

Wichub-Wala

Wichub-Wala is a bustling yet relaxed island. In addition to the usual sandy pathways and cane-and-thatch huts there are some decaying cement structures, including a former swimming pool now full of large tropical fish. To the west, the tiny semi-submerged private coral outcrop of **Ukuptupu** was formerly home to a Smithsonian marine research station until the institute was ejected from the *comarca* in 1998.

Nalunega

Just south of Ukuptupu lies **Nalunega**, "the house of the macaw" in Dulegaya; these brightly coloured birds were resident on the island when it was first colonized. A more appealing village than Wichub-Wala, with a population of around five hundred, it

7

GUNA NAMES AND LANGUAGE

All island communities have a **Guna name**, which often has several variant spellings, and a **Spanish name**. Matters have been further complicated by the standardization of the Guna alphabet in 2011 in which the letters "p", "t" and "k" were removed and replaced by "b", "d" and "g", which are sometimes doubled to give "bb", "dd" and "gg"; the letters "l", "m" and "n" are also doubled in some contexts. However, this standardization has not yet permeated all of Guna society. In the Guide, when introducing a place, we have tried to use the more commonly used name first (be it in Spanish or in Dulegaya) and given the alternative – and sometimes a variant spelling – in parentheses.

GUNA GLOSSARY

The most essential word to grasp in Dulegaya (Guna language) is the versatile "**nuedi**", meaning "hello", "yes" and "it's good/OK" or "welcome". "Nuegambi", meaning "thank you" is also useful. Other key cultural terms include:

absoguedi chanter
Bab Dummad and **Nan Dummad** Great Father and Mother, the creators
Baba Nega heavenly spirit world
boni evil spirits
dule masi traditional Guna fish and plantain stew
Ibeorgun Guna prophet and religion
Innamudigi initial puberty ritual held at a girl's first menstruation
inna nega *chicha* house
innasuid second puberty ritual for girls during which they are officially named
nainumar cultivated lands on the mainland
neg uan burial ground
nele traditional healer or shaman
nuchu (nuchukana) carved wooden totem(s) to ward off evil spirits
Onmagged Dummad Sunmagaled Guna General Congress
onmagged nega meeting house
saila chief
uaga (uagmala) outsider(s)
ulu dugout canoe

has broader streets dotted with shady trees populated with parrots, while traditional cane-and-thatch buildings rub shoulders with occasional aluminium-topped cement structures. At the centre lie a primary school, the meeting hall and the basketball court.

Isla Corbiski

A ten-minute boat ride from El Porvenir, the tiny crowded village-island of **Corbiski** will give you a warm welcome. Overnight visitors will have plenty of opportunities to interact with the local populace and learn about Guna culture, though there's no beach for lounging about.

ARRIVAL AND DEPARTURE — EL PORVENIR AND AROUND

A few charter flights arrive but most visitors arrive by **boat** from Cartí/Barsukum.

ACCOMMODATION

Cabañas Nalunega Nalunega Karina ☎ 6514 9333 or Angelica ☎ 6969 7148, ✉ karinaiglesias0303@gmail.com. Three over-the-water cane cabins, on solid cement bases and with electricity, share a bathroom. Cloth hung on the inside provides a greater measure of privacy than in many such *cabañas* while also letting the breeze through. Meals, tours and transfer from Cartí included. $$

Cabañas Corbiski Isla Corbiski Elias Pérez ☎ 6020 0844, ✉ corbiski@gmail.com. Accommodation is in a handful of comfortable (by *comarca* standards) over-the-water wooden cabins, with decent mattresses, solar-generated electricity and private bathrooms. An excellent choice if you are interested in Guna culture, and not just beach-lounging. Owner Elias is fluent in English. Packages totally all-inclusive including transport from Panama City, taxes, full board, snacks and all excursions. A percentage of the profits go to community projects. $$$

Hotel El Porvenir By the disused airstrip, El Porvenir ⓦhotelporvenir.com. This long-established hotel, offering the only accommodation on the island, is pleasantly situated in grassy grounds with its own veranda bar-restaurant and eleven rather gloomy concrete rooms with tin roof and private cold-water bathrooms. The place is relaxed, and the staff friendly. Rates include full board plus a daily excursion to nearby islands, though transport from the capital can also be arranged. $$$

The Gardi islands and around

The road connecting Panama City funnels backpackers and day-trippers into the Cartí docks. Just a coconut's throw away, the **GARDI (CARTÍ) ISLANDS**, together with the tiny uninhabited palm-covered retreats of **Icodub (Isla Aguja)**, **Achuerdub (Isla Ansuelo)** and **Aridub (Isla Iguana)** nearby, experience the greatest number of day-trippers in the archipelago. The best recommendation is to stay on one of the smaller islands – **Gardi Yandub** if you want to sample Guna village life, or Aridub for the desert-island experience – and drop by **Gardi Sugdub** during the day to visit the excellent museum, or in the evening if there's a community event.

7

Gardi Sugdub

Close to the mainland, densely populated **Gardi Sugdub** forms the stadium-sized hub of this island group and, with around two thousand inhabitants – some of whom have now moved to the new purpose-built (and soulless) mainland community of Isber Yala – is one of the *comarca*'s busiest communities but it's not a desirable place to spend the night.

The centre comprises a few large, functional cement buildings, including a secondary school, medical centre, library and post office, standing amid a maze of cane and thatch. There are a couple of restaurants, and numerous stalls selling soft drinks and snacks. The large number of people passing through and the increasing proliferation of consumer goods has resulted in rubbish piling up in the streets and at the water's edge.

Museo de Cultura y Arte Guna

Centre of the island • Daily 8am–4pm • Charge • ⓣ 669 1390

The main reason to visit Gardi Sugdub is to spend time at the **Museo de Cultura y Arte Guna**. Stuffed full of artefacts, with pictures from floor to ceiling, it covers many aspects of Guna culture – *mola*-making, funerary rites, traditional medicine, religious beliefs – with some bilingual signage in Spanish and English. The place really comes alive through the informative explanations of the curator, Deliano Davies, who is happiest conducting tours in Spanish but can manage some English.

Nurdub

Very close to the coast, four families occupy the tiny outcrop of **Nurdub**, welcoming visitors to their simple *cabañas* (see below). Provided your Spanish is up to the task, this intimate environment is ideal for deepening your understanding of Guna culture. Although there's no beach, daily trips are arranged to beaches.

ARRIVAL AND DEPARTURE — THE GARDI ISLANDS AND AROUND

By boat For independent travellers, there is always transport waiting to transfer passengers to Cartí from the dock (10–20min).

ACCOMMODATION

Cabañas Ariyasaladub Aridub ⓦfacebook.com/Kunaisland. For anyone wanting to experience simple island life, sleeping in traditional cane-and-thatch huts with sandy floors (but modern beds (2–6) with mattresses and bedding). There is, however, a large, more modern over-the-water restaurant. Camping is also permitted. Camping

$$, *cabañas* $$$

★**Cabañas Nurdub** Nurdub ☎6803 7033. Six immaculate cane *cabañas* on a tiny island that allows cultural immersion. Day-trips are offered to Isla Perro Chico (see page 260) and to the beautiful, deserted Piderdub, where you can also choose to camp as part of your stay. Lodgings, meals and one daily beach excursion plus transfer from Cartí are included. $$$

Cayos Limones

Offering perfect tranquillity (provided you don't coincide with a cruise-ship stopover), the gorgeous islands that comprise **CAYOS LIMONES** are clustered east and northeast of El Porvenir. Once dedicated to harvesting coconuts, they now function mainly as prime day-trip and backpacker destinations. At other times, it's worth staying overnight, allowing you to soak up the tranquillity by a campfire and admire the sparkling night sky.

Islas Perro Chico and Perro Grande

7

Community tax/day-pass

Isla Perro Chico (Assudubbibbi) – also known as Perro Uno and not to be confused with its more populated namesake with the airstrip much further east – is the most visited island in the Cayos Limones, and therefore in Gunayala, so can be overwhelmed with day-trippers on summer weekends and holiday periods. It offers the best **snorkelling** in the area, around an accessible reef and a sunken cargo boat in the narrow channel separating it from adjacent Isla Diablos. A further draw is the beachside **restaurant** that offers an a la carte menu, though the two-storey cement structure that houses it (and some upstairs accommodation) is less appealing. The only slightly larger sibling islet, **Isla Perro Grande (Assudubdummad)**, is another popular day-trip destination, also lacking sufficient shade and sand to accommodate all the day-visitors in high season.

Isla Diablos

Community tax/day-pass waived if lunch is eaten at one of the restaurants

A short hop (or strong swim – beware of currents) from the midsummer mayhem and the sunken cargo boat near Isla Perro Chico, **Isla Diablos (Niadub)** has a thin stretch of **beach** with a sheltered swimming area and two backpacker accommodations that are getting increasingly congested, but with relatively good restaurants. The over-the-water restaurant (with TV) attached to *Cabañas Niadup* is popular with day-trippers.

Chicheme Grande

Towards the outer perimeter of the archipelago, the large palm-covered **Chicheme Grande (Wichubdubdummad)**, home to a handful of families, is a popular day-trip destination. In addition, sailing vessels on the Puerto Lindo/Portobelo–Cartagena route (see box, page 24) often stop here for the night. Waves thunder over the protective outlying reef, which prevents rubbish from washing up on the gorgeous beach, and the island's relative size coupled with its isolation engender an away-from-it-all feel – outside peak periods when the music from the Andutu Bar, aimed at entertaining partying Panamanians, can rather spoil the ambiance.

Wailidub

Wailidub, tucked away behind a mangrove-fringed islet, is one of the nicest places to stay in the area. Favoured by passing sailboats, which stop off at the well-known bar-restaurant at *Cabañas Wailidup* (see page 262), it comprises a windward stretch of alabaster sand, shelving into crystalline shallows sprinkled with starfish, and an open grassy patch surrounded by willowy palms. It also has the rare luxury of a fresh water supply. But beware the bugs when the wind drops, and check that day-trippers are not booked onto the island during your planned stay.

LOBSTER AND THE CLOSED SEASON

If you're hoping to sample the succulent **lobster** for which Gunayala is famous, avoid the closed season (*veda*; March–May). During this period conch, crab and octopus are also off-limits. Note that in budget all-inclusive accommodation there is usually a supplement if you want lobster for a meal.

Yansailadub

The smallish island of **Yansailadub** – also referred to as Isla Yanis or Yani – boasts several attractions. Beyond the powdery white sand fringing the island, the shallows host plenty of marine life, such as basking and white-tipped sharks, stingrays and starfish. A natural swimming pool sandbank lies just offshore.

Nugnudub

Named after one of the tallest trees in the rainforest, **Nugnudub (Isla Ceiba)** is a small beach-bar island, where a central palm-shaded grassy patch is sprinkled with seats round low-lying tables. The bar (with music) at the back knocks up a mean cocktail, which you can also enjoy in an over-the-water hammock, and in high season, you'll be subjected to karaoke. Chartered yachts are not allowed. Tented accommodation is available.

Piscinas naturales

Combined with a trip to one of the islands is usually a quick stop at one of the cays' several **piscinas naturales** (natural swimming pools), which are barely submerged sandbanks between the islands. Here you can stand, with water up to your chest, and marvel at the surrounding translucent water.

Misdub

Within sight of Masargandub and within easy striking distance of the Cayos Holandeses, **Misdub (Isla del Gato)** is delightfully pristine, having only relatively recently opened to visitor. With little development – only one cabin (though others are planned) and a restaurant – it's a real treat. Palm trees only cover one third, the rest is scrub and a glorious swathe of white sand, which shelves into very shallow protected water, more for lolling than swimming. Here, you can wade out to lie in over-the-water hammocks and swings, where pelicans, terns and other seabirds hang out. Back on land, you can shelter from the sun in supremely comfortable bed-hammocks.

Masargandub

Just off the eastern end of the Cayos Limones, and about an hour's boat ride from Cartí en route to the Cayos Holandeses, lies **Masargandub**. A gem of an island and one of the largest in the *comarca*, with pristine reefs and impressive birdlife. it takes a full hour to circumnavigate on foot. Starfish, stingrays and dolphins inhabit its translucent waters, iguanas peek out through the undergrowth and hawksbill turtles dig their nests in the soft sand (late April to July). At the time of writing the island was closed to visitors as the congress settles how the three families from different islands should manage the co-ownership. It is expected that some kind of tourism will resume eventually.

ACCOMMODATION AND EATING — CAYOS LIMONES

Cabañas Assudub Bibbi 6003 0551 These attractive raised, thatched wooden cabins come with private sea-facing porches. Containing four comfortable beds (1 double, 2 singles) and a fan, some have private bathrooms, whilst others share. Cheaper still is a bed in a traditional sandy-floor cane hut. Alternatively, book a room upstairs in the two-storey cement building, with access to a shared balcony affording glorious sea views – only a recommended option midweek, outside the holiday season, when the crowds have dispersed. Camping allowed (own tent). Camping $$, dorms $$, cabins $$$

Cabañas Niadub Isla Diablos facebook.com/p/

Cabañas-Niadub-100064022350183, ⓣ6119 1114 (Dennis). The preferred option on the island, with its own sliver of beach and sheltered waters to loll in. They offer dorm *cabañas* for up to ten, tents (equipped with airbeds and sheets) and 12 private *cabañas* – four bang on the beach with private porch and chairs – worth paying extra for. All share tiled-floor bathrooms, which are cleaner than many, and generally have water. There's also a volleyball court and a pleasant over-the-water restaurant (when the loud TV isn't on), open to day-visitors. Lodging, meals, tours and snorkel use included. Camping $$, dorms $$, doubles $$$

★ **Cabañas Wailidup** Wailidub ⓦwailidup.com. Four relatively smart, if basic, en-suite *cabañas* set on the grassy interior, and six superior ones (extra) built on stilts over the water with sea-facing balconies, solar-powered electricity, private bathrooms and aluminium roofs. The bar-restaurant serving succulent seafood is favoured by yachties. Room rates include transfer from Cartí, meals and trips. Transport from Panama City can be included. Snorkel rental available. $$$

Cabañas Wissudub Isla Chicheme Grande ⓣ6846 5217 (Argelio Burgos). The oldest lodgings on the island. A row of brightly painted wooden cabins with wooden floor, aluminium roof and small porch peek through the palm fronds at the sea. The priciest *cabañas* have a fan, electricity and private bathroom. Thatched huts house dorms. Wherever you sleep, you'll hear the waves crashing on the reef at night. Camping is also available, with tents to rent. Toilet and shower facilities are fine, but water shortages are common in high season. Meals – slightly more bountiful and sophisticated than many in this price bracket – are available in a tiled-floor restaurant that has a TV and blaring music. There are kayaks to rent. Cartí transfer $30. Camping $$, dorms $$, doubles $$$

★ **Cabañas Yansailadub** ⓣ6074 7841, ⓔyanifigueroa2001@gmail.com. A row of simple box-like wooden rooms and shared ablutions (using salt water to flush the toilets). There are three more fancy over-the-water cabins, painted inside and out, which contain a double and single bed each, plus a small table with a couple of chairs for the private porch. Camping with your own tent also permitted. Meals are tasty and service is friendly and efficient. Camping $$, double $$$, cabin $$$

Camping Misdub ⓣ6074 7841, ⓔyanifigueroa2001@gmail.com. Groups with their own tents tend to be placed close to the ablution block (kept clean), to keep the noise away from other campers. Camping is in small two-person (occasionally leaky) tents where the inflatable mattress takes up much of the space. Food is adequate, but most of all, it's a magical island, where you can marvel at the stars at night. Camping $$

Camping Nugnudub ⓣ6497 8060. Superior walk-in tents (with mattress and bedding) and a welcome cocktail from the popular day-tripper island bar. Food served at the restaurant (included) includes tasty lobster and jumbo shrimps, and there are kayaks to use. Camping $$

Río Sidra and around

Some 15km east of Cartí, just off the mainland, lies **RÍO SIDRA**; formerly a key portal into the archipelago until its airport was closed a few years ago, it is still an important settlement within the *comarca*. Originally two separate islands, **Urgandi** (which recently changed its name to **Urnaguedub**, meaning "the place to tether boats") and **Mamartupu** combined to make Río Sidra – a community of close on two thousand – by reclaiming the land in between. Each retains its own identity, maintaining separate *sailas*, meeting houses and churches – and each charges a community visitors' tax – though they share a school and basketball court. As you face the town from the main jetty, Urnaguedub lies to the right, Mamartupu to the left; the main drag, a broad sandy boulevard with a number of grocery stores, bisects both, running the length of the island.

The island is convenient for visiting **Nusadub** and **Isla Maquina**, famous for its *molas*, and is a popular village excursion for the backpacker islands of **Senidub**, **Naranjo Chico** and **Isla Pelicano**. Other scenic diversions in the area include the lovely sandy island of **Bigirdub** and starfish haven of **Isla Salar**, while the mainland attractions include a boat trip up the **Río Masargandi**, calling in at the cemetery at its mouth, and a trek through luxuriant rainforest to the once-sacred waterfall of **Saiba**, where you can cool off in the delightful freshwater pool at its base.

Nusadub and Isla Maquina

A small community of around four hundred just across the water from Río Sidra, the unfortunately named **Nusadub (Isla Ratón)** – "Rat Island" – does not harbour any more of these rodents than anywhere else, though sandflies are a major nuisance here in winter (May–Dec). Nearby, diminutive **Isla Maquina (Mor Agedub)**, whose four-hundred-plus inhabitants are less accustomed to visitors, is known for its fine *molas*.

GUNAYALA FESTIVALS

The main party to catch in the *comarca* is the celebration of the **Guna Revolution**, which takes place from February 23 to 25 (Feb 19–21 in Agligandi) in various forms around the archipelago. Skirmishes between Panamanian forces and Guna are re-enacted on land and sea, accompanied by storytelling, parades and drinking. October, meanwhile, sees the splendid dance competitions of the **Feria de Isla Tigre** (see page 266), which also involves a lot of music and cultural events.

Isla Pelicano and Senidub

The postage-stamp-sized islands of **Isla Pelicano (Gorgidub)** and **Senidub (Isla Chiquita)**, crowned with coconut palms and fringed with strips of soft sand, are perennial favourites with backpackers since they offer the cheapest packages in the *comarca* and stays are easily organized through Panama City hostels. As a result there can often be something of a holiday-camp atmosphere on them. Of the two, Senidub is the slightly larger and better tended, and has a lovely stretch of beach at one end, though it's rather cluttered with *cabañas*. Possible **excursions** from both take in the village of Soledad Mirya (Mirya Ubgigandub), which is noted for fine *molas*, or the glorious white-sand beaches of Piderdub.

7

Naranjo Chico

Belying its diminutive tag, **Naranjo Chico (Narasgandubbibi)** is the second largest island in the area after Naranjo Grande (Narasgandubdummad). It is particularly lovely for its distinctive hourglass shape, its gorgeous swathe of white-powder sand – from which you can snorkel – and its vegetation of coconut palms, shrubs and delightful hibiscus flowers, though overdevelopment remains a threat. Several families run lodgings here, but with most *cabañas* set back off the sand, nestled in the undergrowth, the nicest stretch of beach remains relatively unspoilt.

ARRIVAL AND GETTING AROUND — RÍO SIDRA AND AROUND

By boat Río Sidra is a 45min boat ride from Cartí. Senidub, Naranjo Chico and Pelicano are around a 20–30min boat ride northwest of Río Sidra, or 40min from Cartí.

ACCOMMODATION AND EATING

SENIDUB

Cabañas Dubesenika 6768 4075. This a legendary party spot with twenty tightly *cabañas*, some with sandy floors, but a handful of pricier elevated wooden ones bang on the beach. The large cement over-the-water dining room is visited by stingrays in the early evening. Also has a volleyball court. Guests share an oversubscribed, basic communal shower/toilet area, and luxuries such as juice, snacks, beer and cigarettes can be bought at the "office". The generator runs from 6 to 10pm. Rates include basic and sometimes small meals. Dorms $$, doubles $$–$$$

Cabañas Senidub 6657 9300, cabanas_senidub@hotmail.com. Run by a family cooperative from Soledad Miria, this place offers dorm *cabañas* packed with beds plus five private *cabañas*, and even has an occasionally functioning toilet/shower. Though solar-powered electricity illuminates the pleasant dining area, a generator runs between 6 and 10pm. There's a shady volleyball court, too. Meals included. Dorms $$, doubles $$

NARANJO CHICO

Cabañas Isla Narasgandup Naranjo Chico sanblasnarasgandup.com. On the quiet side of the island, this friendly place has three private sandy-floor *cabañas* set back across a patch of grass that also serves as a volleyball court, and three pricier en-suite beachside *cabañas* with wooden floors and a private porch overlooking the sea. All have solar-powered electricity. Rates include Cartí transfer and food, and can include excursions. $$

Cabañas Miro (formerly Robinson) 6764 0728. Probably the nicest of the three inexpensive lodgings on the main beach (three dorms, four private, with new mattresses and mosquito nets) and their patch of island is enlivened by flowers and shells. Avoid the back *cabañas* nearest the generator, and bag a sea-facing cabin. Showers and bathrooms are shared. Rates include meals and an excursion to Senidub or Estrella. Dorms $$, doubles $$

GUNA CEMETERIES

One of the most fascinating tours offered by Guna communities is to their traditional Guna **burial ground** (*neg uan*) on the mainland. From afar the cemetery resembles a miniature village, a mass of thatched rooftops, which turn out to be shelters protecting the graves from the rain. Beneath each one is an elongated mound of earth, representing the pregnant belly of Nabguana (Mother Nature) as she gives birth to the deceased in the heavenly spirit world (Baba Nega), as well as everyday utensils, clothing and food, which are left to accompany the deceased on their journey and serve as gifts for relatives who have already passed away.

Before burial the deceased is bathed in aromatic herbs and dressed in their best clothes, their cheeks painted with the natural reddish dye of *achiote*, a colour believed to ward off the evil spirits (*boni*). After villagers have paid their respects, the body is laid to rest in a deep grave in a hammock oriented towards the rising sun in the east, symbolic of the beginning of new life, which is also sometimes alluded to by laying cotton threads – representing the umbilical cord – across the corpse. A dugout tethered nearby is left to carry the deceased to their ancestors.

Cayos Holandeses and around

Three groups of predominantly **uninhabited cays** forming an equilateral triangle provide the archipelago's most spectacular underwater scenery. At the top of the triangle, marking the outer limit of the *comarca* 30km from shore, **Cayos Holandeses (Maoki)** are the most remote, yet the most visited, of the three. Effectively out of bounds during the frequent fierce winds and high waves of December to the end of February, at other times this chain of around twenty densely forested islands acts as a magnet for yachts drawn to the sheltered anchorage and shallow, translucent waters. The protection is afforded by the outlying **Wreck Reef**, which has ensnared Spanish galleons and the odd drug-smuggling vessel, parts of which still protrude through the pounding surf. The resulting bays form clear natural swimming pools displaying a stunning array of sponges and soft and hard corals – fire, elkhorn, brain, fan – that attract rays, reef sharks, moray eels, starfish and a plethora of polychromatic fish. At the time of writing, overnight **camping** was only allowed in remote **Morodub (Tortuga)** because it has toilet facilities. It also has an attractive grassy interior, shady picnic tables, a gorgeous white-sand beach and crystalline waters offering excellent snorkelling

Cayos Los Grullos and Cayos Coco-Bandero

Strung out along the 30km expanse of sea between Río Sidra and Narganá and Corazón de Jesús, **Cayos Los Grullos** and **Cayos Coco-Bandero (Ordupuquip)** – two clusters of around a dozen or so cays – comprise thin powdery beaches peppered with driftwood encircling densely forested isles and coral-filled shallows. Popular with cruising yachts, they attract Guna dugouts selling *molas* and fresh produce to the visitors.

ARRIVAL AND DEPARTURE — CAYOS HOLANDESES AND AROUND

By boat For budget travellers staying on the inner isles near Cartí or Río Sidra, an excursion to Cayos Holandeses often requires a fuel supplement.

ACCOMMODATION AND EATING — CAYOS HOLANDESES AND AROUND

Camping Morodub ☎ 6100 7883. Bring your own tent or come with a Guna tour company that can provide one. Alternatively, contact the family running the campground, who may be able to provide one, in addition to preparing food. Camping $$

★ **Ibin's Beach Restaurant** Banedub ☎ 6119 4743. Just off the tip of the Cayos Holandeses is arguably the archipelago's best gourmet restaurant, popular with yachties. It has a lovely breezy, over-the-water setting, and serves high-quality fresh seafood – fish, conch, octopus, lobster – served with coconut rice or seasoned potatoes and a smidgen of salad, accompanied by ice-cold beer. There's even vegetable curry. $$–$$$

Central Gunayala

The main appeal of **central Gunayala** lies in **Isla Tigre**, which sustains many traditional Guna practices. Forty kilometres further east, sprawling **Playón Chico** presents an interesting combination of modernity and tradition. The region possesses a handful of delightful sand-fringed coconut isles on which to idle, and though its beaches don't match the breathtaking beauty of many in the western end of the archipelago, the mainland excursions into primeval **rainforest** more than compensate. Consider also a trip up **Río Azúcar (Uwargandub)**, a few kilometres west of Narganá – it is one of the most beautiful rivers in the *comarca*, brimming with birdlife, with the occasional crocodile idling on the bank.

Narganá and Corazón de Jesús

A quick glance round either **Narganá (Yandub)** or **Corazón de Jesús (Aggwanusadub)** and it's easy to forget you're in Gunayala. The paved squares are dotted with benches, lampposts flank wide sandy streets, evening sound systems blast out reggaeton and bachata, and traditionally clad women are conspicuously absent. Some Guna see the twin islands as a warning of the fate of the *comarca* if the spread of *uaga burba* – the spirit of outsiders – proceeds unchecked. On the plus side, the location of the two islands is enchanting, nestled in a bay and fringed with mangroves fronting forest-clad hills. Moreover, if you've been travelling around the *comarca*, you might find Narganá's *Hostal Parks* – with cable TV – a welcome relief (see page 265).

Corazón de Jesús, in keeping with its name, has a **statue of Christ** in its central plaza, which is illuminated at night. Other than that, the island's main features are its airstrip, a handful of government buildings and a church; there's a small cemetery at the northern tip. Most of the action occurs down at the wharf and at its opposite number across the dividing channel of water in Narganá: boats load up with supplies and drop off passengers, and yachts bob at anchor.

Across the bridge in Narganá, the gleaming golden **statue of Carlos Inaediguine Robinson**, educator and major player in the 1925 Guna Revolution, stands as if in defiance at the centre of the main plaza. Spacious sandy streets lead off the square in grid formation, in stark contrast to most Guna communities' cramped, labyrinthine layouts. Cement houses, occasionally surrounded by a hedge or garden, alternate with traditional cane-and-thatch dwellings, sometimes sprouting satellite dishes. Given that the first missionaries to the *comarca* settled in Narganá, it's no wonder the place has four churches.

ARRIVAL AND DEPARTURE — NARGANÁ AND CORAZÓN DE JESÚS

By plane Aero Albrook and Blue Skies Panama both operate charter flights to Corazón de Jesús (see page 254).

By boat Both islands have 5.30am departures for Cartí. Enquire at the wharf in Corazón de Jesús; in Narganá, Paco, who runs the island's fuel depot by his home at the back of the primary school, is a good source of information.

ACCOMMODATION AND EATING

Hostal Parks By the primary school, Narganá ⊕6137 8678, ⊕piolalejandroparks@hotmail.com. Four bland, tiled-floor a/c rooms, with cable TV – overpriced for what they are but it's probably the best option here, and rates are negotiable. Boat tours can also be arranged; a trip up nearby Río Azúcar (Uwargandub) is recommended. $$

Restaurante YEHIS At the eastern tip of Narganá ⊕6046 5422. One of several restaurants on Narganá offering a pleasant view of bobbing yachts and large plates of tasty seafood – mains include octopus, conch, fish and lobster with rice, salad or *patacones*. Service is often indifferent. $$

Isla Tigre

Populous yet spacious, elongated **Isla Tigre (Digir Dubbu)** has the rare luxury of a couple of slender beaches. This island is managing better than most to sustain Guna mores while opening up to tourism. The northern tip of the island has a grassy stretch (former airstrip) where volleyball is played in the late afternoon. Or you can have a beer in the community bar. Possible inexpensive **excursions** include a visit to the mainland cemetery, a three-hour hike to waterfalls or a snorkelling trip around one of the nearby islands, where coconuts are harvested.

Some aspects of **traditional living** are still practised: families rotate to harvest coconuts, and workers take it in turn to staff the community restaurant. The island also has its own NGO and is actively involved in lobster protection and recycling practices. The **Guna dance** – involving men playing panpipes and women shaking maracas – originated here, and during the mid-October **Feria de Isla Tigre** dance troupes from across the *comarca* compete for prizes. You can catch them rehearsing on some evenings and at weekends.

ARRIVAL AND DEPARTURE — ISLA TIGRE

By boat Isla Tigre is a 1hr 30min boat ride from Cartí. The airstrip on nearby Corazón de Jesús is open to charter flights.

7

ACCOMMODATION

Homestay Digir facebook.com/Isladigir, 6892 4635 (tourist coordinator), islatigrekuna@gmail.com. At the time of writing only homestays were the only accommodation on offer, which will probably entail sleeping in a hammock in the home of your host family and sharing the family meal. Get in touch in advance with the tourism coordinator. $$

Playón Chico

Two cemeteries atop hills on the mainland announce your arrival at the sprawling administrative hub of **Playón Chico (Uggubseni)**, home to around three thousand people. A large, flat, coral-filled pancake packed with cane-and-thatch dwellings, interspersed with functional concrete buildings, the island is wrestling to balance traditional customs with modern developments, but is a vibrant and welcoming place for all that.

The wharf opens out onto the main-square-cum-basketball-court, and a painted stage. A concrete pedestrian bridge leads to the **mainland**, where a football pitch, airstrip and several government buildings, including a secondary school, are located. In the early morning, men armed with machetes stride up the path leading to the cultivated lands (*nainumar*). Westernizing influence is evident in the numerous churches scattered round the island, and in the presence of electricity, which allows for a weekend film night at the community hall by the basketball court, and results in the sound of competing TVs penetrating paper-thin walls as you try to sleep.

Attractive **excursions** include hikes into pristine rainforest taking in the cascading waterfall of Saibar Maid; birdwatching up the Río Grande; and lazy sun-lounging, moderate snorkelling and fishing off nearby coconut isles.

ARRIVAL AND INFORMATION — PLAYÓN CHICO

By plane Air Panama and Blue Skies Panama operate charter flights here (see page 254).

By boat In addition to transfers to Cartí, boat transfer to Isla Tigre and Ailigandi is frequent and easy to organize.

ACCOMMODATION AND EATING

Domy's 200m from the basketball court 6038 5157. The engaging Domy and Nilka offer a three-bed budget dorm in the top floor of a two-tiered wooden house, with shower below and a breezy deck with hammocks from which to watch the world go by. Breakfast and tours to a beach or the mainland can be arranged at extra cost. $$

Refresquería Sol 50m from the basketball court 6136 6541. The best place to eat on the island, offering one of the *comarca*'s more varied menus including good-value *almuerzos*. You should book, and choose your dish, in advance – select from fish, langoustines, pork chops or chicken with rice and lentils – since demand often exceeds supply. $$

THE TRADITIONAL GUNA WAY OF LIFE

Historically the Guna have lived collectively and worked cooperatively. Though some hunting was practised, **fishing** and **subsistence agriculture** – yuca, plantain, rice, maize, sugar cane, cocoa, fruit trees and coconuts – were the mainstay of the economy for many years. In the late 1960s, **coconuts** accounted for seventy percent of the *comarca*'s revenue, bartered for dry goods, such as fuel, clothing and cooking oil, sold by the brightly painted Colombian trading vessels that you still see tethered to the main jetty at communities across the region. More than three million coconuts are still harvested annually.

Guna society is traditionally both matrilocal (when a man marries he moves into his in-laws' compound and works for them) and matrilineal (property is inherited down the female line). But these practices are slipping, and while women's views are respected, men play a larger role as chiefs, healers and interpreters in community meetings. Men undertake most of the agricultural labour, and the entire Guna Congress is male.

Families traditionally live in compounds of cane-and-thatch dwellings, the living quarters crammed with hammocks and the rafters laden with clothing, buckets and utensils. Villages without aqueducts bring fresh water by canoe from the mainland. Seafood accompanied by plantain, rice and coconut are staples, and *dule masi* – a fish stew containing boiled green plantains, coconut and vegetables – is effectively the Guna national dish.

At the heart of community life stands the **onmagged nega** (meeting house), where villagers, including children, congregate most evenings, though attendance is dropping off among the young. The *saila* – usually recognizable by his hat – is the leader in all village matters, though some communities now have several *sailas* to fulfil particular functions. A mixture of songs, chants, stories and talk filter through the walls, as Guna history, mythology and religion are as much a part of the reunions as information-giving, public debate and conflict resolution. Another key community building is the **inna nega**, where the *chicha brava* (*inna* in Guna), the potent mind-numbing sugar-cane-based homebrew, is left to ferment in large clay urns for major celebrations such as a young girl's puberty ritual (see box, page 268).

CHANGES TO GUNA SOCIETY

As in any society, Guna life is evolving: numerous communities now have piped fresh water from the mainland; electricity (albeit limited, and often solar) is available on many village-islands; cement block buildings are increasingly common; shops stock canned food, sweets and biscuits, whose wrappers often litter the streets; the use of mobile phones is mushrooming; and the iconic Guna traditional dress is declining among women. That said, *molas* – the colourful, reverse-appliqué, multilayered panels that make up the most distinctive part of their traditional blouses – are still a major source of income for the Guna.

Christian churches have taken root on some islands, on the understanding that they respect traditional **religion**. Despite the Guna authorities' success in insisting on intercultural bilingual **education**, schooling is primarily about preparing young people for a modern industrialized society. In this respect, many Guna hope that tourism, if managed carefully, may help ensure that changes in lifestyle can coexist with more established mores.

Already, tourism has played a pivotal role in the Guna's reluctant but inevitable metamorphosis from a collective barter economy – the word for "money" does not exist in Dulegaya – to a more individualistic cash economy. The resulting **economic inequalities** have put a strain on communities that are already struggling to deal with major social upheavals due to increasing contact with outsiders (*uagmala*) and returning urbanized Guna who are no longer prepared to live as their ancestors did. **Environmental damage** by outsiders and the Guna themselves constitutes a further challenge, often exacerbated by tourism, especially in western Gunayala. Issues include waste disposal, overfishing, particularly of lobster, reef degradation and deforestation of the mainland, and the threat of rising sea levels due to climate change.

San Ignacio de Tupile

Ten kilometres southeast of Playón Chico, midway along the *comarca*, lies the well-organized community of **San Ignacio de Tupile (Dadnaggwe Dubbir)**. As you step out of a boat at the community pier, you are greeted by a statue of the Virgin Mary – an indication of the island's fairly widespread evangelization. Though tourists rarely visit, the vibe among the 1500 inhabitants is relaxed and welcoming, particularly if your visit coincides with the **patron saint festivities** (July 28–31), when you can join in the celebrations marked by rowing races and various competitions.

Beyond the statue stands the primary school, where a wide main boulevard peels off left. The streets are kept spick-and-span, as community regulations mean families are held responsible for disposing of rubbish on the mainland. Rules are equally strict about getting a permit to leave the island, aimed at curbing what elders see to be the moral decline among some of the younger members of the community. Squeezed between two public phone boxes, the strangely whitened face of General Inatikuña, the community's first *saila* following relocation from the mainland to the island in 1903, stares out across the street.

7

Excursions are available to the unremarkable nearby beach on Ilestup ("Isle of the Englishman", after a gent who lived there in the 1700s) and to the Río Yuandub Gandi, where alligators laze on sandbanks and a rainbow of birds flit in and out of the foliage.

ARRIVAL AND DEPARTURE — SAN IGNACIO DE TUPILE

San Ignacio is a 30–40min **boat ride** from Playón Chico, the nearest airstrip.

EATING

Community restaurant By the wharf. The community's only restaurant is up the stairs to the right by the wharf. It serves a decent plate of fried fish with rice and plantain. $$

The eastern isles

What might loosely be described as the **eastern isles** stretch over the whole of the eastern half of the *comarca*, which, outside the sprinkling of lodges near **Achutupu (Assudub)** and **Mamitupu** (Mammidub) sees precious few outsiders beyond the odd yacht and Colombian trading vessel. Here, lacking the protection of an offshore reef, the seas are rough and transport between communities sparse. After storms, rubbish jettisoned from boats will

PUBERTY RITUALS

Although like many Guna customs, **puberty rituals** are becoming less common, If you spend time in one of the more traditional village-islands you may be lucky enough to be invited to attend one. Whereas adolescent boys pass into adulthood unheralded, a **young girl** traditionally undergoes two important ceremonies. The first, **innamudiggi**, at her first menstruation, prompts several days of confinement in a small ceremonial enclosure cloaked in banana leaves (*surba*) within the house, where she is purified in herbal baths and finally painted from top to toe in the indigo *jagua* dye before being allowed to join the festivities outside. The second celebration, **innasuid**, involving the whole village, entails the young woman being officially named and receiving a ceremonial haircut, a protracted affair signifying that she is now available for marriage. Food is shared, pipes are passed and *chicha* abounds – and the presence of cigarettes and seco in some communities reflects the changing times.

Ironically the young woman at the heart of the festivities misses out on most of the fun, remaining in seclusion until the actual hair-cutting. In an increasing fog of rituals, chants, cocoa-bean incense, tobacco and alcohol, the celebrations, aimed partly at affirming the coexistence of the material and spiritual worlds, continue for several days, until the *chicha* has run out, by which time several people have usually passed out.

wash up on the shore in places. Islands of note include **Agligandi** – home of the Guna Revolution – while the twin settlement of **Ogobsucum** and **Usdub** boasts the archipelago's largest population. Marking the eastern limit of the *comarca*, on the mainland, lies the border town of **Puerto Obaldía** and the more appealing mainland community of **Armila.**

Agligandi

Westernmost of the eastern islands, overlooking coastal mangroves (*ailan*), **Agligandi** (previously **Ailigandi**) has its spot firmly cemented in Guna history as the first place of organized resistance in the Guna Revolution of 1925; note the Guna swastika flag (representing an octopus) fluttering proudly above the rooftops. It's a good place to witness the annual revolution celebrations (see box, page 263). A pivotal figure in the rebellion was Chief Olokindibipilelel (Simral Colman), whose **statue** – incongruously clad in suit and bowler hat – claims a central position on the densely populated island of around 1200, next to the obligatory basketball court. A warren of pathways weaves through tightly packed thatched dwellings, in the midst of which is squeezed the tiny **Museo Olonigli**. A small local restaurant lies midway along the central avenue.

Museo Olonigli

No fixed hours • Donations welcome

As with other museums in the *comarca*, **Museo Olonigli** comprises a single room stuffed with artefacts whose significance only becomes clear through the explanations (in Spanish) of the owner-curator, Roy Cortéz Olonigli. He elaborates on traditional culture drawing on his own woodcarvings, which depict Guna symbols and rituals.

ARRIVAL AND DEPARTURE — AGLIGANDI

By boat Agligandi is a 10min boat ride from the Achutupu (Assudub) airstrip (see page 269). The community transport association offers three boats a week (usually Mon, Wed & Fri) to Cartí, which can stop off at other islands including Playón Chico and Isla Tigre en route.

Achutupu and Mamitupu

Five kilometres east of Agligandi, the unusual crescent-shaped island of **Achutupu (Assudub)**, dotted with banana trees and coconut palms, has a deceptively spacious feel. The village has a primary school, health centre and restaurant by the pier, alongside a basketball court. It's inadvisable to swim off the strip of sand that might optimistically be called a beach, due to pollution. There's nowhere to stay on the island itself, but higher-end lodgings are close at hand, and Mamitupu is a short boat ride away. A small restaurant lies midway along the central avenue.

Just a kilometre southeast of Achutupu, **Mamitupu (Mammidub)** has ten *sailas* governing a traditional village of about 1200. Photography is forbidden here, though it is permitted on excursions to the mainland, and residents still need a permit to leave the island.

ARRIVAL AND DEPARTURE — ACHUTUPU AND MAMITUPU

By plane The airstrip, 200m across from Achutupu on the mainland, receives the occasional Air Panama charter flights. Motorized dugouts greet the plane and will ferry you to Achutupu for a few dollars.

By boat There are occasional boats to Cartí, though it can be a 4–5hr haul.

ACCOMMODATION

Akwa Reef Lodge (formerly Akwadup Lodge) West of Achutupu ⓦakwareeflodge.com. A 5min boat ride west of Achutupu, this exclusive (by Guna standards) lodge offers comfort and seclusion in a row of six simple brightly painted over-the-water wooden bungalows. They're set rather close together but nicely decorated, with two double beds with decent mattresses in each, solar-powered ceiling fans and mosquito nets. Rates, which are on the high side, can include meals, lodgings and airport transfer. Community taxes are extra. Accommodation only $$; all-inclusive $$$$

Cabañas Kalu Obaki Mamitupu 6478 4434 (Waica), 6489 9918 (Pablo Nuñez, who speaks English). Set apart from the main village in a palm-shaded grassy end of the island stand four simple huts, with decent mattresses protected by mosquito nets, a good-size table, private washing area (for bucket and water ablutions) and solar-powered electricity. Flush toilets are shared, as is the pleasant *rancho* dining area. Rates include meals and community taxes. $$$

Ogobsucum and Usdub

Beyond Mamitupu, completing the remaining 75km to Puerto Obaldía, you pass the densely matted, thatch rooftops of the *comarca*'s most populous communities: the four-thousand-strong twin settlements of **Ogobsucum** and **Usdub**, renowned for their gold craftwork. The next notable community is the pine-clad **Isla Pino (Dubbag)**, which unlike any other island in the *comarca*, has a large hill; though only a little more than a square kilometre in size, it boasts a couple of forest trails and a picturesque waterside thatched village. Travellers rarely venture this far east to these more traditional communities – you will need to check in with the police and ask **permission** of the *saila* to visit or stay on an island, and dress appropriately (see box, page 257). It is usually possible to negotiate with a family for a hammock or bed, pay for meals and engage the services of someone to explore the rivers and rainforest on the mainland. The seas along this stretch of coastline are particularly rough and should only be navigated in a decent boat, with life jackets, not the shallow dugouts many boatmen use.

7

Puerto Obaldía

PUERTO OBALDÍA is the last major "town" before the Colombian border. Despite a tidy park, a decent playing field, clean streets and a scenic seaside location, it is an unendearing encampment, where the frontier police in combat gear guard against drug runners, Colombian guerrillas and smugglers. Though technically within the *comarca*, the community has a mixed population of Guna, Colombian refugees and non-Guna Panamanians. You could end up with a more intimate knowledge of the town than you would like unless you've booked an air ticket to Panama City in advance, since seats are often oversubscribed.

ARRIVAL AND INFORMATION — PUERTO OBALDÍA

BY PLANE

Air Panama operates mid-morning shared charter flights Tues, Fri & Sun (provided there is demand; check prices with the airline in advance) from Panama City's Albrook Airport to Puerto Obaldía with almost immediate return flights to the capital (1hr). The airstrip is a 2min walk from the centre.

BY BOAT

To Gunayala Regular unscheduled speedboats head west up the *comarca* to Cartí (6–8hr; $110/person) from Puerto Obaldía, usually departing before 9am when they're full; ask around. You should also be able to negotiate a price if you want to be dropped off at another community along the way. Seas can be particularly rough and dangerous over the first three hours (especially Dec–Feb), even when conditions are considered "safe". It is imperative that you check the condition of the boat beforehand (see page 256).

To Colombia Visitors travelling on to Colombia from Puerto

SECURITY IN THE FRONTIER ZONE

The **security situation** in the frontier zone is liable to change at a moment's notice so be sure to check out the latest information on the ground before you head into this area. In addition to the relatively safe boat-hopping route (see above), some travellers take the unofficial overland route from Puerto Obaldía via La Miel, hike across the border to Sapzurro in Colombia, and then head on to Capurganá. However, this is not advisable; although many people make the journey without a hitch, a few never arrive. Importantly, this route (from Colombia to Panama) has now become a popular route for migrants trying to reach the US (see page 25).

Obaldía (see page 24) take a launch (1hr) to the resort town of Capurganá, from where a further ferry to Turbo, or Necoclí, and onward bus to Medellín or Cartagena are possible.

IMMIGRATION

Before crossing the Colombian border, or after arriving from Colombia, you'll need to visit immigration (daily 8am–4pm; a hefty charge to attend at other times), just off the park, for an entry or exit stamp. When arriving in Panama, you may also be asked for proof of onward travel out of the country and evidence of the means to support yourself financially. You then need to swing by the police post, to register and have your belongings searched (see page 25). Searches here are very thorough, from your tube of toothpaste to your underwear.

ACCOMMODATION AND EATING

Hotel Doña Primitiva Near the park. Simple but clean fan-ventilated rooms, with cold en-suite shower, accommodating two to four people. $$

Las Tres "L" Corner of the park. Friendly restaurant with a pleasant patio where you can get a decent breakfast and lunch, though options are limited. Arrive early for lunch, since food often runs out when visitor numbers are high. $–$$

7

Armila

Highly recommended is a detour to the welcoming Guna community of **ARMILA**, which is idyllically located at the base of a forest-cloaked hill where two rivers empty into the sea. Atypically spacious, and run by five *sailas*, the village boasts an intriguing mix of traditional cane *cabañas* and more substantial Afro-Antillean-style wood-and-thatch houses, sometimes painted or on stilts. Beyond, more than 4km of cream-coloured windswept beach extends along the coast. **Turtle watching** is one of several tourist **activities**; others include jungle walks, river trips by dugout and swimming in the local freshwater lagoon. Provided the sea is calm, beach and snorkelling trips can be organized to the lovely Playa Blanca at La Miel, by the Colombian border.

Turtle watching

Armila is one of the world's most important nesting sites for **leatherback turtles**, with several thousand nests protected by the community. The visitor community fee goes towards the conservation and monitoring project. Nesting occurs between February and July, peaking between late April/May and June. There's a major **turtle festival** during the third week in May (Festival Cultural y Ecológico de las Tortugas Marinas), involving traditional music and dancing, during which a three-night package deal is usually offered, and camping is permitted.

ARRIVAL AND DEPARTURE — ARMILA

By plane *Cabañas Ibedi* (see below) has a charter flight deal with Air Panama for a return fare from Panama City of $270.

By boat Although Armila is just a 20min boat ride up the coast from Puerto Obaldía, landing on the beach (there is no jetty) is frequently impossible due to rough waves (especially Dec–Feb and sometimes July and Aug), or water spilling out of the river-mouths following torrential rain.

On foot When conditions are too rough to travel by boat, you will need to make a moderately strenuous uphill hike (1hr 30min–2hr) to reach Armila from Puerto Obaldía, accompanied by a guide.

ACCOMMODATION

★ **Cabañas Ibedi** ibedialnatural.com. Run by Ignacio Crespo, known as "Nacho", an engaging, trained multilingual biologist and conservationist. Three simple, tidy raised cabins of varying sizes with private porches sit among trees and a lovely hibiscus garden. Basic toilet/shower facilities can be shared or private and there's solar-powered electricity at night. Food is tasty and activities varied, including river kayaking, guided hikes, a snorkelling beach excursion and turtle observation (in the season). Food, tours and transfer from Puerto Obaldía are included in the rates. Cheaper deals, in more rudimentary accommodation, can sometimes be negotiated for budget travellers. Minimum two-night stay. $$$

Yaug Galu cabaña 333 2060 (public phone) or 6023 2311. Community *cabaña* attached to the turtle conservation foundation, Fundación Yaug Galu (facebook.com/yauggalu). Dorm beds are available to tourists when the organization is not hosting visiting researchers. $

The Darién and eastern Panama

LAGO BAYANO

The Darién and eastern Panama

Mention of the Darién – Panama's largest province, abutting Colombia – conjures up a host of images, some alluring, others less so; some true, others vastly exaggerated. What is not in dispute is the region's status as one of the last true tropical wildernesses – though even this is under threat – encompassing swathes of mountainous forest containing an astounding array of wildlife. This is most apparent in Parque Nacional Darién, which provides unparalleled opportunities for serious hiking and birdwatching.

The Darién covers a sparsely populated, rugged expanse sprawling across almost twelve thousand square kilometres; it reaches its highest point at Cerro Tacarcuna (1875m) by the border, but includes numerous peaks of more than 1000m. The province also boasts Panama's longest river, the **Río Tuira**, which empties into the Golfo de San Miguel, a vast mangrove-lined body of water that opens out into the Pacific Ocean. Yet travellers are increasingly drawn to the Darién as much by its people as by its compelling scenery; several communities populated by the closely related **Emberá** and **Wounaan** – the region's main indigenous peoples – have opened up to tourists. In the **Comarca Emberá-Wounaan** or in communities just outside the *comarca*, such as **La Marea** and **Mogue**, you can stay overnight in a village and learn about the intricacies of basketry or woodcarving, for which they are world-renowned, or hike through steaming rainforest to spot harpy eagles – the area boasts the greatest concentration of these raptors in the world. **Guna** communities also exist, mainly in **eastern Panama province**, historically considered part of the Darién. Their two small *comarcas* stretch along the shores of **Lago Bayano**, a vast reservoir 100km east of Panama City, which enjoys a picturesque setting in an increasingly deforested landscape, and has an impressive network of caves.

Brief history

The Darién bore witness to some of the bloodiest confrontations between the invading conquistadors, greedy for gold and power, and the indigenous groups desperate to defend their territories – most notably at **Santa María La Antigua del Darién**, the first successful Spanish settlement on the mainland since the time of Columbus (across the border in present-day Colombia). Balboa took Santa María in 1510, and later intercepted an attempt to reclaim the city, led by Cacique **Cémaco**, a pivotal figure in the indigenous resistance; he captured all the alliance's chiefs, bar Cémaco, and had them hanged as an example. It is perhaps only fitting that Balboa, who first espied the Pacific from the Darién, also met his end here – beheaded by Pedrerías Dávila in the coastal town of Acla (in present-day Gunayala) – while Santa María was eventually abandoned by the Spanish in favour of Panama City, and was razed to the ground by indigenous forces in 1524.

The region's population

The indigenous peoples most in evidence today are the **Emberá** and **Wounaan**. Both groups may have migrated from the Chocó regions of Colombia (which is why they are often referred to collectively as Chocós). **Guna** presence is still recalled in some of the place names, notably the snaking Río Tuira, and though most Guna moved to the Caribbean coast, pockets remain in the more recently formed *comarcas* of Madugandi and Wargandi, and in isolated communities in Panama and Darién provinces. The other substantial population, dominant in the regional capital of La Palma and in settlements lining the Golfo de San Miguel, are the **Afro-Darienites**, descendants

YAVIZA RESIDENTS

Highlights

1 Lago Bayano Take a boat ride in search of caiman lurking in the lake's muddy fringes, and venture into the bat-infested Cuevas de Majé. See page 279

2 Parque Nacional Darién On the banks of a picturesque river, the MiAmbiente refuge Rancho Frío provides the main access to the natural wonders of Parque Nacional Darién. See page 283

3 Staying with the Emberá or Wounaan Spend a few nights in the villages of La Marea, Mogue or Playa Muerto, where you can learn about Emberá culture and the surrounding rainforest. See page 286

4 Harpy eagle nests Stake out the nest of the world's most powerful raptor and wait for a parent to swoop into view and deliver a monkey to their needy chick. See page 288

5 Río Sambú A gloriously sinuous river, lined with mangroves and rainforest, and populated with ibis, herons and kingfishers. See page 289

6 The Pacific coast A voyage by boat to Playa Muerto, Bahía Piñas or Jaqué from La Palma hugs a rugged, mountainous coastline, where spectacularly forested steep slopes tumble into the ocean. See page 291

HIGHLIGHTS ARE MARKED ON THE MAP ON PAGE 276

on the whole of the *cimarrones* – escaped enslaved populations brought over by the Spanish, who fled and waged warfare from their own strongholds (*palenques*) in the rainforest, forming strategic alliances with pirates and indigenous groups. Some of their communities are now mixed with Emberá and Wounaan, and, in some parts, with **Afro-Colombian refugees**, who fled the more recent civil conflict across the border. The completion of the Interamericana to Yaviza in 1979 opened the floodgates to **colonos** (the name often given to migrating *mestizo* cattle ranchers and farmers predominantly from the Azuero Peninsula), who have now cleared vast tracts of land along the highway for pasture, and constitute around fifty percent of the total population of Darién province.

Current challenges

Though the joint Comarca Emberá-Wounaan was established in 1983, covering around 25 percent of Darién province, indigenous communities continue to face multiple threats to their lands, livelihoods and cultures. These range from **violent clashes** with *mestizo* settlers encroaching on their territory, to friction with government, fuelled by the territorial overlap with the national park, whose regulations restrict traditional hunting and agricultural practices. Illegal logging, which has escalated in recent years, is also fuelling **deforestation**, and communities are constantly at risk of violence and extortion from **criminal gangs** trafficking

THE EMBERÁ AND WOUNAAN

Two separate but related ethnic groups speaking mutually unintelligible languages, the majority of Panama's **Emberá** (warriors famed for their poisonous blow-darts) and **Wounaan** (more noted for their artistry) inhabit wood-and-thatch huts along the Darién's numerous rivers – though the increasing presence of zinc roofs and cement buildings is indicative of encroaching modernization. As former seminomadic hunter-gatherers, it is only relatively recently that their communities started to live in fixed villages, a government-promoted project primarily to facilitate schooling and access to modern health care; before, family homes, though still sprinkled along the rivers as they are today, formed temporary bases from which to hunt and practise limited slash-and-burn agriculture before moving on, allowing forest to recover.

The groups' wooden **houses** are built on stilts, to protect them from wild animals and unwelcome intruders, as well as rising floodwaters. Semi-open sides permit cooling breezes to enter while preserving a degree of privacy. The platform, accessed by a tree trunk, with notches carved out as steps, constitutes a living space with a fire pit for cooking; crucially, the heat prevents the thatched roof from rotting during the rainy season, and keeps destructive insects at bay. Traditionally, the largest building in the community is the *bujia* or *casa comunal*, a splendid circular construction with a soaring conical ceiling, where meetings are held, guests are received and ceremonies take place. Missionaries have been chipping away at traditional **beliefs** since the time of the conquistadors, and while shamanism persists, villagers are more likely today to head for the government medical centre than put their trust in traditional medicine.

To learn more about Emberá or Wounaan village life, consider **staying the night** (see box, page 286).

arms or cocaine, or smuggling people through the Darien Gap. In the last decade, the flow of US-bound **migrants** through the rainforest – which peaked at over half a million in 2023 – has had a major impact on communities and on the environment. Although the migrant economy has improved some village economies, it has disrupted traditional ways of life, resulting in alcoholism and drug addiction among some male youth, while the huge amounts of human waste have contaminated rivers.

ARRIVAL AND INFORMATION — THE DARIÉN AND EASTERN PANAMA

Few tourists come to Darién and those that do generally visit on a **tour**. That said, it is entirely possible to visit **independently** – though you need to wrestle with Panamanian bureaucracy first (see box, page 278), and have time, money and some Spanish-language skills.

INDEPENDENT TRAVEL

BY PLANE

There are no longer any scheduled flights to the Darién, but Air Panama (airpanama.com) and other companies offer shared charter flights to Jaqué via nearby Bahía Piñas (1hr 15min).

BY BUS AND BOAT

Bus and boat transport in the Darién requires patience and flexibility. Timetables are only loosely adhered to and services may be delayed or cancelled if there are insufficient passengers to warrant a trip. Set out as early as possible from Panama City's Albrook bus terminal to reach your destination the same day. For Darién bus schedules, call 6792 9493 or visit their office in the terminal.

To Yaviza and Metetí Beyond the expensive express bus to Yaviza (midnight; around 5–6hr), most buses bound for the Darién stop at Metetí, where you transfer to a local minibus for Yaviza. Journey times are often dependent on the condition of the paved road, especially in the rainy season. The last daily bus to the Darién leaves Albrook at 5.20pm.

To La Palma To reach La Palma and other destinations in the Golfo de San Miguel, take the bus to Metetí, then a minibus shuttle to nearby Puerto Quimba (see page 281), from where there is a water-taxi to La Palma (see page 285). Some communities also have boats that leave from Puerto Quimba and may bypass La Palma altogether if full.

SAFETY AND RED TAPE IN THE DARIÉN

For many years the rule of thumb for **safety** in the Darién has been to draw an imaginary line from the Caribbean Colombian border, through Yaviza, to Bahía Piñas and Jaqué on the Pacific coast, beyond which you should not travel. Rancho Frío excepted, this still holds; however, due to the occasional flare-up in violence and drug-trafficking-related incidents (see page 43), other places may be temporarily off limits too. Always check before travelling with your consulate, and once on your travels, continue to seek local advice, especially from the frontier police (SENAFRONT) and village authorities. Security is always tightened up again after any major incident.

The restriction that foreign travellers had to obtain a **permit** from SENAFRONT was theoretically lifted in 2016. However, in practice they can still make life difficult for independent travellers (and refuse you access to certain places) if you haven't informed them of your travel plans in advance. If questioned at any control point, you need to give a precise destination and dates, whatever your actual plans (or lack of) might be. You can either go in person to the SENAFRONT office, opposite the Summit on the road to Gamboa, or send an e-mail to Ⓔ dirgeneral@senafront.gob.pa, addressed to the 'Director del SENAFRONT', noting your name, nationality, passport number, dates and destinations. They advise doing this at least three days before you want to travel. You can write in English and if you get no response telephone (Ⓣ 527 1011) since they should send you a permit (free), which you should photocopy and present whenever asked at checkpoints. SENAFRONT maintains a presence in many Darién communities, and you may be required to sign in with them and present your ID on arrival.

8

COMMUNICATIONS

Communication is very difficult and intermittent in the Darién. Some communities have no mobile phone reception; you might need several days and several attempts to make contact either by email or phone, since people may only have access to these services when they visit a large town. Outside Metetí, wi-fi is rarely available; we have indicated in our accommodation listings where it exists. Moreover, unlike in some areas of Panama, virtually nobody will speak any English.

GETTING AROUND

By boat Once in the Darién proper, transport is by boat, usually in a motorized fibreglass boat (*panga*), but in more remote destinations by dugout (*piragua*). Boat travel entails waiting around as many communities are on tidal rivers, only accessible at high tide, especially in the dry season. It's infinitely cheaper, though not always comfortable, to travel in a community boat, or *colectivo*, already heading to your destination (*como pasajero*) than to hire a boat privately (*viaje especial*). One-way *colectivo* fares from Puerto Quimba, for example, range from $5 to La Palma, $25 to Sambú, $40 to Playa Muerto and $70 for as far as Jaqué. For private charter you will have to cover the cost of the fuel (often for the return trip, even if you're only travelling one way), the captain and probably a poleman; find out fuel costs and the amount required for your journey from another source before negotiating a price, and note that if hiring someone's services for an overnight stay in a village, you may need to pay for *their* lodging and food too.

Guides You cannot visit the national park without a guide (see page 279); you will also need to hire a guide in the indigenous villages to explore the surrounding forest. Most villages have local Spanish-speaking guides (around $25–35/day) who will have varying levels of knowledge about the rainforest and its wildlife. One or two may speak a little English.

Panama province

Panama province east of the canal is known less for any sightseeing charms than for rampant deforestation and the continuing urban spread out towards Chepo – an unappealing agro-commercial town and former gateway to the Darién. That said, **Lago Bayano**, some 90km east of Panama City is worth a half-day, while the two adjoining Emberá communities just south of the Interamericana at **Ipetí** provide the other main reason to stop en route to the Darién proper. Popular with day-trippers and budget tours from Panama City, their relatively barren location lacks the rainforest charm of other villages in Darién province. However, if you're keen to drop in, any bus bound for Yaviza, Metetí or Agua Fría will let you off by the roadside, from where it's a twenty-minute walk along a gravel road.

Lago Bayano

Though earmarked for "development", **LAGO BAYANO** remains a picturesque location, perfect for boat rides and picnics, and with a fascinating **cave network** at its southeastern tip. Its apparent charm and tranquillity, however, belie the anger of indigenous communities – displaced when the reservoir was formed in 1976 and still awaiting full compensation from the government – and the acres of forest that were submerged when the Río Chepo (or Río Bayano) was dammed to supply Panama City with more hydropower; dead tree trunks protruding eerily from the water act as poignant reminders. The economic mainstay of the sixteen lakeside communities – including those of the Guna **Comarca de Madugandi**, as well as Emberá, Wounaan and Ladino settlements – is the commercial fishing of tilapia.

Named after Bayano, a charismatic leader of a major settlement of *cimarrones* (see box, page 280), the 350-square-kilometre reservoir is a popular day-trip destination from Panama City; at weekends, families spill out of vehicles at the impressive **Puente Bayano**, which fords the lake's narrowest point, and pile into motor **launches** for island picnics, fishing trips or tours of the lake, on the lookout for caimans, crocodiles and otters slithering around the muddy banks.

ORGANIZED TOURS TO THE DARIÉN

Though **customized itineraries** can also be arranged, **all-inclusive tours** generally leave Panama City (usually Dec–April), and include transport to and around the Darién, as well as accommodation, meals and non-alcoholic drinks, activities and bilingual guiding services with a naturalist guide in Spanish and English. Bear in mind that two days of any trip are spent getting there and getting back from Panama City, so a five-day tour should be a minimum. You may also be able to negotiate a reduction in price if you agree to meet the tour in the Darién itself – usually Yaviza or Puerto Quimba. Daily all-inclusive rates vary enormously from $120–550/person (often sharing), depending on the company, and level of comfort and expertise. Most trips need a minimum of four people to run.

Canopy Camp Border of the Reserva Hidrológica Filo del Tallo, east of Metetí, off the Interamericana ⓦ canopytower.com. Part of the *Canopy* "family", the camp comprises eight luxurious African safari tents (with electricity and fans) laden with local, sustainably sourced teak, on raised platforms that provide private observation decks. Aimed mainly at birders, packages also include excursions of interest to general nature-lovers.

Ecotour Darién C Villa Nueva, Santa Fé ⓦ ecotourdarien.com. Working with local guides and communities, this sound, Darién-based Panamanian ecotour company (with some English-speaking guides) offers several moderately priced multiday tours including to a birding lodge up the Río Chucunaque, to the MIA refuge at Rancho Frío, and a five-day trek across the mountains from Sambú to Playa Muerto, leaving from Metetí.

Jungle Treks ⓦ jungletreks.com. Former ANCON Expeditions guide Rick Morales operates his own trekking outfit with local guides. The "Darién Gap Expedition" (5–12 days) involving days of backpacking and camping. Minimum four people and six-months' notice needed.

Tours Darién ⓦ toursdarien. Emberá director Jairo Cunampio works with several guides with different specialisms, offering tours to indigenous communities or to the national park, including birdwatching and nature walks.

Travel Darién ⓦ traveldarienpanama.com. Indigenously-owned company operating out of the Emberá community of La Chunga, but can include nights in the rainforest sleeping in a hammock, or tours focused on birdwatching.

EL "REY NEGRO BAYANO"

While his origins and date of death remain uncertain, there is no doubt that **El "Rey Negro Bayano"** (also Ballano or Vaino) was the most successful leader of the *cimarrones* and the undisputed king, referred to as such even by the Spanish. Commanding the loyalty of between four hundred and 1200 followers, he constructed an impenetrable hilltop fortress from where he repeatedly attacked Spanish forces and plundered mule trains on the Camino Real. Despite conducting three major campaigns against him (1553–56), the governor of Panama failed to quell the resistance, prompting the viceroy of Peru to charge a certain Captain Pedro de Ursúa with the specific task of crushing the *cimarrones* rebellion. Realizing he couldn't take Bayano's mountain stronghold by force, Ursúa used deceit. Pretending to offer Bayano a peaceful settlement and half the land, the conquistador arranged a celebratory feast. There – so the story goes – he drugged the wine, which stunned Bayano and his men, resulting in their easy capture, thereby ending six years of revolt against the Spanish Crown.

Cuevas de Majé

Southeastern tip of Lago Bayano • Charge

Lago Bayano's most fascinating destination is the **Cuevas de Majé**, comprising a 1km-long system of limestone caverns, replete with colonies of bats clinging to calcitic formations. Towards the end of the dry season, it's possible to wade your way (up to your chest) through the entire system, emerging in a steep-sided verdant gully, dripping with mosses and ferns. At other times, the raised water level means you'll need to go partway in a boat before stepping into the water, and may not be able to make it through on foot. In either case, you'll need a headlamp, footwear with a good grip and a minimum amount of clothing that you're happy to get soaked. Make sure your tour also takes in the impressive **rock walls** that enclose the entrance to the nearby Río Tigre.

Comarca de Madugandi

North of Lago Bayano • Charge for the *comarca*

The indigenous community of **Akua Guna** (or Loma de Piedra) at the western end of the Puente Bayano marks the entry to the Guna **Comarca de Madugandi**, established in 1996, which includes eighty percent of the reservoir's surface area and extends from the forested northern shores of the lake up the mountainous backdrop of the Serranía de San Blas. Well over three thousand Guna inhabit the *comarca*, dispersed among fourteen communities; some, such as **Icanti**, **Pintupu** and **Tabardi**, are open to receiving tourists, but you'll need to stay in someone's home as there's no organized accommodation available as yet. Enquire at Akua Guna if you wish to visit.

ARRIVAL AND TOURS — LAGO BAYANO

Tour companies in the capital offer expensive **bus-and-boat excursions** from the capital (from around $160), though they sometimes include kayaking, but it's easy, and much cheaper, to get there by bus and visit the lake and caves with a local operator.

By bus Buses depart from Albrook bus terminal for Puente Bayano (4am–4.40pm; every 40min; 2hr), which hosts the first of several police checkpoints. Buses from Yaviza and Metetí can also drop you off at the bridge.

Boat tours Reserve your launch in advance (especially at weekends) as organizing a boat and guide on the spot (from $70/boat for up to five) can take time: for lake tours, contact Noy Ortega (T 6744 5300, prefers 24hr notice), who has a house by the bridge.

Bayano Adventures W panamacaves.com, W bayanoadventures.com. A local tour company, with a pleasant lakeside setting on a dairy farm, which runs cave tours. It also offers family-focused fun such as kayaking and farm-based activities. You can camp here in your own tent or in one provided, but avoid weekends and holiday periods if you want some peace and quiet.

The Interamericana to Yaviza

Agua Fría No. 1, a place easily missed were it not for the police checkpoint, marks the entry into Darién province. From here, traffic tends to speed along the remaining 110km of virtually straight (predominantly tarred) road past pastureland, the odd settlement and occasional teak plantation to the end of the tarmac at **Yaviza**, spelling the end of the Interamericana.

Puerto Lara

Five kilometres downriver from the important agricultural community of **Santa Fé** lies **PUERTO LARA**. One of the few communities to receive plenty of technical support and funding, this Wounaan village of around six hundred people has a functioning fishing association, computer centre, basketball court and produces high-quality crafts (see ⓦecoturismowounaan.com). Though both Emberá and Wounaan are renowned for their **basketry** and tagua **carving**, it is the Wounaan who historically have been artists and have the greater reputation; many pieces from Puerto Lara are sent straight to Panama City for sale, but some can still be perused in the village, where workshops in *artesanía* are also held. Beyond the village, **boat trips**, **guided hikes**, **birdwatching** (within a small patch of forest of modest appeal), fishing and traditional dances can all be arranged by contacting the president of the tourism committee (see below).

ARRIVAL AND DEPARTURE — PUERTO LARA

8

TO/FROM METETÍ OR PANAMA CITY

By bus Buses between Panama City and Metetí stop at Santa Fé (every 30min; 40min from Metetí, roughly 4hr 30min from Panama City). Alight at the turn-off to Puerto Lara on the Interamericana, 22km before Metetí. Ask at the house at the junction for a taxi for the 8km drive to Puerto Lara. Occasional *colectivos* leave the village for the Interamericana – the stop for the *colectivo* return trip is on the access road.

ACCOMMODATION AND EATING

Community accommodation Contact the president of the tourist committee, Neldo ⓦecoturismowounaan.com. A plain open-sided wooden "lodge" overlooking the main street offers several partitioned rooms with mattresses and shared toilet and shower around the back (and one pricier, relatively deluxe room with private bath). Visitors pay for food purchases, plus a daily group fee for the tourist coordinator and cook. Doubles $$

Metetí

A police security checkpoint heralds your impending arrival in **METETÍ**, a long, strung-out settlement that is an increasingly important commercial and administrative hub. It's hardly endearing, but if you're travelling around much in the Darién, you're likely to pass through more than once, since it offers good links with Yaviza – from where it's a shortish hop to El Real, the main gateway to the national park – and **Puerto Quimba**, which provides a water-taxi link to La Palma, capital of the Darién and access point for many of the Emberá and Wounaan communities.

The village's de facto centre lies across the bridge at the turn-off to Puerto Quimba, where there's a taxi rank, a handful of warehouse-like shops and a bus station.

ARRIVAL AND INFORMATION — METETÍ

By bus The bus station is 1.5km up the Puerto Quimba road from the main junction. There are direct services to Panama City (2am–5.40pm; every 40min; 5–6hr), or you can flag down a bus from Yaviza at the junction with the Interamericana. Buses to Yaviza (5.30am–6pm; every 30min; 50min, depending on road conditions) usually (but not always) leave from the bus station and also pick up passengers at the junction with the Interamericana. Buses also run to Puerto Quimba (5am–5.30pm; every 30min; 30min), to meet the water-taxi to and from La Palma (5am–6pm; every 30min; 30min).

Taxis Taxis will ferry you from the junction to the terminal for very little, charging slightly more to take you to the bank.

MIA office The Mi Ambiente office is just north of the T-junction (Mon–Fri 8am–4pm).

ACCOMMODATION AND EATING

Crown Darién 500m before the bus station on the Puerto Quimba road instagram.com/crownd_14. This small hotel has more character than other options in Metetí, though rooms need some TLC. Thirteen en-suite rooms – some with balcony – offer tepid showers but are enhanced by a/c and cable TV. The on-site bar-restaurant dishes up a few basic meals. $

Hospedaje Aruba 400m before the bus station on the Puerto Quimba road 6344 2388. Aesthetics are not high on the agenda in this tatty hotel, offering desultory service and bland rooms. But the tiled bathrooms are clean (cold water), the mattresses firm and you get cable TV, a/c and free wi-fi. It's a suitable alternative if the *Crown*'s full. $

Hotel & Restaurante Bellagio Signposted off the Puerto Quimba road facebook.com/bellagiometeti. The best place to eat in town, and in air-conditioned comfort. Dishes are roasted or grilled, a rare pleasure in the Darién. The town's fanciest rooms are overpriced, but there's a sparkling pool, and lower rates can be negotiated. $$

DIRECTORY

Banks One of the Darién's two national banks, with an ATM, is in Metetí, 2km west of the main road junction. Another ATM is by the stop for Panama-bound buses at the T-junction.

8

Yaviza

The gently rolling final 50km of the Interamericana to **YAVIZA** is mercifully slightly more tree-lined than the stretch between Chepo and Metetí. It comes to an abrupt halt at the banks of the Río Chucunaque, hidden behind a high chainlink fence and reams of barbed wire.

Marking the official start of the infamous **Darién Gap** (*Tapón del Darién* – literally Darién cork or plug), the highway hiatus between Central and South America, Yaviza simultaneously exudes a lethargic end-of-the-road torpor and an edgy frontier-town feel. The mixed population of around three thousand (Afro-Darienite, Emberá, Wounaan and *mestizo*) eyes outsiders warily, while gun-toting frontier police officers routinely patrol the town.

Yaviza's only interest to visitors is as a stepping stone to El Real, the gateway to **Parque Nacional Darién**, or to the Distrito Cémaco, the northern segment of the Comarca Emberá-Wounaan, which has been out of bounds to visitors for years on account of the security situation.

During the day, most of the action occurs at the **wharf**, where buses pull in: supplies are loaded onto a flotilla of motorized *piraguas* headed for communities upriver, while mounds of plantain and yuca bound for the city are heaved onto trucks, and the surrounding makeshift *fondas* and restaurants do a thriving trade.

ARRIVAL AND INFORMATION — YAVIZA

By bus Buses for Yaviza, via Santa Fé and Metetí, leave Panama City's Albrook terminal (3.15am–1.30pm; every 40min–1hr; 6–7hr; express bus at midnight). Many stop at Metetí if there are few passengers, where you transfer onto a local minibus to Yaviza (see page 281). Buses leave Yaviza for Panama City (3.15am–4pm; every 40min–1hr) and for Metetí (6am–5.20pm; every 30min).

Police registration On arrival, visit the heavily fortified SENAFRONT headquarters – take the left-hand pavement from the bus stop to register and show your permit.

Parque Nacional Darién HQ 100m beyond the SENAFRONT barracks. You should have paid your park fees online in advance (see page 42) though your guide might have done all the red tape for you and included the fees in the rate. The MIA office (Mon–Fri 8am–4pm; 299 6430) will want to see your passport, the SENAFRONT permit and the bank receipt or screenshot of the online payment to prove that you have paid your park fees. They will also want to know that you have engaged the services of a guide. Alternatively, you can visit the *Áreas Protegidas* office at the park headquarters in Albrook (miambiente.gob.pa/contactenos).

WILDLIFE IN PARQUE NACIONAL DARIÉN

The biodiversity in **Parque Nacional Darién** is staggering even as it is shrinking. More than 450 **bird species** have been recorded, including an array of vibrantly coloured macaws and parrots and strange-named rarities such as the beautiful treerunner, scale-crested pygmy tyrant and Chuck-will's-widow. Mammal species top 168, with numerous endemics and endangered animals lurking in the lush vegetation; the park offers the best chance, albeit slender, of glimpsing any of the big-five cats (see page 311), or a Baird's **tapir** – though spotting their footprints in the early morning mud is more likely – and even the occasional **spectacled bear** has been sighted. Yet the arboreal richness of the **rainforest** in the Darién demands just as much attention, with tracts of primary and secondary growth and a towering canopy of barrigón, spiny cedar and graceful platypodium. A visit in March or April is rewarded with the golden crown of the guayacán, heralding the start of the rains, and the russet bloom of the silvery cuipo trees looking down on the already lofty forest canopy, favourite nesting site of the world's largest concentration of **harpy eagles** (see box, page 288). Most of this can only truly be appreciated from the air, or from breaks in the tree line when ascending the region's peaks. On the forest floor, the scene is very different: dark and dank, and dominated by gnarled tree trunks entwined with vines or studded with vicious spines, vast buttress roots, dangling lianas, ferns and rotting leaf litter.

The park was declared a UNESCO World Heritage Site in 1981 and a Biosphere Reserve in 1983, but the **protection** it is offered in practice is worth little more than the paper it's written on, as illegal hunting, logging, extraction of rare plants and animals, and slash-and-burn agriculture continue unchecked. Ironically, the long list of undesirables that have taken refuge in the rainforest – FARC guerrillas, right-wing paramilitaries, drug traffickers, smugglers and bandits – have acted as unwitting conservationists by frightening off most settlers and major developments, though earlier fighting over the border in Colombia resulted in an influx of refugees, who also cleared land to cultivate. In recent years, the park has also become a major route for migrants fleeing from conflict, poverty and persecution in countries as far away as Bangladesh, Syria and Libya, attempting to reach North America via South and Central America (see box, page 308). This has resulted in substantial environmental damage as well as compounding human misery.

8

ACCOMMODATION AND EATING

Travellers heading to Parque Nacional Darién should note that Yaviza is a better place to stock up with **supplies** than El Real. After 7pm, you'll be unlikely to find anywhere serving food.

Hospedaje Sobia Kirú 60m along the cement path at right angles to the wharf ⓣ 6150 5449. Leticia will give you a warm welcome. Travellers on a shoestring budget can get a couple of single beds in a fan-ventilated room with shared bath for a modest fee but it's worth splashing out on a sparkling more expensive en-suite double (with modern a/c and cable TV). $

Restaurante Oderay 40m along the pavement from the wharf. This reasonable eating option, with a small dining patio, dishes up a decent plate of fried chicken or fish for moderate prices. It is often packed at breakfast, and has a good toilet. $–$$

Parque Nacional Darién

At 5790 square kilometres, **PARQUE NACIONAL DARIÉN** is the most expansive protected area in Central America. Created in 1972, it outranks all of Panama's national parks in both size and reputation, but is nevertheless one of the least visited protected areas in the country – reaching the refuge at Rancho Frío requires considerable organization. That said, the awe-inspiring greenery, laced with rivers and waterfalls and rich in wildlife, is well worth the time and money, providing a truly magical experience.

The park hugs the Colombian border, a forested carpet rising from the mangroves, coastal lagoons and deserted beaches of the **Pacific**, rippling over the volcanic ranges of the **Serranía del Sapo** and **Serranía del Jungurudó** northeast to the park's highest point of **Cerro Tacarcuna** (1875m), on the continental divide of the **Serranía del Darién**, and stopping just short of the Caribbean coast. Numerous important rivers scythe their way through the green mantle, including the Tuira, Sambú and Balsas.

Now that hiking the Darién Gap has been consigned to history, **visiting the national park** these days means hiring a guide and staying at the only permanent camp: MiAmbiente's refuge at Rancho Frío, reached via El Real, though some expeditions go and camp under tarpaulin up on the ridge. At the time of writing, the refuge was in a sad state of disrepair, but the facilities were due to be upgraded in 2025.

ESSENTIALS — PARQUE NACIONAL DARIÉN

Fees At the time of writing the park entry fee was $5, but see page 42. Accommodation fees do not feature on the MIA website but are $6/person for camping and $15 for a bunk in the refuge.

Guides To enter the park and/or stay at the refuge at Rancho Frío – currently the only accommodation in the park – you need to hire a guide. The tourism authority website (atp.gob.pa/industrias/guias-de-turismo-2) has a list of certified guides, including several for the Darién. Or you can go with a tour company (see page 279). The most experienced (and expensive) MIA-recommended local guide and guide co-ordinator is Isaac Pizarro (6245 3606). Other certified Darién guides include Elsie Quintero de León (6510 6838), Balbino Barrio (6204 3131) and Ismael Quiroz M. (6829 3965). All speak some English. Make sure you have the necessary supplies (see box, page 286) – best acquired in Yaviza – including food for the guide. You can also engage a local (and therefore cheaper) guide in Pijibasal (see page 285), but they are unlikely to speak English and may not necessarily have the specialist knowledge you want.

8

El Real

The deceptively fast-flowing waters of the Río Chucunaque snake down 6km from Yaviza through variegated walls of water chestnuts, banana plantations, expansive trees and pastureland to the low-key grassy bank "jetty" of **EL REAL** on the Río Tuira, the jumping-off point for the MiAmbiente refuge at Rancho Frío. From the jetty, it's a sweltering fifteen-minute walk into the town proper – a one-time fortified colonial settlement, now a pleasant if somnolent collection of houses constructed from various combinations of wood, zinc and concrete, and a couple of churches, interwoven with a network of cement pathways.

ARRIVAL AND DEPARTURE — EL REAL

By boat Boats regularly make the 40min journey from Yaviza to El Real, unless delayed by a major downpour; *colectivo* rates are inexpensive.

ACCOMMODATION AND EATING

Until the rumoured new hotel is built, homestay is the only accommodation option in the town.

Casa de Sabina C. Balboa 299655. Currently the best of the homestay options, offering two basic clean rooms containing single beds, firm mattresses shared bathroom (cold water – though outages are common). One is ventilated by a small fan, the other by a rattling old a/c unit. $

Fonda (no name) C Balboa. Breakfast and other fried meals – *patacones* with fried fish or chicken – are available in the only (unnamed) *fonda* in town, next door to Casa de Sabina, for a few dollars. $–$$

Rancho Frío

The only national park refuge still in operation within the park, **Rancho Frío**, is scenically situated on the shady banks of the Río Perescenico, with several **trails** leading off from the camp. These include the serious day- or overnight trek to the cloud forest of **Cerro Pirre** (1200m) – which requires lugging tent, sleeping bag and provisions up the mountain; it can be chilly at night, so pack something warm. There are several flattish spots with plastic tarpaulins, under which you can pitch your tent. The **Sendero**

de las Antennas provides a stiff all-day alternative that culminates in a hilltop police post, affording sweeping views of La Palma and the Golfo de San Miguel, with the Pacific as backdrop. Less strenuous walks can be had closer to camp, but still require a guide – the most popular is the two-hour circular **Sendero Rancho Frío**, which takes in a waterfall and natural *piscina*. During the wet months, the rivers and waterfalls are truly spectacular, though the refuge and mountain trails are often swathed in mist and the quantity of mud to wade through can scarcely be imagined, making even the shortest hike a major physical achievement. In the dry season, paths are easier to hike, views more frequently glimpsed and your chances of spotting mammal life – driven to the river to drink – is greatly enhanced.

ARRIVAL AND DEPARTURE — RANCHO FRÍO

By 4WD In the dry season, the easiest access from El Real is to arrange transport by 4WD as far as the village of Pirre Uno, 12km upriver, from where it is a flattish 5km walk to the refuge. Or you can arrange to be taken by horse from Pirre Uno.

By boat During the rains, you can sometimes get upriver by boat as far as Pijibasal, from where it's an hour's hike to the refuge.

ACCOMMODATION

Rancho Frío On the banks of the Río Perescenico. The basic refuge has limited electricity and at the time of writing was in a state of disrepair. Bring all provisions with you, including bedding and food – and enough for the park warden and/or guide. Be sure to pack bottled water or, better still, a water filter or purifying tablets, since tap water is not drinkable, as well as a torch, first-aid kit etc. A mosquito net is advisable. Camping $̲, dorm $̲

8

Pijibasal

In the buffer zone adjacent to the national park, **Pijibasal** (ⓦpaverte.com/pijibasal-turismo-comunitario) is a welcoming Emberá community, situated in an open grassy area, and well accustomed to receiving visitors. Here you can engage a local guide to explore trails in the surrounding forest and learn about traditional uses for various plants of the area, go birdwatching, or go paddling on a balsa raft on the river (when water levels permit). You could also hire a community guide to take you into the national park, but make it clear if you want a birdwatching expert. Accommodation is in raised wooden huts.

Around Golfo de San Miguel

Stacked up on a hilly peninsula, the ramshackle collection of wooden buildings that constitute the lively provincial capital of **La Palma** jut out into the widening expanse of the Río Tuira as it empties into the **Golfo de San Miguel**, a large bite-shaped body of water penetrating into Panama's southeastern Pacific coastline. Just across the water from La Palma, Isla El Encanto (or Boca Chica) hosts the scarcely visible, crumbling remains of the overgrown **Fuerte de San Carlos de Boca Chica**; though little more than a watchtower, it was a crucial link in a chain of defences that safeguarded the gold mines at Cana. Sprinkled along the coastline amid the mangroves are several predominantly Afro-Darienite communities such as **Garachiné** – comprising a collection of fairly dilapidated buildings and negligible services. The rivers that flow into the Golfo de San Miguel are the means of access to the **Comarca Emberá-Wounaan** and to the villages of **La Marea**, **Mogue**, **La Chunga** and, of course, **Sambú** itself.

La Palma

Resembling no other town in Panama, **LA PALMA**, a predominantly Afro-Darienite settlement of around six thousand, is the regional administrative and commercial hub,

VISITING AN EMBERÁ OR WOUNAAN VILLAGE

Staying overnight in an **Emberá or Wounaan village** is a great way to interact with villagers and learn about their day-to-day activities, as well as giving you access to the rainforest. Accommodation will either be in a traditional communal house (raised, thatched and open-sided) or in a family home. Communities that are used to greeting tour parties tend to offer slightly better **facilities** (showers, flush toilets and maybe even mattresses and mosquito nets), whereas others may provide little more than a wooden floor or a hammock for you to sleep on, and possibly a fire to cook your own food and a bucket of water for washing.

As many settlements are located on tidal rivers only accessible at high tide you may well have to hang around by jetties waiting for the water level to rise – generally, you need to be flexible and organized, taking **food** with you where possible, since many communities expect you to provide the food to cook and village shops are thinly stocked. **Bottled water** – or the means of purifying it – is both necessary and scarce; beer is more widely available, though check on the village etiquette before indulging and be discreet in your drinking, except when the whole village is having a party.

Most visitors head for villages round the **Golfo de San Miguel** or in the **Distrito Sambú** section of the **Comarca Emberá-Wounaan**, where you first need to report to the *comarca* office in Puerto Indio (see page 289) and pay the $10 entry fee. Mobile phone signals are fickle, and some communities have no coverage at all; given the difficulties in communication in the Darién, most independent travellers just turn up. The tourist coordinator (or president) is the person to ask for on arrival. They can tell you the prices and whether money needs to be paid to them (to be disbursed later to the relevant people) or directly to anyone who provides a service. They may also allocate you a personal tourist coordinator (usually $10–20/group – or solo traveller – per day), who will organize all aspects of your stay. Families usually take turns in hosting visitors to ensure that wealth is distributed across the community, but it is essential to sort out what's to be paid to whom from the outset to prevent misunderstandings. **Costs** are charged per person and itemized separately: village community fee ($10); accommodation ($10–15/night); meals ($5); services of a cook ($10/day per group or solo traveller); fishing trips or guided hikes ($10–15; more to a harpy eagle nest); body painting with *jagua* – (dye from the juice of a tropical berry mixed with charcoal; $5–10); and dance performances ($70/group). Assuming you take one excursion and three meals a day, you should budget around $50–60 per person per day, plus **transport** to reach the village ($15–30/person one way, depending on the distance if you manage to catch a *piragua colectivo*; private hire will cost several hundred dollars).

Sales of **handicrafts** are also an important aspect of village visits, displayed in a small shop or by the artisans themselves, and at set prices (usually from $20) that are inevitably lower than in Panama City. If you don't intend to buy anything, alert the tourist coordinator to avoid embarrassment; otherwise, try to spread your purchases round several artisans.

where motorized dugouts from the coastal and riverine communities jostle for position at the narrow and non-too-salubrious main jetty. The town's one sultry street is chock-full of hole-in-the-wall restaurants, bars and hotels, and shops selling welcome piles of fresh produce and other goods that are regularly shipped in from Panama City. Most visitors gravitate to La Palma to connect with transport to Emberá communities such as La Marea and Mogue, or those further afield up the Río Sambú, and you'd be well advised to stock up with supplies while here – the (pricier) village stores are unlikely to provide much beyond tinned fish, rice and biscuits. If you don't have the means to purify **water**, make sure you pick up a flagon or two of the bottled variety.

ARRIVAL AND DEPARTURE — LA PALMA

By water-taxi Water-taxis to La Palma run from Puerto Quimba (daily 5am–5.30pm; every 30min; 30min; $5). The last return water-taxi to Puerto Quimba leaves around 5.30pm.

ACCOMMODATION AND EATING

Hotel Biaquirú Bagará C Principal ⓣ299 6224. This basic, family-run hotel is your best bet, with a dozen neat wood-panelled rooms, some with fan and shared (cold-water) bathroom, others en suite with a/c. There's a shared waterside deck with hammocks. $$

Lola's Grill C Principal, near the basketball court ⓦinstagram.com/restaurant_lolasgrill. The ebullient Lola serves inexpensive seafood with coconut rice or yuca (from $6) in her upstairs restaurant, but like most places in La Palma it can close early and suffer from a lack of provisions.

Pension Tuira C Principal ⓣ299 6316. For shoestring travellers who fancy being in the thick of the noisy action – there's a *cantina* next door – this friendly hotel provides rooms with fan or a/c ($5 extra) and communal balconies overlooking the estuary. $

La Marea

Forty minutes' boat ride southeast from La Palma up the sinuous tree-lined Río La Marea, the small, welcoming community of **LA MAREA** provides a perfect introduction to the Emberá way of life. The "*marea*" (tide) is crucial to village logistics since the place is only reachable at high tide, and even then, at the backend of the dry season, the *piragua* scrapes along the riverbed. Traditional open-sided wood-and-thatch dwellings are dotted across a sloping expanse of neatly trimmed grass ending at the riverbank, where a small *rancho* is used for dance performances and craft displays; opposite this, a tiny shop sells beer and a few tinned essentials.

An infectious tranquillity pervades the settlement – aside from the two hours in the evening when the generator is on – and for most of the night it is illuminated by starlight and kerosene lamps. Unlike in some communities, many of the 160 villagers choose to go about their business clad in traditional attire, except when heading into town. The surrounding forest abounds in **wildlife**, worth exploring with a guide following a trail leading to a waterfall or a lake, or embarking on a substantial hike or a shorter horseride. Otherwise, the days can happily slip by interacting with villagers, getting your body painted in *jagua* dye and cooling off in the river.

8

ARRIVAL AND ACTIVITIES — LA MAREA

To visit the community, contact the tourism coordinator Edison Grajales (ⓣ6742 3615).

By boat *Piraguas colectivas* rarely head for La Marea but it's worth contacting the community in advance, to find out if there's likely to be transport. If no transport is due, you must either hike into the community (3hr) from Chepigana, or pay a substantial sum for a private boat.

Activities The village trail goes straight into the rainforest and guiding services can be provided.

ACCOMMODATION AND EATING

Community accommodation A traditional house is set aside for visitors, with space to hang a hammock or spread a sleeping bag, and a family allocated either to cook food (which they prefer you to provide and costs more, or lend you their fire pit and utensils to prepare your own meals. Rates inclusive of lodging and meals. $–$$

Mogue

There's a *Heart of Darkness* feel about entering the **Río Mogue**, enclosed by forbidding walls of mangroves, flecked with perching white ibis, which eventually clear at a scenic mooring, ten minutes' walk from the village of **MOGUE**. The name derives from Mogadé, a mythical Emberá creature that lived in the mountains and ate people – though Panama City would seem to have devoured more of the dwindling village population as they leave in search of employment. Besides a little tourism, agriculture – plantain, yuca and a variety of other fruits and vegetables – constitutes the economic mainstay of the community, though a minority still fish or hunt iguanas, agoutis and other small animals with traditional arrows or a gun. Another important source of income is **basketry** – especially masks – for which Mogue is justifiably renowned. Mogue is also the most likely community to have

SAVING THE HARPY EAGLE

Instantly recognizable for its splendid slate-grey back, brilliant white chest and distinctive crest, the **harpy eagle** (*águila harpía*) is the largest eagle in the Neotropics and one of the most powerful worldwide, with talons the size of a grizzly bear's claws. The larger female can weigh up to 9kg and be more than 1m long, and despite its vast wingspan of more than 2m, it can reach speeds of up to 80km/h while accelerating through trees to stab its prey.

After declining in numbers for many years due to loss of habitat and hunting, a successful breed-and-release programme has resulted in Panama now having the greatest concentration of harpy eagles in Mesoamerica, with more than two hundred pairs in the Darién alone. It is a long recovery process, though, as harpy eagles are lethargic breeders, laying two eggs once every three years; worse still, once the first egg has hatched, the second is discarded as the pair focuses on nurturing the single chick in the nest for another six months, and taking care of it for a further two years.

Following environmental campaigns with local communities and in schools, public awareness and interest in the harpy eagle has increased. Fittingly, the raptor is now the **national bird**, topping the national coat of arms, and has its own national day on April 10. All this publicity, it is hoped, will help ensure the harpy eagle's continued survival.

For more on the efforts to save this majestic bird, check the Patronato Amigos del Águila Harpía (W aguilaharpia.org). To find out which communities have an active harpy eagle nest in any given year, contact the Darién desk of Áreas Protegidas in the MIA offices in Panama City (see page 42), or contact the Darién communities themselves.

8

an active **harpy eagle nest** (see box), where a willingness to stake the place out for several hours can often be rewarded by a truly special sighting: a parent returning with a monkey in its talons, which is ripped apart, before tiny morsels are fed to the chick with incredible delicacy.

The focus of community life is the zinc-roofed **casa comunal**, where on Saturdays or Sundays the leaders preside over the weekly village gathering. The tri-weekly Evangelical services are also a draw for a large number of the community, while late afternoon the football pitch provides an important social focus for both the men's and women's teams, and visitors are welcome to join in.

ARRIVAL AND ACTIVITIES — MOGUE

By boat Transport to the village makes the journey expensive unless you catch a village boat from La Palma. Enquire at the main jetty, as boats leave with the rising tide most days. Otherwise, contact the *presidente de turismo*, Alberto Rito (T 6056 6309), to arrange a boat pickup in La Palma. Ask for the cool box to be brought along, which you can fill with fish, chicken or shrimp from the market for meals; otherwise your diet will be very limited.

Hiking and birdwatching It takes 15min to reach the more luxuriant rainforest from Mogue, and a further 1hr 30min along a well-trodden trail to an active harpy eagle nest, though there are numerous less-frequented paths to explore with a guide populated with toucans, sloths and monkeys.

Horseriding and fishing These activities can also be organized on the spot.

ACCOMMODATION AND EATING

Community accommodation Visitors can sleep on a mattress in a small tent or in a hammock in the *casa comunal*, whose breezy raised platform, where food is served, affords a prime spot to eavesdrop on village life. $

Reserva Punta Patiño

Established in the early 1990s, **Reserva Punta Patiño** is Panama's first and, at 300 square kilometres, largest private reserve, occupying the entire headland at the tip of the choppy Golfo de San Miguel, just beyond the lively Afro-Darienite fishing village of **Punta Alegre**.

While the landscape is nowhere near as dramatic as the jungle-carpeted peaks of the interior, the regenerating hinterland forest – once devastated by cattle ranching, timber extraction and coconut plantations – is filling up with native hardwoods. Weasel-like tayra and grey foxes live here, as well as the extraordinary-looking capybara, the world's largest rodent, which resembles a giant guinea pig and weighs in at 55kg. The area also covers a stretch of charcoal **beach,** an important expanse of **mangroves**, and mud and **salt flats** that attract an abundance of resident and migratory seabirds.

Managed by the environmental organization **ANCON**, and not open to the general public – only groups of volunteers, the reserve is not without its critics, not least the Emberá, who feel the land should be theirs.

Garachiné

Set against the imposing backdrop of Cerro Sapo (Toad Hill), the small, neglected fishing community of **GARACHINÉ** is only of interest to visitors who intend to hike the overland route to Playa Muerto (see page 291), or are trying to reach Sambú via a bumpy road which then loops back to the coastal Wounaan community of Taimatí. Unless you arrive at high tide, you'll be wading knee-deep across alluvial mud flats to the shore.

ARRIVAL AND INFORMATION — GARACHINÉ

By boat Boats regularly depart from La Palma and Puerto Quimba.

By road Getting a ride to Sambú by road is tricky, with transport only going early in the morning and returning in the afternoon. Wait by the bus shelter (*la caseta*) at the end of the main cement path.

ACCOMMODATION AND EATING

There's little to tempt the palate in Garachiné and the few **fondas** that exist have irregular hours; it's usually a case of looking around to see what's open.

AJ's Hospedaje C Principal ⓣ 6501 3234 or 6506 2097. Behind the hardware store are five surprisingly nice, simple rooms, offering ample space, gleaming tiled floors and bathrooms and comfortable beds, plus a/c and cable TV. $$

8

Río Sambú and the Comarca Emberá-Wounaan

Portal to the twelve communities of the **Distrito Sambú** of the **Comarca Emberá-Wounaan**, 12km up the serpentine **Río Sambú**, the twin settlements of **Sambú** and **Puerto Indio** are generally only reached by river at high tide. The boat trip, sweeping round the river's tortuous bends, causing flocks of white ibis to fly off in unison, is highly atmospheric. As the Río Sambú's waters swell during the rainy season, *piraguas* can penetrate as far upstream as the tiny village of Pavarandó; more easily accessible downriver is the fairly dispersed community of **La Chunga**, which lies a few minutes' paddle up a quiet tributary.

Sambú and Puerto Indio

While **SAMBÚ** and its counterpart **PUERTO INDIO**, connected by a footbridge, are pleasant enough places, they serve more as a gateway to swathes of primeval **forest** and a serpentine waterway leading to **Emberá** and **Wounaan communities** further upriver.

The contrast in mood and architecture between the two villages is striking. In bustling Sambú – where all accommodation and eating options are located – cement pathways wind between tightly packed houses of various architectural styles, accommodating a mixed population of Emberá, Wounaan, *mestizos* and Afro-Darienites. Across the river, quieter Puerto Indio, at the western limit of the Distrito Sambú, of which it is the capital, comprises an indigenous population living in traditional wooden housing raised on stilts, where afternoon social activity centres round the basketball court or football pitch.

TOURS FROM SAMBÚ AND PUERTO INDIO

In **Puerto Indio**, the tourism committee, based in the Oficina del Congreso, offers a range of day **excursions to the Distrito Sambú** (for which you'll need to provide your own food and water). These include a guided walk round the village, taking in a nearby lake, a half-day excursion to a waterfall involving a 45-minute boat ride and a modest rainforest walk, and lengthier ventures to the communities of La Chunga or Pavarandó. In all cases, **overnight stays** can easily be arranged, either in the *casa comunal* or in someone's house. Arquinio Dogirama (E emberaguia@yahoo.es) and Domicilio Cárdena (La Chunga public phone T 333 2516) are **guides** authorized by the *comarca*'s tourism committee, though each village has its own guide.

Sambú guides are not allowed to guide within the *comarca*, but can offer excursions to rainforest and Emberá communities that lie outside the *comarca* boundaries.

ARRIVAL AND INFORMATION — SAMBÚ AND PUERTO INDIO

By boat Boats to Sambú and Puerto Indio ($20 from La Palma, $25 from Puerto Quimba) leave most days.

By boat and 4WD If there isn't a boat going directly to Sambú, in the dry season you could go to Garachiné (see page 289), where you can usually hitch a ride to Sambú along the dirt road in a *colectivo*.

SENAFRONT registration The SENAFRONT checkpoint is halfway down the disused airstrip in Sambú.

Fees The $10 entry fee to the *comarca* should be paid at the Oficina del Congreso in Puerto Indio.

ACCOMMODATION AND EATING

8

Arturo's Close to the airstrip. Greasy breakfasts and filling lunches for a few dollars. Evening meals are a case of what's left over. $–$$

Mi Sueño By the airstrip T 6902 8327. Eleven small, wooden-fan-ventilated rooms with shared bathroom, and a large communal balcony affording a pleasant view of the surrounding hillside. The occasionally functioning restaurant offers cheap meals. Tours to Emberá village of Villa Queresia can also be arranged. $

Villa Fiesta By the airstrip T 6792 9493. Four bright, good-value rooms (two with a/c, two with fan) with excellent beds, private bathroom and fridge; meals can also be arranged. Former Emberá *cacique* Ricardo Cabrera, the genial owner and proprietor of the downstairs shop, is fluent in English and a mine of local knowledge. $$

La Chunga

The shady hamlet of **LA CHUNGA** – named after the ubiquitous palm used for basketry – lies on a small tributary of the same name, which feeds into the Río Sambú, downriver from Sambú/Puerto Indio. Since the tributary is only navigable at high tide, at other times you land at a pontoon on the main river, from where it's a twenty-minute walk along a boardwalk through mosquito-infested swamp to the village. At the time of writing the bridge over Río Chunga had collapsed, meaning you would need to ring the village phone in advance to ensure someone could paddle you across, or wait until the water had receded enough to wade across.

An avenue of cedar trees marks the entrance, opening out onto an overgrown basketball court surrounded by a handful of traditional homes. **Basketry** is still widely practised by the women. Make sure you check out the village **stocks** (*sepo*); miscreants who commit an offence and are unable to pay the fine are placed there for a couple of hours, an experience, which in olden times was made particularly painful by being made to sit on a pile of cooked rice, which attracted vicious ants that tuck in to the penitent's buttocks. These days, since the sale of alcohol is banned in the community, the stocks are rarely used. The Wounaan community of **Semaco**, known for its exquisite basketry, music and dance, is just a two-hour hike away. A village guide can take you **birdwatching** upriver, or perhaps to a **harpy eagle nest**.

ARRIVAL AND ACCOMMODATION — LA CHUNGA

By boat Although La Chunga has its own motorized transport that occasionally travels to and from La Palma on weekdays, you can also catch a ride in the Sambú/Puerto Indio boats, which will drop you at the La Chunga pontoon on the Río Sambú, from where it is a 20min walk.

Community accommodation 333 2516 (public phone). Overnight guests are made comfortable in someone's home on mattresses with mosquito nets and even sheets and pillows. Bathrooms are shared and rudimentary. You pay a daily rate for someone to prepare your three meals. $

The southeastern Pacific coast

The Darién's **Pacific coast** is as remote and unexplored as the jungle-filled interior: to the northwest of the Golfo de San Miguel, the coastline is dominated by mangroves, but to the southeast it comprises kilometres of deserted beaches interspersed with rocky outcrops, cliffs and expanses of pristine forest, with the brooding *serranías* del Sapo and Jungurudó a dramatic backdrop. Three places of interest stand out here: the Emberá village of **Playa de Muerto**; the luxury sport-fishing magnet of **Bahía Piñas** (tropicstar.com), staffed primarily from the adjacent village of **Puerto Piñas**; and **Jaqué**, the last sizeable community before the Colombian border. Note that Bahía Piñas and Jaqué are the only places in the Darién accessible by **plane**.

Playa Muerto

Attractively situated amid serried ranks of coconut palms backing a chocolate swathe of sand, **PLAYA MUERTO** is the only Emberá community on the Pacific coast. Its gruesome name ("Beach of the Dead") derives from the corpses that used to wash ashore following sea-battles between bullion-laden Spanish galleons and pirate ships in colonial times. Isolated, and inaccessible by boat in winter, when the waves are huge, the village is well worth a visit. Beyond the village stocks – which are still used to punish wrongdoers – Playa Muerto has largely lost its traditions (except for cultural performances) but the setting is attractive, and the pace relaxed. You can have your body painted in *jagua* dye, hike through the rainforest or take a short stroll to a nearby waterfall and natural pool. Note also that following a major promotional campaign by the national tourism association and the fact that it is the current favoured endpoint of jungle treks in the Darién, and even on some cruise ship itineraries, you could find yourself with more visitors than you might expect (or want) in such a remote place. So it's worth checking in advance whether the community will be receiving groups when you intend to visit.

8

ARRIVAL AND DEPARTURE — PLAYA MUERTO

By boat Boats from La Palma for Jaqué call in at Playa Muerto provided sea conditions are favourable – they have to land passengers on the beach – as do the occasional cargo boats from Panama City (see page 292). Boats infrequently leave Playa Muerto for La Palma or Puerto Quimba.

On foot A couple of Darién tour operators include the overland two-day trek from Sambú or Garachiné (see page 289), staying in a MIA bunkhouse en route. Alternatively, you can arrange for a local community guide (and mule if you don't want to carry a pack) to meet you in Garachiné or Puerto Quimba, if you prefer, though you'd need to contact the tourism coordinator in Playa Muerto (see below).

ACCOMMODATION

★ **Community accommodation** At the back of the beach 6720 1200 (Rangel Grijales). Choose between a traditional, raised wood-and-thatch building with ocean-facing open sides (sleeps ten), or a smaller, two-person wooden *cabaña* with porch, slightly back from the beach. Sleep on a mattress or in a hammock and watch the pelicans and the sunsets. Shared bathroom with flush toilet and cold-water showers. Simple meals are provided. Accommodation and full board $

Puerto Piñas

Less edgy and much smaller than the neighbouring frontier community of Jaqué, **PUERTO PIÑAS** has a more impressive setting, encircled by forested mountains, in a protected bay – the safest anchorage along this part of the coast – boasting a substantial beach and riverside location. From here you can organize a day-hike over the mountains to the cream-coloured sands of **Playa Blanca**, which offers sheltered **snorkelling**, or to the Wounaan village of **Biroquera,** from where it's a half-hour boat trip down to Jaqué.

Jaqué

Though actually around 40km from the Colombian border, **JAQUÉ** is Panama's Pacific border town, and as such heavily garrisoned – you'll need to check in with SENAFRONT. The three-thousand-strong mixed population, including many Colombians, live around a vague grid of cement paths. Though enlivened somewhat by the generous sprinkling of plantain, mango trees and coconut palms, Jaqué is still an unappealing place: heavily littered, with loud *cantinas* blaring out reggaeton and surprisingly lacking anywhere that serves coffee. Yet the setting is impressive, with the mountains of the Cordillera de Jungurudo forming a distant backdrop, a 4km stretch of beach pounded by surf, and a sweeping river-mouth rich in birdlife. Stroll along the sands, surf the waves, birdwatch or contract a boat to take you upstream to the Wounaan community of **Biroquera**, where you can sort out a place to sling up a hammock, or contract a guide to accompany you on a splendid three-hour **hike** to the fishing hamlet of Piña.

ARRIVAL AND INFORMATION — PUERTO PIÑAS AND JAQUÉ

8

By plane There are no longer scheduled flights, but Air Panama offers shared charter flights to Jaqué via Bahía Piñas.

By boat in Panama It is possible to catch a ride in a boat from La Palma to Jaqué or Puerto Píñas. The sea can be very rough, especially in the rainy season, so be sure to make the relevant safety checks beforehand (see page 28). Every year, there's an accident at sea and people drown. Enquire at Terraplén, by the Mercado de Mariscos in Panama City, about departures of cargo boats, which offer bunk beds and bench seats for the 14–16hr voyage between Panama City and Jaqué (via Playa Muerto and Puerto Piñas) every four or five days, depending on demand and ocean conditions. Snacks are sold on board, but it is best to bring your own food. The boat leaves on the second high tide of the day, so check the departure time the day before. Boat services to Colombia are planned.

By boat from Colombia There is currently no immigration office in Jaqué, so immigration formalities have to be undertaken on arrival in Panama City – at Balboa Yacht Club on the Amador Causeway – but your details will be taken by SENAFRONT at Jaqué's beach (the de facto port) on arrival.

Transfers Jaqué–Puerto Piñas Though only a small headland separates the two communities, a short inexpensive hop by boat.

ACCOMMODATION AND EATING

PUERTO PIÑAS

Fonda Laura 200m down the cement path from the airstrip. You'll get a hearty welcome from the ebullient Laura as well as a tasty plateful of *mondongo* or chicken, rice and beans. She also has rooms to rent, though usually for long-term lets.

Hospedaje Nemecia By the church near the airstrip ☎6802 3808. Four neat, clean tiled-floor rooms, the odd frilly bedspread, plus a/c and satellite TV, and shared cold-water showers. $$

JAQUÉ

Aventuras Jaqué 600m southeast of the SENAFRONT checkpoint ☎6900 5679. Basic, cement block at the outskirts of the community with fan-ventilated rooms containing two single beds. Bring a mosquito net in the rainy season. $–$$

Fonda Alex On the main cement path, near the riverside SENAFRONT headquarters. Like everywhere else in town, you won't get coffee and the menu has few options, but this friendly wood-and-thatch hut is still the pick of the *fondas*, serving reasonable platefuls of fish or chicken with plantain, rice and salad. $–$$

THE GAILLARD CUT, C.1913

Contexts

History

Though the Republic of Panama is only a little over a century old, humans have lived on the isthmus for thousands of years. Its location as a slender bridge between two vast land masses has been as crucial to its development as its eventual link between two expanses of ocean.

Pre-Columbian society

Panama's scarce archeological remains give little clue to the societies that inhabited the region, in part because many early excavations were poorly executed and finds were damaged or looted. Lacking the huge structures and sophisticated carvings that epitomize the Maya, Aztec and Toltec civilizations of Mesoamerica, the trading societies of Central America have always taken a historical backseat. Yet central Panama boasts the earliest traces of **pottery-making** in the Americas with ceramics from Monagrillo, in the northern Azuero Peninsula, carbon-dated to 2500–1200 BC. A nearby fishing village in Sarigua is considered to be the isthmus's **oldest settlement**, dating from around 11,000 BC.

The most sophisticated societies inhabited central Panama, with some of the richest archeological finds in the **necropolis** of Sitio Conté, outside Penonomé. Excavations by American academics in the 1930s opened up around a hundred **tombs** to reveal thousands of intricate **gold pieces of jewellery** alongside sophisticated **polychrome ceramics** and other artefacts dating back to the first century, most of which were shipped off to the States.

At El Caño, near Natá, lies a **ceremonial site and necropolis** for the elite of the Coclé culture, dating from 700 to 1000 AD. Excavations since 2008 have uncovered riches similar to those of Sitio Conté in eight **burial chambers** – as of 2024 – including one unearthed in 2011 containing the remains of an important chief, bedecked in **gold**, and surrounded by the skeletons of 25 carefully arranged bodies, believed to be sacrificial companions for the afterlife. In the Western Highlands, outside Volcán, another important site indicates the existence of what has been termed the **Barriles culture**, at its apogee around 500 to 600 AD, and known for its curious **stone statues** of a figure wearing a conical hat carrying another on its shoulders (see page 195). A large **ceremonial grinding stone**, or *metate*, adorned with human heads – also in the museum – has led to speculation about human sacrifice. Sprinkled round Sitio Barriles and elsewhere in western and central Panama on moss-covered boulders are numerous **petroglyphs**; the largest unearthed so far is La Piedra Pintada outside El Valle.

Arrival of the Spanish

The first European credited with setting foot on the isthmus was the Spanish aristocratic notary **Rodrigo Galván de Bastidas**, who in 1501 made a low-key arrival, trading his way peacefully up the Caribbean coast as far as present-day Colón. In contrast, **Christopher Columbus** (Cristóbal Colón), who arrived a year later on his

11,000 BC	2500–1200 BC	500–600 AD
The first settlement is established on the isthmus, a fishing village, in the Azuero Peninsula	The earliest traces of pottery-making in the Americas are also found in the Azuero Peninsula	An eruption by Volcán Barú is thought to have brought an end to the Barriles culture – one of the most important pre-Columbian societies

CACIQUE URRACÁ

The most famous of three Guaymí (forefathers of the Ngäbe) heads in western Panama – the others being Natá and Parita, after whom the Spanish named settlements – was the mighty indigenous chief **Urracá**, who provided the colonizers' fiercest resistance over a nine-year period. Managing to unite community leaders who were traditional enemies, he conducted guerrilla-type raids from his mountain stronghold above Santa Fé de Veraguas. After repeatedly failing to defeat Urracá, the Spanish resorted to deception, luring him down to Natá under the pretence of negotiating a peace settlement. Here he was immediately seized and taken in chains to Nombre de Dios, from where he was to be deported to Spain. Managing to escape, he returned to his people, vowing to fight the invaders to the death. By this stage, however, the Spanish were so afraid of his warriors that they avoided conflict with them whenever possible, while the chief continued his resistance until he died in 1531.

fourth and final voyage to the "New World", headed for the western and central Caribbean coast, keen to lay his hands on the legendary gold. He attempted to establish the first European settlement on the isthmus, provoking violent conflicts with indigenous populations. Though relations between Columbus and the local chief or *cacique*, **Quibián**, known as "El Señor de la Tierra", were initially friendly, the mood changed once it was clear the Spanish intended to stay and plunder. When Columbus left his garrison at Santa María de Belén (in present-day Veraguas) to seek reinforcements, Quibián rallied local leaders to destroy the settlement but was captured by Columbus's brother Bartolomé, who had been left in charge. While being transported as a prisoner downriver to Belén, the chief dived out of the dugout and was presumed drowned. He survived, however, and went on to lead an assault against the invaders, forcing them to flee.

The respite was short-lived. In 1505 the king of Spain, Ferdinand II, intent on expanding his empire, dispatched two men to take charge of what had been named "*Tierre Firme*" (extending from present-day Venezuela to Panama): **Alonso de Ojeda** was to govern the land between Cabo de la Vela in present-day Colombia through to the Golfo de Urabá, known as Nueva Andalucía, while **Diego de Nicuesa** was to oversee the west from the gulf to Gracias a Dios on what is now the border between Honduras and Nicaragua (and was known as Castilla de Oro, after its supposed riches). Both campaigns ended in disaster.

Though estimates of the indigenous population at the time of the Spanish conquest vary from two hundred thousand to two million, what is not in dispute is the speed at which the local communities were decimated, as much by **disease** brought by the conquistadors as through **massacre** and **enslavement**. The remainder retreated to inhospitable remote mountain areas, where they either lay low or continued their resistance against the invaders. The Spanish instituted a feudal-style system of **encomiendas**, theoretically entrusting "free" indigenous peoples to the stewardship of colonizers for their well-being and instruction in the Catholic faith in return for labour; in practice, workers were more often treated like slaves. Though the system was abolished in 1720, it did not spell the end of intense hardships for many of the rural population.

1501–02	**1505**	**1513**
Spanish explorers Rodrigo de Bastidas and Christopher Columbus visit modern-day Panama	The Spanish conquest intensifies; indigenous populations are massacred or enslaved, though some resist	Vasco Núñez de Balboa crosses Panama, becoming the first European to see the Pacific Ocean

Balboa and the Mar del Sur

There's little in **Vasco Núñez de Balboa**'s inauspicious early life to suggest he would rise to prominence. After setting foot on the isthmus as a member of Bastidas's expedition, he settled on Hispaniola, where, failing as a pig-farmer, he fled his creditors by stowing away on a boat bound for the mainland. Upon discovery, he was saved from being thrown off the ship thanks to his knowledge of the isthmus. As the incipient Spanish settlements struggled to survive, including the new regional centre **San Sebastián de Urabá**, founded by Ojeda, Balboa recommended relocating across the gulf. **Santa María de la Antigua del Darién** (on the other side of the current Panama–Colombia border) was thus established on a site that had been seized from followers of Cacique **Cémaco**, a pivotal figure in the indigenous resistance. It was the first successful Spanish settlement on the isthmus, eventually becoming the capital of **Castilla de Oro** until the seat transferred to Panama City in 1524.

Meanwhile Balboa continued his acquisition of power by subjugating, negotiating and making peace with local populations. Hearing from the locals about another sea to the south and land dripping in gold and pearls, Balboa found a route through the forests of the Darién to become the first European to look out onto the **Pacific Ocean** on September 25, 1513. Several days later, in true imperialist fashion, Balboa waded into the water in full body armour, sword in one hand, statue of the Virgin Mary in the other, and claimed possession of the "Mar del Sur" in the name of the king of Spain. Yet he received scant reward for his "discovery" – in 1519 his jealous superior **Pedro Arias de Ávila**, known as Pedrarias the Cruel or *Furor Domini* (Wrath of God), the first governor of Castilla de Oro, had him beheaded.

Panama City and the Camino Real

In the face of appalling losses from disease, Pedrarias moved his base from the Caribbean side to the slightly more salubrious Pacific coast, where he dispossessed more indigenous populations of their land to **found Panama City** (Panamá La Vieja) in 1519. The new settlement became the jumping-off point for further Spanish inroads north and south along the coast, and, after the conquest of Peru in 1533, it began to flourish as the transit point for the fabulous riches of the **Incas** on their way to fill the coffers of the Spanish Crown. From Panama City, cargo was transported across the isthmus on mules along the paved **Camino Real** to the ports of Nombre de Dios and later Portobelo, on the Caribbean coast. A second route, the **Camino de Cruces**, was used to transport heavier cargo to the highest navigable point on the Río Chagres, where it was transferred to dugout canoes to be carried downriver to the coast.

The flow of wealth attracted the attention of Spain's enemies, and the Caribbean coast was under constant threat from European **pirates**, the first of whom, the Englishman **Francis Drake**, successfully raided Nombre de Dios. He received support from the **cimarrones**, communities of escaped enslaved Africans who lived in the jungle and often collaborated with pirates in ambushing mule trains and attacking the Spanish. In the most daring assault, in 1671, Welshman **Henry Morgan** and his men sailed up the Río Chagres, having destroyed the fortress at San Lorenzo at the river-mouth en route, and crossed the isthmus to ransack Panama City. Though Morgan is generally blamed

1519

Panama City is founded on August 15 by conquistador Pedro Arias de Ávila (known as Pedrarias)

1533

The Camino Real flourishes as the main transit route for plundered riches from South America bound for Spain

1595–1739

The Spanish are constantly threatened by European pirates and privateers; Henry Morgan sacks Panamá Viejo in 1671

THE WATERMELON WAR

The completion of the **Panama Railroad** left many Panamanian labourers, including the new immigrant workforce, unemployed and resentful of their well-paid US counterparts, some of whom showed scant respect for their hosts or local customs. On April 15, 1856, tensions spilled over. An intoxicated (white) American named Jack Oliver, who had been killing time in the bars waiting for the boat, grabbed a slice of **watermelon** from a local (black) stallholder and refused to pay. When the trader drew a knife, Oliver's mate tossed a dime at him, further enraging the merchant, and as he advanced on Oliver, the latter drew a gun. An attempt to disarm the American resulted in a bystander getting shot, prompting a full-scale anti-US **riot**. Many Americans holed up in the railway depot and gunfire was exchanged with the crowd, which was attempting to batter down the door. Rather than control the situation, the **police** joined in the affray, which continued until a trainload of the vigilante **Isthmus Guard** arrived to disperse the mob. While the number of casualties in the so-called "Watermelon War" – seventeen dead and 29 wounded, predominantly American – was not disputed, blame for the violence was. Amid claims and counterclaims of racism, the US government dispatched two **warships** to Panama and occupied the railway station – albeit only for three days – but their demand for total control of the railroad was refused.

for the fire that then engulfed the place, it was more likely due to the detonation of the city's gunpowder supplies ordered by the defeated Spanish governor.

The city was rebuilt in 1673 on today's Casco Viejo behind defences so formidable that it was never taken again, but the raiding of the Caribbean coast continued until finally in 1746 Spain rerouted the treasure fleet around Cape Horn. With the route across the isthmus all but abandoned, Panama's importance to the imperial project diminished.

Independence from Spain

By the turn of the nineteenth century, independence movements in South America, headed by **Simón Bolívar** and **José de San Martín**, were gathering pace. Though the isthmus initially remained fairly detached from the process, it was not devoid of nationalist sentiment. On November 10, 1821, the tiny town of La Villa de Los Santos unilaterally declared that it would no longer be governed by Spain, in what was known as the *Primer Grito de la Independencia* (First Cry for Independence); the rest of the country followed suit, declaring **independence** on November 30. It retained the name of Panama, as a department of what historians have subsequently termed "Gran Colombia"; with the secession of Ecuador and Venezuela it quickly became Nueva Granada. Almost immediately conflicts emerged between the merchants of Panama City, eager to trade freely with the world, and the distant, protectionist governments in Bogotá, leading to numerous, if half-hearted, attempts at separation. As the century wore on, US influence asserted itself, most notably in the 1846 **Mallarino-Bidlack Treaty**, which granted the US government rights to build a railroad across the isthmus and, significantly, accorded them power to intervene militarily to suppress any

1746	**1821**	**1830**
Spain reroutes the treasure fleet around Cape Horn, resulting in economic decline	Panama declares independence from Spain, and joins the confederacy of Gran Colombia (Bolivia, Peru, Ecuador, Venezuela, Colombia and Panama)	Panama becomes a province of Colombia after the dissolution of Gran Colombia

secessionist uprisings against the New Granadan government – a theoretically mutually beneficial accord that was to seriously backfire on Bogotá.

The **discovery of gold** in California in 1849 sparked an explosion in traffic across the isthmus. Travel from the US east coast to California via Panama – by boat, overland on foot, and then by boat again – was far less arduous than the trek across North America, and thousands of "Forty-niners" passed through on their way to the goldfields. In 1850 a US company began the construction of a **railroad** across Panama. Carving a route through the inhospitable swamps and rainforests proved immensely difficult – thousands of the mostly Chinese and West Indian migrant workers died in the process – but when the railroad was completed in 1855, the Panama Railroad Company proved an instant financial success, earning $7 million in profit in the first six years, despite having cost $8 million to construct. The railroad also marked the beginning of a new era in foreign control: within a year, the first **US military intervention** in Panama had taken place (see box, page 297).

The French canal venture

In 1869 the opening of the first transcontinental railway in the US reduced traffic through Panama, but the completion of the **Suez Canal** that same year made the long-standing imperialist dream of a canal across the isthmus a realistic possibility. Well aware of the strategic advantages such a waterway would offer, the French secured a concession to **build a canal**, as well as purchasing the Panama Railroad, from the New Granadan government. In 1881, led by ex-diplomat **Ferdinand de Lesseps**, the driving force responsible for the Suez Canal, the Compagnie Universelle du Canal Interocéanique began excavations.

Despite de Lesseps' vision and determination, the "venture of the century" proved to be a disaster, not least because of his technical ignorance and arrogance. In the face of impassable terrain – forests, swamps and the shifting shales of the continental divide – the proposed sea-level canal proved unfeasible, while yellow fever, malaria and a host of other unpleasant diseases ravaged the workforce. In 1889 the Compagnie collapsed; $287 million had evaporated as a result of financial mismanagement and corruption, implicating the highest levels of French society. Hundreds of thousands of ordinary French investors lost everything.

The War of the Thousand Days

At the end of the nineteenth century the simmering feud between the Conservative and Liberal parties erupted into a bloody three-year **civil war** called the **War of the Thousand Days** (*Guerra de los Mil Días*). Though there were ideological differences – ruling elite **Conservatives** supported strong central government, limited voting rights and close bonds between Church and State, whereas the merchant class and educated **Liberals** wanted more decentralized, federal government, universal voting rights and a greater division between Church and State – there were also many factions within each party. The violence was triggered by alleged election fraud by the landed Conservatives in their bid to remain in power, but by the time the bloody conflict had ended in 1902, claiming a hundred thousand lives, it was hard

1850–55

The California Gold Rush prompts construction of the Panama Railroad across the isthmus

1881

French architect Ferdinand de Lesseps begins excavations for the Panama Canal. Some twenty thousand workers die before the venture is abandoned in 1889

PEDRO PRESTÁN AND THE FIRE OF COLÓN

One of the uglier episodes in the factional feuding between Liberals and Conservatives occurred in 1885, with the public hanging of **Pedro Prestán**. Prestán, a Liberal revolutionary, had taken advantage of the absence of Colombian troops in Colón – they had headed over to Panama City to quell an attempted coup – by seizing control of the city. After looting businesses to raise money, he and his band of rebels purchased arms from the US, which arrived on a steamship anchored in the bay. When the ship agent refused to unload the arms, Prestán took the agent, US consul and several other Americans **hostage**, threatening to kill them if the US naval vessel stationed nearby landed troops and the arms were not handed over. Though the weapons were promised and the hostages released, the Americans reneged on the deal. Fleeing to Monkey Hill outside the city, Prestán and his poorly armed combatants got caught up with the Colombian troops now back from Panama City. The rebels were routed and the **city caught fire**; built of wood, it was totally destroyed, killing eighteen and leaving thousands homeless. Prestán, who had fled by boat to his native Cartagena, became the scapegoat. Many of his men were rounded up and **executed** while Prestán himself was captured, tried and convicted by a partisan jury, and left to hang above the railway tracks in Colón.

to pinpoint what much of the fighting had actually been about. It's also unclear whether key Liberal protagonists were motivated more by the desire for separation than social justice; regardless, most Liberals were subsequently elevated to the status of nationalist heroes.

The initial Liberal revolt was led by **Belisario Porras**, the popular exiled lawyer, who later won three periods of office as president of Panama. With the support of the presidents of Nicaragua and Ecuador, Porras entered western Panama on March 31, 1900, with an invasion force commanded by Colombian **Emiliano Herrera**, at the insistence of President Zelaya of Nicaragua. Their antagonism was a major factor in the ultimate Liberal failure. Moving towards Panama City, they gathered numerous supporters, but slow progress allowed reinforcements to arrive from Colombia. On arrival outside the capital, Herrera rejected Porras's attack plan and led a botched single-pronged assault on the city in which a thousand died. Though the Conservatives reasserted their authority, small bands of Liberal sympathizers ran riot in the interior, especially in the central rural areas under the leadership of **Victoriano Lorenzo**, a local official of mixed heritage from Coclé and a champion of the indigenous population.

In 1901, a second Nicaraguan-backed Liberal force managed to take Colón and effectively immobilize the railway, forcing the Colombian government to ask the US to broker an armistice. The Liberals, fearing intervention by the US government, agreed to the peace conditions but Lorenzo refused to accept the terms. In a sordid collusion between both Conservative and Liberal social elites, Lorenzo was tricked into capture. In disregard of the amnesty detailed in the accord, he was summarily tried and executed by firing squad on May 15, 1903, in the Plaza de Armas (today's Plaza de Francia, where a plaque commemorates the event) of Panama City. Six months later Panama separated from Colombia.

1902

End of three-year civil war between the Conservative and Liberal parties – La Guerra de los Mil Días – which claimed one hundred thousand lives

1903

Backed by the US, Panama declares separation from Colombia but essentially hands the US control of the future Canal Zone "in perpetuity"

Separation from Colombia

Despite the French canal debacle, the dream of an interoceanic waterway remained as strong as ever. US President **Theodore Roosevelt**, in particular, felt that the construction of a canal across Central America was an essential step to becoming a major sea power. At first the favoured route was through Nicaragua, but the persuasive lobbying of Philippe **Bunau-Varilla**, former acting director and major shareholder in the French company, swung the Senate vote in Panama's favour. His masterstroke was to buy ninety Nicaraguan stamps that showed an erupting volcano – a major argument against the Nicaragua route – and send one to each senator just three days before the vote. In 1903 a **treaty** allowing the US to build the canal was negotiated with the Colombian government, whose senate refused to ratify it, understandably wary that the US would not respect their sovereignty. Outraged that "the Bogotá lot of jackrabbits should be allowed to bar one of the future highways of civilization", Roosevelt gave unofficial backing to Panamanian secessionists.

In the event, the **separation** was a swift almost bloodless affair with only one casualty. The small Colombian garrison in Panama City was bribed to switch sides and a second force that had landed at Colón agreed to return to Colombia without a fight after its officers had been tricked into captivity by the rebels. On November 3, 1903, the **Republic of Panama** was declared and immediately recognized by the US, whose gunship standing offshore prevented Colombian reinforcements from landing to crush the rebellion.

The Canal

A new **canal treaty** was quickly negotiated and signed on Panama's behalf by the slippery Bunau-Varilla, who had managed to get himself appointed a special envoy, theoretically only with negotiating powers. The Hay-Bunau-Varilla Treaty gave the US "all the rights, power and authority … which [it] would possess and exercise as if it were the sovereign", in perpetuity over an area of territory – the **Canal Zone** – extending five miles (8km) either side of the canal. In return, the new Panamanian government received a one-off payment of $10 million and a further $250,000 a year. (Of particular interest to Bunau-Varilla was the $40 million the French canal company received for all its equipment and infrastructure.) Even American secretary of state John Hay admitted the treaty conditions were "vastly advantageous to the US and we must confess … not so advantageous to Panama". Panama's newly formed national assembly found the terms outrageous, but when told by Bunau-Varilla that US support would be withdrawn were they to reject it – a claim he invented on the spot – they ratified the treaty, and work on the Panama Canal began.

It took ten years, 56,000 workers from 97 countries – though primarily from Barbados – and some $352 million to complete the task, an unprecedented triumph of organization, perseverance, engineering and, just as crucially, sanitation, during which time chief medical officer Colonel **William Gorgas** established a programme that **eliminated yellow fever** from the isthmus and brought malaria under control. As a result, the **death toll** – though still numbering some 5600 workers, predominantly of West Indian descent – was substantially lower than it would otherwise have been.

1914	1925	1936
The Canal is completed. Around 56,000 people from 97 countries have a hand in its Construction	The successful Dule Revolution results in the Guna people being promised a measure of cultural autonomy	Despite a treaty limiting US rights, tensions continue to build between Panama and the US territory of the Canal Zone

Meanwhile the two men in charge, **John Stevens**, a brilliant railway engineer, and his successor **George Goethals**, a former army engineer, managed to solve the problems that had stymied the French. The idea of a sea-level canal was quickly abandoned in favour of constructing a **series of locks** to raise ships up to a huge artificial lake formed by damming the mighty Río Chagres. Stevens was responsible for maximizing the potential of the railway, devising an ingenious pulley system that enabled them to excavate over 170 million cubic metres of earth and rock, three times the amount removed at Suez. The 13km **Gaillard Cut**, which ran through the continental divide, required a mind-boggling 27,000 tonnes of dynamite. The end result, overseen by Goethals, was the largest concrete structure, earth dam and artificial lake that the world had ever seen, accomplished with pioneering technology that set new standards for engineering. On August 15, 1914, the SS *Ancón* became the first ship to officially transit the Canal, which was completed six months ahead of schedule. In all the triumphant celebrations, the 40,000 people who were displaced in the making of the canal, their homes and livelihoods destroyed, were largely forgotten.

An enormous **migrant workforce**, at times outnumbering the combined populations of Panama City and Colón, was imported to work on the Canal's construction, and many of these workers – Indians, Europeans, Chinese and above all West Indians – stayed on after its completion, indelibly transforming the racial and cultural make-up of the country. Work was carried out under an apartheid labour system, where white Americans were paid in gold and the rest – the vast majority of whom were black – in silver. Employees were "**gold roll**" or "**silver roll**", a categorization that permeated every aspect of life. The gold roll employees and their families enjoyed higher wages, superior accommodation, better nutrition, health care and schooling; even toilets and drinking fountains were set aside for the exclusive use of one group or the other. Unsurprisingly, the mortality rate among black workers was four times higher than among whites.

The New Republic

Though their economy boomed during the Canal's construction, it was soon apparent to Panamanians that they had exchanged control by Bogotá for dominance by the US. The government, largely controlled by a ruling **oligarchy** known as the "twenty families", was independent in name only; the US controlled everything – trade, communications, water and security. Moreover, the de facto sovereignty and legal jurisdiction that the US enjoyed within the Canal Zone made it a strip of US territory in which Panamanians were denied the commercial and employment opportunities enjoyed by the US "**Zonians**", a situation that lasted well beyond the completion of the Canal. The US agreement to guarantee Panamanian independence came at the price of intervention whenever the US considered it necessary to "maintain order", a right they exercised on several occasions.

One such action followed the Dule or **Guna Revolution** in 1925, an eventual result of the Panamanian government refusing to recognize the relative autonomy granted by the Colombian authorities in 1870 through the Comarca Dulenega. Pressure mounted when outside groups were given concessions to plunder Guna resources and persistent

1940

Fascist president Arnulfo Arias Madrid sets about disenfranchising Afro-Antillean and Chinese-Panamanians while pursuing racist immigration policies

1953

The first *comarca* is legally established in Panama under the authority of the Guna General Congress violent attempts made to suppress Guna culture. Following an **armed revolt** led by Sailas (chiefs) Nele Kantule and Olokindibipilele (Simral Colman), which resulted in around twenty fatalities on each side, the Guna declared independence. Forestalling government retaliation, the US – concerned for the safety of the canal – stepped in and mediated a **peace agreement** that granted the Guna the semiautonomous status they still retain.

The Republic of Panama's first president, the respected Conservative **Manuel Amador Guerrero**, was actually from Colombia, but the first Panamanian president of real impact was **Belisario Porras**, elected to office in 1912 for the first of three terms (1912–16, 1918–20 and 1920–24). A trained lawyer and prominent Liberal leader from the War of a Thousand Days, he is largely credited for establishing the basic infrastructure necessary for a newly independent state – roads, bridges, hospitals, schools, libraries, a legal system, communication networks and even the cherished national lottery.

The rise of nationalism

Despite a **new treaty** limiting the US right of intervention in 1936, resentment of American control became the dominant theme of Panamanian politics and the basis of an emerging sense of national identity. **Arnulfo Arias Madrid**, a fascist and Nazi-sympathizer – earning him the nickname "Führer Criollo" – exploited this while going on to become one of the country's most popular leaders. Of middle-class farming stock from Coclé, and a Harvard graduate, he founded Acción Communal, the political precursor to the Partido Nacional Revolucionario and present-day **Partido Panameñista (PP)**, which espoused his nationalistic and initially racist doctrine of **Panameñismo**. After assisting his older brother Harmodio Arias Madrid to the presidency in 1932, he won office himself in 1940, for the first of three periods (1940–41, 1949–51 and 1968).

During his first term he set about disenfranchising Afro-Antillean and Chinese-Panamanians and pursuing **racist** immigration policies. On the positive side he instigated the social security system, improved many workers' rights (a policy strand abandoned in his later term), modernized banking and gave the vote to women. Crucially, he was adamant about pushing for a better deal with a US government intent on expanding its military defences outside the Canal Zone. But the US-backed Panamanian Policía Nacional (National Police) and its successor, the Guardia Nacional (National Guard), made sure that no president who challenged the status quo lasted long in office and Arias was ousted by military coup each time, the last after only two weeks.

Nevertheless, **anti-US riots** erupted periodically over the next thirty years. The ten-thousand-strong protest in 1947 against the US attempt to extend the lease on World War II-era bases outside the Canal Zone helped persuade the deputies not to ratify the proposal. By 1948, the US military had withdrawn from outside the Zone. The most infamous disturbances, however, were the so-called **flag riots** of 1964. The flying of flags was a trivial but symbolic battleground for Panamanian-US antagonism. When the US flag was flown on its own for two days in succession in Balboa High School – not along with the Panamanian flag, as had been agreed – two hundred Panamanian students arrived at the school to rectify the situation. A skirmish broke out and the

1964

"Martyrs' Day" flag riots leave 21 Panamanians dead and more than five hundred injured

1968

Omar Torrijos, chief of the National Guard, overthrows President Arnulfo Arias and imposes a military dictatorship

1977

Torrijos secures a new canal treaty with US president Jimmy Carter, who agrees to transfer the Canal to Panamanian control in 1999

Panamanian flag was torn, prompting full-scale mob violence. The 21 Panamanians who died were later elevated to the status of **national martyrs**, commemorated annually on January 9, *Día de los Mártires* (Martyrs' Day).

Omar Torrijos and the new canal treaty

After a brief power struggle following the coup to oust Arnulfo Arias in 1968, Lieutenant Colonel **Omar Torrijos** of the National Guard established himself as leader of the new military government. Fracturing the political dominance of the white merchant oligarchy (known disparagingly as the *rabiblancos*, or "white tails") in his pursuit of a pragmatic middle way between socialism and capitalism, he was a charismatic, populist leader. Over twelve years he introduced a wide range of reforms – a new constitution and labour code, nationalization of the electricity and communications sectors, expanded public health and education services – while simultaneously maintaining good relations with the business sector, establishing Colón's **Zona Libra** and initiating the banking secrecy laws necessary for Panama's emergence as an international financial centre. Rather more darkly, he was extremely intolerant of political opposition and his critics were often imprisoned or simply "disappeared". Several **mass graves** from the period were unearthed during a Truth Commission instigated by President Moscoso, though there was no evidence of Torrijos' direct involvement in the atrocities.

Central to Torrijos' popular appeal was his insistence on gaining Panamanian control over the Canal. After lethargic negotiations with the Nixon and Ford administrations, Torrijos signed a new canal treaty with US president Jimmy Carter on September 7, 1977. Under its terms the US agreed to a gradual withdrawal, passing complete control of the Canal to Panama on December 31, 1999; in the meantime it was to be administered by the **Panama Canal Commission**, composed of five US and four Panamanian citizens. Even so, the US retained the right to intervene militarily if the Canal's neutrality was threatened. Under pressure from Washington to democratize, Torrijos formed a political party, the **Partido Revolucionario Democrático (PRD)**, and began moving Panama towards free democratic elections. In 1981, however, he died in a plane crash, which was rumoured to have been plotted by the **CIA** or Colonel **Manuel Noriega**, Torrijos' former military intelligence chief.

Manuel Noriega and the US invasion

After a period of political uncertainty, Noriega took over as head of the National Guard, which he restructured as a personal power base and renamed the Fuerzas de Defensa de Panamá (**Panama Defence Forces** or **PDF**), becoming the de facto military ruler in 1983. Although the 1984 elections gave Panama its first directly elected leader in nearly two decades, Nicolás Ardito Barletta, the real power lay in the hands of **Noriega**, backed by the US government.

A career soldier, Panama's new military strongman had been on the US Army's payroll as early as the 1950s and the CIA's from the late 1960s, before becoming chief of intelligence for the National Guard in 1970. In the early 1980s, Noriega assisted the US by supporting its interests elsewhere in Central America, especially

1983

Colonel Manuel Noriega becomes de facto military ruler. He is initially supported by the US, but also cultivates drug-cartel connections

1988

US charges Noriega with rigging elections, drug smuggling and murder; Noriega declares state of emergency, dodging a coup and repressing opposition

PANAMA'S INDIGENOUS POPULATION

While Panama's national economy enjoys one of the highest growth rates in Latin America, the distribution of wealth remains highly skewed, the poorest twenty percent living below the poverty line, receiving less than 1.5 percent of the earnings. This includes most of Panama's 698,000 **indigenous citizens**, who comprise around seventeen percent of the total population according to the 2023 census. Some have been assimilated to varying degrees into urban life; most, though, inhabit the rural regions, with around 37 percent living in the various *comarcas* – semiautonomous areas demarcated by the state over the last sixty-plus years – many without access to clean water, health care, electricity, decent schooling or paid employment.

Panama has eight indigenous groups, the most numerous by far being the **Ngäbe** (445,000), who share a vast *comarca* in western Panama, spanning Bocas del Toro, Chiriquí and Veraguas, with the less numerous **Buglé** (almost 24,000). The groups are culturally similar but speak mutually unintelligible languages. The first *comarca* established was Guna Yala in 1953, the result of a revolution by the **Dule** (or **Guna**) people (112,000) in 1925, which stretches out along the coastal strip of eastern Panama to the Colombian border, incorporating more than four hundred tiny islands. Much later, the smaller inland *comarcas* of Wargandi and Madugandi were added. The **Emberá** (52,000) and **Wounaan** (eleven thousand) inhabit the forests of the Darién, though some live in the Chagres river basin nearer Panama City. Around a fifth remain within the *comarca* boundaries; many others are scattered among around forty riverside communities across the province, or have gone to the city. At the other end of the isthmus in Bocas del Toro province, the **Naso**, also known as the Teribe, number nearly seven thousand and live around Changuinola and along the rivers heading up into the mountains. After years of lobbying, the Naso were finally granted their own *comarca* in 2019. A few kilometres north, on the banks of the Río Sixaola, live the **Bri-Bri** (just over seven hundred). The often forgotten **Bokota**, which number less than seven hundred, are often mistakenly considered Buglé since they speak Buglere; they live around the Bocas–Veraguas provincial boundary in the Comarca Ngäbe-Buglé.

Suffering the highest levels of poverty in the *comarca*, some Ngäbe and Buglé migrate for

Nicaragua. Whereas Torrijos had supported the leftist Sandinistas in Nicaragua's civil war, Noriega allegedly provided covert US military support for the Contras, helping to funnel money and weapons to the guerrilla force – a charge he denied. At the same time, Noriega was busy building relations with the Colombian cocaine cartels in Medellín. Although this extracurricular activity was ignored by the US for years, in 1986 the **Iran-Contra Affair** – in which the US government sold weapons illicitly to Iran and used the proceeds to fund the Contras – brought an unwelcome glare of publicity on the cosy arrangement between Noriega and the CIA. Deciding it was politically expedient to drive Noriega from power, the US government began economic sanctions in 1987, followed by Noriega's indictment on drug charges in the US in February 1988.

On December 20, 1989, US president George H.W. Bush launched the ironically named "**Operation Just Cause**", and 27,000 US troops invaded Panama. They quickly overcame the minimal organized resistance offered by the PDF. Bombers, helicopter gunships and even untested stealth aircraft were used against an enemy with no air

1989

US troops invade Panama and oust Noriega, but also kill and leave homeless thousands of civilians

1992

US court finds Noriega guilty of drug charges, sentencing him to forty years in prison seasonal jobs on banana, coffee and sugar plantations to earn cash to sustain them the rest of the year. Guna, Emberá and Wounaan women, in particular, earn an income from their fine craftwork – though villages in remote areas more or less compete with each other for the small percentage of visitors who venture past Panama City and the Canal. Some indigenous Panamanians move to and from the capital city and the *comarcas* depending on casual employment opportunities.

Although the *comarcas* cover a fifth of Panama's land, these territories as well as those of indigenous communities residing outside their boundaries are under constant **threat**. Some lands lie within national parks and reserves, which has enabled government, generally through its environment arm, to apply restrictions on traditional lifestyles in the name of conservation, while simultaneously allowing mining or hydroelectric projects to go ahead often with minimal or no consultation with indigenous authorities and no compensation to those forced to move. Government and big business are not the only threats: poor cattle farmers, *colonos*, desperate for fresh grazing land, have been encroaching on indigenous lands for years, particularly in eastern Panama. In the Darién, in particular, you can add drug traffickers, people smugglers and paramilitaries to the list (see page 276).

By far the most **organized politically** are the Guna, who have had the greatest success in defending their rights against the state and have had greater representation (including women) at government level. The other main indigenous groups have tended to follow the Guna model, electing a **General Congress** consisting of a *cacique* and community representatives. Leaders from indigenous parties have begun working together to tackle attempts to marginalize them or incorporate them into models of development they do not espouse. There have been several notable legal victories, including at the Inter-American Commission on Human Rights (IACHR), and most recently, in 2023, the government was forced to close the copper mine affecting numerous Ngäbe communities (see page 222). But these successes have been the only bright lights in an otherwise bleak narrative.

defences, and hundreds of explosions were recorded in the first twelve hours. The poor Panama City barrio of El Chorrillo was heavily bombed and burned to the ground, leaving some fifteen thousand people homeless; a Human Rights Watch report noted that civilian deaths were more than four times higher than military casualties among the PDF. Noriega himself evaded capture and took refuge in the papal nunciature, before being forced to surrender on January 5 after a round-the-clock diet of ear-splitting heavy metal and rock music blasted from the car park. He was taken to the US, **convicted of drug trafficking** and sentenced to forty years in a Miami jail.

Estimates of the number of Panamanians killed during the invasion vary from several hundred to as many as ten thousand. The invasion's illegality, however, was clear, condemned by the United Nations and the Organization of American States, both of which demanded the immediate withdrawal of US forces. Despite most Panamanians being relieved to see the back of Noriega, they were outraged at the excessive use of force and America's blatant disregard for Panamanian sovereignty.

1999

Mireya Moscoso, widow of Arnulfo Arias, becomes the country's first female president, and presides over the handover of the Canal to Panama in December

2004

Martín Torrijos, son of former dictator Omar Torrijos, is elected president; plans for a Panama Canal expansion plan are passed with an overwhelming majority

THE MULTIBILLION-DOLLAR GAMBLE: EXPANDING THE CANAL

Two years overdue and a couple of billion dollars over budget, the **Panama Canal expansion** was finally inaugurated on June 26, 2016 amid much fanfare, fireworks and flag waving. The bold investment aimed to accommodate Post-Panamax vessels (ships that are too big to fit into the original Canal lock chambers) through two larger sets of locks and by widening the Culebra Cut, thereby tripling the size of the ships it can accommodate and doubling the Canal's capacity. But the project has not been without its setbacks: for a start, the Panamanian government and some of the Spanish and Italian contractors are still involved in legal wrangles about who should pay for the cost overruns. Of greater concern is the huge amount of water needed to ensure the smooth passage of the vast container ships through the Canal. Although the new Cocolí and Agua Clara locks include water-recycling devices, overall the Canal now needs twice the amount of water than it did previously – an issue that came to the fore in 2024, when a severe drought caused Lago Gatún to almost dry up, resulting in an annual reduction in shipping transits by almost a third. Faced with the likelihood of future droughts due to climate change, the government plans to sink a further $1.6 billion into a new reservoir in Río Indio, which runs parallel to the Canal. Yet the project is already facing protests, not least from the 2,000 people who would be displaced. Add to that the economic uncertainty in world shipping and Donald Trump's ambitions to regain control of the Canal, and it remains to be seen whether the $5.4 billion gamble to expand the canal will ultimately pay off.

The dawn of the twenty-first century

In an interesting twist, the presidential elections of 1999 were contested between Martín Torrijos, illegitimate son of the former military ruler, and the widow of Arnulfo Arias (the man Torrijos ousted in 1968), **Mireya Moscoso**, who became Panama's first female leader. On December 31 she presided over the seamless **handover of the Canal**, which is now efficiently managed by the independent Autoridad del Canal de Panamá. The US withdrawal was a mixed blessing for Panama's economy: many jobs disappeared with the closure of the bases, but the valuable real estate and infrastructure Panama inherited created investment opportunities. Still, a number of the former US buildings lie abandoned, and relations with the US remain complex.

Moscoso's term in office got off to a rocky start when, before the first budget vote, she gave Cartier watches and jewellery as "Christmas presents" to the 72 members of the legislative assembly. It set the tenor for the presidency, which was scarred with accusations of **corruption** and incompetence. Her term ended in similarly controversial fashion as she tried to push through construction of a tarred road linking Boquete and Cerro Punta through the national park of Volcán Barú. Opposition to the outrageous plan successfully united numerous national and international environmental groups and became a major election issue allowing **Martín Torrijos**, heading the PRD, to become president.

Though Torrijos junior was elected on a platform of "zero corruption" it did not take long before scandals started to emerge; nor was his administration's record on the environment particularly memorable, approving countless hydroelectric projects in Chiriquí and Bocas del Toro provinces with scant environmental assessment

2009

Right-wing supermarket magnate Ricardo Martinelli becomes president after a landslide victory. Meanwhile, the government ignores a landmark IACHR ruling in favour of the Ngäbe, and continues working on the Río Changuinola dam

2011

Silvia Carrera is elected the first female cacique of the Ngäbe studies and little negotiation with the indigenous populations most affected. In his biggest gamble, he green-lighted the **Canal expansion** project (see box, page 306).

The Canal expansion, Odebrecht and the "Panama papers"

The elections in May 2009 broke the political stranglehold that the PRD and PP had enjoyed for the previous seventy years as conservative multimillionaire supermarket magnate **Ricardo Martinelli** swept to power. Head of the new **Cambio Democrático** (Democratic Change; CD) party, he immediately launched popular initiatives, increasing the minimum wage, establishing pensions and ensuring free books and uniforms for school children. Panama enjoyed sustained economic growth – though the gap between the "haves" and "have-nots" continued to increase – and the government spent a staggering $20 billion on roads, schools and bridges across the country. In the capital countless skyscrapers sprang up, the new Metrobus and metro systems were established and the Cinta Costera – an ambitious land reclamation project – was extended, including a highly controversial ring-road round Casco Viejo.

However, as with Martinelli's predecessors, corruption scandals flourished and his increasingly autocratic ruling style, curtailment of the press and overuse of police force – especially against indigenous communities – provoked much criticism at home and internationally. In the 2014 elections, Martinelli's estranged vice-president, **Juan Carlos Varela**, who had fallen out with his former ally after being dismissed as foreign minister, won a surprising victory for the Partido Panameñista.

Meanwhile, the inauguration of the delayed and overbudget **Canal expansion** in June 2016 (see box, page 306) was overshadowed by a series of **huge corruption scandals**. Involving many of the country's elite, they ranged from the "**Panama Papers**" – a massive leak of Panama's offshore financial dealings that implicated numerous world leaders, criminals and celebrities in tax evasion – to revelations about successive governments' widespread acceptance of millions of dollars in kickbacks in awarding mega-construction contracts to the Brazilian construction giant, Odebrecht. Former presidents Martiń Torrijos, Ricardo Martinelli and Juan Carlos Varela, and hundreds of others, were all implicated, though many charges were subsequently dropped. In the wake of the scandals, 2017 witnessed widespread anticorruption and antigovernment street protests.

Covid-19 and persistent protests

The **Covid-19 pandemic** reached Panama in March 2020, with far-reaching effects. Under the stewardship of then president **Laurentino Cortizo**, the country experienced the region's highest per-capita infection rates, long periods of lockdown, multiple job losses and one of the world's longest school closures – almost eighteen months. The global economic fallout from the pandemic, combined with the war in Ukraine, increased the cost of living, especially the price of fuel, food and medicine. With unemployment rising and increasing levels of informal and inadequately paid jobs, many have struggled to cope and are demanding better health, education and other services. For most of July 2022 angry Panamanians took to the streets in the biggest **protests and strikes** in decades, forcing Cortizo to reduce the price

2012

Countrywide protests by the Ngäbe and Buglé over mining and hydroelectric concessions on their land end in police violence, leaving thousands wounded and three dead

2016

The new Panama Canal locks are inaugurated

2020–22

Covid-19 hits the poorer 50 percent working in the informal sector very hard, widening inequalities of fuel, agree to food caps on certain items and sign agreements on employment reform with various trade unions. But the peace was short-lived. With no evidence of change, by August 2023 protests and strikes had begun again, intensifying in October as the **Interamericana was blockaded** for almost two months, and the economy effectively paralyzed. This time the trigger was the fast-tracked extension agreement for the First Quantum **copper mine** (see page 315), which united protest from many groups, including teachers, nurses, constructors, indigenous groups and environmentalists. Four people were killed, over a hundred injured and the government suffered billions of dollars of lost revenue. The Supreme Court eventually judged the mine agreement to be unconstitutional, the mine was closed and Cortizo was forced to sign into law an indefinite moratorium on new mining concessions. At the same time, he struggled to deal with the worst **drought** in decades, which imperilled the Panama Canal.

In the 2024 elections, mining, corruption, employment and the economy were key issues. Former president Ricardo Martinelli was the frontrunner, as voters were nostalgic for the economic boom times that he represented – even though he'd been convicted of money-laundering, and was holed up in the Nicaraguan embassy, to avoid prison. After being disqualified from standing, however, Martinelli's votes were transferred to the CD stand-in candidate and eventual winner, **José Raúl Mulino**. He reneged on his election promise to commute his former ally's sentence but has managed to "close down" the migrant highway through the Darién Gap (see page 276) – with the assistance of Donald Trump.

But Mulino is in for a bumpy presidency as ordinary Panamanians are fed up with being ignored and maltreated. Protests have resumed in 2025, with additional grievances including the privatization of the social security system, the new reservoir for the Canal (see page 306) and US influence in the country. It remains to be seen whether more mass protests will succeed in kick-starting real social change.

2024

Four months of nationwide protests and blockades across the Interamericana cause massive economic disruption and force government to close down a large copper mine. Unprecedented drought reduces the Canal's capacity by 40 percent

2025

US President Trump threatens to "take back" control of the Canal

Wildlife

One of Panama's major attractions is its varied and abundant wildlife. For its diminutive size – slightly larger than the Republic of Ireland, smaller than the US state of South Carolina – Panama's biodiversity and level of endemism is astounding. Located at the barely touching fingertips of two continents, the country hosts fauna from both land masses: deer and coyotes more readily associated with temperate North America as well as jaguars and capybaras from the tropical South, and a cornucopia of astounding marine life. The flora is equally diverse: an estimated ten thousand vascular plant species grow on the isthmus, predominantly in the country's luxuriant tropical rainforests, which cover an estimated 45 percent of the land.

Flora

Panama's **tropical wet forests**, or **rainforests**, which by definition receive an annual rainfall of more than 2m and can receive up to three times that amount on some of the Caribbean slopes, are what most excite nature-lovers. **Primary** rainforests – original, undisturbed growth – are highly prized for their greater biodiversity, comprising seventy percent of the country's forested area. In these complex ecosystems most animal and plant activity occurs in the forest "roof" or **canopy** and the **sub-canopy**, where dangling vines and lianas provide vital transport links. Poking out of the canopy, which filters out more than ninety percent of the sunlight, are a sprinkling of robust **emergent trees**, generally around 60–70m tall, able to withstand being buffeted by storms and scorched by sunlight. Most easily recognized, and visible from a great distance, is the ringed silvery grey trunk of the **cuipo** (*cavanillesia platanifolia*), which exhibits a bare umbrella-like crown during the dry season; particularly abundant in the Darién, it is a favourite nesting site of the harpy eagle. Equally distinctive from above is the lofty **guayacán** (*tabebuia guayacan*), whose brilliant golden crown stands out against the dense green canopy carpet, blooming a month in advance of the first rains. Not atypically, both species drop their leaves in the dry season to reduce water loss through evaporation. From the forest floor, the vast buttress roots of the **ceiba** (silk-cotton or kapok tree; *ceiba petandra*), or thinner versions on the **Panama tree** (*sterculia apetela*), are more striking; so, too, the vicious protective spines on the **spiny cedar** (*pachira quinata*), or the swollen midsection of the aptly named **barrigón** (*pseudobombax septenatum*) – *barriga* meaning "pot belly" in Spanish – which can double its waist size to store water and whose pretty pompom flowers open for evening pollination.

Dominated by vines, ferns, saplings and shrubs typically 10–25m tall, the forest **understorey** and **forest floor** below are relatively sparsely populated in the cathedral-like primary forest, in contrast to the dense and tangled vegetation of **secondary** forest. It's in these lower layers that you'll come across the pinkish hues of **heliconias**, such as the vividly named **lobster's claw** (*heliconia rostrata*), edged with yellow, and the more solid **beefsteak** (*heliconia mariae*), a "medium-rare" dark pink, or the pouting scarlet bracts of the Warholian **hotlips** (*psychotria poeppigiana*), which lure butterflies and hummingbirds to the almost invisible central flowers.

Topping the higher mountainous ridges, especially in western Panama, and almost permanently enveloped in mist, are dense patches of eerie fern-filled **cloud forest**, characterized by shorter, stockier trees covered in **lichen** and dripping with **mosses**. Boughs here are more heavily laden with **epiphytes**, including many of Panama's thousand-plus species of delicate **orchid** and **bromeliads**, whose leaves trap moisture, providing water for numerous tree-dwelling organisms. Back down on the coast, some

1700 square kilometres of mostly **red**, **white** and **black mangroves** constitute a vital buffer zone, serving both terrestrial and marine ecologies.

Fauna

Though most visitors yearn to catch sight of a jaguar or tapir, you'll likely have to settle for smaller **mammals** and the less elusive members of the **avian** and **amphibian** populations, which can be just as fascinating.

Birds

Panama lays claim to around a thousand recorded species of **bird**, more than Canada and the US combined, and greater than any Central American state. The 17km Camino del Oleoducto (Pipeline Road) in the former Canal Zone alone boasts a species list of more than four hundred. Even Panama City harbours egrets to elaenias, parakeets to pelicans: avian-rich locations within the greater city boundaries include the Metropolitan and other parks, Panamá Viejo, the Amador Causeway and round Cerro Ancón and Balboa.

Acting as a continental funnel, Panama sees many **migrants**, with numbers peaking in September and October and returning in more dispersed fashion from March to May. During this period, more than a million shore birds carpet the Pacific coastal mud flats, though it is the **raptor migration** that captures the imagination. Hundreds of thousands of **turkey vultures**, interspersed with **Swainson's** and **broad-winged hawks**, ride the thermals, wheeling their way along the isthmus (late Oct to Nov), a spectacular sight best appreciated from the summit of Cerro Ancón or one of Gamboa's several canopy lookouts.

While twitchers may get excited locating a dull-coloured rare endemic in the undergrowth, average nature-lovers will be more impressed by the visually dazzling birds. The cloud forests of Chiriquí afford an unparalleled opportunity to spot the iridescent emerald-and-crimson **resplendent quetzal** – especially visible and striking during spring courtship displays – while the Darién jungle maintains a similar reputation for the **harpy eagle**, Panama's gigantic national bird and arguably the world's most powerful raptor, with its distinctive tousled crest and ferocious giant talons (see box, page 288). Other glamour birds include the country's multicoloured, raucous **parrots** (*loros*), including five species of endangered **macaw** (*guacamaya*). Sadly depleted through the pet trade, loss of habitat and hunting – their flashy tail feathers make a customary adornment for some traditional costumes and dances – they have been forced into more remote areas, with the **scarlet macaw** making its last stand on the island of Coiba. Panama's seven varieties of **toucan** (*tucán*), including toucanets and aracaris, are another psychedelic feature of the landscape; their oversized rainbow-coloured bills help pluck hard-to-reach berries and regulate body temperature. Abundant in the Canal area and round Cerro Ancón, they are most easily spotted croaking in the canopy early morning or late afternoon. Panama's 59 types of **hummingbird** (*colibrí*) are spellbinding as they hover round flowers and feeders as if suspended in air, or whizz past your ear at some 50km/h. Lustrous **tanagers**, smart **trogans** and the distinctive racquet-tailed **motmots** will also turn heads.

Some birds are more notable for their behaviour: **jacanas**, whose vast, spindly feet enable them to stride across floating vegetation, are nicknamed "lily-trotters"; minute fluffy **manakins** conduct manic acrobatic courtship displays in their communal mating arenas known as *leks*; and the prehistoric-looking **potoo** is a nocturnal insectivore that camouflages itself on the end of a tree stump during the day, invisible to would-be predators. Spend enough time in the Western Highlands, especially in the breeding season (March–Sept), and you're likely to hear the distinctly unbell-like metallic "boing" of the strange-looking **three-wattled bellbird** complete with what look like strands of liquorice hanging from its beak; audible from almost a kilometre away, it is considered one of the loudest bird songs on earth. Mention should also be made of the ubiquitous **oropendola** (gold pendulum); these large, generally russet-toned birds, with outsize pointed beaks and golden tails, are renowned for their colonies of skilfully woven hanging nests, which dangle from tall trees like Christmas decorations.

Terrestrial mammals

Spotting any of Panama's 230-plus mammal species – half of which are small **bats** – requires luck and persistence and is nigh on impossible when it comes to Panama's "big five" wild cats, which in descending size order are the **jaguar**, **puma**, **jaguarundi**, **ocelot** and **margay**. Nocturnal and shy at the best of times, from years of human predation, they are most numerous in the country's two remaining wilderness areas at either end of the isthmus: the Darién and Amistad.

Spotting tracks in the morning mud is the closest you're likely to get to a jaguar in the wild. Referred to as a "*tigre*" (tiger) by indigenous populations and revered as a symbol of power and strength, the jaguar is the world's third largest feline after the lion and tiger, weighing in at around 60–90kg, and with leopard-like markings. It's more probable you'll encounter its dinner, be it **deer** (*venado*), the raccoon-like **coati** (*gato solo*) or large rodents such as the **agouti** (*ñeque*) or the nocturnal **paca** (*conejo pintado*, literally "painted rabbit" on account of its white spots). Panama also harbours the world's largest rodent, the **capybara**, which can tip the scales at 65kg; resembling a giant guinea pig, it wallows in the shallows round Gamboa and grazes at Punta Patiño, in the Darién. A more ambitious feature of the jaguar's diet is the **peccary**, a kind of wild boar. Two barely distinguishable species forage through the rainforest undergrowth in Panama: the more frequently seen **collared** peccary (*saíno*), which lives in small herds, and the elusive, aggressive **white-lipped** peccary (*puerco de monte*), which can travel in battalions of several hundred and be dangerous when threatened.

One of the largest, most extraordinary-looking mammals in the Neotropics is **Baird's tapir** (*macho de monte*). Another endangered nocturnal creature, it resembles an overgrown pig with a sawn-off elephant's trunk stuck on its face, which is actually a stubby prehensile nose and upper lip used to grip branches and eat the leaves and fruit. Though the adults are dull brown, baby tapirs have spotted and striped coats for camouflage. More commonly espied are **sloths** (*perezosos*) and **anteaters** (*hormigueros*), both of which arrived on the planet shortly after the demise of dinosaurs. Panama's **two-toed** and **three-toed** sloths spend much of their time literally hanging around treetops, either curled round a branch camouflaged as an ants' nest, or gripping with their long curved claws, doing everything in slow motion to conserve energy. Inexplicably, they make a near-suicidal descent to ground level once a week to defecate. In contrast, the **northern tamandua**, a type of anteater, moves nimbly along the branches, hoovering up ants and termites. Not an uncommon sight in the Metropolitan Park, even though mainly nocturnal, they are widespread across the country, whereas the wholly terrestrial **giant anteater** is verging on extinction nationally, as is the **spectacled bear**, named after the cream-coloured markings around its eyes.

Monkeys are an almost guaranteed sighting in Panama, which hosts all seven Central American species. A distinctive feature of the tropical landscape, the large, shaggy **mantled howler monkey** (*aullador negro*) is more likely to be heard before being seen; the ape's stentorian cries travel for kilometres, with large troops announcing dawn and dusk and even the onset of heavy rain. The other two more widespread species are the cherub-like **Geoffroy's tamarin** (*mono tití*), found in central and eastern Panama, and the larger, highly intelligent **white-throated capuchin** (*mono cariblanco*). Named for their physical resemblance to brown-robed Capuchin friars, though also somewhat misleadingly dubbed "white-headed" or "white-faced", the monkey's pink anthropomorphic face makes it a popular pet. Catching sight of a troop of **black-headed spider monkeys** (*mono araña negro*) – one of several types of endangered Panamanian spider monkey – elegantly gliding through the canopies of eastern Panama is a magical experience. At the other end of the isthmus, the **owl** or **night monkeys** (*mono de noche*), with their saucer-like eyes, are restricted to the Caribbean lowlands of Bocas, while over on the Pacific side, the delicate **squirrel monkey** (*mono ardilla*) is occasionally sighted in the Burica Peninsula in southwestern Chiriquí.

Reptiles

Mention the fact that you intend to hike in the jungle, and someone is bound to alert you to the dangers of **snakes**, though a relatively small percentage are venomous and snakebites are rare – most serpents are as wary of humans as humans are of them. The most feared, accounting for almost all fatal snakebites in Panama, is the **fer-de-lance** pit viper, which inhabits a variety of lowland habitats. Commonly dubbed "*equis*" ("X") for the markings on its well-camouflaged brown, cream and black skin, it often exceeds 2m in length. The female gives birth to fifty to eighty live young, which incredibly are already 30cm, not to mention venomous, when born. Initially arboreal, feeding on frogs and lizards, they become terrestrial with age. The world's largest pit viper, the dangerous **bushmaster**, can reach 3m, but fortunately is only encountered in remote forests and, like most pit vipers, is nocturnal. In contrast, Panama's various species of **coral snake**, both venomous and benign, all possess striking black, red and yellow-banded markings; since it's difficult to differentiate among them, it's best to assume danger. Positively mellow in comparison – though packing a powerful bite if provoked – the giant **boa constrictor** is Panama's only endangered snake, hunted for its prized skin.

Similarly threatened is the **green iguana**, which ranges from lime-green to dusty brown in colour and is pursued for its eggs and tasty meat, earning it the nickname "*gallina de palo*". Despite its dragon-like appearance, it is a docile forest-living herbivore that likes to be near water; the large flaps of skin under its chin (dewflaps) are used to regulate body temperature and for courtship and territorial displays. The tetchier, charcoal-grey **spiny-tailed** or **black iguana** is most commonly found on the Azuero Peninsula. The world's fastest lizard, it escapes predators by hitting speeds of up to 35km/h; the miniature version, a 30cm **basilisk**, takes flight across water on its hind legs and partially webbed feet, earning it the nickname **"Jesus Christ" lizard**.

In Panama's mangrove-filled estuaries and mud-lined waterways, including around Lago Gatún and Lago Bayano, **crocs** and **caimans** lurk. The endangered, aggressive **American crocodile** has actually increased its numbers here, as has the smaller, more docile **spectacled caiman**.

Amphibians

Of all Panama's amphibians, **frogs** are the most compelling. The country's emblematic and revered **golden frog** (see box, page 136) has been declared extinct in the wild, due to the **chytrid fungus**, which has been decimating amphibians worldwide. Since 2009, an Amphibian Ark rescue mission (Ⓦamphibianrescue.org) has been capturing and breeding species in captivity, in the hope that they can be released into the wild in the future. The brilliantly coloured miniature **poison dart frogs**, with markings as varied as wallpaper, are relatively easy to see, especially in Bocas del Toro (see box, page 233), as they hop around the leaf litter under trees by day. But the rainforests harbour other equally extraordinary specimens, less visible since they're primarily nocturnal: the tiny lime-green **glass frog**, whose inexplicably transparent belly affords you the dubious pleasure of observing its viscera and digestive processes; the **flying frog** with giant webbed feet that help parachute it through the air; and the **milk frog** – so named after the toxic mucous it secretes when threatened – which possesses two giant vocal sacs either side of the head that also act as buoyancy aids in water.

Insects and arachnids

Although **insects** don't generally set the pulse racing, **butterflies** are the exception. With sixteen thousand species, Panama hosts approximately ten percent of the world's Lepidoptera, from the enormous **owl butterfly**, so-called after the large "eyes" on its mottled brown wings, to the tiny delicate **glasswing**, whose translucent wings are reminiscent of a stained-glass window. Most magnificent of all, is the iridescent **blue morpho**, whose drunken zigzagged flight makes it particularly hard to photograph.

Ants can be found in abundance; tiny Isla Barro Colorado alone has 225 species. Most distinctive are the packed highways of industrious **leafcutter** ants bearing enormous segments of leaf to their vast underground complex, where they are pulped to cultivate a "fungus garden", which in turn feeds the ants. Also easy to spot is the enormous black **bullet ant**; the size of a large grape and prevalent in low-lying forests, it holds the dubious distinction of causing the world's most painful insect sting.

Panama also possesses more than a thousand species of **spider**, a fair proportion of which are poisonous though rarely lethal to humans. One such is the innocuous-sounding **wandering spider** – until you realize its scientific name derives from the Greek for "murderous" (*phoneutes*) – which is a hairy arachnid that stalks the forest floor at night rather than ambushing prey in a web or lair. It is often mistaken for the stockier, hairier and relatively harmless **black tarantula**; also a night-time predator, it can be seen poking out of its lair, in a hollowed-out log or semi-submerged under leaf litter, during the day. Worth avoiding is the female **black widow spider**; recognizable by the glossy black abdomen and red hourglass mark on the underbelly, she has a potent venom with which to inject her prey. The **golden silk orb-weaving spider** makes the largest web; a magical sight on a sunlit morning in the rainforest, it really does glisten like gold thread.

Marine life

With coastlines on two oceans, Panama's marine biodiversity is impressive, especially where warm ocean currents and upwellings of cool nutrient-rich waters converge along the Pacific's Golfo de Chiriquí. Humpback **whales** calve in this area (July–Oct) and can also be sighted off the Pearl Islands and the tip of the Azuero Peninsula. These 15m giants are exciting to behold though whale watching in Panama is in its infancy. Earlier in the year (Feb–July), you may be lucky enough to catch sight of the gargantuan but placid whale shark, the world's largest fish, as it moves submarine-like through the waters round Coiba. Hammerhead and tiger **sharks** are occasionally spotted though white-tipped reef sharks are more common. The distinctive black-and-white killer whales, or orcas – actually the world's largest dolphin – prey on younger and weaker marine mammals, but aren't as widespread as bottle-nosed **dolphins**. From October to December schools of diamond-shaped golden rays glide like floating autumn leaves, occasionally leaping 2m into the air, as do more solitary manta rays; boasting a colossal 6m wingspan, one weighs as much as a small car.

In general, the Pacific coast boasts a greater number of large fish – **blue** and **black marlin**, **amberjack**, **wahoo**, **dorado** and **tuna**, to name a few – while the **coral reefs** on the Caribbean side, particularly around the archipelago of Bocas del Toro and parts of Gunayala, are populated with a greater variety of soft and hard corals. These feed and shelter aquatic life from sinuous **moray eels** and spiky **sea urchins** to delicate **sea horses** and a rainbow of dazzling fish. Iridescent **parrot fish** (30–50cm) are among the most distinctive, named less for their technicolour coats than for their serrated parrot-like "beaks" that gnaw algae and coral polyps off the reef. The ground coral is digested and excreted as sand – up to an estimated 90kg per fish annually – a major factor in the formation of Panama's glorious **white-sand beaches**. The Caribbean's other mammalian draw is the **manatee**, or sea cow, an amiable elephantine herbivore with a paddle-like rudder and flabby fleshy snout, found in the Humedales de San San Pond Sak in Bocas del Toro.

Five species of **marine turtle** lay their eggs on both Atlantic and Pacific shores, roughly between March and October/November – timings depend on species and location (see box, page 237). In the Caribbean, Bocas del Toro is the easiest place to visit **hawksbill**, **leatherback** and, to a lesser extent, **green** turtle nesting sites while **loggerheads** frequent the shallows. On the Pacific side, Isla de Cañas, off the Azuero Peninsula, is renowned for the mass **olive ridley** nesting (May–Nov), though the other species also deposit their eggs there in smaller numbers.

Environmental issues

As elsewhere in the tropics, the rainforests of Panama are disappearing at an alarming rate, threatening wildlife and, ultimately, human survival. While 45 percent of the country is still covered in forest, and deforestation rates have slowed since the millennium, the country is losing around one percent of its species-rich primary growth a year. A third of the land lies in national parks and reserves, but many of these are "paper parks" since the perennially underfunded Ministry of the Environment is short of cash and, in some cases, political clout and/or the will to enforce the regulations.

Deforestation

Although the large-scale extraction of mahogany, cedar or purpleheart destined for European and North American markets has come under greater control in recent years, the timber industry continues to be a major contributor to **deforestation** as illegal logging, and more insidiously, selective thinning continues.

By far the main driver of deforestation is **colonization**, clearing the land for cattle ranching and subsistence agriculture, and more recently, palm oil cultivation. Having already denuded the entire Azuero Peninsula and most of the Pacific slopes of central and western Panama, *colonos*, or "colonists", have been moving into eastern Panama in recent years along the Darién highway and Caribbean coast, sometimes into protected areas, often with the collusion of government officials. Despite the richness of tropical forests, the layer of nutritious topsoil is particularly thin so that once cleared it soon becomes worthless, forcing farmers to move on to fell new areas. Though usually contesting this encroachment onto their lands, some indigenous communities are also contributing to deforestation thanks to population increases and forced changes in lifestyle: in some cash-strapped settlements they are even leasing land to farmers for cattle grazing or colluding with illegal timber extraction. Panama's coastal mangrove forests – considered to be the most extensive, healthiest and most diverse in all Central America – are critically threatened, from agricultural expansion and coastal development on the mainland and water pollution, overfishing and sedimentation on the islands and marine areas.

Small-scale initiatives across the country aim to improve **environmental awareness**, ranging from assistance for micro-enterprises such as plant nurseries and agroforestry projects to tree-planting and recycling, often backed by NGOs and international environmental organizations. One such programme, started in 2003, was supported through Fundación Nacional Parque Chagres, the result of a "debt-for-nature" swap whereby $10 million of debt to the US government was eradicated over a 14-year period in return for the Panamanian government banks spending $700,000 annually on green-oriented projects and education. Of course it's no coincidence that the focus was the Chagres river basin, which is vital to the functioning of the Panama Canal, the lifeblood of Panama's economy and not insignificant to the US.

Reforestation programmes in Panama have become more common in the last few years. Initially they were all teak plantations, which arguably further degrade the soil, do nothing to sustain biodiversity and, being a monoculture, are more susceptible to disease; however, there has been a positive recent move towards more sustainable mixed plantations of native species. The Azuero Earth Project (Ⓦazueroearthproject.org), another Panama–US collaboration, is attempting to establish a biological corridor in the Azuero Peninsula, working with local landowners to regenerate tropical dry forest, as well as carry out community outreach and education programmes.

Mining and hydroelectric projects

Another area of environmental concern is the **mining industry**. After the hiatus in mineral exploitation during the 1990s due to its unprofitability, prices have begun to rise again, and the threat looms once more. In 2008, Panamanian environmental watchdog CIAM (Centro de Incidencia Ambiental) revealed that the amount of land involved in mining concessions that had either already been granted or were awaiting consideration totalled three times the country's surface area. Though many projects have not yet been realized or have stalled since then, significant degradation has been caused by those mining operations that have been pushed through. Top of the list of offenders is the vast Petaquilla open-cast copper and gold mine in Colón province, which restarted operations despite still owing $2 million in fines and damages for environmental negligence and trampling on local people's rights. Although the mine is now bankrupt and its CEO, "father of Panamanian mining" Richard Fifer, is behind bars for non-payment of employees' social security, the damage has been done.

Cerro Colorado, potentially one of the world's largest copper mines, lies in the middle of the Comarca Ngäbe-Buglé, where the indigenous population is also defending its territory against the many **micro-hydroelectric projects** underway or planned for western Panama – more than seventy in Chiriquí at the last count – one of which has already resulted in intervention by the Interamerican Human Rights Commission. In 2012, the Ngäbe and Buglé managed to bring the country's economy to a standstill by blocking the Interamericana for six days, though the protest ended in violence as the police were sent in, leaving at least three dead and many wounded.

Thankfully, Panama is now also looking towards alternative, more renewable energy sources, establishing its first wind farm outside Penonomé in Coclé province in 2015 – the largest in Central America – as well as a huge photovoltaic power station on the Azuero Peninsula.

Tourism and environmental impact

It's a difficult balance between promoting tourism and limiting its environmental and social impact. **Indigenous communities** are being encouraged to engage in **cultural ecotourism**, inviting visitors to learn about their traditional ways of life and selling their handicrafts. With little financial support from the government, some groups have benefited from assistance from NGOs or local Peace Corps workers. Emberá communities along the Chagres, in particular, have gained valuable income from cruise-ship tours and day-trip groups from travel agencies in Panama City because of their proximity to the capital. But the long-term effect when large groups swamp small villages in high season, eroding the land and tramping en masse down the same rainforest trail, is more difficult to gauge. Moreover, the impact on the marine environment of the cruise-ship industry – the area of tourism in which the government has invested most heavily – is also unknown.

Visitor numbers are small in most indigenous communities that engage with tourism, except in the western end of **Gunayala**. This is partly due to the road across the cordillera from the Panamerican Highway, which has allowed faster, cheaper access. Day-tripping Panamanians and beach-loving backpackers make up the bulk of the visitors: for small, overpopulated islands with inadequate sanitation and often ad hoc waste disposal, there's untold pressure on the natural resources. The beautiful islands of **Bocas del Toro**, the most visited region outside the capital and Canal area, suffer from similar problems as water, sanitation and electricity systems struggle to cope with pressure from high visitor numbers and the substantial expat population. On the positive side, turtle watching is taking off here, and in other areas of Panama, which as an income-generating project might eventually help protect their nesting sites.

Books

There are very few bookshops in Panama, and even fewer have a substantial section of books in English. In Panama City (see page 86), a couple stock a small, pricey selection in English. The colossus of contemporary Panamanian literature is Enrique Jaramillo Levi – internationally acclaimed short-story writer, poet, essayist, editor and critic, who, despite such accolades, has had relatively few works translated into English. New authors, such as Afro-Panamanian Melanie Taylor Herrera, have short stories and poetry translated into English, scattered around various journals, some of which are accessible online.

THE CANAL

Rosa Maria Britton and Eduardo Montaina *The New Panama Canal: A Breathtaking Journey Between the Pacific and Atlantic Oceans*. Expensive coffee-table book published to mark the 2016 opening of the Canal expansion, offering spectacular colour photos and stunning views.

William Friar *Portrait of the Panama Canal: Celebrating Its History and Expansion.* Updated edition to include the recent Canal expansion, this readable account by former Zonian and *New York Times* journalist is a paperback coffee-table offering containing a few wonderful historical photos as well as some more mundane contemporary glossies of the Canal and Panama.

★ **Julie Greene** *The Canal Builders: Making America's Empire at the Panama Canal.* Long overdue focus on the men and women who, in dreadful conditions and facing all sorts of discrimination, worked to achieve the realization of America's grandiose dream of empire. You also meet the big players whose ambition ignored the human cost.

Ulrich Keller *The Building of the Canal in Historic Photographs.* A clear case of pictures speaking louder than words, as 164 detailed black-and-white photos evoke the lives of both rich and poor engaged in the monumental struggle to build the Canal.

★ **Marixa Lasso** *Erased: The Untold Story of the Panama Canal* An excellent counterpoint to the dominant narrative of the canal being a colossal achievement, this award-winning book by a Panamanian history professor focuses on the negative impacts the canal had on the histories, livelihoods and ways of life of the 40,000 people who were displaced during its construction.

★ **David McCullough** *The Path Between the Seas: The Creation of the Panama Canal, 1870–1914.* Though this is a detailed scholarly work of seven hundred pages, the plot-twisting narrative and larger-than-life characters sweep the reader along, together with a focus on understanding the underlying causes of events.

★ **Matthew Parker** *Hell's Gorge: The Battle to Build the Panama Canal* (also published as *Panama Fever*). A gripping account of the struggle with jungle, disease, engineering impossibilities and disastrous ignorance, which is a meticulously researched yet wide-ranging narrative that focuses on the oft-neglected labour force that lived and died digging the Big Ditch.

OTHER HISTORY AND POLITICS

Kevin Buckley *Panama: The Whole Story* Written by a former *Newsweek* correspondent, this inevitably isn't "the whole story" but Buckley does well in looking of events leading up to the US invasion of Panama in 1989 from various angles. He vividly brings to life the complex web of corruption and political intrigue on both sides.

Peter Earle *The Sack of Panama: Captain Morgan and the Battle for the Caribbean.* Swashbuckling account of the real-life pirates of the Caribbean and the Spaniards' efforts to defeat them, focusing on the Welsh privateer Henry Morgan and his exploits, culminating in the sack of Panama in 1671.

John Esquemeling *The Pirates of Panama: True Account of the Famous Adventures and Daring Deeds of Sir Henry Morgan and Other Notorious Freebooters.* Based on a lively firsthand account originally written in Dutch, the first English edition was published in 1684. The author was barber surgeon to Henry Morgan and accompanied him on his notorious expedition against Panama City.

Aims McGuinness *Path of Empire: Panama and the Californian Gold Rush.* A look at the key role played by the isthmus during the Gold Rush in the mid-1800s as the fastest link between New York and San Francisco, the consequences of building the Panama Railroad and the first of many military interventions by the US.

Bastian Obermayer and Frederik Obermaier *The Panama Papers: Breaking the Story of How the Rich and*

Powerful Hide Their Money. Both gripping and disheartening in equal measure. Insights into the exposé on how the global political, commercial and celebrity elite use perfectly legal offshore accounts for tax avoidance, while their funds are used to launder drug money.

John Lindsay Poland *Emperors in the Jungle: The Hidden History of the US in Panama*. A human-rights campaigner and investigative journalist explores the role of the US military in Panama and the dubious uses to which it put the land it acquired.

John Prebble *The Darien Disaster*. Highly detailed and often turgid exploration of the doomed attempt by the Scots to colonize the Darién. The minutiae, such as the numbers of cases of rum loaded onto the ships, obscure the depth of the tragedy that bankrupted Scotland.

Sonja Watson *The Politics of Race in Panama: Afro-Hispanic and West Indian Literary Discourses of Contention*. This thoughtful, scholarly work, which examines the way that race and identity are inscribed differently by authors from the Afro-Caribbean and Afro-Hispanic communities, leads you to wish more of these authors' writings were more widely available in English.

John Week and Phil Gunson *Panama: Made in the USA*. Written in 1991, this much-praised analysis of the 1989 American invasion of Panama and its historical background deals with the legal implications and political consequences, while shining a light on the part Noriega played leading up to the attack

GUNA CULTURE

Edith Crouch *The Mola: Traditional Kuna Textile Art* Lavishly illustrated – with almost 900 images – this book explores the aesthetics, symbolism and shifting influences on a hundred years of *mola*-making by the Guna women.

James Howe *Chiefs, Scribes and Ethnographers: Kuna Culture from Inside and Out*. Written by a professor of anthropology who has spent considerable time among the Guna over a 35-year period, this book deals with accounts that the Guna chiefs themselves have given of their life and culture. Like his previous books – *A People Who Would not Kneel: Panama, the United States and the San Blas Kuna* and *The Kuna Gathering: Contemporary Village Politics in Panama* – it's a serious but rewarding read, and is available on Kindle.

★ **Salvador Mary Lyn (ed.)** *The Art of Being Kuna: Layers of Meaning among the Kuna of Panama*. Glossy coffee-table book (though also available in paperback) full of fascinating photos and scholarly insights on the interweaving of Guna art, culture and environment.

Joel Sherzer *Stories, Myths, Chants and Songs of the Kuna Indians*. The author, a linguistic anthropologist, lived among the Guna people photographing and recording their oral tradition of songs and ritual performances. He reveals their close association with plants and animals and their belief in myths and magic.

Jorge Ventocilla, Heraclio Herrera and Valerio Nuñez *Plants and Animals in the Life of the Kuna*. Written by two Guna biologists and a Panamanian colleague, this book is aimed at the Guna reader as well as outsiders, providing fascinating insights into the Guna perspective on ecology and cosmology as they relate to environmental issues.

FICTION

Iain Banks *Canal Dreams*. More nightmare than dream, in which an unloveable, famous Japanese cellist is trapped on a ship in the Panama Canal that is captured by guerrillas. The violence she and her lover suffer at their hands leads her to an equally violent revenge.

Jane Bowles *Two Serious Ladies*. An avant-garde classic of 1943, this story follows two women seeking freedom from the confines of social convention. On holiday in Panama, one falls in love with a young sex worker and leaves her husband to live in the brothel in Colón. Offering a glimpse of the city's red-light district, it also includes a scene in the historic *Washington Hotel*.

Cristina Enríquez *The World in Half*. Debut novel from US author who draws on her Panamanian heritage to narrate a young woman's search for identity as she leaves her ailing mother to find in Panama the father she never knew. Though the book is heavy-handed with the geological symbolism, the protagonist's physical and existential journey keep the pages turning. The same author's award-winning *Come Together Fall Apart* contains a novella and a handful of short stories, which provide deft close-ups of a range of Panamanian characters in the turbulent 1980s, just before the fall of Noriega. *The Great Divide* is her most recent offering, a bold attempt at an epic novel, following multiple fictional characters labouring on the Canal – so many that it's hard to get attached to any of them.

Douglas Galbraith *The Rising Sun*. A detailed, somewhat rambling historical novel about the Scottish expedition to the Darién, fuelled by human greed but leading to unbelievable hardship and the eventual bankruptcy of Scotland. It is difficult to warm to the main character who tells the story, but the horror comes across.

James Stanley Gilbert *Panama Patchwork Poems*. A fascinating collection, published between 1901 and 1937, by a one-time employee of the Panama Railroad Company. Though "Poet Laureate of the Isthmus" may be a tad exaggerated, his accessible verse provides a powerful evocation of pre-Canal hardships for settlers in Colón.

Robert Hatting *Murder in Panama*. Though it won't win any awards for writing, this first of a trilogy of Kindle thrillers set in Panama will happily pass time on the plane, or a beach, taking you round the country at a breathless pace.

★ **John Le Carré** *The Tailor of Panama*. With an explicit nod to Graham Greene's *Our Man in Havana*, this satirical spy thriller is a classic. Set just before the US handover of the Canal, a young unscrupulous British agent embarks on an elaborate fiction of intrigue, which spirals out of control. While both American and British intelligence services are lampooned as much as Panamanian high society, the novel, nevertheless, caused some upset in Panama upon publication.

Enrique Jaramillo Levi *The Shadow: Thirteen Stories in Opposition*. Short stories by Panama's pre-eminent (post) modern writer, though some tales are scarcely more than vignettes. You'll either be seduced by the originality of his imagination and fluid prose or left baffled and irritated as meaning slips through your grasp. More accessible is his edited collection of short stories by Costa Rican and Panamanian women, *When New Flowers Bloomed*, tackling a range of subjects from gender relations to political events.

William Penn *The Panama Conspiracy*. A thriller that manages improbably to link all the US's enemies, from Fidel Castro through Red China to Osama Bin Laden, in a complex plot culminating in a plan to blockade the Panama Canal.

★ **Eric Zencey** *Panama*. All but the first chapter is actually set in Paris, with a deftly drawn cast of real and imagined characters woven into a historically intriguing murder mystery that centres on the financial scandal surrounding the Panama Canal debacle.

BIOGRAPHY AND MEMOIR

Darrin DuFord *Is There a Hole in My Boat? Tales of Travel in Panama Without a Car*. The author set out in 2006 to explore Panama using public transport or hitching a lift, by dugout or on foot, aiming to get closer to the life and culture of the people than the average tourist; he never seems to turn down a new experience.

Christian Giudice *Hands of Stone: The Life and Legend of Roberto Durán*. Meticulously researched biography of Panama's most famous boxer and one of the sport's all-time greats, drawing on plenty of fascinating, original interview material. A warts-and-all rags-to-riches tale that tracks his rise to fame from the slums of Panama City, giving a view of his contradictory character inside and outside the ring.

Graham Greene *Getting to Know the General: The Story of an Involvement*. Greene provides a personal slant on Omar Torrijos, the country's most charismatic leader, whom the author befriended during his time in troubled late 1970s and early 1980s Panama.

Malcolm Henderson *Don't Kill the Cow Too Quick: An Englishman's Adventures Homesteading in Panama*. Entertaining and informative, especially for expats thinking of following a dream, this book follows a couple's retirement in Bocas in the late 1990s, where they eventually established an organic farm.

Leo Mahon *Fire Under My Feet: A Memoir of God's Power in Panama*. The moving memoir of a compassionate Roman Catholic priest sent in 1963 to a poverty-stricken town in Panama to found a church.

Martin Mitchinson *The Darien Gap: Travels in the Rainforest of Panama*. An entertaining account of eighteen months spent in the trackless jungle trying to retrace the route to the Pacific made by the first European, Balboa, in 1513. It's a successful blend of personal experience, history and local lore.

Manuel Noriega and Peter Eisner *America's Prisoner: The Memoirs of Manuel Noriega*. The other side of the story of a leader who was vilified, arrested and put on trial by the US. A controversial book, it is worth reading for its revelations about the American attitude to Panama and Latin America.

WILDLIFE

★ **George R. Angehr and Robert Dean** *The Birds of Panama: A Field Guide*. In need of updating, but this is still the best available field guide for identifying birds.

George Angehr, Dodge Engleman and Lorna Engleman *A Bird-finding Guide to Panama*. You need to read the title carefully – this excellent, detailed guide tells you where to find the birds and how to get there by car, but is not a bird identification manual. Details updated on the web at Ⓦ audubonpanama.org.

Rainforest Publications *Panama Field Guides* (numerous titles). This company has produced an excellent series of illustrated laminated concertina-style pocket field guide pamphlets on Panama's flora and fauna, giving scientific, Spanish and English names. Available in Panama or online (Ⓦ rainforestpublications.com).

Jorge Ventocilla and Dana Gardner *A Guide to the Common Birds of Panama City* (Smithsonian Tropical Research Institute & Panama Audubon Society). Excellent, beautifully illustrated pocket book aimed at the average nature-lover – perfect for anyone basing their stay in the capital and wanting to identify the city's surprisingly abundant birdlife.

Language

Spanish is the national and official language of Panama and the first language of more than two million of the population. A recorded thirteen other first languages are spoken across the country, including English, which is used by many black Afro-Antilleans (see page 45) – though outside Panama City and the touristy areas of Bocas del Toro and Boquete, it's not widely spoken. Learning at least the basics of Spanish will make your travels considerably easier and reap countless rewards in terms of reception and understanding of people and places.

Pronunciation and word stress

In Spanish, each word is **pronounced** as written according to the following guide:

A somewhere between the "A" sound of "back" and that of "father"
E as in "get"
I as in "police"
O as in "hot"
U as in "rule"
C is soft before E and I, otherwise hard; *cerca* is pronounced "SERka".
G works the same way – a guttural "H" sound (like the "ch" in "loch") before E or I, a hard G elsewhere; *gigante* is pronounced "HiGANte".
H is always silent.
J is the same sound as a guttural "G"; *jamón* is pronounced "ham ON".
LL sounds like an English Y; *tortilla* is pronounced "torTIya".
N is as in English, unless there is a "~" over it, when it becomes like the N in "onion"; *mañana* is pronounced "maNYAna".
QU is pronounced like an English "K" as in "kick".
R is rolled, **RR** doubly so.
V sounds like a cross between B and V, *vino* almost becoming "beano".
X is a soft "SH", so that *Xela* becomes "SHEla"; between vowels it has an "H" sound – *México* is pronounced "ME-hi-ko".
Z is the same as a soft C; *cerveza* is pronounced "serVEsa".

Getting the **word stress** right makes a big difference: *PAgo* means "I pay", *paGÓ* she/he paid. The rule is simple: if a word ends in a vowel, "s" or "n", the stress is on the syllable before last. If it ends in any other consonant, the stress is on the last syllable. Exceptions are marked with an accent on the vowel of the stressed syllable.

Latin American Spanish lacks the lisp common in Spain, where *cerveza* is often pronounced "therVEtha". One feature of the speech of many Panamanians which makes understanding more difficult is the aspiration of the "S" sound at the end of a syllable or word, such that the word *cascada* is pronounced more like "cahcada". Also, words containing a "ch" such as *muchacho* may sound more like "mushasho". Generally the Spanish of indigenous Panamanians is easiest to understand.

Formal and informal address

For English-speakers one of the most difficult things to get to grips with is the distinction between formal and informal address. Generally speaking, the third-person **usted** indicates respect and is used in business, for people you don't know and for those older than you. Second-person **tú** is for children, friends and contemporaries in less formal settings. (Remember also that in Latin America the second-person **plural** – *vosotros* – is never used, so "you" plural will always be *ustedes*.)

Verbal courtesy is an integral part of speech in Spanish and one that – once you're accustomed to the pace and flow of life in Panama, especially out of the city – should become instinctive. Saying *Buenos días/Buenas tardes/Buenas noches*, or the abbreviated *buenos* or *buenas*, and waiting for the appropriate response is usual when asking for something at a shop or ticket office, for example, as is adding *señor* or *señora* (in this instance similar to the US "sir" or "ma'am").

On meeting, or being introduced to someone, people are likely to say *con mucho gusto*, "it's a pleasure", and you should do the same. On departure you will more often than not be told *¡Que le vaya bien!* – literally meaning "May all go well with you", it often translates better as "Take care" or "Travel safely".

BASIC WORDS

a lot mucho
afternoon tarde
and y
bad mal(o)/a
big gran(de)
boy chico
closed cerrado/a
cold frío/a
day día
entrance entrada
exit salida
girl chica
good bien/buen(o)/a
he él
her ella
here aquí
his suyo
hot calor/caliente
how much cuánto
if si
later más tarde/después
less menos
ma'am/missus señora
man señor/hombre
maybe talvez
miss señorita
more más
morning mañana
night noche
no no
now ahora
open abierto/a
or o
please por favor
she ella
sir/mister señor
small pequeño/a
thank you gracias
that eso/a
their suyo/de ellos
there allí
they ellos
this este/a
today hoy
tomorrow mañana
what qué
when cuando/cuándo
where dónde
with con
without sin
yes sí
yesterday ayer

BASIC PHRASES

Hello ¡Hola!
Goodbye Adiós
See you later Hasta luego
Good morning Buenos días
Good afternoon Buenas tardes
Good evening/night Buenas noches
Sorry Lo siento/Discúlpeme
Excuse me Con permiso/Perdón
How are you? ¿Cómo está (usted)?/¿Qué tal?
Nice to meet you Mucho gusto
Not at all/You're welcome De nada/para servirle
I (don't) understand (No) Entiendo
Do you speak English? ¿Habla (usted) inglés?
I (don't) speak Spanish (No) Hablo español/castellano
What (did you say)? ¿Mande?/¿Cómo?
Could you… please? ¿Podría…por favor?
…repeat that …repetirlo
What's your name? ¿Cómo se llama usted?
My name is… Me llamo…
Where are you from? ¿De dónde es usted?
I'm from… Soy de…
How old are you? ¿Cuántos años tiene? (usted)
I am…years old Tengo…años
I don't know No sé
Do you know…? ¿Sabe…?
I want/I'd like Quiero/Quisiera
What's that? ¿Qué es eso?
How much is it? ¿Cúanto es/Cuesta?
What is this called in Spanish? ¿Cómo se llama este en español/castellano?
There is (is there)? Hay (?)
Do you have…? ¿Tiene…?

What time is it? ¿Qué hora es?
May I take a photograph? ¿Puedo sacar una foto?
It's hot/cold Hace calor/frío

BASIC NEEDS, SERVICES AND PLACES

ATM cajero automático
Bank banco
bathroom/toilet baño/sanitario
beach playa
border crossing frontera
church iglesia
internet café cibercafé
laundry lavandería/lavamático
map mapa
market mercado
money dinero/plata
museum museo
pharmacy farmacia
post office el correo
restaurant restaurante
supermarket supermercado
telephone teléfono
tourist office oficina de turismo

NUMBERS (NÚMEROS), MONTHS (MESES) AND DAYS (DÍAS)

1 un/uno/una
2 dos
3 tres
4 cuatro
5 cinco
6 seis
7 siete
8 ocho
9 nueve
10 diez
20 veinte
21 veintiuno
22 veintidos
30 treinta
40 cuarenta
50 cincuenta
60 sesenta
70 setenta
80 ochenta
90 noventa
100 cien
1000 mil
first primero/a
second segundo/a
third tercero/a
January enero
February febrero
March marzo
April abril
May mayo
June junio
July julio
August agosto
September septiembre
October octubre
November noviembre
December diciembre
Monday lunes
Tuesday martes
Wednesday miércoles
Thursday jueves
Friday viernes
Saturday sábado
Sunday domingo

GETTING AROUND

bus autobús
minibus buseta/colectivo
bus station terminal de autobuses
bus stop parada de autobús
boat barco/lancha/panga
dugout canoe cayuco/piragua
dock/pier muelle
airplane avión
airport aeropuerto
car carro/auto(móvil)
engine motor
4WD/4X4 doble tracción/cuatro por cuatro
taxi taxi
lorry/truck camión
pickup camioneta
bicycle bicicleta
motorcycle moto
petrol/diesel/gas gasolina
ticket billete/pasaje
ticket office taquilla/ventanilla
I'd like a ticket to… (Necesito) un billete (pasaje) para…
…one way …sólo ida
…return/round trip …ida y vuelta
I would like to rent a… Me gustaría alquilar un/una…
Where does…to…leave from? ¿De dónde sale… para…?
What time does the…leave from? ¿A qué hora sale**…** para…?

What time does the...arrive in...? ¿A qué hora llega...en...?

DIRECTIONS

Where is...? ¿Dónde está...?
How do I get to...? ¿Por dónde se va a...?
I'm lost Estoy perdido/a
Is it far? ¿Está lejos?
left/right izquierda/derecha
straight ahead derecho/recto
north norte
south sur
east este
west oeste
street calle
avenue avenida
block cuadra
corner esquina
(main) road carretera

ACCOMMODATION

Is there (a)...nearby? ¿Hay...aquí cerca?
...hotel ...un hotel
...cheap, small hotel ...una pensión/un hospedaje
...hostel ...un hostal
Do you have...? ¿Tiene...?
...a room ...un cuarto
...with two beds ...con dos camas
...a double bed ...con cama matrimonial
...a dorm room ...cuarto colectivo/dormitorio
...a cabin ...una cabaña
It's for Es para
...one person ...una persona
...two people ...dos personas
...for one night ...una noche
...one week ...una semana
Does it have... ¿Tiene...?
...a shared bath ...baño compartido
...a private bath ...baño privado
...hot water ...agua caliente
...air conditioning ...aire-acondicionado
... a fan ... abanico
...a mosquito net ...mosquitero
May I see a room? ¿Puedo ver un cuarto?
May I see another room? ¿Puedo ver otro cuarto?
Yes, it's fine Sí, está bien

FOOD AND DRINK

BASIC DINING VOCABULARY

almuerzo lunch
cafetería self-service restaurant
carta menu
cena dinner
comedor basic restaurant
comida corriente cheap set menu, usually lunch
comida típica traditional cuisine
cuenta bill
desayuno breakfast
fonda inexpensive, informal local restaurant
menú del día cheap set menu
menú ejecutivo a fancier and pricier set menu than the *menú del día*
mesa table
plato fuerte main course
plato vegetariano vegetarian dish
silla chair
vaso glass
Soy vegetariano/a I'm a vegetarian
Tengo hambre/sed I'm hungry/thirsty

BASIC FOOD VOCABULARY

aceite oil
ajo garlic
arroz rice
azúcar sugar
chile chilli
galletas biscuits/crackers
hielo ice
huevos eggs
mantequilla butter
mermelada jam
miel honey
natilla sour cream
pan (integral) bread (wholemeal)
pimienta pepper
queso cheese
sal salt
salsa de tomate tomato sauce

FRUTAS (FRUIT)

aceitunas olives
chirimoya custard apple
coco coconut
fresa strawberry
guanábana soursop
guayaba guava

guineo banana
limón lemon
manzana apple
maracuyá passionfruit
marañon cashew
melón melon
mora (zarzamora) blackberry
naranja orange
papaya papaya
piña pineapple
plátano plantain
sandía watermelon
uva grapes

LEGUMBRES/VERDURAS (VEGETABLES)

aguacate avocado
cebolla onion
champiñón (hongo) mushroom
ensalada salad
espinaca spinach
frijoles beans
gallo pinto mixed rice and beans
lechuga lettuce
lentejas lentils
maíz sweetcorn/maize
menestra bean/lentil stew
papa potato
papas fritas chips/French fries
tomate tomato
zanahoria carrot

CARNE (MEAT), AVES (POULTRY) AND MENUDO (OFFAL)

bistec/lomo steak
carne beef
cerdo pork
chuleta pork chop
jamón ham
mondongo tripe and chorizo stew
patas trotters
pollo chicken
res beef
ropa vieja shredded spicy beef and rice
sancocho thick red meat or chicken soup with root vegetables

MARISCOS (SEAFOOD) AND PESCADO (FISH)

almejas clams
anchoa anchovy
atún tuna
calamares squid
camarón shrimp
cangrejo crab
ceviche raw seafood marinated in lime juice with onions
concha conch
corvina sea bass
langosta lobster/crayfish
langostina king prawn
mejillónes mussels
mero grouper
pargo rojo red snapper
pulpo octopus
trucha trout

BOCADOS OR BOCADITOS (SNACKS)

carimañola mashed boiled yuca stuffed with beef
carne en palito meat on a little stick
churro ribbed, tubular doughnut-cum-waffle
empanada cheese-/meat-filled pastry
emparedado sandwich
hamburguesa hamburger
hojaldre deep-fried doughypancake
patacones fried green plantains
platanitos plantain crisps
salchichas sausages
tortilla thick fried maize patty
tortilla de huevos omelette
tostada toast

BEBIDAS (DRINKS)

agua mineral mineral water
...con gas ...sparkling
...sin gas ...still
agua potable drinking water
aromática herbal tea
batido fresh fruit milk shake
café coffee
cerveza beer
chicha maize and/or fruit drink
chicha fuerte fermented maize drink
chicheme ground maize drink made with milk, vanilla and cinnamon
jugo juice
jugo natural pure fruit juice
leche milk
licuado fresh fruit shake
pipa fresh coconut juice
raspados flavoured ice shavings
refresco/soda (cold) soft drink
ron rum
seco rough sugar cane spirit
té tea
té de manzanilla camomile tea
vino blanco/tinto white/red wine

COOKING TERMS

a la parrilla barbecued
a la plancha griddled
apanado breaded
asado roast
encocado in coconut sauce
frito fried
picante spicy hot
puré mashed
revuelto scrambled

Glossary and acronyms

ACP Autoridad del Canal de Panamá (Panama Canal Authority)

Afro-Antillano Panamanian of African heritage from the West Indies

Afro-Colonial Panamanian of African heritage from the Spanish colonial era

Afro-Panameño/a Panamanian of African heritage from all eras

ANCON Asociación Nacional para la Conservación de la Naturaleza Panama's most prominent environmental NGO

artesanías traditional handicrafts

ATP Autoridad de Turismo Panamá

barrio neighbourhood; suburb

bohío see *rancho*

bomba pump at a petrol station, often shorthand for the petrol station itself

cacique chief (originally a colonial term, now used for elected leaders/figureheads of indigenous *comarcas*)

campesino peasant farmer

cantina local, hard-drinking bar, usually men-only

chiva rural bus, which may be a converted pickup

colectivo shared taxi/minibus, usually following a fixed route (can also be applied to a boat – *lancha colectiva*)

colono generally a *mestizo* farming settler who originated from the Azuero Peninsula and central areas and moved to colonize other parts of the country

comarca semiautonomous area demarcated for the major indigenous peoples

cordillera mountain range

diablo rojo colourful painted buses being phased out, but still evident in some parts of Panama City and along the Caribbean coast

feria fair (market); also a town fête

finca ranch, farm or plantation

gringo/gringa any light-skinned foreigner, particularly a North American

guardaparque park warden

huaca pre-Columbian gold treasure buried with the dead in a tomb

INAC Instituto Nacional de Arte y Cultura (government department in charge of museums and preservation of cultural heritage)

indígeno/a an indigenous person (also used adjectivally)

ladino a vague term – applied to people it means Spanish-influenced as opposed to indigenous, and at its most specific defines someone of mixed Spanish and indigenous blood

mestizo person of mixed indigenous and Spanish blood, though like the term *ladino* it has more cultural than racial significance

metate pre-Colombian stone table used for grinding corn

MiAmbiente Catchy name for the Ministerio del Ambiente (Ministry of the Environment), also shortened to MIA

mochilero backpacker

montuno traditional male costume consisting of a loose cotton shirt and knee-length trousers

(fiestas) patronales patron saint festivals enjoyed by every town or village

pollera embroidered dress with full skirt considered to be the national costume of Panama

quincha adobe

rancho open-sided (wooden) structure with palm-thatched roof (see *bohío*)

STRI Smithsonian Tropical Research Institute

Small print and index

ABOUT THE AUTHOR

A freelance researcher, writer and educator, **Sara Humphreys** has toiled, travelled and tarried in various countries in sub-Saharan Africa, Latin America and Europe, including a year living in Opuwo, northwest Namibia, helping untangle post-independence curriculum changes. When not travelling, she can be found swinging in a hammock in Barbados.

A ROUGH GUIDE TO ROUGH GUIDES

Published in 1982, the first Rough Guide – to Greece – was a student scheme that became a publishing phenomenon. Mark Ellingham, a recent graduate in English from Bristol University, had been travelling in Greece the previous summer and couldn't find the right guidebook. With a small group of friends he wrote his own guide, combining a contemporary, journalistic style with a thoroughly practical approach to travellers' needs.

The immediate success of the book spawned a series that rapidly covered dozens of destinations. And, in addition to impecunious backpackers, Rough Guides soon acquired a much broader readership that relished the guides' wit and inquisitiveness as much as their enthusiastic, critical approach and value-for-money ethos. These days, Rough Guides include recommendations from budget to luxury and cover more than 120 destinations around the globe, from Amsterdam to Zanzibar, all regularly updated by our team of roaming writers.

Browse all our latest guides, read inspirational features and book your trip at **roughguides.com**.

Rough Guide credits

Senior Editor: Rachel Lawrence
Cartography: Carte
Picture Editor: Piotr Kala
Picture Manager: Tom Smyth
Layout: Claire Armstrong
Publishing Technology Manager: Rebeka Davies
Production Operations Manager: Katie Bennett
Head of Publishing: Sarah Clark

Publishing information

Fourth edition 2025

Distribution
UK, Ireland and Europe
Apa Publications (UK) Ltd; mail@roughguides.com
United States and Canada
Two Rivers; ips@ingramcontent.com
Australia and New Zealand
Woodslane; info@woodslane.com.au
Worldwide
Apa Publications (UK) Ltd; mail@roughguides.com

Special Sales, Content Licensing and CoPublishing
Rough Guides can be purchased in bulk quantities at discounted prices. We can create special editions, personalized jackets and corporate imprints tailored to your needs. mail@roughguides.com.

roughguides.com

EU Representative
LOGOS EUROPE, 9 rue Nicolas Poussin, 17000, LA ROCHELLE, France; Contact@logoseurope.eu; +33 (0) 667937378

Printed by Finidr in Czech Republic

ISBN: 9781835292518

This book was produced using **Typefi** automated publishing software.

A catalogue record for this book is available from the British Library.

Help us update

We've gone to a lot of effort to ensure that this edition of **The Rough Guide to Panama** is accurate and up-to-date. However, things change – places get "discovered", transport routes are altered, restaurants and hotels raise prices or lower standards, and businesses cease trading. If you feel we've got it wrong or left something out, we'd like to know, and if you can direct us to the web address, so much the better.

Please send your comments with the subject line "**Rough Guide Panama Update**" to mail@roughguides.com. We'll send a copy of the next edition (or any other Rough Guide if you prefer) for the very best emails.

Acknowledgements

Thanks to the many Panamanians who assisted in my investigations, including the helpful staff in the ATP offices of Portobelo and Pedasí, various MiAmbiente park wardens, and Feliciano González for updates on and around Boquete. Muchas gracias too to Raffa Calvo for accompanying me on recces round the Azuero and the Costa Arriba, and for insights and info on various other parts of the country. A big shout out also goes to Nick Egerton-King for providing the low-down on hostels and nightlife in Bocas, Santa Catalina and Panama City.

Back at Rough Guides, a sincere thanks goes to my editor, Rachel Lawrence, for her encouragement and support, and to both Rachel and Katie Bennett (in Cartography) for their flexibility around deadlines. Appreciation, as ever, is due to Val Humphreys for seeking out new book titles, and to Adrian for moving house on his own while I was living it up in Panama, and for keeping me fed and watered during late-night write-ups.

Photo credits

(Key: T-top; C-centre; B-bottom; L-left; R-right)

All images **Shutterstock**

Cover: Red-eyed tree frog **Shutterstock**

Index

D

E

N

U

W

Z

Map symbols

The symbols below are used on maps throughout the book

Listings key

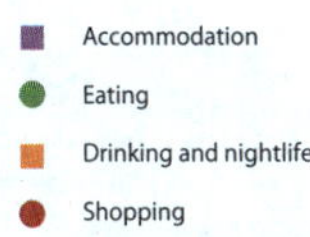

BENEFITS OF PLANNING AND BOOKING AT ROUGHGUIDES.COM/TRIPS

PLAN YOUR ADVENTURE WITH LOCAL EXPERTS

Rough Guides' English-speaking local experts are hand-picked, based on their experience in the travel industry and their impeccable standards of customer service.

SAVE TIME AND GET ACCESS TO LOCAL KNOWLEDGE

When a local expert plans your trip, you save time and money when you book, even during high season. You won't be charged for using a credit card either.

MAKE TRAVEL A BREEZE: BOOK WITH PEACE OF MIND

Enjoy stress-free travel when you use Rough Guides' secure online booking platform. All bookings come with a money-back guarantee.

WHAT DO OTHER TRAVELLERS THINK ABOUT ROUGH GUIDES TRIPS?

This Spain tour company did a fantastic job to make our dream trip perfect. We gave them our travel budget, told them where we would like to go, and they did all of the planning. Our drivers and tour guides were always on time and very knowledgable. The hotel accommodations were better than we would have found on our own. Only one time did we end up in a location that we had not intended to be in. We called the 24 hour phone number, and they immediately fixed the situation.

Don A, USA

Our trip was fantastic! Transportation, accommodations, guides – all were well chosen! The hotels were well situated, well appointed and had helpful, friendly staff. All of the guides we had were very knowledgeable, patient, and flexible with our varied interests in the different sites. We particularly enjoyed the side trip to Tangier! Well done! The itinerary you arranged for us allowed maximum coverage of the country with time in each city for seeing the important places.

Sharon, USA

PLAN AND BOOK YOUR TRIP AT
ROUGHGUIDES.COM/TRIPS